# mylabschool™
## Where the classroom comes to life!

*Fr... classroom* video footage of teachers and students interacting to building standards-based lessons and web-based portfolios . . . from a robust resource library of the "What Every Teacher Should Know About" series to complete instruction on writing an effective research paper . . . **MyLabSchool** brings together an amazing collection of resources for future teachers. This website gives you a wealth of videos, print and simulated cases, career advice, and much more.

Use **MyLabSchool** with this Allyn and Bacon Education text, and you will have everything you need to succeed in your course. Assignment IDs have also been incorporated into many Allyn and Bacon Education texts to link to the online material in **MyLabSchool** . . . connecting the teachers of tomorrow to the information they need today.

**PEARSON** AB

**VISIT www.mylabschool.com to learn more about this invaluable resource and Take a Tour!**

## Here's what you'll find in mylabschool™
### Where the classroom comes to life!

### VideoLab ▶
Access hundreds of video clips of actual classroom situations from a variety of grade levels and school settings. These 3- to 5-minute closed-captioned video clips illustrate real teacher–student interaction, and are organized both topically *and* by discipline. Students can test their knowledge of classroom concepts with integrated observation questions.

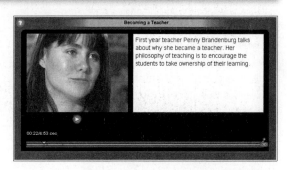

Becoming a Teacher

First year teacher Penny Brandenburg talks about why she became a teacher. Her philosophy of teaching is to encourage the students to take ownership of their learning.

00:22/4:53 sec

### ◀ Lesson & Portfolio Builder
This feature enables students to create, maintain, update, and share online portfolios and standards-based lesson plans. The Lesson Planner walks students, step-by-step, through the process of creating a complete lesson plan, including verifiable objectives, assessments, and related state standards. Upon completion, the lesson plan can be printed, saved, e-mailed, or uploaded to a website.

# Here's what you'll find in mylabschool™

## Simulations ▶

This area of MyLabSchool contains interactive tools designed to better prepare future teachers to provide an appropriate education to students with special needs. To achieve this goal, the IRIS (IDEA and Research for Inclusive Settings) Center at Vanderbilt University has created course enhancement materials. These resources include online interactive modules, case study units, information briefs, student activities, an online dictionary, and a searchable directory of disability-related web sites.

## ◀ Resource Library

MyLabSchool includes a collection of PDF files on crucial and timely topics within education. Each topic is applicable to any education class, and these documents are ideal resources to prepare students for the challenges they will face in the classroom. This resource can be used to reinforce a central topic of the course, or to enhance coverage of a topic you need to explore in more depth.

## Research Navigator ▶

This comprehensive research tool gives users access to four exclusive databases of authoritative and reliable source material. It offers a comprehensive, step-by-step walk-through of the research process. In addition, students can view sample research papers and consult guidelines on how to prepare endnotes and bibliographies. The latest release also features a new bibliography-maker program—AutoCite.

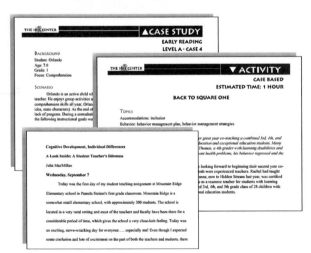

## ◀ Case Archive

This collection of print and simulated cases can be easily accessed by topic and subject area, and can be integrated into your course. The cases are drawn from Allyn & Bacon's best-selling books, and represent the complete range of disciplines and student ages. It's an ideal way to consider and react to real classroom scenarios. The possibilities for using these high-quality cases within the course are endless.

# A Course *for* Teaching English Learners

## Lynne T. Díaz-Rico

California State University, San Bernardino

PEARSON

Boston ■ New York ■ San Francisco
Mexico City ■ Montreal ■ Toronto ■ London ■ Madrid ■ Munich ■ Paris
Hong Kong ■ Singapore ■ Tokyo ■ Cape Town ■ Sydney

**Executive Editor:** Aurora Martínez Ramos
**Series Editorial Assistant:** Lynda Giles
**Marketing Manager:** Krista Clark
**Editorial Production Service:** Omegatype Typography, Inc.
**Composition Buyer:** Linda Cox
**Manufacturing Buyer:** Linda Morris
**Electronic Composition:** Omegatype Typography, Inc.
**Interior Design:** Omegatype Typography, Inc.
**Photo Researcher:** Omegatype Typography, Inc.
**Cover Administrator:** Kristina Mose-Libon

For related titles and support materials, visit our online catalog at www.ablongman.com.

Between the time website information is gathered and then published, it is not unusual for some sites to have closed. Also, the transcription of URLs can result in typographical errors. The publisher would appreciate notification where these errors occur so that they may be corrected in subsequent editions.

ISBN-10: 0-205-51050-7
ISBN-13: 978-0-205-51050-4

**Library of Congress Cataloging-in-Publication Data**
Díaz-Rico, Lynne T.
   A course for teaching English learners / Lynne T. Díaz-Rico.
      p.   cm.
   Includes bibliographical references and index.
   ISBN 0-205-51050-7 (pbk.)
   1. English language—Study and teaching—Foreign speakers.   2. English language—Study and teaching—United States.   3. English language—Study and teaching—Handbooks, manuals, etc.
I. Title.
   PE1128.A2D448   2008
   428.2'4—dc22
                                                                                          2006052777

Printed in the United States of America

10   9   8   7   6   5   4   3              11   10   09   08

**Photo Credits:**
p. 2: © Mary Kate Denny / PhotoEdit; p. 10: Karen A. Heath; p. 34: © Tony Freeman / PhotoEdit; p. 46: © Will Hart / PhotoEdit; p. 63: © Michael Newman / PhotoEdit; p. 92: © Tony Freeman / PhotoEdit; p. 131: Lindfors Photography; p. 141: © Michael Newman / PhotoEdit; p. 169: © Myrleen Ferguson Cate / PhotoEdit; p. 180: © Will Hart / PhotoEdit; p. 189: © Michael Newman / PhotoEdit; p. 211: © Spencer Grant / PhotoEdit; p. 261: Nancy Sheehan Photos; p. 276: © Michael Newman / PhotoEdit; p. 341: Karen A. Heath

**Lynne Díaz-Rico** is Professor of Education at California State University, San Bernardino. She has worked with public and private teacher education institutions and agencies around the world to prepare teachers for classrooms with diverse students and English-language pedagogy. Her books *Crosscultural, Language, and Academic Development Handbook* and *Strategies for Teaching English Learners* are widely used to educate English-language development teachers. Her research interests are in pedagogies for multilingual classrooms; creative, innovative English teaching strategies; critical discourse analysis; and visual literacy.

# CONTENTS

Preface    xv

## PART ONE    Teaching English to English Learners

## INTRODUCTION
## Teaching English Learners    1

English Learners in U.S. Schools    1

Teaching with Integrity    4

The Professional Preparation of Teachers to Educate English Learners    8

## CHAPTER ONE
## Language Structure and Use    11

Ah, Language!    11

Language Universals    11
   All Languages Have Structure    12
   Language Is Dynamic    12
   Language Is Complex    12

Phonology: The Sound Patterns of Language    13
   Phonemes    13
   Stress    16
   Pitch and Rhythm    17
   Intonation Patterns    18
   Teaching Pronunciation    18

Morphology: The Words of Language    20
   Morphemes    20
   Word-Formation Processes    21
   Using Morphemes in Teaching    21

Syntax: The Sentence Patterns of Language    23
   Explicit Teaching of Syntax    24

Semantics: The Meanings of Language    26
   Semantic Challenges    26
   Acquiring Vocabulary    28
   Academic Vocabulary    28
   Vocabulary Teaching and Concept Development    28
   Semantic Shifts    30

**Language Functions    30**

Academic Language Functions    30
Functions and Classroom Routines    31
Cognitive Academic Language Proficiency    32
A Curriculum That Promotes Academic Language    32
Evaluating Curricula for Academic Language    32

**Discourse    33**

Academic Discourse    33
Oral Discourse in the Classroom    34
Discourse That Affirms Students' Voices    38

**Pragmatics: The Influence of Context    39**

Appropriate Language    39
Nonverbal Communication    41
Evaluating the Pragmatic Features of School Programs    42

**Dialects and Language Variation    43**

Dialects and the Education of English Learners    43
Common Features That Constitute Dialects    44
How Dialects Exhibit Social and Ethnic Differences    45
Attitudes toward Dialects    45
Dialects and Style    46
Vernacular Dialects and Language Teaching    47

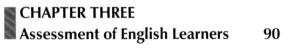

## CHAPTER TWO
## First- and Second-Language Development and Their Relationship to Academic Achievement    49

**Processes and Stages of Language Acquisition    49**

First-Language Acquisition    49
Second-Language Acquisition    51
First- and Second-Language Acquisition: Commonalities    52

**Theories and Models of Second-Language Acquisition    54**

Former Theories That Still Influence Current Practice    54
Current Theories of Language Development    56

**Factors That Influence Second-Language Acquisition    67**

Psychological Factors: The Learner's Background    70
Psychological Factors: Social–Emotional    74
Psychological Factors: Cognitive    77
Sociocultural and Political Factors That Influence Instruction    81

## PART TWO    Assessment and Instruction

## CHAPTER THREE
## Assessment of English Learners    90

**Principles of Standards-Based Assessment and Instruction    90**

Standards-Based Education: Federal Government Mandates    90
Standards for English-Language Development    91

**Role, Purposes, and Types of Assessment    95**

Assessment-Based Instruction    95
Identification, Placement, Instruction, Progress Tracking, and
Redesignation/Reclassification of English Learners    95
Issues of Fairness in Testing English Learners    101
Types of Classroom Assessments for English Learners    103
Selecting and Using Appropriate Classroom Assessments    107
Assigning Grades to English Learners    107
Test Accommodation    108

**Language and Content Area Assessment    108**

Combining Language and Content Standards and Learning Strategy Objectives    108
English-Language Development Assessments    110
Interpreting the Results of Assessment    110

**Special Issues in Assessment    111**

Academic and Learning Problems That English Learners May Experience    111
Identification, Referral, and Early Intervention of English Learners
with Special Needs    112
Teaching Strategies for the CLD Special Learner    114

# CHAPTER FOUR
# Programs for English Learners    117

**The History of Multilingual Competency in the United States    117**

Early Bilingualism in the United States    118
The Struggles for Language Education Rights in the Twentieth Century    118
Legal and Legislative Mandates Supporting Language Education Rights    120

**Federal and State Requirements for ELD Services    124**

No Child Left Behind    124
Proposition 227    125
*Williams et al. v. State of California*    126
*Lau v. Nichols*    126

**The Politics of Bilingual Education    127**

Support for Heritage-Language Proficiency    127
Support for Two-Way (Dual) Immersion    127
English-Only Efforts    128
What Is "Fully Qualified" under NCLB?    129

**Empowerment Issues Related to English Learners    129**

**Equity and Policy Issues Related to English Learners    130**

**Components of ELD Programs    131**

Dual-Language Development Programs (Additive Bilingualism)    131
Transitional Bilingual Education    134
Structured English Immersion    135
Newcomer (Front-Loaded) English    135
English-Language Development Programs    137

**English-Language Development and Academic Instruction**    **140**

The SDAIE-Enhanced Content Classroom    140
A Model for SDAIE    140

**Parental Rights and Communicating with Families**    **144**

Parental Rights    144
School–Community Partnerships    145

# CHAPTER FIVE
# English-Language/Literacy Development and Content Instruction    147

**Foundations of English-Language Literacy**    **147**

Connections between Oracy, Literacy, and Social Functions    147
Personal Factors Affecting Literacy Development in English    149
Promoting Literacy Development in English Across the Curriculum    155
Scaffolding Strategies in English Literacy Across the Curriculum    155

**Instructional Planning and Organization for ELD and SDAIE**    **162**

Planning for Standards-Based ELD and Content Instruction    162
Organizing the Environment to Enhance Interaction    167
Grouping for Student Success    168
Teaching Collaboratively    174

**Differentiated Instruction in ELD and SDAIE**    **176**

Bridging: Accessing and Building Prior Knowledge    176
Appealing to Diverse Learning Modalities    178
Access to Cognitive Academic Language    179
Teaching with SDAIE Strategies    181
Modifying Language without Simplification    181
Scaffolding: Temporary Support for Learning    182
Guided and Independent Practice That Promotes
    Students' Active Language Use    184
Formative Assessment and Reteaching    185
Summative Assessment, Culminating Performance, and Metalearning    185
Reflective Pedagogy    185

**Effective Resource Use in ELD and SDAIE**    **186**

Selecting and Using Appropriate Materials    186
Modifying Materials for Linguistic Accessibility    187
Culturally Appealing Materials    187
Technological Resources to Enhance Instruction    188

**Teacher Commitment**    **190**

# CHAPTER SIX
# English-Language Development    191

**The Focus on Communicative Interaction**    **191**

What Is Communicative Competence?    191
The Cognitive Perspective    192
An Interlanguage Perspective    192

**The Role of Grammar      193**

  Benefits of Explicit Instruction of Language      194
  The Role of Feedback in Explicit Teaching      195
  The Supplemental Role of Implicit Learning      196
  Teaching Grammar      196

**Content-Based English-Language Development      197**

  Collaboration and Reciprocity      197
  CBI-ELD: Lesson Planning      197

**English-Language Oracy Development      199**

  Basic Interpersonal Communication Skills      199
  Listening Processes      200
  Speaking, Communication Skills, and the ELD Standards      206

**English-Language Literacy Development      214**

  Reading First in the Primary Language      215
  ELD and ELA Standards in Reading      215
  Purposes for Reading      216
  Standards-Based Reading Instruction      217
  Developing Word Analysis Skills      217
  Developing Reading Fluency      221
  Reading Processes      223
  Developing Reading Comprehension      226
  Developing Literary Response and Analysis Skills      230
  Secondary-Level Content Reading      230
  Writing and the English Learner      231
  Generation 1.5 and College Writing      232
  Writing as a Social Construction      232
  Stages of Writing Development for Young English Learners      232
  Handwriting in English      233
  The Writing Workshop      234
  Issues with ESL Writing      236

## CHAPTER SEVEN
## Planning and Implementing SDAIE-Based Content Instruction      239

**Planning SDAIE Lessons      239**

  Setting Objectives      239
  Selecting and Modifying Materials      242

**Differentiated Instructional Delivery in the Content Domains      244**

  Bridging: Accessing Prior Knowledge and Building Schemata      244
  Vocabulary Front-Loading      247
  Strategic Teaching Using Multimodalities      247
  Access to Cognitive Academic Language Across the Content Areas      248
  Modifying Language without Simplification in Content Delivery      250
  Scaffolded Content Instruction      251
  Guided and Independent Practice That Promotes Students'
    Active Language Use      256

Resources for Independent Practice     257
Formative Assessment and Reteaching Content     260
Summative Assessment of Content Lessons     261

**Instructional Needs beyond the Classroom     264**


# PART THREE     Culture and Inclusion


# CHAPTER EIGHT
# Culture and Cultural Diversity and Their Relationship
# to Academic Achievement     266

**Cultural Concepts and Perspectives     266**

What Is Culture?     266
Key Concepts about Culture     268
Looking at Culture from the Inside Out     275
Cultural Diversity: Historical and Contemporary Perspectives     277
Political and Socioeconomic Factors Affecting English Learners and Their Families     278
Educational Issues Involving English Learners beyond the Classroom     280

**Cultural Contact     286**

Fears about Cultural Adaptation     287
Processes of Cultural Contact     287
Psychological and Social–Emotional Issues Involving Cultural Contact     288
Resolving Problems of Cultural Contact     289

**Cultural Diversity in the United States and California     292**

The Demographics of Change     292
Migration and Immigration in the United States and California     293
Contemporary Causes of Migration and Immigration     294
The Cultural and Linguistic Challenges of Diversity     298

**Intercultural Communication     302**

Cultural Diversity in Nonverbal Communication     302
Cultural Diversity in Verbal Communication     304
Strategies for Intercultural Communication in the School and Classroom     307
Teaching Intercultural Communication     308

**Investigating Ourselves as Cultural Beings     309**

The Personal Dimension     309
Cultural Self-Study     309
Participating in Growth Relationships     311


# CHAPTER NINE
# Culturally Inclusive Instruction     312

**The Role of Culture in the Classroom and School     312**

Acknowledging Students' Differences     312
The Alignment of Home and School     312

The Value System of the Teacher and Cultural Accommodation    313
Adapting to Students' Culturally Supported Facilitating or
    Limiting Attitudes and Abilities    323

**Educating Students about Diversity    323**

Global and Multicultural Education    323
The Multicultural Curriculum: From Additive to Transformative    324
Validating Students' Cultural Identity    326
Promoting Mutual Respect among Students    327

**Learning about Students' Cultures    327**

Ethnographic Techniques    327
Students as Sources of Information    329
Families as Sources of Information    329
Community Members as Sources of Information    330
The Internet as an Information Source about Cultures    330

**Culturally Inclusive Learning Environments    330**

What Is a Culturally Supportive Classroom?    330

**Family and Community Involvement    333**

Value Differences in Family and Community Support for Schooling    333
Issues in Family Involvement    333
Myths about Families and Other Communication Barriers    334
Enhancing Home–School Communication    334
Family–Teacher Conferences    334
How Families Can Assist in a Child's Learning    336
Internet Resources for Family Involvement    337
A Model of Home–School Relationships    337
Family Members as Cultural Mediators    337
The Home–School Connection    340
Involving the Family and Community in School Governance    341

**Bibliography    343**

**Name Index    363**

**Subject Index    369**

# PREFACE

To educate English learners, teachers need both basic principles and also specific practices and methods. This book is designed to help teachers to be more effective in expanding English learners' access to the core curriculum, instructing all students with a rich and demanding curriculum, and making crosscultural connections by means of teaching practices and curricular content. This includes a broad foundation in second-language acquisition issues and techniques, the influence of culture on schooling, the cultural practices of schooling, and the sociopolitical context of education, as well as strategies for teaching content subjects such as mathematics, sciences, and social studies.

A *Course in Teaching English Learners* offers an opportunity for educators to access in a single volume the information necessary to educate practicing and prospective teachers in principles for working with students who are English language learners. Not only teachers, but also program coordinators, curriculum developers, administrators, and materials designers can use up-to-date research and methods to work successfully with English language learners.

This work contains the most recent teaching techniques, cultural knowledge, and language proficiency assessment strategies now available, and offers activities to help teachers learn about their English language learners, their families, their communities, their language and cultures. Readers of this book not only learn about theories of language acquisition but also how the theories are applied in the classroom, highlighting successful features of English Language Development programs and drawing examples from the classrooms of practicing teachers.

The California Teachers of English Learners (CTEL) Test, along with the credential and certification efforts of other states, is the chief means by which school districts can be assured that professionals are prepared to meet the needs of English language learners. The *Course* is designed to be a comprehensive review and preparation manual for this certification.

After a brief Introduction that surveys the demographics of English learners across the United States as well as the extent of the need for qualified teachers, Chapter 1 offers fundamentals in the nature of language, including its structure, function, and variation. Chapter 2 introduces language learning, comparing first and second language acquisition processes. Essentials of assessment follow in Chapter 3, which addresses issues of standardized testing under federal mandates and weighs the pros and cons of testing English learners for purposes of placement and evaluation.

Chapter 4 compares program models for educating English learners and includes a discussion of controversies about current legal requirements, best practices, and school reform efforts in the area of bilingual education. Chapters 5 through 7, on specially designed academic content instruction in English (SDAIE) and English language development, offer frameworks within which teachers can plan, implement, and assess their lessons. Chapters 8 and 9, on cultural diversity and culturally inclusive instruction, bring to the fore best practices in motivating English learners toward high academic achievement in line with the values and practices of home and community.

An exciting feature of the book is the inclusion of the end-of-chapter learning activities based on MyLabSchool videos. This encourages practicing and prospective educators to listen to and observe the work of experts in the field of English language development and to model their practice on key ideas that have proven successful in a variety of classrooms.

Teachers who can plan and carry out effective instruction that incorporates knowledge of intercultural communication can be expected to build a base of personal knowledge about the ways in which language, content knowledge, culture, schooling are connected. This book is designed to offer a solid foundation in core techniques, in a manner that balances a growth in theoretical understanding with exposure to effective practice. One goal of this course is to increase teachers' confidence in their teaching ability. Simultaneously, a focus on issues of social justice and a moral commitment to democracy within the context of cultural values and individual rights and responsibilities brings to this book the themes that have sustained and inspired me throughout my professional life. I offer my thanks and tribute to colleagues in the profession of teaching English learners who have shared with me their like-minded dedication.

The methods and strategies included in this course reflect current practice in the field of teaching English learners. Use of a carefully structured tool kit of strategies, with a clear process for use, permits educators to act clearly and consistently as professionals. The complex texture of native and target cultures, native languages, social and political situations, socioeconomic status, and individual differences in learners that one faces when teaching English learners demands continuous innovation and experimentation with teaching and learning strategies.

This book features specific, anecdotal documentation of the use and success of specific strategies in the context of the classroom. Examples in the book are drawn from classrooms in levels kindergarten through high school, across a variety of contexts. I hope that the reader as practitioner can apply these strategies with both immediate and long-term success.

Due to constraints of time and space this book does not include an in-depth coverage of second-language acquisition theory, the complexity of which remains a fascinating subjects of intensive empirical sand theoretical study. I hope instead that the reader will become curious about the issues and research in this field and seek further education in this area.

## MYLABSCHOOL

**mylabschool** is a collection of online tools for your success in this course, on your licensure exams, and in your teaching career. Visit www.mylabschool.com to access the following:

- Video footage of real-life classrooms, with opportunities for you to reflect on the videos and offer your own thoughts and suggestions for applying theory to practice
- An extensive archive of text and multimedia cases that provide valuable perspectives on real classrooms and real teaching challenges
- Allyn & Bacon's Lesson and Portfolio Builder application, which includes an integrated state standards correlation tool
- Research paper assistance using Research Navigator™, which provides access to three exclusive databases of credible and reliable source material: EBSCO's

ContentSelect Academic Journal Database, The *New York Times* Search by Subject Archive, and "Best of the Web" Link Library
■ Career Center with resources for Praxis exams and licensure preparation, professional portfolio development, and job search and interview techniques

## ACKNOWLEDGMENTS

This book was made possible through the help of many people. I credit my editor Aurora Martínez with the vision to foresee the publications needed by teachers of English learners. I wish to thank my colleagues in the field of teaching English to speakers of other languages and applied linguistics for their encouragement, including Larry Selinker, Gertrude Tinker-Sachs, Suchada Nimmannit, Shelley Wong, Connie Williams, Su Motha, Ena Lee, Ryuko Kubota, Natalie Hess, Lia Kamhi-Stein, Suzanne Medina, Stephen Stoynoff, Charles S. Amorosino, Jr., Jun Liu, Sandy Briggs, Elliot Judd, Mabel Gallo, Michele J. Sabino, Liz England, Christine Coombe, Kim-Marie Cole, and so many others. I acknowledge the support of my students, who gave me feedback on early drafts. Thanks to my colleagues at California State University, San Bernardino for their collegial support, including Dr. Bonnie Piller, Jennifer Valleley, Peggy Marcy, and Starley Dullien.

My sincere thanks goes to the editorial staff at Allyn and Bacon, including Lynda Giles, and Diana Neatrour and the team at Omegatype Typography. Also my deep thanks to the reviewers, Laura Alamillo, CSU, Fresno; Emilio Garza, CSU, Bakersfield; and Constance Olivia Williams, for their dedication and diligence.

# INTRODUCTION

# Teaching English Learners

Teachers in elementary and secondary schools in the United States face an unprecedented challenge—educating the growing number of students whose families speak a language other than English or whose backgrounds are culturally diverse. In addition to educating recently arrived immigrants with limited English proficiency, schools need to offer a high-quality, college-bound curriculum to English-speaking students whose heritage is Native American or who are second-generation immigrants.

In the face of this diverse linguistic and cultural terrain, the responsibilities of the U.S. educator have become increasingly complex. Teachers must now modify instruction to meet the specific needs of culturally and linguistically diverse (CLD) students, especially English learners, using English-language development (ELD) techniques and other instructional adaptations to ensure that all students have access to an excellent education. In turn, educators find that these diverse cultures and languages add richness and depth to their teaching experience. The core of the teaching profession in the United States remains the monolingual teacher who can benefit from teacher education that includes specialized methods and strategies for the effective education of CLD students.

Language learning is a complex process that forms the foundation for academic skills. Competence in more than one language is a valuable skill. Students who come to school already speaking a home language other than English have the potential to become bilingual if schooling can preserve and augment their native-language proficiency. One exciting trend is the spread of two-way immersion (TWI) programs, which enable monolingual English-speaking students to learn a second language in the company of English learners.

This book uses the term *English learner* to mean "students whose first (primary, native) language is not English and who are learning English at school." This chapter offers an overview of the demographics of English learners.

## ENGLISH LEARNERS IN U.S. SCHOOLS

### Demographics of English Learners in the United States

The National Clearinghouse for English Language Acquisition and Language Instruction Educational Programs (NCELA, 2004) put the number of English learners (K–12) in the United States at 4.7 million for 2001–2002. Nearly half of the nation's children under age five (45 percent) are racial or ethnic minorities (Cohn & Bahrampour, 2006), and the percentage is increasing mainly because the Hispanic population is growing so rapidly. This accounted for

1

*English learners comprise a growing proportion of school children in the United States.*

49 percent of the country's growth from 2004 to 2005, driving 70 percent of the growth in children younger than five. Of the population under age five, 22 percent is Hispanic.

In 2004, California, with a school enrollment of approximately 1.6 million English learners, led the states in need for English-as-a-second-language (ESL) services at the K–12 level (California Department of Education [CDE], 2006b). Services were delivered in California for students of fifty-six primary languages, including Khmu, Albanian, Marshallese, and Chamorro, with the largest number of students speaking Spanish (85.3 percent) and Vietnamese (2.2 percent).

## Spanish-Speaking English Learners

Given these data, it is not surprising that the majority of households in the United States in which English is not spoken is Spanish-speaking (28.1 million); this represents an increase of 62 percent over the decade 1990 to 2000. Latinos are the fastest-growing segment of the population, with a 3.3 percent growth rate, fueled largely by births rather than immigration (Gaouette, 2006). In 2005, 42.7 million Latinos resided in the United States, constituting 16 percent of the total U.S. population (the terms *Hispanic* and *Latino* are used interchangeably in the census reports). Of the Spanish-speaking households, 66.1 percent are from Mexico or of Mexican-American origin; 14.5 percent from Central or South America; 9 percent from Puerto Rico or of Puerto Rican origin; 4 percent from Cuba or of Cuban-American origin; and 6.4 percent from other Hispanic/Latino origin. Latinos make up more than 30 percent of the population of New York City (Wallraff, 2000) and 39.5 percent of the population of California.

Nearly half of all Latinos live in a central city within a metropolitan area (46.4 percent); more than 45 percent live in the West. Moreover, many Spanish speakers are poor—in 1999, 22.8 percent of all Latinos were living in poverty (compared to 7.7 percent of non-Latino Whites). In addition, Latino children under age eighteen were more likely than non-Latino White children to be living in poverty (30.3 percent versus 9.4 percent) (U.S. Census Bureau, 2000).

## Asian/Pacific English Learners

The second largest non-English-speaking population comprises Asians and Pacific Islanders. In July 2005, the Asian and Pacific Islander population in the United States numbered 14.4 million, constituting 4.8 percent of the population. (*Asian* refers to those having origins in any of the original peoples of the Far East, Southeast Asia, or the Indian subcontinent, including Cambodia, China, India, Japan, Korea, Malaysia, Pakistan, the Philippine Islands, Thailand, and Vietnam. *Pacific Islander* refers to those having origins in any of the original peoples of Hawai'i, Guam, Samoa, or other Pacific islands.)

Like Spanish speakers, the Asian and Pacific Islander population (3.6 percent of the United States) lives in metropolitan areas (nearly 96 percent), with 45 percent living in central cities, double the proportion for non-Hispanic Whites (22 percent) (U.S. Census Bureau, 2001a). Approximately 2.4 percent of these Asians are Chinese speakers, about two million speakers of Chinese (Mandarin). Four out of five of these report that they prefer to speak Chinese at home (Wallraff, 2000).

By and large, then, in the United States, those who educate English learners are more likely to find employment in California, New Mexico, New York, or Texas, in central city schools, serving Hispanics or Asian/Pacific Islanders. Aside from this employment likelihood, however, demographics indicate that services for English learners are needed in every state and large city.

To educate these students, resources are badly needed. However, inner-city schools are faced with large numbers of poor children, fewer books and supplies, and teachers with less training and experience. Thus, excellence in education for English learners is frequently compromised by the fact that such students may be poor and attending underfunded and poorly equipped schools.

## Putting Faces to Demographics

English learners in the United States present a kaleidoscope of faces, languages, and cultures:

Hayat, eleventh grade, refugee from Afghanistan, living in Oakland, California . . .

Rodica, eighth grade, adoptee from Romania, living in Kansas City, Missouri . . .

Viviana, third grade, second-generation Mexican American living in Prescott, Arizona, whose parents speak no English . . .

Muhubo, sixth grade, immigrant from Somalia, living in Lewiston, Maine . . .

Hae Lim, second grade, visitor from Pusan, Korea, "temporarily" living with an aunt in Torrance, California . . .

Lei Li, kindergartner, attending a neighborhood school in Amherst, Massachusetts, while her mother is an international student at a nearby university . . .

Tram, tenth grade, living in inner-city San José, whose parents speak Vietnamese but who has lived in the United States since he was two years old . . .

Augustín, fourth grade, a Trique Indian from San Juan Copala in the Oaxaca state in Mexico, who speaks Spanish as a second language and is learning English as a third language . . .

Juan Ramon, second grade, whose mother recently moved from San Juan, Puerto Rico, to live with relatives in Teaneck, New Jersey . . . .

Some of these students may be offered primary-language instruction as a part of the school curriculum, but those students whose language is represented by few other students in the school district face structured English immersion, with little support in their native language.

### English Learners with Learning Challenges

Some English learners face academic learning challenges in addition to the need to acquire a second language. They may be diagnosed with learning disabilities and referred to special education services; they may suffer culture shock during the process of acculturation; or they may experience other difficulties that require counseling services or situations in which their families are not able to meet their social, emotional, or health needs.

Like their counterparts who are native English speakers, English learners may require special services, including referral to gifted-and-talented programs, resource specialists, reading-resource programs, counseling, or tutoring.

## TEACHING WITH INTEGRITY

This book takes a critical perspective on the education of English learners—one that looks at dual-language proficiency and language policy in the context of broader issues of social equity and social justice. Teachers who develop a deeper understanding of the effects of culture and language on the success—or disenfranchisement—of CLD students through school culture, curricula, and instructional methods are better prepared to promote social change. Teachers with a critical perspective look within, around, and beyond educational issues; ask probing questions about the role of educators in the struggle to attain fairness, justice, equity, and equal opportunity in the world; and work toward social equity and justice as a part of their role as language educators.

One of the major challenges for those who teach English learners is to motivate them to achieve the highest possible level of school achievement. In this process, teachers work to create a classroom environment characterized by equal opportunity and a democratic process so that English learning represents a positive experience for English learners. A second challenge for teachers of English learners is to respect the native language and the rights of its speakers. Teachers who make sincere attempts to learn the languages of their students and build English on students' prior language expertise serve as intercultural and interlingual educators. Only in the context of full support for the bilingual, bicultural learner does the teaching of English respect the learner's linguistic and cultural heritage.

Critical educators are those who teach with integrity (Balderrama & Díaz-Rico, 2006). Their passion for teaching and learning fosters within their students the capacity for joyful lifelong learning, a sense of respect for and pride in their own culture, and a sense of curiosity regarding human diversity. Colleagues can undertake together the task of achieving social justice: equal access to, and opportunity for, quality education for all students. Critical educators advocate an inclusive society in which language, literacy, and culture are integrated with respect and not compromised in any way.

Teachers are intellectual workers, knowledge professionals with cultural expertise. As such, the role of teachers is to help students attain the wisdom and skills the whole community needs in order to prosper. Teachers of English learners teach academic content and English-language development while upholding high professional standards within a context that is humane, academically challenging, grounded in academic knowledge, ethical, upholds intercultural relationships, and promotes educational equity. Teaching with integrity includes six elements. Each is discussed in turn.

## The Willingness to Be Fully Human

First, teachers must be willing to be human and to treat others with humanity. This is partially fulfilled when the teacher deeply believes—and communicates the belief—that teachers and students have equal civil rights in the classroom as well as parity as fellow human beings. One way of looking at the humanity of teaching is to examine the ways in which teachers and students mutually socialize one another in classroom interaction. Cole (2003) has called this *intersubjectivity*—the co-creation of joint activity. Intersubjectivity in the classroom features communication of mutual respect, shared activity, nonverbal immediacy, nonthreatening ways of regarding students, shared pacing, shared space, and the enjoyment of shared cultural commonplaces.

This does not mean teachers act as "buddies" to students, but rather as fully actualized human beings who are able to apologize when wrong, seek peer help when unsure, and grow and learn alongside students. Teachers with integrity have compassion at their core because they are conscious of others' misfortunes and distress and have an active desire to alleviate such hardships.

## High Expectations for Students

A second facet of teaching with integrity is having high academic expectations for students, a deep commitment to the idea that all students can achieve academic success. Teacher expectations operate as a cycle of teacher–student mutual perceptions: Teachers and students form perceptions of each other, and then communicate these to each other, causing both to respond in positive or negative ways (Jussim, 1986).

Recognizing, addressing, and understanding these expectations and how they operate are therefore an integral part of examining the role of a teacher's integrity toward English learners. Teachers must learn to avoid prejudgments and stereotypes so that such negativity does not produce a self-fulfilling prophecy of low achievement. If students have internalized low expectations for themselves, teachers who strive to change students' low academic performance can sow seeds of improved self-esteem. The strongest teachers are those who believe in students' success more than students believe in their own failure. Teachers with flexible expectations readily revise their impressions when direct information about student achievement is available.

## Being "Fully Qualified"

A third aspect of teaching with integrity is *expertise in content.* The No Child Left Behind federal education legislation (2001) specifically requires schools to employ teachers who are fully qualified in the areas they will instruct. Two areas of content expertise related specifically to English learners that are not often required—but should be—are the following: (1) theories and pedagogy relevant to teaching English learners academic literacy and (2) some degree of proficiency in the primary language of their students.

Given the existing linguistic diversity prevalent in U.S. classrooms, these two areas of expertise are central to the implementation of content knowledge. The widely accepted mythology in the United States that a person can be well educated and remain monolingual is questionable with regard to being "fully qualified" as an educator. The Latino population has become the largest minority in the United States, and educators who are able to augment their teaching using both second-language acquisition principles and Spanish-language skills are increasingly needed.

## Maintaining Professional Ethics

A fourth aspect of teaching with integrity is ethical teaching. The educator with ethics upholds the morals of the profession of teaching, which include believing in the worth and dignity of each human being and recognizing the supreme importance of democratic principles (National Education Association, Code of Ethics of the Education Profession, 1975). Teachers with integrity are educators with ethics who recognize the importance of professional conduct and are willing to accept a role in protecting the freedom to teach and learn, and they work toward providing equal educational opportunity for all.

The code of ethics includes aspects of the teacher's commitment to the student. For example, teachers shall not knowingly distort subject matter relevant to the student's progress; grant advantage or deny benefit on the grounds of race, color, creed, sex, national origin, marital status, political or religious beliefs, family, social or cultural background, or sexual orientations; or use professional relationships with students for private advantage (such as receiving money for private tutoring after school the same students they teach during the day—this represents a conflict of interest).

Other aspects of ethical behavior address an educator's commitment to the profession. These ethical principles, for example, forbid misrepresentation of one's qualifications, disclosing information about colleagues obtained during the course of professional service, and receiving gifts or favors that might compromise one's professional decisions. *Ethical Issues for*

*ESL Faculty* (Hafernik, Messerschmitt, & Vandrick, 2002) touches on problematic issues that may arise when students come from countries with social norms that are quite different than those in the United States.

## Being an Intercultural Educator

Fifth, a teacher with integrity has an intercultural repertoire. The ability to communicate effectively with people from other cultures is the hallmark of the intercultural educator. According to Smith, Paige, and Steglitz (1998), a person with an *intercultural perspective* has incorporated a set of core elements into hisor her repertoire that facilitate, and form the foundation for, intercultural communication. These core elements are complex and subtle, yet represent a clear and useful body of knowledge, skills, and dispositions that educators need to function professionally in a diverse society.

These elements are as follows. Intercultural educators engage in face-to-face interactive communication that shows sensitivity to the different ways in which individuals construct their social reality, involves the whole person in a compassionate manner, and takes into consideration the social context of the communication. Intercultural educators recognize that they must work on themselves in order to progress from ethnocentric to ethnorelative views. An individual's culture provides tools to interpret reality only one way; intercultural educators must move beyond this limitation. Intercultural education is further discussed in Chapter 9.

## Clarity of Vision

The sixth and last facet of integrity is clarity of vision: being able to see clearly the social and political realities surrounding teaching. Fundamental questions surround the teaching of English learners. Why do individual students achieve, whereas others fail academically? Why is there disproportionate academic failure between groups of students, particularly between majority Whites and African Americans, Latinos, English learners, or low-income students, for example? Why do those with European-American origin, or who are White, monolingual-English-speaking students, including those who come from high-income groups, succeed disproportionately? Thinking teachers interrogate those processes that affect their teaching and professional performance; and, in turn, they sustain political and ideological insight about the process of schooling and their role as teachers.

This political clarity is important if teachers are to act with power and facilitate student empowerment. First and foremost, teachers can function as more conscientious professionals when they understand the larger social and political forces that affect their professional lives. With this understanding, teachers can confront social and political forces with the tools to change those aspects of society that undermine educational success, particularly for low-status student groups such as English learners.

As suggested in the definition of political clarity, teachers must be cognizant that they do not teach in a vacuum, but that instead their work is interconnected with broader social processes that affect their teaching. Commonly accepted belief systems explain and rationalize the existing social order. How do teachers explain the fact that multilingualism is facilitated for the privileged but not encouraged for those students who come from lower socioeconomic backgrounds? The ideology of unexamined beliefs affects teaching and schooling practices at the level of microinteractions of daily classroom life.

Social institutions such as schools play major roles in maintaining and perpetuating social processes important to society. Certain groups manage to dominate others and determine how people in positions of privilege maintain those positions with the support and approval of the disempowered—a process Leistyna, Woodrum, and Sherblom (1996) define as *hegemony,* the unexamined acceptance of the social order—even when the social classes in power make decisions that disempower others.

Beliefs about language are powerful hegemonic devices, intimately connected to social position. For example, hegemonic beliefs about second-language acquisition in the United States privileges French above Spanish as a preferred foreign language of study and stigmatizes non-native speakers of English in the role of English teachers, privileging native speakers of English. However, at every opportunity, teachers with integrity oppose attitudes based on hegemonic ideas or folk beliefs, upholding professional practices that are substantiated by research or infused with clarity of vision about the all-too-hidden processes that perpetuate unequal power relations and inequality.

Teaching with integrity means wholeness in all that teachers do. This implies a genuine vision of social justice in the classroom. Teachers with integrity are able to sustain their humanity in the face of potentially dehumanizing forces that would reduce teaching and learning to mechanical enterprises devoid of intrinsic interest and personal investment (Freire, 1970; Bartolomé, 1994; Giroux, 1988). As suggested earlier, teaching English learners is a challenging and complex task requiring both integrity in teaching and pedagogical skills and knowledge along various dimensions of instruction. Teaching with integrity provides a model for a professional approach that is humane, student-centered, and equitable.

## THE PROFESSIONAL PREPARATION OF TEACHERS TO EDUCATE ENGLISH LEARNERS

School districts seeking highly qualified teachers for English-language development programs employ teachers with bilingual certification who can deliver primary-language education, in recognition of the fact that these teachers have additional preparation and expertise relevant to their position. These teachers are expected to deliver ELD instruction along with primary-language instruction in literacy and in content areas. In states where structured English immersion (content delivery in English without support for primary-language literacy) is the specified model for English learners, teachers use specially designed academic instruction in English (SDAIE) strategies in addition to ELD.

The availability of employment as a teacher in the United States, then, depends on local population demographics, the role of ELD teaching in relation to bilingual education, and the local need for teachers qualified for ELD. One fact, however, remains a constant: the current shortage of teachers in U.S. classrooms. The United States is expected to need from two to four million teachers by 2010 (Chan, 2004). The teacher shortage is particularly acute in urban areas, where 40 to 50 percent of English learners are found. Almost half of new teachers leave the profession within five years, and the rate is even higher in low-income communities (National Commission on Teaching and America's Future, 2002). Districts are setting aside funds for training new teachers, raising starting salaries for teachers, and recruiting teachers for bilingual education. The employability outlook has never been better for teachers who specialize in teaching English learners.

## Career Preparation for Teachers

To prepare for teaching English learners, an individual can pursue various levels of precareer preparation, from BA programs with a special emphasis, to post-BA teacher credential programs, to MA programs that include teacher certification. The website of the organization Teachers of English to Speakers of Other Languages (TESOL, Inc., www.tesol.org) has a link (www.tesol.org/careers/seekers-faq1.html#2) that may help to clarify these terms and the important differences that distinguish these preparation programs and levels of career training. Despite the widely varying career ladders available to educators, the demand for English-language teaching professionals has steadily grown, not only in the United States but also throughout the world.

Because each state has the authority to set its own requirements for the certification of teachers, states vary in their professional requirements for teachers of English learners. The website www.ncela.gwu.edu/policy/states/index.htm offers a complete listing of requirements for teaching English learners by state.

The field of teaching English learners is equally open to those whose native language is English and those who are non-native speakers. An individual who has learned English as a speaker of another language and has achieved some measure of bilingual competence is uniquely qualified to understand the needs of English learners (see Brutt-Griffler & Samimy, 1999). TESOL's Nonnative English Speakers in TESOL (NNEST) Caucus (http://nnest.moussu.net) can provide more information about this topic.

The Internet can help to provide a broad picture of the possibilities available to those who specialize in teaching English learners. The Center for Research on Education, Diversity, and Excellence at the University of California, Santa Cruz offers a range of resources, including research articles and teaching guides (online at www-rcf.usc.edu/~cmmr/crede.html). The Center for Multilingual Multicultural Research at the University of Southern California contains links to scholarships and teacher training programs (online at www.usc.edu/dept/education/CMMR).

## Professional Organizations for Teachers

Teachers of English learners choose as their major professional affiliation such organizations as the National Association for Bilingual Education (NABE, online at www.nabe.org), Teachers of English to Speakers of Other Languages (TESOL, Inc., online at www.tesol.org), National Council of Teachers of English (NCTE, online at www.ncte.org), International Reading Association (IRA, online at www.ira.org), or state, regional, or local affiliates of these organizations. These organizations increasingly include a focus on English learners in their publications and conference sessions. However, NABE and TESOL are the only U.S.-based professional organizations with the teaching of English learners as their central mission.

## Information about Teaching English Learners

The professional information available from the National Clearinghouse for English Language Acquisition (online at www.ncela.gwu.edu) includes an archive of newsletters, a conference calendar, links to scholarly journals, statistics about English learners, and resources on heritage languages. For Tagalog, for example, NCELA's website offers links to Tagalog (Filipino) curriculum materials, multilingual books in Tagalog, and lists of language and cultural resources, Web resources and organizations, and a listing of colleges and universities in North America that teach Tagalog.

*It is not necessary to be a native English speaker to teach English learners.*

For ELD teaching, Dave's ESL Cafe (www.eslcafe.com) is a popular site for English learning, featuring chatrooms, an online bookstore, job listings, and sections on slang, idioms, and other language-teaching tips. The site also includes 3,020 links to other topics (flash cards, multicultural issues, lesson plans, online help, newsgroups, and tongue twisters, to name a few categories).

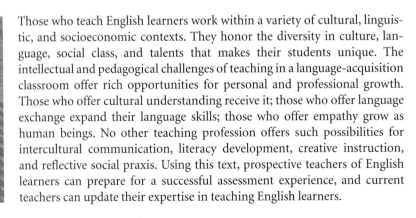

Those who teach English learners work within a variety of cultural, linguistic, and socioeconomic contexts. They honor the diversity in culture, language, social class, and talents that makes their students unique. The intellectual and pedagogical challenges of teaching in a language-acquisition classroom offer rich opportunities for personal and professional growth. Those who offer cultural understanding receive it; those who offer language exchange expand their language skills; those who offer empathy grow as human beings. No other teaching profession offers such possibilities for intercultural communication, literacy development, creative instruction, and reflective social praxis. Using this text, prospective teachers of English learners can prepare for a successful assessment experience, and current teachers can update their expertise in teaching English learners.

# CHAPTER ONE

# Language Structure and Use

## AH, LANGUAGE!

Verbal language is unique to human beings. It allows us to express our deepest feelings, our broadest concepts, our highest ideals. It takes us beyond the here and now, and even beyond the possible—by means of language, we might join the attackers at the siege of Troy or journey through the looking glass with Alice. Language can connect humans as children listen to stories before the fireplace on a cold winter night; or it can, together with culture, divide two peoples into bitter sectarian warfare. Language communicates the heights of joy and the depths of despair.

Language equalizes—preschoolers as well as professors can be considered native speakers of their first language. Alternatively, language reflects inequality—dialect distinctions often demarcate social class. Almost all aspects of a person's life are touched by language. Language is universal, and yet each language has evolved to meet the experiences, needs, and desires of that language's community.

Understanding language structure and use provides teachers with essential tools to help students learn. All languages share universal features, such as the ability to label objects and to describe actions and events. All languages are divided into various subsystems (phonology, morphology, syntax, semantics, and pragmatics). What is most amazing is that language users learn all these subsystems of their first language without realizing it—native speakers are not necessarily able to explain a sound pattern, a grammatical point, or the use of idiomatic expression. To them, that is "just the way it is." Language, then, is a system that works even without conscious awareness, an inborn competence that unfolds and matures when given adequate stimulation from others.

This chapter explores these various aspects of language and provides suggestions to help English-language development (ELD) teachers identify student needs and provide appropriate instruction. Knowledge about language structure and use also helps teachers recognize the richness and variety of students' language skills in both first and second languages. Linguistic knowledge—not only about English but also about the possibilities inherent in languages that differ from English—helps teachers view the language world of the English learner with insight and empathy.

## LANGUAGE UNIVERSALS

At last count, 6,912 languages are spoken in today's world (SIL International, 2000). Although not all of these have been intensely studied, linguists have carried out enough investigations over the centuries to posit some universal facts about language.

## All Languages Have Structure

All human languages use a finite set of sounds (or gestures) that are combined to form meaningful elements or words, which themselves form an infinite set of possible sentences. Every spoken language also uses discrete sound segments—phonemes—such as /t/, /m/, or /e/, and has a class of vowels and a class of consonants.

All grammars contain rules for the formation of words and sentences of a similar kind, and similar grammatical categories (for example, nouns and verbs) are found in all languages. Every language has a way of referring to past time; the ability to negate; and the ability to form questions, issue commands, and so on.

Although human languages are specific to their places of use and origin (for example, languages used by seafaring cultures have more specific words for oceanic phenomena than do languages used by desert tribes), semantic universals, such as "male" or "female," are found in every language in the world. No matter how exotic a language may appear to a native English speaker, all human languages in fact share the same features, most of which are lacking in the language of apes, dolphins, or birds.

## Language Is Dynamic

Languages change over time. Pronunciation (phonology) changes—across 400 years, for example, Shakespeare's plays often feature scene-ending couplets whose words may have rhymed in his day but do not rhyme in modern translations. We recognize that pronunciation in English has altered over time, because the spelling of some words is archaic: We no longer pronounce the /k/ in *knight* or the /w/ in *write*. Semantics change over time: Words disappear, such as the archaic English words *bilbo, costermonger, fluey,* and *shew.* Words expand their meanings, such as *geek* and *mouse.* New words appear, such as *supermegapixel* and *paraspam.* Some languages change more than others: Written Icelandic has changed relatively little since the thirteenth century, whereas writers for *Wired,* a New York–based technology magazine, coin an average of 30 new words in English with each month's edition.

Teachers who respect the dynamic nature of language can take delight in learners' approximations of English. When Chinese speakers fail to produce past-tense markers (*Yesterday I download a file),[1] they may be speaking the English of the future, when the past-tense morpheme (-d, -ed, -t) may be dropped, just as the second-person inflection (-est, as in "thou goest") has disappeared.

## Language Is Complex

Without question, using language is one of the most complex of human activities, yet it provides the human race with a psychological tool unmatched in power and flexibility. It is normal for humans no matter what their native language to be able to communicate a wide range of concepts, both concrete and abstract. All languages are equally complex, capable of expressing a wide range of ideas, and expandable to include new words for new concepts. Motu, one of 715 indigenous languages in Papua New Guinea, has a complex vocabulary for indigenous plants,

---

[1]An asterisk (*) before a word or a sentence indicates that it is phonetically or grammatically incorrect.

whereas Icelandic has an elaborate system of kinship names that allows people to trace their ancestry for hundreds of years.

Language is arbitrary, meaning that we cannot guess the meaning of a word from its sound (except for a few words such as *buzz*)—there is no inherent reason to link the sound and meaning of a word. Because the meaning–symbol connection is arbitrary, language gains an abstracting power removed from direct ties to the here-and-now of objects or events. Moreover, language is open-ended—an infinite set of sentences can be produced in any language.

Even though language is complicated, every healthy child—regardless of racial, geographical, social, or economic heritage—is capable of learning any language to which he or she is exposed. By the age of five, most children have learned how to make well-formed sentences in their native language and are thus considered native speakers. Although some students may be shy or their language skills delayed in development, it is incorrect to say that a young child "doesn't have language."

# PHONOLOGY: THE SOUND PATTERNS OF LANGUAGE

Phonology is that part of a language describing sounds and sound changes. Phonetics is that part of linguistics that deals with the following: (1) speech sounds, (2) how these are made vocally, (3) sound changes that develop in languages, and (4) the relation of speech sounds to the entire language process (Heilman, 2002, p. 4).

---

**▌ DID YOU KNOW**
**Is It English?**

These activities illustrate the characteristics of the English sound system:

- Which of the following are *possible* English words and which would be *impossible* because they do not fit the English sound system? *stgmonic, chetelogo, ndele, tassitic*

  (Answer: not *stgmonic* and *ndele*—they contain non-English-like consonant clusters)

- Products are often brought to the market with names that use phonemic enhancement: The gasoline company and product Esso was renamed Exxon in 1973 in part because test marketing showed that people responded more strongly to the looks and sound of the double *X* then the double *S*.

---

## Phonemes

Phonemes are the individual sounds in a language, the distinctive units that "make a difference" when sounds distinguish words. For example, in English the initial consonant sounds /p/ and /b/ are the only difference between the words *park* and *bark* and thus are phonemes. The number of phonemes in a language ranges between twenty and fifty; English has a high average count, from thirty-four to forty-five, depending on the dialect. Hawai'ian, in contrast, has one of the lowest phoneme counts, with eight consonants and ten vowels. Table 1.1 lists the phonemes in English (using the International Phonetic Alphabet) with example words.

**TABLE 1.1**    Phonemes in English: Vowels and Consonants

| Vowels | Examples | Consonants | Examples |
|---|---|---|---|
| /A/ | wake, pain, tray | /b/ | bet, habit, rub |
| /a/ | pat | /k/ | cake, naked, lack |
| /E/ | be, beat, flee | /d/ | do, sadder, wed |
| /e/ | set | /f/ | far, offer, half, phony |
| /I/ | I, tie, by | /g/ | gone, digger, beg |
| /i/ | if, tin | /h/ | head, behold |
| /O/ | no, moat, stone | /j/ | jam, tragic, stage, ledge |
| /o/ | pot | /l/ | light, willow, well |
| /U/ | futile, Tuesday | /m/ | mine, dim |
| /u/ | cup, dumb | /n/ | none, fun, Lynne |
| /OO/ | to, rue, chew, boot | /p/ | push, topple, step |
| /oo/ | soot, put | /kw/ | quiet |
| /oi/ | toil, boy | /r/ | rope, Larry, bar |
| /ou/ | pout, how, mouse | /s/ | sip, hustle, miss |
| /aw/ | saw, call, caught | /t/ | tip, after, bat |
| /ar/ | far | /v/ | vet, hover, gave |
| | | /w/ | wag, away |
| | | /ks/ or /gz/ | sox, exit |
| | | /y/ | your, yet |
| | | /z/ | zip, noisy, buzz |
| | | /sh/ | shout, lotion, wash |
| | | /hw/ | what |
| | | /ch/ | chop, pitch |
| | | /th/ | thing, southside, north |
| | | /th/ or $\partial$ | that, mother, soothe |
| | | /ng/ | wing, running |
| | | /zh/ | genre, collision, pleasure |

If phonemic variations do not distinguish words, they are considered variations of one phoneme rather than completely different phonemes. For example, in English—at least in the Pittsburgh dialect—the name "Lynne" is pronounced with the tongue to the back of the roof of the mouth, whereas when pronouncing the name "Linda" the tongue is tipped farther forward. However, both are acceptable versions of the /l/ phoneme because this difference alone does not distinguish two word meanings, as does the difference between *pan* and *ban*.

English learners' aural comprehension and pronunciation may be affected when English words contain phonemes that are unfamiliar to them. The schwa (the sound of the "e" in the phrase "the hat") is often difficult for Spanish speakers because Spanish vowels rarely alter their sound quality in unaccented syllables. A digraph—a pair of letters used to write one sound or a combination of sounds that does not correspond to the written letters combined—may confuse the English learner who attempts to separate the digraph into two separate phonemes. The concept of diphthong (defined as a vowel blend with two adjacent vowels, each of which is sounded) may transfer in principle from another language, although the diphthongs may differ from language to language. Mandarin has diphthongs (*shyueh*), as does Spanish (*hay*).

---

**▌ DID YOU KNOW?**

**English Phonemes Not Found in Other Languages**

Certain phonemes in English do not exist in certain other languages. English learners from these backgrounds might experience difficulty in hearing and producing these sounds.

Not in Japanese: /dg/ /f/ /i/ /th/ /oo/ /v/ /schwa/

Not in Spanish: /dg/ /j/ /sh/ /th/ /z/

---

*Phonemic sequences* are the permissible ways in which phonemes can be combined in a language. Languages also have permissible places for these sequences: initial (at the beginning of a word), medial (between initial and final position), and final (at the end of a word), or in a combination of these positions. In English, /spr/ as in *spring,* /nd/ as in *handle,* and /kt/ as in *talked* are permissible phonemic sequences, but neither /nd/ nor /kt/ can be used initially (*ndaft* is not permissible). English uses /sp/ in all three positions—*speak, respect, grasp*—but uses /pt/ in only one—*apt* (the word *optic* splits the phonemes into two syllables; the word *pterodactyl* has a silent *p*).

Phonemes can be described in terms of their characteristic point of articulation (tip, front, or back of the tongue), the manner of articulation (the way the airstream is obstructed), and whether the vocal cords vibrate or not (voiced versus voiceless sounds). Table 1.2 shows the English stops (phonemes that are produced by completely blocking the breath stream and then releasing it abruptly). The point placements given in the chart relate to the positions in the mouth from which the sound is produced. Not all languages distinguish between voiced and voiceless sounds. Arabic speakers may say "barking lot" instead of "parking lot" because to them /p/ and /b/ are not distinguishable.

**TABLE 1.2** Point of Articulation for Voiced and Voiceless English Stops

| | Labial | | | Dental | | |
|---|---|---|---|---|---|---|
| **Point** | **Bilabial** | **Labiodental** | **Interdental** | **Alveolar** | **Palatal** | **Velar** |
| voiceless | *p* | | | *t* | | *k* |
| voiced | *b* | | | *d* | | *g* |

## CLASSROOM GLIMPSE: Pronunciation Bingo

*While studying the unit "Our Community," Mrs. Fogarty has the students generate the names of the streets on which they live. Students then write these street names on blank bingo cards. Various students serve as "callers" to pull the street names from a container and read them to their classmates. Correct pronunciation distinguishes between similar sounding names (First versus Fourth Streets). As the caller pronounces the street name, the rest of the class practices auditory discrimination.*

## BEST PRACTICE: Pronunciation Self-Correction

The teacher can encourage pronunciation self-correction in the following ways:

- Writing overheard utterances on the board (without identifying the student) for the class as a whole to practice
- Pointing to a wall chart with typically mispronounced items (for example, the pronunciation of *-ed* and *-s* endings, *r/l* errors, basic word stress rules, and sentence intonations)
- Offering students pronunciation software that has a recording feature so students can receive feedback (Goodwin, Brinton, & Celce-Murcia, 1994)

Even though pronunciation practice is essential, teachers should not stigmatize English learners or require them to repeat phrases aloud in front of other students. Pronunciation practice should be private.

### Stress     *Betonung / Lautstärke*

Characteristics of language sounds beyond the phoneme are stress, pitch/tone, and intonation. Stress, the amount of volume a speaker gives to a particular sound, operates at two levels: word and sentence. Stress is a property of syllables—stressed syllables are longer and louder than unstressed syllables. In some languages, stress is predictable; in Czech, stress is usually on the first syllable of a word; in French, on the last syllable of a phrase. Stress is difficult to learn in English because there are "no consistent rules" (Dale & Poms, 2005, p. 84). Incorrect stress can alter the meaning of words. Within words, specific syllables are stressed. In the following examples, the stressed syllable is indicated by the accent mark ´:

| | |
|---|---|
| *désert* | noun, "dry region" |
| *dessért* | noun, "sweet foods after the main meal" |
| *ínvalid* | noun, as in "person with long-term, debilitating illness" |
| *inválid* | adjective, as in "null, void" (Dale & Poms, 2005, p. 84) |

Stress can further be used at the sentence level to vary emphasis. For example, the following sentences all carry different emphases:

Kímberly walked home. (It was Kimberly who walked home.)

Kimberly wálked home. (She walked; she did not ride.)

She walked hóme. (She walked home, not to Grandma's house.)

In some cases, the wrong stress on a word completely undermines comprehension.

## CLASSROOM GLIMPSE: A Misplaced Word Stress

*Rashid sat down, shoulders slumped. "I'm beginning to get discouraged. People don't understand my speaking."*

*"Give me an example," I suggested.*

*Rashid continued, "At lunch my friend was eating something mashed. I said 'That looks like potty toe.' She gave me a strange look."*

*"Potty toe?" I asked. "What in the world do you mean? You'd better write down the word." (He wrote the word.)*

*"Oh!" I exclaimed, looking at the paper. "Potato!"*

Students who learn a second language sometimes have difficulty altering the sound of a word in the context of whole sentences. Thus, teachers are better served by teaching words in context rather than in lists.

### Pitch and Rhythm          Tonhöhe

Beyond the phoneme, other sound qualities are important in oral speech. Pitch at the word level or at the sentence level is one of the phonological components of a language that plays an important role in determining meaning. *Tone languages* use the pitch of individual syllables to contrast meanings (examples are Thai, Mandarin, Vietnamese, Zulu, Apache, Navajo, and Kiowa). "Eva is going," as a statement, is said with a rise on the syllable "go," followed by "-ing" with a falling pitch; but said as a question, the pitch rises at the end.

Pitch interacts with word stress to produce prosody, the underlying rhythm of the language. The way an individual word fits into a sentence may change the stress. For example, in the sentence "He's my uncle—Uncle Bob," the first use of "uncle" is heavily stressed on the first syllable because the syllable is placed in the first clause at the climax of the prosodic contour, just before the final pitch drop. During the second "uncle," neither syllable is stressed, because the name "Bob" carries the emphasis, hence the stress.

Because English words are pronounced with different phonemes depending on their place in a sentence, in contrast to Spanish, in which the vowels are more apt to maintain their sound values irrespective of their place in the sentence, Spanish speakers may have difficulty achieving the prosody of the native speaker of English.

Typical problems in oral speech are pronouncing all words with equal emphasis, avoiding contractions (thus sounding stilted), and pausing incorrectly between words. To achieve proper prosody, words in phrases are blended together and functional words are reduced in emphasis ("How are you" sounds like "Howaru?"), and sounds are linked across words, so that "We've eaten" sounds like "We veaten." Smooth prosody is a combination of phrasing and pausing: "Please//do your chores//before you go out."

## Intonation Patterns

The use of pitch to modify the sentence meaning is called *intonation*. Each language has a distinctive sound flow across the sentence. English has a pattern characterized by accented and unaccented syllables, the same patterns that are found in English poetry. The *iamb* is a beat with one unaccented syllable followed by an accented one, as in the phrase "too late to go." An *anapest* is a beat with two unaccented syllables followed by an accented one: "in the heat of the night." Most sentences in English combine accented and unaccented syllables in an undulating rhythm until just before the end of the sentence, at which time the pitch rises and then drops briefly.

In contrast, Cantonese, as a tonal language, has intonation variation that distinguishes words by tone, but an entire sentence does not have a rise-and-fall curve. Because English requests, for example, make use of a questioning intonation to soften the demanding tone ("Could you sit down over there?"), a Cantonese speaker may sound impolite to English ears ("Could! You! Go! Sit! Down! Over! There!"). Intonation matters a great deal when language fulfills social functions.

*Contrastive analysis*—paying careful attention to phonemic differences between languages and then spending more time teaching those phonemes that differ—has been found to be relatively nonproductive as a teaching methodology. There is little evidence that learners will find genereal phonemic differences between languages to be difficult. *Error analysis*, however, can guide teachers; making careful note of a learner's difficulties can provide evidence about the need for specific interventions. Empirical teaching—teaching guided by data—helps to focus phonological training directly on the learner's difficulties.

## Teaching Pronunciation

Correct pronunciation, including phoneme production, stress, pitch, and prosody, is one of the most difficult features of learning a second language. Native speakers acquire the phonology of their native language by listening to and producing speech. The same is true to some degree in a second language, but by using audiolingual methods (see Chapter 2) there is a role for such phonemic drills as minimum pair work (*bit/pit, hill/hail, dog/dock*). Beyond word-level pronunciation, students can practice sentence-level intonation.

Teachers can help students practice intonation by leading choral reading, one clause at a time, repeated once. This differs from a regular read-aloud because the explicit purpose here is to practice prosody. Learners may benefit from looking at a chart representing a normal sentence curve. As a declarative sentence is read aloud, the teacher—or a lead student—traces the progression of the intonation pattern across the curve. A question would require a different demonstration curve. This helps English learners listen for and replicate the desired prosody.

## CLASSROOM GLIMPSE: Pronunciation, Intonation, and Stress

*Primary-grade teachers use chants, rhymes, and songs as a natural part of their teaching. In the higher grades, many teachers invite students to write their own songs based on the current topic of study. For example, when studying geometry, one teacher taught students to distinguish types of triangles using the following song to the tune "Clementine": "Equilateral, has the sides equal/ Isosceles has a pair/ Scalene—angles all acute/ Right—one angle like a square." Table 1.3 offers some games that can be used to teach intonation and prosody in English.*

**TABLE 1.3**    Activities to Teach Intonation in English

| Name of Activity | Description | Language-Acquisition Level |
|---|---|---|
| Consonant Memory | One student completes a sentence with a target consonant sound. The next student repeats the sentence and adds another word containing the same sound. ("I went on vacation and packed a dog [doll, dish].") | Beginning, Early Intermediate |
| Plural Practice Bragging | Students make up closets full of clothes, refrigerators full of food, or garages full of vehicles. ("I have twelve cars and ten bicycles.") | Beginning, Early Intermediate |
| Three Verb Tag | Prepare lists of three past-tense verbs at a time, one of which has a different ending sound (*baked, cleaned, cooked*—answer is *cleaned*). See how many "odd" verbs each student can "tag." | Beginning to Intermediate |
| Yes/No Interview | Students formulate questions to ask one another that are answered by brief affirmative or negative sentences. ("Do you like school?" "Yes, I like it a lot.") | Early Intermediate, Intermediate |
| Tongue Twister | Students make up their own tongue twisters using words from the dictionary with the target consonant in the initial position. | Early Intermediate to Advanced |
| Found a Dog | Students write fake ads about finding a dog that contain two or three sentences. Each student gets a turn reading aloud his or her dog description. | Early Intermediate to Advanced |
| Contraction Interview | Students interview each other for five facts. When they present these facts about their partner aloud to the class, they must use three contractions. ("He's on a soccer team.") | Early Intermediate to Advanced |

*Source:*    Adapted from Dale & Poms (2005).

Teachers who overemphasize exact pronunciation when learners are in the early stages of learning English may hinder the innovative spirit of risk-taking that is preferable when a learner is trying to achieve fluency. Teaching intonation through fun activities such as chants and songs brings enjoyment to language learning. On the other hand, at higher levels of proficiency it is essential to provide the learner with corrective feedback.

If an older learner has serious accent issues—to the point of unintelligibility—computer software such as that available from Auralog (www.auralog.com) can provide individualized tutoring. Such pronunciation software is excellent for the specific, repetitive drills needed to develop a more native-sounding accent. Many such programs allow the user to record speech and then compare the recording with a norm; some even show a graphic representation of the speech tone for purposes of comparison. Students can work in privacy at a listening center or in a computer laboratory.

Learners of English can look for phonological cues in word structure only when the pronunciation is regular. For example, knowing the pronunciation for *bad* will help with *had*, *Dad*, *pad*, and *fad*, but not with *wad*. Still, many phonics-based reading approaches carefully control the learner's exposure to vocabulary, focusing on words that are phonetically regular during the learner's early reading phase. This can lead to some contrived text, such as Learning Pyramid's *Miss Nell Fell in the Well* (Whitman, 1994). One solution would be to balance the use of controlled readers with read-aloud texts that expose the learner to a broader range of phonemes during listening comprehension.

To ensure that adequate attention is paid to phonology, two principles to keep in mind when evaluating ELD programs are the following: First, does the program offer the teacher an ample set of tools to explain, practice, and review pronunciation in a structured way? Second, does the program balance texts based on strict sound–symbol correspondence with texts that expose the reader or listener to a naturally occurring set of phonemes, a set that mirrors the distribution of phonemes in everyday speech?

## ■■■ MORPHOLOGY: THE WORDS OF LANGUAGE

Morphology is the study of the meaning units in a language. In some cases in English, individual words constitute these basic meaning units (e.g., *chase*). However, many words can be broken down into smaller segments—morphemes—that still retain meaning.

### Morphemes

Morphemes, small units that cannot be further subdivided, are the basic building blocks of meaning. *Fundamentalists* is an English word composed of five morphemes: *funda* + *ment* + *al* + *ist* + *s* (root + noun-forming suffix + adjective-forming suffix + noun-forming suffix + plural marker). Morphemes can be represented by a single sound, such as /a/ (as a morpheme, this has two meanings; "a" can be a stand-alone, or free, morpheme meaning an indefinite article ["a girl"], or it can be a bound morpheme (["a-"] meaning *without*, as in *amoral* or *asexual*). Morphemes can be a single syllable, such as the noun-forming suffix *-ment* in *amendment*, or two or more syllables, such as in *lion* or *parsley*. Two different morphemes may have the same sound, such as the *-er* in dan*cer* ("one who dances") and the /er/ in fanc*ier* (the comparative form of *fancy*). A morpheme may also have alternate phonetic forms: The regular plural *-s* can be pronounced either /z/ (*bags*), /s/ (*cats*), or /iz/ (*bushes*).

Morphemes are of different types and serve different purposes. Free morphemes can stand alone (*envelope, the, through*), whereas bound morphemes occur only in conjunction with others (*-ing, dis-, -ceive*), either as *affixes* or as *bound roots*. Affixes at the beginning of words are *prefixes* (*un-* in the word *unafraid*); those added at the end are *suffixes* (*-able* in the word *believable*); and *infixes* are morphemes that are inserted between other morphemes (*s-* in *mothers-in-law*).

Part of the power and flexibility of English is the ease with which longer English words are formed by adding prefixes and suffixes to root words (cycle, cyclist; fix, fixation). The predictability of meaning carried by standard affixes can make it easier for students to learn to infer words from context rather than to rely on rote memorization.

## BEST PRACTICE: Working with Morphemes

To generate interest in science concepts, at the beginning of each general science unit Mrs. Silvestri selected several roots from a general list (*astro, bio, geo, hydr, luna, photo, phys, terr*). She then asked students to work in pairs to search their texts for words with those roots from the relevant chapter in the science text. Next she handed out a list of prefixes and affixes and asked each pair to generate five to ten new words, including definitions. Students wrote each new word and its definition on two index cards and played a memory matching game with their card decks.

### Word-Formation Processes

English has historically been a language that has borrowed extensively from other languages or coined new ones from existing words. Studying how new words are formed—largely from existing morphemes—helps English learners understand morphemes. Table 1.4 displays new words that have been published in *Wired* magazine in recent years. Each word is derived in part from an existing word in English.

**Clipping**   Clipping is a process of shortening words, such as *prof* for *professor* or the slangy *teach* for *teacher*. If students learn both the original and the clipped version, they gain the sense that they are mastering both colloquial and academic speech.

**Acronyms**   In English, *acronyms* are plentiful, and many are already familiar to students—USA, CNN, and NASA, for example. A list of acronyms helps students increase their vocabulary of both the words forming the acronyms and the acronyms themselves. Who can resist knowing that *laser* is light amplification by stimulated emission of radiation?

**Blends**   Words formed from parts of two words are called blends—for example, *chortle* from *chuckle* + *snort*, and *travelogue* from *travel* + *monologue*. Students can become word detectives and discover new blends (*Spanglish, jazzercise, rockumentary*) or create their own blends (a hot dog in a hamburger bun can be a *hotburger*).

### Using Morphemes in Teaching

Students can add to their enjoyment of learning English by finding new words and creating their own. Those who play video games can make up new names for characters using morphemes that

**TABLE 1.4**    Neologisms (New Words and Phrases) from *Wired* Magazine (April 2006)

| New Word | Derivation | Meaning |
|---|---|---|
| @homer | @ = at + home + er | one who stays at home |
| funkatizing | funk + atize + ing | making something funky |
| geekonomics | geek + economics | finance for computer aficionados |
| geek-year | geek + year | like "dog year"; different timescale for nerds |
| middleware | middle + ware as in hardware ↔ software | hybrid form of hardware-software |
| office-chairy | office chair + like | adj. form of office chair |
| paraspam | para = almost + spam | something like spam |
| transgenic | trans = across + genic = life | hybrid species |
| trigger species | trigger = early tip-off | the first species to be affected, as by global warming |
| übergroovy | über = over the top + groovy | supercool |
| viral video | viral = contagious + video | video that is rapidly disseminated via the Internet |

evoke pieces of meaning. Advertising copywriters and magazine writers do this on a daily basis; the word *blog* is a combination of the free morphemes *web* and *log*; then came *vlog* (*video* added to *blog*). The prefixes *e-* and *i-* have combined to form many new words and concepts over recent decades (e.g., *e-pets* and *i-tunes*). The study of morphology is fun and increases word power.

Depending on the student's first language, some morphemes are easier to acquire than others. For example, the prefix *en-*, meaning "to bring about, to make, or to put into," is more often used to make verbs from nouns or adjectives that derive from the Anglo-Saxon side of English; that is, words that are not directly related to cognates in Romance languages. For example, one can say "enjoy" but not "*enmuse." In contrast, words ending in the noun suffix *-ion* are relatively easy for Spanish speakers because they are usually words that have cognates in Spanish. Therefore, students may not as easily acquire the words in Table 1.5 as they might the words in Table 1.6.

**TABLE 1.5**    Words with Morpheme *en-* as Prefix

| | | |
|---|---|---|
| enjoy | enact | enliven |
| enlarge | enclose | ensure |
| enrich | encourage | entrust |
| entrap | entangle | enroll |
| enable | encrust | enforce |

**TABLE 1.6**    Words with Morpheme *-ion* as Suffix

| | | |
|---|---|---|
| transportation | division | translation |
| action | succession | comparison |
| examination | combination | validation |
| preparation | signification | respiration |
| certification | termination | separation |

Attention to morphemes in the classroom can accelerate language acquisition if students are exposed to families of words across parts of speech; that is, if *courage* is taught alongside *courageous, discourage,* and *encourage,* or *ice* is taught with *icy, ice cream, icicle, ice age,* and *iceberg.* Instead of defining new words, students may enjoy separating new words into morphemes and finding other words that match these morphemes. This activity is consonant with a key principle of brain-based learning (see Chapter 2): The brain learns faster when engaged in pattern-matching or pattern-finding activities.

## BEST PRACTICE: Working with Morphemes

The teacher can encourage awareness of comparatives and superlatives using the following game, called Speed Search.

Students circulate around the room to see how many people they can find who fit the description on the slip of paper they have drawn from a box. After two minutes, they draw another slip for a second round of play. Students win if they have the most points after a designated number of rounds. Sample descriptions: Find a person who believes that dogs are less intelligent than cats. Find a person who has more than two brothers. Find a person who is the oldest child in the family. (Kealey & Inness, 1997, pp. 24–25)

A similar game can be used to teach subject–verb agreement. Two sets of sentence beginnings are distributed to half the class. Set A has beginnings such as "When I get up in the morning, I . . ." and "When something scares me, I . . . ." Set B has stems such as "Just before guests arrive, my mother . . ." and "When we shop for groceries, my family . . . ." The other half of the class receives two kinds of sentence completion phrases; one kind uses verbs with third-person endings (". . . cleans up the house") and one is without the *s* (". . . get jumpy"). Each person with a third-person subject needs to find a matching third-person verb. (Rinvolucri, 1984, pp. 102–103)

## SYNTAX: THE SENTENCE PATTERNS OF LANGUAGE

Syntax refers to the rules that govern the formation of phrases and sentences. The words in a language have semantic properties that entail their use in a sentence in some ways and not in others. A well-formed sentence is more than the sum of the meaning of the words; in English the position of the word in a sentence is an important part of the overall meaning. Sentence A, "The teacher asked the students to sit down," has the same words as sentence B, "The students asked the teacher to sit down," but not the same meaning. Not every sequence of words is a sentence: Sentence C, "*Asked the the teacher to down students sit," violates syntactic rules in English and thus has no meaning.

Native speakers of a language have syntactic proficiency—they can distinguish syntactically correct from incorrect combinations of words, even though they may not be able to explain what syntactic rules have been violated. Even very young English-speaking children know that sentences A and B are meaningful but sentence C is not. The mind is a strong organizing force, constantly striving to gain meaning, so speakers of a language can comprehend even imperfectly formed sentences.

Whereas syntax refers to the internally constructed rules that make sentences, *grammar* looks at whether a sentence conforms to some standard. An important distinction, therefore, is the one between standard and colloquial usage. Many colloquial usages feature acceptable sentence patterns in English, even though their usage is not standard—for example, "I ain't got a pen" is acceptable English syntax but not standard usage. Teachers who are promoting the standard dialect need to be aware that students' developing competence will not always conform to that standard.

Besides grammaticality and word order, speakers' syntactic knowledge helps them understand three other sentence features. Double meaning, or *ambiguity*, occurs in sentences such as "She is a Korean karate expert" or the frequently seen "Please wait for the hostess to be seated." On the other hand, sentences can have different structures but mean the same thing: "He is hard to please," "Pleasing him is hard," "It is hard to please him." Finally, speakers can understand and produce novel utterances, the *creative* aspect of language.

## Explicit Teaching of Syntax

In the late twentieth century, it was widely believed that students could acquire a second language without explicit teaching of syntactic structures. However, because the mind seeks to acquire patterns, and syntax is a pattern, creative and systematic teaching of syntax can accelerate language learning. Grammar books that teach students to label the parts of speech and build up sentence structures from simple to complex are useful. Balancing this systematic instruction with grammar games and creative language engagement such as poetry—even Mad Libs, the game that has students blindly providing nouns, adjectives, and verbs without knowing the story plot—helps students to learn the parts of speech. Figure 1.1 presents a simple card for teaching sentence syntax.

A pocket chart in a learning center can be used to teach sentence structure. Students can work in pairs to assemble meaningful sentences using packs of sentence components. Words in the same sentence should be on the same color of index card so that multiple sentences can be kept separated as students work. A trick to checking students' work quickly is for each set of cards to spell out a word on the back of the cards if the cards are in the correct order (see Figure 1.1).

Some students have more *metalinguistic knowledge* than others—that is, they have the vocabulary to talk about grammar because they learned the grammar of their native language. As with other kinds of learning, the wise teacher assesses students' prior knowledge to learn where to begin instruction.

**FIGURE 1.1**   A Quick-Check Method for Syntax Learning Center Activity

The following cards are given to students in random order:

| The | quick | fox | ran | from | the | fire |
|-----|-------|-----|-----|------|-----|------|

Each card has a single letter on the back. If the cards are in the right order, the teacher can pick up each finished deck and quickly check to see if they spell a word or phrase. This one is as follows:

| F | O | X | F | I | R | E |
|---|---|---|---|---|---|---|

Describing the characteristic differences between languages—contrastive analysis—is useful to some degree in predicting what kinds of syntax errors students make (see Box 1.1 for Mandarin and Box 1.2 for Spanish). However, direct instruction must be balanced with rich, authentic exposure to English sentences, both spoken and written, and the learner must be allowed time for syntactic structures to be absorbed, consolidated, and deployed in many situations before a given structure can be said to be a stable feature of the learner's repertoire.

---

### Box 1.1 English Syntax Contrasted with Chinese (Mandarin)

English learners with Chinese as a mother tongue may need additional teacher assistance with the following aspects of English:

- Verb tense: *I see him yesterday. (In Chinese, the verb form is not changed to mark the time during which the action occurred—the adverb, not the verb, signals the time. Conjugating the verb form in English may prove to be difficult for the learner.)
- Subject–verb agreement: *He see me. (In Chinese, verbs do not change form to create subject–verb agreement.)
- Word order: *I at home ate. (In Chinese, prepositional phrases usually come before the verb—the rules governing adverb placement in English are difficult for many learners.)
- Plurals: *They give me 3 dollar. (In Chinese, like English, the marker indicates number, but the noun form does not change to indicate plural; in English the noun form changes.)
- Articles: *No one knows correct time. (Chinese uses demonstrative pronouns [this one, that one] but not definite or indefinite articles [a, the]. The rules for such use in English are complex.)

---

### Box 1.2 English Syntax Contrasted with Spanish

English learners with Spanish as a mother tongue may need additional teacher assistance with the following aspects of English:

- Verb conjugation: Spanish has three groups of regular verbs, in contrast to one group in English (those that add -ed or -d), but English has more classes of irregular verbs (wildly irregular go/went/gone versus mildly irregular like send/sent, break/broke, etc.).
- Subject–verb agreement: In Spanish, first-, second-, and third-person forms must be changed from the base form to create subject–verb agreement. It is sometimes hard to remember that in English only the third-person form is changed.
- Noun/Adjective order: In Spanish, adjectives come sometimes before and sometimes after the noun (un buen día, un día Linda). These alterations, however, obey regular rules.
- Articles: Spanish, like English, uses both definite and indefinite articles, but with different rules (for example, languages need the definite article, el ingles). Both definite and indefinite articles must match the noun to which they refer (unos muchachos, las mujeres).

*Source:* Spinelli (1994).

## ██ SEMANTICS: THE MEANINGS OF LANGUAGE

Semantics is the study of the meanings of individual words and of larger units such as phrases and sentences. Speakers of a language learn the "agreed-upon" meanings of words and phrases in their language; these meanings must be shared, or communication becomes impossible. However, English is a flexible language that is responsive to the needs of a dynamic culture, and new concepts emerge daily that require new words; so English learners must acquire vocabulary continuously in order to keep up with the semantic demands.

Some words carry a high degree of stability and conformity in the ways they are used (*slap* as a verb, for example, must involve the hand or some other flat object—"He slapped me with his ball" is not semantically meaningful). Other words carry multiple meanings (e.g., *scrap*), ambiguous meanings (*bank*, as in "They're at the bank"), or debatable meanings (*marriage*, for example, for many people can refer only to heterosexual alliances, whereas others might apply it to nonheterosexual contexts).

### Semantic Challenges

In second-language acquisition, there are three basic semantic challenges. First is the process of translating—finding words (lexical items) in the second language that correspond to those already known in the first. The second challenge is learning words for ideas and concepts that are new in the second language for which there is no first-language counterpart (for example, the Polish term *fúcha* has no equivalent in English ["to use company time and resources to one's private ends"]) (de Boinod, 2006). The third challenge is found in encountering a word that is similar in the second language to one in the first but whose meaning is different in small or large ways. Table 1.7 lists words that are cognates in English and Spanish—their meaning is identical. Table 1.8 lists near cognates, and Table 1.9 lists false cognates—those for whom the similar appearance is misleading.

Another challenge is that English is extraordinarily rich in synonyms. One estimate of English vocabulary places the number at over three million words; the *Oxford English Dictionary* contains some 290,000 entries with some 616,500 word forms. Fortunately, only about 200,000 words are in common use, and an educated person draws from a stock of about 20,000 to use about 2,000 in a week (Wilton, 2003). The challenge when learning this vast vocabulary is to distinguish denotations, connotations, and other shades of meaning.

**TABLE 1.7**   Examples of English–Spanish Cognates
(Same meaning, same spelling; may be pronounced differently)

| | |
|---|---|
| club | plural |
| director | radio |
| hotel | rural |
| hospital | salmon (Spanish salmón) |
| mineral | sofa (Spanish sofá) |
| postal | tenor |
| perfume | violin (Spanish violín) |

**TABLE 1.8** Examples of English–Spanish Near Cognates
(Same meaning, slightly different spelling; may be pronounced differently)

| English | Spanish | English | Spanish |
|---------|---------|---------|---------|
| February | febrero | tranquil | tranquilo |
| March | marzo | reserved | reservado |
| April | abril | salt | sal |
| May | mayo | violet | violeta |
| June | junio | second | segundo |
| July | julio | intelligent | inteligente |
| August | agosto | problem | problema |
| button | botón | cream | crema |
| visit | visitar | check (bank) | cheque |
| much | mucho | deodorant | desodorante |
| office | oficina | garden | jardin |
| courtesy | cortesía | map | mapa |
| lamp | lámpara | paper | papel |
| medal | medalla | use | uso |

**TABLE 1.9** Examples of English–Spanish False Cognates
(Close in sound; slightly different spelling; different meaning)

| Spanish | Meaning in Spanish | English False Cognate | Meaning in English |
|---------|--------------------|-----------------------|--------------------|
| blando | soft | bland | Soothing; not stimulating or irritating |
| blanco | white | blank | Colorless; free of writing |
| campo | country | camp | Place for tents or temporary shelter |
| codo | elbow | code | A system of signals |
| despertador | alarm clock | desperate | Almost beyond hope |
| dirección | address | direction | The way to go; authoritative instruction |
| cola | tail | cola | Drink |
| plata | silver | plate | Sheet of metal, food dish |

## BEST PRACTICE: Nuances of Meaning

- For adolescent learners, the teacher provides a list of a dozen common emotions (love, anger, fear, and fright are the big four; a few others are thankfulness, doubt, guilt, surprise, contempt, delight, hunger, nervousness).
- Students, working in pairs, make up situations that would engender the emotion.
- Rich discussion about nuances of meaning might result!

### Acquiring Vocabulary

What does it mean to "know" a word? Recognizing a word involves matching stored meaning with meaning derived from context. In addition, knowing a word includes the ability to pronounce the word correctly, to use it grammatically in a sentence, and to know with which morphemes it is appropriately connected. This knowledge is acquired as the brain absorbs and interacts with the meaning in context. This may be due to the important role that context plays in forming episodic memory—memory that is tied to emotionally rich experience.

Nation (1990) lists the following as the types of word knowledge that are necessary if one is to be considered to have complete knowledge of a given word: its spoken form, written form, grammatical behavior, collocational behavior (what words are frequently found next to the word), frequency, stylistic register constraints (such as formal/informal contexts), conceptual meaning, and word associations (such as connotations).

Three types of vocabulary knowledge are *passive, controlled active,* and *free active* (Laufer & Paribakht, 1998). Passive knowledge involves understanding the most frequent meaning of a word (e.g., "break"—He breaks a pencil). Controlled-active knowledge involves cued recall (e.g., The railway con_____ the city with its suburbs), and free-active knowledge involves spontaneous use of the word. These three types of knowledge develop at different rates, with passive the fastest and active (free active) the slowest. Passive vocabulary is always larger than active vocabulary.

### Academic Vocabulary

Acquiring the vocabulary of schooling is essential to school success; it is a large part of what Cummins (1979, 1980) called cognitive academic language proficiency (CALP). This vocabulary has been compiled into lists by various researchers (c.f., Bromberg, Liebb, & Traiger, 2005; Huntley, 2006). Although no exhaustive list exists of academic terms by grade level, Table 1.10 presents academic terms by approximate grade level. Table 1.11 displays examples of academic vocabulary.

### Vocabulary Teaching and Concept Development

Many methods have been used to teach vocabulary during second-language acquisition; using rote memorization of lists or flash cards with words and meanings is probably the least effective, even if picture cues are provided. Having rich experience of new words in the

**TABLE 1.10**   Examples of Cognitive Academic Words by Approximate Grade Level

| Grade 1 | Grade 2 | Grade 3 | Grade 4 | Grade 5 | Grade 6 |
|---------|---------|---------|---------|---------|---------|
| connect | measure | indent | define | summarize | minimum |
| check | width | proofread | method | evidence | initial |
| ruler | margin | paragraph | highlight | energy | estimate |
| period | dictionary | hyphen | environment | positive | factor |
| capital letter | schedule | topic | exhibit | gender | percent |
| grade | label | graph | layer | nuclear | simulate |
| mistake | draft | edit | region | source | transfer |
| chalk | chart | ignore | research | substitute | variable |
| file | margin | select | style | theme | volume |

**TABLE 1.11**   Examples of Academic Vocabulary

| | | | | |
|---|---|---|---|---|
| access | available | component | element | sufficient |
| adjust | capacity | confirm | emphasis | supplement |
| alter | clarify | consistent | instance | survey |
| approach | comment | contrast | random | undergo |
| aspect | complex | core | specific | visible |

*Source:*   From Huntley (2006).

context of their use is the way words are usually acquired in the first language. Games such as Pictionary and Total Physical Response are useful when objects and actions are simple. More nuanced or complex knowledge requires careful work at all the levels described earlier by Nation (1990).

## BEST PRACTICE: Key Principles for Teaching Vocabulary

- Vocabulary taught with collocations—words that appear commonly co-appear (for example, the verb *lose* is presented as "lose your way," "lose your temper," "lose your keys," etc.)
- Vocabulary taught within its grammatical environment (for example, verbs are always introduced with *to*—"to apply," "to return")
- Emphasis on register (teach where, when, with whom a word is used; in a formal or informal setting?)
- Emphasis on word form (does it include a prefix or suffix as a clue toward meaning?)
- Emphasis on connotation (nuances of meaning differentiating one word from another) (Daloğlu, 2005)

**TABLE 1.12**    Semantic Shifts When Writing

| Informal Register | Formal Register |
| --- | --- |
| you know | it is evident |
| a lot of, a whole bunch of | multiple |
| getting (dark, warm) | becoming |
| a piece of | a component of |
| to take a chance | to attempt |
| to make an offer | to offer |
| to keep on doing | to continue |

### Semantic Shifts

Language users must make semantic shifts when writing. It may be understandable when a speaker overuses the colloquial "you know" when telling a story, but in written English, one must shift toward more formal expression. Learning to make this shift is an important part of cognitive academic language. Only in certain types of writing—such as literature when a colloquial dialect is expressed, or in gonzo journalism, a flamboyant, first-person genre—is the colloquial form acceptable.

Teachers can emphasize this semantic shift by, for example, using a chart that compares "talk written down" with "more thoughtful writing." Table 1.12 contrasts these two writing styles as semantic shifts.

Semantics is a domain in which growth must be sustained at every level of schooling and in every content domain. Teacher education, for example, has its own lexicon; prospective teachers are asked to master such terms as *assertive discipline, wait-time, manipulatives, mind mapping, retelling, writing genre, mini-lesson,* and so forth. Demonstrating proficiency in these and similar terms is a measure of professionality.

## LANGUAGE FUNCTIONS

Language proficiency is not an end in itself; language is used for various purposes—to solve problems, communicate feelings, or keep records as people go about their daily routines. Halliday (1978) has distinguished seven different functions for language: *instrumental* (getting needs met), *regulatory* (controlling others' behavior), *informative* (communicating information), *interactional* (establishing social relationships), *personal* (expressing individuality), *heuristic* (investigating and acquiring knowledge), and *imaginative* (expressing fantasy or possibility).

A curriculum might encourage students to perform a wide variety of functions such as reporting, evaluating, questioning, and critiquing. Many other functions are not necessarily encouraged by schools but take place in schools nonetheless: interrupting, shifting the blame, threatening, accusing, arguing, demanding, and making excuses. Learners must acquire written as well as spoken competence in the effort to match forms with functions.

### Academic Language Functions

Academic language functions include explaining, informing, justifying, comparing, describing, proving, debating, and so forth. There is some overlap in the terminology of academic functions and of thinking skills. Academic English—also called cognitive academic language proficiency, or CALP—is designed for abstract, decontextualized performance across a variety of content domains, which requires a long period of successful schooling, exposure to academic language, feedback and support in its use by students, and explicit instruction in vocabulary, morphology, syntax, and cognitive strategies.

Providing English learners with opportunities to engage in the various functions is critical for enabling them to develop a full range of proficiency in English. In school, however,

TABLE 1.13   Phrases Associated with Academic Functions of Language

| Function of Language | Sample Phrase(s) |
| --- | --- |
| Indicating cause and effect | Therefore, as a result, gradually |
| Providing example | For instance, that is, one sample, such as, in fact |
| Comparing | Like, likewise, similarly, in much the same way, equally |
| Emphasizing | Moreover, chiefly, above all |
| Indicating sequence | In the first place, starting with, consequently, finally |
| Summarizing | To conclude, in other words, thus |

rarely do teachers allow students to practice "out of school" social functions; the emphasis is usually on language functions necessary for the work of learning. Table 1.13 aligns academic language functions with typical phrases that are used during that function.

### Functions and Classroom Routines

In every situation, participants are expected to use language to carry out specific routines. One of the important tasks of kindergarten and first-grade teachers is to teach children how to respond appropriately in the school setting. Confusion and a sense of alienation can arise for English learners who are used to the school routines in their own countries and face the unexpected in U.S. schools. A knowledgeable teacher recognizes that these students are acting according to the routines with which they are familiar. It may take time—and explicit coaching—for students to learn the set of behaviors appropriate for a U.S. school context.

## BEST PRACTICE: Acquiring Language Functions

- *Instrumental:* Students practice a list of ways to request actions of others, including "Could you . . ." "Would you mind . . . ."
- *Regulatory:* Students take turns acting as timekeeper and taskmaster in cooperative groups.
- *Informative:* Students keep records of classroom pets, weather patterns, or commonly misspelled words on a bulletin board.
- *Interactional:* Students work together to plan field trips, social events, and classroom and school projects.
- *Personal:* Students use personal language in a journal and then share their thoughts and opinions on a voluntary basis.
- *Heuristic:* During projects, students brainstorm questions about which no one knows the answer.
- *Imaginative:* Students "play" with language—the sounds of words and the images they convey.

*Source:* Adapted from Pinnell (1985).

## Cognitive Academic Language Proficiency

During the school years, students need to acquire cognitive academic language proficiency (CALP), which comprises academic language functions. In contrast, basic interpersonal communication skills (BICS) constitute the language used for social interaction. For English learners, BICS has been found to approach nativelike levels within two years of exposure to English, but five or more years may be required for minority students to match native speakers in CALP (Collier, 1987; Cummins, 1981a; Hakuta, Butler, & Witt, 2000). Students need skills in both kinds of language.

CALP is the language needed to perform school tasks, which are often abstract and decontextualized. Because it provides few concrete cues to assist comprehension, Cummins (1984) calls CALP *context-reduced* communication. CALP also involves systematic thought processes, the cognitive toolbox needed to categorize, compare, analyze, and accommodate new experiences. CALP is key to acquiring the in-depth knowledge needed in a complex modern society.

CALP requires a growth from the simple *use* of language to the more complex ability to *think and talk about* language—metalinguistic awareness (Scarcella & Rumberger, 2000). Precise differentiation of word meaning and the ability to decode complicated sentences require a gradual understanding of the cultural and social uses of the language to which they are exposed. CALP is not gained solely from school or solely from the home—one reinforces the other. However, CALP is highly dependent on the assistance of teachers because, for the most part, CALP is learned in school. (See Chapter 2 for more on CALP.)

## A Curriculum That Promotes Academic Language

Teachers can promote the use of CALP by ensuring that students understand and use specific content vocabulary. When comparing two numbers, a teacher might ask, "Which number is greater?" The term *greater than* is specific to mathematics because it eventually corresponds to the symbol ">"; *bigger* as a synonym is not as useful. Keeping a personal glossary of terms used academically is also useful for all students.

Some teachers confuse the terms *BICS* and *CALP* with *correct* versus *incorrect* usage of English. CALP is *not* just hypergrammatical BICS. Teachers can help students to acquire CALP by analyzing the conceptual and critical thinking requirements of the grade-level curriculum *and* taking the time to ensure that all students are explicitly taught such requirements. Good teachers use CALP with their students; but excellent teachers ensure that students can use CALP themselves.

Without this explicit attention to teaching CALP, one of three outcomes is all too common. First, students who come to school already having acquired CALP as a benefit of a privileged home environment may outshine English learners. Second, the curriculum for English learners may be watered down due to the assumption that those who lack CALP cannot perform academically at a high cognitive level. Third, students lacking CALP in English are not able to participate knowledgeably and are often given a skills-based, direct instruction approach that does not encourage a constructivist learning environment.

## Evaluating Curricula for Academic Language

Academic materials that incorporate CALP teach not only content but also the cognitive skills to acquire content. *High Point* (Schifini, Short, & Tinajero, 2002) makes CALP explicit by listing CALP terminology to be covered in each unit. For example, Level C Unit 4 Theme 1 (A Fork in the Road) presents words such as *choice, decision, advantages,* and *disadvantages, pros,* and *cons* to accomplish the academic function: justifying (p. 223). Level C Unit 5 Theme 2 (Moving Forward) offers CALP terms such as *responsible, avoid, accept,* and *solve a problem;* subsequent vocabulary work teaches *denotation, connotation, thesaurus, substitute,* and *synonym.* Thus, *High Point* is an exemplar of a CALP-equipped curriculum.

## DISCOURSE

Discourse is classified using various dimensions. One dimension is *written versus spoken;* another is *register* (formal versus informal); *genre* (a combination of communicative purpose, audience, and format); and *monologic, dialogic,* or *multiparty* (how many are involved) (Celce-Murcia & Olshtain, 2001). Many kinds of analysis have been used in the study of discourse: studies of information structure, coherence, cohesion, turn-taking, and critical discourse analysis.

Discourse analysis can be defined as the analysis of language "beyond the sentence" (Tannen, 2001). Discourse might be characterized as "language associated with a particular activity, a particular kind of knowledge, a particular group of people or a particular institution" (Peim, 1993). The study of discourse looks at language in its larger units, such as oral text (classroom talk, speeches, casual conversation) and written text (magazine articles, school assignments, signs, and posters). Discourse specialists have looked at such behavior as how people take turns, how speakers use contextual cues as they interact, and how people show others they are listening. These features are heavily influenced by culture.

In school, language is used differently than it is in the experiences of everyday life. As students acquire a second language—English—they are exposed to a distinct set of language functions that are specially adapted for school. This can work to the benefit of English learners if educators can affirm the voices that students bring to school and encourage them to build the second language on the knowledge they have gained in their first language, thus increasing their academic potential.

### Academic Discourse

What does it mean to use language for academic purposes? An educated person lives in a world in which discourse is used for a wide range of purposes. For many, literacy at work has become highly computer dependent, with word processing, databases, telephone number files, e-mail, and Web-based activities, as well as paper dependent, with piles of various folders containing information, along with books, journals, and newsletters. At home, personal literacy may include cookbooks, hobby materials, newsmagazines, correspondence, and bill-paying. All these reading materials have their own place, time, and task orientation.

Literacy practices are activities that form discourses within the culture or society at large. By the time a student enters undergraduate education, the discourse demands are intense: reading course syllabi, textbooks, study guides, handouts, laboratory manuals, tests, online materials, and reference materials; listening to lectures and peer discussions; writing tests, research papers, and other notes; making formal oral presentations; and informally contributing orally in class or in group working sessions. English learners must prepare for these discourse registers and activities in elementary and secondary school programs.

*Classroom discourse patterns involve students as active language users.*

**Academic Competence: Psychological Factors**   Producing and understanding academic discourse are demanding because they are dependent not only on acquiring cognitive academic language proficiency, but also on developing qualities such as persistence; the ability to achieve rapport with one's teachers; attunement to demands of the task; and the ability to seek, obtain, and benefit from help. These personality features help the individual to accommodate to the demands of the situation.

**Academic Competence: Sociocultural Factors**   Success in previous schooling makes present and future accommodations easier. The peer culture must sustain patterns of academic activity; the parental/cultural standards of achievement must also be appropriately demanding and supportive; and the school must enforce high educational standards, with expert management, well-certified staff, and adequate resources. In this way, the individual is situated within a social and cultural context that sustains academic activity.

## Oral Discourse in the Classroom

Classroom discourse is a special type of conversation. Intonation, pausing, and phrasing determine when one person's turn to speak is over and the next person's turn begins. Markers signal the circulation of power. As Foucault (1979) noted, discursive practices in the modern world prepare the individual for power. Schooling can shape an average person into a "good" student using discourse.

Good language learners are able to gain access to a variety of conversations in their communities. The communities of practice (Lave & Wenger, 1991) in which they participate—even peripherally—provide access to the utterances of others and the cultural practices they need to become engaged in community life. This means that the community of practice in a classroom does as much to create a good learner as the individual's cognition and striving.

Linguistic features are useful ways to examine classroom discourse. Turn markers governing who takes the floor signal speaking and listening. Some listeners nod frequently, and others offer eye contact or feedback such as "hmm," "uh huh," and "yeah." If a teacher is speaking, the type of listening that a learner signals is an important part of that learner's image in the mind of the teacher. If someone seems uninterested or uncomprehending (whether or not they truly are), the speaker tends to slow down, repeat, or overexplain, giving the impression of "talking down."

**The Recitation Pattern: A Typical Learning Encounter**  Classrooms in the United States often follow a model of instruction based on recitation (Mehan, 1979). Typically, the pattern has three parts, called the IRE sequence. First, the teacher initiates (I) an interaction by asking a question. A student responds (R), and the teacher follows up with evaluation (E). Alternatively, this may be called the IRF pattern by replacing the term *evaluation* with the term *feedback*, which consists not only of praise or disguised evaluation but also of reformulation, repetition of the student's answer, and summarizing or delivering information.

The IRF pattern shares characteristics of other kinds of teacher talk. The teacher not only produces the most language but also takes the most turns. Questions asked in this way usually call for simple information recall, and the responses are limited to this type of thinking. The teacher tends to ask "known-answer" questions in which students' responses can be easily evaluated (Pridham, 2001). The IRF pattern is easy to identify, partially because of its prevalence.

*I*nvitation to respond:
> **Teacher:** Who knows why names are capitalized? (Some students are wildly waving their hands, begging to be chosen to respond; others are averting their eyes, hoping *not* to be called on) Alma?

*R*esponse:
> **Alma:** It's somebody's name.

*E*valuation or *F*eedback:
> **Teacher:** That's true. Good, Alma.

*I*nvitation to respond: (pattern repeats) . . .
> **Teacher:** But who can tell me what the term for that is?

The IRF is not the only discourse pattern in which the teacher dominates, but it is the most frequent. In *teacher-fronted* classrooms in general (Harel, 1992), the teacher takes the central role in controlling the flow of information, and students compete for attention and permission to speak. English learners are dependent on their ability to understand the teacher's explanations and directions.

Clearly the IRF pattern has positive instructional features. This pattern can activate students' prior knowledge about a topic, review material already covered, present new information, calm a noisy room, check on the general state of group knowledge on a topic, and evaluate the discipline and cooperation of individual students. This evaluation of the student seems to shape a teacher's academic expectations for that student. Many features of the recitation pattern work for the benefit of instruction, although the same features that benefit some students may create difficulties for English learners (see Table 1.14).

**TABLE 1.14**    Positive and Negative Features of the IRF for English Learners

| Positive Features | Possible Negative Features for English Learners |
|---|---|
| *Invitation to Bid* | |
| Teacher waits for silence and imposes order on student behavior. | English learners may not appear as attentive as English speakers because they might have difficulty comprehending instruction. |
| Teacher controls the scope of the lesson by asking selected questions. | English learners may need more time than English speakers to understand questions and frame responses. |
| Teacher determines order and importance of information by posing questions. | |
| Teacher controls the level of language displayed in class by choice of lexicon and complexity of sentence structure. | Students with creative and individualistic thinking may wish to contribute related ideas outside the scope of the immediate topic. |
| Teacher controls pace and rhythm of discourse. | Instructional language, including vocabulary, may be too complex for English learners. |
| | Pace and rhythm of discourse may be different in students' native language, causing discomfort. |
| *Response* | |
| Teacher evaluates behavior of individuals by looking to see who is willing and ready to participate. | English learners may be reluctant to bring attention to themselves because they are insecure about their oral language, see such an action as incompatible with group cohesiveness and cultural norms, or are reluctant to display knowledge in front of others. |
| Teacher controls potential for reward by choosing respondent. | |
| By acting eager to answer, students can demonstrate responsivity to instruction, attention, and cooperation even if they do not really know the answer the teacher expects to hear. | Students may lack experience in particular topics under discussion, although their background may be rich in topics that are not curriculum related. |
| Teacher controls behavior by calling on students who may not be attentive. | Students from cultures in which children do not make direct eye contact with adults may not appear attentive during instruction. |
| Students can practice risk-taking by volunteering to answer. | English learners may be reluctant to volunteer to answer if they are not 100% sure their idea is correct and their culture does not reward ambiguity. |
| Students can show knowledge whether from prior instruction or experience. | |
| *Evaluation (Feedback)* | |
| Teacher is able to evaluate students' level of oral participation. | Students may need prior language development in oral participation, including turn-taking, listening, and speaking. |
| Teacher is able to use teacher approval as a reinforcer. | Students from certain cultures may not depend on teacher for approval. |
| Teacher is able to establish public recognition for those who answer correctly. | |

**TABLE 1.14**   *(Continued)*

| Positive Features | Possible Negative Features for English Learners |
|---|---|
| Teacher may use the evaluation turn to correct sentence grammar. | Individual public recognition may be taboo in some cultures. |
| Teacher can withhold negative evaluation by partially accepting an incomplete answer. | Research shows that second-language grammar is not improved by public correction of grammar, but by gradual acquisition of forms during language input and output. |
| Teacher can avoid direct negative evaluation by asking one student to "help" another to improve an answer. | |
| Teacher may evaluate students' success in the recitation pattern as an indicator of facility with "display knowledge" cultural pattern. | Indirect negative evaluation may be confusing for some students, leaving them with unclear concept formation. |
| Teacher can elaborate on answer and expand a concept by delivering direct instruction at this point. | Students who are unfamiliar with "display knowledge" cultural pattern may appear uncooperative. |
| Teacher can improve a poor answer by substituting more correct terminology or restating a sentence in more correct grammar. | Students who are not rewarded by encouragement of more complex questions and responses gradually receive fewer hours of attention and instruction. |
| As teacher evaluates students' responses, he or she determines what question comes next. | |

**Recitation Pattern: Questioning Strategies**   Through skilled questioning, teachers lead discussions and ascertain students' understanding. Questions should be framed to match students' proficiency levels and to evoke the level of critical or creative thinking sought in the response. Teachers who are sensitive to varying cultural styles are aware that in some cultures students are reluctant to display knowledge before a large group. The teacher must organize other means for students to demonstrate language and content knowledge, such as small-group discussions.

A hierarchy of question types can be matched to students' proficiency levels. Beginning English learners in the "silent period" may be asked a question requiring a nonverbal response—a head movement, pointing, or manipulating materials. Once students begin to speak, either/or questions allow them merely to choose the correct word or phrase to demonstrate understanding: "Is the water evaporating or condensing?"; "Did explorers come to the Americas from Europe or Asia?" Once students can produce language, *wh-* questions are appropriate: "What is happening to the water?"; "Which countries sent explorers to the Americas?"; "What was the purpose of their exploration?"

If a teacher is seeking evaluative responses requiring critical thinking by means of questioning strategies, more wait-time is necessary for students to understand the question and frame a thoughtful response. Bias is avoided if all respondents are given equal feedback and support in increasing the cognitive complexity of the answer.

Teachers of English learners cannot help using teacher-fronted discourse patterns to some extent, because of the legacy of traditional teaching discourse. However, awareness of its strengths (in summary, ease of use, usefulness in controlling attention and behavior, and diagnosis of a learner's responsiveness) and weaknesses (for example, limited learner oral production, limited peer interaction, and inequity of reinforcement) may encourage teachers to limit the use of teacher-fronted discourse in teaching English.

**Cooperative Learning as a Discourse Alternative**   The way discourse is organized is important for second-language acquisition in content classes. Classrooms that feature flexible grouping patterns and cooperative learning permit students greater access to the flow of information as they talk and listen to their peers, interact with the teacher or another adult in small groups, and use their home language for clarification purposes (Wells, 1981).

In cooperative-learning classrooms, the style of teacher talk often changes: Teachers assist students with the learning tasks, give fewer commands, and impose less disciplinary control (Harel, 1992). The teacher plans tasks so that students use language in academic ways. Students are placed in different groups for different activities. Teachers work with small groups to achieve specific instructional objectives (e.g., in literature response groups or in instructional conversations, discussed next).

**The Instructional Conversation as a Discourse Alternative**   An instructional discourse format called the *instructional conversation* is one alternative to a teacher-fronted classroom. With a group of six to eight students, the teacher acts as a discussion leader, following up a literature, social studies, or math lesson with a directed conversation that invites a deeper understanding of the issues raised (Tharp & Gallimore, 1991). The focus is on assisted understanding of complex ideas, concepts, and texts, permitting a more satisfying intellectual relationship between teacher and students.

Learning to manage and appreciate the instructional conversation takes time, but many teachers find that the increased attention paid to students' assisted thinking reaps great benefits in teachers' increased understanding of students' thought processes as well as in students' sense of instructional co-ownership. It is difficult for most teachers to keep silent and let students think and volunteer their thoughts in good time, to move the conversation forward by building on students' ideas rather than the teacher's, to select topics that students find genuinely interesting and comprehensible, and to have patience with English learners' struggle to find the words for their thoughts. However, the rewards are great—a satisfying instructional conversation is the event for which, at heart, every good teacher yearns.

## Discourse That Affirms Students' Voices

Throughout this book, the emphasis is on the co-participation of the learner in learning. It is imperative that teachers encourage the language that is needed and desired by the student, and if that desire does not exist, to evoke those emotions and motivations as an integral part of instruction. Instruction—particularly in a second language—that is not meaningful and motivating to the learner becomes empty.

What kind of participation enhances motivation and promotes acquisition? *Co-construction of meaning* permits the learner to plan, choose, and evaluate knowledge in relation to personal needs and goals. *Participatory genres* help the student to bridge the home–school divide. For example, the "talk-story" of Hawai'ian culture, when brought into the classroom, opened up the discourse around reading (Jordan, Tharp, & Baird-Vogt, 1992). By working in acknowledgment of, rather than at cross-purposes to, these community patterns of discourse, teachers can choose modifications to teacher-fronted discourse that will be successful for a particular group of learners.

In summary, using the tools of ethnography and community participation, teachers can learn how to help the learner participate in meaningful English-language instruction. A study of how the community uses discourse can help teachers pattern their classroom activities in ways that increase the likelihood that students' English proficiency will grow.

## PRAGMATICS: THE INFLUENCE OF CONTEXT

Pragmatics is the study of communication in context. It includes three major communication skills. The first is the ability to use language for different functions—greeting, informing, demanding, promising, requesting, and so on. The second is the ability to appropriately adapt or change language according to the listener or situation—talking differently to a friend than to a principal, or talking differently in a classroom than on a playground. The third ability is to follow rules for conversations and narrative, knowing how to tell a story, give a book report, or recount events of the day.

Linguists who study pragmatics examine the ways that people take turns in conversation, introduce topics of conversation and stay on topic, and rephrase their words when they are misunderstood, as well as how people use nonverbal signals in conversation: body language, gestures, facial expressions, eye contact, and distance between speaker and listener. Because these pragmatic ways of using speech vary depending on language and culture (Maciejewski, 2003), teachers who understand these differences can help learners adjust their pragmatics to those that "work" when speaking English.

### Appropriate Language

To speak appropriately, the speaker must take into account the gender, status, age, and cultural background of the listener. For example, the teacher's assistant in a classroom may be an older woman who shares the language and culture of the children and who addresses students in a manner similar to the way she interacts with her own children, whereas the teacher might use more formal language. Similarly, when a teacher who formerly taught second grade takes a job at the sixth-grade level, he or she must learn to adjust the tone of voice to one appropriate for older students.

**Language Contexts and Register Shifts** Various *language registers* match language-use contexts—whether the classroom, a social event, a store, or different types of written correspondence—that require a formal or informal tone, specific vocabulary and sentence structures, or even vocal pitch changes. Language registers are in turn enveloped by other verbal and nonverbal clues. For written genres, for example, the paper and ink quality varies according to the purpose and content of the written message; for oral genres, variation can be found in the distance between speakers, the roles of men versus women, and the tone and pitch of the voice.

There is a great contrast, for example, in the pitch of a kindergarten teacher's voice when reading a story aloud versus a high school football coach's instruction on the gridiron. These differences are adapted to the verbal and nonverbal—sometimes physical—features of the context. Factors that affect a speaker's or writer's choice of pragmatic features are cultural and social norms; the social and physical setting; goals and purpose of the language used; the identities of the participants; the role of the speaker or writer vis-á-vis the audience; and the subject matter involved.

## CLASSROOM GLIMPSE: Learning to Be Appropriate

*In preparation for a drama unit, Mrs. Morley has her students develop short conversations that might occur with different people in different situations, such as selling ice cream to a child, a teenager, a working adult, and a retiree. Pairs of students perform their conversations and the class critiques the appropriateness of the language. Students develop a feel for appropriate expressions, tones, and stances before working on plays and skits.*

**Teaching Oral Register Shifts**    Registers may involve conventions of intonation, vocabulary, or topic that meet the needs of the people and the tasks to be performed in that situation. For example, car advertising commercials filmed locally often use "car commercial register," a kind of frenzied tone performed by a man speaking loudly and quickly, whereas airline pilots who use the public address system of the airplane adopt a folksy tone, reassuring and paternal—"captain register"? Kindergarten teachers who read fairy tales aloud use *storytelling register*, featuring the tone of wonder and suppressed excitement. A *register shift* enables a language user to adapt to these rules.

Formal oral presentations, for example, may resemble written language, with scholarly sounding words, passive voice, or use of the subjunctive, because many speakers write out a presentation in advance. Informal, casual speech often features contractions, slang, and incomplete sentences (Cipollone, Keiser, & Vasishth, 1998). Table 1.15 displays a variety of registers that students might master for use in a classroom.

## BEST PRACTICE: Training Students in Oral Register Shifts

- Set up opportunities for situated practice, require oral presentations, stage dramatic events, and engage older students in storytelling to children.
- Offer repeated trials with feedback to help students improve the ability to shift registers.
- Let students take the initiative in creating settings and events for a variety of register usages that require leadership and talent in language use.
- Apply strategies for identifying and addressing difficulties English learners may encounter in comprehending regional dialects or other varieties of English.
- Create an instructional environment that respects English learners' home language and variety of English.

**TABLE 1.15**  Typical Oral Registers in the Classroom

| Register | Description or Example |
|---|---|
| Student response register | A firm tone, spoken confidently, that reaches all other students in the room |
| Leadership register | The voice of roll call, the call to line up for lunch, or the call to be quiet and listen |
| Classroom presentation register | Involves eye contact with an audience, confident bearing, pleasing and varied tone of voice, and an inviting sense of two-way communication with listeners |
| Dramatic register | Spoken dialogue in a play, in the role of narrator or announcer; it is "larger than life," with exaggerated emotion and voice |
| Storytelling to children | Features simplification and a sense of warmth and intimacy, no matter what the size of the crowd |
| Cooperative work register | The "ten-inch voice"; able to be heard within one's group but not by the next group |

**Turn-Taking**  A key aspect of learning to be appropriate is learning how to take turns. Native speakers of a language have internalized guidelines for when to speak, when to remain silent, how long to speak, how long to remain silent, how to give up "the floor," how to enter into a conversation, and so on, and how to show respect when doing so. Linguistic devices such as intonation, pausing, and phrasing are used to signal an exchange of turns. Some groups of people wait for a clear pause before beginning their turn to speak, whereas others start while the speaker is winding down.

In some cultures, overlapping a turn with the speaker is acceptable; in other cultures, this is considered rude and causes feelings of unease or hostility. Some children can interrupt instruction without receiving negative sanction, whereas other children are chided for frequent interruption. Punishing some students while letting others take unwarranted turns is tantamount to linguistic discrimination. To avoid this, a skilled teacher instructs second-language students about how to get turns and monitors instruction to ensure fairness. (It is difficult to see one's own behavior in this; it is best for the teacher to ask a peer to observe.)

## Nonverbal Communication

An important part of the pragmatic dimension of language is the complex nonverbal system that accompanies, complements, or takes the place of the verbal: "An elaborate and secret code that is written nowhere, known by none, and understood by all" (Sapir, quoted in Miller, 1985). This nonverbal system, estimated to account for up to 93 percent of communication (Mehrabian, 1969), involves sending and receiving messages through eye contact, facial expression, gesture, posture, and tone of voice.

Everyone is adept at sending and receiving these nonverbal messages, but, as in oral language, people are often unconscious of the information they are receiving. Because this nonverbal system accounts for a large part of the emotional message given and received, awareness of its various aspects helps teachers to recognize when students' nonverbal messages may not fit with expected school norms.

**Body Language**   The way one holds and positions oneself—one's body language—is one way that people communicate. Body language can convey power and confidence, or submission and timidity, merely by the tilt of the head, the position of the shoulders, or the grip of a handshake.

Gestures—expressive motions or actions made with hands, arms, head, or even the whole body—are ways to add meaning to verbal language, or they can take the place of words. Through the use of eyebrows, eyes, cheeks, nose, lips, tongue, and chin, people nonverbally signal any number of emotions, opinions, and moods.

Eye contact is another communication device that is highly variable. Many folk sayings express the idea that "the eyes are the windows of the soul," and it is important for some that the gaze be direct but not too bold. Eyes can reveal or hide emotions; not only the gaze but the shape of the eye, and even the size of the pupil convey emotions.

**Conceptions of Space and Time**   People's distance between themselves and others, the invisible "bubble" that defines an individual's personal space, varies according to relationships. People usually stand closest to relatives, close to friends, and farther from strangers. Coming too close can be interpreted as aggressive behavior; conversely, staying too far away may be perceived as cold. Teachers with students of many cultures in their classes may have the opportunity to observe many spatial facets of communication.

Use of time, even daily rhythms, varies across cultures. Hall (1959) pointed out that for speakers of English, time is treated as a material object—a commodity—rather than an objective experience. English expressions include "saving time," "spending time," and "wasting time." Teachers often reprove students for idling and admonish students to "get busy." Standardized tests record higher scores for students who work quickly. In fact, teachers correlate rapid learning with intelligence.

With an awareness of mainstream U.S. conceptions of time, teachers become more understanding of students and their families whose time values differ from their own. Some students may need more time to express themselves orally because the timing of oral discourse is slower in their culture. Parents who were raised in cultures with radically different concepts of time may not be punctual for parent conferences. One group of teachers allowed for this by designating blocks of three hours when they would be available for conferences, letting parents arrive when they could without fixed appointment times. Thus, teachers' accommodation to the intercultural pragmatics of the situation was key to an improved school climate.

## Evaluating the Pragmatic Features of School Programs

Intercultural pragmatics often involves concepts, feelings, and attitudes that are difficult for teachers and school administrators to discuss. Some teachers, lacking a more nuanced vocabulary, focus on teaching students *manners*, a term that carries a variety of meanings, from interpersonal respect to reliance on traditional, hierarchical adult–child rituals. Seeing others' beliefs, values, and behaviors through the lens of one's own culture often means that others' culturally based behavior—that of students and their families—is viewed as wrong, maladapted, or rude. Teachers who avoid the trap of "right" versus "wrong" can set an open and accepting tone.

Making the pragmatic features of the school and other settings explicit for English learners helps students engage in oral and written discourse that is appropriate for a given context, purpose, and audience. One teacher wrote a Welcome Book for newcomers to the classroom that explained routines, procedures, expected behaviors, and shared values. A student's "buddy" would have the chance every day to go over sections of the manual with the newcomer, and a copy was sent home. This helped students and their families know what to expect.

## DIALECTS AND LANGUAGE VARIATION

The language used in a certain context varies not only according to pragmatic factors of register shift (cultural and social norms; social and physical setting; goals; purpose; participants; audience; and subject matter) but also in long-term variations that influence the way people produce language. An oral dialect is evinced when people talk a certain way in order to feel appropriate within a given context. Teachers who take such variation into consideration communicate respect and understanding of contextual influences on English-language use.

Within the first few seconds of listening to the voice of a stranger, native speakers can usually identify not only whether the speaker's voice is familiar but also a host of other information about that person. As Wolfram (1991) noted, "It is surprising how little conversation it takes to draw conclusions about a speaker's 'background'—a sentence, a phrase, or even a word is adequate to trigger a regional, social, or ethnic classification" (p. 1). *Dialect* refers to "any variety of language which is shared by a group of speakers" (p. 2). Dialect varies with region, social class, and ethnic origin.

### Dialects and the Education of English Learners

Language educators cannot help being influenced by dialect considerations. Wolfram (1995) emphasized the importance of dialect issues for educators of English learners:

> The standard version of English provided in most ESL curricula aims unrealistically at a dialect-neutral variety of English. At the same time, the majority of ESL learners are surrounded by an array of dialects, including some well-established vernacular dialects for those who live in economically impoverished conditions. The socialization of many ESL learners into US culture may lead them to adopt the same uncharitable, biased opinion of vernaculars that is often found among native speakers of English. . . . It thus seems appropriate to incorporate dimensions of language variation into the ESL curriculum. (p. 1)

A student's dialect may affect teacher expectations. The ESL teacher may be tempted to oversimplify classroom language to match students' acquisition level. Finding the appropriate balance of language knowledge, pedagogical skill, dialect accommodation, and standard-language modeling is a challenge for teachers of English learners.

One important question is whether ESL teachers should model Standard English. In many urban schools, bilingual (Spanish–English) teachers are in demand in elementary schools, and personnel administrators do not seem to see Spanish-accented English as a negative in this context. However, some personnel administrators still seem to prefer to hire high school English teachers who are native speakers, or who speak the English language without a "foreign" accent.

A central issue, that of honoring the dialect of the learner, means finding the appropriate balance between respecting the home dialect of the student and modeling and teaching Standard English. Prejudice may be an issue in ESL contexts. Speakers of a regional dialect (for example, a Mexican-American dialect in Fresno) may not be accorded the same respect as speakers of Standard English. Yet within a specific community, a dialect may be the norm. Should English teachers enforce Standard English even if it is not the norm in the students' community? Thus, dialect issues are also issues of social power and status in society.

Students who speak nonstandard dialects are very aware when they have difficulty acquiring standard forms for academic writing and avoiding stereotyping and discrimination (Nero, 1997). But they are also aware that their very identity and deepest values are linked to their language, leading to potential conflicts in self-evaluation and acculturation—but also to possible positive biculturality (Bosher, 1997; LePage & Tabouret-Keller, 1985). The role of dialect is complex. This section examines dialect from a linguist's point of view: common features of dialects, how dialects reflect social and ethnic differences, what types of attitudes people have toward dialects, and how dialects affect style.

## Common Features That Constitute Dialects

Why do languages have dialects? Language differences go hand-in-hand with social differentiation. People can speak differently because they are physically separated (regional dialects) or because they are socially separated (by means of economic ecology and social stratification). A third explanation is based on linguistic differences between the dialects themselves.

**Regional Dialects**    Sometimes physical terrain keeps dialects isolated and intact. In the United States, the geographic isolation of some southern communities has given rise to the so-called Appalachian English (Wolfram, 1991). The overall dialect terrain of the United States is an example of regional dialects. The four distinct dialects that most Americans find recognizable in the United States today can be roughly characterized as (1) New York City, (2) New England, (3) the South, and (4) everyone else. The use of these dialects often has cultural implications.

**Social-Stratification Dialects**    Within social groups, language establishes and maintains social distinctions. If people want to be considered a part of a particular social group, they consciously or unconsciously adopt the vocabulary items, pronunciation, and grammatical patterns of that group. This is easy to see in the case of teenage slang. Even when people's language receives negative social evaluation from mainstream English speakers, they continue to use the language of their in-group. Features of the dialect may be associated with ethnic solidarity, whereas speaking like a mainstream person may cause loss of friends or weakening of family ties. It is not uncommon for speakers to try to live in two or more worlds.

**Deeper Syntactic Causes for Dialects**    The third explanation for the origin and persistence of dialects is based on linguistic analysis. Double negation within a sentence, as in the Southern U.S. dialect construction "The dog didn't like nobody," is also found in European languages. Deletion of the copula ("You ugly") is a feature of African-American Vernacular English (AAVE) but also of Chinese and other languages. Lack of the 's in the possessive structure ("that man hat") in AAVE is true for other possessive structures in English ("her hat"); similarly, the lack of the noun plural ending ("four girl") in AAVE is common in many languages. Thus, dialects persist based on the ways in which languages are constructed.

## How Dialects Exhibit Social and Ethnic Differences

Whether dialects have a regional, social, or linguistic explanation, speakers acquire a dialect of English based on the language used by others of their region, social class, and native language. The most obvious form of dialect usage is in the sound of the language—the *accent*. People use accent to make judgments on a range of personal qualities and capabilities, such as innate intelligence, morality, and employability (Wolfram, 1991). Just because someone speaks with an accent does not mean he or she is less competent in the language. In fact, as Lippi-Green asserts,

> [D]egree of accentedness, whether from LI interference, or a socially or geographically marked language variety, cannot predict the level of an individual's competency in the target language. In fact . . . high degrees of competence are often attained by persons with especially strong L2 accents. (1997, p. 70)

Standard pronunciation (an accent known as General American or Midwestern) has become associated with high-status occupations, such as doctors, lawyers, professionals, and executives of large companies. Thus, language variation is associated with a person's economic activity. Economic discrimination based on language is enforced by means of informal, often invisible, social networks that intersect with social-class stratification.

Many people live in communities in which people are multidialectic, code-switching back and forth easily between multiple languages, each with its own repertoire of styles. To overcome the negative effects of social stratification, many people who are non-native speakers of English seek to lose the accent that they feel hinders them from assimilating into the mainstream. On the other hand, in many cultures the dialect they speak *is* the mainstream, and to acquire any other accent risks social stigma. In some cultures, being bilingual is acceptable only to a limited degree.

## Attitudes toward Dialects

People who are forbidden by law from discriminating against others on the basis of race or ethnicity may use accent as a means of social stigmatization or exclusion (Lippi-Green, 1997). Teachers may unwittingly communicate a negative social evaluation to a non-native-English-speaking student by speaking louder, using shorter sentences, slowing speech, restricting vocabulary and range of topics, or signaling a patronizing attitude (curiously enough, this is also done to the elderly). This puts the non-native speaker in a position of lower status.

Americans, consciously or unconsciously, view certain "foreign" languages as less prestigious than others. Because of racism, the French spoken by Haitians may not be evaluated as positively as French spoken by a Canadian. Status issues are prevalent in dialect differences among native speakers of English. In many parts of the world, the prestige form of British English is considered a preferable dialect to any form of American English.

Language is central to the identification of self and group. Teachers can damage the teacher–student relationship through prejudice or impair students' academic success through lower academic expectations. Student who are made to feel inferior for reasons of accent may internalize the shame associated with discrimination or maintain a negative attitude toward learning English. As Lippi-Green (1997) states, "When an individual cannot find any social acceptance for her language outside her own speech communities, she may come to denigrate her own language, even when she continues to use it."

## Dialects and Style

A speaker's or writer's choice of language variation for a given discourse may be influenced by the context or setting of the discourse and by the speaker's age, gender, culture, level of education, social class, or vocation. Formal settings call for formal language; a

*Students speaking a non-standard dialect of English are a rich source of language input to English learners in urban schools.*

student skilled in making this distinction may be chosen for public speaking at school assemblies.

Male–female differences have been shown in women's greater pitch changes to show emotion, higher overall pitch, and greater use of expressive adjectives and intensifiers (Brend, 1975). Characteristics of female speech are related more to powerlessness than gender, suggesting that women have learned to use these linguistic forms because they have traditionally been relegated to relatively powerless social positions (O'Barr & Atkins, 1980). English educators may find that male and female learners acquire different dialects of English, transferring to English the different roles and speech patterns in the native language. For example, female students may be more reticent to speak than male students, or vice versa. In these cases, a teacher might openly discuss the differences and find ways to equalize speaking opportunities.

## Vernacular Dialects and Language Teaching

Because accent and intonation patterns are important in second-language acquisition, students need to understand four basic truths about dialect usage in English: (1) one's dialect, if widely used by the surrounding racial, ethnic, or cultural community, is equally valid as a subset of English as any other dialect; (2) dialects are often used as a basis for discrimination, combined with underlying issues of power and race relations; (3) it is common for individuals all over the world to learn more than one dialect of English and to switch from one dialect to another depending on the context; and (4) such features of dialect as accent can be altered, if so desired, by specific, albeit time-intensive, drill.

**Teaching Standard English: Whose Standard?**   In a language as varied as English, there are naturally some who feel that it is important to establish a standard, or norm, against which usage is measured. Experts who publish grammar and usage books usually prescribe correct or standard language forms, but in English, in fact no such standard exists. Generally speaking, Standard American English is a composite of several subdialects spoken by the educated professional middle class. People seeking success in school and in the job market tend to adopt the language used by people in positions of power.

Many educators feel it is their right and privilege to enforce Standard English on their students. Teachers may subordinate the language of their students using a variety of messages, both overt and covert. Some teachers believe it is their right to correct students in public, to reprimand them for incorrect usage, or to refuse to communicate until a standard is reached ("You must answer in a complete sentence," "I can't understand you—say it again") (Lippi-Green, 1997).

Varieties of language are a result of normal social processes rather than of inadequacies on the part of individual speakers. The unique voice of the student is lost if educators insist on the use of Standard English exclusively in the classroom. Just as the worldview of the Native American is lost if the indigenous language dies away, so is the interlanguage of the student lost if no one listens. By balancing the need to teach Standard English with the zest and delight in each individual's vernacular, education can become a reservoir of English-language diversity.

In summary, language affords rich and dynamic expression. Familiarity with the structures and functions of language helps teachers to promote English-language development while supporting students' self-expression in their primary languages. Teachers with knowledge about the various subsystems of language can recognize the effort involved in developing English ability and incorporate students' language development objectives into all facets of the daily program.

Language is accompanied by a nonverbal system that surrounds and supports grammatical competence. Knowledge about and skill in nonverbal communication help teachers to enhance rapport with students. Understanding the basics of language helps to make language learning a meaningful, purposeful, and shared endeavor.

### VIDEO WORKSHOP: "An ESL Vocabulary Lesson"

In this video, a first-grade teacher demonstrates ESL strategies for teaching vocabulary and word identification in isolation.

To access the video, log on to MyLabSchool at www.mylabschool.com, enter Assignment ID **ENV3** into the **Assignment Finder**, and select the video entitled "An ESL Vocabulary Lesson." Watch the video, complete the questions that follow, and e-mail your responses to your professor for credit.

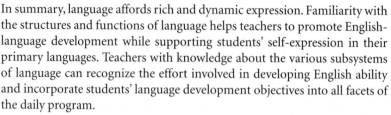

# CHAPTER TWO

# First- and Second-Language Development and Their Relationship to Academic Achievement

Attending school in a second language is a challenge. English learners' futures—their dreams, identities, and expectations of success—are enhanced if they have a successful school experience. By knowing about how language is acquired, teachers can recognize and use communication strategies that help students succeed. As an introduction to the study of language acquisition and learning, this chapter presents an overview of historical and contemporary theories that provide an orientation to English-language development.

## PROCESSES AND STAGES OF LANGUAGE ACQUISITION

Learning a language—the first or the second (second-language acquisition means learning any language after the first, whether it is the second, third, etc.)—is only partially a conscious activity. Most people retain very little awareness of having actually learned the first language. In contrast, people tend to remember learning the second language, especially if it is learned in school. Often learners are self-conscious about second-language acquisition. Even so, some of the same unconscious processes that helped us acquire the first language continue to underlie acquisition of the second.

Learning a language, even for children, requires a fully functioning mind. The mind processes a vast amount of verbal and nonverbal input and extracts meaning. Perceptual processes (listening and looking at the world and listening to ourselves) operate together with automatic language centers (involving phonemic awareness, linear-syntactic assembly, emotional circuits, and speech production), which in turn are synthesized with higher-order thinking (cognitive processes such as memorization, categorization, generalization and overgeneralization, and metacognition) to produce and understand language.

### First-Language Acquisition

By the age of five, a normal child can operate in the world with a full range of phonemic, syntactic, semantic, and pragmatic skills. The pronunciation resembles that of other speakers of the first language; the sentence structure is adequate; vocabulary amounts to several thousand words; and discourse skills include command of basic conversational skills, such as talking about a variety of topics with different audiences. Although parental input is useful for developing a large vocabulary, children learn language from other speakers, whether other children, neighbors, or television.

**The Innateness Hypothesis**   A child not only imitates the language in the environment but also seeks out patterns and tests rules by creating novel sentences. Lenneberg (1967) claimed that language is a biologically controlled behavior that develops from within, triggered by age and environment. Direct teaching and intensive practice have little effect on this "unfolding," but there are characteristic stages associated with language development. From birth to age two is a critical period for language emergence, during which crucial brain structures must develop. A second critical period, from the ages of ten to sixteen, allows the individual to learn language easily but not with native-speaker competence (Cipollone, Keiser, & Vasishth, 1998).

**Stages of First-Language Acquisition**   After only a few weeks of crying, infants begin to coo in vowel-like sounds such as "oooooh" or "aaaaah" in addition to crying. At around three or four months, infants start to add consonant sounds to their cooing, and they begin to babble at between four and six months of age using consonant and vowel sounds together. By the end of the first year, infants develop a sense of the role of language in communication (Lu, 2000).

When children first speak, they seem to utter single words to represent the whole meaning of an entire sentence, the so-called holophrastic utterance (Shaffer, 1999); for example, "ball" can mean "Throw me the ball" or "Where did the ball go?" Children's first words are contextual and identify people or things or express needs. In their second year, children begin to produce two-word phrases; later, this expands to three or more words, generating simple sentences in "telegraphic speech" that contain mainly the essential content words, such as verbs and nouns, but omit the function words, such as articles, auxiliary verbs, prepositions, and pronouns. Although these first sentences seem to be ungrammatical in terms of adult standards, they have a structure of their own.

As children's use of simple sentences increases, their sentences become increasingly elaborate and sophisticated. Language development, especially vocabulary growth and conversational skills, continues at a rapid pace throughout the preschool years. The development of conversational skills requires children to interact actively with other people. Through interacting with other, more experienced language users, children modify and elaborate their sentences in response to requests for more information, learn to take turns in speaking, and adjust their messages to their listeners' level of understanding.

**The Role of the First Language in Schooling**   Research has shown that proficiency in the first language helps students to achieve in school. To learn about a student's strengths in the first language, a teacher, primary-language-speaking aide, or parent who is fluent in the language of the student might observe a student working or playing in the primary language and take notes on the child's language behavior. Some schools may test students' first-language (L1) proficiency using such measures as the Bilingual Syntax Measure (BSM), which measures oral proficiency in English and/or Spanish grammatical structures. Knowledge about the student's linguistic and academic abilities may assist the teacher in second-language (L2) academic content instruction.

## BEST PRACTICE: First-Language Proficiency in School

- Monitor students' fluency in their primary languages and share concerns with parents if a student appears to be dysfluent in the home language.
- In cooperative groups, allow use of the first language so that students can discuss concepts.

### Second-Language Acquisition

How many people can say they are truly fluent in more than one language? In many parts of the world, people undergo schooling in multiple foreign languages as a widely accepted component of being well educated. In Canada and elsewhere, the ability to communicate, read, and write in two languages is encouraged. Millions of people around the world are *multicompetent language users* (Cook, 1999), meaning their bilingualism or trilingualism acts as an asset to them or to their society.

The United States is one of the few countries in which a young person can graduate from secondary school without ever studying a second language. Yet many young people enter schooling fluent in a primary language other than English, a proficiency that can function as a resource. Ideally, schools can help students whose families speak a language other than English to sustain fluency and develop academic competence in their heritage language while acquiring fluency and literacy in English.

**Types of Bilingualism**   Cummins (1979) analyzed the language characteristics of the children he studied and suggested that the level of bilingualism attained is an important factor in educational development. *Limited bilingualism,* or subtractive bilingualism, can occur when children's first language is gradually replaced by a more dominant and prestigious language. In this case, children may develop relatively low levels of academic proficiency in both languages. *Partial bilingualism,* in which students achieve a nativelike level in one of their languages, has neither positive nor negative cognitive effects. The most positive cognitive effects are experienced in *proficient (additive) bilingualism,* when students attain high levels of proficiency in both languages.

## BEST PRACTICE: Promoting Additive Bilingualism

Skilled teachers help students build English proficiency on a strong first-language foundation. They:

- Encourage families to preserve the home language
- Stock classroom libraries with books in the home language(s)
- Welcome classroom visitors and volunteers who speak the home language and ask them to address the class about the importance of proficiency in two languages

**Simultaneous Dual-Language Acquisition**   Preschool bilingual programs are pushing the age ever lower for children to acquire a second language: almost at the same time as the first language. Parents and teachers sometimes express concern about children's ability to become proficient simultaneously in two languages. What does research indicate about such a process? Does this negatively affect first-language acquisition?

Before the age of three, children have acquired the basic elements of grammar: how words go together to make meaning. Bilingual children may sometimes mix the grammar and vocabulary of their two languages, but such errors are temporary; however, they rarely use phonemes of one language in the other unless their pronunciation models have an accent. For example, if young speakers of Spanish are exposed to English with a standard (U.S. Midwest) accent, they will acquire that accent; if they learn English from speakers who speak English with a Spanish accent, they will learn English with that accent.

Some phonemes in both languages develop later even for native speakers (the /th/ in *thin*, for example, for native English speakers, and the trilled /r/ in *arroz* for Spanish speakers), so it is to be expected that some second-language speakers will show the same kind of development. Most important, by the age of five or six, bilingual speakers show great progress in two languages: They can use and repeat complex sentences; they have mastered 90 percent of the sound systems; and they can use prepositions correctly, use slang and make jokes, modify their speech if necessary to talk to younger children, and take conversational turns without being seen as interruptive or rude. These are impressive advances in language and well worth any temporary confusion along the way.

**Proficiency Levels of Second-Language Acquisition as Identified in the CELDT** The main purpose of the California English Language Development Test (CELDT) is to identify new students who are English learners in K–12, to determine their level of English proficiency, and to annually assess their progress toward becoming fluently English proficient. The CELDT covers four skill areas: listening, speaking, reading, and writing. Students in kindergarten and grade 1 are assessed only in listening and speaking. Students in grades 2 through 12 are assessed in all four areas.

The CELDT contains five proficiency levels: beginning, early intermediate, intermediate, early advanced, and advanced, along the four dimensions of language (listening, speaking, reading, and writing). Table 2.1 describes in general the five levels of the CELDT and the language proficiency associated with each level.

Because the CELDT is aligned with California's English Language Development standards (California Department of Education, 1999) and closely tied to the state's language arts standards, a teacher can use an English learner's CELDT level(s) as a guide to match specific language objectives in the lesson plan with the linguistic needs of the student.

### First- and Second-Language Acquisition: Commonalities

Language acquisition is furthered when the learner is immersed in a stimulating environment. Language knowledge builds on prior knowledge of concepts and is vocabulary intensive. The brain operates as a pattern-seeking processor with a high motivation to understand communication it deems important. Accompanying verbal language is a rich and informative system of nonverbal communication, supplying and interpreting the underlying emotions and gestural components. All language learning is time consuming, with an accumulation of skill that cannot be rushed.

A second language is built on the foundation of the first language; this is the only way the learner can make sense of the world. This development is cultural as well as linguistic. Therefore,

**TABLE 2.1**   CELDT Levels and Associated Proficiency Descriptor

| Level | | Proficiency Descriptors |
|---|---|---|
| Beginning | Listening/Speaking | May be able to recognize and speak a few isolated words and phrases |
| | Reading | May be able to recognize a few isolated words |
| | Writing | May be able to write a few isolated words |
| Early Intermediate | Listening/Speaking | Can produce words or phrases; can separate spoken sounds into words and respond to questions using simple vocabulary |
| | Reading | Can recognize words and phrases in print and match words to pictures |
| | Writing | Can respond to a writing prompt with a simple sentence |
| Intermediate | Listening/Speaking | Can produce relevant sentences using increasingly complex vocabulary |
| | Reading | Can read text with basic comprehension |
| | Writing | Can respond to a writing prompt with sentences or write a story with a sequence of events |
| Early Advanced | Listening/Speaking | Can understand instructional delivery and respond relevantly |
| | Reading | Can read text using skills of inferencing, drawing conclusions, and making predictions |
| | Writing | Can write with well-formed sentences and paragraphs, communicating ideas with organization |
| Advanced | Listening/Speaking | Can understand and respond to instructional delivery on increasingly complex topics |
| | Reading | Can read narrative and expository texts with comprehension requiring a range of thinking skills |
| | Writing | Writing is fluent and accurate, communicating ideas with organization, few grammatical errors, and specific vocabulary |

supporting the learner's meaning-making efforts furthers English acquisition. Providing linguistic and cultural support for the learner is a major theme of this book.

**Separate or Common Underlying Proficiency**   Some critics of bilingual education claim that educating children in the primary language reduces their opportunity to acquire English. This argument assumes that proficiency in English is separate from proficiency in a primary language and that content and skills learned through the primary language do not transfer to English—a notion that Cummins (1981b) has termed *separate underlying proficiency (SUP)*. In contrast, Cummins asserted that cognition and language, once developed in the primary language, form a basis for subsequent learning in any language. This position assumes a *common underlying proficiency (CUP)*, the belief that a second language and the primary language have a shared foundation, and that competence in the primary language provides the basis for competence in the second language.

For example, children learning to read and write in Korean develop concepts about print and the role of literacy that make learning to read and think in English easier, despite the fact that these languages do not share a similar writing system. The surface differences in the languages are less important than the deeper understandings about the function of reading and its relationship to thought and learning. According to Cummins (1981b), students do not have to relearn in a second language the essentials of schooling: how to communicate, how to think critically, and how to read and write.

# THEORIES AND MODELS OF SECOND-LANGUAGE ACQUISITION

Various theories and methods of second-language teaching have been used throughout recorded history, each based on an underlying rationale or set of beliefs about how language is best learned. These range in type from traditional to innovative. This chapter provides a historical context, with a focus on contemporary theories and models that underlie current instructional models.

## Former Theories That Still Influence Current Practice

Latin was the model for grammar throughout the Middle Ages, even though it was not an appropriate model for most European languages. Some current grammar-centered teaching practices sustain this model. Similarly, outdated practices of language teaching carry the legacy of now-discredited theories. Table 2.2 presents an overview of historical methods of language acquisition, the underlying theoretical premises of these methods, and their legacy of beliefs and justification for current teaching practices.

**Grammar Translation**   When Latin was the focus of second-language schooling, teachers translated and drilled on vocabulary, verb tenses, and parts of speech. The grammar-translation method of instruction is still widely used in settings in which the main goal is reading and grammar knowledge. Students learn in a carefully controlled curriculum and are rewarded for memorization. However, students have little choice in what they learn, little contact with actual speakers of the language they are acquiring, almost no actual use of the language in a social context, and little stimulation of curiosity, playfulness, and exploration—aspects of learning that are intrinsic to the nature of the mind. In contrast, current second-language teaching, especially in the elementary school, features extensive social interaction and active language use (Takahashi, Austin, & Morimoto, 2000).

**Focus on Structure**   The descriptive and structural linguistics of the nineteenth century led to the comparison of languages for the purpose of teaching. *Contrastive analysis* is the theory that comparing the first and second languages can predict what might be easy or difficult for

TABLE 2.2    Historical Methods of Second-Language Acquisition, Underlying Theoretical Premise, and Contribution to Second-Language Teaching

| Method of Instruction | Underlying Theory | Legacy in Current Beliefs about Second-Language Teaching |
| --- | --- | --- |
| Grammatical analysis | Learning a language is equivalent to knowing about the structure of the language. | Emphasis on following rules of grammar |
| Grammar translation | Second language is learned by translating second-language structures into first language, emphasizing grammar and vocabulary. | Focus on vocabulary memorization |
| Structural linguistics and contrastive analysis | Second language is learned by classifying similar languages into groups and comparing the structures of two languages with each other to note similarities and differences. | Language comparison as a teaching methodology |
| Behaviorism as audiolingualism | Second language is learned by habit formation, especially by training in correct pronunciation. | Used to justify repetitious, structured practice in which learners are drilled on correct pronunciation |
| Behaviorism as direct teaching and mastery learning | Second language is learned by dividing what is to be learned into small units and using rote repetition, with much drill and practice. | Used to justify scripted lessons with controlled vocabulary and extensive testing |

the learner. However, its central premise—that the more similar two languages are, the more easily a speaker of the first will learn the second—was impossible to prove (Gass & Selinker, 2001), and contrastive linguistics has been largely an ineffectual way to teach a second language except in small areas such as cognates.

**Behaviorism**    When behaviorism dominated learning theory, it greatly influenced second-language teaching. Principles of repetition and reward led to classroom methodologies of drill and practice. Three aspects of behaviorism are still used in contemporary language teaching: audiolingualism, direct teaching/mastery learning, and total physical response (TPR).

The audiolingual method of language learning is behavioral, emphasizing oral practice such as oral pattern drills of specific grammatical forms ("It's cold today, *isn't it?*"). The goal for the learner is to learn new habits of speech, including correct pronunciation, in the second language through repetitious training directed and controlled by the teacher. Errors are corrected immediately to discourage "bad" habit formation. Reading and writing are often delayed until the student has an adequate oral base. The strength of the audiolingual method is its repetitious drill to achieve correct pronunciation, although two drawbacks are that it limits exposure to the target culture and fails to emphasize self-motivated language acquisition.

Direct teaching and mastery learning are also forms of behaviorist instruction, and their widespread use in classrooms of English learners through reading programs such as Open Court and Direct Instruction demonstrates that behaviorism is still widely practiced. Direct teaching incorporates explicit instructional objectives for students and promotes the learning of facts, sequenced steps, or rules. The instructor uses carefully scripted lessons divided into small units with specific objectives that move at a lockstep pace. Students are regularly tested over the material that is covered and receive immediate remediation if performance lags.

An advantage of direct teaching and mastery learning is the focus on the subskills of language, including word recognition and low-level comprehension skills. The weakest part of direct teaching is that students are seldom asked to set their own goals in learning or pursue their own interests, and they have little time to explore language creatively. Balancing the strengths and weaknesses of behavioral-based pedagogy, one might conclude that these teaching approaches have a distinct, yet limited, role in instruction.

**Total Physical Response (TPR)**   In TPR, students respond to an oral command that is simultaneously being modeled. For example, the teacher says "Stand" while standing up and "Sit" while sitting down, and students follow along (Asher, 1982). The instructor repeats the commands followed by the appropriate action until students perform without hesitation. The instructor then begins to delay his or her own action to allow students the opportunity to respond and thus demonstrate understanding. Eventually, the students, first as a whole group and then as individuals, act on the instructor's voice command alone. The number of commands is gradually increased. Students continue to respond in a nonverbal manner until they feel comfortable issuing their own commands.

Reading and writing can also be introduced through commands. The instructor may write on the board "Stand" and gesture to the students to perform the action. After practice with the written form in class, students can be given lists of familiar commands that they can then manipulate in their own fashion. The concrete, hands-on methodology recommended by Asher (1982) is associated with early stages of second-language learning and is recommended by Krashen and Terrell (1983) for promoting comprehension in a low-anxiety environment.

## Current Theories of Language Development

Starting in the mid-twentieth century, several important theories have shaped current understanding of language acquisition and development. In 1959, Chomsky criticized the prevailing belief that language is learned through constant verbal input shaped by reinforcement. He claimed that language is not learned solely through a process of memorizing and repeating, but that the mind contains an active language processor, the language acquisition device (LAD), that generates rules through the unconscious acquisition of grammar. This led to a cognitive emphasis, focusing on the role of the mind.

The idea of communicative competence—that the *use* of language in the social setting is important in language performance—directed attention away from the structural analysis of language toward a more anthropological or cultural approach. Halliday (1975) emphasized the role of social relations in language. Vygotsky was a prime mover in social interactionist theories of learning. Current conceptions of language have thus moved away from the merely linguistic components of a language to the more inclusive realm of language in use, which includes its psychological, social, and political domains.

**Transformational Grammar**   Chomsky envisioned language as a set of rules that human beings unconsciously know and use. He postulated that human beings, once exposed to the language(s) of their environment, use their innate ability to understand and produce sentences they have never before heard, because the mind has the capacity to internalize and construct language rules. The rules help native speakers distinguish whether a group of words forms a sentence in their language. The goal of transformational grammar is to understand and describe these internalized rules. Much of Krashen's monitor model can be traced to Chomsky's influence.

**Communicative Competence**   Hymes (1972) introduced the term *communicative competence*, meaning the ability that enables language users to "convey and interpret messages and to negotiate meanings interpersonally within specific contexts" (Brown, 1987). Rather than merely knowing grammatical forms, the competent speaker is one who knows when, where, and how to use language appropriately, including producing and understanding in different social contexts. As Taylor (1987) noted,

> Real communication is a shared activity which requires the active involvement of its participants. . . . We have a responsibility to create an atmosphere in which communication is possible, one in which students can feel free to take communicating initiative and are motivated to do so. Making classes "student-centered" can contribute to creating such an atmosphere. (p. 49)

Communicative language teaching involves social functions of language, such as requesting, agreeing, refusing, telling a story, expressing disappointment, and so forth. Even at the beginning level of English, students learn how to meet their needs through communication. At the early intermediate CELDT level, students might listen to and repeat conversations or role-play a situation in which someone makes a complaint ("Sorry to bother you, but . . .") or an apology ("I'm sorry"), working to expand their repertoire of common phrases, such as "How's it going?"; "I hope so"; "I doubt it"; and a hundred other useful expressions (see Spears, 1992).

Communicative language teaching has also led to greater use of games and communicative activities that lighten the spirit of learning, reduce anxiety, add excitement to a lesson, and make review and practice more fun. Box 2.1 offers a variety of resources for communicative games.

## BEST PRACTICE: Enhancing Communicative Competence

In a high school ESL class, Mr. Thurmond demonstrates grammatical, sociolinguistic, strategic, and discourse competence to students by having them role-play a job interview. As students conduct and analyze the interview situation, they identify such aspects as the need for forms of politeness and the inappropriate use of slang. In one such activity, the final winner was the applicant who, having at first been turned down, used strategic competence—she asked to be put on a waiting list and then got the job when the first-choice candidate accepted "a better offer"!

> ## Box 2.1    Resources for Communicative Games
>
> Blair, R. W. (Ed.). (1982). *Innovative approaches to language teaching*. Boston: Heinle and Heinle.
> Danesi, M. (1985). *A guide to puzzles and games in second language pedagogy*. Toronto: Ontario Institute for Studies in Education.
> Lewis, G., & Bedson, G. (1999). *Games for children*. Oxford: Oxford University Press.
> Lewis, M. (1997). *New ways in teaching adults*. Alexandria, VA: Teachers of English to Speakers of Other Languages.
> Maculaitis, J. (1988). *The complete ESL/EFL resource book: Strategies, activities, and units for the classroom*. Lincolnwood, IL: National Textbook Company.
> Nation, P. (1994). *New ways in teaching vocabulary*. Alexandria, VA: Teachers of English to Speakers of Other Languages.
> Omaggio, A. (1978). *Games and simulations in the foreign language classroom*. Washington, DC: Center for Applied Linguistics.

Chesterfield and Chesterfield (1985) found that students used communicative strategies to enhance their second-language competence. Table 2.3 presents these in order of their development.

These communication strategies are employed for transmitting an idea when the learner cannot produce precise linguistic forms. Brown (2000) groups communication strategies into five main categories: avoidance (evading sounds, structures, or topics that are beyond current proficiency); use of prefabricated patterns (memorizing stock phrases to rely on when all else

**TABLE 2.3**   Second-Language Communication Strategies

| Strategy | Description |
|---|---|
| Repetition in short-term memory | Imitating a word or structure used by another |
| Use of formulaic expressions | Using words or phrases that function as units, such as greetings ("Hi! How are you?") |
| Use of verbal attention-getters | Using language to initiate interaction ("Hey!" "I think") |
| Answering in unison | Responding with others |
| Talking to self | Engaging in subvocal or internal monologue |
| Elaboration | Providing information beyond that which is necessary |
| Anticipatory answers | Responding to an anticipated question or completing another's phrase or statement |
| Monitoring | Correcting one's own errors in vocabulary, style, and grammar |
| Appeal for assistance | Asking another for help |
| Request for clarification | Asking the speaker to explain or repeat |

*Source:* Chesterfield & Chesterfield (1985).

fails); use of cognitive and personality styles to compensate for unknown language structures; appeals for help; and language switch (falling back on the primary language for help in communication).

This last strategy, often called *code-switching*, has been studied extensively because it permeates a learner's progression in a second language. Code-switching—the alternating use of two languages on the word, phrase, clause, or sentence level—is used by many bilingual speakers for a variety of purposes, not just as a strategy to help when expressions in the second language are lacking.

Baker (1993) lists ten purposes for code-switching: (1) to emphasize a point, (2) because a word is unknown in one of the languages, (3) for ease and efficiency of expression, (4) as a repetition to clarify, (5) to express group identity and status or to be accepted by a group, (6) to quote someone, (7) to interject in a conversation, (8) to exclude someone, (9) to cross social or ethnic boundaries, and (10) to ease tension in a conversation. Code-switching thus plays a key role in bilingual communicative competence.

## CLASSROOM GLIMPSE: Code-Switching

*Jennifer Seitz, a third-grade teacher, uses Alicia's primary language, Spanish, as a way to help Alicia learn English. A recent immigrant to the United States, Alicia has acquired whole phrases or words in English from a fellow student and intersperses these when speaking Spanish to gain access to her peer group. On the playground, she has been heard to repeat in Spanish something just said in English, perhaps to clarify what was said or to identify with two groups. She often uses English when learning concepts in the classroom but uses Spanish when she is discussing the concept with another student or when the conversation involves a personal matter. The content of the instruction and the interpersonal link between speakers seem to be the main factors in her language choice.*

Although language purists look down on language mixing, a more fruitful approach is letting children learn in whatever manner they feel most comfortable so that anxiety about language will not interfere with concept acquisition. In fact, a teacher who learns words and expressions in the students' home language is able to use the students' language to express solidarity and share personal feelings when appropriate.

**Sociocultural Models of Second-Language Acquisition**   Schools, as institutions of learning and socialization, represent the larger culture. Culture, though largely invisible, influences instruction, policy, and learning in schools (Trueba, 1989). Knowledge of the deeper elements of culture—beyond superficial aspects such as food, clothing, holidays, and celebrations—can give teachers a crosscultural perspective that allows them to educate students to the greatest extent possible.

Anthropologists have joined with educators to view closely the culture of schooling and the language learning that takes place therein. Intensive studies of Hawai'ian and Native-American cultural practices of learning helped Mehan (1981), Tharp (1989), and other educational researchers (Philips, 1972; Phillips, 1978) recommend ways in which schools could institute culturally compatible practices (see Chapter 9).

Learning is not a separate and independent activity of individuals but an integral part of participation in a community (Lave & Wenger, 1991). Children return to dynamic and interactive communities after a day at school. Teachers must come to know and respect what the community offers students and encourage knowledge to travel a two-way path as it circulates from school to home and back to school. Thus, learning is both an individual and communal activity. The "funds of knowledge" approach (Moll, 1992; González, Moll, & Amanti, 2005) sees the cultural practices of households and communities as resources that can be connected in a meaningful way to the school curriculum.

**The Interactionist Model**    Extending the notion of communicative competence, Long (1980) developed the interactionist model. Using peer conversation as a means of enriching a student's exposure to language maximizes the opportunity for a student to hear and enjoy English; teachers need to provide many opportunities for English learners to engage in discourse with native speakers of English, in a variety of situations. ELD programs that restrict English learners to certain tracks or special classrooms, without incorporating specific opportunities for native/non–native-speaker interaction, do a disservice to English learners.

Interaction theorists have analyzed conversation to understand how meaning is negotiated. According to them, face-to-face interaction is a key to second-language acquisition. By holding conversations, non-native speakers acquire commonly occurring formulas and grammar as they attend to the various features in the input they obtain. Through their own speech output, they affect both the quantity and the quality of the language they receive. The more learners talk, the more other people will talk to them. The more they converse, the more opportunity they have to initiate and expand topics, signal comprehension breakdowns, and try out new formulas and expressions.

## BEST PRACTICE: Encouraging Native-Speaker/Non–Native-Speaker Interaction

- Students can interview others briefly on topics such as "My favorite sport" or "My favorite tool." The responses from the interviews can be tallied and form the basis for subsequent class discussion.
- English learners can interact with native English speakers during school hours through cross-age or peer interactions.

**Constructivist Views of Learning**    Constructivism is an offshoot of the cognitivist tradition in which complex, challenging learning environments help students take responsibility for constructing their own knowledge. As students deal with complex situations, the teacher provides support. Thus, students and teachers share responsibility for the knowledge construction process, collaborating on the goals of instruction and the planning needed for learning to take place (Fosnot, 1989; Wells & Chang-Wells, 1992).

Key elements of constructivist learning are the encouragement of student autonomy and initiative, the expectation that student responses will drive lesson content and instructional strategies, learning experiences that provoke discussion, a focus on students' concept understanding rather than teachers' concept explanation, and an emphasis on critical thinking and student dialogue. Constructivist methods make minimal use of rote memorization and instead focus on problem solving. Students discuss, ask questions, give explanations to one another, and present ideas and solve problems together.

Constructivist learning in the elementary years helps students maintain their curiosity and zest for learning. Typical constructivist environments are children's museums, rich worlds in which children can be exposed to many different stimuli. At the middle and high school levels, students use research resources featuring various types of information representation. Conducting research need not be a solitary occupation; project-based learning, for example, is a constructivist technique in which teams of students pool resources and expertise in the service of large undertakings.

## BEST PRACTICE: Promoting Students' Knowledge Construction

- Instructional objectives are compelling and comprehensible.
- Complex problems require teachers to become learners as well as students.
- Students are exposed to a variety of representational formats for knowledge (text, visual, oral, figurative, etc.).
- Working in teams, students learn conflict resolution skills as well as receptive and productive language skills.

**Social Constructionist Views of Language Learning**　The Russian psychologist Lev Vygotsky emphasized the role of social interaction in the development of language and thought: Language joins with thought to create meaning (Wink, 2000). Interaction occurs in a cultural, historical, and institutional context that shapes the availability and quality of the tools and signs that mediate higher mental functions. Vygotsky recognized that all teaching and learning takes place within the context of the memories, experiences, and cultural habits found within families.

According to Vygotsky (1981), teaching must take into consideration the student's *zone of proximal development*, defined as "the distance between the actual developmental level as determined by independent problem solving and the level of potential development . . . under adult guidance or in collaboration with more capable peers" (p. 86). Social interaction between adults and students operates within this zone. Mediation of learning—assisting students' performance—requires teachers to adapt to the level of the student, provide help when needed, and help students to work with one another and the teacher to co-construct meaning.

## BEST PRACTICE: Using Social Interaction to Learn English

The social uses of language are advanced when students engage in communicative pair or group tasks. Students benefit from communication with one another, members of the school community, and members of the community at large. They

- Practice reader's theater with other students
- Develop interview questions for a community survey
- Plan an exhibition of art or written work to which the public will be invited

**Interlanguage Theory**   In second-language learning, learners use four kinds of knowledge: (1) knowledge about the second language, (2) competence in their native language, (3) ability to use the functions of language, and (4) their general world knowledge. The language they produce is an *interlanguage*, an intermediate system they create as they attempt to achieve nativelike competence.

Selinker's interlanguage hypothesis (1972, 1991) asserted that the learner's language should be viewed as creative, with rules unique to itself, and not just a borrowed or incomplete form of the target language. Although this may be imperfect compared to target-language proficiency, it represents a learner variety of the target language. The view that learners have intermediary language modes that are natural and normal ways of learning offers a refreshing opportunity for teachers to view second-language learning as a productive pathway whose features have unique interest.

**Krashen's Monitor Model**   Krashen (1981, 1982) proposed a theory of second-language acquisition called the monitor model, which in five distinct hypotheses claimed that languages are acquired best when language acquirers comprehend messages and lower the mental and emotional blocks that can prevent them from fully comprehending input. Although the monitor model has been extensively criticized, it has nonetheless provided the theoretical base for the Natural Approach, which has had an extensive impact on changing the nature of second-language instruction in the United States. Each of the five hypotheses is described in the following paragraphs.

In the *acquisition-learning hypothesis*, Krashen (1985) defined second-language *acquisition* and *learning* as two separate processes. Learning is "knowing about" a language (formal knowledge). Grammar teaching promotes learning by providing the learner with explicit knowledge about the rules of a language. Acquisition, on the other hand, is an unconscious process that occurs when language is used for real communication. Acquirers gain a "feel" for the correctness of their own utterances as their internal monitor is gradually adjusted, but they may not be able to state any specific rules about why such utterances are "correct." Krashen considered acquisition more important than learning.

This hypothesis has its detractors. Some find the distinction between learning and acquisition vague, difficult to prove, or misleading (Af Trampe, 1994; Ellis, 1986; McLaughlin, 1990). Despite these criticisms, for the classroom teacher, Krashen's distinction between acquisition and learning is important in that teachers acknowledge the fact that students will produce some language structures unself-consciously and will need rules and help for others.

Krashen's *natural order hypothesis* states that there appears to be a predictable order of acquisition of English morphemes. The order is slightly different for second-language learners from the first-language order, but there are similarities. For example, children learn how to express a negative structure in the first and second languages in a similar way, first putting the negative marker outside the sentence (L1, "No Mom sharpen it"; L2, "Not like it now"); then putting the negative marker between the subject and the verb (L1, "I no like this one"; L2, "This no have calendar"); and finally, putting the negative marker in the correct position (L1, L2, "I don't like this one"). This example illustrates the idea that children acquire correct usage of grammatical structures in their second language gradually.

The *monitor hypothesis* postulates an error-detecting mechanism, the monitor, which scans an utterance for accuracy and edits—that is, confirms or repairs—the utterance either before or after attempted communication. However, the monitor cannot always be used. In a situation involving rapid verbal exchange, an individual may have little time to be concerned with correctness.

The monitor hypothesis is not without flaws. The monitor is difficult, if not impossible, to observe or distinguish during its use (Shannon, 1994). Krashen's claim that children are more successful language learners because they are not burdened by the monitor is disputed by McLaughlin (1987), who argues that adolescents are more successful learners than are children. Therefore, several theorists dispute the usefulness of the monitor as a construct.

The *input hypothesis* claims that language is acquired in an "amazingly simple way—when we understand messages" (Krashen, 1985, p. vii). Contrary to popular belief, simply immersing a learner in a second language is not sufficient. Language must contain what Krashen calls "comprehensible" input. Krashen introduced the expression $i + 1$, where $i$ stands for the current level of the acquirer's competence and 1 is the next structure due to be acquired in the natural order. Input needs to contain structures at the $i + 1$ level for the acquirer to advance.

Critics have pointed out that there is in fact no way of measuring the $i + 1$ level. Therefore, it is impossible to tell what "comprehensible input" really means, and, as Marton (1994) pointed out, Krashen's emphasis on comprehensible input ignores the active role of the learner in communicating and negotiating useful and understandable language. Nonetheless, when working with English learners, teachers need to use a variety of techniques and modalities, including visual and kinesthetic, to ensure that their speech is comprehensible.

The *affective filter hypothesis* addresses emotional variables, including anxiety, motivation, and self-confidence. These are crucial because they can block input from reaching the

*Language is acquired best when students are actively engaged in interesting, comprehensible activities.*

language acquisition device. If the affective filter blocks some of the comprehensible input, less input enters the learner's LAD, and thus less language is acquired. A positive affective context increases the input. These emotional variables are discussed later in this chapter.

Like others of Krashen's hypotheses, the affective filter is virtually impossible to define operationally. Most teachers understand, however, that a nonthreatening and encouraging environment promotes learning, and that it is important to increase the enjoyment of learning, raise self-esteem, and blend self-awareness with an increase in proficiency as students learn English (see "Reducing Excessive Student Anxiety" later in this chapter).

**Cummins's Theories of Bilingualism and Cognition**   Jim Cummins's work (1981b) falls within the cognitive approach to language, with its emphasis on the strengths the learner brings to the task of learning a second language. The cognitive approach to learning is based on the premise that learners already have considerable knowledge of the world. Cummins's research has furthered the belief that being bilingual is a cognitive advantage and that knowledge of the first language provides a firm foundation for second-language acquisition. Moreover, Cummins's concept of cognitive academic language proficiency helps teachers identify and teach the type of language that students need to acquire for academic success.

Cognitive academic language proficiency requires a complex growth in many linguistic areas simultaneously. This growth is highly dependent on the assistance of teachers because, for the most part, CALP is learned exclusively in school. The complexity of CALP can be captured by examination of the five Cs: communication, conceptualization, critical thinking, context, and culture (see Table 2.4). Many of the skills that are a part of CALP are refinements of basic interpersonal communication skills (BICS), whereas others are more exclusively school-centered.

## BEST PRACTICE: Teaching Students to Use CALP

A look at an elementary classroom shows the integrated work that takes place across the five CALP areas.

Mrs. Gómez found in her second-grade transitional bilingual class that although the students were fairly fluent English conversationalists they were performing poorly in academic tasks. Students seemed to understand English when pictures and other visual clues were present. However, when she gave instructions or briefly reviewed concepts, the students appeared lost. She realized that students needed lessons that eased them along the continuum from their interpersonal language use to the more abstract academic requirements. When Linda and several of her classmates were jumping rope during recess, Mrs. Gómez wrote down many of the patterned chants the girls were reciting. She transferred these to wall charts and read and recited them with the children.

Next she introduced poems with more extensive vocabulary on wall charts, supplementing the charts with tapes that children could listen to in learning centers. At the same time, the class was studying the ocean. Mrs. Gómez set up other learning centers with shells, dried seaweed, fish fossils, and other ocean objects. The instructions for these centers featured patterned language similar to that already encountered in the rhymes and poems. Gradually Mrs. Gómez was able to record more complex and abstract instructions in the learning centers. This progression and integration of activities helped the children move along the continuum from BICS to CALP.

**TABLE 2.4** Components of Cognitive Academic Language Proficiency (CALP)

| Component | Explanation |
|---|---|
| Communication | Reading: Increases speed; uses context cues to guess vocabulary meaning; masters a variety of genres in fiction (poetry, short story) and nonfiction (encyclopedias, magazines, Internet sources) to "read the world" (interprets comics, print advertising, road signs). |
| | Listening: Follows verbal instructions; interprets nuances of intonation (e.g., in cases of teacher disciplinary warnings); solicits, and profits from, help of peers. |
| | Speaking: Gives oral presentations, answers correctly in class, and reads aloud smoothly. |
| | Writing: Uses conventions such as spelling, punctuation, report formats. |
| Conceptualization | Concepts become abstract and are expressed in longer words with more general meaning (*rain* becomes *precipitation*). |
| | Concepts fit into larger theories (*precipitation* cycle). |
| | Concepts fit into hierarchies (rain → precipitation cycle → weather systems → climate). |
| | Concepts are finely differentiated from similar concepts: (*sleet* from *hail*, *typhoons* from *hurricanes*). |
| | Conceptual relations become important (opposites, subsets, causality, correlation). |
| Critical thinking | Uses graphic organizers to represent the structure of thought (comparison charts, Venn diagrams, timelines, "spider" charts). |
| | Uses textual structures (outlines, paragraphing, titles, main idea). |
| | Uses symbolic representation (math operators [$<$, $>$, $+$, $=$]; proofreading marks; grade indications; [10/20 points, etc.]). |
| | Reads between the lines (inference). |
| | Detects bias; separates fact from opinion; tests validity of sources. |
| | Plans activities, monitors progress, evaluates results, employs self-knowledge (metacognition). |
| | Increases variety and efficiency in use of learning strategies. |
| Context | Nonverbal: Uses appropriate gestures (and is able to refrain from inappropriate); interprets nonverbal signs accurately. |
| | Formality: Behaves formally when required to do so. |
| | Participation structures: Fits in smoothly to classroom and schoolwide groups and procedures. |
| Culture | Draws on experience in mainstream culture (background knowledge). |
| | Uses social-class markers, such as "manners." |
| | Moves smoothly between home and school. |
| | Marshals and controls parental support for school achievement. |
| | Deploys primary-language resources when required. |
| | Maintains uninterrupted primary-culture profile ("fits in" to neighborhood social structures). |
| | Develops and sustains supportive peer interactions. |

**Meaning-Centered Approaches**    Researchers (Goodman, 1986; Smith, 1983) looking at children learning to read in naturalistic settings noticed that they actively seek meaning. They work to make sense of text. They combine text clues with their own prior knowledge to construct meanings. The theory called *whole language* arose from the idea that meaning plays a central role in learning and that language modes (speaking, listening, reading, writing) interact and are interdependent. Whole language, a philosophy of reading instruction, complemented many of the findings of studies in first- and second-language acquisition.

Meaning-centered systems of language acquisition (also called *top-down* systems—see Weaver [1988]) support the view of language as espoused by Halliday (1978)—that language is a complex system for creating meanings through socially shared conventions. The notion of *meaning-making* implies that learners are generating hypotheses from and actively constructing interpretations about the input they receive, be it oral or written. Language is social in that it occurs within a community of users who attach agreed-upon meaning to their experiences.

**Semiotics**    Not all second-language acquisition depends on verbal language. Semiotics is a discipline that studies the ways in which humans use signs, symbols, icons, and indexes to create meaning. Signs—and the meanings they carry—vary across cultures and languages, adding richness to the study of second language that words alone seldom express fully.

Semiotics provides a perspective for examining human development through the interplay of multiple meaning systems. Semiotics has become increasingly important within the last decade, as sophisticated computer art, animation, and graphics programs available through the Internet have opened up a language of two-dimensional shape and color that supplements, if not replaces, text as a source of information and experience for many young people. For those interested in knowing more about this field, see Chandler (2005), Kress and Van Leeuwen (1995), and Scollon and Scollon (2003).

### BEST PRACTICE: Using Semiotics to Acquire a Second Language

- Students can view themselves, other students, teachers, the community, and culturally authentic materials (phone books, voicemail messages, advertising brochures, music videos, etc.) to examine ways that meaning is communicated using both verbal and nonverbal messages.
- Students can engage in a variety of purposeful cross-media activities—produce music, create collages, and write poems, journal entries, or advertising slogans—to display their identities, values, or ideas.
- Students can "people-watch" using semiotics to read nonverbal messages sent by dress styles, posture, demeanor, and so forth as a way to increase their interactions with one another at all levels of language proficiency. (Díaz-Rico & Dullien, 2004)

**Contributions of Research about the Brain**    A basic question concerning second-language acquisition is "What is the role of the brain in learning language?" Neurolinguists attempt to explain the connection between language function and neuroanatomy and to identify, if possible, the areas of the brain responsible for language functioning. Recent studies have looked at the role of emotions and visual and gestural processing in second-language acquisition, tracing the brain processing of not only verbal language but also nonverbal input such as gestures, facial expressions, and intonation (Schumann, 1994).

Several contemporary educators have developed learning methods that take into consideration brain processing. According to their research, learning is the brain's primary function. Many parts of the brain process reality simultaneously, facilitating language acquisition (see Table 2.5). For further information about brain-based learning, see *Brain/Mind Learning Principles in Action: The Fieldbook for Making Connections, Teaching, and the Human Brain* by Caine, Caine, McClintic, and Klimek (2004); Jensen's *Teaching with the Brain in Mind* (1998); Lyons and Clay's *Teaching Struggling Readers: How to Use Brain-Based Research to Maximize Learning* (2003); and Smilkstein's *We're Born to Learn* (2002).

## BEST PRACTICE: Using Principles of Brain-Based Learning in Oral Presentations

### Before a Presentation

- Have students lower anxiety by taking a few deep breaths, visualizing success, and repeating positive self-talk phrases (brain-based principle 2: Learning engages the entire physiology).
- Remind students to review the structure of the information, especially how the parts of the presentation fit together (brain-based principle 6: The brain processes parts and wholes simultaneously).

### During the Presentation

- The speaker concentrates on the task while staying tuned to the needs of the audience (brain-based principle 7: Learning involves both focused attention and peripheral perception).
- Tenseness that is redefined as "eustress" ("good stress") supplies energy for learning rather than inhibits performance (brain-based principle 11: Learning is enhanced by challenge and inhibited by threat).

### After the Presentation

- Students evaluate their accomplishment, ask for feedback and tune in to the reactions of others, identify problem areas, and make a plan for improvement (brain-based principle 10: Learning occurs best when facts and skills are embedded in natural, spatial memory—including the memory of positive performance).

## FACTORS THAT INFLUENCE SECOND-LANGUAGE ACQUISITION

Learners do not learn language in a vacuum. They learn it by interacting with others. Psychological and sociocultural factors play important roles in a learner's acquisition and use of a second language (see Figure 2.1). Each learner is simultaneously an individual and a member of a group. An individual's character traits enable him or her to function in specific ways. As a

**TABLE 2.5**    Principles and Implications for Brain-Based Instruction

| Principle | Implications for Instruction |
| --- | --- |
| 1. The brain can perform multiple processes simultaneously. | Learning experiences can be multimodal. As students perform experiments, develop a play from the text of a story, or take on complex projects, many facets of the brain are involved. |
| 2. Learning engages the entire physiology. | Stress management, nutrition, exercise, relaxation, and natural rhythms and timing should be taken into consideration during teaching and learning. |
| 3. The search for meaning is innate. | Language-learning activities should involve a focus on meaning; language used in the context of interesting activities provides a situated, meaningful experience. |
| 4. The brain is designed to perceive and generate patterns. | Information is presented in a way that allows brains to extract patterns and create meaning rather than react passively. |
| 5. Emotions are crucial to memory. | Instruction should support the students' backgrounds and languages. Interaction should be marked by mutual respect and acceptance. |
| 6. The brain processes parts and wholes simultaneously. | Language skills, such as vocabulary and grammar, are best learned in authentic language environments (solving a problem, debating an issue, exploring) in which *parts* (specific language skills) are learned together with *wholes* (problems to be solved). |
| 7. Learning involves both focused attention and peripheral perception. | Music, art, and other rich environmental stimuli can enhance and influence the natural acquisition of language. Subtle signals from the teacher (processed peripherally by students) communicate enthusiasm and interest. |
| 8. Learning always involves conscious and unconscious processes. | Students need opportunities to review what they learn consciously so they can reflect on, take charge of, and develop personal meaning. |
| 9. There are at least two types of memory: spatial memory and rote learning systems. | Teaching techniques that focus on the memorization of language bits—words and grammar points—use the rote learning system. Teaching that actively involves the learner in novel experiences taps into the spatial system. |
| 10. Learning occurs best when facts and skills are embedded in natural, spatial memory. | Discrete language skills can be learned when they are embedded in real-life activities (demonstrations, field trips, performances, stories, drama, visual imagery). |
| 11. Learning is enhanced by challenge and inhibited by threat. | Teachers need to create an atmosphere of acceptance. Learners are taken from the point they are at present to the next level of competence through a balance of support and challenge. |
| 12. Each brain is unique. | Teaching should be multifaceted. English learners can express developing understanding through visual, tactile, emotional, and auditory means. |

*Source:* Caine, Caine, McClintic, & Klimek (2004).

**FIGURE 2.1** English Learner Profile

**Psychological Factors: Learner's Background**

Learner's name _____ Age _____ Gender (M / F)

Grade _____ L1 proficiency _____

Type of bilingualism _____

Previous L2 experience _____

Assessed L2 level: Reading ____ Writing ____ Listening ____ Speaking ____

Academic success _____

Likes/dislikes _____

**Social–Emotional Psychological Factors**

Self-esteem _____

Motivation _____

Anxiety level_____

Attitudes toward L1/L2 _____

Attitudes toward the teacher and the class _____

**Cognitive Psychological Factors**

Stage of L2 acquisition _____

Cognitive style/learning style _____

Learning strategies _____

**Sociocultural Factors**

Family acculturation and use of L1 and L2 _____

Family values _____

Institutional support for L1 _____

Sociocultural support for L1 in the classroom environment _____

_____

member of a group, a person—largely unconsciously—adopts rules for interaction and takes on roles appropriate for effective functioning in that group. Teachers who are aware of these individual (psychological) and group (sociocultural) factors are able to adapt instruction to meet the individual needs of the learners so that each student can achieve academic success. Figure 2.1 offers an outline that can help teachers organize the factors they know about a given learner.

Psychological factors are traits specific to individuals that enable them to acquire a second language (L2). Learners use their personalities to process the language they hear and to create meaningful responses. Psychological factors can be divided into three categories: *background* factors, *social–emotional* factors, and *cognitive* factors. A learner's age, prior language experience, and prior schooling affect current school performance. As they learn, the sense of mastery of a language creates an affective–emotional response: enjoyment, pride, and competence. The work of mastering a second language can be considered cognitive. Teachers can help students be aware of those psychological factors that further their language learning and can work with students to ensure that these factors promote rather than impede their learning.

## Psychological Factors: The Learner's Background

**Naming Practices and Forms of Address**    A learner's name represents the individual as well as a family connection. People feel validated if their names are treated with respect. Teachers who care make an effort to pronounce students' names accurately. Taking extra time to talk privately with a student is preferable to practicing the student's name in public, which may be embarrassing for the student.

Naming practices differ across cultures. In the United States, people use a first (or given), middle, and last (or family) name. Around the world, naming practices vary. In Taiwan, for example, the family name goes first, followed by given names. In Vietnam, names are also ordered as family name, middle name, and given name. Puerto Ricans, as well as other Hispanics, generally use three names: a given name, followed by the father's surname, and then the mother's surname. If one last name must be used, it is generally the father's surname. Thus, Esther Reyes Mimosa can be addressed as Esther Reyes. If the first name is composed of two given names (Hector Luis), both are used.

In many cultures, adults are referred to by their function rather than their name. In Hmong, *xib fwb* means "teacher," and Hmong children may use the English term *teacher* in the classroom rather than a title plus surname, as in "Mrs. Jasko." Middle-class European-American teachers may consider this to be rude rather than realizing this is a culturally based practice.

## BEST PRACTICE: Students' Names

- Understand the use and order of names but also pronounce them correctly.
- Work with the student privately to practice his or her name.
- Don't change a student's name, apply a nickname, or use an "English" version of a student's name (even at the student's request) without first checking with a member of the student's family.

**Age**    Second-language acquisition (SLA) is a complex process that occurs over a long period of time, and the optimum age for its inception has been widely debated. Many people believe that children acquire a second language more rapidly than adults, but recent research counters this notion. Although it is true that the kind of instruction varies greatly according to the age of the learner—how formal the treatment of grammar and rules can be and what kind of communicative activities are appropriate—there is little evidence to indicate that biology closes the door to learning a second language at certain ages (see Singleton and Ryan [2004] and Han [2004] for further discussion of age-related issues in SLA, as well as Box 2.2 on page 71).

**First-Language Proficiency**    Research has shown that proficiency in the first language helps students to achieve in school. To learn about a student's strengths in the first language, a

## Box 2.2   What Is the Best Age for Second-Language Acquisition?

For adults, learning a second language can be a frustrating and difficult experience. In contrast, it seems so easy for children. Is there a best age for learning a second language?

### *Point:* Children Learn Second Languages Easily

Those who argue the *critical period hypothesis* believe that a child can learn a second language more rapidly than an adult because the brain has a language-acquisition processor that functions best before puberty (Lenneberg, 1967)—despite the fact that the critical period hypothesis has not been proved.

Evidence from child second-language studies indicates that the language children speak is relatively simple compared to that of adults, with shorter constructions and fewer vocabulary words, and therefore appears more fluent. Moreover, adults are often unaware that a child's silence indicates lack of understanding or shyness, and they underestimate the limitations of a child's second-language acquisition skills. One area that seems to be a clear advantage for children is phonology: The earlier a person begins to learn a second language, the closer the accent may approach that of a native speaker (Oyama, 1976).

### *Counterpoint:* Adults Learn Languages More Skillfully Than Children

Research comparing adults to children has consistently demonstrated that adolescents and adults outperform children in controlled language-learning studies (e.g., Snow & Hoefnagel-Hoehle, 1978). Adults have access to more memory strategies; are, as a rule, more socially comfortable; and have greater experience with language in general. The self-discipline, strategy use, prior knowledge, and metalinguistic ability of the older learner create a distinct advantage for the adult over the child in language acquisition.

Marinova-Todd, Marshall, and Snow (2000) analyzed misconceptions about age and second-language learning and reached the following conclusions: "Older learners have the potential to learn second languages to a very high level and introducing foreign languages to very young learners cannot be justified on grounds of biological readiness to learn languages" (p. 10). "Age does influence language learning, but primarily because it is associated with social, psychological, educational, and other factors that can affect L2 proficiency, not because of any critical period that limits the possibility of language learning by adults" (p. 28).

### Implications for Teaching

Teachers need to be aware that learning a second language is difficult for children as well as for adults. Helping children to feel socially comfortable reduces their anxiety and assists acquisition.

teacher, primary-language-speaking aide, or parent who is fluent in the language of the student might observe a student working or playing in the primary language and take notes on the child's language behavior. Knowledge about the student's linguistic and academic abilities may assist the teacher in first- or second-language academic content instruction.

Acceptance of the first language and use of the first language to support instruction promote a low-anxiety environment for students. A lower anxiety level in turn promotes increased learning.

**Previous L2 Experience**    English learners in the same grade may have had vastly different prior exposure to English, ranging from previous all-primary-language instruction to submersion in English—including students with no prior schooling at all. Moreover, no two students have been exposed to exactly the same input of English outside of class. Therefore, students' prior exposure to English and attainment of proficiency are often highly varied. Teachers may need to ascertain what degree of L2 instruction students have previously attained in order to design English-language instruction at the appropriate level.

Students who have not had a positive experience when first learning English may have "shut down" and be unwilling to speak. It may take time for a more positive approach to L2 instruction to produce results, combined with a positive attitude toward L1 maintenance.

## BEST PRACTICE: Equalizing Prior L2 Experience

- If students in the same class have drastically different prior experience in L2, it may be necessary to group students who are at about the same level of English skills (homogeneous grouping) for targeted ELD instruction.
- Heterogeneous groups—each group containing students who are at different levels of English proficiency—can be used for cross-level language stimulation.
- For students who seem unwilling to speak English, small-group language games within homogeneous groups may lower anxiety and increase fluency.

**Assessed L2 Level**    An important part of the knowledge about the learner that a teacher amasses as a foundation for instruction is the student's assessed level of proficiency in listening, speaking, reading, and writing in English. This can be obtained during the process of assessment for placement. In California, the California English Language Development Test (online at www.cde.ca.gov/ta/tg/el) is the designated placement instrument. Other states have other ways to assess proficiency (see each state's Department of Education website). No matter the source of information, the student's L2 level is the beginning point of instruction in English.

## BEST PRACTICE: Assessing L2 Proficiency Levels

- Be aware that a student's listening and speaking proficiency may surpass that of reading and writing, or vice versa.
- Assess each language skill independently.
- Use a measure such as the Student Oral Language Observation Matrix (SOLOM) to assess students' oral proficiency.
- Use *The English–Español Reading Inventory for the Classroom* (Flynt & Cooter, 1999) to provide a quick assessment of reading levels in two languages.

**Stages of Second-Language Acquisition**   Second-language learners vary greatly in their acquisition of a second language. However, there are generally accepted stages of development through which all learners progress. These stages include *preproduction, early production, speech emergence*, and *intermediate fluency*. In preproduction—also called the silent period— the learner is absorbing the sounds and rhythms of the new language, becoming attuned to the flow of the speech stream, and beginning to isolate specific words. In this stage, the learner relies on contextual clues to understand key words and generally communicates nonverbally. For the most part, learners in the silent period feel anxious when expected to produce speech. This stage corresponds to the beginner level of the CELDT.

Once a learner feels more confident, words and phrases are attempted—the early production stage (CELDT's early intermediate stage). Responses can consist of single words ("yes," "no," "OK," "come") or two or three word combinations ("where book," "don't go," "teacher help"). Students can sometimes recite simple poems and sing songs at this point. In the third stage, speech emergence (CELDT's intermediate stage), learners respond more freely. Utterances become longer and more complex, but as utterances begin to resemble sentences, syntax errors are more noticeable than in the earlier stage ("Where you going?" "The boy running"). At CELDT levels of early advanced or advanced, students begin to initiate and sustain conversations and are often able to recognize and correct their own errors.

Regardless of the way one labels the stages of second-language acquisition, it is now recognized that, in natural situations, learners progress through predictable stages, and learners advance through them at their own pace. Undue pressure to move through the stages rapidly only frustrates learners and retards language learning.

## BEST PRACTICE: Matching Instruction to Students' L2 Levels

Ideally, classroom activities match the students' second-language acquisition levels.

### Beginning Level
- Provide concrete activities featuring input that is augmented by pictures, real objects, carefully modified teacher speech, and frequent repetition of new vocabulary.

### Early Intermediate and Intermediate Levels
- Ask questions that produce single words and brief phrases.
- Provide opportunities for students to use their primary language as they acquire the second language.

### Early Advanced Level
- Engage students in opportunities to speak with greater complexity, read several pages of text even though they have limited comprehension, and write paragraphs.
- Offer a curriculum that supports and explicitly teaches learning strategies.

**Academic Success**   A valid predictor of school success is prior academic success. By reading a student's cumulative academic record, a teacher should get a sense of the student's strengths and weaknesses. This can be augmented by observations of the student during academic activities, as well as interviews with family members and former teachers. It is important for the current teacher to assemble as complete a record of students' prior schooling as possible to best inform instructional decisions.

**Likes/Dislikes**    Inquiring about students' favorite academic subjects, television shows, and extracurricular activities is one way of bridging adult–child, teacher–student, or intercultural gaps. Getting-to-know-you activities can be based on the following questions: Who/what is your favorite [native-language/culture] singer? Actor? Video game? Outdoor game? Storybook? Holiday? What do you like about it? Students can write about favorite subjects, and teachers can then use these culturally familiar ideas in classroom math story problems and other content. This conversation may need to occur using the home language.

## Psychological Factors: Social–Emotional

The affective domain, the emotional side of human behavior, is the means through which individuals respond to their environment with feeling. Some affective factors pertain specifically to individuals' feelings about themselves, whereas other factors pertain to their ability to interact with others. This emotional dimension helps determine how language acquisition and communication take place. Those affective factors discussed here are self-esteem, motivation, anxiety, and learner attitudes.

**Self-Esteem**    Many teachers intuitively recognize that self-esteem issues play important roles in their classrooms, and they encourage students to feel proud of their successes and abilities. Efforts to empower students with positive images of self, family, and culture may facilitate language learning. Teachers also strive to ensure that learners feel good about specific aspects of their language learning (e.g., speaking, writing) or about their success with a particular task.

Self-esteem is particularly at risk when an individual is learning a second language, because so much identity and pride are associated with language competence. Schools that honor the primary languages and cultures of students and help students to develop additive bilingualism foster strong identities, whereas schools in which students face disrespect and discrimination hinder students' social and emotional development (Cummins, 1996).

## CLASSROOM GLIMPSE: Building Self-Esteem

*Anita Álvarez was a Spanish-speaking first-grade student at the beginning stages of English-language acquisition. She was shy and retiring, and Mrs. Figueroa noticed that she seldom took advantage of opportunities to chat with her peers. Anita seemed to have good sensorimotor abilities and to be particularly adept at building three-dimensional models following printed diagrams. When Mrs. Figueroa observed that Mary, another student in the class, had a lot of difficulty in constructing objects, she teamed Anita with Mary, and, with Anita's help, Mary completed her project successfully.*

*Noting this success, Mrs. Figueroa "assigned competence" to Anita by publicly praising her to the class and referring students to her for help. This boosted Anita's feelings of worth—her "task" self-esteem—and the effects transferred to academic areas. Mrs. Figueroa was pleased to see that, subsequently, Anita talked more with other students and seemed to acquire English at a faster rate.*

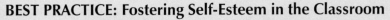

Many classroom activities can be used to enhance students' self-esteem. One activity, Press Release, asks students to write a news story about an incident in which they achieved a victory or reached a goal. A second activity, Age Power, asks students to think positively about their age and answer the question, "What do you like about being your present age?" (Moskowitz, 1978).

In the Name Game, students introduce themselves by first name, adding a word that describes how they are feeling that day, a word that begins with the same letter as the first name (the teacher may provide English learners with an alphabetized list of adjectives). Each subsequent person repeats what the others have said in sequence. Another activity, Name Interviews, lets students work in pairs to use a teacher-provided questionnaire. This includes questions such as "What do you like about your name? Who named you? Were you named for someone? Are there members of your family who have the same name?" and more (Siccone, 1995).

## BEST PRACTICE: Fostering Self-Esteem in the Classroom

If classroom teachers can foster students' self-esteem, students will . . .

- Feel free to express their minds, with respect, and without any attack in response
- Expect the best from others, but also accept imperfections
- Contribute freely to ideas and feel valued in small teams and in class
- Show positive attitudes to others' different ideas, even when they disagree
- Apologize whenever offense is taken by any member of the group
- Laugh at themselves and shake off personal offense if they [feel insulted]. (Adapted from Weber, 2005, p. 16)

Related to self-esteem is the concept of *inhibition,* a term that suggests defensiveness against new experiences and feelings. Emphasizing fluency over accuracy in the first stages of language learning may help students feel less inhibited.

The ability to take risks, to "gamble," may facilitate second-language acquisition. Educators believe that those who are willing to guess at meaning when it is not clear and to be relatively unconcerned about making errors will progress in language skills more rapidly than their more inhibited colleagues. As Brown (2000) pointed out, however, students who make random guesses and blurt out meaningless phrases have not been as successful. It appears that moderate risk-takers stand the best chance at language development.

**Motivation**   "The impulse, emotion, or desire that causes one to act in a certain way" is one way to define motivation. Various individual, sociocultural, and instructional factors affect motivation. Gardner and Lambert (1972) postulated two types of motivation in learning a second language: *instrumental*, the need to acquire a language for a specific purpose such as reading technical material or getting a job, and *integrative*, the desire to become a member of the culture of the second-language group. Most situations involve a mixture of both types.

## BEST PRACTICE: Motivating Students

- Give pep talks to remind students that anything worth doing may seem difficult at first.
- Provide students with a list of encouraging phrases to repeat to themselves as self-talk.
- Make sure a student's peer group consists of academic achievers.

**Anxiety Level**    Anxiety when learning a second language can be seen as similar to general feelings of tension that students experience in the classroom. Almost everyone feels some anxiety when learning a new language—that is, feelings of self-consciousness, desire to be perfect when speaking, and fear of making mistakes. Using a foreign language can threaten a person's sense of self because speakers know they cannot represent themselves fully in a new language or understand others readily (Horwitz, Horwitz, & Cope, 1991).

Because anxiety can cause learners to feel defensive and can block effective learning, language educators strive to make the classroom a place of warmth and friendliness, where risk-taking is rewarded and encouraged and where peer work, small-group work, games, and simulations are featured. In such contexts, student-to-student communication is increased. Classroom techniques can teach students to confront anxiety directly.

## CLASSROOM GLIMPSE: Discussing Anxiety

*In a series of lessons, Mr. Green has students write a letter to an imaginary advice columnist, relating a particular difficulty they have in language learning and asking for advice. Working in groups, the students read and discuss the letters, offer advice, and return the letters to their originators for follow-up discussion.*

*In a second exercise, students collect mistakes over a number of class periods and, in groups, assess the errors. They then rate the errors on a scale of 1 to 3 for such qualities as amusement, originality, and intelligibility, and they tally points to reward the "winning" mistake. Again, class discussion follows. By working together and performing interviews in pairs, students begin to feel more comfortable because they have the opportunity to get to know a classmate and to work with others.*

## BEST PRACTICE: Reducing Excessive Student Anxiety

- Monitor activities to ensure that students are receiving no undue pressure.
- Use competitive tasks in which students have a reasonable chance to succeed.
- Avoid having anxious students perform in front of large groups.

- When using a novel format or starting a new type of task, provide students with examples or models of how the task is done.
- Occasionally make available take-home tests to lower unnecessary time pressures for performance.
- Teach test-taking skills explicitly and provide study guides to help students who may need extra academic preparation.
- To increase energy levels in class, give students a brief chance to be physically active by introducing stimuli that whet their curiosity or that surprise them. (Adapted from Woolfolk, 2003, p. 367)

**Attitudes of the Learner**   Attitudes play a critical role in learning English. Attitudes toward self, toward language (one's own and English), toward English-speaking people (particularly peers), and toward the teacher and the classroom environment affect students (Richard-Amato, 2003). One's attitude toward the self involves cognition about one's ability in general, the ability to learn language, and self-esteem and its related emotions. These cognitions and feelings are seldom explicit and may be slow to change.

Attitudes toward language and those who speak it are largely a result of experience and the influence of people in the immediate environment, such as peers and parents. Negative reactions are often the result of negative stereotypes or the experience of discrimination or racism. If English learners are made to feel inferior because of accent or language status, they may have a defensive reaction against English and English speakers. Students may also experience ambivalent feelings about their primary language. This can cause problems within the family and create a backlash against English or English speakers.

Attitudes toward the teacher and the classroom environment play an important role in school success in general and English acquisition in particular. Families may promote positive attitudes toward school, thus influencing their children's success. In contrast, parents who have experienced discrimination and had negative experiences at school may subconsciously mirror these same attitudes, adding to their children's ambivalent attitudes toward education. Some theorists have postulated that students' refusal to learn what schools teach can be seen as a form of political resistance, which promotes misbehavior, vandalism, and poor relationships with teachers (Nieto, 2004).

Teachers can do much to model positive attitudes toward the students' primary language. A teacher–family conference may be advisable if a student continues to show poor attitudes toward the first or second language or the school. Chapter 9 offers strategies for involving the family in schooling.

## Psychological Factors: Cognitive

The cognitive perspective helps educators understand language learners as people who are active processors of information. Language is used in school in expanded ways: to create meaning from print, to encode ideas into print, to analyze and compare information, and to respond to classroom discussion. All of these activities involve cognitive factors. Students learn in many different ways using a variety of strategies and styles. This section addresses students' learning styles and learning strategies.

**Learning Styles** Many researchers have documented differences in the manner in which learners approach the learning task: "Learning styles are the preferences students have for thinking, relating to others, and for particular types of classroom environments and experiences" (Grasha, 1990, p. 23). These preferences serve as models for instructors in their efforts to anticipate the different needs and perspectives of students. Knowing these preferences can help instructors anticipate the different needs and perspectives of students, help students to understand themselves as learners, and use the information to plan and to modify certain aspects of courses and assignments.

Keefe (1987) divided learning style variables into four categories: physiological, affective, incentive, and cognitive. *Physiological* variables influence personal nutrition, health, time-of-day preferences, sleeping and waking habits, need for mobility, and needs for and response to varying levels of light, sound, and temperature. *Affective* variables include how much structure or supervision students need, what anxiety and curiosity they display, and what degree of persistence they use to pursue a task in the face of frustration. *Incentive* variables cover students' personal interests; levels of achievement motivation; enjoyment of competition versus cooperation; risk-taking versus caution; reaction to rewards and punishment; social motivation arising from family, school, and ethnic background; and locus of control (internal, seeing oneself as responsible for one's own behavior, or external, attributing circumstances to luck, chance, or other people). Table 2.6 sums up the learning style typologies according to Keefe (1987).

*Cognitive* learning style variables, for Keefe (1987), include field independent versus field dependent; conceptual/analytical versus perceptual/concrete; broad versus focused attention; easily distracted versus capable of controlled concentration; leveling (tendency to lump new experiences with previous ones) versus sharpening (the ability to distinguish small differences); and high cognitive complexity (accepting of diverse, perhaps conflicting input) versus low cognitive complexity (tendency to reduce conflicting information to a minimum).

Sonbuchner (1991) referred to learning styles as *information-processing styles* (preferences for reading, writing, listening, speaking, visualizing, or manipulating) and *work environment preferences* (differences in motivation, concentration, length of study sessions, involvement with others, level of organization, prime times for study, amount of noise, amount of light, amount of heat, and need for food or drink).

Gardner's theory of multiple intelligences (1983) has made a huge impact on current thinking about differentiating instruction. Assuming that students show a strong predilection for verbal, spatial, logical, interpersonal, intrapersonal, musical, kinesthetic, or nature-based thinking gives the teacher eight ways to think about diversifying teaching and learning. Silver, Strong, and Perini (2000) offer a valuable summary of ways to integrate learning styles and multiple-intelligence theories, including a distinction between *content* of learning (multiple intelligences) and *process* of learning (learning styles) and a four-part learning style way to look at content areas (using mastery, interpersonal, understanding, and self-expression as four delivery modalities for each content type).

**TABLE 2.6** Variables That Constitute Learning Style Differences

| Cognitive | Affective | Incentive | Physiological |
|---|---|---|---|
| ■ Field independent v. field dependent<br><br>■ Scanning (broad attention) v. focusing (narrow)<br><br>■ Conceptual/analytical v. perceptual/concrete<br><br>■ Task constricted (easily distracted) v. task flexible (capable of controlled concentration)<br><br>■ Reflective v. impulsive<br><br>■ Leveling (tendency to lump new experiences with previous ones) v. sharpening (ability to distinguish small differences)<br><br>■ High cognitive complexity (multidimensional discrimination, accepting of diversity and conflict) v. low cognitive complexity (tendency to reduce conflicting information to a minimum) | ■ Need for structure<br><br>■ Curiosity<br><br>■ Persistence<br><br>■ Level of anxiety<br><br>■ Frustration tolerance | ■ Locus of control (internal: seeing oneself as responsible for own behavior; or external: attributing circumstances to luck, chance, or other people)<br><br>■ Risk-taking v. caution<br><br>■ Competition v. cooperation<br><br>■ Level of achievement motivation (high or low)<br><br>■ Reaction to external reinforcement (student needs rewards and punishment v. does not) | ■ Gender-related differences (typically, males are more visual–spatial and aggressive, females more verbal and tuned to fine-motor control)<br><br>■ Personal nutrition (healthy v. poor eating habits)<br><br>■ Health<br><br>■ Time-of-day preferences (morning, afternoon, evening, night)<br><br>■ Sleeping and waking habits<br><br>■ Need for mobility<br><br>■ Needs for and response to varying levels of light, sound, and temperature<br><br>■ Social motivation arising from family, school, and ethnic background (high or low)<br><br>■ Personal interests (hobbies, academic preferences) |

*Source:* Keefe (1987).

Table 2.7 provides a list of learning style websites that feature learning style information, diagnostic checklists, and ideas for adapted instruction. Although lessons throughout the school day cannot be adapted for all learning styles, the teacher who builds variety into instruction and helps learners to understand their own styles can enhance students' achievement.

**TABLE 2.7**   Websites That Feature Learning Style Information, Diagnostic Inventories, and Ideas for Adapted Instruction

| Website | Source | Content |
|---|---|---|
| www.chaminade.org/inspire/learnstl.htm | Adapted from Colin Rose's *Accelerated Learning* (1987) | Users can take an inventory to determine whether they are visual, auditory, or kinesthetic and tactile learners. |
| www.engr.ncsu.edu/learningstyles/ilsweb.html | North Carolina State University | Users can take a learning styles questionnaire with 44 items to self-assess. |
| http://volcano.und.nodak.edu/vwdocs/msh/llc/is/4mat.html | Living Laboratory Curriculum | Explains how to use McCarthy's 4-MAT system. |
| www.usd.edu/trio/tut/ts/style.html | University of San Diego | Learn about learning styles (auditory, visual, and kinesthetic); identify your own learning style. |
| http://web.indstate.edu/ctl/styles/learning.html#STYLES | Indiana State University | Types of learning styles, using learning styles to teach, and applying learning styles to complex projects; links to online learning styles inventories. |

## BEST PRACTICE: Teaching to Diverse Learning Styles

Although in the typical classroom it is not possible to tailor instruction precisely to meet each individual's needs, some modifications can be made that take learning styles into account.

- Students who are dependent may benefit from encouragement to become more independent learners. The teacher might offer a choice between two learning activities, for example, or reduce the number of times a student can ask the teacher for help. In contrast, students who are highly independent might be provided activities and assignments that encourage collaboration and teamwork.
- Students who show little tolerance for frustration can be given a range of tasks on the same skill or concept. If the student can complete the first task with no errors, subsequent tasks can slowly increase in complexity, with the student gradually gaining skill and confidence but accepting the fact that he or she may not always be correct.

**Learning Strategies**   Aside from general language-acquisition processes that all learners use, learners adopt individual strategies to help them in the acquisition process. Learning strategies include the techniques a person uses to think and to act in order to complete a task. Chamot and O'Malley (1994) have incorporated specific instruction in learning strategies in their Cognitive Academic Language Learning Approach (CALLA). In CALLA, learning strategies are organized into three major types: metacognitive, cognitive, and social-affective. (See Chapter 5 for further discussion.)

## Sociocultural and Political Factors That Influence Instruction

Language learning occurs within social and cultural contexts. Proficiency in a second language also means becoming a member of the community that uses this language to interact, learn, conduct business, and love and hate, among other social activities. Acting appropriately and understanding cultural norms is an important part of the sense of mastery and enjoyment of a language. Learners adapt patterns of behavior in a new language and culture from their home culture as they learn a new language. These patterns of behavior can be helpful but also limiting.

Culture includes the ideas, customs, skills, arts, and tools that characterize a given group of people in a given period of time (Brown, 2000). (See Chapter 8 and Chapter 9 for further discussion on culture.) An individual's original culture operates as a lens that allows some information to make sense and other information to remain unperceived. When two cultures come into contact, misunderstandings can result because members of these cultures have different perceptions, behaviors, customs, and ideas. Thus, sociocultural factors—how people interact with one another on a daily basis—play a large role in second-language acquisition.

If, as many believe, English can be learned solely through prolonged exposure, why do so many students fail to master cognitive academic language? Some clues to this perplexity can be found beyond the language itself, in the sociocultural context. Do the students feel that their languages and cultures are validated by the school? Do the patterns of schooling mirror the students' modes of cognition? A well-meaning teacher, even with the most up-to-date pedagogy, may still fail to foster achievement if students are socially and culturally uncomfortable and alienated. Sociocultural issues are explored here with a view toward helping teachers bridge culture and language gaps between home and school.

**Family Acculturation and Use of the First and Second Languages**   Acculturation is the process of adapting to a new culture. Acculturation depends on factors beyond language itself and beyond the individual learner's motivation, capabilities, and learning style; it usually is a familywide phenomenon. Moreover, acculturation may not be a desirable goal for all groups.

Why do some students from certain minority backgrounds do better in school than others? Ogbu (1978) drew a distinction between various types of immigrant groups. *Castelike minorities* are those minority groups that were originally incorporated into society against their will and have been systematically exploited and depreciated over generations through slavery or colonization. Because of discrimination, castelike minorities traditionally work at the lowest paying and least desirable jobs, from which they cannot rise regardless of talent, motivation, or achievement. Therefore, academic success is not always seen as helpful for members of these groups.

On the other hand, immigrant minorities who are relatively free of a history of depreciation, such as immigrants to the United States from El Salvador, Guatemala, and Nicaragua, may view the United States as a land of opportunity. These immigrants do not view education as irrelevant or exploitative but rather as an important investment. Therefore, the internalized attitudes about the value of school success for family members may influence the individual student.

In support of his acculturation model, Schumann (1978) asserted, "the degree to which a learner acculturates to the target language group will control the degree to which he acquires the second language" (p. 34). He concluded that if the following factors are in place, acculturation will take place:

- Members of the primary-language and English-language groups view each other with positive attitudes, are of equal status, and expect to share social facilities.
- The primary-language and the English-language groups have congruent cultural patterns, and the English-language group desires that the primary-language group assimilate.
- The primary-language group is small and not very cohesive, and members expect to stay in the area for an extended period.

Schumann's model demonstrates that the factors influencing a student's L1 and L2 use are complicated by sociocultural variables stemming from society at large.

## BEST PRACTICE: Learning about Family Acculturation

- If possible, visit the student's home.
- Observe the family's degree of acculturation.
- Note the family's media consumption: What television shows does the family watch, in which language? Do family members read books, magazines, or newspapers? In which languages?

A family's use of L1 and L2 is also influenced by the relative status of the primary language in the eyes of the dominant culture. In modern U.S. culture, the social value and prestige of speaking a second language vary with socioeconomic position; they also vary depending on which second language is spoken.

Many middle-class parents believe that having their children learn a second language benefits their children personally and socially and will later benefit them professionally. In fact, it is characteristic of the elite group in the United States who are involved in scholarly work, diplomacy, foreign trade, or travel to desire to be fully competent in two languages. However, the languages that parents wish their children to study are often not those spoken by recently arrived immigrants (Dicker, 1992). This suggests that a certain bias exists in being bilingual—that being competent in a "foreign" language is valuable, whereas proficiency in an immigrant language is a burden to be overcome.

## BEST PRACTICE: Recognizing Biases

- Recognize areas in which there may be differences in language use and in which those differences might create friction because the minority group's use may be deemed "inferior" by the majority.
- Be honest about your own biases, recognizing that you communicate these biases whether or not you are aware of them.
- Model correct usage without overt correction and the student in time will self-correct—*if* the student chooses Standard English as the appropriate sociolinguistic choice for that context.

**Family Values and School Values**   As student populations in U.S. schools become increasingly diversified both linguistically and culturally, teachers and students have come to recognize the important role that attitudes and values play in school success. At times the values of the school may differ from those of the home. Not only the individual's attitudes but also the family's values and attitudes toward schooling influence a child's school success.

## CLASSROOM GLIMPSE: Family Values

*Amol is a third-grade student whose parents were born in India. As the only son in a male-dominant culture, he has internalized a strong sense of commitment to becoming a heart surgeon. His approach to classwork is painstaking, slow, and careful, and often he is the last one to finish an assignment during class. His teacher's main frustration with Amol is that he cannot quickly complete his work. However, when talking with Amol's family, the teacher notes that his parents seem pleased with his perfectionism and not at all concerned with his speed at tasks. In this respect, home and school values differ.*

In this example, the teacher epitomizes a mainstream U.S. value: speed and efficiency in learning. This value is exemplified in the use of timed standardized testing in the United States. Teachers often describe students of other cultures as being lackadaisical and uncaring about learning, when in fact these students may be operating within a different time frame and value system.

Other values held by teachers and embodied in classroom procedures have to do with task orientation. The typical U.S. classroom is a place of work in which students are expected to conform to a schedule, keep busy, maintain order, avoid wasting time, conform to authority, and achieve academically in order to attain personal worth (LeCompte, 1981). Working alone is also valued, and children often spend a great deal of time in activities that do not allow them to interact verbally with other people or to move physically around the room.

Children need to find within the structure and content of their schooling those behaviors and perspectives that permit them to switch between home and school cultural behaviors and values without inner conflict or crises of identity (Pérez & Torres-Guzmán, 2002). Teachers who examine their feelings about such values as cooperation versus competition, aggression versus compliance, anonymity versus self-assertion, sharing time versus wasting time, and disorder versus order can use this examination to develop a more flexible cultural repertoire.

The danger of excluding the students' cultures from the classroom is that students may become oppositional. Ogbu and Matute-Bianchi (1986) attributed achievement difficulties on the part of some Mexican-American children to a distrust of academic effort, a reflection of the destructive patterns of subordination and social and economic deprivation of the minority group. Segregated schools that offered inferior education resulted in a general mistrust of schooling, and students had difficulty in accepting, internalizing, and following school rules, leading to a lack of achievement. This element of resistance or opposition often takes the form of mental withdrawal, high absenteeism, or reluctance to do classwork.

Schools with high concentrations of English learners may deprive children of the use of their cultural knowledge and experience. If teachers consistently use examples drawn from the dominant culture and not the students', use literature that displays pictures and photographs of one culture only, and set up classroom procedures that allow some students to feel less comfortable than others, English learners become alienated from their home, family, and culture. This is unfair and damaging. The implementation of a rich and flexible cultural repertoire can encourage students to draw on their culture to promote achievement.

**Institutional Support for the Primary Language and Those Who Speak It**   Educators may view a student's ability to speak a home language other than English as an advantage or as a liability toward school success. Those who blame bilingual students for failing in school often mistakenly believe that students and/or their parents are uninterested in education and unwilling to comply with teacher-assigned tasks, are handicapped in learning because they have not acquired sufficient English, or suffer from "cultural mismatch" between the ways children learn at home or among their peers and the ways they are expected to learn at school.

In fact, schools often operate in ways that advantage certain children and disadvantage others, causing distinct outcomes that align with social and political forces in the larger cultural context. Institutional support for the primary language and students who speak it is a prime factor in school success for these students. This avoids the outcome of maintaining the poor in a permanent underclass and of legitimizing inequality (Giroux, 1983), with schooling used to reaffirm existing class boundaries.

## CLASSROOM GLIMPSE: The Way Schools Use Language to Perpetuate Social-Class Inequality

*The fourth-grade class was electing student council representatives. Mrs. Lark called for nominations. Mary, a monolingual-English-speaking European-American student, nominated herself. Mrs. Lark accepted Mary's self-nomination and wrote her name on the board. Rogelio, a Spanish-speaking Mexican-American child with limited English proficiency, nominated Pedro. Mrs. Lark reminded the class that the representative must be "outspoken." Rogelio again said "Pedro." Mrs. Lark announced to the class again that the representative must be "a good outspoken citizen." Pedro turned red and stared at the floor. Rogelio did not pursue Pedro's nomination. No other Mexican-American child was nominated, and Mary won the election. Pedro and Rogelio were unusually quiet for the rest of the school day and avoided making eye contact with the teacher. (Adapted from Erickson, 1977, p. 59)*

Incidents like the one in Mrs. Lark's classroom are generally unintentional on the teacher's part. Teachers have specific ideas and guidelines about appropriate conduct, deportment, and language abilities that stem from their own cultural patterns. A beginning step in helping all students feel fully integrated into the class and the learning environment is for teachers to become sensitive to their own cultural and linguistic predispositions.

Nieto (2004) identified numerous structures within schools that affect student learning: tracking, testing, the curriculum, pedagogy, the school's physical structure and disciplinary policies, the limited roles of both students and teachers, and limited parent and community involvement.

*Tracking*, the practice of placing students in groups of matched abilities, despite its superficial advantages, in reality often labels and groups children for years and allows them little or no opportunity to change groups. Secondary school personnel who place English learners in low tracks or in nonacademic ESL classes preclude those students from any opportunity for higher-track, precollege work. In contrast, a supportive school environment offers equal education opportunity to all students, regardless of their language background.

*Testing* results determine the kinds of curricula taught to various groups. Students who respond poorly on standardized tests are often given "basic skills" in a remedial curriculum that is essentially the same as the one in which they were not experiencing success. A supportive school is one that offers testing adaptations for English learners as permitted by law; for example, academic testing in the primary language, extended time for test taking, and fully trained testing administrators.

*Curriculum design* is often at odds with the needs of learners. Only a small fraction of knowledge is codified into textbooks and teacher's guides, and this is rarely the knowledge that English learners bring from their communities. Moreover, the curriculum may be systematically watered down for the "benefit" of children in language-minority communities through the mistaken belief that such students cannot absorb the core curriculum. As a result, students' own experiences are excluded from the classroom, and little of the dominant culture curriculum is provided in any depth. A supportive environment is one that maintains high standards while offering a curriculum that is challenging and meaningful.

*Pedagogy*, the way students are taught, is often tedious and uninteresting, particularly for students who have been given a basic skills curriculum in a lower-track classroom. The pressure to "cover" a curriculum may exclude learning in depth and frustrate teachers and students alike. Pedagogy that is supportive fully involves students—teachers make every effort to present understandable instruction that engages students at high levels of cognitive stimulation.

*The physical structure of the school* also affects the educational environment. Many inner-city schools are built like fortresses to forestall vandalism and theft. Rich suburban school districts, by contrast, may provide more space, more supplies, and campuslike schools for their educationally advantaged students. Supportive schooling is observable: Facilities are humane, well cared for, and materially advantaged.

*Disciplinary policies* may result in certain students being punished more often than others, particularly those who wear high-profile clothing, have high physical activity levels, or tend to hold an attitude of resistance toward schooling. Rather than defining students as deviant or disruptive, teachers can design cooperative groups that allow children to express themselves and learn at the same time, thus supporting rich cultural and linguistic expression.

*The limited role of students* may exclude them from taking an active part in their own schooling, and alienation and passive frustration may result. However, in addition to language barriers, cultural differences may preclude some students from participating in ways that the mainstream culture rewards. The following Classroom Glimpse illustrates the ways in which students' culturally preferred participation styles differed from the teacher's.

## CLASSROOM GLIMPSE: Culturally Preferred Participation Styles

*In classrooms on the Warm Springs (Oregon) Reservation, teacher-controlled activity dominated. All the social and spatial arrangements were created by the teacher: where and when movement took place; where desks were placed and even what furniture was present in the room; and who talked, when, and with whom. For the Warm Springs students, this socialization was difficult. They preferred to wander to various parts of the room, away from the lesson; to talk to other students while the teacher was talking; and to "bid" for one another's attention rather than that of the teacher.*

*For the Native-American children, the small-reading-group structure in which participation is mandatory, individual, and oral was particularly ill fitting. They frequently refused to read aloud, did not utter a word when called on, or spoke too softly to be audible. On the other hand, when students controlled and directed interaction in small-group projects, they were much more fully involved. They concentrated fully on their work until it was completed and talked a great deal to one another in the group. Very little time was spent disagreeing or arguing about how to go about a task. There was, however, explicit competition with other groups.*

*A look at the daily life of the Warm Springs children revealed several factors that would account for their willingness to work together and their resistance to teacher-directed activity. First, they spend much time in the company of peers with little disciplinary control from older relatives. Community life encourages accessible and open community-wide celebrations. No single individual directs and controls all activity, and there is no sharp distinction between audience and performer. Individuals are permitted to choose for themselves the degree of participation in an activity. Schooling became more successful for these students when they were able to take a more active part. (Adapted from Philips, 1972, pp. 370–394)*

*The limited role of teachers* may exclude them from decision making just as students are disenfranchised. This may lead teachers to have negative feelings toward their students. A supportive environment for English learners should be supportive of their teachers as well.

*Limited family and community involvement* may exclude families from participation in their children's schooling. Parents may find it difficult to attend meetings, may be only symbolically involved in the governance of the school, or may feel a sense of mismatch with the culture of the school just as their children do. In circumstances like these, it is simplistic to characterize parents as being unconcerned about their children's education. School personnel, in consultation with community and parent representatives, can begin to ameliorate such perceptions by talking with one another and developing means of communication and interaction appropriate for parent and school communities.

## CLASSROOM GLIMPSE: Building Home–School Partnerships

*When students began skipping classes in high school, several teachers and staff became concerned. The district's ESL and bilingual staff and several school principals met individually with students and parents to search for the reasons the school system wasn't working. Community meetings were held with parents, teachers, school principals, central office administrators, and the school superintendent to strengthen the home–school partnership. The community meetings rotated among the elementary, middle, and high schools and included informal potluck suppers and teacher- and parent-facilitated roundtable discussions. Numerous suggestions and positive actions came from these meetings—including the powerful links that were made between the district and the families. (Zacarian, 2004)*

A supportive classroom environment for CLD students is less effective if the environment or practices of the school are discriminatory. Teachers can exercise influence within the school and society at large to support the right of CLD students to receive an effective education.

**Sociocultural Support for L1 in the Classroom Environment**   Various sociocultural factors influence the support that is offered for the primary language and its speakers in the classroom. If students are seated in rows, with the teacher instructing the whole group, many students may not be productive. They may benefit more from the opportunity to interact with peers as they learn, speaking their primary language if necessary to exchange information.

Cooperative learning has had positive results in the education of CLD students (Johnson & Johnson, 1995). Positive race relations among students and socialization toward pro-social values and behaviors are potential outcomes of a cooperative learning environment. Students may gain psychological support from one another as they acquire English, and this support can help the students work with the teacher to achieve a workable sociocultural compromise between the use of L1 and L2 in the classroom.

## BEST PRACTICE: Supporting the Primary Language

- Feature the primary language(s) of students on bulletin boards throughout the school and within the classroom.
- Showcase primary-language skills in written and oral reports.
- Involve primary-language speakers as guests, volunteers, and instructional assistants.

**Political Factors**   Why is there disproportionate academic failure between groups of students, particularly between majority White and African Americans, Latinos, English learners, or low-income students, for example? Why do those of European-American origin, or those who are White, monolingual-English-speaking students, including those who come from high-income groups, succeed disproportionately? Thinking teachers interrogate those processes that affect their teaching and professional performance and, in turn, sustain political and ideological insight about the process of schooling and their role as teachers.

All societies in the world have a system of social stratification, meaning that the social system is hierarchically arranged and that some groups have different access to power, resources, and even perceived social worth. The United States, as a complex society, is also stratified, and its social stratification processes are influenced by class, race, occupation, income, and level of education, along with race, gender, age, region of residence, and, in some cases, national origin and levels of English-language proficiency.

Teachers are themselves members of a social class, race, or gender whose perceptions of specific groups, such as English learners, are influenced by their worldviews and preconceptions. Teachers who are clear about the ways in which social-class affiliations influence students' behavior, sense of identity, and academic performance can gain insight, for example, into why low-status students may initially resist the authority of a middle-class teacher.

## CLASSROOM GLIMPSE: Blaming the Students

*One beginning teacher admitted that 70 percent of the students in her sixth-period high school English class were failing. Notice that she could not say, "I have failed 70 percent of my students," or "due to academic tracking, 70 percent of students who cannot meet current standards of performance in English were placed in one class." Admitting that grading and tracking practices are partly to blame for students' failures prevents teachers and administrators from solely blaming the students.*

*Institutional racism* is a set of practices and policies condoned by the school that privileges some students and discriminates against others (see also Chapter 8). Ways to counteract institutional racism are for teachers of English learners to act informally to recruit teachers from underrepresented minorities as colleagues, to monitor the academic quality of life available to English learners, to volunteer to organize clubs that can effectively recruit English learners, and to involve parents and the community in cooperative endeavors.

*Linguistic racism,* discrimination based on language, is taking the place of discrimination once based exclusively on race. For instance, each day millions of Americans are denied their right to speak in their own words. Santa Ana (2004) suggested that this linguistic racism is most evident in schools where the largest silenced group is the millions of American schoolchildren who do not speak English. He stated that although racism based on skin color has been publicly discredited, linguistic discrimination remains largely unexamined by most people in the United States. Teachers with integrity oppose any act that systematically silences students or punishes those for speaking their native or home language.

Political clarity can help teachers act together as professionals to question and interrupt unfair and unjust practices in their individual classrooms as well as their schools. Unfortunately, teachers are often isolated in the job, working alone, with few opportunities to work collegially to address common concerns. However, when teachers remove barriers of isolation, they can compare notes about their collective experiences. They may begin to see that individual concerns are not chance occurrences but are instead related to wider social issues. Teaching with integrity means working collectively with other colleagues and community members to name and oppose institutionalized practices that dehumanize and disempower people based on their racial or linguistic backgrounds.

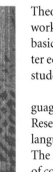 Theories of second-language acquisition provide the rationale and framework for the daily activities of instruction. Teachers who are aware of the basic principles of contemporary language acquisition and learning are better equipped to plan instruction and explain their practices to peers, parents, students, and administrators.

Although the teacher's role is valuable as students learn a second language, actually learning the language is the responsibility of the learner. Research on cognitive processes shows that learners construct and internalize language-using rules during problem solving or authentic communication. The shift from *what the teacher does* to *what the learner does* is a characteristic of contemporary thinking about learning in general and language acquisition specifically and has wide implications for teaching English learners.

**VIDEO WORKSHOP:   "Culture and Self-Esteem"**

In this video, teachers emphasize the importance of culture in their classrooms and discuss strategies for maintaining self-esteem among students for whom English is not a first language.

To access the video, log on to MyLabSchool at www.mylabschool.com, enter Assignment ID **ENV1** into the **Assignment Finder**, and select the video entitled "Culture and Self-Esteem." Watch the video, complete the questions that follow, and e-mail your responses to your professor for credit.

**(mylabschool**
Where the classroom comes to life!

# CHAPTER THREE

# Assessment of English Learners

Human beings have been learning for millennia. The traditional proof that learning had taken place was in the product—people could clearly see that a field was plowed productively or a house was built in a sturdy manner. Classroom learning differs because the outcomes are often more abstract and difficult to measure. Assessment is a way of ensuring that students are making progress and that instructional activities are designed wisely. The use of standards helps educators to agree on the expectations and content of English-language instruction and be certain that the school successes of ELD learners are clearly documented. Using these standards, assessment becomes the measure of whether students have acquired the desired skills and knowledge.

Some assessments are informal means of checking to see whether students understand instruction, whereas the purpose of others is to report to the government whether students have met predetermined standards. The emphasis on standards dovetails with outcome-based learning, a philosophy of education that relies on an explicit connection between specific goals and actual outcomes. Under the federal No Child Left Behind Act of 2001, states must measure student progress on statewide achievement tests. The role of teachers is to describe in detail what students are expected to accomplish in terms of these standards, and then to design learning activities that will enable students to meet the standards.

This chapter addresses the various kinds of assessments, the different educational contexts in which assessments take place, and ways that these assessments can be used to evaluate student learning. Included in this chapter are implications of assessment for English learners and a description of the role of teachers in the assessment process.

## PRINCIPLES OF STANDARDS-BASED ASSESSMENT AND INSTRUCTION

### Standards-Based Education: Federal Government Mandates

At the 1989 Education Summit in Charlottesville, Virginia, President George H. Bush and the nation's governors proposed a long-term national education strategy (often referred to as Goals 2000). The call went out for national professional organizations to articulate clear, high standards for what students should know (content standards) and how well they should know it (performance standards). Then the states were supposed to establish delivery standards, a description of what all schools must provide for students to achieve these standards. All students were to be measured at intervals (say, fourth, eighth, and tenth or twelfth grade).

These standards and assessments together constitute a voluntary accountability system. This accountability system was incorporated into law in 2001.

The No Child Left Behind Act (NCLB) requires that all students be "proficient" in reading and mathematics by the school year 2013–14. Beginning in 2005–06, all public school students in grades three through eight must be tested annually, using state achievement tests. This group includes English learners, who must be assessed in a valid and reasonable manner that includes reasonable accommodations and, to the extent practicable, testing in the primary language. Those students who have completed thirty months of schooling must, however, be tested in English reading (special exemptions can be applied for on a case-by-case basis, and students living in Puerto Rico are automatically exempted). States must establish baseline proficiency goals to which yearly progress is compared.

In the current climate of standards-driven instruction, the results of student assessment are often used to assess the effectiveness of the teacher's instruction. Often, funds are augmented for schools that show increased test scores or, conversely, withheld from schools in which test scores have not risen over a given period. Under NCLB, schools that fail to make acceptable yearly progress (AYP) for two years in a row are subject to corrective action. This is "high-stakes" assessment—the reputation and resources of schools and teachers rest on students' test performance.

## Standards for English-Language Development

The aim of using standardized measures is to ensure that all students are held to the same level of performance. Yet the net result is often to penalize schools whose English learners do not score well on tests designed for native English speakers. This poses a dilemma: On the one hand, high standards across schools do not permit school districts to lower academic standards for schools with high percentages of English learners. On the other hand, forcing students to undergo frustrating experiences of repeated testing in English when they are not ready can discourage them. Alternatively, testing students in their primary language is not effective if schools do not offer primary-language instruction.

Many states, including California, have adopted standards to guide the process of teaching English to English learners. Two purposes of English-language development standards are to provide teachers with consistent measures of English learners' progress and to ensure that English learners can eventually, like English-speaking students, meet and exceed standards for English-language arts content. Access to high-quality instruction is accomplished by aligning assessment with instruction so that each student can be taught at the appropriate level. Teachers assess, plan, teach appropriately, and reassess to keep students moving forward. Thus, assessment takes into consideration the assessment of both ELD skills and content area knowledge.

English-language development takes place in stages. Rather than using the four stages introduced in the Natural Approach (preproduction, early production, speech emergence, and intermediate fluency), the California English Language Development Standards (California Department of Education [CDE], 1999a) are divided into five levels: beginning, early intermediate, intermediate, early advanced, and advanced. The ELD standards describe expected proficiency on the part of the English learner in each of six key domains of language (listening and speaking, reading/word analysis, reading fluency and systematic vocabulary development,

Standardized tests are increasingly used to measure educational outcomes.

reading comprehension, reading literary response and analysis, and writing strategies and application).

For example, in the domain of listening and speaking, expected language proficiency increases gradually from beginning to advanced levels. Table 3.1 depicts the expectations for each of the five levels.

**Advantages of Standards-Based Instruction for English Learners**    An advantage of establishing content and performance standards for English learners is that teachers can use these standards to focus on what students need to know. Rather than following the traditional ELD emphasis on sentence structure, grammar, and the learning of discrete vocabulary terms,

**TABLE 3.1** Listening and Speaking Expectations in the California English Language Development Standards for English Learners at Five Levels

| ELD Level | Expectations |
|---|---|
| Beginning (K–2) | Begins to speak with a few words or sentences, using some English phonemes and rudimentary English grammatical phrases. |
| | Answers simple questions with one- or two-word responses. |
| | Responds to simple directions and questions using physical actions and other means of nonverbal communication. |
| | Independently uses common social greetings and simple repetitive phrases. |
| Early Intermediate | Begins to be understood when speaking, but may have some inconsistent use of Standard English grammatical forms and sounds. |
| | Asks/answers questions using phrases or simple sentences. |
| | Retells familiar stories and short conversations by using appropriate gestures, expressions, and illustrative objects. |
| | Orally communicates basic needs. |
| | Recites familiar rhymes, songs, and simple stories. |
| Intermediate | Asks/answers instructional questions using simple sentences. |
| | Listens attentively to stories/information and identifies key details and concepts using both verbal and nonverbal responses. |
| | Can be understood when speaking, using consistent Standard English forms and sounds; however, some rules may not be in evidence. |
| | Actively participates in social conversations with peers and adults on familiar topics by asking and answering questions and soliciting information. |
| | Retells stories and talks about school-related activities using expanded vocabulary, descriptive words, and paraphrasing. |
| Early Advanced | Listens attentively to stories/information and orally identifies key details and concepts. |
| | Retells stories in greater detail including characters, setting, and plot. |
| | Is understood when speaking, using consistent Standard English forms, sounds, intonation, pitch, and modulation, but may have random errors. |
| | Actively participates and initiates more extended social conversations with peers and adults on unfamiliar topics by asking and answering questions, restating and soliciting information. |
| | Recognizes appropriate ways of speaking that vary based on purpose, audience, and subject matter. |
| | Asks and answers instructional questions with more extensive supporting elements. |

*(Continued)*

**TABLE 3.1** *(Continued)*

| ELD Level | Expectations |
|---|---|
| Advanced | Listens attentively to stories/information on new topics and identifies both orally and in writing key details and concepts. |
| | Demonstrates understanding of idiomatic expressions by responding to and using them appropriately. |
| | Negotiates/initiates social conversations by questioning, restating, soliciting information, and paraphrasing. |
| | Consistently uses appropriate ways of speaking and writing that vary based on purpose, audience, and subject matter. |
| | Narrates and paraphrases events in greater detail, using more extended vocabulary. |

*Source:* Adapted from the California English Language Development Standards, online at www.cde.ca.gov/re/pn/fd/englangart-stnd-pdf.asp.

teachers can pursue an articulated sequence of instruction, integrating the teaching of English into increasingly sophisticated levels of language and meaningful discourse, fluent communication skills, and cognitive academic language proficiency.

The use of standards avoids what has been too-frequent practice in the past: the use in ELD of materials and practices designed for younger students or for special education students (Walqui, 1999). Gándara (1997) reported vast discrepancies between the curricula offered to English speakers and to English learners. The use of standards can alter this practice. A standard becomes useful to teachers when they can identify when the standard has been met or progress is being made toward meeting it (Jametz, 1994). Moreover, students can use these standards to evaluate their own performance.

**Disadvantages of Standards-Based Instruction for English Learners** Although the overall goal of standards-based education is noble—devising a set of very broad standards for all students and measuring success according to a common set of criteria—the ongoing needs of English learners require that school districts remain flexible about the specific means for addressing standards and determining student achievement (Nelson-Barber, 1999). The heavy emphasis on high-stakes testing—and the attendant punitive consequences for schools with low test scores—places English learners at risk of failure.

In fact, schools across the United States report low test scores for students who are linguistically "nonmainstream." Math test scores on the California Achievement Test show a gradual decline for English learners compared to all students, from a 14 percent gap in grade 2 to a 26 percent gap in grade 10 (Bielenberg & Wong Fillmore, 2004/2005). The emphasis on testing leaves little time for teachers to focus on teaching the academic subjects and the language that English learners need to acquire to perform well on high-stakes tests.

The answer to this dilemma is for school districts to invest in high-level, late-exit primary-language instruction and to allow students to be tested in their primary language. The catch is the NCLB requirement that students be tested in English reading after three years of schooling. This regulation pressures schools to begin English reading early. English learners, then, are assumed to attain grade-level expectations in English reading that are set for native English speakers, resulting in pressure toward submersion—or, at best, early-exit transition bilingual education programs—as a preferred model.

If testing has become an index used to compare schools competitively, wisdom suggests that high-quality education requires more than high standards. It also requires a high level of resources to accomplish such mandates. In a sense, the whole community must invest in the learning that takes place in a classroom, for the whole community suffers if the learning impetus of the young is misdirected, quashed, or squandered.

# ROLE, PURPOSES, AND TYPES OF ASSESSMENT

What are the components of the assessment picture for English learners? Some assessments used with English learners are required by government programs and legal mandates, and others are a part of standard classroom practice. Ideally, assessment provides information about students' abilities that teachers can use to advance students' academic and personal development.

## Assessment-Based Instruction

Assessment is the beginning of instruction. With a valid evaluation of the current level of a learner's knowledge, a teacher knows where to start. Assessment also takes place at intervals in order to modify or improve the learner's performance. Assessment informs educators about the strengths and needs of the language learner so that students are properly placed and appropriately instructed, and also informs school authorities, parents, or other concerned parties of the student's progress. A final use of assessment is to compare student achievement against national goals and standards, which poses a significant problem for English learners.

Assessment should not be used merely to place students and design remediation. The best use of assessment is to advance students' understanding and abilities as an integral part of education.

## Identification, Placement, Instruction, Progress Tracking, and Redesignation/Reclassification of English Learners

English learners move through standards-based education in a systematic way. First, procedures are in place in each school district for identifying English learners as they enroll in school. Placement assessment determines the appropriate level of instruction, and, using this placement level as a guideline, teachers design instructional activities and monitor students' progress until they can be reclassified—considered ready to participate in mainstream instruction. The fundamental principle is that English learners be given high-quality English-language education.

**Universal Access to the Language Arts Curriculum**   California, for example, has its own set of education standards. In the area of English-language arts, the draft *Reading/Language Arts Framework* was adopted by the state Board of Education in April 2006. This framework is aligned with the English language arts (ELA) standards. The ELD standards support the ELA standards in two ways: They are aligned with the ELA standards by using similar terminology and categories, and they prepare English learners to advance to the level to which the ELA standards can be used to guide their learning.

Chapter 7 of the *Reading/Language Arts Framework,* "Universal Access to the Language Arts Curriculum," describes the procedures that must be in place in the classroom to ensure that English learners can make adequate yearly progress to meet the standards outlined for mainstream English language arts. These procedures include the following:

- The use of assessment for placement, planning, and monitoring instruction
- Modification of curricula to meet the needs of English learners
- Deployment of a variety of resources and teaching methods adapted to the individual needs of English learners
- Differentiation of instruction in such areas as depth, complexity, and emphasis to ensure students' mastery of key concepts
- Use of flexible grouping strategies according to students' needs
- Marshaling of help from school personnel when appropriate

**Identifying the English Learner**    Various methods are used to identify English learners needing services. The *home language survey,* a short form administered by school districts to determine the language spoken at home, is among the most frequently used methods of identifying students whose primary language is not English. *Registration* and *enrollment* information collected from incoming students can be used to identify those with a home language other than English. A teacher or tutor who has informally observed a student using a language other than English often does identification through observation. Interviews may provide opportunities to identify students, as may *referrals* made by teachers, counselors, parents, administrators, or community members.

One difficulty with the home language survey is that some parents simply indicate that the home language is English, a misdirection that usually stems from the desire that the student receive English-only instruction. The resulting submersion in English-only instruction is difficult for both the learner and the teacher, but placement is the parents' decision.

**Assessment for Placement**    Once students are identified, their level of English proficiency needs to be determined. School districts are required by state and federal mandates to administer a placement test before assigning a new student to an instructional program if a home language survey indicates that the student's primary language is not English. The assessment should be done by staff with the language skills to communicate in the family's native language. Parents and students should be provided with orientation about the assessment and placement process and the expectations and services of the school system. Most important, the school staff needs to be trained in, aware of, and sensitive to the cultural backgrounds and linguistic needs of the student population.

Various states in the United States use a mixture of measures to evaluate students for ELD services. These include the following: oral proficiency tests, teacher judgment, parent request, literacy tests in English, prior instructional services, writing samples in English, achievement tests in English, teacher ratings of English proficiency, oral proficiency tests in the native language, and achievement tests in the native language (Hopstock & Stephenson, 2003).

Table 3.2 lists a variety of tests that are used for identification and placement of English learners in various states.

**TABLE 3.2** Tests Used for Identification and Placement of Language-Minority Students

| | |
|---|---|
| BINL | Basic Inventory of Natural Language |
| BOLT | Bilingual Oral Language Tests |
| Brigance-C | Brigance Comprehensive Inventory of Basic Skills—English and Spanish |
| Brigance-D | Brigance Diagnostic Assessment of Basic Skills—Spanish |
| CAT | California Achievement Test |
| CELT | Comprehensive English Language Test |
| CTBS | Comprehensive Test of Basic Skills |
| FLA | Functional Language Assessment |
| IPT | IDEA (Oral Language) Proficiency Test |
| ITBS | Iowa Test of Basic Skills |
| LAB | Language Assessment Battery |
| LAS | Language Assessment Survey |
| MAP | Maculatis Assessment Program |
| MAT | Metropolitan Achievement Test |
| MRT | Metropolitan Readiness Test |
| PIAT | Peabody Individual Achievement Test |
| PPVT | Peabody Picture Vocabulary Test |
| QSE | Quick Start in English |
| SAT | Stanford Achievement Test |
| SRA | Science Research Associates, Inc. |
| TAP | Total Academic Proficiency |
| WRAT | Wide Range Achievement Test |

*Source:* Adapted from DeGeorge (1987–1988).

## BEST PRACTICE: Learning about Students' Language Abilities

- Observe students in multiple settings, such as classroom, home, and playground.
- With the help of a trained interpreter if necessary, obtain histories (medical, family, previous education, immigration experience, home languages).
- Interview current or previous classroom teachers for information about a student's learning style and classroom behavior.
- Seek information from other school personnel (e.g., counselor, nurse), especially if they are capable of assessing the home language.
- Ask the student's parents to characterize the student's language and performance skills in the home and the community. (Cheng, 1987)

Educators who draw from a variety of information sources can see the students' needs in a broader context and thus design a language program to meet these needs. Teacher-devised checklists and observational data gathered as students participate in learning activities can be used to confirm or adjust student placement (Lucas & Wagner, 1999).

**The California English Language Development Test**    Matched to the California English Language Development Standards is the California English Language Development Test, used to identify new students who are English learners in grades K–12, determine their proficiency, and annually assess their progress in English skills. This test is administered yearly by school-site specialists, either the ELD teacher, an aide, or a program coordinator. California mandates that the CELDT be given within thirty days of enrollment. The CELDT meets the federal mandate that a state receiving funds under Title III of NCLB define annual measurable achievement objectives (AMAOs) for monitoring the progress of English learners toward attaining proficiency in English. Each school district is responsible for submitting annual assessment reports based on CELDT scores.

Students earn a raw score for proficiency in listening/speaking, reading, and writing (grades kindergarten and 1 are tested in listening/speaking only). These raw scores are converted into scaled scores, which can be used to compare proficiency across repeated administrations of the test. The scaled scores also represent weights; in grades 2 through 12, listening/speaking is 50 percent of the test, and reading and writing are weighted at 25 percent each. Charts are used to convert scores into the five proficiency levels from beginning to advanced for each grade level. Accommodations in scheduling, setting, aids, equipment, and presentation format are available for English learners with disabilities.

**Assessment-Based Instruction**    Teaching methods that ensure differentiated standards-based instruction for English learners should take into account the range of English proficiency levels represented in the classroom (as measured by the CELDT), ranging from beginner to advanced fluency. Although students are retested annually using the CELDT, teachers routinely use multiple means to measure and document the progress of an English learner.

English learners' achievement in English is made possible by a linkage between standards, placement testing, instruction, and careful record keeping. Placement tests such as the CELDT that are directly linked to standards-based classroom instruction for English learners permit teachers to begin using targeted instructional practices as soon as students enter the classroom and provide a seamless system that helps teachers track students' continuous progress toward mainstream instruction. Each linkage—from standards to assessment to instruction and back to assessment—is explained in the following sections.

Ideally, each content lesson in which the student participates has not only a content objective, derived from the relevant content standard, but also a language objective designed to meet one of the ELD standards still to be achieved. The ELD standard is based on the students' CELDT level(s); that is, if a group of students has placed in the early intermediate level of the CELDT in reading, the reading objective(s) is drawn from the intermediate level, the level still to be attained. In addition, to promote cognitive academic language proficiency, each lesson should have a learning strategy objective. These objectives are further described in Chapter 5.

One might think that moving from assessment to objective is reverse thinking—indeed, Wiggins and McTighe (1998) call it "backwards" lesson planning—but if the goal is to demonstrate progress in English acquisition, one must first determine what ELD standard a student needs to meet and pair that standard with some assessment that would provide the required evidence that the student has met the standard. Thus, assessment is the flip side of setting objectives—one cannot exist without the other. According to curriculum experts (Contra Costa County Office of Education, 2006), the process of instruction consists of the following:

- Aligning curriculum (both teacher-created and textbook assignments) with grade-level standards and students' assessed level(s) (also called *curriculum calibration*)
- Using grade-level formative (in-process) and summative (final) assessments to improve student achievement
- Applying effective instructional strategies to ensure student mastery of the standards taught

## BEST PRACTICE: "Backwards" Planning

Sheni Chen plans a lesson for sixth-grade students at the intermediate and advanced ELD levels. She plans to address two literacy response and analysis (reading) standards from the California ELD standards: (Intermediate) "Read text and use detailed sentences to respond orally to factual questions about brief prose" and (Advanced) "Read a literary selection and orally explain the literary elements of plot, setting, and characters by using detailed sentences." Three objectives result:

1. (Intermediate) Students will work in groups to use complete sentences to make a sequence chain of ten events in the story "Something to Declare" by Julia Alvarez (see Schifini, Short, & Tinajero, 2002, pp. 120–125).
2. (Advanced) Students will work in groups, using complete sentences to fill out a plot/setting/character matrix chart about the story "Something to Declare."
3. (Intermediate and Advanced) Students will use their charts to play a quiz game with other groups at their level.

Formative Assessment: The teacher will circulate to help the groups plan and complete their charts.

Summative Assessment: Students will receive one point for each of ten questions their group can answer based on their chart.

In subsequent chapters, lesson plans and teaching strategies are presented that differentiate between English learners at various levels of proficiency. Because classrooms invariably include students from more than one level, each lesson plan must include participation for students whose scores represent more than one ELD level. This is the challenge of differentiated instruction.

**Differentiating Instruction to Meet Standards**   In designing universal access to the language arts curriculum, Kame'enui and Simmons (2000) proposed that teachers treat students as members of one of three distinct groups: a benchmark group, a strategic group, or an intensive group. Interventions are tailored to the needs of these groups (see Table 3.3).

**TABLE 3.3**    Interventions Tailored to Three Need-Based Groups

| Group | Characteristics | Interventions |
|---|---|---|
| Benchmark | May be experiencing minor difficulties. | Reteach concepts. Provide additional learning time. Offer support, such as a reading tutor. Use SDAIE techniques. |
| Strategic | Test results show 1–2 standard deviations below the mean. | Provide specific additional assignments to be done with supervision. Schedule extended language arts time. Use SDAIE techniques; modify curriculum. May be referred to school Student Success Team for intervention strategies; may require a 504 plan for targeted interventions. |
| Intensive | Extremely and chronically low performance in one or more measures. | Refer to Student Success Team for evaluation. Special education placement may entail additional resources or instructional support. Student, if placed in special education, will be given an individualized education program (IEP). |

*Source:* California (draft) *Reading/Language Arts Framework* (2006), pp. 410–412.

When interpreting this grouping, it is important to note that the process of acquiring English is not a disability. Just because a student is at the early stage of learning English does not mean that student is in need of intensive intervention. Learning a second language is a social and cognitive achievement that requires time. However, if a student has made no significant progress over a period of four or five months, a referral for a speech/language evaluation may be in order. In bilingual populations, the incidence of special education needs is normally distributed in the same proportion as in the mainstream population.

Gregory (2003) offered strategies for differentiating instruction, particularly in response to standards mandates. Strategies address a range of aspects from learning styles to classroom management.

**Progress Tracking**    In many school districts, each English learner has a progress file in which the yearly CELDT score is recorded. The speaking/listening, reading, and writing standards are listed in the folder, with boxes to check when the student meets each standard. In this file are also stored writing samples that provide evidence that the writing standards have been met. As this folder travels with the student class by class, it is evident which standards are yet to be met. This documentation serves as the step-by-step proof that the English learner is making progress toward transition to the ELA standards for the mainstream learner.

**Redesignation/Reclassification/Exit**   When English learners score a certain level on the CELDT, among other criteria, they are considered ready to participate with English-speaking students in the mainstream classroom. The process for redesignation varies across districts and states. Some districts organize bilingual education advisory committees to ensure parent representation and participation in implementing redesignation criteria that are reliable, valid, and useful. Some states set score targets on language and achievement tests that are used as criteria for proficiency, but in other states the individual districts set their own reclassification criteria. The reclassification process in California uses four criteria:

- CELDT score
- Teacher evaluation of a student's academic performance, based on report card grades, grade point average, or another measure used by the school district
- Consultation with parent or guardian
- Performance in basic skills, as measured by the student's California English Language Arts Standards Test

## BEST PRACTICE: Criteria for Redesignating English Learners

Verdugo Hills High School (Tujunga, California) has various criteria for redesignating students. The school first asserts that "[r]edesignated students speak at least two languages. They learned English as a Second Language and proved their command of English by passing a redesignation test." The students must pass the following:

- CELDT (California English Language Development Test)
- The ELA (English Language Arts) section of the CST (California Standards Test) with a score of basic or higher
- Math and English or ESL 3/4 classes with a C or higher
  (Verdugo Hills High School, 2006)

### Issues of Fairness in Testing English Learners

Tests play a significant role in placing and reclassifying English learners. However, standardized tests are not necessarily well suited as measures of language ability or achievement for English learners. In fact, some have argued that the very use of tests is unfair because tests are used to deprive people of color of their place in society. The goal of tests notwithstanding, both the testing situation and the test content may be rife with difficulties for and bias against English learners.

One might ask just how fair it is to test an English learner whose proficiency is at the earliest levels using assessments that are designed for native English speakers.

Zacarian (2006) relayed the following anecdote about a student who was tested in the Massachusetts Comprehensive Assessment System (MCAS). Clearly, this test failed to connect in a positive way to classroom instruction.

> One year ago, An moved from Vietnam to the United States. She could not speak English and required a translator to meaningfully understand all her instructional program. Her motivation to learn and do well in school was quite strong.

A year after An arrived, she was required to take the MCAS. Her translator was not allowed to assist her.

Faced with the MCAS test, An broke down in tears. She fled the exam site and sought out her tutor. Speaking Vietnamese, she sobbed uncontrollably about how bad she felt about not being able to take the test. During the ensuing week, her attitude toward learning dramatically shifted from one of open-minded risk-taker to that of timid, tentative learner. (p. 11)

Factors within the context of testing such as anxiety, lack of experience with testing materials, time limitations, and rapport with the test administrator may cause difficulties.

**Test Anxiety**    All students experience test anxiety, but this anxiety can be compounded if the test is alien to the students' cultural background and experiences. Certain test formats such as multiple-choice and think-aloud tasks may provoke higher levels of anxiety because students may fear that these assessments inaccurately reflect their true proficiency in English (Scarcella, 1990).

**Time Limitations**    Students may need more time to answer individual questions because of the time needed for mental translation and response formulation. Students from other cultures do not necessarily operate under the same conception of time as do European Americans. Some students may need a time extension or should be given untimed tests.

**Problematic Test Content**    For the most part, language placement tests are well suited for assessing language. Other tests, however, particularly achievement tests, may contain translation problems or bias that affects the performance of English learners. Translating an English-language achievement test into another language, or vice versa, to create equivalent vocabulary items may cause some lack of correspondence in the frequency of the items.

*Geographic bias* might occur when test items feature terms used in particular geographic regions that are not universally shared. *Dialectical bias* occurs when a student is tested using expressions relevant to certain dialect speakers that are not known to others. *Language-specific bias* is created when a test developed for use with one language is used with another language. *Cultural bias* may occur if the test content represents content from the dominant culture that may be understood differently or not at all by English learners. Common European-American food items such as bacon, musical instruments such as a banjo, even nursery rhymes and children's stories may be unfamiliar. Test content may represent a *class bias;* for example, the term *shallots* appeared on a nationally administered standardized achievement test, but only students whose families consume gourmet foods are likely to be familiar with the term.

**Validity**    A test is *valid* if it measures what it claims to be measuring. A test has *content validity* if it samples the content that it claims to test in some representative way. For example, if a reading curriculum includes training in reading for the main idea, then a test of that curriculum would include a test item about reading for the main idea. *Empirical validity* is a measure of how effectively a test relates to some other known measure, such as subsequent success or performance, or with another measure used at the same time.

**Reliability**    A test is *reliable* if it yields predictably similar scores when it is taken again. Although many variables can affect a student's test score—such as error introduced by fatigue, hunger, or poor lighting—these variables usually do not introduce large deviations in students' scores. Ideally, test results should not vary from one day to the next.

**Practicality**   A test may be valid and reliable but cost too much to administer either in time or money. A highly usable test should be relatively easy to administer and score. For example, if a portfolio is kept to document student progress, issues of practicality would be that the portfolio be easy to maintain, accessible to students, and easily scored with a rubric agreed on by teachers and students.

## BEST PRACTICE: In Testing

The following checklist can be used to monitor testing practices for English learners:

- Does the assessment of what has been learned closely match what has been taught? The test content should reflect the curriculum, with the same type of material being tested as was presented during instruction, with the same language and student interaction.
- Do the conditions for assessment resemble that of instruction? The use of similar conditions helps students access and remember what they have learned.
- Does the assessment build on the experiences of students? Is it relevant to their lives, and can it be matched to their developmental level?
- Is the atmosphere positive, avoiding distractions?

### Types of Classroom Assessments for English Learners

Assessment instruments can be used for a number of purposes: to make decisions about student placement, to make day-to-day instructional decisions such as when to provide a student with additional mediation, to make resource decisions such as allocation of instructional time or materials, and to measure student achievement against standards. Teachers who use assessment skillfully can choose which methods of assessment are most useful for classroom decision making; develop effective grading procedures; communicate assessment results to students, parents, and other educators; and recognize unethical, illegal, and otherwise inappropriate assessment methods and uses of assessment information (Ward & Murray-Ward, 1999).

**Test Types**   Various types of tests are used for various purposes. Each has its purposes, features, and limitations.

*Textbook tests* are provided by the textbook publisher and designed to correlate with text content. On the plus side, such tests provide a direct measure of what was presented in the text. Another positive feature is the fact that such a text is probably state adopted because of its match with state standards (Linn, 2000). This makes it easier to compare one class with another. One limitation may be the lack of relevance of this content to the student or the culture of the community.

*Performance-based tests* use a product or a performance as an outcome measure. When schools communicate performance standards to students, the students will be aware of the expectations for their work. Outcome-based performance assessment is designed to provide information about students' proficiency (Marzano, 1994), including the ability to analyze and apply, rather than simply recognize or recall information. Performance-based testing procedures can be based on tasks that students are asked to do, including essays, demonstrations, computer simulations, performance events, and open-ended problem solving.

## BEST PRACTICE: Performance Assessment

An ideal performance test for reading would meet the following criteria:

- Contain materials similar to that found in real books rather than to reproduced paragraphs written with a controlled vocabulary
- Be administered by a concerned adult who is usually present to help (the teacher, or classroom parent volunteer)
- Be observational and interactional, but also valid and reliable, and available for comparison and reporting purposes
- Offer a picture of the student's reading strengths and weaknesses
- Be motivating and fun, so that students, by taking it, would be encouraged to read more (based on Bembridge, 1992)

A positive aspect of performance-based assessment is that it delivers targeted feedback to students on their work in a way that encourages them to compare their work to specific standards. In this way, assessment can provide information about which aspects of instruction need to be redesigned so that both student and teacher performance improves.

*Curriculum tasks* measure the success of activities performed in class. An advantage is that an add-on assessment is not necessary; the class activities themselves can be scored and graded. A limitation is that when students have been given extensive help to complete tasks using formative assessment, it is difficult to assess the skill level they have attained independently of help.

*Authentic tests* measure proficiency on a task commonly found outside the classroom. Examples of authentic assessment include the use of portfolios, projects, experiments, current event debates, and community-based inquiries. Assessments are considered authentic if they stem directly from classroom activities, allow students to share in the process of evaluating their progress, and are valid and reliable in that they truly assess a student's classroom performance in a stable manner (Hancock, 1994; O'Malley & Pierce, 1996).

The advantage of authentic assessment is that it is directly related to classroom performance and permits teachers to design and offer the extra mediation students may need as determined by the assessment. Although such real-world relevance is useful to students in the long run, practically speaking it may be difficult to simulate real-world conditions inside the classroom.

## CLASSROOM GLIMPSE: Authentic Assessment

*At International High School in Queens, New York, authentic assessment is deeply embedded in all activities. In the Global Studies and Art interdisciplinary cluster, students researched a world religion that was unfamiliar to them. Their assignment was to create or re-create a religious artifact typical of the religion.*

*To begin the project, the film* Little Buddha *was shown, and students brainstormed possible research questions. Other project activities included visiting a museum that exhibits religious artifacts, researching in dyads, and communicating their research in progress to peers.*

*On the day of the final performance, students sat at tables of six, shared their findings, asked questions, and clarified what they had learned. The culminating activity was an informal conversation in yet another grouping so that students could expand their perspectives. Although students had their written reports at hand, they could not rely on them for their initial presentations or during the discussion. (Walqui, 1999, p. 74)*

*Teacher-made tests* are often used to determine report card grades. They may contain features of performance-based or other kinds of testing, the distinction being that they are teacher-created. Teacher-made language tests can assess skills in reading comprehension, oral fluency, grammatical accuracy, writing proficiency, and listening. Teacher-constructed tests may not be as reliable and valid as tests that have been standardized, but the ease of construction and administration and the relevance to classroom learning make them popular.

**Assessments That Supplement Tests**   *Portfolio assessments* can be used to maintain a long-term record of students' progress, to provide a clear and understandable measure of student productivity instead of a single number, to offer opportunities for improved student self-image as a result of showing progress and accomplishment, to recognize different learning styles, and to provide an active role for students in self-assessment (Gottlieb, 1995). Portfolios can include writing samples (compositions, letters, reports); student self-assessments; audio recordings (retellings, oral think-alouds); photographs and video recordings; semantic webs and concept maps; and teacher notes about students (Glaser & Brown, 1993).

## CLASSROOM GLIMPSE: Using Portfolio Assessment

*Mr. Zepeda uses a running record to assess students' reading level as he listens to them read individually. In addition, he schedules individual conferences to learn about students' interests. He sets up a schedule so that he is collecting material for student portfolios on a regular basis, and he encourages the students to be involved actively in selecting work for their portfolios.*

*By the time of parent conferences, student portfolios contain writing samples; anecdotal records; photos; periodic running records; periodic math assessments; records of books the student has read; a complete writing project including prewriting, drafts, and final, published copy; a summary of the student's progress; and a list of goals set and accomplished. In preparation for the conference, Mr. Zepeda tells the students, "I want you to select the one piece of work that you feel best about. Write a one-page note to your parents explaining why you are proud of that piece of work and what you learned from doing it." (Herrell, 2000, p. 160)*

*Observation-based assessment* is used by a teacher to makes notes of students' learning behavior as they interact and communicate using language. Observations can be formal (e.g., miscue analyses) or informal (such as anecdotal reports to record students' telling a story, giving a report, or using oral language in other ways). Observations should extend across all areas of the curriculum and in all types of interactional situations to show students' progress. An observation checklist allows the teacher to circulate among students while they are working and monitor specific skills, such as emergent literacy skills, word identification skills, and oral reading (Miller, 1995).

## BEST PRACTICE: Anecdotal Observations

Mrs. Feingold keeps a pad of 3″ × 3″ sticky notes in the pocket of her jacket. When she observes a student's particular use of language, use of a particular learning style, or other noteworthy behavior, she jots the information on a note, including the student's name, date, and time of day. She then transfers this note to a small notebook for safekeeping. Periodically, she files the notes by transferring them to a sheet of paper in each student's file. Just before parent conferences, she duplicates this page—which contains as many as twelve notes side by side—as a permanent observational record of the student's language behaviors.

*Questionnaires and surveys* can help teachers learn about many students' skills and interests at once. These can be given at intervals throughout the year and stored in a student's portfolio.

*Scoring rubrics* created by teachers or obtained commercially can be determined in advance of an assignment and assist both teacher and student by communicating in advance the basis for scoring (Jasmine, 1993).

## BEST PRACTICE: Developing a Scoring Rubric

Rubrics are straightforward to develop.

1. First, the teacher identifies desired results. What should students *know* and *be able to do* at the end of the lesson/unit?
2. Then the teacher determines what is considered to be acceptable evidence: What performance (task) will the students do?
3. Finally, the connection to grading is set. What are the criteria for judging—the point values connected to each aspect of the work?
4. If time permits, examples of excellent, acceptable, and poor work help students visualize the grading criteria.
5. The use of a rubric encourages students to check their work against the criteria in a formative way before final grading.

**Checking for Comprehension**    How does the teacher assess who understands instruction? One part of formative, or in-process, assessment is the use of teacher questions to check an

English learner's comprehension. Depending on the listening skills of the learner, the teacher must ask questions differently for differentiated levels of English proficiency.

At the beginning level, a learner can be asked questions that require a nonverbal answer, or a simple yes/no response: "Is this the Atlantic Ocean?" (pointing to a map). At the early intermediate level, a student can be asked a question requiring a one- or two-word response, or a simple phrase: "Is this the Atlantic or the Pacific Ocean?" At the intermediate level, students can answer in a sentence. "What happened when Columbus first landed?" At the early advanced and advanced levels, the teacher can follow up a single question with another to clarify the students' response or to ask for additional information. Thus, questions are tailored to the student's listening and speaking skills.

## Selecting and Using Appropriate Classroom Assessments

How does a teacher know what, when, and how to test English learners? Tests must be aligned with district curriculum requirements so that test results measure student progress on preselected benchmarks.

Empirical teaching is the foundation for providing additional mediation when necessary to promote the achievement of English learners. Using a variety of assessments the teacher ascertains the factors that contribute to a student's success or difficulties and then designs teaching methods linked to students' needs.

## Assigning Grades to English Learners

Grading and assessment issues concern teachers of all students, but teachers of English learners face additional challenges. English learners' limited English affects their ability to communicate their content knowledge. Should there be two standards of achievement, one for English learners and one for native speakers? Teachers and English learners may have different expectations and interpretations of the grade (Grognet, Jameson, Franco, Derrick-Mescua, 2000). Answers to these issues are not easy. But by working collaboratively with other teachers in the school, an overall schoolwide plan can be developed.

A variety of approaches have been used to assign grades to English learners. Some schools that assign a *traditional A–F grade scale* in accordance with grade-level expectations do not lower performance standards for English learners in sheltered classes, although assignments are adjusted to meet the students' language levels. A *modified A–F grade scale* is used to assess students' work with an A–F grade based on achievement, effort, and behavior, and with report card grades modified by a qualifier signifying work performed above, at, or below grade level. A third type of grading system is the *pass/fail grade scale* used by schools whose English learners are integrated into the regular classroom. This scale avoids comparing the English learners with English-proficient classmates (From the Classroom, 1991).

Some schools have begun to assign a numerical grade according to a student's knowledge of state standards. For example, in second grade, if a child is required to "read fluently and accurately and with appropriate intonation and expression," the number grade reflects the mastery of this standard. Such ancillary factors as attendance and class participation do not influence this grade.

## BEST PRACTICE: A Grading and Assessment Plan

- Ensure that the school or school district has a fair policy for grading English learners that everyone follows.
- Grade a combination of *process* and *product* for all students.
- Early in the class, explain to students what and how you grade. Show examples of good, intermediate, and poor work.
- Use rubrics.
- Involve students in developing criteria for evaluating assignments and help them use these criteria to evaluate their own work
- Use a variety of products to assess (some less dependent on fluent language skills, such as art projects, dramatizations, portfolios, and graphic organizers).
- Adapt tests and test administration (allow more time for English learners; read the test aloud).
- Teach test-taking skills and strategies.
- Grade beginning English learners as satisfactory/unsatisfactory or at/above/below expectations until the end of the year. Then assign a letter grade for the year.
- Put a note on the report card or transcript to identify the student as an English learner. Write comments to clarify how the student was graded. (Adapted from Grognet et al., 2000)

### Test Accommodation

Under certain conditions, the testing situation can be accommodated for English learners. Extended time, large-print format, audio cassette recording, or changes in presentation format may provide English learners with access to the test content without compromising test security or integrity.

## LANGUAGE AND CONTENT AREA ASSESSMENT

Teachers with a flexible repertoire of assessment strategies can design instruction to provide a range of evidence that English learners are advancing in English proficiency and accessing the core curriculum. In an integrated lesson format, each lesson combines language development objectives aligned with the ELD standards, subject matter objectives aligned with content standards, and learning strategy objectives designed to teach cognitive academic language proficiency and thinking skills.

### Combining Language and Content Standards and Learning Strategy Objectives

Objectives are necessary to guide teaching. A lesson with a clear objective focuses the instruction by concentrating on a particular goal and guides the teacher to select those learning activities that accomplish the goal. Once objectives are clearly stated, the teacher selects material that will help students achieve those objectives.

**FIGURE 3.1** Liberty: Content, Language, and Learning Strategy Objectives

**Social Studies Content Objectives**

The students will . . .

Examine the causes and course of the American Revolution and the contributions of South Carolinians

Identify and explain historical, geographic, social, and economic factors that have helped shape American democracy

Describe the means by which Americans can monitor and influence government

**English-Language Development Objectives**

The students will . . .

Listen to, speak, read, and write about subject matter information

Gather information both orally and in writing

Select, connect, and explain information

**Learning Strategy Objectives**

The students will . . .

Apply basic reading comprehension skills (skimming, scanning, previewing, reviewing text)

Take notes to record important information and aid their own learning

Determine and establish the conditions that help them become effective learners (when, where, how to study)

*Source:* Adapted from Majors (n.d.).

**Assessing Content Objectives**    Figure 3.1 displays an example lesson with three types of objectives: content, language, and learning strategy. State agencies, district planners, and school officials have developed curricular maps matched to state standards for each content area. Each lesson contains content area objectives drawn from these standards, with assessment to match the objectives.

For example, in a grade 2 science lesson, the objective might be to learn about balance in nature by sequencing the life cycle of the butterfly. This objective addresses the following California life science standard: "Plants and animals have predictable life cycles. As a basis for understanding this concept: Students know the sequential stages of life cycles are different for different animals, such as butterflies, frogs, and mice" (California Department of Education, 2006c, n.p.). The assessment would be designed to determine whether the students understood this concept.

**Assessing Language Development Objectives**    Each content area has specific language demands. The teacher considers the various tasks that language users must be able to perform in the different content areas (e.g., describing in a literature lesson, classifying in a science lesson, justifying in a mathematics lesson, etc.). In selecting the language objectives, the teacher reviews the target ELD levels of the students and selects objectives that are compatible with the language required in the content lesson. All four language modes (listening, speaking, reading, writing) should be included in the planning across the period of a week. Assessment for these would allow the teacher to "check off" these objectives for each student.

**Assessing Learning Strategy Objectives**   Learning strategies help students learn *how* to learn. Chamot and O'Malley (1994) divided strategies into three areas: cognitive, metacognitive, and social-affective. Each lesson should teach students a skill that helps them learn better. Whether or not they learn this skill should be assessed like any other objective.

## English-Language Development Assessments

Various types of informal and formal ELD assessments are used depending on the language skill involved. In the domain of reading instruction, for example, teachers use a variety of assessment tools, including informal reading inventories, literacy skill checklists, running records, miscue analysis, guided observations, and portfolio assessment (Swartz et al., 2003). The goals of reading instruction, in general, are to expand word recognition, comprehension, and analytic skills.

The goals of writing are similar; vocabulary usage, organization of thought, and ability to master conventional usage in punctuation and grammar are paramount. To this end, assessments in writing balance three major areas: attention to sentence and paragraph structure and organization of ideas, originality and depth of thought, and mechanics (Swartz, Klein, & Shook, 2002).

Listening and speaking skills are the most difficult to assess because in the case of listening the skill is receptive, and hard to measure. Often, however, a student's listening affects classroom behavior directly, in that a student with underdeveloped listening skills may misunderstand oral directions and appear distracted or unresponsive. To assess speaking skills, teachers can plan specifically for oral interchange between students or between teacher and student, and can use simple rubrics to record performance in such areas as pronunciation, fluency, and intelligibility.

## Interpreting the Results of Assessment

Using a three-level rubric, a teacher can scale a student's performance on any objective, including the skills stipulated by the ELD standards. Either the student achieves a secure proficiency in the skill and can move on, or the student needs more guided or independent practice, or he or she cannot perform the skill even with assistance. In the last case, it may be necessary to revisit the same skill at a lower level of the ELD framework; a student may need to be regrouped with others at a lower proficiency level until the preceding level of skill is secure and the student is ready to advance.

**Need-Driven Classroom-Based Interventions**   Students who are not meeting the ELD standards may need individual interventions that can be performed in the regular classroom by the teacher. These include teaching the student using modified input, such as multimodalities (audio-recording a reading passage, using manipulatives, or increased use of primary-language instruction). Other resources might be offered to the learner, such as a simplified text, additional review, study outlines, computer-assisted skill drills, or the services of an instructional aide. These interventions modify and differentiate instruction to address individual learning needs. More modifications are described in a following section for pre–special education intervention.

**Scaffolding Assessments** Scaffolding means building a temporary structure to support learning that is removed once learning takes place. Assessments are sometimes scaffolded to get students started or to help them focus on the desired outcome. At a physical level, this can mean supplying a map with the major rivers already drawn for a geography test, or supplying a chart for $x$ and $y$ values on an algebraic graphing test. More commonly, test questions are scaffolded by underlining key terms, dividing a test question into subsections, or providing direct reference to prior knowledge. These are considered temporary aids, in that a student will not need such assistance every time.

## SPECIAL ISSUES IN ASSESSMENT

A variety of associated issues surrounds the education of English learners. Some of these issues pertain to the skills and abilities of the individual learner, whereas other issues have their origin in larger social or political factors. These include the placement of English learners in special education as well as issues of under- and overachievement in schools.

### Academic and Learning Problems That English Learners May Experience

English learners and students with learning disabilities may experience similar difficulties. This creates a challenge to determine whether a learning impairment is due to the students' second-language acquisition process or to an underlying learning disability that warrants a special education placement. Gopaul-McNicol and Thomas-Presswood (1998) noted the following possible characteristics of English learners and culturally different students that may cause them to resemble students with learning disabilities.

**Perceptual Disorders** If an English learner's home language is nonalphabetic, he or she may have difficulty with alphabetic letters. If a student was not literate in L1, he or she may have difficulty with sound–symbol relationships.

**Receptive Language Disorders** A student may experience difficulty processing language, following directions, and understanding complex language.

**Metacognitive Deficits** English learners without CALP may process information slowly. If from a nonliterate background, the student may lack preliteracy behaviors and strategies, such as regulatory mechanisms (planning, evaluating, monitoring, and remediating difficulties), or not know when to ask for help.

**Memory Difficulties** Lack of transfer between the first and second language or limited information retention in the second language may be present.

**Motor Disorders** Cultural differences and lack of previous education can influence motor performance such as graphomotor (pencil) skills.

**Low Social–Emotional Functioning** English learners may experience academic frustration and low self-esteem. This may lead to self-defeating behaviors such as learned helplessness.

Limited second-language skills may influence social skills, friendships, and teacher–student relationships.

**Difficulty Attending and Focusing**    English learners may exhibit behavior such as distractibility, short attention span, impulsivity, or high motor level (e.g., finger tapping, excessive talking, fidgeting, inability to remain seated). These may stem from cognitive overload when immersed in a second language for a long period of time.

**Culture/Language Shock**    Students experiencing culture or language shock may show uneven performance, not volunteer, not complete work, or seek constant attention and approval from the teacher. The emotional reactions to long-term acculturation stress may lead to withdrawal, anger, or a pervasive sense of sadness.

**Reading Dysfunctions**    English learners may exhibit a variety of reading problems, including slow rate of oral or silent reading (using excessive lip movement or vocalization in silent reading); short perceptual span (reading word by word rather than in phrases); reading without expression; mispronunciation of words (lack of word attack skills or random substitutions); omission, insertion, or substitution of words and letters in oral reading; excessive physical movement when reading (squirming); reversals or repetition of words or groups of words in oral reading; lack of comprehension; inability to state the main idea or topic or to remember what has been read; failure to reread or summarize; lack of skill in using information tools such as table of contents; and lack of interest in reading in or out of school.

**Written Expression Skill Deficits**    Writing may present an additional area of difficulty for English learners, at the level of grammar and usage or at the level of content. Teachers often judge writing as "bad" if it lacks the following characteristics: variety in sentence patterns; variety in vocabulary (choosing correct words and using synonyms); coherent structure in paragraphs and themes; control over usage, such as punctuation, capitalization, and spelling; and the ability to detect and correct one's own errors. These writing skills take years to develop. One cannot expect a newcomer to English to demonstrate proficiency in these skills immediately. Some writing skills may not be a part of the student's native culture, and acquiring these requires acculturation as well as second-language acquisition.

## Identification, Referral, and Early Intervention of English Learners with Special Needs

Classroom teachers, along with parents and other school-site personnel, are responsible for identifying English learners with special instructional needs. When a classroom teacher initially identifies a student who may need additional mediation, a phase of intensive focus begins that may or may not result in a placement in special education. The classroom teacher's primary concern is to determine whether a student's academic or behavioral difficulties reflect factors other than disabilities, including inappropriate or inadequate instruction.

**The Referral Process**    The school screen team, school-site assessment council, or otherwise-named entity is a school-site committee that bears responsibility for receiving and acting on an initial referral by the classroom teacher for a student who is in need of additional mediation in learning. The team reviews the classroom teacher's specific concerns about the student and makes suggestions for modifying the learning environment for the student within the regular classroom. This process of gathering data and implementing changes in the educational environment for the student before testing is called the period of initial intervention.

How can the classroom teacher decide whether a student might have a disability requiring referral to special education? Friend and Bursuck (2002) offered these questions as a means to assist the decision-making process:

- What are specific examples of a student's needs that are as yet unmet in the regular classroom?
- Is there a chronic pattern that negatively affects learning? Or, conversely, does the difficulty follow no clear pattern?
- Is the student's unmet need becoming more serious as time passes?
- Is the student's functioning significantly different from that of classmates?

**Early Intervention**    If a student is not responsive to alternative instructional or behavioral interventions over a period of several weeks or months, there is more of a chance that a placement in special education will be necessary (Ortiz, 2002; García & Ortiz, 2004). A key to the diagnosis of language-related disorders is the presence of similar patterns in both the primary and the second languages. Poor oral language/vocabulary development, difficulties with writing, and poor comprehension in both languages often indicate learning disabilities. The classroom teacher implements strategies over a period of time and documents the effect these innovations have on the student.

## BEST PRACTICE: Instructional Modifications for English Learners

Although many of the following recommended strategies are appropriate for all students, they are particularly critical for English learners suspected of a learning disability:

- Teach skills and strategies explicitly.
- Provide instruction through all learning channels—visual, auditory, and tactile.
- Monitor the student for fatigue.
- Provide "wait-time" and "think-time."
- Respond positively to communication attempts.
- Use questions appropriate to students' second-language acquisition stage.
- Check frequently for comprehension.
- In bilingual classrooms, use the preview-view-review technique. (Adapted from Nemmer-Fanta, 2002)

**Continued Services during and after Placement**    Working directly with the student, the classroom teacher may tutor or test the child in the curricular material used in the classroom; chart daily measures of the child's performance to see if skills are being mastered; consult with other teachers on instructional interventions; devise tests based on the classroom curriculum; and train older peers, parent volunteers, and teacher aides to work with the student as tutors.

If the evaluation process results in the recommendation of special education services, the classroom teacher may help to write the student's individual education program (IEP). Collaboration between the classroom teacher, special educators, parents, and the student is vital to the drafting and approval of an IEP that will result in academic success.

## Teaching Strategies for the CLD Special Learner

Modified instruction can accommodate different instructional needs within the classroom and foster learning across academic content areas. *Inclusion* is a term often used to describe the provision of instruction within the conventional or mainstream classroom for students with special needs or talents. Although primarily associated with the education of exceptional students, this term has also been used for the varying degrees of inclusion of CLD learners in the mainstream classroom.

The mainstream classroom of an included student is a rich, nonrestrictive setting for content instruction and language development activities. The three components of an exemplary program for CLD learners—comprehensible instruction in the content areas using primary language and SDAIE, language arts instruction in English, and heritage- (primary) language maintenance or development—are present.

The teacher makes every effort to help the student be "as dynamically a part of the class as any student that is perceived as routinely belonging to that class" (Florida Department of Education, 2003, n.p.). Overall, teaching for inclusion features teaching practices that showcase learners' strong points and support the areas in which they may struggle. By using a variety of interactive strategies, teachers have ample opportunity to discover which methods and activities correspond to student success.

The task for the teacher becomes more complex as the increasingly varied needs of students—those who are mainstream (non-CLD/non–special education), mainstream–special education, CLD learner, CLD learner–special education—are mixed in the same classroom.

Such complexity would argue that an inclusive classroom be equipped with additional educational resources, such as teaching assistants, lower student-to-teacher ratio, and augmented budget for instructional materials. The chief resource in any classroom, however, is the breadth and variety of instructional strategies on which the experienced teacher can draw. The following sections suggest multiple strategies in the areas of listening skills, reading, and writing.

**Adapting Listening Tasks**    Techniques for teaching listening skills have been grouped in Table 3.4 into the three phases of the listening process: before listening, during listening, after listening.

**Adapting Reading Tasks**    Reading assignments for inclusion students listed in Table 3.5 follow the three-part division of the reading process (before reading, during reading, and after reading).

**Adapting Writing Tasks**    Writing is used in two main ways in classrooms: to capture and demonstrate content knowledge (taking notes, writing answers on assignments or tests) and to express creative purposes. If the acquisition of content knowledge is the goal, students can often use a variety of alternatives to writing that avoid large amounts of written work (both in class and homework). In general, teachers of students with special needs in inclusive settings change the response mode to oral when appropriate (Smith, Polloway, Patton, & Dowdy, 2003).

**TABLE 3.4** Strategies for Additional Mediation of the Listening Process for Included Students

| Phase | Strategies |
|---|---|
| Before Listening | ■ Directly instruct listening strategies.<br>■ Arrange information in short, logical, well-organized segments.<br>■ Preview ways to pay attention.<br>■ Preview the content with questions that require critical thinking.<br>■ Establish a listening goal for the lesson.<br>■ Provide prompts indicating that the information about to be presented is important enough to remember or write down. |
| During Listening | ■ Actively involve students in rehearsing, summarizing, and taking notes.<br>■ Use purposeful, curriculum-related listening activities.<br>■ Model listening behavior and use peer models.<br>■ Teach students to attend to teacher cues and nonverbal signs that denote important information.<br>■ Use verbal, pictorial, or written prelistening organizers to cue students to important information.<br>■ Teach students to self-monitor their listening behavior using self-questioning techniques and visual imagery while listening. |
| After Listening | ■ Discuss content. Use teacher questions and prompts to cue student response (e.g., "Tell me more").<br>■ Integrate other language arts and content activities with listening as a follow-up. |

*Source:* Adapted from Mandlebaum & Wilson (1989).

**TABLE 3.5** Strategies for Additional Mediation of the Reading Process for Included Students

| Phase | Strategies |
|---|---|
| Before reading | ■ Preview reading materials to assist students with establishing purpose, activating prior knowledge, budgeting time, and focusing attention.<br>■ Explain how new content to be learned relates to content previously learned.<br>■ Create vocabulary lists and teach these words before the lesson to ensure that students know these vocabulary words rather than just recognize them.<br>■ Ensure that readability levels of the textbooks and trade books used in class are commensurate with the students' language levels.<br>■ Locate lower-reading-level supplements in the same topic so that tasks can be adapted to be multilevel and multimaterial.<br>■ Rewrite material (or solicit staff or volunteers to do so) to simplify the reading level, or provide chapter outlines or summaries.<br>■ Tape text reading or have it read orally to a student. Consider the use of peers, volunteers, and/or paraprofessionals in this process. |

*(Continued)*

**TABLE 3.5** (*Continued*)

| Phase | Strategies |
|---|---|
| During reading | ▪ Highlight key words, phrases, and concepts with outlines or study guides.<br>▪ Reduce extraneous noise.<br>▪ Use visual aids (e.g., charts and graphs) to supplement reading tasks. |
| After reading | ▪ When discussing stories, paraphrase material to clarify content.<br>▪ Encourage feedback from students to check for understanding.<br>▪ Reteach vocabulary to ensure retention.<br>▪ Provide the page numbers where specific answers can be found in a reading comprehension/content assignment.<br>▪ Use brief individual conferences with students to verify comprehension. |

*Source:* Adapted from Smith, Polloway, Patton, & Dowdy (2003).

Overall, the classroom teacher with a wide repertoire of strategies for instructing English learners will be able to employ these techniques to augment mainstream instruction whenever necessary. One caution, however: Learning English is not a compensatory endeavor, not a handicap. English learners are doing on a daily basis what the average resident of the United States cannot do—function in two languages. When successful, it is an intellectual triumph.

Regardless of how valid, reliable, and practical an assessment may be, if it serves only the teachers' and the institution's goals, the students' language progress may not be promoted. Assessment must instead be an integral part of a learning environment that encourages students to acquire a second language as a means to fulfill personal and academic goals.

### NEW YORK TIMES EDUCATION NEWS FEED: Read and Report

The New York Times Education News Feed is a collection of education-related stories from the New York Times, updated hourly. You can access the New York Times Education News Feed directly by logging on to www.mylabschool.com, and entering Assignment ID **NYTNF** into the **Assignment Finder.**

Your assignment is to return to the news feed once a day for a week, and read as many articles as appear on the subject of educational assessment, English language learners, or both. Make notes on each article as you read them. At the end of the week, look over your notes and write a page describing the things you learned that were new to you, with comments on how you think this new information will help you become a better classroom teacher. Bring your work in to share with the class, or submit it to your professor for credit.

**(mylabschool**
Where the classroom comes to life!

# CHAPTER FOUR

# Programs for English Learners

English learners enter schooling fluent in a primary language other than English, a proficiency that can function as a resource. In many parts of the world, including Canada, second-language instruction is considered either a widely accepted component of being well educated or a legal mandate in an officially bilingual country. Acquiring a second language is not easy, especially to the level of using that language to succeed in postsecondary education. English learners face that challenge daily.

A growing number of schools in the United States offer two-way immersion programs that help English learners develop academic competence in their heritage language while acquiring fluency and literacy in English—while at the same time native-English-speaking students develop speaking fluency and academic competence in the home language of the English learners. These programs showcase the idea that *multicompetent language use* (Cook, 1999, p. 190) is a valuable skill. Proficiency in multiple languages is also a career enhancement in the modern world of global commerce.

The classrooms of the United States are increasingly diverse, with students coming from many countries of the world. The challenge to any English-language development program is to cherish and preserve the rich cultural and linguistic heritage of the students as they acquire English.

This chapter addresses the history, legality, and design of program models that induct speakers of other languages into English instruction. Although most of these programs take place at the elementary level, an increasing number of students immigrate to the United States at the middle and high school levels, and programs must be designed to meet their needs as well. The program models presented in this chapter vary greatly on one key dimension—how much encouragement is offered to students to maintain their primary language and how much instructional support they receive to accomplish this.

## THE HISTORY OF MULTILINGUAL COMPETENCY IN THE UNITED STATES

Bilingualism has existed in the United States since the colonial period, but over the more than two centuries of American history it has been alternately embraced and rejected. The immigrant languages and cultures in North America have enriched the lives of the people in American communities, yet periodic waves of language restrictionism have virtually eradicated the capacity of many U.S. residents to speak a foreign or second language, even those who are born into families with a heritage language other than English. For English learners,

English-only schooling has often brought difficulties, cultural suppression, and discrimination even as English has been touted as the key to patriotism and success. This section traces the origin and development of, and support for, language services for English learners in the United States.

### Early Bilingualism in the United States

At the time of the nation's founding, at least twenty languages could be heard in the American colonies, including Dutch, French, German, and numerous Native-American languages. In 1664 at least eighteen colonial languages were spoken on Manhattan Island. Bilingualism was common among both the working and educated classes, and schools were established to preserve the linguistic heritage of new arrivals. The Continental Congress published many official documents in German and French as well as in English. German schools were operating as early as 1694 in Philadelphia, and by 1900 more than 4 percent of the United States' elementary school population was receiving instruction either partially or exclusively in German. In 1847, Louisiana authorized instruction in French, English, or both at the request of parents. The Territory of New Mexico authorized Spanish–English bilingual education in 1850 (Crawford, 1999). Table 4.1 surveys the early history of language use and policy in America.

Although there were several such pockets of acceptance for bilingual education, other areas of the country effectively restricted or even attempted to eradicate immigrant and minority languages. In 1879, however, the federal government forced Native-American children to attend off-reservation, English-only schools where they were punished for using their native language. In the East, as large numbers of Eastern Europeans immigrated, descendants of the English settlers began to harbor resentment against these newcomers. New waves of Mexican and Asian immigration in the West brought renewed fear of non-English influences (Crawford, 1999).

## BEST PRACTICE: Early Cherokee Language Rights

Under an 1828 treaty, the U.S. government recognized the language rights of the Cherokee tribe. Eventually, the Cherokees established a twenty-one-school educational system that used the Cherokee syllabary to achieve a 90 percent literacy rate in the native language. About 350,000 Aniyunwiya (Cherokee) people currently live primarily in Oklahoma and North Carolina, and about 22,000 speak the language (which today is known as Tsalagi). (www.native-languages.org/cherokee.htm)

### The Struggles for Language Education Rights in the Twentieth Century

World War I brought anti-German hysteria, and various states began to criminalize the use of German in all areas of public life. Subsequently, fifteen states legislated English as the basic language of instruction. This repressive policy continued during World War II, when Japanese-language schools were closed. Until the late 1960s, "Spanish detention"—being kept after

**TABLE 4.1**   Early History of Language Use and Policy in America

| Date | Event | Significance |
|---|---|---|
| Pre-1492 | North America is rich in indigenous languages. | Linguistic diversity is a type of biodiversity, encoding millennia of information about the physical and social environment. |
| 16th century | Spain establishes missions in what is now California. | Spanish rulers decree the replacement of indigenous languages by Spanish. |
| 1781 | U.S. Articles of Confederation are written in English, French, and German. | Early acknowledgment of U.S. multilingualism on the part of the Founding Fathers. |
| 1800s | European Americans settle Western U.S. | Mexicans and Indians are excluded from whites-only schools. |
| 1828 | U.S. government signs a treaty with Cherokee tribes. | The U.S. government recognizes the language rights of the Cherokee tribes. Eventually, a 21-school educational system achieves a 90% literacy rate in Cherokee. |
| 1839 | Ohio adopts bilingual education. | Schools could operate in German and English at request of parent. |
| 1848 | Mexican territory is annexed to the United States in the Treaty of Guadalupe Hidalgo. | Mexican residents of appropriated territory in what are now California, Arizona, New Mexico, Texas, Utah, and Nevada are promised the right to use Spanish in schools, courts of law, employment, and everyday life. |
| 1864 | The federal government forces Native-American children to attend off-reservation schools. | Schools are English only. Native Americans are punished for using their native language. |
| 1888 | First antibilingual education legislation is passed. | Wisconsin and Illinois attempt to institute English-only schooling. |
| 1898 | U.S. wins Spanish–American War and colonizes Puerto Rico and the Philippines. | Public and private schools are forced to use English as the language of instruction. Submersion in English is a sustained policy in Puerto Rican schools until the 1950s. |

school for using Spanish—remained a formal punishment in the Rio Grande Valley of Texas, where using a language other than English as a medium of public instruction was a crime (Crawford, 1999).

Although the U.S. Supreme Court, in the *Meyer v. Nebraska* case (1923), extended the protection of the Constitution to everyday speech and prohibited coercive language restriction on the part of states, the "frenzy of Americanization" (Crawford, 1999) had fundamentally changed public attitudes toward learning in other languages. European immigrant groups felt strong pressures to assimilate, and bilingual instruction by the late 1930s was virtually eradicated throughout the United States. This assimilationist mentality worked best with northern European immigrants. For other language minorities, especially those with dark complexions, English-only schooling brought difficulties. Discrimination and cultural repression became associated with linguistic repression.

After World War II, writers began to speak of language-minority children as being "culturally deprived" and "linguistically disabled." The cultural deprivation theory pointed to such environmental factors as inadequate English-language skills, lower-class values, and parental failure to stress educational attainment. On the basis of their performance on IQ tests administered in English, a disproportionate number of English learners ended up in special classes for the educationally handicapped.

Bilingual education was reborn in the early 1960s in Dade County, Florida, as Cuban immigrants, fleeing the 1959 revolution, requested bilingual schooling for their children. The first program at the Coral Way Elementary School was open to both English and Spanish speakers. The objective was fluency and literacy in both languages. Subsequent evaluations of this bilingual program showed success both for English-speaking students in English and for Spanish-speaking students in Spanish and English. Hakuta (1986) reported that by 1974 there were 3,683 students in bilingual programs in the elementary schools nationwide and approximately 2,000 in the secondary schools.

## Legal and Legislative Mandates Supporting Language Education Rights

Progress in English-language development services in the United States has taken place on three fronts: cultural, legislative, and judicial. Culturally, the people of the United States have seemed to accept bilingualism when it has been economically useful and to reject it when immigrants were seen as a threat. Legislative and judicial mandates have reflected this ambivalence.

After the civil rights era, the provision of services for English learners has been viewed as a right. This is consonant with the Universal Declaration of Linguistic Rights signed in Barcelona in June 1996, the 1948 Universal Declaration of Human Rights, and the Declaration on the Rights of Persons Belonging to National, Ethnic, Religious and Linguistic Minorities of the General Assembly of the United Nations (1992). The May 25 Memorandum from the Office for Civil Rights (also called the Lau Remedies) mandated that school districts with more than 5 percent national-origin minority children must offer special language instruction for students with a limited command of English. It prohibited the assignment of students to classes for the handicapped on the basis of their English-language skills, prohibited placing such students in vocational tracks instead of teaching them English, and mandated that administrators communicate with parents in a language parents can understand.

Because the states reserve the right to dictate educational policy, services for English learners have depended on the vagaries of state law. When the U.S. Congress enacted legislation to begin Title VII of the Elementary and Secondary Education Act, federal funding became available for bilingual education programs. Almost simultaneously, the courts began to rule that students deprived of bilingual education must receive compensatory services. Together, the historical precedents, federal legislative initiatives, and judicial fiats combined to establish bilingual education in the United States (see Tables 4.2 and 4.3).

**TABLE 4.2** The Early Twentieth Century: Language Use and Policy Are Contested in the United States

| Date | Event | Significance |
|------|-------|-------------|
| 1906 | Congress passes English requirement for naturalized citizenship. | First national English-language requirement |
| 1917–1918 | The governor of Iowa bans the use of any foreign language in public: Ohio passes legislation to remove all uses of German from the state's elementary schools. | With German speakers as the target, mobs raid schools and burn German textbooks. Subsequently, 15 states legislate English as the basic language of instruction. |
| 1920s–1970s | Ku Klux Klan members in Maine, numbering 150,141 in 1925, burn crosses in hostility to French Americans. | French is forbidden to be spoken in schools in Maine. |
| 1923 | *Meyer v. Nebraska* | The Supreme Court bans an English-only law in a case brought by German Americans. |
| 1930 | *Del Rio Independent School District v. Salvatierra* | A Texas superior court finds that the Del Rio Independent school district cannot segregate Mexican students, but a higher court rules that the segregation is necessary to teach English to Mexican students. |
| 1931 | *Lemon Grove v. Álvarez* | A state superior court rules that school segregation is against the law in California. |
| 1936 | Massive IQ testing of Puerto Ricans in New York is used to justify widespread school placement of Spanish-speaking children 2–3 years below grade level. | Thousands of New York Puerto Ricans launch a campaign for bilingual education. |
| 1941 | Japanese-language schools are closed. | Japanese are incarcerated in internment camps with English-only schools. |
| 1946, 1947 | *Méndez v. Westminster School District* | The U.S. Ninth District Court applies the 14th Amendment to schools, insisting "schools must be open to all children . . . regardless of lineage." |
| 1961 | Immigrants fleeing the Cuban revolution demand Spanish-language schooling. | Dade County, Florida, implements Spanish–English bilingual education. |
| 1968 | 10,000 Chicanos boycott schools in Los Angeles demanding bilingual education and more Latino teachers; boycotts spread across U.S. | Leaders of Los Angeles boycott are arrested; two years later charges against them are declared unconstitutional. |

**TABLE 4.3** Key Legislation and Court Cases in the Struggle for English Learners' Language Rights

| Date | Event | Significance |
| --- | --- | --- |
| 1964 | The Civil Rights Act: Title VI | Prohibits denial of equal access to education on the basis of race, color, national origin, or limited proficiency in English in the operation of a federally assisted program. Compliance is enforced through the United States Office for Civil Rights. |
| 1968 | ESEA Title VII offers funding for bilingual education programs. | First bilingual kindergarten in New York City; first bilingual education major at Brooklyn College. |
| Early 1970s | Bilingual programs reach only one out of every forty Mexican-American students in the Southwest. | Based on these data, the U.S. Office of Civil Rights begins enforcing compliance with judicial mandates. |
| 1972 | *Serna v. Portales Municipal Schools* | The first federal court enforcement of Title VI of the Civil Rights Act. A federal judge orders instruction in native language and culture as part of a desegregation plan. |
| 1973 | *Keyes v. School District No. 1, Denver, Colorado* | Latinos must be covered by *Brown v. Board of Education*—Mexicans cannot be labeled "white" and used to create falsely desegregated schools containing only blacks and Latinos. |
| 1974 | The Equal Education Opportunities Act (EEOA) (U.S. Congress) | "No state shall deny equal educational opportunities to an individual on account of his or her race, color, sex, or national origin by the failure of an educational agency to take appropriate action to overcome language barriers that impede equal participation by its students in its instructional programs." |
| 1974 | *Lau v. Nichols* (414 U.S. 563) | U.S. Supreme Court establishes the right of students to differential treatment based on their language minority status, but it does not specify a particular instructional approach. |
| 1975 | Lau Remedies—guidelines from the U.S. Commissioner of Education | Standardized requirements for identification, testing, and placement into bilingual programs. Districts are told how to identify and evaluate children with limited English skills, what instructional treatments to use, when to transfer children to all-English classrooms, and what professional standards teachers need to meet. |
| 1977 | *Ríos v. Read* | A federal court rules that a bilingual program must include a cultural component. |

**TABLE 4.3**   *(Continued)*

| Date | Event | Significance |
|------|-------|--------------|
| 1981 | *Castañeda v. Pickard* | The Fifth Circuit Court tests the 1974 EEOA statute, outlining three criteria for programs serving EL students: District programs must be: (1) based on "sound educational theory," (2) "implemented effectively" through adequately trained personnel and sufficient resources, and (3) evaluated as effective in overcoming language barriers. Qualified bilingual teachers must be employed, and children are not to be placed on the basis of English-language achievement tests. |
| 1983 | *Keyes v. School District #1* | Due process is established for remedies of EEOA matters. |
| 1987 | *Gómez v. Illinois State Board of Education* | State school boards can enforce state and federal compliance with EEOA regulations. Districts must properly serve students who are limited in English. |
| 1992 | *Plyler v. Doe* | The U.S. Supreme Court decides that a state's statute that denies school enrollment to children of illegal immigrants "violates the Equal Protection Clause of the Fourteenth Amendment." |
| 1994 | California passes Proposition 187, which makes it illegal to provide public education to illegal immigrants. | Proposition is overturned in the courts because it violates *Plyler v. Doe.* |
| 1998 | California voters approve Unz Initiative Proposition 227 (ED Code 300-340). | Requires that K–12 instruction be overwhelmingly in English, restricting use of primary language as a means of instruction. Subsequent measures pass in Arizona and Massachusetts, but French speakers vote down similar initiative in Maine. |
| 2001 | No Child Left Behind Act, Title III | Federal funding is available to support schools in educating English learners. |
| 2004 | Individuals with Disabilities Education Improvement Act of 2004 (IDEA), Public Law 108-446 | Congress aligns education of children with disabilities with NCLB to mandate equity and accountability. |
| 2004 | *Williams v. State of California* | California schools must provide equitable access to textbooks, facilities, and teaching staffs, including teachers of English learners. |

*See also Crawford (2004, pp. 96–97) for expanded timeline, "Linguistic Diversity in America."

*Sources:* Cockcroft, 1995; Wiese & García, 1998; Crawford, 1999.

## BEST PRACTICE: Indigenous Language Rights

Times have changed for Native-American-language speakers. In the United States, 281,990 families speak an American-Indian home language (www.infoplease.com/ipa/A0192523.html). The most-spoken Native-American language is Navajo, with 150,000 speakers. In 1990 the U.S. Congress passed Public Law 101-477, which sustains the right of Native Americans to express themselves through the use of Native-American languages in any public proceeding, including publicly supported education programs. Among the goals of this law are the following:

- Preserve, protect, and promote the rights and freedom of Native Americans to use, practice, and develop Native-American languages
- Increase student success and performance
- Increase students' awareness and knowledge of their culture and history
- Increase student and community pride

# FEDERAL AND STATE REQUIREMENTS FOR ELD SERVICES

Successive authorizations of the federal Elementary and Secondary Education Act in 1968, 1974, 1978, 1988, and 1989 incorporated federal recognition of the unique educational disadvantages faced by non-English-speaking students. In 1968, Congress authorized $7.5 million to finance seventy-six bilingual education projects serving 27,000 children. In 1974, Congress specifically linked equal educational opportunity to bilingual education, allowing Native-American and English-speaking children to enroll in bilingual education programs, and funding programs for teacher training, technical assistance for program development, and development and dissemination of instructional materials.

In 1978, Congress added to the definition of bilingual education, stipulating that instruction in English should "allow a child to achieve competence in the English language." Additionally, parents were included in program planning, and personnel in bilingual programs were to be proficient in the language of instruction and English. In 1988, Congress increased funding to state education agencies, placed a three-year limit on participation in transitional bilingual programs, and created fellowship programs for professional training. Developmental bilingual programs were expanded to maintain the native language of students in the reauthorization of 1989.

When the Elementary and Secondary Education Act of 1965 was amended and reauthorized in 1994, it was within the framework of Goals 2000, with the goal to "educate limited-English-proficient children and youth to meet the same rigorous standards for academic achievement expected of all children and youth" ([7102][b]). This emphasis on standards was the linchpin of the 2001 reauthorization, the No Child Left Behind Act, in which all schools are required to provide qualified teachers, and all students are required to pass standardized tests.

### No Child Left Behind

Under the No Child Left Behind Act, states must measure student progress on statewide achievement tests. Title III of this act, titled "Language Instruction for Limited English Proficient and

Immigrant Students," proposes to measure the progress of English learners against common expectations for student academic achievement by aligning academic assessments, teacher preparation and training, curriculum, instructional materials, and state academic standards.

The purpose of Title III is to upgrade schooling for low-achieving children in highest-poverty schools, including limited-English-proficient children. The goal is to hold schools, local educational agencies, and states accountable for improving the academic achievement of all students, potentially by closing underperforming schools or providing high-quality educational alternatives to students in such schools.

Because English learners must be tested annually after thirty months of schooling (with few exceptions), and because the continued existence of the school is predicated on annual improvement, English learners experience high-stakes pressure to test well. No second-language acquisition theory in existence makes the claim that the high anxiety of testing furthers language learning. Often, "teaching to the test" leaves little room for teaching English. NCLB, then, appears to be an unfortunate fit with what is known about effective second-language learning.

## Proposition 227

In 1998, California, with a school enrollment of approximately 1.4 million limited-English-proficient children, passed Proposition 227, a measure rejecting bilingual education. The proposition stipulates that

> all children in California public schools shall be taught English by being taught in English. In particular, this shall require that all children be placed in English language classrooms. Children who are English learners shall be educated through sheltered English immersion during a temporary transition period not normally intended to exceed one year. . . . Once English learners have acquired a good working knowledge of English, they shall be transferred to English language mainstream classrooms. (California State Code of Regulations [CSCR], 1998, Article 2, 305)

Article 3, Provision 310 of the CSCR provided parents with waiver possibilities if their children met criteria spelled out in the law: "Under such parental waiver conditions, children may be transferred to classes where they are taught English and other subjects through bilingual education techniques or other generally recognized educational methodologies permitted by law." Before parents can ask for a waiver, however, a student must sit through thirty days of structured English immersion (SEI). Potentially one-ninth of a school year could pass before an English learner at the beginning level could comprehend instruction. Unfortunately, expecting children to learn English (along with academic subjects) in a single year flies in the face of contemporary research on language acquisition (Collier, 1987).

Empirical evidence is lacking that indicates any benefit to language-minority students from passage of Proposition 227. A summary of findings from ten studies conducted by research institutes and scholars affiliated with major California universities found that Proposition 227 had demonstrated considerable disruption to the education of language-minority students with no demonstrable benefits in terms of improved teaching and learning conditions or academic achievement (García, 2000).

A study released by the University of California's Linguistic Minority Research Institute (Gándara, Maxwell-Jolly, García, Asato, Gutiérrez, Stritkus, & Curry, 2000) described the implementation of Proposition 227 in sixteen school districts and twenty-five schools throughout the state. The report documents wide variation in the ways school districts have interpreted 227's requirements. School districts with a strong English-only stance before passage showed a mean decrease in primary-language instruction from 17 percent in 1998 to 2 percent in 1999. In contrast, districts with strong primary-language instruction programs experienced only a 2 percent lower rate of use of Spanish, from 33 to 31 percent, because parents applied for and were granted waivers.

### Williams et al. v. State of California

In 2000, in a class action lawsuit, a group of plaintiffs, including Eliezer Williams, represented by the Mexican American Legal Defense and Educational Fund (MALDEF) sued the State of California, the California Department of Education, the California Board of Education, and the California Superintendent of Public Instruction on behalf of 75,000 public school students, alleging that substandard conditions in California schools were causing deprivation in violation of the equal protection clauses of the California Constitution. The lawsuit claimed that the students in question had suffered from poorly trained teachers, serious overcrowding, inadequate physical conditions for schooling (filthy bathrooms, leaky roofs, and nonfunctioning heating and cooling systems), and insufficient or outdated textbooks.

A settlement was reached requiring the State of California to pass legislation requiring that every school district provide a uniform complaint process for complaints regarding insufficient instructional materials, unsafe or unhealthy facility conditions, and teacher vacancies and misassignments. Such a law was signed into effect in 2004. Funding was also provided for facilities repair, new instructional materials, upgraded education for teachers of English learners, and phasing out of multitrack schools in the lowest-performing schools. In return for these provisions, the plaintiffs in *Williams v. California* agreed not to initiate lawsuits for redress until a period of four years had elapsed.

This lawsuit should inaugurate a renewed emphasis on the preparation of teachers for classrooms of English learners, as well as improve the learning conditions in California's underperforming schools.

### Lau v. Nichols

In 1973 a group of non-English-speaking Chinese students sued San Francisco Unified School District officials, claiming that "sink or swim" instruction (denial of language development services) was a violation of their civil rights under Title VI of the Civil Rights Act of 1964. Lower federal courts had absolved the school district of any responsibility for minority children's "language deficiency." But a unanimous Supreme Court ruled as follows: "There is no equality of treatment merely by providing students with the same facilities, textbooks, teachers, and curriculum, for students who do not understand English are effectively foreclosed from any meaningful education"—essentially stating that imposing the requirement that a child must have basic skills in English before effectively participating in the educational program is "to make a mockery of public education" (414 U.S. 563).

Although *Lau v. Nichols* did not specify what type of program a school district must offer, the Chinese parents who sued the San Francisco Unified School District formed an advisory committee, and eventually a program emerged that satisfied the requirements set forth by the court. In 1975 the so-called Lau Remedies published by the U.S. Commissioner for Education provided standardized requirements for identifying and evaluating children with limited English skills, for the instructional treatments to use, for procedures to transfer children to all-English classrooms, and for professional standards teachers need to meet. To be in compliance with *Lau v. Nichols,* the Lau Remedies are still used as the required elements in most states.

## THE POLITICS OF BILINGUAL EDUCATION

Perceptive teachers realize that the topic of provision of services for English learners is surrounded by political debate. Given the fact that few Americans engage in controversy about second-language acquisition, it is obvious that the underlying arguments for or against bilingual education probably have to do with attitudes about immigration and the role of language in public life. This controversy will continue as Spanish speakers surpass African Americans as the largest minority population in the United States. These arguments treat three main topics: the wisdom of supporting heritage-language proficiency, the role of the native English speaker in bilingual education, and the movement to establish governmental English-only policies.

### Support for Heritage-Language Proficiency

Developmental bilingual programs are designed for students who enter schooling with a primary language other than English. The goals of developmental bilingual programs are maintenance and full development of the student's primary language; full proficiency in all aspects of English; grade-appropriate achievement in all domains of academic study; integration into all-English-language classrooms; and positive identification with both the culture of the primary- and the majority-language group (Cloud et al., 2000).

Monolingual English voters outnumber bilingual voters—for example, 61 percent of voters in California are white (presumably monolingual), whereas only 16 percent of voters are Hispanic, despite the fact that Hispanics make up 30 percent of the population. Changing the political climate from its current position of hostility to bilingual education will take a commitment on the part of English-only voters to foster heritage-language skills. Many heritage-language speakers enjoy and seek to preserve their primary language as a cultural and economic resource. Because Spanish is the third most widely spoken language in the world, Spanish–English bilingualism is a distinct competitive advantage in the local and global marketplace, a valuable asset not only for bilingual individuals but also for society as a whole.

### Support for Two-Way (Dual) Immersion

For parents of English speakers to start their child's second-language instruction in elementary school, they must seek to maintain or establish two-way immersion (TWI) language programs in conjunction with parents of language-minority students. In this model, English learners from a single language background are taught in the same classroom with approximately equal numbers of English-speaking students. Grade-level-approximate curriculum is provided in both languages. Speakers of each language develop proficiency in both their native and second language, achieve academically through and in two languages, and come to appreciate each others' languages and cultures (Lindholm, 1994).

One advocate of TWI found that this model promises "mutual learning, enrichment, and respect"; is "the best possible vehicle for integration of language minority students, since these students are grouped with English-speakers for natural and equal exchange of skills"; and is "particularly appealing because it not only enhances the prestige of the minority language but also offers a rich opportunity for expanding genuine bilingualism to the majority population" (Porter, 1990, p. 154). Cummins (2000a) argued that "a major advantage of two-way bilingual programs . . . is that they overcome segregation in a planned program that aims to enrich the learning opportunities of both minority- and majority-language students" (p. 142).

The politics of TWI are such that two distinct types of parents have sought and attained such programs in their communities. The first are the liberal, middle-class whites who have seen the success of Canadian schools in promoting dual-language competence in English and French and have forged alliances with Spanish-speaking parents (for example, in Long Beach, California; Evanston, Illinois; and Alexandria, Virginia) or French-speaking parents (in the International School of Tucson French Program). The second group comprises parents who are not heritage speakers of a language but who want their children to regain the heritage language (for example, Spanish in Ontario-Montclair School District, California, or in San Antonio, Texas; Cantonese in San Francisco; or Navajo in Chinle, Arizona).

Parents of native-English-speaking children who advocate for the establishment of such a program for their children become advocates for language maintenance on the part of English learners. These parents see advantages in their children learning academic and social skills in two languages, and parents of English learners see that the home language is valued.

## English-Only Efforts

The politics of the U.S. English-only movement are driven by an assimilationist model in the belief that for many immigrants the ability to speak English is a necessity for access to the American middle class. However, as Mora (2002) noted, "this outdated image of the assimilation process ignores the multiple patterns of acculturation for different ethnic groups, many of whom enjoy and preserve their bilingualism as an important cultural and economic resource" (n.p.). Therefore, the idea that the majority should enforce monolingualism on a linguistic minority amounts to linguistic authoritarianism.

English-only bills in the U.S. Congress have repeatedly been defeated. Crawford (2006) described English-only efforts as the politics of fear:

> English Only has always been about fear. Fear of demographic and cultural change, as American communities are transformed by immigrants. Fear of strangers speaking Spanish in public places or posting business signs in Chinese. Fear among Anglos about losing their majority status and, with it, their political dominance. Fear of "the other." (n.p.)

Evidence has shown repeatedly that English learners are more successful when given a firm foundation in their primary language (c.f. Ramírez, 1992) and that bilingualism offers a cognitive advantage (Cummins, 1976). To insist that the United States revert to an outmoded model of monolingualism is to attempt to turn back the clock to an era of language restrictionism, a poor move in a world in which bilingual skills are in increasing demand.

## What Is "Fully Qualified" under NCLB?

It is imperative that teachers are able to understand fundamental principles about second-language acquisition and to communicate, to some degree, with those students acquiring English. Therefore, for teachers to be fully qualified as required by the No Child Left Behind legislation, one might ask, "To be considered 'fully qualified' should teachers acquire at least a basic linguistic competency in the languages that students speak?"

The convenient and widely accepted mythology in the United States that a person can be well educated and remain monolingual is questionable with regard to being "fully qualified." The Hispanic population has become the largest minority in the United States, and educators who are able to augment their teaching using both second-language acquisition principles and Spanish-language skills are increasingly needed. Furthermore, teachers with linguistic competence can enhance the stature of the U.S. educational system in the eyes of the world, as U.S. citizens will no longer be viewed by linguistically multicompetent world citizens as being linguistically handicapped by monolingualism.

# EMPOWERMENT ISSUES RELATED TO ENGLISH LEARNERS

Despite the fact that research has shown the effectiveness of educational programs that support and develop a student's primary language, very few students have ever been fully served with bilingual education programs; for example, in California only 8 percent of students received bilingual education services before Proposition 227 (Mora, 2002). Therefore, one must ask, in a social climate that does not support primary-language programs for students, how can English learners nonetheless be supported? How can communities empower themselves to ensure that language-minority students receive educational equity?

One answer—equivalent to the real estate mantra "location, location, location"—is politics' mantra "lawyers, lawyers, lawyers." MALDEF's victory in *Williams et al. v. State of California* has provided school district–based means for families to submit grievances about poor facilities and resources. Moreover, authorities can respect parent program choices by encouraging parents to seek out primary-language maintenance programs and by staffing such programs in each neighborhood school rather than forcing families to bus their children to magnet programs.

In addition to supporting families in gaining access to equivalent resources by means of the *Williams v. California* remedies, school authorities can do much to create a positive affective environment for all students, including English learners, in the classroom and the school. The positive involvement of family and community members (see Chapter 9) does much to communicate that school and the family are partners in education.

Cummins (1989, 1996) contrasted educational practices that serve as *collaborative* relations of power with those that are *coercive*. Cummins cautioned that children who enter schools in which diversity is *not* affirmed soon perceive that their "difference" is not honored. Often English learners are not encouraged to think critically, to reflect, and to solve problems. This attitude on the part of teachers communicates a sense of reduced worth, resulting in poor motivation to achieve.

Pressuring students to conform to schooling practices that are unfair or discriminatory results in a loss of their identity as human beings. Teachers who are dedicated to social change must help students develop the confidence and motivation to succeed academically; they must also be aware of the ways in which spoken and unspoken language can encourage positive attitudes, building strong personal and social identities.

## EQUITY AND POLICY ISSUES RELATED TO ENGLISH LEARNERS

Achieving high-quality education for English learners has been a centuries-long struggle in the United States. Judging from many measures (e.g., achievement gap, dropout rates, expulsion and detention rates, retention/promotion, tracking, access to AP classes, segregation, length of program, special education placements, gifted education placements, teacher qualifications, teacher retention, and funding and resources), the struggle is by no means over (Rumbaut, 1995; Donato, 1997; Mora, 2000).

Among the indicators that language-minority students have not done well in schools is the fact that nationally Latino students (30.3 percent of whom are limited-English-speaking) are behind their peers in grades 4 and 8, with more than 50 percent below the basic level in reading and math. Latino students are being taught by less qualified teachers, have less access to high-level rigorous classes, are enrolled in fewer college prep courses, and receive fewer state and local funds. More than 40 percent of the teachers teaching English-as-a-second language/bilingual classes are not certified to teach bilingual education or ESL (Gutierrez & Rodríguez, 2005). Only 9.9 percent of Hispanics/Latinos have a college degree, and 48.5 percent do not have a high school diploma. The average income is $14,000 (www.asian-nation.org/demographics.shtml).

Statistics show poor progress as well for Cambodian, Hmong, and Laotian students (44.3 percent of whom are limited-English-speaking); 52.7 percent of this population have no high school diploma and have a median personal income of $16,000. Pacific Islanders also show poor school achievement—13.6 percent have a college degree (compared with 25.3 percent for Whites). The Vietnamese have a 40.4 percent rate of "not English proficient" and have a 13.8 percent rate of attaining a college degree, while 37.8 percent lack a high school diploma (www.asian-nation.org/demographics.shtml).

However, not all language minorities in the United States have done poorly in school. Available data show that 31.3 percent of Chinese are not proficient in English, yet 46.3 percent have college degrees; 32.9 percent of Koreans are not proficient in English yet have a 43.6 percent rate of attaining a college degree (www.asian-nation.org/demographics.shtml).

There is no question that the public climate of support affects the supply of teachers with expertise in educating English learners. Gándara and colleagues (2000) found that between 1997–98 and 1998–99, the year of implementation of Proposition 227 in California, the number of credentialed bilingual teachers in California using their bilingual credential in a teaching assignment with language-minority students dropped by 32 percent. In 1998, 10,894 teacher candidates had bilingual certification; in 1999, that number was reduced to 5,670. The number of teacher candidates earning a credential with a crosscultural, language, and academic development (CLAD) endorsement, meanwhile, rose only 11 percent (Gándara et al., 2000). This does not bode well for staffing the classrooms of English learners, at least in California.

## COMPONENTS OF ELD PROGRAMS

In the widely varied climate of support from area to area in the United States, educational programs range from those that promote additive bilingualism to those that in effect eradicate primary-language proficiency. At the same time as learning English, the language-minority student must gain adequate access to academic content, so a comprehensive program must make provisions for both English and academic learning (and, ideally, a primary-language maintenance component to ensure content and language development in L1). A representative set of the main program types is offered as follows, with the acknowledgment that local implementations might result in a mix of program models, or in outcomes that are not optimal.

### Dual-Language Development Programs (Additive Bilingualism)

In two-way immersion classrooms (also called two-way maintenance bilingual classrooms), English learners from a single language background are grouped in the same classroom with approximately equal numbers of English-speaking students. Grade-level-approximate curriculum is provided in both languages. Speakers of each language develop proficiency in both their native and second language, achieve academically through and in two languages, and come to appreciate each other's languages and cultures (Lindholm, 1994). This enhances the status of the students' primary language, promoting self-esteem and increased cultural pride (Lindholm-Leary, 2000), leading to increased motivation.

*Dual-language programs encourage students from two different languages to teach one another their languages.*

Two-way immersion programs had been implemented in 329 schools in the United States by 2006 (www.cal.org/twi/directory/), with the number of schools growing yearly. Sites were located in twenty-nine states ranging from Alaska to Florida, with the largest numbers in California and New York. Nearly all schools (308) are Spanish–English in design, although other schools immersed students in Cantonese–English, Japanese–English, Navajo–English, Mandarin–English, and German–English. The grade levels served were predominantly K–6, but thirty-four of these schools are middle schools and nine are high schools.

Careful attention to a high-quality bilingual program in the context of primary-language maintenance is key to the success of dual immersion programs (Veeder & Tramutt, 2000). The National Clearinghouse for English Language Acquisition has a wealth of information about two-way programs at www.ncela.gwu.edu, as does a website from the California Department of Education (www.cde.ca.gov/sp/el/ip/faq.asp).

### BEST PRACTICE: Two-Way Immersion

An example of a highly successful dual-language program is that in the Valley Center–Pauma Joint Unified School District in Valley Center, California, a program in existence for over twenty years that promotes language proficiency in English and Spanish. The schools with the program are those with very high populations of English learners (ranging from 25 to 50 percent). Both English learners and Spanish learners are held to the same high standards of achievement, and in fact students in the program have an 80 percent pass rate on the California high school exit examination.

"Project FLUENT focuses on the development of Spanish as a second language utilizing rich activities which incorporate the National Foreign Language Standards K–8th grade and effective use of age-appropriate computerized curriculum and a focus on careers in Mass Communications and Technology." (www.languagepolicy.org/flap04.html)

TWI is predicated on beginning literacy instruction for students in both languages. Reading in a foreign language above the level of emergent literacy takes place by using both literature and subject area content, following many of the same principles as reading in the native language. Time is given in class for reading so that students working in groups can facilitate one another's comprehension. To appeal to students' varied interests, all types of content are used (magazines, newspapers, plays, novels, stories, and poems), depending also on the proficiency level of students and the level of language studied. In this way, students are assured of receiving a challenging academic program in both languages.

Critics have alleged that TWI delays English learning and that these programs fail to teach English to English learners. Amselle (1999) argued, "dual immersion programs are really nothing more than Spanish immersion, with Hispanic children used as teaching tools for English-speaking children" (p. 8). Experts concede that the greatest challenge in two-way bilingual programs is to "reduce the gap" between the language abilities of the two groups (English learners and second-language learners [SLLs]). This gap appears when content classes in English are modified (slowed down) for English learners to "catch up," or when content delivery in the primary language is slowed for SSLs. Table 4.4 features program elements of two-way immersion programs.

**TABLE 4.4** Program Components of Two-Way Immersion

| Program Elements | Program Features |
|---|---|
| Philosophy | Bilingualism as a resource |
| Goal | Additive bilingualism for English learners and native English speakers |
| Purpose | Cognitive academic language proficiency achieved through grade-level-appropriate instruction in both languages |
| Ideal Outcome | Additive bilingualism for English learners and native English speakers |
| Grade/Proficiency Level(s) | Usually begins in kindergarten, with cohort staying together throughout elementary or middle school |
| Placement Criteria | Parental exemption waiver |
| Exit Criteria | Parental choice |
| Program Length | Parent choice (usually K–6) |
| Class Composition | Ideally, 50/50 English native speaker and English learner |
| Language Components | English-language development and primary-language maintenance for English learners; English language arts (ELA) and primary-language-as-a-second-language instruction for native English speakers |
| Limitations | ELD and ELA must be taught separately, as must primary-language maintenance versus primary-language-as-a-second-language instruction for native English speakers, or both groups will be slowed in achievement in their native languages |

Not all primary-language maintenance programs are two-way immersion, but two-way immersion programs featuring native English speakers often enjoy more community support. The following vignette illustrates the public pressure faced by one such school that offers primary-language maintenance.

## CLASSROOM GLIMPSE: Semillas del Pueblo

*A primary-language maintenance chapter school in El Sereno (part of Los Angeles), Academia Semillas del Pueblo, found itself in the center of controversy when a local talk radio station and a conservative Internet blog made assertions that the school espoused a covert separatist ethos. Principal Minnie Ferguson said that despite low test scores, other measures of achievement are more encouraging, showing Semillas del Pueblo students advancing to English fluency at a greater rate than Los Angeles Unified students overall.*

*The Academia held an open house in June, during which groups of children in brightly colored red and yellow shirts sat in circles and played games as others listened intently to teachers reading history lessons in Spanish or sang songs in Mandarin. The curricular emphasis is on multicultural values, with enrollment in 2005–06 that included White, Black, Latino, Asian-American, American-Indian, and native Hawai'ian or Pacific Islander children. (Rivera, 2006)*

## Transitional Bilingual Education

Transitional bilingual education (TBE) programs support the use of students' home language in academic settings only during the period in which they acquire enough English proficiency to make the transition into English-only education. This supports a subtractive view of bilingualism, in effect requiring that English learners discontinue the use of their native language as they increase their fluency in English (Nieto, 2004). In these programs, students receive initial instruction in most, if not all, content areas in their home language while they are being taught English.

There are numerous problems with a TBE program. It may be perceived as a remedial program or another form of segregated, compensatory education. TBE rests on the common misconception that two or three years is sufficient time to learn a second language for schooling purposes, but in fact this is not long enough for students to build cognitive academic language proficiency (CALP) either in their native tongue or in English. As a consequence, they may not be able to carry out cognitively demanding tasks in English or their home language.

Another shortcoming of transitional bilingual education is the effect that English-only schooling has on home-language use. After transition to English, students frequently switch to English as their primary language of communication, and conversational fluency in the home language tends to erode. This retards rather than expedites academic progress in English, primarily because children and parents lose the benefit of a shared language for such purposes as homework help. For these and other reasons, TBE programs have not led to school success for many students (see Medina & Escamilla, 1992) (see Table 4.5).

**TABLE 4.5**   Program Components of Transitional Bilingual Education

| Program Elements | Program Features |
| --- | --- |
| Philosophy | Bilingualism as a bridge to English proficiency |
| Goal | Bilingualism for English learners only until replaced by English as the language of instruction |
| Purpose | Cognitive academic language proficiency achieved through grade-level-appropriate instruction in English |
| Ideal Outcome | Educational parity for English learners and native English speakers |
| Grade/Proficiency Level(s) | Usually K–2, from beginning through advanced proficiency |
| Placement Criteria | Parental exemption waiver |
| Exit Criteria | (See Chapter 3 on Reclassification.) |
| Program Length | Usually three years (K–2) |
| Class Composition | Usually Spanish-speaking, but in California bilingual teachers have been certified in twenty languages |
| Language Components | Content instruction in the primary languages, combined with ELD instruction |
| Limitations | Lack of programmatic support after transition often leads to subtractive bilingualism |

## Structured English Immersion

Structured English immersion (SEI) programs are those in which students are taught solely in English supplemented with strategies designed to increase their understanding of the content, and teachers are not necessarily fluent in the L1 of the students. Many of the teaching techniques used for SEI programs were developed for use in multilingual, often urban, classes where there is not a single primary language shared by the learners. In these classes, the use of L1 was not feasible, or was strongly discouraged because of the belief that L1 would interfere with learning L2.

SEI programs are designed to address the learning needs of English learners whose English is at the intermediate level of fluency or above. Unfortunately, this approach is too often used for beginning English learners. The chief element of "structure" built into these programs is the use of Specially Designed Academic Instruction in English (SDAIE), also called "sheltered instruction." SDAIE incorporates specific teaching (not language) modifications to make a lesson understandable to students.

Students obtain access to core curriculum subjects when the content is modified using SDAIE, and thus they can maintain parity with native-English-speaking classmates. Even literature classes can be modified with SDAIE so that English learners are not relegated to ELD programs whose course credits may not be considered college preparatory in nature. However, teachers need to be trained in SDAIE techniques.

SEI programs have one key advantage: All teachers are responsible for the education of English learners and must be knowledgeable about language development issues and techniques. Students are not linguistically segregated, which too often occurs in secondary school settings.

Although supporters of SEI programs promote increased time spent immersed in English as a way to increase classroom learning, SEI is based on an erroneous assumption: that more time spent immersed in a foreign language will somehow compensate for a lack of comprehension. Even with an elaborate set of SDAIE techniques designed to augment—in reality, substitute for—verbal explanation, few experts would agree that a student subjected to SEI achieves the same level of comprehension that same student would achieve if taught in the primary language.

A key factor is missing in the SEI approach—the opportunity is lost for additive bilingualism. The same drawbacks that can be identified in the TBE model also hold true for SEI programs: There is no development of the primary language, resulting in subtractive bilinguality (see Table 4.6).

## Newcomer (Front-Loaded) English

The goal of newcomer programs is to foster in recent immigrants rapid English learning during the period of early acculturation (Short & Boyson, 2004). Newcomer centers, like Newcomer High School in San Francisco, are more common at the secondary level than in the elementary grades. Newcomer programs may be organized as centers, as separate programs in their own locations, or as programs within a school (Genesee, 1999).

The chief rationale for newcomer programs is that students must learn English before they can be educated in English. A second rationale is that students need social and emotional support during the time in which they may experience culture shock. A third rationale is that there are not enough teachers for the number of English learners, so they must be grouped for educational services.

**TABLE 4.6**    Program Components of Structured English Immersion

| Program Elements | Program Features |
|---|---|
| Philosophy | Bilingualism as a bridge to English proficiency |
| Goal | Bilingualism for English learners only until replaced by English as the language of instruction |
| Purpose | Cognitive academic language proficiency achieved through grade-level-appropriate instruction in English |
| Ideal Outcome | Educational parity for English learners and native English speakers |
| Grade/Proficiency Level(s) | Possibility for all grades, all CELDT levels |
| Placement Criteria | CELDT score level of beginner through advanced |
| Exit Criteria | (See Chapter 3 on Reclassification.) |
| Program Length | Varies depending on individual progress |
| Class Composition | Mixed CELDT levels |
| Language Components | Content instruction in SDAIE-enhanced English combined with ELD instruction |
| Limitations | Access to core academic content depends on SDAIE skills of teachers |

Programs vary in length of day; some are full day, in which students have various content courses along with ELD, whereas others are half-day or after school. Students may be enrolled for a year, four years, or only one semester (Short, 1998). The curriculum is designed to help students move into the regular language support program as soon as possible while helping them gain an understanding of U.S. schools and educational expectations. SDAIE techniques predominate in content classes, if offered. Increasingly, however, the newcomer model is called "front-loading." This means that only English-language development is offered, on an intensive basis, during the newcomer period, with students' having limited access to the core curriculum during this time.

However, research has repeatedly cast doubt on the argument that students must learn English before they can be educated in English. Major disadvantages of the newcomer approach are, first, the idea that newcomers should be separated from the mainstream, English-speaking population during their period of early adjustment. The U.S. Supreme Court, in the ruling *Brown v. Board of Education* (1954), has ruled that separate educational programs, however well meaning, are inherently unequal in implementation. The idea that immigrants should be educated separately—at any stage—promotes segregation in a nation whose school facilities are increasingly ethnically separate (Orfield & Lee, 2005).

A second drawback is that the newcomer approach is based on subtractive bilingual education. Academic support in the primary language is seldom offered, much less primary-language development. It is probably helpful for students to receive counseling and other assistance to help with culture shock, but no amount of humanistic socioemotional "support" in English during students' adjustment period can realistically take the place of genuine support—receiving mediation in the primary language.

**TABLE 4.7**  Program Components of Newcomer (Front-Loaded) Programs

| Program Elements | Program Features |
|---|---|
| Philosophy | Intensive English is the key to English proficiency |
| Goal | Intensive English for English learners must take place before English can be used as the language of instruction |
| Purpose | Cognitive academic language proficiency achieved through grade-level-appropriate instruction in English |
| Ideal Outcome | English learners can participate in SDAIE-enhanced content instruction. |
| Grade/Proficiency Level(s) | Newcomer programs are usually implemented in secondary schools, but front-loading can be done at any grade or level, beginning through intermediate proficiency |
| Placement Criteria | Varies—CELDT score level of beginner or early intermediate plus parental choice |
| Exit Criteria | (See Chapter 3 on Reclassification.) |
| Program Length | Varies |
| Class Composition | Mixed CELDT levels |
| Language Components | Content instruction in SDAIE-enhanced English combined with ELD instruction |
| Limitations | Access to core academic content depends on SDAIE skills of teachers; segregative |

A third drawback is that content vocabulary cannot be learned effectively in a front-loaded manner because it is an integral part of learning content concepts. Unfortunately, students are inevitably slowed in their educational advancement when forced to halt academic learning until their English is developed to some arbitrary point. Moreover, if basic interpersonal skills take two years of exposure to English to develop, and cognitive academic language takes five or more years to develop (Cummins, 1981a; Hakuta et al., 2000), then theoretically two to five years of "boot camp" English would be required, an inordinate amount of time for newcomers to be segregated. Thus, the newcomer, or front-loading, model is ill advised (see Table 4.7).

## English-Language Development Programs

English is taught to English learners in a variety of ways, and studies have shown varying degrees of student success depending on the program model (Thomas & Collier, 1997). Whereas it may be true that extensive exposure to a high-quality English-language development program is a necessity, it is a fallacy to believe that total immersion in English is effective. When students are provided with a solid foundation in their primary language, faster English acquisition takes place. The following four models are the norm for teaching English to English learners.

**Pull-Out ELD**  When English learners must leave their home classroom and receive instruction in vocabulary, grammar, oral language, or spelling for separate half-hour to one-hour-a-day classes with a trained ELD teacher, they are said to be "pulled out." Such instruction rarely is integrated with the regular classroom program, and when students return to the home classroom, they usually are not instructed on curriculum they missed while they were gone. This lack only exacerbates an already difficult learning situation. Of the various program models, ELD pull-out is the most expensive to operate because it requires hiring an extra resource teacher (Chambers & Parrish, 1992). It has, however, been the most implemented, despite being the least effective model (Thomas & Collier, 1997).

**ELD Class Period**    Although pull-out ELD is normally found at the elementary level, students in the secondary school often have separate ELD classes that help them with their English skills. Unfortunately, these classes often focus entirely on the English language and do not help students with their academic subjects. Moreover, in some school districts students who are placed in separate ELD classes at the high school level do not receive college-entrance-applicable credits for these classes. In other words, to be placed in an ELD class is to be denied the chance for college admission. This unfortunate policy is avoided if students are placed in SDAIE-enhanced high school English classes that do bear college-entry credit value.

**Content-Based ELD**    Although content-based ELD classes are still separate and contain only English learners, students learn English through academic content in a curriculum organized around grade-level academic objectives. The most effective of these models is when the ELD teacher collaborates with content area teachers to organize learning objectives around academic subjects in order to prepare students to master grade-level curricula (Ovando & Collier, 1998). Content-based ELD classes develop not only language proficiency but also content knowledge, cognitive strategies, and study skills. Teachers familiarize students with the difference in the style and structure of texts and the type of vocabulary featured in the particular discipline.

Content-based instruction can be of great benefit if content instructors and language teachers work together to provide learners with comprehensible input, as well as to design tasks that are both comprehensible and important. Systematic, planned instruction must present vocabulary, concepts, and structures that are required for mastery of the content (Snow, 1993). The content to be taught, general instructional goals, and time available for instruction are negotiated with the content teacher.

Learning English through content is a worldwide means of English instruction (Brinton & Master, 1997), whether for purposes of business, engineering, medicine, or science. It is most effective when content teachers take an interest in language development and ELD teachers take more responsibility for content.

**Universal Access to the Language Arts Curriculum**    As described in Chapter 3, the goal of ELD programs is for English learners to make the transition from the ELD standards to the standards outlined in the *Reading/Language Arts Framework* and the ELA standards so they can be instructed in a mainstream classroom. This is accomplished through implementing principles of Universal Instructional Design (UID).

With an augmented emphasis on learning styles and other learner differences, UID promotes access to information, resources, and tools for students with a wide range of abilities, disabilities, ethnic backgrounds, language skills, and learning styles. Burgstahler (2002) noted that "Universal Instructional Design principles . . . give each student meaningful access to the curriculum by assuring access to the environment as well as multiple means of representation, expression, and engagement" (p. 1).

Table 4.8 offers an overview of the principles of UID and some suggested applications of these principles in the education of English learners. UID does not imply that one universal strategy fits all but rather that a diversity of opportunities will work for many different students.

**TABLE 4.8** Principles of Universal Instructional Design Applied to English Learners

| Principle | Definition | Application |
|---|---|---|
| Inclusiveness | A classroom climate that communicates respect for varying abilities | Use bilingual signage and materials; welcome and respect aides and assistants; supply multiple reading levels of texts. |
| Physical access | Equipment and activities that minimize sustained physical effort, provide options for participation, and accommodate those with limited physical abilities | Use assistive technologies such as screen readers and online dictionaries to assist in translation; make online chatrooms available for students in two languages. |
| Delivery methods | Content is delivered in multiple modes so it is accessible to students with a wide range of abilities, interests, and previous experiences. | Employ a full range of audiovisual enhancement, including wireless headsets and captioned video; build in redundant modes (e.g., audiotaped read-along books, typed lecture notes, and study guides). |
| Information access | Use of captioned videos and accessible electronic formats; in printed work, use of simple, intuitive, and consistent formats | Ensure that information is both understandable and complete; reduce unnecessary complexity; highlight essential text; give clear criteria for tests and assignments. |
| Interaction | Accessible to everyone, without accommodation; use of multiple ways for students to participate | Set up both heterogeneous groups (across second-language ability levels) and homogeneous groups (same language-ability level); instruct students on how to secure a conversational turn. |
| Feedback | Effective prompting during an activity and constructive comments after the assignment is complete | Employ formative assessment for ongoing feedback. |
| Demonstration of knowledge | Provision for multiple ways students demonstrate knowledge—group work, demonstrations, portfolios, and presentations | Offer different modes to all students so that English learners are not the only ones with alternatives. |

*Source:* Adapted from Burgstahler (2002), Egbert (2004), & Strehorn (2001).

The recommended model for delivery of ELD is that it be integrated with content instruction in a classroom in which the English learner has access to native speakers of English as language models. However, because the English learner is still acquiring basic English skills, ELD instruction cannot provide grade-level-appropriate content. To accomplish this, academic instruction and ELD must go hand in hand.

# ENGLISH-LANGUAGE DEVELOPMENT AND ACADEMIC INSTRUCTION

English learners can succeed in content area classes taught in English. If they can follow and understand a lesson, they can learn content material, and the content area instruction—if modified to include English-language development—becomes the means for acquiring English. Basically, SDAIE addresses the following needs of English learners: (1) to learn grade-appropriate content, (2) to master English vocabulary and grammar, (3) to learn "academic" English, and (4) to develop strategies for learning how to learn.

## The SDAIE-Enhanced Content Classroom

Specially designed academic instruction in English combines second-language acquisition principles with those elements of quality teaching that make a lesson understandable to students. SDAIE is, ideally, one component in a program for English learners that includes ELD instruction, primary-language instruction in content areas (so that students continue at grade level as they learn English), and content-based ESL classes.

An SDAIE classroom has content objectives identical to those of a mainstream classroom in the same subject but, in addition, includes language and learning strategy objectives. Instruction is modified for greater comprehensibility. The distinction between SDAIE and content-based ELD instruction is that SDAIE features content instruction taught by content area teachers with English-language support. Content-based ELD, taught by ELD teachers, features the use of content area materials as texts for ELD lessons.

## A Model for SDAIE

A model for SDAIE originally developed at the Los Angeles Unified School District in 1993 had four components—content, connections, comprehensibility, and interaction. Often, however, teachers could be technically proficient in many of the SDAIE elements yet not be successful with English learners. Discussion and observation revealed that the teacher's attitude played such a critical part in the success of the class that it needed to be explicitly incorporated into the model. Therefore, teacher attitude was added as an overarching component (see Figure 4.1).

Teachers often find that they do not use every aspect of the model in every lesson, but by working within the overall frame they are more assured of providing appropriate learning opportunities for their English learners. The following sections explain and illustrate each of the five SDAIE components.

*Depending on their assessed English level, students can participate in SDAIE-enhanced content lessons.*

**FIGURE 4.1**  A Model of the Components of Successful SDAIE Instruction

**Teacher Attitude**
The teacher is open and willing to learn from
  students.

**Content**
Lessons include subject, language, and learning-
  strategy objectives.
Material is selected, adapted, and organized with
  language learners in mind.

**Comprehensibility**
Lessons include explicit strategies that aid
  understanding:
  • Contextualization
  • Modeling
  • Teacher speech adjustment
  • Frequent comprehension checks through
      strategies and appropriate questioning
  • Repetition and paraphrase

**Connections**
Curriculum is connected to students'
  background and experiences.

**Interaction**
Students have frequent opportunities to

  • Talk about lesson content
  • Clarify concepts in their home language
  • Represent learning through a variety of ways

**Teacher Attitude**    Teachers are no different from the rest of the population when faced with something new or different. Many recoil, dig in their heels, and refuse to change. But teachers have also chosen to work with people, and they frequently find delight and satisfaction in their students' work, behavior, and learning. It is this sense of delight that is important to capture in working with all learners, particularly English learners.

Three aspects characterize a successful attitude in working with second-language learners:

- Teachers believe that all students can learn.
- Teachers are willing to nurture language development.
- Teachers recognize that a person's self-concept is involved in his or her own language and that at times students need to use that language.

### BEST PRACTICE: Positive Teacher Attitudes

An ELD teacher observed and interviewed her colleagues at her school. She discovered that accomplished teachers set up effective learning environments for the English learners. They understood the needs of their culturally and linguistically diverse students and created an atmosphere in the classroom that helped newly arrived students integrate into the life of the school. For example, they would pair each English learner with a buddy. They encouraged friendships by asking a classmate to stay with the English learner at lunch. They provided appropriate instruction for their English learners and applauded their successes. This environment helped relieve much of the beginners' anxiety. (Haynes, 2004)

**Content**    *Content objectives* are necessary to guide teaching. A lesson with a clear objective focuses the instruction by concentrating on a particular goal and guides the teacher to select learning activities that accomplish the goal. Teachers may have to be selective in choosing only the most essential content standards to address in the time allotted.

### BEST PRACTICE: Organizing Content for the Theme of "Acculturation"

Content materials for the social studies theme "acculturation" might include primary documents, personal histories, and literature. Students who research specific concepts related to acculturation, such as immigration assimilation, culture shock, job opportunities, or naturalization, may find that each document features a unique voice. A government document presents a formal, official point of view, whereas a personal or family story conveys the subject from a different, more intimate perspective. In addition, numerous pieces of literature, such as Eve Bunting's *How Many Days to America?* (1988) or Laurence Yep's *Dragonwings* (1975), offer yet other points of view.

**Connections**    Students engage in learning when they recognize a connection between what they know and the learning experience. Therefore, a critical element of the SDAIE lesson is the deliberate plan on the teacher's part to elicit information from and help make connections for the students. This can be accomplished in several ways: through *bridging*—linking concepts and skills to student experiences or eliciting/using examples from students' lives—and by *schema building*—using scaffolding strategies to link new learning to old.

**Comprehensibility**   A key factor in learning is being able to understand. Through all phases of a lesson, the teacher ensures that students have plenty of clues to understanding. This is one of the aspects of SDAIE that makes it different from mainstream instruction. Teachers are aware that they need to present concepts in a variety of ways. They increase the comprehensibility of lessons in four ways: *contextualization* (strategies that augment speech and/or text through pictures, realia, dramatizations, etc.); *modeling* (demonstration of the skill or concept to be learned); *speech adjustment* (strategies to adjust speech from the customary native speech patterns); and *comprehension checks* (strategies to monitor listening and reading comprehension). Table 4.9 provides a list of both object and human resources that can help contextualize classroom content.

**Interaction**   The organization of discourse is important for language acquisition in content classes. In "teacher-fronted" classrooms (Harel, 1992), the teacher takes the central role in controlling the flow of information, and students compete for the teacher's attention and for permission to speak. More recent research (Gass, 2000), however, points to the role of the learner in negotiating, managing, even manipulating conversations to receive more comprehensible input. Instead of English learners being dependent on their ability to understand the teacher's explanations and directions, classrooms that feature flexible grouping patterns permit students to have greater access to the flow of information.

The teacher orchestrates tasks so that students use language in academic ways. Students are placed in different groups for different activities. Teachers themselves work with small groups to achieve specific instructional objectives (e.g., in literature response groups, as discussed in Chapter 6, or in instructional conversations, discussed in Chapters 2 and 6).

In planning for interaction in the SDAIE lesson, the teacher considers opportunities for students to talk about key concepts, expects that students may clarify the concepts in their primary language, and allows a variety of means through which students can demonstrate their understanding.

**TABLE 4.9**   Media, Realia, Manipulatives, and Human Resources to Contextualize Lessons

| Object Resources | Human Resources |
| --- | --- |
| Picture files | Cooperative groups |
| Maps and globes | Pairs |
| Charts and posters | Cross-age tutors |
| Printed material: | Heterogeneous groups |
|   Illustrated books | Community resource people |
|   Pamphlets | School resource people |
|   News articles | Parents |
|   Catalogs | Pen pals (adult and child) |
|   Magazines | Keypals |
| Puzzles | |
| Science equipment | |
| Manipulatives: | |
|   M&Ms | |
|   Buttons | |
|   Tongue depressors | |
|   Gummy bears | |
| Costumes | |
| Computer software | |
| Internet | |

## CLASSROOM GLIMPSE: Interaction

*In one fifth-grade class, the students produced a news program with a U.S. Civil War setting. The program included the show's anchors; reporters in the field interviewing generals, soldiers, and citizens; a weather report; and reports on sports, economics, and political conditions. There were even commercial breaks. The students engaged in much research in order to be historically accurate, but enthusiasm was high as they shared their knowledge in a format they knew and understood. In addition, students were able to work in the area of their particular interest.*

SDAIE offers English learners an important intermediate step between content instruction in the primary language, an environment in which they may not advance in English skills, and a "sink-or-swim" immersion, in which they may not learn key content-related concepts. In most effective instruction for English learners, ELD methods and SDAIE are used together to provide language development and achievement of core content standards for English learners, depending on the program model used and the specific needs of the students. SDAIE is covered in more depth in Chapters 5 and 7.

## PARENTAL RIGHTS AND COMMUNICATING WITH FAMILIES

"Strong parent involvement is one factor that research has shown time and time again to have positive effects on academic achievement and school attitudes" (Ovando & Collier, 1998, p. 270). Yet, for various reasons on the part of both schools and communities, parent involvement has sometimes been an elusive goal. The growing number of English learners in the school system, however, clearly requires that efforts continue to establish communication, develop partnerships, and involve parents, families, and communities. Fortunately, over the past decade successful programs have developed and various guidelines are available to help school personnel, parents, and communities work together to ensure parental rights, parental involvement, successful programs, and school–community partnerships that benefit students.

### Parental Rights

Parents have numerous rights that educators must respect and honor in spite of the challenges they may present to the school. These include (1) the right of their children to a free, appropriate public education; (2) the right to receive information concerning education decisions and actions in the language parents comprehend; (3) the right to make informed decisions and to authorize consent before changes in educational placement occur; (4) the right to be included in discussions and plans concerning disciplinary action toward their children; (5) the right to appeal actions when they do not agree; and (6) the right to participate in meetings organized for public and parent information (Young & Helvie, 1996).

Parents have the right to choose in which language development program options their child will participate (e.g., waiver process) and have the right to be contacted about such rights in an appropriate and effective medium (e.g., bilingual phone calls, home visits, primary-language materials, videos). The *Williams et al. v. State of California* remedies offer several mechanisms by which parents can exert more influence on school procedures.

A fundamental right that all parents have is support in school for the home language. To deny access to native-language literacy exploits minorities (Cummings, 1989). It is important that teachers help families understand the advantages that bilingualism provides to the individual, connecting students to their heritage culture; adding a cognitive dimension by expanding and deepening students' thinking; and, later in life, expanding career opportunities. Family support for bilingualism helps to establish expectations for high academic performance in two languages (Molina, Hanson, & Siegel, 1997). Chapter 9 continues this definition of family involvement.

## School–Community Partnerships

In addition to developing partnerships with parents, schools are reaching toward communities for help in educating all children. Community-based organizations (CBOs)—groups committed to helping people obtain health, education, and other basic human services—are assisting students in ways that go beyond traditional schooling. Adger (2000) found that school–CBO partnerships support students' academic achievement by working with parents and families, tutoring students in their first language, developing students' leadership skills and higher education goals, and providing information and support on issues such as health care, pregnancy, gang involvement, and so on.

Communities can foster a climate of support for English learners by featuring articles in local newspapers and newsletters about these students' achievements in the schools and prizes they have won, by sponsoring literature and art exhibitions that feature students' work, and by publishing their stories written in both languages. Students can be invited to the local library to offer their stories, books, and poetry to other students, again in both English and the primary language. In this way, support for bilingualism and bilingual education programs is orchestrated in the community at large. Working with families and communities is further detailed in Chapter 9.

Many people feel that any tolerance of linguistic diversity undermines national unity. However, others hold the view of the United States as a "salad bowl," which features a mixture of distinct textures and tastes, instead of a "melting pot," in which cultural and linguistic diversity is melted into one collective culture and language. The best educational programs for English learners are explicitly bicultural as well so that students' native cultures as well as heritage languages can be fostered. With these programs in place, the United States will benefit from the rich language resources of all its people.

**VIDEO WORKSHOP:**    **"A Bilingual Navajo School"**

Rockpoint Community School is a bilingual school with a large Navajo population. In this video, a school administrator discusses why it is important for his students to learn in both English and Navajo, and then we see an elementary teacher teach a lesson in English.

To access the video, log on to MyLabSchool at www.mylabschool.com, enter Assignment ID **ENV2** into the **Assignment Finder,** and select the video entitled "A Bilingual Navajo School." Watch the video, complete the questions that follow, and e-mail your responses to your professor for credit.

**ʿmylabschool™**
Where the classroom comes to life!

# CHAPTER FIVE

# English-Language/Literacy Development and Content Instruction

## ▓▓ FOUNDATIONS OF ENGLISH-LANGUAGE LITERACY

The greatest challenge in teaching today is to communicate content in English to students whose English is under development. Research has shown that students learn best in their primary language, but in most schools, primary-language instruction is not an option. Students today are expected to learn not only English but also science, mathematics, social studies, and other subjects in English. How is this possible? Instruction must be systematically modified so that teachers can make academic content more accessible to learners.

Specially designed academic instruction in English (SDAIE) comprises a set of techniques for adapting instruction for English learners. For English learners, ELD instruction is guided by a careful progression through the ELD standards, and SDAIE is used to make academic instruction comprehensible. Without ELD and SDAIE, students are mainstreamed without access to the curriculum—the sink-or-swim approach.

### Connections between Oracy, Literacy, and Social Functions

How do speaking and listening connect to reading and writing? Vygotsky (1981) believed that children learn to engage in higher-level thinking by learning first how to communicate. The more students can use language in the classroom environment, the more they will learn. The language that students bring from home is the foundation not only for the language used at school but also for the process of learning itself. Thus, both English proficiency and learning in the content areas are furthered by a solid base of primary-language proficiency.

Writing and reading, like speech, are social acts. This means that the natural sociability of children in their first language is the foundation for their intellectual development. This chapter presents ways in which literacy and oracy develop within a social context and are enhanced by strategic teaching of language functions. Students need opportunities to engage with English in natural interactional contexts and for a variety of purposes: to establish and maintain social relationships; to express reactions; to give and seek information; to solve problems, discuss ideas, or teach and learn a skill; to entertain or play with language; or to display achievement.

While teaching, observant educators take note of what activities "light a fire" in learners and take care to balance students' receptive and productive skills within a learning environment that respects culture, human interests, and imagination.

**English for Empowerment**    Teachers of English must become aware that oral language is inextricably joined with cultural identity and social differences, and the individual's relationship to institutions and sociocultural contexts affects opportunities to listen and speak. As Peim (1993) puts it, it is not the case that any oral activity in class simply and directly enhances language development. Direct connections to the community and to the circulation of power (Foucault, 1980) strengthen the chance that an individual's efforts to speak and listen will actually enhance his or her social and cultural prospects in life.

Banks (1991) set empowerment in the context of personal and social change:

> A curriculum designed to empower students must be transformative in nature and help students to develop the knowledge, skills, and values needed to become social critics who can make reflective decisions and implement their decisions in effective personal, social, political, and economic action. (p. 131)

However, Wink (2000) cautioned that the verb *empower* should not be used with a direct object, because it is patronizing to believe that one can empower someone else.

Take the contrasting examples of two parent newsletters sent home by a school. The first newsletter is part of the school's open house packet distributed with about six other papers, some of which are in Spanish. The newsletter is a word-for-word primary-language translation of the reverse side, a letter to English-speaking parents. There are no illustrations—merely a page consisting of ten paragraphs, each explaining a different homework tip. This newsletter assumes that the parents welcome the advice of the school authorities and that the parents' role is to help the students complete the assignments sent home by the teachers.

In contrast, another teacher works with students to write Homework Help manuals, six-page "little books" composed by students themselves in cooperative groups. Each group decides on a title for their book and brainstorms the book's content. Will it be in both Spanish and English? Will it include recommendations of a special place to study at home? Will it mention adequate lighting? Will it discuss how to deal with the distractions of television or of siblings? Will it advise students how to solicit help from parents? Each group adds the ideas that the members choose. When the books are ready, the teacher asks each student to take the book home, discuss it with the family, and then come back to class with feedback about whether the suggestions are apt, plus additional ideas.

Looking at these two products, which would benefit students more? Which is more likely to be a focal point for discussion at home? One must admit that the student product is more likely to influence attitudes and behavior toward studying than the administrator's version, no matter the difference in expertise. Moreover, what social functions of language were involved in the student project (interpersonal, representational, heuristic)? In the process of creating the manual, the students naturally used speaking and listening together with reading and writing. This is an example of a transformative literacy that served an institutional purpose.

**An Integrated Approach**    The idea that speaking and listening must precede literacy is outdated. Oral language proficiency promotes literacy and vice versa. Most people are visual learners—memory of a new word, for example, is enhanced when the word can be seen as well as heard. So an integrated approach to English language arts (Pappas, Kiefer, & Levstik, 2006) is recommended, not only at the elementary level but also for content area instruction at the secondary level. Speaking and listening should be combined with reading and writing, and content instructors should integrate the teaching of English with subject matter instruction.

To integrate oracy with literacy, English learners need environments that help them to meet the social, emotional, cognitive, and linguistic demands of learning. Students need a positive *emotional setting*, a climate of trust and respect. Teachers can encourage students to respect the language of their peers and can model respectful listening when students speak. Students need a flexible *physical setting* for interaction: round or rectangular tables, clusters of desks, workstations, and centers. In addition, classrooms need to contain *things to talk about*: nature displays, flags, maps, artifacts, a variety of print material, and a challenging, interesting curriculum. Finally, students need *frequent opportunities to interact*: flexible grouping that allows work with a variety of classmates, cross-age tutors, the teacher, aides, volunteers, other adults at school, guests, and so on (Dudley-Marling & Searle, 1991).

Speaking can be integrated with literacy and oracy activities in many ways (Morgan, 1992). Students can listen to the sharing-time stories of others and use these as starting points for their own "adventures." Inviting community elders to tell stories in class provides rich stimuli, and when the visitors are gone, the students can finish these stories to continue the entertainment or write other stories in response. Older students can write response comments to their peers' oral presentations, share notes from class lectures with a group, or create group research reports. Negotiating, co-creating, responding, and giving presentations help to integrate speaking, listening, reading, and writing.

## Personal Factors Affecting Literacy Development in English

Similar factors influence literacy in English as those that affect second-language acquisition in general (see Chapter 2). An understanding of these factors can help teachers support students' process of learning to read in English.

**Primary-Language Literacy Level**    The more advanced the native-language competency, the more rapid the progress made in English, providing the student is motivated and the social context is supportive. Each year of schooling adds sophistication. In the early grades, a child with concepts about print in the first language has an advantage (including the ideas that print carries a message; that books are organized with a cover, title, and author and are held in a certain way for reading; that reading in English flows in a particular and consistent direction, left to right and top to bottom; that printed language consists of letters, words, sentences, punctuation marks, and case markers (upper- and lowercase, title case, etc.). Successful beginning readers build on their emergent literacy that starts before formal schooling.

In later grades, students who have learned in their primary language how discourse works have an advantage. For example, they can scan text for key ideas or specific details, they can read picture captions to interpret visual information, and they can use text aids such as the table of contents or a glossary. In addition to concepts about print and basic literacy skills, students bring a wealth of reading strategies. Most important, however, is metastrategic knowledge—being able to choose the right strategy for the task from a repertoire of strategies. In addition, students with oracy skills can use their listening and speaking productively in understanding task directions, asking clarifying questions, or displaying knowledge in response to the teacher's questions.

For the most part, primary-language literacy means that the student is familiar with the culture of schooling, including the need to sit still and focus, to follow classroom procedures, and to use pragmatic skills such as manners to act as a productive member of the class. Having the intellectual self-discipline instilled by schooling accompanied by literacy skills in the primary language bodes well for success in English literacy.

**Transfer of Primary-Language Literacy**    Language transfer occurs when the comprehension or production of a second language is influenced by the way the first language has been acquired (Odlin, 1989). Sometimes learners use rules from their first language that are not applicable to the second (*negative transfer*). As an illustration, Natheson-Mejia (1989) describes substitutions that Spanish speakers make when writing in English. These include *es* for /s/ as in *estop, d* for /t/ or /th/ as in *broder, ch* for /sh/ as in *chort, j* for /h/ as in *jelper,* and *g* for /w/ as in *sogen* (*sewing*).

What transfers from the first language? Training in literacy enhances *phonological awareness,* the ability to distinguish units of speech. The ability to focus on syllables and words is a foundational reading skill, which helps students read and in turn is advanced as they read. Moreover, *phonemic awareness* is a key factor that distinguishes good from poor readers (Stanovich, 1986); this is the ability to work with phonemes—to separate phonemes; to add, delete, or substitute phonemes in words; and to blend or split syllables. Students who are practiced in perceiving and manipulating phonemes are better at using letter sounds to apply phonics rules to decoding text as they convert written marks into sound.

Students can transfer sensorimotor skills (eye–hand coordination, fine muscle control, spatial and directional skills, visual perception and memory; auditory skills (auditory perception, memory, discrimination, and sequencing); common features of writing systems (alphabets, punctuation rules); comprehension strategies (finding the main idea, inferring, predicting, use of cueing systems); study skills (taking notes, using reference sources); habits and attitudes (self-esteem, task persistence, focus) (Cloud et al., 2000); the structure of language (speech–print relationships, concepts such as syllable, word, sentence, paragraph); and knowledge about the reading process (Thonis, 1983).

Aside from the preceding skills, students can transfer direct linguistic content. Of course, names for concrete objects in the first language must be relearned, but a few cognates can transfer from Spanish to English (cognates are words in two languages that look alike and have the same or similar meaning; see Garrison [1990]; Nagy, García, Durgunoglu, & Hancin-Bhatt, [1993]). Recognizing a similar word with a similar meaning makes learning new vocabulary easier. Even more important than concrete nouns and cognates are abstract concepts that can transfer. Students have to learn such concepts as proofreading or photosynthesis only once; they can then transfer that knowledge into the second language. The more concepts stored in the first language, the more enabled the student during ELD.

In addition to language labels, phonological awareness, and discourse skills, students can transfer *metalinguistic awareness*—knowledge about the structural properties of language, including sounds, words, grammar, and functions (Gombert, 1992), or the ability to use language as a tool, to step outside of the use of language to think about the language itself. Much more powerful than recognizing random cognates between Spanish and English is the use of metalinguistic knowledge to trace many predictable relations between Spanish and English words. For example, almost all nouns in English that end in *ion* have a Spanish cognate stemming from the -*ar* series of verbs in Spanish—*preparation* (*preparación,* from *preparar*); *communication* (*communicación,* from *communicar*); *attention* (*atención,* from *atentar*); and *action* (*acción,* from *actuar*), to list a few. Powerful language learning is available at the metalinguistic level.

Metalinguistic awareness may develop alongside first-language acquisition or during middle childhood as the child learns to think about the linguistic system (Tunmer, Herriman, & Nesdale, 1988). A third view is that metalinguistic awareness is a result of schooling, particularly of learning to read. Metalinguistic ability is a function of age—to a point—and students vary in this ability. Bilingual individuals outperform monolinguals on tasks requiring metalinguistic abilities (Hamers & Blanc, 1989). To summarize best practice in promoting metalinguistic awareness, knowledge, and skills, Table 5.1 divides these into four components and prescribes practices that enhance these components.

**TABLE 5.1**   Practices That Promote Metalinguistic Awareness

| Component of Metalinguistic Awareness | Definition | Suggestions to the Teacher to Enhance Awareness |
|---|---|---|
| Metaphonological | Identifying the phonological components in linguistic units and intentionally manipulating them | • Teach sound–symbol connection (phonics).<br>• Teach word segmentation into syllables, and onset-rime awareness (the idea that rhymes occur when the ending phonemes are the same sounds, even when beginning phonemes vary). |
| Metasyntactic | The ability to reason consciously about the syntactic aspects of language and to exercise intentional control over the application of grammatical rules | • Teach students to separate the correctness of a sentence from its truth value; teach critical literacy (everything written is not necessarily true).<br>• Have students make good/bad judgments on the correct form of sentences (could use peer editing). |
| Metapragmatic | Concerned with the awareness or knowledge one has about the relationships that obtain between the linguistic system and the context in which the language is embedded | • Help students judge the adequacy of messages and their context.<br>• Point out ironic, sarcastic, humorous, and polite forms of language. |
| Metasemantic | Refers both to the ability to recognize the language system as a conventional and arbitrary code and the ability to manipulate words or more extensive signifying elements, without the signified correspondents being automatically affected by this | • Teach students about word denotation and connotation and nuance of meaning.<br>• Expand vocabulary of synonyms and antonyms.<br>• Explore word oddities.<br>• Help students find cognates between languages. |

*Source:* Gombert, 1992, p. 15; Gombert, 1992, p. 39; Pratt & Nesdale, 1984, p. 105; Gombert, 1992, p. 63.

Teachers can transform language transfer into a learning strategy by helping students become aware of ways in which they can draw from prior knowledge of how language works to make English easier. Explicit attention to transfer, both in teacher attitude (welcoming dual-language use, understanding code-switching, providing support for literacy in multiple languages, and honoring primary languages) and in specific strategies, will help students build second-language acquisition on a firm foundation of first-language proficiency.

**Level of English-Language Proficiency** A student's CELDT score, combined with other measures of proficiency such as teacher observation and reading assessment, determines the appropriate level of instruction for that student. Table 5.2 displays English-language development objectives for listening and reading comprehension at five CELDT levels. The complexity of the standards increases gradually as expectations increase for language proficiency.

A student's CELDT level in grade 2 and beyond is represented as three scores: listening/speaking, reading, and writing. Because of individual differences, students will have mixed skill proficiency levels; one person may be at the early advanced level in speaking/listening, the intermediate level in reading, and early intermediate level in writing. Each proficiency requires distinct objectives.

**TABLE 5.2** Expectations for Listening and Reading Comprehension at Five CELDT Levels

| CELDT Level | Listening Comprehension | Reading Comprehension |
| --- | --- | --- |
| Beginning | Responds to simple directions and questions using physical actions | Responds orally to stories read aloud by answering factual comprehension questions using one- or two-word responses |
| Early Intermediate | Asks/answers questions and makes statements using phrases or simple sentences | Responds to stories read aloud by answering factual comprehension questions using phrases or simple sentences |
| Intermediate | Asks/answers instructional questions using simple sentences | Uses simple sentences to respond to stories by answering factual comprehension questions in the language experience approach (LEA) and guided reading |
| Early Advanced | Comprehends detailed information with minimal contextual clues on unfamiliar topics | Restates facts and details from content area texts |
| Advanced | Identifies orally and in writing key details and concepts from information/stories on unfamiliar topics | Locates and uses text features such as title, table of contents, chapter headings, diagrams, and index |

It would be relatively easy to plan instruction if students at a grade level were homogeneous in English ability, but that is seldom the case. More frequently, English learners with four or five levels of proficiency are mixed in the same class. Therefore, planning must accommodate twenty to thirty students at up to five CELDT levels, with many students at mixed levels. How is this possible?

The answer is differentiated instruction that develops students at two CELDT levels at a time. If a lesson is geared to accomplish writing objectives at the early intermediate and early advanced levels, the beginning-level students may listen while the early intermediate students read aloud what they have written; intermediate and advanced writers may act as peer tutors. In this way, students can participate in lessons although their particular objectives are not addressed on that day.

**Meeting Learners' Needs at Various ELD Levels**   Students at varying levels of English-language development require distinct kinds of instructional planning, organization, and delivery. Box 5.1 displays literature strategies in three stages (before, during, and after reading) that match strategies to students' CELDT levels.

**Motivation**   Maintaining a high level of interest and participation from all students is a key factor in promoting English-language development. Motivation radiates outward across the curriculum from activities at the core—those that students find both comprehensible and interesting. Because it is frustrating and mentally fatiguing to function in another language, the sheer joy of learning must be paramount. Learning does not have to be fun to be motivating, but it does have to be meaningful.

Teachers need to know what children do intellectually in the everyday context of their neighborhood and families. Teachers who interview community members and parents become familiar with the local expertise in many areas, and they use this knowledge to teach in ways that make sense to students. This helps students feel a closer connection and increased respect for community members.

In the "funds of knowledge" program, teachers visited homes to document the family's knowledge in such areas as farming, animal care, construction, trade, business, and finance. By asking questions about these domains, the teacher–investigators opened up new channels of communication between home and school (González, Moll, & Amanti, 2005). Researchers found that practical activities (auto repair, music, etc.) provided rich possibilities for learning to occur. Community members, teachers, and university researchers working on the project met periodically to weave knowledge about family and school matters into academic content and lessons.

## CLASSROOM GLIMPSE: Funds of Knowledge

*One teacher, aware that members of the community often built or remodeled their own homes, created a sixth-grade thematic unit on construction. Over twenty parents and community members visited the class, sharing their knowledge and skills on various aspects of construction. As the unit culminated, students wrote and gave oral reports on their design of a model community. These authentic, relevant activities drew from students real communication and problem-solving skills, adding excitement, authenticity, and a community connection to the classroom. (Moll, 1992)*

## Box 5.1    Strategies by ELD Level of Student for Use Before, During, and After Reading

### Students' ELD Level as Measured by CELDT

| Before, During, and After Reading | Beginning | Early Intermediate    Intermediate | Early Advanced    Advanced |
|---|---|---|---|
| Before Reading | *Visual and kinesthetic prompts:* Pictures, art, movies, physical objects relating to the reading selection that students identify and discuss. | *Anticipation/reaction guides:* A short list of statements to which students agree or disagree. | *Selected read-alouds:* Passages that pique students' interest in the selection. |
| During Reading | *Read-along tapes:* Tapes encourage slower readers, allow absent students to catch up, and provide auditory input for students. | *Image/theme development:* Charts, graphs, pictures, and symbols can trace the development of images, ideas, and themes. | *Visual summaries:* Groups of students create chapter reviews, character analyses, or problem–solutions on overhead transparencies. |
| After Reading | *Character review:* Specific students become a character and provide background for other students' questions about the reading. | *Critic:* "Journalists" write reviews of literature works for the school or classroom newspaper or act as movie critics and review the film version of a text studied in class. They can then compare the differences and draw conclusions about the pros and cons of the different media. | *Genre switch:* Favorite parts of selections can be rewritten as a play and enacted for other classes as a way to encourage other students to read that piece of literature; students can plan a mock television show and devise various formats that include ideas from the literature studied. For example, a game show host can ask contestants to answer questions or to act as characters or objects in the story. |

Of course, in today's schools the ninety minutes each week devoted to this unit would be used to train students to fill in test bubbles. Many such activities are being moved to after-school compensatory programs. How sad that students have to wait until the school day is over before learning something meaningful to the community.

## Promoting Literacy Development in English Across the Curriculum

Ideally, English-language development is not confined to one period of the school day but is instead a part of content area instruction. Each content area has a specialized knowledge base, vocabulary (consider, for example, the different meanings of *foot* in mathematics, biology, geography, furniture construction, poetry, theater), and particular graphic and verbal means for organizing information. Each content area has standards that guide curriculum development that must be addressed along with ELD standards. Table 5.3 offers suggestions for implementing ELD in a variety of ways across the curriculum.

Using content area standards as the basis for content instruction combined with level-specific ELD standards ensures organized, systematic, explicit progress in language proficiency. A language-rich environment adds literacy to meaningful and purposeful instruction in key content knowledge and skills, and integrates listening, speaking, reading, and writing with content objectives.

## Scaffolding Strategies in English Literacy Across the Curriculum

In education, scaffolding is used to help the learner construct knowledge (Berk & Winsler, 1995). During scaffolding, the teacher helps to focus the learner's attention on relevant parts of the task by asking key questions that help to determine the zone of proximal development for that student on that task. Questions and verbalizations give students the opportunity to think and talk about the task.

Dividing the task into smaller, manageable subcomponents and sensitively withdrawing assistance when it is no longer required furthers success (Díaz, Neal, & Vachio, 1991). The teacher who uses scaffolding skillfully does so in a form of dynamic assessment, evaluating and teaching at the same time. Table 5.4 presents scaffolding strategies in various content areas.

Another way to scaffold is to make verbal information visual. Graphic organizers are visual frames used to represent and organize information—"a diagram showing how concepts are related" (McKenna & Robinson, 1997, p. 117). Many kinds of graphic organizers can also be used to help students focus their thoughts and reactions—for example, as they read a literature selection. Because graphic organizers balance visual with verbal representation, they can help to make visible the conceptual structures that underlie content. This helps students make models for understanding ideas and outcomes.

Graphic organizers are particularly useful in content instruction. By using mind maps or other information organizers, students can interact with the concepts presented in various content areas in a way that supplements verbal text (Flynn, 1995). Thus, English learners can access core content even when their reading skills are weak. This results in students becoming more engaged in their learning.

**TABLE 5.3**    Examples of English-Language Development in Content Areas

| Facet of Literacy Development | Examples |
| --- | --- |
| Creating a language-rich environment | Teachers can provide new experiences that arouse interest in and attention to a topic: field trips, guest speakers, fiction and nonfiction films, experiments, classroom discovery centers, music and songs, poetry and other literature, computer simulations, and so on. |
| Meaningful and purposeful literacy activities | After students have had the opportunity to learn new material in a meaningful way, they can transform that knowledge through other means, such as illustrating, dramatizing, creating songs, dancing, rewriting stories. Students can share their learning in a variety of ways—in learning centers; through dramatic, visual, or oral presentations; by staging a reader's theater; by developing slide, video, or computer-based audiovisual shows; or through maps and graphs. |
| Using standards-based thematic unit organization | After demonstrating the basic tools associated with mathematics (rulers, protractors, calculators, computers, etc.), the teacher provides students with a real-life opportunity to use them. Students are told that the classroom needs to be recarpeted. They first have to estimate the area, then check their estimates with the actual tools (using both standard and metric measuring instruments), and then use calculators to find the percentage of error in their estimates. This fits with ELD standards relating to negotiating/initiating oral activities. |
| Selecting appropriate reading materials | Teachers can choose to have one primary content source or a package of content-related materials (chapters from various texts, video- and audiotapes, magazine and newspaper articles, encyclopedia entries, literary selections, Internet sources, software programs, etc.). Regardless of what is chosen, the teacher must consider two main criteria: Are the content objectives for the lesson adequately presented by the material? Is the material comprehensible to English learners? |
| Providing organized, systematic, explicit instruction in key skills | Students identify key words in mathematics problem solving and determine how other words are linked to the key words. For example, in the problem "Five times a number is two more than ten times the number," students must recognize that "a number" and "the number" refer to the same quantity. However, in the problem "The sum of two numbers is 77. If the first number is ten times the other, find the number," students need to know they are dealing with two different numbers (Dale & Cuevas, 1992). |
| Adapting instruction and materials for English learners | Some learners may need special textual material, such as excerpts taken from textbooks, advance organizers for the text that highlight the key topics and concepts in outline form, focus questions, concept maps, or tape-recorded text passages. |

**TABLE 5.3**   (*Continued*)

| Facet of Literacy Development | Examples |
|---|---|
| Integrating listening, speaking, reading, and writing | During the first week of the solar system unit, the names of the planets were tossed into a hat. Each of nine pairs of native-English-speaking and English-learning students selected one planet and developed a poster session about their planet based on resources in the school library. After each pair presented their planet, the teacher combined pairs into small groups. Each group was to create a tenth planet based on what they had learned and present that planet to the class. |

Graphic organizers have at least three major applications. First, *representative/explanatory* organizers are used to increase content understanding, either by building background knowledge before students read a text, or to synthesize new information that is gained from a text. Second are *generative* organizers, used to promote ideas related to content. Students can talk or write about the information presented on a chart. Third, *evaluative* organizers are used to explain understanding of content. Figure 5.1 displays these three types.

**TABLE 5.4**   Scaffolding Strategies for Use in Content Areas

| Scaffolding Strategy | Description of Use in the Content Class |
|---|---|
| Previewing vocabulary | Before beginning a social studies lesson, students in pairs skim the chapter and look up definitions in the glossary. |
| Prereading activities | Students make collages with pictures of vegetables cut from magazines before reading in the health book about the vitamins found in common foods. |
| Language experience approach | After performing a laboratory experiment, students interview one another and write down a report of the experiment results. |
| Interactive journals | Students describe personal exercise goals and write daily results in a journal; their peer "personal trainer" reads and provides feedback and encouragement. |
| Shared reading | Students "buddy read" encyclopedia entries as they write a group science research report. |
| Learning logs | In a mathematics center, students make entries into a group log as they try to solve a weekly puzzle. |
| Process writing | Students working on a monthlong family history project share their rough drafts with family members to gain input before final revision. |
| Graphic organizers | To evaluate ideas for a class fundraiser, students make a pro/con comparison chart with strong and weak aspects of each moneymaking idea. |

**FIGURE 5.1**    Three Types of Graphic Organizers

*Representative/Explanatory*
- Sequential
- Compare/contrast circles
- T-chart
- Comparison chart
- Embedded
- Whole/part
- Cause/effect
- Classification

*Generative*
- Concept development
- Mind map
- Spider map
- K-W-L

*Evaluative*
- Grade scale
- Likert scale

**FIGURE 5.2**    Sample Sequential Organizer: Story Sequence Chart

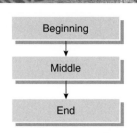

A *sequential organizer* is an explanatory diagram that shows items in order, such as parts of a book, a letter, or an essay; events in a story plot; or steps in written directions (Kagan, 1998, 1999). Figure 5.2 shows a sequential organizer used to list the beginning, middle, and end of a story. Figure 5.3 shows the problem–solution chain in a Native-American "coyote" story. If the events repeat, a cycle graph might be used. A sequence can be a cartoon, a picture strip, or a timeline.

*Compare/contrast organizers* can be used to compare characters in the same story or in different stories, types of correspondence (business versus friendly letters), or genres of reading (fiction versus nonfiction). Visually, comparison charts can be of various types: compare/contrast circles (Venn diagram, see Figure 5.4), T-charts (see Figure 5.5), or comparison charts (see Figure 5.6).

Other *relational organizers* can show information that is embedded (see Figure 5.7), whole/part (see Figure 5.8), or cause/effect (see Figure 5.9).

*Classification organizers* are used to create hierarchies, matrixes, or other concept relations that show specific structures. Figure 5.10 shows a hierarchy format, Figure 5.11 shows a

**FIGURE 5.3**    Sample Sequential Organizer: Problems and Solutions in a Story

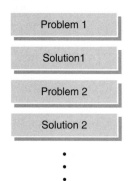

**FIGURE 5.4**    Sample Compare/Contrast (Venn) Diagram Used for the Questions, "How Are Two Things Alike? How Are They Different?"

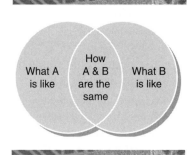

**FIGURE 5.5**    Sample T-Chart: Comparison of Same and Different

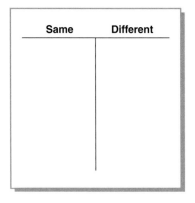

**FIGURE 5.6**   Sample Comparison Chart Showing Comparison by Attributes

**Comparison of Civilizations**

|  | *Egypt* | *United States* |
|---|---|---|
| Duration | More than 4000 years | About 400 years |
| Political structure | Towns united by centralized government | Hierarchy: towns, counties, states, federal government |
| Religion | Pharaonic, later Islam | Predominantly Protestant Christian, then Catholic Christian, then Jewish, Islam, other |

etc.

**FIGURE 5.7**   Sample Relational Organizer Showing Embedded Concepts (Teacher's Phenomenal Field of Personal Relations in the Role of Teacher)

**FIGURE 5.8**   Sample Relational Organizer Showing Whole/Part (Parts of the Atom)

**FIGURE 5.9**   Sample Relational Organizer Showing Cause/Effect (Possible Causes of Lightbulb Nonfunctioning)

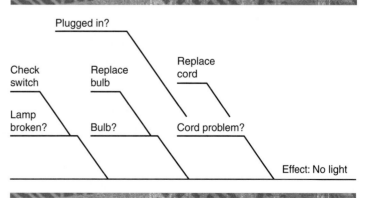

**FIGURE 5.10**   Sample Classification Chart Showing Main Ideas

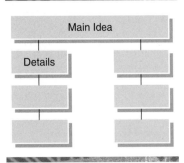

**FIGURE 5.11**   Sample Classification Chart Showing a Matrix

|  | Boys | Girls | Totals |
|---|---|---|---|
| Blue-eyed | 4 | 7 | 11 |
| Brown-eyed | 13 | 10 | 23 |
| Totals | 17 | 17 | 34 |

**FIGURE 5.12**   Sample Classification Chart Showing Dimensions (Learning Styles)

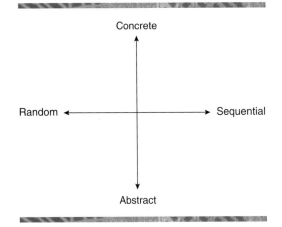

matrix, Figure 5.12 shows a two-dimensional plot, and Figure 5.13 shows an alternative way to display a hierarchy.

*Concept development organizers* are used to brainstorm. They do not display information that is already related. The K-W-L chart is used to introduce a theme, a lesson, or a reading. It can help generate student interest in a topic and help students use their prior knowledge as they read. Students can enter K (what we Know) and W (what we Want to know) in advance, and L (what we Learned) at the end of the unit or lesson (see Figure 5.14). The mind map is basically a circle with the topic in the center, and around it are lines or other connectors that tie students' ideas to the topic (see Figures 5.15 and 5.16).

*Evaluation organizers* show degree of positivity (Kagan, 1998). These can be grade scales (A to F); Likert scales (1 = strongly disagree and, at the other extreme, 7 = strongly agree); or rubric scales (needs work→ satisfactory→ good→ excellent); or they can comprise two boxes ("I like/agree with" versus "I dislike/disagree with") or three boxes, indicating plus/maybe/minus.

Once students and teachers become familiar with graphic organizers, they become a help to English learners in grasping basic concepts without dependence on language as the sole source of understanding. An excellent source is Parks and Black's *Organizing Thinking: Graphic Organizers* (1990).

## CLASSROOM GLIMPSE: Tutoring with Graphic Organizers

*Semantic mapping proved to be a successful approach for the three English learners, two boys ages five and nine and their sister, age ten, whom Judy was tutoring. She searched for an interesting topic that would increase their vocabulary in English. The children chose "Halloween." Starting with words they knew in English (skeleton, witch), Judy wrote the words on chart paper and the children copied the words in their notebooks. The children gave other words in Spanish, and Judy found the English equivalents and wrote them too.*

    *Using a fresh piece of chart paper, Judy asked the students how the list of words could be grouped into categories. The activity continued until the words had been grouped into the cate-gories Animals, Monsters, and Trick-or-Treat. Judy followed up this activity by reading a book on* Halloween, Rotten Ralph's Trick or Treat. *When they came to a word on the chart, Judy pointed this out for reinforcement. (Brisk & Harrington, 2000, pp. 71–72)*

**FIGURE 5.13**   Sample Classification Chart Showing Hierarchy

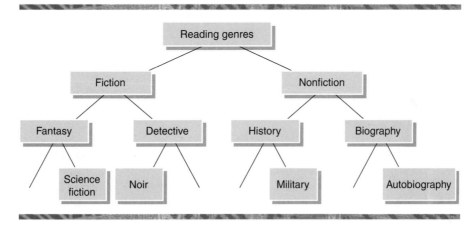

**FIGURE 5.14**   Sample Concept Development Chart: K-W-L

| What We Know | What We Want to Know | What We Have Learned |
| --- | --- | --- |
| | | |

**FIGURE 5.15** Sample Concept Development Chart: Mind Map or Idea Web

**FIGURE 5.16** Sample Concept Development Chart: Character Trait Web

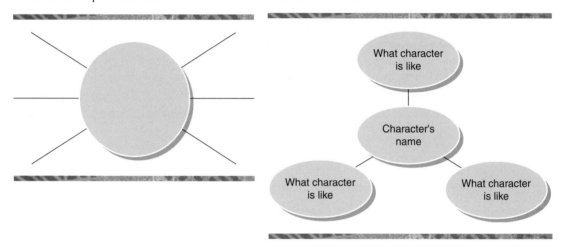

# INSTRUCTIONAL PLANNING AND ORGANIZATION FOR ELD AND SDAIE

Careful planning and a well-organized classroom, combined with effective teaching, are keys to success for English learners. The cycle of instruction consists of the following four phases: (1) the teacher becomes familiar with the characteristics of the students (age, grade level, language-acquisition level); (2) the teacher plans instruction using state and local curriculum standards and textbooks as guides; (3) the teacher delivers instruction using formative assessment to monitor progress; and (4) the teacher employs summative assessment to give grades and make information available about student progress.

This cycle is repeated throughout the school year. Based on assessment data, the teacher modifies instruction for the class as a whole or for individual students, groups, and regroups students, and acquires additional resources as needed. Over this entire classroom-based cycle is the spector of standardized testing, which reports to the community at large, including federal, state, and local authorities, sometimes with the threat of dire consequences to the school if expectations are not met. This is the contemporary context for planning and instructional delivery.

## Planning for Standards-Based ELD and Content Instruction

Lesson planning involves the careful planning of content, language, and learning strategy objectives and the selecting, modifying, and organizing of materials and text that support those objectives. Objectives are necessary to guide teaching. A lesson with a clear objective focuses instruction by concentrating on a particular goal and guides the teacher to select those learning activities that accomplish the goal. Once objectives are clearly stated, the teacher selects materials that will help students achieve those objectives. Finally, assessment provides evidence that learning has, or has not, taken place.

This chapter provides an introduction to ELD and SDAIE teaching. Chapter 7 reviews these concepts in more detail, with specific content area examples.

**Objectives**   What is a lesson objective? The objective states, in behavioral terms, what the student will be capable of doing at the close of the lesson. Such verbs as *contrast, identify, list, summarize, compare, predict, survey*, and *outline* are specific, describing a behavior that can be measured or has a tangible product. In contrast, such verbs as *learn, look at, evaluate, think about, know, review*, and *become aware* are not specific or measurable. Moreover, some verbs do not specify a goal but merely a process or activity. Such terms as *listen to, reflect, practice*, and *work in groups* describe activities, not goals. Hence it is difficult to measure what is accomplished. In contrast, *draw, map, record data, plan*, or *punctuate* are terms that result in a product that can be assessed.

An optimal lesson for English learners has three types of objectives:

- *Content objective:* knowledge, skill, or disposition in a subject area or domain of communicative competence
- *Language objective:* knowledge or skill in some facet of English
- *Learning-to-learn objective:* knowledge, skill, or learning strategy that teaches the student how to acquire or process information

Objectives can include more than one content area. Middle school as well as elementary school instruction is increasingly featuring thematic units that integrate content areas. The teacher considers the various tasks that language users must be able to perform in the unit (listening, speaking, reading, writing) and makes provisions for students to learn the vocabulary and concepts needed in the discourse of the content areas involved.

**Objectives and Standards**   How are objectives chosen? Schools, school districts, or state agencies publish standards documents that spell out what students should know and be able to do. These furnish goals for each grade. A classroom teacher plans instruction using curriculum guides at the specific grade level. Units may be organized based on a theme or, if the course is text-driven, based on chapters in the text (instructional planning is presented in greater detail later in this chapter). Units or chapters are further divided into specific lessons containing the essential content area objectives. The classroom teacher is responsible for presenting the material in an understandable way, arranging for students to participate in learning activities, and then measuring the extent of the students' mastery of the material. Thus, instruction and assessment are linked.

The chosen objectives must be matched to specific performance that students will demonstrate. This is central to the contemporary focus on accountability because the specific performance expected of the student as a learning outcome can be directly linked to some standard for the performance. Together, these constitute *standards-based learning.*

A standard becomes useful to teachers only when they can identify when the standard has been met or progress is being made toward meeting it. Moreover, when schools communicate performance standards to students, students know what is considered important that they be able to do, and they can judge where they stand in relation to the standard. Students must be prepared to receive targeted feedback on their work in a way that encourages them to compare their work to specific standards. Assessment should provide information on what students already do well and pinpoint what they still need to learn; this provides information about what aspects of instruction need to be redesigned (Jametz, 1994).

**Content Standards** Each content domain has standards suggested by the professional organization that represents expertise in the field, such as the National Council for the Social Studies, National Council of Teachers of Mathematics (NCTM), and National Association for Sport and Physical Education (NASPE). In turn, the state departments of education (such as the California Department of Education) incorporate these standards into state content standards, designed to define the knowledge, concepts, and skills that students should acquire at each grade level. These are in turn incorporated into curriculum frameworks (blueprints for implementing the content standards) that are then used by individual school districts to determine what instructors in each grade level should teach. When these goals are met, standardized testing should provide evidence that students are learning.

**Content Objectives** The teacher begins planning by first specifying learning goals and identifying competencies students must develop. The teacher divides these overall goals for the year into units. These units are further divided into specific lessons. Each lesson contains one or more essential content area objectives.

In developing their sequence of content objectives, teachers want to keep two important questions in mind: (1) Have I reviewed the objectives for the year and organized them for thematic flow? (2) Have I considered the sequence of objectives and rearranged them, if necessary, putting more concrete concepts before more abstract ones (i.e., those that can be taught with hands-on materials, visuals, and demonstrations before those that are difficult to demonstrate or that require more oral and/or written skills)? The following are examples of the movement from standards to objective.

## CLASSROOM GLIMPSE: Matching an Objective to a Standard

*Emil Chantal's fourth-grade class read* Amelia's Road *(Altman, 1993) as a focal point for studying the regions of the state of California where certain crops grow. He based this lesson on History Social Science Content Standard 4.1: "Students demonstrate an understanding of the physical and human geographic features that define places and regions in California," specifically, 4.1.3: "Identify . . . and describe the various regions of California, including how their characteristics and physical environments (e.g., water, landforms, vegetation, climate) affect human activity," and 4.1.5: "Use maps, charts, and pictures to describe how communities in California vary in land use, vegetation, wildlife, climate, population density, architecture, services, and transportation."*

*The content objective for this lesson was "Using a map of California, link regions and crops to the plot of* Amelia's Road.*"*

*Using a map of California's farm regions (http://score.rims.k12.ca.us/score_lessons/ amelia_road/map.html), students located where Amelia was born, as well as the locations described in the book. On a study sheet, they also answered questions such as, "What grew in the area in which Amelia went to school?"*

**Language Standards** The California *English Language Development (ELD) Standards* (California Department of Education, 1999a) require that English learners develop proficiency in both the English language and the concepts and skills contained in the English language arts (ELA) content standards (California Department of Education, 1997). Like the ELA standards, the California ELD standards are organized in areas of reading, writing, and listening/speaking. The California English Language Development Test is aligned with the standards as a placement and achievement test. Using the ELD and ELA standards, teachers can work with students through a developmental framework that stipulates the requirements of each proficiency level.

**Language Objectives** Each content area has specific language demands. Language objectives take these into account. The teacher considers the various tasks that language users must be able to perform in the different content areas (e.g., describing in a literature lesson, classifying in a science lesson, justifying in a mathematics lesson, etc.). A language objective takes into account not only vocabulary but also the language functions and discourse of the discipline.

In reviewing language objectives, a teacher can keep the following questions in mind:

- What is the concept load of the unit and what are the key concepts to demonstrate and illustrate?
- What are the structures and discourse of the discipline and are these included in the language objectives?
- Are all four language modes included in the planning (listening, speaking, reading, writing)?

## CLASSROOM GLIMPSE: Language Standards

*In a content-based, intermediate/advanced ELD high school social studies class, standards-based instruction was incorporated into the unit Exploring World Religions. Students used a word web journal to define religion; used reading passages and journals combined with discussions about religion; and read library and Internet research to identify important religious figures. Final portfolios were used to archive students' essays and other writings. Through the unit, note-taking skills, outlines, timelines, maps, games, and other knowledge technologies were incorporated into group research, oral presentations, paragraph writing, and grammar work. (Riles & Lenarcic, 2000)*

**Strategic Learning** The cognitive revolution in learning turned the spotlight on how people transform, elaborate, store, and recover information. According to the cognitive view, people are active learners who initiate experiences, seek out information, and reorganize what they already know in order to achieve new insights, pursue goals, solve personally relevant problems, and attempt to make sense of the world (Bruner, 1986).

Cognitive training includes the use of learning strategies, study skills, memory enhancement, text processing skills, note taking, research skills, test-taking skills, problem solving, transfer, graphic organizers, and information processing tips, as well as learning the characteristics of the brain. A cognitivist view of learning means teaching students *how* to learn.

Teachers motivate students best when they provide course activities and projects that tap students' natural abilities and interests and develop their confidence in their ability to think. Teachers who ask thought-provoking questions and use concrete examples, activities, and demonstrations stimulate students' imaginations and develop their critical thinking skills. This includes metacognition in the form of cognitive self-knowledge (multiple intelligences, learning styles), goal setting, planning, self-monitoring, and self-evaluating.

**Learning Strategy Objectives**   A cognitive lesson needs one or more learning strategy objectives. A *learning strategy objective* can be defined as acquisition or practice of a direct or indirect strategy that increases ease in acquiring a new skill or information (Díaz-Rico, 2004). Learning strategies can be distinguished from content objectives by a simple test: Is the objective one that can be applied outside the specific lesson? Is it a skill that can be used again and again as part of a learner's "mental toolkit"?

**Cognitive Academic Language Learning Approach (CALLA)**   Learning strategies are being recognized more and more as an integral part of teaching, an idea made explicit in Chamot and O'Malley's Cognitive Academic Language Learning Approach (CALLA) (1994). CALLA, designed for English learners at the early intermediate to advanced levels of English-language proficiency, incorporates explicit teaching of learning strategies within academic subject areas. The CALLA model includes three components: topics from the major content subjects, the development of academic language skills, and explicit instruction in learning strategies for both content and language acquisition (Chamot & O'Malley, 1994).

The content topics, aligned with the all-English curriculum, are introduced gradually, emphasizing those that have extensive contextual supports or reduced language demands. The second component, academic language skills, includes all four language modes in daily content lessons. Students learn not just vocabulary and grammar but also important concepts and skills using academic language. In addition, they learn language functions important for the specific curricular areas, such as analyzing, evaluating, justifying, and persuading.

The third—and central—component is instruction in learning strategies. These strategies are divided into three major categories: *metacognitive, cognitive,* and *social-affective.* The metacognitive strategies help students to plan, monitor, and evaluate their learning processes. Teachers help students learn to preview the main concepts in material to be learned, plan the key ideas that must be expressed orally or in writing, decide in advance what specific information must be attended to, check comprehension during listening or reading, and judge how well learning has been accomplished when the lesson is completed.

Cognitive strategies include using reference materials resourcefully; taking effective notes; summarizing material adequately; applying rules of induction or inference; remembering information using visual images, auditory representation, or elaboration of associations to new knowledge; transferring prior skills to assist comprehension; and grouping new concepts, words, or terms understandably. Social-affective strategies teach how to elicit needed clarification, how to work cooperatively with peers in problem solving, and how to use mental techniques or self-talk to reduce anxiety and increase a sense of personal competency.

## CLASSROOM GLIMPSE: Learning Strategy Objectives

*The high school ELD classroom just got three new computers. Mrs. O'Dale knew that several students had computers at home, but nevertheless she wanted to make sure that all the students had basic word-processing skills. Before beginning a unit on autobiography, she identified a set of skills that are useful in word processing. In addition to such content objectives as identifying a topic, using descriptive details, and using time sequence connectors, each lesson in the writing unit would have an objective relating to word processing, beginning with saving and retrieving files, moving text within a file, and spellchecking. Thus, the acquisition of computer skills became learning strategy objectives.*

Skillful lesson planning includes integrating content, learning strategy, and language development objectives. A unit on bacteria would include a learning strategy objective on the use of microscopes and a language objective relating to writing a brief summary (of laboratory observations). In contrast, a social studies lesson would use the reading selection as content but a comprehension-enhancing technique such as "using a cause-and-effect organizer" as a learning strategy.

## CLASSROOM GLIMPSE: Integrating Three Types of Objectives

*The Most Beautiful Place in the World is an instructional unit based on the book by the same title (Cameron, 1988) about a young boy in Guatemala who longs to attend school and learn to read (Levine, 2000). Levine found that the Spanish words, foods, and other cultural aspects incorporated in the novel were particularly appropriate for her students, who were all from Spanish-speaking families. The unit also integrated social studies curricular goals as students studied map locations, compass directions, and cultural comparisons.*

To fulfill language arts goals, Levine's students read for comprehension and enjoyment, read for specific information, predicted and inferred from text, answered questions using oral and written sentences, and acquired academic vocabulary. To meet affective goals, they learned to listen and show respect to peers, help one another learn, and feel secure and successful. Toward study skills goals, they learned specific techniques to learn vocabulary. Assessment included content knowledge, the use of reading strategies, map work, and vocabulary acquisition.

### Organizing the Environment to Enhance Interaction

Teachers can do much to design spaces that make it easier for students to acquire English. The design is in the physical as well as the socioemotional elements.

**Physical Setting**   The arrangement of space in the classroom provides an invitation to interact. Because the verbal presentation of a lesson is supplemented by the use of manipulatives, realia, media, and visual backup, students need to be able to see graphs, pictures, maps, and other physical props, either through imaginative use of the overhead projector or use of a computer hooked to a projector. Acoustics in the classroom should support clear auditory input. There should be ample room for kinesthetic involvement (drama, skits, and "gallery" walks). The room should have tables with chairs to support group work.

**Language-Rich Environment**   The display and use of a variety of print materials in the primary language and English stimulate students' interest in language. These materials might include alternative numbering systems as well as alphabets from the world's languages. Students need to be able to decorate their own bulletin boards with topics that relate to their interests. The display and use of content-related objects such as prints, maps, puzzles, and artifacts offer stimuli for conversations.

## Grouping for Student Success

Many teachers include opportunities for students to talk about key concepts. Teachers ensure that students have numerous conversational partners and opportunities to interact with the content of lessons. A noncompetitive environment can be established through cooperative learning activities, both formally and informally structured. Heterogeneous groups encourage language development as students talk about learning experiences with one another.

Material presented in a mainstream class may be difficult for English learners if the topics are cognitively complex and highly language dependent. Using cooperative learning, English learners have increased opportunities to verify their comprehension by receiving explanations from their peers and sharing prior knowledge. This helps them clarify and familiarize themselves with the lesson content.

Probably more was written on cooperative and collaborative learning in the last twenty years of the twentieth century than in all the previous history of education. David and Robert Johnson (c.f. Johnson, Johnson, & Holubec, 1993), Robert Slavin (1991), and others advocated the use of cooperative learning for elementary students. Others documented the success of cooperative learning with elementary school English learners (c.f. Kessler, Quinn, & Fathman, 1992; Johns, 1992; Cohen, 1994; Johnson & Johnson, 1994) as well as with secondary school ELD students (Faltis, 1993).

**Benefits to English Learners**   Small-group learning provides English learners with a rich discourse environment and multiple opportunities for face-to-face interaction. This is particularly necessary when students must exchange information about academic content and procedures. When students are collaborating in small groups, they have substantially more chances to practice language—without worrying about whether their production is exactly right. This lowers their anxiety and lets them concentrate on the content of learning. They can hear and say key words and phrases and repeat them in a variety of ways until they feel comfortable with their language mastery (Faltis, 2001). Cooperative grouping also increases the possibility that English learners will feel a part of the culture of the classroom as a whole.

**Guidelines for Cooperative Learning**   Developing cooperative skills requires a focus in the classroom on communication and teamwork. Kluge (1999) emphasized the following elements:

- *Positive interdependence:* Members of a group depend on one another, and no one is exploited or left out.
- *Face-to-face interaction:* Students work in proximity to one another.

*Cooperative learning helps to build a sense of community in the classroom.*

- *Individual accountability:* Each group member bears full responsibility for the work performed by the group.
- *Social skills training:* The teacher explicitly explains and models the kind of communication and cooperation that is desired.
- *Group processing:* The teacher makes time for reflection on how the group is working together and helps the group set goals for improvement. (n.p.)

Table 5.5 summarizes the instructional use of cooperative learning with English learners. This information represents a synthesis of tips and guidelines from Bassano and Christison (1995), Cantlon (1991), and Kagan (1998, 1999). (Sources are identified with number keys.)

Even under the best of circumstances, cooperative learning has its challenges. Table 5.6 sets these forth, offering tactics for teachers to address these issues.

Many types of tasks have been designed that feature cooperative structures. These range from simply pairing students for discussion to more elaborate setups requiring extensive time for preparation and monitoring. Table 5.7 presents a few cooperative structures and tasks. (Sources are identified with number keys.)

The jigsaw model of cooperative learning is particularly useful in that students are individually accountable for learning their own material and for sharing their information effectively with other group members. In the jigsaw method, each member (A, B, C, or D) of the base team (I, II, III, or IV) attends an expert group session (all the As huddle together) to study one aspect or section of the topic and thus has one piece of the knowledge puzzle (hence the name "Jigsaw"). Then the individuals return to their base team to share what they have learned. The ultimate

**TABLE 5.5** Instructional Use of Cooperative Learning

| Component of Cooperative Learning | Explanation or Example |
| --- | --- |
| Definition | "An approach to education and a repertoire of teaching strategies based on the philosophy that students can learn effectively in small groups. Cooperative learning restructures the traditional classroom into small, carefully planned learning groups to provide opportunities for all students to work together and to learn from one another." (Source: 5, p. 3) |
| Rationales for using cooperative learning | Practice speaking and listening. Share information. Create things together. Learn democratic processes. Practice negotiating and compromising. (Source: 1, p. 29) Develop leadership, communication, decision-making, and conflict management skills. (Source: 2) Promote real-world team skills. **T**ogether **E**veryone **A**chieves **M**ore (TEAM)! Builds positive interpersonal relations. Transcends differences (cliques). (Source: 4) |
| Roles in teams | Language Monitor, Task Monitor, Timekeeper, Secretary, Clarifier, Encourager, Reporter. (Source: 1, page 29) Materials Monitor, Quiet Captain. (Source: 3) |
| Optimal team size | For initial start-up, dyads (teams of two) are most successful. (Source: 2) If teams of three are necessary, have them sit side by side. (Source: 2) Teams of four are ideal, small enough for active participation and split evenly for pair work. (Source: 3) |
| Frequency of use of cooperative structures | Minimum of three times a week; but simple structures (pair/share) can be used more often. (Source: 2) |
| Room and seating arrangements | Partners should sit side by side. If students are in fours, provide two sets of materials. No student's back should be to the teacher. (Source: 2) |
| Role of the teacher | Source of task; arranger of materials; accountable authority; partner in learning. (Source: 1) |
| Team composition | Heterogeneous (mixed gender, ethnicity, ability); teacher-assigned, long term; this is preferable. (Source: 3) To form heterogeneous ability groups, list students in ability from high to low (1–28), divide into quartiles, then form one group from 1, 8, 15, 22; next group 2, 9, 16, 23, etc. (Avoids highest grouped with lowest.) Random (randomly mixed ability, etc.); breaks up the monotony; short term. (Source: 3) Random teams may be a problem if all high achieving are in one group, or two students create mutual discipline problems. (Source: 2) Random grouping: Use colored marbles or slips with group numbers in a jar; group students by month of birth; count off around class. (Source: 1) |
| Team management | Inform students how much time is allotted to task; have an agreed signal to stop working (clap pattern, ringing a bell, countdown, etc.). (Source: 2) |

**TABLE 5.5**   *(Continued)*

| Component of Cooperative Learning | Explanation or Example |
| --- | --- |
| Rationale statement | Teacher explains why work is done in a team, what the benefits are, and what behavior is expected. (Source: 2) |
| Necessary group skills | Forming into groups quickly.<br>Participating with muted voices.<br>Establishing turn-taking routines.<br>Involving more hesitant members in group processes. (Source: 1) |
| Trust building/ bonding | Rapport building; discuss favorite foods, hobbies, likes, dislikes.<br>Nonacademic fun activities: games, puzzles.<br>Academic tasks: partner reading, checking homework together (staple papers together, teachers correct top paper). (Source: 2) |
| Teaching social skills | Teacher models behavior: quiet voices, taking turns, everyone participating, encouraging partner, signal to stop. (Source: 2) |
| Appreciation statements by peers at debriefing | "(*Name*), you helped the team by _____."<br>"(_____), you did a great job of _____."<br>"(_____), I appreciated it when you _____."<br>"(_____), you are very good at _____."<br>(Source: 2) |
| Clarification statements by peers | "I don't understand."<br>"Excuse me?"<br>"Speak more slowly, please."<br>"Okay?" (Source: 1, p. 29) |
| Procedural statements by peers | "It's my/your/his/her turn."<br>"Quickly! We have four minutes."<br>"You first, then me." (Source: 1, p. 29) |
| Peers asking for/ offering help | "Are you finished?"<br>"I need help."<br>"Do you need help?" (Source: 1, p. 29) |
| Individual accountability | Students have progress conferences with instructor.<br>Groups are rated by teacher using monitoring chart.<br>Groups monitor themselves periodically using rating charts. (Source: 1) |
| Rewards (nonmaterial); avoid message that reward involves escape from work (extra recess) | Elementary: Happygrams, applause, display group work, AV treat, play a special game.<br>Middle/high school: library passes, computer time, daily announcements recognition, newsletter recognition, display work, special privileges, team picture displayed. (Source: 2) |
| Feedback | At the close of activity, teammates write on 3″ × 5″ card: "Which question/problem gave you difficulty?" "Give examples of what you might do differently next time." "List ways in which your partners helped the team to reach its goal." (Source: 2) |

*Sources:* (1) Bassano & Christison (1995); (2) Cantlon (1991); (3) Kagan, S. (1998); (4) Kagan, S. (1999); (5) Coehlo, Winer, & Olsen (1989).

**TABLE 5.6**  Challenges to Cooperative Learning and Tactics to Meet Them

| Challenge | Tactics for Teachers |
|---|---|
| Students cannot get along. | Keep activities short and simple while students are learning how to work together.<br>Group students wisely; place a socially immature student with two who are more mature.<br>Teach social skills and review regularly. |
| Student prefers to work alone. | Provide encouragement by emphasizing importance of working in a group, giving examples from teacher's work.<br>Give bonus points to class for working well together.<br>Provide individual work occasionally as "safety valve." |
| Student is unmotivated. | Use interest inventory to discover student's likes and dislikes.<br>Ask previous teachers what works for the student.<br>Give student a role in the group in which he or she will succeed. |
| Student cannot keep up with others. | Let student prepare some part of task prior to group work.<br>Provide a modified worksheet for slow student.<br>Provide an alternate way for student to perform. |
| Group finishes before others. | Provide an extension or enrichment task that extends the activity.<br>Two groups who finish first can compare their products. |
| Group finishes last. | See if task can be modified so all groups will finish together.<br>Teacher or member of early-finishing group can spend some time to help slow group.<br>Let individuals take home tasks. |
| Too much noise. | Monitor groups and commend those who are quiet and on-task.<br>Use a standard signal for noise such as blinking room lights.<br>Assign a member of each group as noise control. |

*Source:* Ellis & Whalen, 1992.

learning goal is for each member of the base team to have the whole set of information, so each member must communicate what has been learned in the expert group.

## CLASSROOM GLIMPSE: Jigsaw Cooperative Learning

*In one use of the jigsaw model, intermediate ELD students studied the use of persuasion in advertising by looking at three different types of ads in three expert groups and completing worksheets with questions such as, "How is the ad trying to persuade you? Is it using reason, an appeal to the emotions, or an appeal to a feeling of right or wrong? Is the advertisement effective? Why or why not?" Returning to their base group, group members described the ad they studied and completed a second worksheet summarizing the types and effectiveness of persuasion used in various ads. Students then worked cooperatively to write their own ads. (Weatherly, 1999, p. 79)*

**TABLE 5.7** Sample Cooperative Learning Activities

| Name of Activity | Description of Activity |
|---|---|
| Relay | Four students learn a skill; they teach it to four others; eight teach it to eight more, until everyone knows it. (Source: 1) |
| Group Memory | In groups of six, give each group a line to memorize. Group members receive extra credit if everyone can say it when time is up. (Source: 1) |
| Listen Please (also called Information Gap) | In this paired activity, student A has words on various cards and student B has a matching set of picture cards. Listening to the description on a card, student B must pick out the matching card. (Source: 1) |
| Sequencing Task | Students put a cut-up sequence in correct order. Example: scrambled dialogue from a phone call to a friend. (Source: 1) |
| Scavenger Hunt | With a stack of newspapers, group finds one of each: some good news, some bad news, weather map, letter to editor, overseas news, etc. (Source: 1) |
| Round Robin | Each person does a problem (using one color ink) and then passes paper to next team member, who does the next problem. Teacher corrects one sheet. (Source: 2) |
| Jigsaw | Students receive number and letter (Ex.: I–IV, A–D). Base teams: I, II, III, IVs. Students exit base team; all As group to study one aspect, etc., then return to base team to share expertise. (Source: 2) |
| Numbered Heads Together | Each student in the group has a number (1–4); students huddle to make sure all can respond, then a number is called and that student responds. (Source: 3) |
| Rotating Review | Students visit wall charts; each chart has different review question; they write answers, then rotate to next chart. (Source: 3) If they agree with what is already written, they mark with asterisk. |
| Send-a-Problem | Groups create problems that are sent around the class for other teams to solve. (Source: 3) |
| Pairs Compare | Pairs come up with ideas to solve a problem. When pairs are through, two pairs make a team of four and compare ideas, generating more ideas. (Source: 4) |
| 4S Brainstorming | While brainstorming solutions to an open-ended prompt, team members take one of four roles: Speed Sergeant: Encourages many responses quickly; Sultan of Silly: Tries to come up with silly ideas; Synergy Guru: Helps members build on one another's ideas; and Sergeant Support: Encourages all ideas, suspends judgment. (Source: 4) |
| Group Memory | Students write everything they know about a topic they plan to study, including unanswered questions that come to them. In groups of three, they read the paper to the group, and everybody adds ideas to their list. The group compiles unanswered questions and turns in a Group Memory Sheet. (Source: 5) |
| Partner Prediction | Teacher preidentifies places in a literature story where the students can stop and predict what happens next. They share predictions with a partner. They must then share aloud what the partner predicts. |

*(Continued)*

**TABLE 5.7** (*Continued*)

| Name of Activity | Description of Activity |
| --- | --- |
| 2/4 Question Some More | Teacher identifies key points in a read-aloud story. Partners talk about the story so far, then discuss what questions occur to them. They share these in a team of four, then with the class. (Source: 5) |
| Panel of Experts | Students read selected passages, taking notes of possible comprehension questions. In a group, students agree on four questions. One group in the room forms a panel, and others question them. Play continues until panel gets two right or one wrong; then questioning group becomes panel. (Source: 5) |
| Picture Dialogue | Before reading, teacher displays a picture from the book or sets a mental image using words. Working in pairs, students take character A or B and write a dialogue that characters say to each other. They read them aloud. (Source: 5) |

*Sources:* (1) Bassano & Christison (1995); (2) Cantlon (1991); (3) Kagan, S. (1998); (4) Kagan, S. (1999); (5) Whisler & Williams (1990).

## Teaching Collaboratively

Team teaching, peer tutoring, working with a mentor, and working with bilingual paraprofessionals are different means of supporting student learning. All individuals working with the teacher provide a challenge in planning activities and monitoring student achievement. Teachers who value the help provided by assistants and peers must be willing to invest time in both planning and supervising for such teamwork to be employed effectively.

**Teaching with Peers** Peer collaboration is "a style for direct interaction between at least two coequal parties voluntarily engaged in shared decision making as they work toward a common goal" (Friend & Cook, 1996, p. 6). This definition pinpoints several necessary principles: Professionals must treat one another as equals; collaboration is voluntary; a goal is shared (that of finding the most effective instruction for the students under consideration); and responsibility is shared for participation, decision making, and resources, as well as accountability for outcomes. These are predicated on a collegial working environment of mutual respect and trust.

If the ELD teacher is a specialist, he or she and the classroom teacher act as helpful colleagues, sharing expertise about L2 acquisition effects, lesson planning, or potential crosscultural misunderstandings. They collaborate to resolve conflicts, work with translators, and draw on community members for information, additional resources, and parental support. Some schools assign mentor teachers to work with beginning teachers, offering support and feedback.

**Working with Paraprofessionals** Paraprofessional educators may be instructional aides, volunteers from the parent community, tutors from other grades, high school students, or senior citizens and other community volunteers. Involving paraprofessionals requires careful organization to recruit skillful helpers and to use them effectively. Prudent planning is needed to maintain high-quality instruction and to ensure that assistants in the classroom feel valued.

A paraprofessional works alongside the teacher to assist in preparing materials, doing clerical work, monitoring small groups of students, giving tutorial help, or providing basic instruction under teacher supervision. The quasi-instructional duties, such as tutoring and assisting small groups of students, provide an extension of teacher expertise. It is the teacher's responsibility to see that the aide is effective in promoting student achievement and that students receive high-quality instruction.

Classroom teachers have responsibility for all instruction and classroom behavior. The tasks carried out by the aide should be planned by the teacher—paraprofessionals should not be expected to plan and prepare materials without teacher supervision. Instruction provided by the aide likewise is valid and important and should be considered as such by the students. Moreover, student achievement should not be evaluated solely by the paraprofessional; this is a responsibility of the classroom teacher.

Paraprofessionals should have a classroom space provided for their tutoring or group work. The number of students for which an aide is responsible may vary, from one-to-one tutoring to supervising the entire class while the teacher is involved in conferences or individual student contact. Should the aide be unavailable, the teacher must have backup plans so that the day's activities can be modified.

Often, teacher assistants who are brought into the classroom to offer primary-language instruction share the students' cultural background. These individuals can provide valuable linguistic and emotional support for students as they learn English. On the other hand, such aides may subtly modify the teacher's educational intentions.

## CLASSROOM GLIMPSE: The Aide Has Her Own Ideas

*Mr. Burns, a fifth-grade teacher in a bilingual classroom, had a Cambodian aide, Sarit Moul, who was the mother of four students in the school. While working in cooperative groups, the students were expected to exchange ideas and information, as well as compose and deliver group reports. Mr. Burns began to notice that the Laotian students did not speak voluntarily but waited to be called on. In observing Ms. Moul work with these students, he found that she discouraged students from speaking unless they received permission to do so. In conferring with her, Mr. Burns discovered, to his chagrin, that she believed that speaking out undermined the teacher's authority. A compromise had to be negotiated that would encourage students to develop speaking proficiency.*

It is not easy to be a classroom assistant and to work under someone else's supervision. Making the aide feel part of the instructional team is an important aspect of morale. For this to happen, aides need to be engaged in meaningful work from which they can derive a sense of accomplishment and not be relegated to tedious and menial tasks. They need to be given clear directions and understand not only what is expected of them but also what is expected of the students. It is important that they participate in instructional planning and be involved in seeing certain activities through to closure. Aides are also a source of valuable feedback to the teacher on students' needs and accomplishments. For their efforts, paraprofessionals deserve appreciation, whether it is a spoken "thank you" and a pat on the back or

> ### Box 5.2    Guidelines for Working with and Supervising a Paraprofessional Teaching Assistant
>
> - Develop a daily schedule of activities.
> - Inform your paraprofessional about your expectations of him or her.
> - Demonstrate and verbally explain specific teaching tactics to be used for particular lessons and students.
> - Be open to suggestions from the paraprofessional.
> - Take time to observe the aide's performance, providing praise or corrective feedback for specific actions.
> - Provide remedial attention for any documented weak areas and keep a record of effort spent working on these areas.
> - Do not criticize the paraprofessional in front of the students.
>
> *Source:* Adapted from Westling & Koorland (1988).

an occasional gift or token of esteem. Box 5.2 provides guidelines for teachers who are working with a paraprofessional.

## DIFFERENTIATED INSTRUCTION IN ELD AND SDAIE

To make academic content comprehensible for English learners, SDAIE teachers provide a context for instruction that is rich in opportunities for hands-on learning and student interaction. Teachers devote particular attention to communication strategies. By altering the means of presenting material to make it more accessible and understandable, the teacher maintains a challenging academic program without watering down or oversimplifying the curriculum. In general, SDAIE incorporates fundamental principles of good teaching—the ability to communicate, to organize instruction effectively, and to modify complex information to make it understandable to students. Box 5.3 outlines the basic elements of the SDAIE lesson plan. Each part is described in turn.

### Bridging: Accessing and Building Prior Knowledge

In the teaching context, prior knowledge refers to knowledge that students bring with them that can be tapped and built on during the lesson. This prior knowledge consists of students' existing concepts, understandings, and relevant experiences. Some prior knowledge may include misconceptions, so some "unlearning" may have to take place. Also, some prior knowledge may be based on experiences and conceptualizations of the students' home cultures that are beyond the teacher's experience.

Brain-based theory postulates that learners are engaged when the brain is able to create meaning by blending knowledge from previous experiences with that of present experiences. Effective teachers thus orchestrate meaning by making connections, instead of leaving this to

---

## Box 5.3 Fundamental Elements of the SDAIE Lesson Plan

I.  Setting objectives

   Content: Activity goals linked to grade-level standards

   English-Language development:
      Speaking
      Listening
      Reading
      Writing

   Learning strategy: Augmenting long-term cognitive, metacognitive, or social-affective abilities

II.  Preparing modified materials

III.  Differentiated instruction

   Bridging: Accessing and building prior knowledge

   Appealing to diverse learning modalities

   Access to cognitive academic language

   SDAIE techniques

   Scaffolding: Temporary support for learning

   Guided and independent practice that promotes students' active language use

   Formative assessment and reteaching

IV.  Summative assessment of objectives

V.  Reflective pedagogy

---

chance. These connections can be made by connecting to students' lives, connecting to previous academic knowledge, and, finally, by linking or anchoring previous knowledge to new knowledge.

## BEST PRACTICE: Tapping into Previous Knowledge

The following strategies elicit information from students and help the teacher understand the extent of students' understanding:

- Brainstorming
- K-W-L (What do I *know?* What do I *want* to learn? What have I *learned?*)
- Mind maps
- Pretests
- Questionnaires
- Interviews

If students have little prior knowledge about the topic at hand, teachers can help students build schema or schemata—that is, construct a framework of concepts that shows the relationships between old and new learning and how they are connected. Semantic mapping and webs are ways of presenting concepts to show their relationships. After a brainstorming session, the teacher and students could organize their ideas into a semantic map, with the main idea in the center of the chalkboard and associated or connected ideas as branches from the main idea. Alternatively, a teacher could be more directive in creating a map by writing the central topic and branching out from it with several major subtopics. Students could provide information that the teacher then writes into the appropriate category.

## CLASSROOM GLIMPSE: Building Schemata

*Mrs. Figueroa read* Cloudy with a Chance of Meatballs *(Barrett, 1978) to her second-grade students. Using a concept map with the words junk food in the center, they brainstormed on the questions "What is junk food?"; "What junk food can you think of?"; and "What is in junk food that our bodies don't need?" Students then grouped in pairs to write an adventure story with junk food as the villain.*

### Appealing to Diverse Learning Modalities

The nature of teaching requires some kind of standardization and grouping because class sizes are usually too large to treat each student in a unique manner. The reality in U.S. classrooms, however, is that students are increasingly heterogeneous in an array of ways beyond language: religion; mainstreamed students with disabilities; race/ethnicity (one-third of the U.S. school population is nonwhite; see Marlowe & Page [1999]); and mobility (43 million people in the United States move every year; see Hodgkinson [1998]). The challenge is clear: How can curriculum, instruction, and assessment be responsive to this learner diversity?

**Learning Styles Applied to the ELD/SDAIE Classroom**    The use of learning styles is based on a few basic hypotheses: (1) that every learner—and teacher—has a learning style preference; (2) that all styles are equally valid, although the educational context may value some more than others; (3) that learning about one's preferences, and acquiring styles other than one's preference, may assist students in learning; and (4) that learning strategies are linked to learning styles (Reid, 1995). Teachers can reduce the complexity of the learning style typologies by surveying various systems, analyzing themselves, and settling on one or two systems that both explain individual differences and offer a relatively easy way to accommodate instruction to learner differences.

**Adapting Instruction to Learning Styles**    In the typical classroom, some modification may be made that takes learning styles into account. If students as a group are both competitive and dependent, for example, assignments that enhance other characteristics (such as collaborative and independent learning) might be developed. Teachers can use a variety of learning activities to accommodate distinct learning styles. Students' awareness of their learning style preferences constitutes a metacognitive strategy (see the following Best Practice box). Once aware of their own preferences, students can use this knowledge to support their learning.

A comprehensive source for the incorporation of learning styles into second-language acquisition instruction is Reid's (1995) *Learning Styles in the ESL/EFL Classroom*, a compendium of articles on research and practice in this area. The book features various inventories of learning styles; suggestions for learners with visual, auditory, and haptic preferences; and a look at crosscultural implications.

## BEST PRACTICE: Incorporating Learning Styles into Instruction

- Diagnose your own learning style preferences so you understand yourself as a teacher.
- Settle on one or two systems that help you to be aware of students' learning style diversity.
- Find a way to add variety to instructional plans that makes a difference on this set of preferences.

**Using Realia, Manipulatives, and Hands-On Materials**   Student learning activities should develop students' interactive language but not disadvantage an English learner. Collaborative problem-solving teams include member roles that provide a variety of input and output modalities to balance the English skills and nonverbal talents of students. English learners can benefit from the use of media, realia, science equipment, diagrams, models, experiments, manipulatives, and other modalities that make language more comprehensible and that expand the means and modes by which they receive and express information.

### Access to Cognitive Academic Language

Cummins (1979, 1980) has posited two different yet related language skills: basic interpersonal communication skills (BICS) and cognitive academic language proficiency (CALP). BICS involves those language skills and functions that allow students in school to communicate in everyday social contexts that are similar to those of the home: to perform classroom chores, chat with peers, or consume instructional media as they do television shows at home.

BICS is *context embedded* because participants can provide feedback to one another, the situation itself provides cues that further understanding, and factors apart from the linguistic code can furnish meaning. In contrast, CALP, as the name implies, is the language needed to perform abstract and decontextualized school tasks successfully. Students must rely primarily on language to attain meaning.

Both BICS and CALP are clearly more than words. BICS involves the totality of communication that takes place between two or more people in their everyday activities. Some exchanges with people involve no words at all; for instance, a nod of the head while passing in the hallway at work may serve the same communicative purpose as a greeting. CALP, on the other hand, is more difficult to define. Beyond words, it also involves systematic thought processes. It enables the human brain systematically to categorize, compare, analyze, and accommodate new experiences.

*Pictures and hands-on activities help students to gain basic interpersonal communicative skills as well as academic language.*

CALP represents the cognitive toolbox—entire systems of thought as well as the language to encode and decode this thought. Without the acquisition of CALP—that is, not only specific terminology but also the clarity of thought provided by the classification and organization inherent in academic language and thought processes—students are incapable of acquiring the in-depth knowledge that characterizes the well-educated individual in a complex modern society.

## CLASSROOM GLIMPSE: Developing CALP

*Mrs. Álvarez found in her second-grade structured English immersion class that, although the students were fairly fluent in English when chatting with one another, they lacked the vocabulary to perform on academic tasks. When she gave instructions or briefly reviewed concepts, the students appeared lost. She became aware that students needed to move along the continuum from their everyday English usage to more abstract academic language.*

*The class was studying the ocean. Mrs. Álvarez set up learning centers with shells, dried seaweed, fish fossils, and other ocean objects. The instructions for these centers featured patterned, predictable language tied to the concrete objects, with words such as* group, shape, *and* size. *Gradually Mrs. Álvarez tape-recorded more complex and abstract instructions for use in the learning centers, such as* classify, arrange, *and* attribute. *This progression and integration of activities helped the children move along the continuum from BICS to CALP.*

## Teaching with SDAIE Strategies

English learners need scaffolding strategies as support to enable them to successfully complete tasks that require academic language proficiency. SDAIE means a curriculum that teaches content first and English second. Bell (2002) explained the rationale for such classes at the high school level:

> Students, parents, teacher, and counselors were concerned when we proposed [SDAIE] classes because they felt they might not match the curriculum, and they might affect acceptance into four-year colleges and universities. We explained that our English language development classes would focus on English language acquisition at the student's proficiency level. The SDAIE classes would focus on teaching the same curriculum as the regular courses, with added support materials.
>
> My students were so relieved to be in these classes. They have struggled with lowered self-esteem from lowered grades in previous years. In English 10, they learn the themes, symbols, and plot of important literature. In history they learn the key events, the important political concepts, and key people from the time period. They can understand and keep up with the materials, getting grades that reflect their knowledge in the SDAIE classroom. (p. 15)

SDAIE strategies include making increased use of cooperative learning, modifying instructional delivery and sometimes modifying the textbooks, checking for understanding, monitoring and formatively assessing students, and providing supportive resources. These are addressed in turn as follows.

## Modifying Language without Simplification

Teachers must ensure that students understand what is said in the classroom. Teachers in SDAIE classrooms devote particular attention to four communication strategies: *language contextualization, teacher's speech modification, use of repetition and paraphrase,* and *use of patterned language.*

**Language Contextualization**    Teaching should be focused on the context of the immediate task, augmenting vocabulary with gestures, pictures, realia, and so forth to convey instructions or key words and concepts. This provides a rich visual and/or kinesthetic (e.g., through drama and skits) environment. Verbal markers are used to organize the lesson, such as *note this* to denote importance, or *now, first, second,* and *last* to mark a sequence. To help with directions, teachers can determine the ten most frequently used verbal markers and teach these through mini-total physical response (TPR)-type lessons. The teacher might also learn how to say simple directions in the students' language(s).

**Teacher's Speech Modification**    To be understandable to those who do not speak or understand English well, the teacher must adjust speech from the customary native speech patterns. This takes place at many linguistic levels—phonological (precise articulation); syntactic (shorter sentences, with subject–verb–object word order); semantic (more concrete, basic vocabulary; fewer use of idioms); pragmatic (frequent and longer pauses; slower delivery; and exaggerated intonation, especially placing more stress on important new concepts); and discourse (self-repetition; main idea easily recognized and supporting information following immediately). Teachers in SDAIE classrooms also talk less in the classroom, encouraging students to talk.

As students become more proficient in English, teachers again adjust their speech, this time increasing speed and complexity. Ultimately, English learners will need to function in an all-English-medium classroom; therefore, over time, SDAIE teachers need to reduce the speech modification scaffolds they use to accommodate their students' evolving proficiency.

**The Use of Repetition and Paraphrase**     Verbal repetition can be employed to increase comprehensibility (for example, using the same type of directions throughout various lessons), as can organizational repetition (lessons that occur at specific times, lessons with clearly marked verbal and nonverbal boundaries, such as "Now it's time to . . . ," or the use of specific locations for specific content). Concepts are presented numerous times through various means. Elaboration, in which the teacher supplies redundant information through repetition and paraphrase, may prove effective (Nunan, 1991).

**Use of Patterned Language**     It is helpful for teachers to signal the beginning and ending of lessons clearly, using stock phrases (e.g., "Math time is over. Put away your books"). Procedures and classroom routines should be predictable so that English learners do not feel they have to be ever vigilant for a change in rules. This reduces stress and gives students a feeling of security. Table 5.8 summarizes the modifications teachers can make in speech and instructional delivery to make their teaching more comprehensible.

Although SDAIE teaching involves presentation of subject matter in English, opportunities are available throughout the lesson for students to clarify their understanding using their primary language, supplemented whenever possible by primary-language resources (print, electronic, personnel) that can help students with key concepts.

The scope of this book does not permit an exhaustive discussion of SDAIE. For an excellent in-depth treatment, refer to *Making Content Comprehensible for English Language Learners: The SIOP Model* (Echevarria, Vogt, & Short, 2000).

**Clarification of Concepts in the Primary Language**     In SDAIE classrooms, students are afforded opportunities to learn and clarify concepts in their own language. When possible, the teacher provides primary-language resources (print, electronic, personnel) that can help students with key concepts. Although SDAIE teaching involves presenting subject matter in English, teachers continue to provide opportunities throughout the lesson for students to clarify their understanding using their primary language.

Use of the primary language is still a controversial issue, and many teachers shy away from it on the mistaken belief that primary-language use detracts from developing English proficiency. However, research continues to show that when students are able to use their first language, they make more academic gains in both content and language than if they are prohibited from using it (Collier, 1995).

## Scaffolding: Temporary Support for Learning

A teacher's role is to provide support for learning. This support continually shifts as students learn. The teacher must become skilled at supporting and then withdrawing support while coaxing the student to perform at a continuously higher level, and then in turn supporting that higher level.

**TABLE 5.8**  Teachers' Language Modification in SDAIE

| Type of Modification | Definition | Example |
|---|---|---|
| Precise articulation | Increased attention to enunciation so that consonants and vowels in words are understandable | "Trade your *homework* with the person *beside* you." |
| Use of gestures | Showing with hands what is to be done | Make a swapping gesture with papers to act out "trading homework." |
| Intonation | Increased stress on important concepts | "The number of *correct* answers goes at the top of the page." |
| Simplified syntax | Shorter sentences, with subject-verb-object word order | "Mark the papers. Give them back." |
| Semantic clarity | More concrete, basic vocabulary; fewer use of idioms | "Turn in your work. I mean, give me your homework." |
| Pragmatic distinctness | Frequent and longer pauses; slightly slower delivery | "Check the chemicals. . . . Check the list. . . . Be sure your team has all the chemicals for your experiment." |
| Use of discourse markers | Careful use of transition words, emphasis, and sequence markers | "Note this" to denote importance, or "now," "first," "second," and "last" to mark a sequence. |
| Use of organizational markers | Clearly indicating change of activity | "It's time for recess. . . . Put away your books." |
| More structured discourse | Main idea easily recognized and supporting information following immediately | "Today we are learning about mole weight. . . . I will show you how to calculate mole weight to make the correct solution." |
| Use of clarification checks | Stopping instruction to ask students if they understand; monitoring students' comprehension | "Hold your thumb up in front of your chest if you understand how to use the formula for acceleration." |
| Soliciting written input | Having students write questions on index cards | "I have a card here asking for another explanation of longitude degrees and minutes. OK . . . ." |
| Repetition | Revisiting key vocabulary terms | "*Precipitation* means overall rain or snowfall; we are going to study the precipitation cycle." |
| Use of mini-TPR lessons to preteach key terms | Acting out terms to increase understandability | " 'On the other hand' ": Carlos, stand over here, and Elena, stand here—you are on one hand, he is 'on the other hand.' " |
| Use of primary language | Saying simple directions in the students' language(s) | "*tsai jher*, over here, *tsai nar*, over there" (Mandarin). |

**Clarification Checks**    Teachers monitor listening and reading comprehension at intervals to gain a sense of the students' ability to understand. The teacher might pause to ask a question requiring a simple response, such as "Show me how you are going to begin your work," or ask individual students to restate the instruction using their own words.

Questions at the literal level are designed simply to check whether students understand directions, details, or procedures. During formal presentations, teachers often use strategies such as asking students to "vote" on their understanding of what has been said by a show of hands. This helps to maintain interest and check for understanding. Depending on student response, teachers may need to rephrase questions and information if the students do not initially understand.

**Using Questions to Promote Reflection**    Effective questioning techniques can probe for students' abilities to infer and evaluate. Teachers need to be patient when asking questions—to wait for students to understand the question before calling on individuals. Even after nominating a student to answer, wait-time is necessary to allow an English learner to compose and deliver a response. He or she may know the answer but need a little more processing time to say it in English.

Effective mediational questions—those that promote reflection—focus on the process of thought rather than on low-level details. The following questions or requests provoke thought:

- Tell me how you did that.
- What do you think the problem is?
- What's another way we might approach this?
- What do you think would happen if . . . ?
- What might you do next? (Adapted from Costa & Garmston, 2002)

If a student has the correct answer and is basically understandable, it is not necessary to insist on correct grammar. Accepting the answer and letting the student know it is correct, or delivering corrective feedback on the content, is helpful.

Skilled questioning using a linguistic hierarchy of question types helps teachers ascertain students' understanding. To reiterate: For students in the "silent period," questions elicit a nonverbal response—a head movement, pointing, or manipulation of materials. Once students begin to speak, they can choose the correct word or phrase to demonstrate understanding of either/or questions: "Does the water expand or contract to form ice?" "Did Russians come to California from the west or the north?" Once students are more comfortable producing language, *wh-* questions are used: "What is happening to the water?" "Which countries sent explorers to California?" "What was the purpose of their exploration?" Skillful teachers can ask questions requiring critical or creative thinking even at the beginning level; students at advanced English levels are not the only ones capable of inferential thinking.

## Guided and Independent Practice That Promotes Students' Active Language Use

Modeling and demonstrating skills, use of cooperative learning and collaborative teaching, use of interesting and culturally appealing materials (including materials in students' primary language[s]), and skillful employment of technological resources are means of enhancing instruction as guided or independent practice. A fundamental principle is the idea that English learners must produce language, and that their developmental interlanguage must be supported with encouragement and appropriate feedback.

## Formative Assessment and Reteaching

As students are learning, the teacher can help them maintain momentum and solve ongoing problems through a process of formative assessment. This involves progress checks, helping students to evaluate their efforts in the light of their goals and to stay on track. The teacher may require formal weekly progress reports, ask for partial products at predetermined times, or set deadlines for circulation of rough drafts. Formative evaluation can permit much valuable ongoing readjustment of the learning process. The responsibility for this monitoring is shared between teacher and learners, but much of the responsibility for adjustment falls on the learner.

Teachers exercise patience in helping students monitor and adjust their learning to meet the desired performance standards; vanquish students' habits of sloth or procrastination, if these are a problem; conquer the students' lack of faith in themselves by providing encouragement, structure, and guidelines; overcome students' impatient desire to improve instantly, as they perhaps try and fail several times before succeeding; help students accept the disappointment of failure if there is some aspect of a complex problem that eludes solution; or make themselves available during students' basic struggle to use English as a means of expression.

Not all learning is successful. Sometimes problems that are worth addressing are beyond comprehension, and sometimes problems that are comprehensible are simply not interesting. Most teachers do everything possible to facilitate successful learning. But, in the last analysis, it is not the teacher's job to rescue students from disappointment or failure; these are a part of authentic learning. Sometimes metalearning—the wisdom about learning—comes after the learning has been attempted, in a process of reflection and hindsight.

## Summative Assessment, Culminating Performance, and Metalearning

A final performance on a certain day—such as a play with other students as audience or an exhibit for parents—helps students understand the real world of promise and fulfillment. Despite the satisfaction these culminating events offer, the substance of assessment remains with the content standards that have been achieved. Peer evaluation, self-evaluation, and teacher evaluation together garner the final evidence: Was the learning successful? What was learned about the content? What was learned about the process? And most excitingly, what is still not known? What remains to be discovered?

## Reflective Pedagogy

Pausing to reflect is the final step in lesson delivery; it occurs at the end of instruction for English learners and in turn reactivates the cycle of teaching and planning. Some questions teachers may use to frame their critical contemplation of their teaching are listed in Box 5.4.

> ## Box 5.4    Critical Reflection in Lesson Planning
>
> - What were the strengths in the lesson?
> - Were content, learning, and language objectives clearly stated to students?
> - Were students, including English learners, engaged in the lesson?
> - How many opportunities were provided for English-language development?
> - What evidence do I have to demonstrate that lesson adaptations for English learners were adequate?
> - Which evidence demonstrated learning by English learners?
> - Which opportunities allowed students to self-assess and be responsible for their own learning?
> - What areas require changes for lesson improvement?
>
> *Source:* Balderrama & Díaz-Rico (2006).

## EFFECTIVE RESOURCE USE IN ELD AND SDAIE

A key to success in the SDAIE classroom is the provision of resource-rich teaching to expand the modalities in which English learners can receive information. But which materials? And how to select them?

### Selecting and Using Appropriate Materials

Choosing the right genre is one way to help English learners develop their conceptual and linguistic schemata. The literature curriculum, for example, can be a planned sequence that begins with familiar structures of folktales and myths and that then uses these as a bridge to more complex works of literature. Myths and folktales from many cultures are now commonly available in high-quality editions with vibrant illustrations. Students can move from these folktales and myths to selected short stories by authors of many cultural backgrounds, then to portions of a longer work, and then to entire works.

## CLASSROOM GLIMPSE: A Variety of Materials

*William Pruitt (2000, pp. 31–49) describes how his students move from studying different versions of a folktale to studying other kinds of tales.*

*One of the goals of the story unit is for students to examine how the same story may differ as it appears in different perspectives, media, and cultures, and to compare and contrast these forms. Over the course of the two-week unit, we read and compare and contrast an original (translated) version of "Beauty and the Beast," a poem entitled "Beauty and the Beast," and three video versions of the story. Once students have gained experience with this folktale and understand the pattern of activities, we move to other texts that have film adaptations, for example,* Tuck Everlasting *(Babbitt, 1976).*

Materials used in the classroom are most accessible when they match the age, language ability, and prior content knowledge of the students. Materials in the primary language can supplement content delivery in English. In fact, with a rich theme, materials from around the world can be featured in instruction.

## BEST PRACTICE: Materials for a Rich Theme

A good example of the use of a rich theme is "Tool Use" (*Into English*, Level C, pp. 58–71). Students identify, graph, and discuss their use of tools; they can investigate what tools are used at home or at their parents' workplaces; they can explore tools used for everyday life such as in cooking; they can brainstorm new uses for tools and learn the names of common academic tools. This unit can incorporate crosscultural study (Chinese abacus) and total physical response (a game of charades acting out tool use). Classroom visitors can discuss the tools they use in their work. (Tinajero & Schifini, 1997)

### Modifying Materials for Linguistic Accessibility

The teacher selects, modifies, and organizes text material to accommodate the needs of English learners. In modifying text, the goal is to improve comprehensibility through such means as providing study guides or defining new content vocabulary by showing vocabulary pictorially. Focus questions or concept maps serve as advance organizers. Selected passages can be tape-recorded for students to listen to as they read along in the text. These adaptations increase readability. As students' language proficiency increases, so should the complexity of their reading material. The goal is to move students toward the ability to work with unmodified texts (Richard-Amato & Snow, 1992).

### Culturally Appealing Materials

Multicultural materials are a rich source of language and content area learning, including books and other print media, visual aids, props, realia, manipulatives, materials that access other modalities, and human resources. Students may be able to bring in pictures, poems, dances, proverbs, or games; new ways to do math problems; or maps that show a different perspective than that given in the textbook. Shen's Books (www.shens.com) carries a wide selection of multicultural materials, including those on such themes as multicultural Cinderella stories and other fables; music around the world; foods of the world; immigrant life, adoption, and interracial families; Arabic and Islamic culture; Southeast Asia; and alphabets around the world.

The Internet is also a rich source of multicultural content. Students can search for their own primary-language content. However, it's possible that the teacher who does not speak or read the primary language of the student may not be able to screen for inappropriate content. Family or community members may be able to assist in finding educationally relevant content.

Sources for multicultural viewpoints and materials for various curriculum areas are presented in Table 5.9.

**TABLE 5.9** Multicultural Materials: Sources for the Content Areas

| Content Area | Suggested Material |
| --- | --- |
| Mathematics | *Multicultural Mathematics: A More Inclusive Mathematics.* Accessed July 27, 2006, from www.ericdigests.org/1996-1/more.htm. |
| Social Studies | Multicultural history and social studies sites. Accessed July 27, 2006, from www.edchange.org/ multicultural/sites/history.html. |
| Literature | *Multicultural Children's Literature.* Accessed July 27, 2006, from www.lib.msu.edu/corby/ education/multicultural.htm. |
| Science | *Multicultural Science and Math Connections: Middle School Projects and Activities.* Accessed July 27, 2006, from http://fermat.nap.edu/html/rtmss/5.72.html. |

## Technological Resources to Enhance Instruction

Computer-assisted instruction (CAI) has been available for classroom use since the earliest days of word processing (late 1970s), with large-scale tutoring systems available in the 1980s that enabled the individual user to attempt repeated answers and receive error feedback without public embarrassment. Computer-mediated communication (CMC) and more sophisticated computer-simulated learning environments have come into use in the twenty-first century (see Herring, 1996; Bitter, Pierson, & Burvikovs, 2004).

**Tools for Instruction and Communication**   The digital revolution is changing the way people learn (Murray, 2000). Websites offer lesson plans, quizzes, chatrooms, and bulletin boards that allow the learner to sample English idioms, prepare for standardized tests, or connect with English learners in other parts of the world. Many teachers have access to Internet hookups in the classroom. Students can interact with others meaningfully, writing informal e-mails with "keypals" in different areas of the world or using writing-based chatrooms online in real time (Warschauer, 1995).

The instant communication available through the Internet connects students with other parts of the world, with speakers of English, and with rich sources of information. The World Wide Web delivers authentic materials, including texts, images, sound recordings, videoclips, virtual reality worlds, and dynamic, interactive presentations. Students can listen to live radio stations from around the world or hear prerecorded broadcasts of music, news, sports, and weather (LeLoup & Ponterio, 2000). Search engines (e.g., Google, Yahoo!, Altavista) help the student find authentic materials on classroom, group, or individual research topics.

Today's teachers are educated to maximize the instructional and communicative use of the Internet, CD-ROM-based software, and other CMC tools, including audio and video production using computers, although in the process, older, non-computer-based tools of multimedia production are falling by the wayside (see Herrell, 2000, pp. 134–138, for tips on the use of a variety of multimedia formats, including camcorder and overhead projector). Some

*Students who are literate in their native language can use the computer to access primary-language content information as they learn English.*

teachers are also skilled in using computer-managed instruction (CMI) techniques such as grade book programs and database management.

**Computers Support Language Learning** Word processing supports the formal writing process by allowing students to electronically organize, draft, revise, edit, and even publish their work. Students can develop oral skills by using presentation or authoring software to create professional-looking oral presentations, and they can use both aural and oral skills in Web-enabled telephone conversations.

Software programs are available for ELD that include traditional drill-and-practice programs focusing on vocabulary or grammar; tutorials; games; simulations that present students with real-life situations in the language and culture they are learning; productivity tools, such as word processing, databases, spreadsheets, graphics, and desktop publishing (DTP); and presentation or authoring programs. Material from encyclopedias and even *National Geographic* is available on CD-ROM.

The computer is a powerful learning tool that requires the teacher to organize, plan, teach, and monitor. Egbert and Hanson-Smith (1999) found that computer technology can provide students with the means to control their own learning, to construct meaning, and to evaluate and monitor their own performance.

## CLASSROOM GLIMPSE: Computer-Assisted English Learning

*Abdul uses the Internet in a high school content-based ELD class to research current events for world history. To practice pronunciation for his ELD class, he uses software that enables him to click on a word or sentence to hear it repeatedly, look up a meaning, see a related picture or videoclip, and/or read a related text; or listen to a sentence, compare his voice to a computer model of the correct response, and have the computer judge the accuracy of his attempts.*

Computer-assisted language learning teachers help students carefully plan and organize learning experiences, rehearse useful language, and understand the physical operation of the Internet. For a well-organized, highly readable guide for using the computer in the language classroom, see *Internet for English Teaching* (Warschauer, Shetzer, & Meloni, 2000).

## TEACHER COMMITMENT

Although technological tools and techniques for ELD and content area teaching are changing rapidly, what remains constant is the need for English learners to receive high-quality instruction that permits them access to the cognitive academic language they need for school success. Teachers who are dedicated to student achievement are key.

In SDAIE classrooms, it is not only the students who are learning. Successful teachers themselves are open, not only *willing* to learn but also *expecting* to learn.

English-language development and content learning go hand in hand in classrooms that support high-quality instruction for English learners. These classrooms feature multiple modalities for instruction and a rich mix of stimulating materials and linguistic interaction. Most of all, classrooms that foster high achievement are those in which the teacher is committed to enriching language and promoting a high level of content learning using SDAIE to make instruction comprehensible and meaningful.

# CHAPTER SIX

# English-Language Development

## ■■■ THE FOCUS ON COMMUNICATIVE INTERACTION

English-language development is a specialty that is essential for English learners, who must improve their English while learning grade-level academic content. ELD includes speaking/oral language development and listening, reading (both content area reading and literature), and writing. To develop learners' English, teachers need an array of strategies.

Current research emphasizes that meaningful and purposeful communicative interactions (both oral and written) promote learners' English-language development and content area learning. Second, the language that is *learned* takes precedence over the language that is *taught*. Assessment plays a key role in documenting what is actually learned. Finally, the learner's interlanguage is the basis for instruction. Empirical teaching takes note of learners' needs and instruction is planned accordingly. Each of these ideas is explored in turn.

### What Is Communicative Competence?

In 1972, Hymes introduced the term *communicative competence* to emphasize the idea that the *use* of language in a social setting is the key to language performance. Current theories of language have moved away from a grammatical view of language to the more inclusive concept of language for communicative purposes. The competent speaker is recognized as one who knows when, where, and how to use language appropriately.

Canale (1983) identified four components of communicative competence. *Grammatical competence* focuses on the skills and knowledge necessary to speak and write accurately. *Sociolinguistic competence* involves knowing how to produce and understand language in different social contexts, taking into consideration such factors as the status of participants and the purposes and conventions of interaction. *Discourse competence* is the ability to combine and connect utterances (spoken) and sentences (written) into a meaningful whole. *Strategic competence* helps the language user repair breakdowns in communication and enhance the effectiveness of communication.

## CLASSROOM GLIMPSE: Discourse Competence in Kindergarten Students

*An example of discourse competence can be seen in the following conversation between two kindergarten boys, one a native English speaker and the other an English learner. Rolando responds*

**191**

*appropriately (though not kindly) to Andrew's request and adds information about his decision at the proper moment. This conversation shows that Rolando has discourse competence.*

> **Andrew:** *Can I play?*
> **Rolando:** *No.*
> **Andrew:** *There're only three people here.*
> **Rolando:** *Kevin went to the bathroom.*
> **Andrew:** *Can I take his place 'til he comes back?*
> **Rolando:** *You're not playing.*

## The Cognitive Perspective

Current language teaching is being shaped by several important ideas. First, the shift toward a cognitive paradigm means that *learning* has taken precedence over *teaching*. What the student learns is the important outcome of the teaching–learning process, not what the teacher teaches. Second, learning is maximized when it matches what takes place naturally in the brain. Third, thematic integration across content areas unifies the language processes of reading, writing, speaking, listening, thinking, and acting. Therefore, current perspectives on second-language learning align with brain-compatible instruction.

The cognitive perspective emphasizes assessment as the way to ensure that learning has taken place. Additionally, one sees the strong push to develop students' CALP as a cognitive focus. Last, the emphasis on acquisition of cognitive tools—learning strategies—as a key part of each lesson is a cognitive perspective. The idea of cognitive tools plays an increasing role in current understanding of literacy (Egan & Gajdamaschko, 2003).

## An Interlanguage Perspective

Learners of a second language have only one starting point: their primary language. Therefore, every understanding they have of the second language is filtered through their existing knowledge. As they become more familiar with the second language (in this case, English), they move toward learning that builds on their new knowledge base. Until they have that new knowledge, however, the language they produce is a hybrid form, an interlanguage (Selinker, 1972, 1991). The term *interlanguage* means that when a person learns a second language, the language that he or she produces will have the quality of intermediacy; it is a transitional phenomenon that may or may not develop into proficiency in the target language.

Interlanguage theory asserts that the learner's language should be viewed as creative and rule governed. An ELD curriculum that elicits the learner's creativity allows the learner to show the current state of his or her interlanguage. The view that learners have intermediary language modes that are not flawed misrepresentations of English, but rather are natural, creative expressions of the learner's innate language "genius," offers a refreshing opportunity for teachers to view second-language learning in a positive light.

Second, the errors that the learner makes (systematic errors that show a pattern of thinking, not random mistakes) are a necessary part of the learning process and provide a source of information for the teacher. Thus, the learner's interlanguage (and no two learners' interlanguages are identical) is the foundation for ELD teaching that respects and delights in individual creativity, channeled through the ELD standards.

Contemporary English-language development teaching is woven of three parts—the emphasis on communication, the need to develop the learner's cognitive academic language, and support for the learner's developmental interlanguage. These theoretical trends are amalgamated into a solid foundation for ELD.

## THE ROLE OF GRAMMAR

Following Chomsky's lead, linguists envision grammar as a set of rules that human beings unconsciously know and use. They believe that human beings, once exposed to the language(s) of their environment, use their innate ability to understand and produce sentences they have never before heard, because the mind has the capacity to internalize and construct language rules. The rules help native speakers determine whether a group of words forms a sentence in their language.

If use of the rules of sentence formation is largely unconscious, what role does explicit teaching of grammar play? There are two ways to think about this. First, linguists are not clear on how first- and second-language acquisition of grammar differ. Krashen's acquisition hypothesis (see Chapter 2) claimed that second-language syntax was acquired in the same order as that of the first language, but it is not clear if the same internal brain mechanisms are involved (for a discussion of this issue, see Gass and Selinker [2001]). Second, if second-language acquisition follows different brain pathways (and in most people's subjective experience, this is true—learning a second language is more difficult than learning the first, which is why more people are not bilingual), then there is a role for explicit teaching of grammar.

Krashen (2003) has a few current words to say on this topic:

> I do not think that grammar teaching should be at the core of curriculum, but there are good reasons for including it. First, grammar teaching can be an excellent introduction to the study of linguistics, which has obvious value, e.g., the study of universals, language change, and dialects. Second, even with massive reading, complete acquisition of the conventions of writing may not take place. . . . [T]hese gaps are typically small and rarely interfere with the clarity of the message. Conscious knowledge of grammar rules can help fill at least some of these gaps, and can be used in the editing stage of the composing process, after ideas are on the page. (n.p.)

Another author has a slightly different view:

> In determining how much grammar to teach explicitly, how much accuracy to demand, and at what stages and in what contexts: one size does not fit all. Teachers must juggle three important elements: (1) the goal of instruction/time for instruction, (2) the structure of the target language, and (3) the style of the learner. (Robin, 2006, n.p.)

Robin goes on to explain that grammar has a larger role to play in second-language acquisition if the learner intends to achieve advanced proficiency, if the language has highly difficult morphology, and if a highly structured environment fits the learner's cognitive style.

One might argue that the older and more disciplined the learner, the larger a role explicit instruction in grammar could play.

### Benefits of Explicit Instruction of Language

Second-language acquisition, as a domain of learning, is difficult. To attain linguistic and cultural proficiency requires precise control of meaning, careful attunement to intonation, and mastery of behavioral subtlety. Explicit instruction usually means direct instruction (with goals, activities, and assessment strictly determined by the teacher or other authorities) combined with precise error correction or other overt feedback.

The earliest type of language teaching was grammar-translation pedagogy, in which the instructor explained the meaning of vocabulary words and the structure of sentences, and students' access to the target language was limited to a carefully controlled curriculum. The strengths of this methodology are that those skilled in traditional school behaviors—memorization and rote learning—receive good grades. Moreover, the explaining and translating involve the first language—little of this instruction takes place directly in the target language. Therefore, students are more likely to find the explanations and translations comprehensible.

There are drawbacks to this direct instruction. There is often little independent language acquisition, limited access to the target language and culture, and little social interaction with target-language speakers. Speaking and listening—the foundations of the brain's acquisition of language—are limited, and oral proficiency is seldom achieved. Grammar-focused lessons that are not communicatively based can be boring, cumbersome, and difficult for students.

Explicit teaching may be required when some basic feature of English is so illogical or dissimilar to the L1 that it is not easily understood, even in context. Aspects of English grammar that may offer exceptional challenge to English learners include use of word order, determiners (*this, that, these, those, a, an, the*), prepositions (*in, on, at, by, for, from, of*), auxiliaries (*do, be, have*), conjunctions (*but, so, however, therefore, though, although*), interrogatives, intensifiers (*some, any, few, more, too*), and distinctions among modal verbs (*can, could, would, should, may, might, must*). Phrasal verbs (*look over, pick up*) also present considerable difficulty to Spanish speakers learning communicative English.

## CLASSROOM GLIMPSE: Explicit Feedback during Reading Tutoring

*The following exchange during the tutoring of reading shows explicit teaching of the sound–symbol connection in English:*

> **Pedro:** *Miscle?*
> **Tutor:** */mus/ . . .*
> **Pedro:** */muskl/*
> **Tutor:** Muscle *has what is called silent /c/; you see it but you don't pronounce it.* Muscle *without /c/ sounds like /musl/.*
> **Pedro:** *Muscle.*

### The Role of Feedback in Explicit Teaching

Feedback is essential to the knowledge and performance of any new skill. Feedback usually means explicit error correction, but it can also mean indirect hints. A teacher's job is to understand the conditions under which feedback works best. For example, a teacher needs to know that students benefit from the time teachers spend providing extensive feedback on writing. But what is known about feedback in language learning? Under what conditions are the different forms of feedback effective for particular learners? The answers to such questions would enable teachers to predict what feedback is likely to work best.

Feedback is integrated differently into different types of practice. For example, communicative activities tend to be low in feedback as long as participants are understandable; grammar instruction tends to invite right/wrong correction; and oral presentations invite feedback on clarity, organization, and audibility. Modality of language use (e.g., written, oral, computer-mediated) influences the type of feedback—people are usually more anxious about feedback on their oral performances than on their written products, and most people are not at all upset about feedback received during computerized tutoring.

Although research on feedback is still underway, some general principles are well known, such as the idea that highly anxious learners need positive as well as corrective feedback. To date, there has been scarce research on the characteristics of learners that enable them to learn from feedback. This is a promising avenue for further investigation. Whatever research is carried out on this subject should be combined with formative assessment, as feedback can be considered a kind of formative assessment.

## BEST PRACTICE: Error Correction Guidelines

Systematic errors, such as the Chinese learners' omission of past-tense declension in the verb ("Yesterday he drinks"), are a window into the learner's thinking. A thoughtful awareness of error is the best teacher. The more language is produced, the more errors are made, the more learning can occur. The goal is to have the learner produce as much language as possible and create awareness about errors.

At the beginning ELD level, learners need to listen to and look at language but not be required to produce it in public, where errors are an embarrassment. Individual or paired practice is useful, including high-interest activities with lots of visuals, controlled vocabulary, and simple sentence structures.

At the early intermediate and intermediate levels, high-interest activities in which errors do not impede the communication of meaning are useful. Tasks are structured to accomplish focused growth in measurable ways, balanced by language activities in which the learner is interested and successful.

At the early advanced and advanced levels, error correction focuses on learner self-correction, balanced by targeted teacher feedback. Emphasis is equal across grammatical, strategic, sociolinguistic, and discourse functions.

Because assessment is such an important part of the contemporary emphasis on learning, error correction and formative assessment as feedback are featured in the discussions that follow on the teaching of each specific modality (listening/speaking, reading, and writing).

### The Supplemental Role of Implicit Learning

In addition to explicit instruction, implicit learning has a role in second-language acquisition. By providing grammar in context in an implicit manner, we can expose students to substantial doses of grammar study without alienating them from the learning of English. One can teach short grammar-based sessions, immediately followed by additional function-based lessons in which the new grammar or structure is applied in context, and trust that the brain will absorb the grammar point while communication takes place.

Current studies have combined explicit and implicit instruction under the term *focus-on-form* approach. Gascoigne (2002) discussed the arguments for and against explicit teaching of grammar and suggested the use of such methods as boldfacing target grammar forms in a text, raising the learner's consciousness about forms through various noticing activities, and careful choice of activities that involve correcting language forms.

### Teaching Grammar

Grammar is taught explicitly by using a grammar book that presents systematic reference and explains grammar points with a suitable degree of accuracy. An example is Byrd and Benson's *Problem-Solution: A Reference for ESL Writers* (1994), an excellent resource that covers grammar points with clear explanation and examples.

A focus on correct usage and sentence structure—including spelling, capitalization, and punctuation—is important for English learners, although this should not be taken to the extreme. Often, mainstream teachers base their estimation of students' academic potential on a few key features of written production—namely, the look of writing, such as legible handwriting, correct spelling of basic words, and well-formed sentences. Therefore, as students write—for purposes of critical thinking, reaction to literature, or project-based learning—some products of their writing should be taken to the final, corrected draft stage.

**Working with Syntax**    Awareness of sentence structure can be enhanced by having students work creatively with sentences. They can *expand* sentences by adding details to a simple sentence ("I went home for lunch" becomes "I skipped home with my mama's tortilla at the tip of my tongue"). They can *link* sentences by taking an element from a simple sentence and using it to create an image-rich subsequent sentence ("My cat brought me a lizard in her mouth" [The idea = something about the lizard] "I couldn't tell if that lizard was dead or just pretending"). They can *rearrange* sentences by moving internal phrases to the opening slot ("Lisa drives her tricycle out front to meet Papa when he comes home from work"/"When Papa comes home from work . . .").

**Writing for Grammar**    Writing tasks can incorporate correct usage. One example is a tongue-in-cheek book that students produced about points of interest in the surrounding neighborhoods, *The Homegirls' Guide to South Seventh Street*. Key stores, names of streets, and even car brands were correctly capitalized. For a class meal, another group collected recipes from home that featured the imperative form of the verb ("Slice cucumbers thinly") (Shoemaker & Polycarpou, 1993). Thus, correct usage and grammar can be an integral part of learning activities. Correct usage such as punctuation, capitalization, and paragraph structure is emphasized in the context of composition, allowing grammar to be taught in an integrated way, which includes a special focus on difficult features when necessary.

# ▒▒ CONTENT-BASED ENGLISH-LANGUAGE DEVELOPMENT

Content literacy is "the ability to use reading and writing for the acquisition of new content in a given discipline" (McKenna & Robinson, 1997, p. 8). In content-based instruction (CBI) ELD classrooms, ELD educators, in collaboration with content teachers, organize learning objectives around academic subjects to prepare students to master grade-level curricula. This is a supplement to the students' English class.

Content literacy is more than "having knowledge" in a particular discipline; it represents skills needed to acquire knowledge of content and make it easier for the student to read and write in the discipline. This literacy is content specific; an individual who can read and write about science may not be able to do so in mathematics. However, being able to think clearly, understand key concepts, and express oneself are cognitive skills that do generalize across disciplines, so efforts to promote content literacy in one subject can positively affect learning in other subjects.

CBI-ELD classes develop not only language proficiency but also content knowledge, cognitive strategies, and study skills. Teachers familiarize students with the difference in the style and structure of texts and the type of vocabulary featured in the particular discipline. Reference might be made to background knowledge that is restricted to that discipline (Addison, 1988), along with abstract, specialized, and difficult vocabulary.

## Collaboration and Reciprocity

Content-based instruction can be of great benefit if content instructors and language teachers work together to provide comprehensible input to the learner, as well as to design tasks that are both understandable and important. Systematic, planned instruction must present vocabulary, concepts, and structures that are required for mastery of the content. Whether an *adjunct* model—having the language teacher assist in content teaching by providing additional contact and support (Snow & Brinton, 1988)—or a *collaborative* model—with the ELD teacher co-teaching the content course—is chosen, providing English instruction coupled with content-specific instruction increases the likelihood of academic success.

Is the collaboration between ELD and content instructors reciprocal? If ELD teachers teach content, then the content teachers should also include language development objectives along with content objectives. If this is not the case, then content-based ELD unfortunately positions ELD teachers as adjunct content instructors, which leads instructors of other disciplines to believe that ELD is not a content domain in its own right. This tends to undermine the professional status of ELD. The collaboration with content instructors should be two way, with both types of classes having language and content objectives.

## CBI-ELD: Lesson Planning

In CBI-ELD, the content to be taught, general instructional goals, and time available for instruction are negotiated with the content teacher. One important factor in the success of CBI-ELD is the ELD teacher's past experiences in teaching similar content or ability to transfer knowledge gained from teaching similar concepts in other disciplines.

Five types of reading lesson plans are commonly used in content-based ESL (McKenna & Robinson, 1997). Table 6.1 describes the five lesson types in detail.

**TABLE 6.1**    Types of Reading Lesson Plans in ELD Content-Based Instruction

| Lesson Plan Type | Directions to Teacher |
| --- | --- |
| **Directed Reading Activity**<br>Advantages:<br>• Flexible, purposeful<br>Disadvantage:<br>• May be too teacher-directed | Establish readiness for reading, relating to students' prior knowledge and preteaching vocabulary or specialized skills (maps or charts, etc.).<br>Set purposes for reading (analyze goals and communicate these goals to students).<br>Arrange for students to read silently.<br>Discuss the reading.<br>Extend students' understanding by using supplementary materials or by assigning a writing task. |
| **Directed Reading–Thinking Activity**<br>Advantages:<br>• Emphasizes the reading/thinking connection<br>• Encourages students to set own purposes<br>Disadvantage:<br>• Not well suited to new or unfamiliar material | Help students set purposes for reading; check students' prior knowledge, preteaching concepts if necessary; encourage students to predict content using cues.<br>Facilitate reasoning as students read.<br>Help students test their predictions, locating and discussing bases for conclusions. |
| **K-W-L** (what students *k*now, *w*ant to learn, and *l*earn)<br>Advantages:<br>• Activates prior knowledge<br>• Establishes group purposes<br>Disadvantage:<br>• Not well suited to unfamiliar material | Brainstorm with students to elicit prior knowledge of the topic, then discuss, grouping ideas into subtopics.<br>Select subtopics of interest based on what they need to know; have students write out their interests.<br>Assess what was learned by the reading. |
| **Explicit Teaching**<br>Advantage:<br>• Permits clear-cut, sequential planning<br>Disadvantages:<br>• May encourage overreliance on teacher for direction<br>• Literacy activities may be avoided when planning | Create readiness by a positive introduction and by communicating objectives clearly.<br>Teach concepts directly, checking for understanding, reteaching if needed.<br>Provide opportunities for guided and independent practice. |
| **Listen-Read-Discuss**<br>Advantages:<br>• Effective with low-ability readers<br>• Does not appear to encourage voluntary reading<br>Disadvantages:<br>• May encourage overreliance on teacher for direction<br>• Highly teacher-directed | Present complete text through lecture and demonstration.<br>Give students a chance to read the material silently.<br>Conduct a discussion of the selection. |

*Source:* McKenna & Robinson (1997).

TESOL, Inc. has published a series of four volumes (*Integrating the ESL Standards into Classroom Practice* [Agor, 2000; Irujo, 2000; Samway, 2000; and Smallwood, 2000]) that demonstrate CBI-ELD.

# ENGLISH-LANGUAGE ORACY DEVELOPMENT

Oracy in English—learning to speak and listen—makes it possible for students to succeed in school. English learners already know a great deal about using oral language in their primary language. They know how to share their thoughts and opinions with others and how to use language strategically to get what they want, get attention, take turns, and so forth. Bourdieu (1977) called this knowledge "linguistic capital," a part of the resources that English learners bring to schooling.

Of course, if English learners acquire a dialect characteristic of the middle class and are backed by a houseful of cultural tools such as atlases, encyclopedias, magazines, and other reference materials, the oral language they use is even more valuable as linguistic capital. The knowledge about life coded in the L1 is worth quite a lot, however, if the teacher views this knowledge as a resource that can be used to promote academic success. Oracy that is directly connected to the community strengthens an individual's cultural capital.

## CLASSROOM GLIMPSE: Connecting Oracy to the Community

*Each student in Nora Bryce's ELD class created a short presentation about some aspect of his or her native culture. They practiced giving the presentations to one another during class. As "cultural ambassadors," various students went with Nora in pairs to a local breakfast Kiwanis meeting once a month before school. The Kiwanis members became so interested in the students' presentations that they devoted their fundraising activity to awarding college scholarships to class members. In this way, community connections enhanced the students' cultural capital and vice versa.*

Children's intellectual development is built on verbal interaction in the first language. According to Vygotsky (1981), children learn to engage in higher-level thinking by first listening and speaking. This has profound implications for the education of English learners: The more that students use language within the social context of the classroom, the better they will learn how to think. Teaching strategies provide imaginative ways to use oral language to further develop students' intellects. The following sections discuss ways to teach English oracy.

### Basic Interpersonal Communication Skills

A newcomer to the English language needs to learn basic interpersonal communication skills (BICS) that permit adjustment to the routines of schooling and the comforts of peer interaction. The importance of BICS is that students can begin to understand and communicate with their teacher, develop and fine-tune their interpersonal skills, and begin to overcome culture shock. School-age children use BICS to communicate basic needs to others or to share informal social interactions with peers. The focus in BICS is on getting across a message, with little regard for sentence structure and word choice.

BICS is clearly more than words—some exchanges with people involve no words at all; for instance, a glance from the teacher may nonverbally warn a student about misbehavior. Cummins (1984) called BICS *context embedded* because factors apart from the linguistic code can furnish meaning. For example, one student asks another for an eraser: "Mine's gone. You got one?" The student points to the pencil eraser and beckons for a loan. The item itself, rather than the language, provides the context. Other cues that add meaning to BICS in this situation are the tone of voice (requesting) and the "give me" gesture.

**Time to Attainment of BICS**   Fluency in BICS often leads students, parents, or other adults to assume that the child has mastered English. In a poll taken in 2000, 86 percent of children ages five to seventeen whose home language was Spanish reported that they spoke English "well" or "very well," and 90 percent of youths whose home language was Asian or Pacific Island reported that they spoke English "well" or "very well" (U.S. Census Bureau, 2001c). However, students who may appear to be fluent enough in English to survive in an all-English classroom may in fact have significant gaps in the development of academic aspects of English.

**Helping Students Acquire BICS**   Teachers can encourage newcomers' acquisition of basic social language in several ways. First, pairing a new student with a bilingual buddy who speaks the same primary language as well as English eases the pain of culture shock. Seating newcomers so that they can be involved with other pupils and participate with other students can help to keep the new students alert and interactive.

A "Newcomer Handbook" is helpful during the earliest stages of BICS acquisition. Students can help to create this orientation guide. Sections of this guide might feature simple school rules and procedures, English phrases to use for various social functions (asking for help, volunteering for class jobs, etc.), and guides for homework help. Pages might be included that present a simple map of the school with bilingual labels.

Cooperative tasks of all kinds provide opportunities for students to speak with one another. Cooperative groups with mixed abilities permit students some measure of participation even though it may not include a role requiring a high level of verbal ability in English. Students are assigned well-defined roles that rotate among all members. Box 6.1 summarizes ways to help students develop BICS in the classroom.

## Listening Processes

Although listening may be seen as a "receptive" skill, it is by no means a passive act. According to the sociocognitive approach to learning, listening is an act of constructing meaning. Listeners draw on their store of background knowledge and their expectation of the message to be conveyed as they actively comprehend a conversation or oral presentation. The role of the

**Box 6.1**   Ways to Develop Basic Interpersonal Communication Skills (BICS) in the Classroom

Encourage friendships between English-speaking students and newcomers.

- Classroom grouping is linguistically heterogeneous.
- Playground activities are structured for heterogeneity.
- Students may work on group projects and make new friends.
- Encourage parents to make friends (perhaps in after-school clubs).
- Younger siblings may be included.

Use flexible grouping for academic work.

- Students are exposed to a variety of linguistic models.
- If one speaker dominates the group, variety will give others a chance to be heard.
- Students can speak with others who speak more or less fluently.
- Structure groups so that everyone talks, including through presentations.

Project-based learning allows students to discuss plans together.

- Projects may permit different intelligences to shine.
- English learners may be strong contributors in nonverbal ways (e.g., drawing).
- Projects promote collaboration and sharing.

Cross-age tutoring encourages language growth.

- Students gain fluency by reading to younger children.
- Older students can read to younger students who need language models.
- Older students can supervise classroom learning centers.
- Cross-age combinations can be useful (sixth grader + third grader + two kindergartners).

Instructional conversations can help develop students' speaking skills.

- When the teacher is a conversant, conversations are more academic.
- The teacher is the best model for thinking skills.
- A skilled conversation leader can draw out shy speakers.
- The conversation models literate, intellectual behavior.

Interviews can encourage English use at home.

- A variety of survey formats are available.
- Students can survey friends and neighbors.
- Writing up the results or graphing allows students to practice other skills.

teacher is to set up situations in which students can develop their own purposes and goals for listening, acquire the English that is most useful in their daily lives, feel a sense of purpose, and engage in real communication. Over 40 percent of daily communication time is spent listening

(Burely-Allen, 1995), and teachers are becoming more aware that listening skills should be taught, rather than assuming that the skill develops itself.

Listening can be divided into conversational listening and academic listening (Long, 1987). For purposes of simplification, listening activities are discussed here under the categories of listening for beginning comprehension, listening to repeat, listening to understand, and listening for communication.

**Listening for Beginning Comprehension**     At the beginning level of language acquisition, the ELD objectives focus on demonstrating comprehension through active participation. During the initial "silent period," learners actively listen as they segment the sound stream, absorb intonation patterns, and become comfortable with English. They demonstrate comprehension through nonverbal means. With this methodology, academic subjects can be included.

Listening is for the purpose of comprehension. For example, students can view a poster of animals in a barn. The teacher might ask a student in the beginning stage, "Are people *safe* around these tame animals?" (pointing to the sheep, cat, and calf). A nod as a response to the word *safe* indicates comprehension. The teacher could ask a student who is in the beginning stage, "Which odors do you like?" (pointing to the Sense of Smell poster). The student can show comprehension by pointing.

A "listening area" can be set up in which English learners can listen to books on tape, with picture books or models set up to support understanding of what is heard. Two such stations might be set up side by side so students can share this listening experience with a friend. It might be comforting to a child if the person recording the tape speaks English that is accented the same way that people from the primary-language community sound.

**Listening to Repeat**     At the early intermediate stage, the ELD standards indicate a student should be able to "participate in recitation, singing, and dramatics." Teachers use poems, nursery rhymes, and songs to introduce rhyming words, asking students to fill in the blanks at the end of lines. In addition, teachers can read aloud wordplay books, alliterative books, and books with tongue twisters, encouraging students to talk about how the author manipulates words. Other listening activities could include listening for focal stress or for syllables (Kozyrev, 1998). Such activities help students hear the language and develop phonemic awareness.

Chants provide rhythmic presentations of the sentence intonation patterns of English. "The rhythm, stress, and intonation pattern of the chant should be an *exact* replica of what the student would hear from a native speaker in natural conversation" (Graham, 1992, p. 3). Graham (1988) has put fairy tales into jazz chant form, giving younger and less proficient students the opportunity to work with longer texts.

Actions can accompany songs, chants, and poems. It is easy to make up simple hand, arm, or body movements. To the poem "Here Is the Beehive," one first-grade teacher made up a series of hand motions: "Here is the beehive, where are the bees? / Hidden away where nobody sees. / Watch and you'll see them come out of the hive, One, two, three, four, five" / Bzzzzz" (close fingers into a fist, hold it up, open it up one finger at a time, wave fingers in the air) (Linse, 2006).

## BEST PRACTICE: Listening to Repeat

Level C of Hampton Brown's *Into English* features many ways to develop oral fluency by listening and repeating.

*Chant/rap.* "Rainy Day": "The sky is dark / The sky is gray. / I think it's going / To rain today." (p. 153)

*Choral rendition.* Using Poster 13 of the poem "Corn," the teacher forms three groups; group 1 says the first line of the poem, group 2 the second line, and so forth.

*Story/book echo.* Using Little Books, the teacher reads the book and students echo after each pause. (Tinajero & Schifini, 1997)

**Listening to Understand: The Task Approach** Students are asked to demonstrate comprehension by performing tasks such as writing the correct response or selecting the correct answer. To be successful, they must listen carefully. Typical classroom tasks are listening to an audiotape and completing true/false exercises based on the content, listening to a prerecorded speech and circling vocabulary items on a list, and listening to a lecture and completing an outline of the notes. Students may be asked to listen for the main idea, for specific information, for synonyms, or for vocabulary in context. Teachers in content classes in which English learners are mainstreamed especially need to attend to the listening skills of these students to make sure they are understanding the content.

To enhance listening for understanding, students listen to stories and information, responding appropriately using both verbal and nonverbal responses; they listen for main ideas, details, and sequences; they listen for implied meaning; and they apply knowledge of vocabulary, idiomatic expressions, discourse markers, organization, and tone to further their understanding.

## CLASSROOM GLIMPSE: Listening for Understanding

*Daniela Panferov's eighth-grade ELD class invited the artist Yi Kai to their class to talk about his art training in mainland China and the group to which he belongs, Global Harmony Through Arts. Mrs. Panferov and students discuss the topic of the upcoming talk and brainstorm questions and comments the students might like to ask or make. During the talk, students listen for answers to their questions. The talk is tape-recorded and the tape subsequently put into a listening center. Students are able to relisten, making note of ideas they may have missed. (Sholley, 2006)*

**Listening for Communication** One emphasis at the early advanced and advanced levels is listening for communication: developing students' abilities to communicate fluently and accurately by integrating listening, speaking, and pronunciation practice, as well as developing skills in anticipating questions, understanding suggestions, and note taking. In the communicative approach, once listeners are beyond the initial stage, interviews are often used to augment listening skills. Listening can also be used in problem-solving situations by means of riddles, logic puzzles, and brainteasers as well as more traditional mathematical problems. Listening, far from being a mere receptive skill, can be successfully combined with other language modes as part of an integrated approach to English acquisition. Table 6.2 provides sample listening comprehension activities within each ELD level.

**Before Listening**    Explicit instruction in listening can be organized as "before," "during," and "after listening" in a similar fashion as in reading instruction (see Chapter 3). Prelistening tasks can include a preview of vocabulary, a brief chat to assess schemata and prior knowledge, a cue to the type of text organization expected (such as chronological order), or attention to a map that cues a spatial setting for the listening task. Unit 5, Chapter 1 ("The American Civil War") of Dunkel and Lim's *Intermediate Listening Comprehension* (1994) offers a prelistening preparation task defining *civil war,* introducing key vocabulary, and previewing the text structure of causal explanation. At a more advanced level, Dunkel, Pialorsi, and Kozyrev's *Advanced Listening Comprehension* (1996) presents a preview of the content of the listening tasks and also a lengthy outline to assist the listener in previewing the textual organization of the excerpt.

**During Listening**    Students can follow an outline as they listen, take notes cued by a set of questions, or take notes in a variety of ways, using idea maps, outlines, paragraphs, or lists. They can listen several times, with slightly different purposes: for detection of transition words, key content terms, the main idea, supporting details, or the attitude of the speaker.

If the teacher feels the need to lecture, a helpful strategy for English learners is to have the lesson videotaped while students simply listen to the lecture, concentrating on understanding and writing down only questions or parts of the lecture they do not understand. Later, the videotape is played and the teacher and several students take notes on the board. The teacher can model the type of outline that indicates the main ideas and supporting details. After a few minutes, the videotape is stopped and the discussion then highlights various note-taking strategies and provides new strategies. This activity can be used on a periodic basis to enhance students' ability to comprehend lectures and take effective notes (Adamson, 1993).

**After Listening**    Many kinds of activities can follow up a listening task. Students can write, discuss, read, draw, or act out their interpretation of the content. They can attend to the linguistic aspects of what they have heard by completing worksheets on word meaning, idiomatic usage, formal versus informal English, words that compare/contrast, or words that introduce causal statements. The focus can be on cultural aspects of the reading, content applications across the disciplines, or critical thinking, including problem solving.

The postlistening time offers the most authentic activities—most conversation takes place after listeners have shared a talk, movie, or similar event. The postlistening phase can host critical conversation on the main ideas and a genuine sharing of opinions. This is one of the pleasures of real conversation (Miller, 2004).

**TABLE 6.2**   Activities for Listening Comprehension by ELD Level

| Level | Example Listening Activity |
|---|---|
| Beginning | Hearing sound patterns:<br>　Rhyming poems<br>　Songs<br>　Couplets<br>Comprehending narratives<br>　Read-aloud stories<br>　Small-group sharing-time anecdotes |
| Early Intermediate | Hearing sound patterns:<br>　Tongue twisters<br>　Jingles<br>　Jazz chants<br>　Alliterative poems and books<br>Listening to sentences:<br>　Dialogues<br>　Skits<br>　Open-ended sentences<br>　Conversation starters<br>Playing games:<br>　Twenty questions<br>　Pictionary<br>　Password? |
| Intermediate | Listening to answer factual questions orally or in writing:<br>　Dialogues<br>　Talks<br>　Arguments<br>Listening to discourse:<br>　Books on tape<br>　Classroom dramatics, plays<br>　Instructional conversations |
| Early Advanced | Listening to make notes:<br>　Class lectures<br>　Taped content readings<br>　Movies and computer files<br>Cooperative problem-solving activities:<br>　Group work<br>　Logic puzzles<br>　Brainteasers |
| Advanced | Listening to make notes:<br>　Guest lecturers<br>　Whole-class presentations<br>Cooperative problem-solving activities:<br>　Riddles<br>　Logic puzzles<br>　Brainteasers |

*Source:* Adapted from Díaz-Rico & Weed (2006).

## CLASSROOM GLIMPSE: Listening to a Recording

*Mr. Geller's American History class is going to listen to a recording of F. D. Roosevelt's radio Fireside Chats. Here is what he will say:*

- *Before listening: "Today we are going to listen to President Roosevelt address the nation. What do you think he might talk about? Why does a president talk directly to the people?"*
- *During listening: "While you listen to the program, try to listen for the main idea. Also, try to listen for the emotional tone."*
- *After listening: "Let's group into threes. In your group, complete these two tasks. Summarize the talk. Describe the emotional tone."*

**Authentic Tasks in and out of the Real World** An effective listening curriculum exposes students to a variety of speakers, for a variety of tasks, on a variety of topics, for a variety of purposes. The test of real listening skill is going out into the real world. Listeners must bring a relatively sophisticated set of understandings to bear: what to expect from the speaker, the setting in time and place, the topic, the genre of the text, and the co-text, or accompanying clues to meaning (Morley, 1995). Students can be encouraged to interview classmates and community members; attend movies, plays, and concerts; participate in hobby groups; or work in community service.

Despite the complexity of listening tasks and the emphasis on communicative approaches, however, listening is only half the work—one must also learn to speak.

### Speaking, Communication Skills, and the ELD Standards

Speaking involves a number of complex skills and strategies. In spoken discourse, words must not only be strung together in proper grammatical sequence, but they must also make sense in form, meaning, purpose, and function. Part of the role of the teacher is to help students assimilate and produce discourse not only for the purpose of basic interpersonal communication (informal) but also for the comprehension and production of cognitive academic language (formal). In addition, the teacher provides opportunities for students to express themselves in the wide range of language functions.

The emphasis on communicative methodology mandates that teachers try to get English learners to talk. In K–12 classrooms in U.S. schools, large numbers of English learners are mainstreamed into contexts that render them silent. Language learners develop best when they have opportunities to interact (Wells, 1998). It is therefore vital that teachers help students develop their speaking abilities.

**ELD Standards** Listening and speaking are the only skills assessed on the CELDT during kindergarten and first grade. The emphasis in speaking at the early intermediate level is on asking and answering questions and making simple statements, retelling stories, and participating in classroom oral language events; consistent use of correct grammar and intonation are not expected. At the intermediate level, the expectation is for English learners to use English sounds and grammar more consistently and expand vocabulary as they continue to ask and answer questions, retell stories, and participate in conversations. At early advanced and advanced levels, students are expected to produce academic language, with more precise vocabulary, details, and concepts across a range of tasks, using nativelike English. Clearly these goals require extensive oral practice.

**Developing Oral Language**   Morgan (1992) offers a host of ways that teachers can develop oral language in the classroom. An encouraging classroom climate helps students to feel confident, to be able to speak freely and make mistakes, and to believe that their way of speaking is respected and their opinions taken seriously. A noncompetitive atmosphere encourages sharing ideas through interaction, especially at a dedicated sharing time every day. A "productively talkative" work environment is not so noisy that a timid child feels overwhelmed. Even in a "normally noisy" class, a shy student may need a "home corner" where he or she can listen to tapes in the primary language or engage in nonverbal play in which English is not necessary. This allows rest from the stress of foreign language immersion.

## BEST PRACTICE: Strategies to Develop Students' Speaking Skills

- Academic opportunities for talking and working together range from low structure (work-related chitchat) to highly structured (for example, each person in a cooperative group is responsible for one section of an oral report).
- Listening to students with enthusiasm and interest communicates that their thoughts are valued.
- A pocket chart with slots for every student can be filled with a paper flower after they have spoken at sharing time, with no student receiving a second turn until everyone has had a chance to volunteer a personal anecdote.
- Make sure a quiet area is available where a child can "escape" English for a while.

**Situations for Speaking**   Students need opportunities to talk in natural interactional contexts and for a variety of purposes: to establish and maintain social relationships; to express reactions; to give and seek information; to solve problems, discuss ideas, or teach and learn a skill; to entertain or play with language; or to display achievement. In addition, students need to learn to interact with a variety of conversational partners: other students, the teacher, other adults at school, cross-age peers, guests, and so on.

Speaking reinforces listening comprehension. The content or SDAIE teacher, to ensure comprehension, needs to solicit feedback from students about the course content. To find out who is comprehending the material, the teacher must ask. If no one asks questions, the teacher finds other ways to check for understanding. Cooperative speaking activities are a part of every SDAIE lesson. Some instructors stop for a pair/share break every so often, so each student can ask a partner one question.

If structured public speaking is important in the content of the class, students are given a tight outline and timetable for each presentation. The teacher might invite students to meet outside of class before the presentation to rehearse. Other students can help by participating in a peer-scoring rubric in which content is emphasized over understandability. It is wise not to surprise students with requests for extemporaneous speaking.

## CLASSROOM GLIMPSE: Creating Conversation-Friendly Environments

*The kindergarten teacher transformed her room into a rain forest by putting artificial trees in the center, placing several live plants and a small inflatable plastic pool underneath them, putting more live plants in the water-filled pool, hanging photographs of the rain forest throughout the room, placing area rugs near the display, and posting a question in large letters: "Why are rain forests important?" Whole-group instruction occurred early in the morning, before lunch, and at the end of the school day. At other times, students worked in small groups on the area rugs.*

*A high school teacher, for the Civil War unit, displayed flags of the period and a Confederate uniform crafted by the students, involved students in a letter-writing project imagining they were Confederate solders writing home during the war, and grouped the desks into clusters, each one representing a regiment of soldiers or a home community. (Adapted from Zacarian, 2005)*

**Resources for Spoken Discourse**    Opportunities for oral discourse range from those that are carefully constructed to those that are completely student generated. Several kinds of speaking activities can be included in daily lessons, including problem solving in small groups, practicing persuasive or entertaining speeches, role-plays, interviews, chain stories, talks, problems, and discussions (c.f. Zelman, 1996). *Discussion Starters* (Folse, 1996) offers speaking activities that build oral fluency using exercises specifically designed for group participation. The discussion prompts are based on role-play, "finish-the-story" situations, problems that can be solved only if members of a group work together, and real court cases for groups to play "judge."

Table 6.3 organizes representative oral activities into the three categories suggested by Allen and Vallette (1977). These categories range from tightly structured on the left to freely constructed on the right.

**TABLE 6.3**    Formats for Oral Practice in the ELD Classroom

| Guided Practice | Communicative Practice | Free Conversation |
|---|---|---|
| Formulaic exchanges | Simulations | Discussion groups |
| Greetings | Guessing games | Debates |
| Congratulations | Group puzzles | Panel discussions |
| Apologies | Rank-order problems | Group picture story |
| Leave taking | Values continuum | Socializing |
| Dialogues | Categories of preference | Storytelling/retelling |
| Mini-conversations | Opinion polls | Discussions of: |
| Role-plays | Survey taking | Films |
| Skits | Interviews | Shared experiences |
| Oral descriptions | Brainstorming | Literature |
| Strip stories | News reports | |
| Oral games | Research reports | |
| | Storytelling | |

*Source:* Díaz-Rico & Weed (2006).

**Improving Pronunciation**    English learners need proficiency in the English sound system. Pronunciation involves the correct articulation of the individual sounds of English as well as the proper stress and pitch within syllables, words, and phrases. Longer stretches of speech require correct intonation patterns. However, the goal of teaching English pronunciation is not necessarily to make second-language speakers sound like native speakers of English. Some English learners do not wish to have a nativelike pronunciation but prefer to retain an accent that indicates their first-language roots and allows them to be identified with their ethnic community. Still others may wish to integrate actively into the mainstream culture and therefore are motivated to try to attain a native accent in English. Teachers need to recognize these individual goals and enable learners to achieve pronunciation that does not detract from their ability to communicate.

Students' attempts to reproduce correct word stress, sentence rhythm, and intonation may improve by exposure to native-speaker models. The teacher's role, in this case, is to create a nonthreatening environment that stimulates and interests students enough that they participate actively in producing speech. Teachers may also take a more direct role in improving pronunciation. Clarification checks can be interjected politely when communication is impaired. Teacher correction or sentence completion can be given after the teacher has allowed ample wait-time. Older students might be given the task of comparing speech sounds in their native language with sounds in English in order to better understand a contrastive difference.

### BEST PRACTICE: A Game to Practice Linking Words

"Syl/la/bles and Linking" is an activity proposed by Benson (1999) to raise awareness about the need to smoothly link syllables across words. To prepare for the game, students in pairs practice separating words into syllables by clapping along with the instructor as words are said in syllables. Then students receive a written paragraph and mark the syllables as the instructor reads. To play the game, students stand together in pairs. The instructor reads a list of word phrases, some of which have linked words and some of which do not. Students link arms if the words are linked. Students are out of the game if they link arms incorrectly.

### BEST PRACTICE: A Game for Stress and Sentence Intonation

Working in pairs, students receive a card containing a dialogue. In pairs, student A mimics the stress and intonation of one of the sentences on the card using a nonsense syllable. Student B tries to guess which is the target sentence (Cogan, 1999). Another game for practicing stress is Stress Clapping. A student comes to the front of the room, pulls a sentence written on a folded overhead transparency strip out of a box, and displays the sentence on the overhead projector (sentences are taken from song lyrics, poems, or limericks). The student must read the sentence aloud and clap each time there is a stressed word. The student's team receives a point for each stressed word correctly identified (Mahoney, 1999b).

Using a computer program for practice is a self-tutoring way in which students can improve their pronunciation. Such programs as Tell Me More (available from Auralog, www.auralog.com) are fun and easy to use.

**Before Speaking**    Prespeaking activities warm the students to the topic and activate or provide some prior knowledge. In Kehe and Kehe's (1998) Unit 11 ("Your Hometown and

Childhood Home"), students write their answers to several questions about their hometown before beginning the discussion. In Huizenga and Thomas-Ruzic's (1992) *All Talk,* Unit 13 ("Pick Your Perfect Vacation"), students warm up to the task of interviewing a partner by circling new words in vacation ads. These activities help students practice vocabulary and survey the content terrain before speaking.

Students can prepare for an impromptu speech on the subject of a news story by watching the evening news on television, listening to a news radio station, reading a newspaper or newsmagazine such as *Time* or *Newsweek,* and/or talking to people outside of class about selected issues. Students who must prepare for a formal public presentation need a more structured approach, with an attention-getting opener, a preview of what will be said, a substantive main body of the speech, a summary of the main points, and a memorable conclusion. An outline helps the student keep the presentation on topic. Rehearsal in advance of delivery—whether aloud to oneself, onto an audio- or videotape, or before a critical audience—helps students pace the delivery, create a natural tone, and practice difficult pronunciation (Wong, 1998).

**While Speaking**    Teachers working in mixed-ability classrooms can plan group activities that help students in different ways. Students can work in homogeneous groups when the goal of the activity is accuracy and in heterogeneous groups when the goal is fluency.

## BEST PRACTICE: Story Retelling at Four ELD Levels

First-grade students at the beginning ELD level can listen to a reading of "The Three Little Pigs" and recite the wolf's "I'll blow your house down!" along with the reader. A group of early intermediate students can retell the story using pictures and then talk about the pictures. Intermediate students can retell the story to the teacher or a cross-age tutor who can write their story for them, and then students can reread, illustrate, and rearrange the story from sentence strips. Early advanced English learners can create a new ending for the story.

Informal class discussions are a low-key way to practice speaking. While speaking, a student makes eye contact with listeners and adjusts the volume to an appropriate distance between the speakers. A speaker usually does not use notes when chatting with a classmate, but sometimes such notes are available from a previous brainstorming session. Turns are usually shared in small groups, and one person does not monopolize discussion.

Students making a public speech or formal presentation require a more formal approach, with a neat public appearance that shows respect for the situation and audience. Visual aids in the form of charts or overhead projections help listeners to see as well as hear the presentation. Memorizing the presentation is not advisable, for it may lead to a stiff and forced delivery. Stance should be facing the audience, with hands and feet appearing calm and under control (Wong, 1998).

Correction while a person is speaking is seldom appropriate. If the teacher makes such corrections, the speaker may become tense and unable to be fluent or creative. If the speaker is genuinely unable to be understood, the teacher can be honest about it. However, the teacher impedes communication if he or she expects an imperfect sentence to be repeated correctly. Reformulation is the best alternative; if the teacher hears an incorrect utterance, a similar sentence can be repeated to the student naturally and in the context of the conversation without embarrassing the student (Bartram & Walton, 1994).

Oral presentations can be assessed using *holistic scoring,* with a three-level score (good/ excellent/superior) based on content (clear purpose, vivid and relevant supporting details), organization (well-structured introduction, body, and conclusion), and delivery (skillful verbal and nonverbal language, with clear, appropriate, and fluent speech). Alternatively, *analytic scoring* gives point values to each aspect of content, organization, and delivery, and the speaker receives as a grade the sum of the points for each aspect (see Chaney and Burk [1998], for examples of each type of scoring).

**After Speaking**   Many kinds of activities can follow up a speaking task. As in the listening task, students can write, discuss, read, draw, or act out their interpretation of the content, attending to the linguistic or cultural aspects of what they have heard. For the most part, oral discussion is a vital part of any other task and should be developed as a top priority. When students have been outside the classroom on a service-learning project, debriefing is needed so that students can reflect on and share with one another what they have learned.

*English learners can use drama as an extension activity in a reading lesson.*

Strategic speaking involves a combination of cognitive, social, and emotional factors. Table 6.4 offers a compendium of strategies to enhance English learners' oral presentations.

**Speaking Games and Tasks**   Table 6.5 describes three kinds of tasks by ELD level that enhance listening and speaking. The game-style format reduces speaking anxiety.

**Oral Discourse and the Instructional Conversation**   Contemporary educators have sought discussion formats that engage students in critical thinking and intellectually pro-

**TABLE 6.4**   Some Strategies Useful for English Learners in Speaking

| Phase of the Speaking Process | Sample Strategies |
| --- | --- |
| Before speaking | English learners can . . . Lower anxiety by taking a few deep breaths, visualizing success, repeating positive self-talk phrases. Review the purpose of the talk; ask for clarification if unsure of goal. Activate background knowledge; make associations with similar situations. Predict what will happen and what language is needed; practice difficult vocabulary in advance. Plan the talk, using an outline, rehearsing with a partner if it is a joint presentation. |
| While speaking | Ask for clarification or help if necessary. Concentrate on the task, avoiding distractions. Stay involved with others; negotiate meaning with listeners. Monitor speech, paying attention to vocabulary, grammar, and pronunciation; try new words; back up and fix mistakes if necessary. Compensate for vocabulary shortcomings by using cognates, synonyms, gestures, or guesses; simplify message if necessary; base talk on information about which speaker has some prior knowledge. |
| After speaking | Self-reward with positive affirmations. Evaluate accomplishment, reviewing goals and strategies, asking for feedback and tuning in to the reactions of others. Identify problem areas, looking up grammar and vocabulary that were troublesome. Make a plan for improvement, noting strategies of classmates or instructor's suggestions. Ask for help or correction from more proficient speakers. Keep a learning log, writing down reflections, strategies, reactions, and outcomes. |

*Source:* Adapted from Alcaya, Lybeck, Mougel, & Weaver (1995).

**TABLE 6.5** Three Activities for Listening and Speaking

| Name of Activity | ELD Level | Directions for the Teacher |
|---|---|---|
| Shadow Tableaux | Beginning | Pass around a bag and have each student put in a small personal object. Spread these out on an overhead projector so only their shadow can be seen. Have students work in pairs to name all the objects. (Mahoney, 1999a) |
| Give Me a Word That . . . | Early Intermediate | Students form three groups (A, B, C). Prepare index cards (one for each student) with vocabulary questions starting with the phrase, "Give me . . . ." For example, "Give me a word that dances . . ." (*ballerina, Madonna*) A word that runs. (*runner, river*) A blue word (*sky*) A cold word (*ice, winter*) Student A reads a word; group B has 30 seconds to give an answer; if not, group C can answer. Whichever is correct wins that round. (Mansour, 1999) |
| Headline News | Intermediate | Cut out interesting headlines and their corresponding photographs from newspapers. Cut the headlines in half (do not split word phrases). Paste the beginnings and ending of the headlines onto index cards. Students in group A receive photographs, group B, headline beginnings, and group C, headline endings. Students move around the room, asking one another (not showing) the content of their card. The first set to identify its three parts wins the game. (Hetherton, 1999) |

ductive social interaction. In the instructional conversation (IC), the instructor functions as "thinker-leader" while encouraging voluntary oral participation. The IC model developed by Goldenberg and Gallimore (1991) has both instructional and conversational elements. The most important instructional element is the thematic focus. Themes are drawn from text that participants read in common before beginning the conversation. A good theme is one that is flexible and grows out of the ideas of the participants, without being superimposed by the leader. This flexibility creates shared responsibility for the discussion by the participants.

The conversation elements include aspects that defuse anxiety and promote interaction. It is helpful, for example, to talk while seated in a circle of chairs, which facilitates eye contact and allows individuals equal access to turns. Disagreement and difference of opinion are protected; part of the challenging atmosphere is for students to find a way to evaluate one another's viewpoints. In the IC format, turns are voluntary—no one is called on to speak. Grammar is not corrected. Group members talk with one another in everyday English on topics that elicit opinions without necessarily requiring expertise or prior knowledge.

To support the conversational elements of the IC, the thinker-leader asks open-ended questions, responds positively to student ideas, and weaves ideas that are volunteered by class members into the instructional content. A tone of challenging, nonthreatening, intellectual give-and-take promotes critical thinking and speaking. As one student speaks, others listen. Teachers might offer lunch-hour discussions with interested students on a voluntary basis on selected topics of interest to students.

**Media Literacy**     Critical media analysis is an excellent way to stimulate English learners' listening and speaking skills. Being able to sort out information and critically research, analyze, and understand the media are becoming more and more important. *Media literacy* has been used as an umbrella term for the analysis of Internet information, computers, art, graphics, images, text, advertising, and so forth. From a critical perspective, students can respond to questions such as, "What media do you watch? Is there a 'best' way to get your information? Do advertising techniques have an impact on you or someone you know? How accurate is the content? What biases can be spotted?" (see http://lsb.syr.edu/projects/media/cml.html).

Speaking and listening are ends in themselves and do not always have to be linked to reading and writing. But such links, both planned and unplanned, demonstrate that language is a whole, and proficiency in one skill mutually reinforces others.

## ENGLISH-LANGUAGE LITERACY DEVELOPMENT

Literacy instruction is a crucial aspect of K–12 schooling in the United States. The topic of how best to instruct English learners has been a part of the debates over the best ways to help students learn to read and read to learn (see Wolfe & Poynor [2001] for a discussion of the politics of reading instruction). However, a complicating factor that is sometimes not considered by reading researchers is the varying background experiences that English learners bring to the reading task. California TESOL (CATESOL, 1998) provided the following five classifications for English learners that help teachers understand the differences in English learners according to their literacy background:

- Young learners (K–3) whose beginning literacy instruction is in their primary language
- Young learners (K–3) acquiring initial literacy in English because they do not have access to primary-language reading instruction
- Older learners with grade-level primary-language literacy who are beginning to develop literacy in English
- Older learners with limited formal schooling in their home country

- Older learners with inconsistent school history, with limited development of either the primary language or English (p. 1)

This complex terrain, with English learners coming from a wide range of backgrounds and achieving a wide range of scores on the CELDT, suggests it is unlikely that a one-size-fits-all approach to reading instruction will be suitable. Instead, a differentiated instruction model is necessary.

## Reading First in the Primary Language

Study after study has demonstrated that the degree of children's native-language proficiency is a strong predictor of their progress in ELD. Hurrying young children into reading in English without adequate preparation in their own language is counterproductive. The report of the National Research Council (Snow, Burns, & Griffin, 1998) recommended that language-minority children who arrive at school with no proficiency in English but speaking a language for which there are instructional guides, learning materials, and locally available proficient teachers should be taught how to read in their native language while acquiring oral proficiency in English and subsequently taught to extend their skills to reading in English.

The Reading First program established by the No Child Left Behind Act enacted a new "high-quality evidence-based program" for U.S. students (see www.ed.gov/programs/readingfirst/index.html). No recommendations were made, however, for specific reading instruction for English learners, although in 2000 these students represented 9.3 percent of total public school enrollment (Antuñez, 2002).

## ELD and ELA Standards in Reading

The California English Language Development Standards correspond to the California English Language Arts Standards in reading. The same categories are used so that as English learners progress, their skills are developed in the categories that will be used for evaluation in the mainstream class. These categories are as follows: Reading Word Analysis, Reading Fluency and Systematic Vocabulary Development, and Reading Literary Response and Analysis. Although the subskills that make up these categories become progressively more challenging across the five ELD levels, even at the beginning level students are exposed to literature and asked to respond ("Listens to a story and responds orally or in drawings").

The chief difficulty in teaching reading to English learners is that for native English speakers, reading is a matter of recognizing on paper the meaning that already exists in oral language. Those who do not understand English, however, must first learn the language before decoding its written form.

The difficulty, then, is that when working with English learners, teachers have to teach English as they teach how to read English. Most teachers of reading are aware that students do not understand everything they read—even native English speakers need to acquire vocabulary as well as the thinking skills (comprehension, inference) that accompany literacy. English learners need to learn thousands more words just to reach the starting point of the linguistic knowledge that native speakers learned before starting school. This catch-up must take place at school. ELD reading and ELA reading fundamentally differ in that there is a double burden on the English learner. Therefore, the ELD standards precede the mainstream ELA standards.

## Purposes for Reading

During the advent of the era of television, critics asked, "Is reading dead?" With the advent and proliferation of the Internet, people are asking the same question as they see young people inundated with images and sounds that flout classic print conventions. At the same time, however, more individuals are expected to be literate than ever before, as employment in modern technology requires advanced reading and writing skills.

However, in the midst of calls for enhanced literacy to benefit the workplace, Corley (2003) cautioned that this functionalist approach ignores the need for critical literacy: "The practice of helping learners make sense of what they are learning by grounding it in the context of their daily lives and reflecting on their individual experiences, with an eye toward social action" (p. 1). McLaren (1995) called for media studies to be a central focus of school curricula so that learners can be educated beyond a functional literacy that serves the purpose of the school but perhaps not the purpose of the individual (Barton, Hamilton, & Ivanič, 2000).

The search for reading strategies that fit the generic learner quickly runs afoul not only of current calls for situated literacy but also of the impossibility of finding a "best" method. Certainly, contextual and instructional variation complicates matters. Older learners need different reading instruction than do children, learners' prior schooling creates diverse starting points for instruction, and learners' goals deviate from official policy mandates. In spite of these shortcomings, it is clear that instruction in reading can be applied situationally and experimentally until some wisdom is reached about best practices for the particular context and learners.

Most people learn new skills in an integrated way, starting from the need to learn for some purpose. May and Rizzardi (2002) emphasize that most learners read and write because they see others doing it—reading directions, newspapers, or road signs for information, or reading novels, just to pass the time. However, many English learners do not see their families reading or writing. Therefore, it takes a leap of imagination for them to see themselves as readers. It is important, then, that the classroom as a community be a place in which reading is enjoyable. A context of shared enjoyment is the key to making literacy an everyday part of life.

One reading expert summarizes the issues that characterize current thinking about the teaching of reading:

> One thing that we know is that reading is a complex act. It seems easy once you know how to do it, but reading requires the coordination of a number of processes: knowing letters and sounds, spelling patterns, the meaning of words being read, how collections of words combine to form phrases and longer pieces of text and how to apply what you know in order to understand what you read. A reading program that ignores any of these is unlikely to be successful. "Back to basics" fans like to trumpet the fact that "phonics works." But they're only partly right. Phonics in a vacuum—in the absence of purpose and meaning, in other words, interesting things to read and hear and talk about—won't help children learn to read well. (Goldenberg, 2001, B11)

## CLASSROOM GLIMPSE: A Purpose for Reading

*The SAIL program, a grades 1–6 reading intervention program in Montgomery County, Maryland, was designed to deliver meaning-centered instruction to the lowest-achieving students. Rather than looking for deficits in these students, in effect blaming them for not reading, educators developed an integrated-skills, strategies-based program. Before having students read, teachers probed for personal commitment by asking each student, "Why do you want to become a better reader?" Answers varied: "I want to read to my little brother," "I want to get smart," or "I want to be an astronaut." These are places to begin—to find the fit between curriculum and personal aspirations. (Bergman & Schuder, 1993)*

## Standards-Based Reading Instruction

New basal readers on the market reflect the current emphasis on standards-based instruction. For example, *Launch into Reading, Level I* (Heinle & Heinle, 2002a, 2002b), an ELD reader, refers to the specific California English Language Arts Standard to which each lesson is connected. Lesson 13, "Flowers (A Poem by E. Greenfield)" addresses Reading Standard 6, 3.4, "Define how tone or meaning is conveyed in poetry." Follow-up exercises ask students to use a continuum scale to rank "five ways you can learn about people's feelings and ideas" (short story, poem, magazine or newspaper article, movie or TV program, and conversation), which addresses Reading Standard 2, 2.7, "Interpret information from diagrams and charts."

Later in the lesson, students are asked to find the rhyming words in the poem "Flowers" (Reading Standard 1, 1.6, "Create and state a series of rhyming words") and then work with a partner to interpret a poem (Writing Standard 6, 2.4, "Write responses to literature: Organize the interpretation around several clear ideas, premises or images"). All teaching materials, the teacher's resource book, the student workbook, and the student reading book contain explicit references to standards on each page.

High Point from Hampton-Brown (Schifini et al., 2002) is an excellent ELD series, complete with teaching tips designed to facilitate comprehensible input, decodable small books, learning strategies for enhancing cognitive academic language, ways to increase reading fluency, writing support for students with non-Roman alphabets, and cultural tips. The introductory material in the teacher's edition (p. 12) states that curriculum standards provided the foundation for the design of the book. The texts themselves do not contain ELD standards, however, leaving the integration of standards and instruction to a separate supplemental document.

## Developing Word Analysis Skills

What characterizes literacy instruction for English learners? The natural developmental processes that children undergo in learning their first language (oral and written) also occur in second-language acquisition (oral and written). For reading, these processes include using knowledge of *sound–symbol relationships* (graphophonics), *word order and grammar* (syntax), and *meaning* (semantics) to predict and confirm meaning, and using background knowledge about the text's topic and structure along with linguistic knowledge and reading strategies to make an interpretation (Peregoy & Boyle, 2005). The following sections specifically detail the major tenets of current reading pedagogy and practice.

**Emergent Literacy**    A key insight of emergent literacy theory is that children learning to read already understand quite a bit about print. Most young children have had much exposure to print in the culture at large and may have engaged in various informal kinds of reading. Even homes without books often have magazines and the ubiquitous advertising on television, which includes product names. Therefore, it is the teacher's job to build on these nascent skills so students can "grow into reading."

Emergent literacy involves a combination of components. Emergent readers must learn to . . .

- Draw on their prior knowledge of the world to connect the printed word with its semiotic meaning (for example, the red octagonal sign at a street corner means "stop")
- Enhance their phonemic awareness by linking sounds with symbols
- Recognize a set of sight words that are not phonetically predictable (*the* is not "ta-ha-ay")
- Acquire reading behaviors, such as handling books and focusing on text
- Participate in a culture of reading, reading for enjoyment, sharing their pleasure in reading with others, borrowing and returning books to the class library, and working in the company of others to acquire meaning from books

**Concepts about Print**    Students need a foundation of basic ideas about print. They may already intuit some of these, or they may need schooling to gain these concepts. This knowledge involves practice with print (see www.ncrel.org/sdrs/areas/issues/content/cntareas/reading/li1lk11.htm).

- Where to begin writing or reading, going from left to right.
- Where to go after the end of the line (return sweep).
- The print, not the picture, carries the message.
- Word-by-word pointing (one-to-one correspondence).
- Concept of a letter, word, sentence.
- Concept of first and last part (of the word, sentence, story).
- Letter order in words is important.
- There are first and last letters in words.
- Upper- and lowercase letters have purpose.
- Different punctuation marks have meaning.

Other authors have called this *skill with print,* which includes the preceding concepts listed with a few additional insights (Gunning, 2005):

- Language is divided into words.
- Words can be written down.
- Space separates written words.
- Sentences begin with capital letters and end with punctuation.
- A book is read from front to back.
- Reading goes left to right and top to bottom.
- Words, not pictures, are read.
- A book has a title, an author, and sometimes an illustrator.

## BEST PRACTICE: Fostering Emergent Literacy in Children

- Provide an accessible, appealing literacy environment with attractive reading and writing materials.
- Classroom reading materials should include extra copies of books read aloud by the teacher or books by the same author, commercial books, student-written books, comic or cartoon books (with words), magazines, encyclopedias, and bilingual, age-appropriate dictionaries.
- Encourage children to role-play or playact reading and writing activities.
- Incorporate shared book experiences using Big Books or enlarged text.
- Follow up shared reading with independent reading, small-group review of the Big Book, or work with language skills such as phonics.
- Bolster reading with chanting or singing based on reading the lyrics together. (Adapted from Gunning, 2005)

**Phonemic and Morphemic Awareness**   The ability to hear and manipulate sounds in words is called *phonemic awareness.* The basic insight is that spoken language consists of identifiable units—utterances are composed of spoken words, which in turn consist of syllables, which in turn have distinct sound units (Chard, Pikulski, & Templeton, n.d.). Phonemic awareness is an auditory skill and does not involve words in print. The following are phonemic awareness exercises:

- Blending: What word am I trying to say? Ppppppiiiiiii n.
- Segmentation (first sound isolation): What is the first sound in *pin*?
- Segmentation (last sound isolation): What is the last sound in *pin*?
- Segmentation (complete): What are all the sounds you hear in *pin*?

## BEST PRACTICE: Activities to Help Learners Develop Phonemic Awareness

- *Wordplay* (What is left if I take away the *b* in *bright*? *right.*)
- *Rhyming games* (One, two, buckle your shoe)
- *Nursery rhymes* (Jack and Jill went up the hill)
- *Picture books with rhymes*

*Morphemic awareness* is the understanding that the smallest elements of meaning contained in words play a role in word recognition. Readers advance in skill when they can combine their knowledge of spelling and meaning patterns with sound–symbol correspondence (Ehri, 1997). Both of these concepts are taught explicitly in direct approaches to reading.

**Vocabulary and Concept Development**   The prior knowledge most useful for reading is largely word knowledge (vocabulary). This is the chief hurdle faced by English learners because reading a word successfully depends on knowing the word in the first place. Once students start to read, vocabulary acquisition accelerates because general comprehension of a text allows readers to predict and infer meaning of unknown words they encounter. The teacher's job is to help students develop background knowledge through the use of other books, oral discussion, exposure to media, or use of pictures or other visual prompts, combined with text, in order to build schemata—that is, construct a framework of concepts that shows the relationships of old and new learning and how they are connected.

**Decoding** Incomplete or inaccurate decoding limits comprehension—decoding is essential to reading. Students with phonemic awareness can use this skill in phonics instruction as they come to understand that there is an orderly relationship between written letters and speech sounds. Attempting to read an unfamiliar word is a process of trying to connect the letter with its sound and then to affirm the meaning from the context.

Using *sight words* (those that do not conform to phonetic rules—about 10 percent of English written words), the learner relies on visual memory to match sound with writing. Using *phonics,* the learner explicitly constructs the sound–symbol connection. Each of these techniques has its place in learning basic words. Lists of sight words can be obtained from reading texts. These include frequently used words with nonpredictable spelling, such as *the, might, could,* and so forth. Phonics can be taught using the synthetic method (bottom up), with students learning phonemes in isolation, then learning to blend them, and finally seeing them in the context of words. Or students can learn using the analytic method, beginning first with contrasting words that contain the target phonemes and then having students generate similar words. The analytic method is illustrated in Box 6.2.

---

### Box 6.2   Teaching Reading via the Analytic Method of Phonics

1. **Planning:** Make a list of easy words that includes the target phonic element, for example the digraph /sh/: *cash, crash, mash, dish, fish,* and so forth. Write simple, meaningful sentences for each one, or a little story, if possible, that contains the words. Find pages in a common reading book that has these or other *sh-* words, including /sh/ as a final sound.
2. **Teaching:** Read the sentences aloud to the students in a smooth and informal fashion. Have the students echo-read the sentences—repeating after the teacher, then repeating each underlined target word after the teacher, looking to see what sound the words have in common.
3. **Guided practice:** Students each make the target sound and look again at the letters that make the sound. Have students say other words with the same sound. Students choral-read the sentences and then take turns reading them aloud.

*Source:* May & Rizzardi (2002, p. 177).

Books designed for phonics instruction as much as possible use words with a regular sound–symbol correspondence. This does not always lend itself to engaging prose. Because English as a language has changed in sound–symbol correspondence in the 550 years since the printing press was first used, its basic, everyday prose often features the most irregular, least phonics-amenable words. Unfortunately, then, in English, sometimes the more interesting the text, the less phonics-friendly the words.

The International Reading Association finds that phonics is an important part of a beginning reading program but states explicitly that phonics instruction needs to be embedded in a total reading/language arts program (International Reading Association, 1997). Today, teachers introduce phonics through mini-lessons and gamelike activities such as making words and word sorts rather than by having students mark letters and words on worksheets.

**From Letter to Word Recognition**　Written English is based on the alphabetic principle, and children need to understand that sounds correspond to letters. Prereading activities help to develop visual discrimination, including such tasks as matching pictures and patterns, sequencing story cards in a meaningful order, and matching uppercase letters to lowercase letters. Teaching letters phonetically takes place in a sequence. First, alphabet cards introduce the name of each consonant letter and the sound it makes. Matching objects and pictures to letters helps learners to identify initial sounds. Ending sounds can be treated in a similar way. Then short vowels are introduced, usually in the order *a, i, o, u,* and *e;* this is followed by the short vowels blended with consonants. Simple stories featuring short vowels help students find early success with reading. Long vowels and vowel blends are taught next, followed by digraphs (consonants which together make a single sound, like /th/).

However, reading based on phonetic awareness alone may not be the best approach for English learners (Flood, Lapp, Tinajero, & Hurley, 1997). Hamayan (1994) cites four reasons why structural approaches (phonics based and grammar based) are not sufficient to meet the needs of preliterate English learners: (1) They do not meet the learner's need to acquire an understanding of the functional aspects of literacy, (2) literacy is forced to emerge in an unnatural way and in an artificial form, (3) a focus on form without a functional context makes learning abstract, meaningless, and difficult, and (4) literacy becomes a boring chore.

Teachers of English learners are encouraged to provide students with rich language experiences, including wordplay, which lead them to understanding sound–symbol correspondences. During and after read-alouds, for example, teachers point out specific sound and letter patterns that occurred in the texts. According to Peregoy and Boyle (2005), specific instruction in sound–symbol correspondence emerges best through students' own writing. Their invented or temporary spelling represents "an important step on the way to conventional spelling while providing individualized phonics practice that will assist both reading and writing development" (p. 153).

## Developing Reading Fluency

The ability to decode rapidly, accurately, and efficiently is known as fluency. The *Literacy Dictionary* (Harris & Hodges, 1995) defines *fluency* as "freedom from word-identification problems that might hinder comprehension in silent reading or the expression of ideas in oral reading" (p. 85). Because human beings have limited attention capacity, decoding words needs to become so automatic that it can be accomplished with minimal active attention. This theory of automaticity (Laberge & Samuels, 1974) posits that if a reader has to devote sizable attention to decoding, insufficient attention will be available for that constructive, critical reading comprehension. Chard and colleagues (n.d.) put it this way: "Although fluent decoding is not sufficient for high levels of reading comprehension, it is definitely a prerequisite for comprehension" (n.p.).

Through careful attention to print in sequential decoding, readers begin to notice that patterns of letters, such as -*ing* and -*ike,* occur in many words. Helping them focus on these patterns and recognize these repeated patterns in words can help readers to process or "chunk" the letters as a single unit. When readers are able to do this, they are able to more rapidly identify and process words during reading, increasing fluency.

One would like to believe that extensive use of context cues makes reading more fluent, as the reader does not have to pause to define an unfamiliar word. However, even if a reader correctly identifies a word using context, there is no guarantee the word will be recognized the next time it is encountered in print. Without the letter-sound connection, the contextual advantage is lost. If a reader can decode a word using other skills, context can provide a useful "check" or confirmation of the word—but only after the word has been tentatively decoded.

**Reading Aloud**   A learner's specific approach to decoding can be analyzed by listening to him or her read aloud. When attempting a sentence with an unknown word, various readers use distinct strategies. One type of reader uses *semantic knowledge.* If the sentence reads, "Joey pushed open the door of the haunted . . . ," a reader might guess that the next word is not *hose,* because the meaning would not make sense. Another type of reader might use *syntactic knowledge* on the sentence "Joey drives a small . . ." to reject the word *care* as the wrong choice for that part of the sentence. Still a third type of reader might use *orthographic shape* in the sentence "Joey drove a load of trees to the paper mill," knowing that the words *pap* and *paperwork* look wrong. A single reader might use these three types of meaning-making equally often, or the teacher might detect a preference for one type of decoding. Interventions would be designed accordingly (Newman, 1985).

**Seeking Meaning**   The need to understand is natural to the mind. The goal of the reading instructor is for students to come away from a reading passage with meaning. Because the reader constructs this meaning, there will always be some imperfect match between the meaning as intended and the meaning as attained by each reader. The richest of text evokes the most fundamentally meaningful, yet passionate and idiosyncratic response. Anything less is reductionistic—to be doomed to accept the exact understandings of others rather than to glory in our own, however unique. This is the chief reason for the existence of literature.

**Systematic Vocabulary Development**   Throughout one's schooling, acquiring vocabulary is a constant. One important research question that remains unresolved concerns whether adequate vocabulary in a second language can be acquired through reading (Nagy, 1997) or is more likely to result from some kind of direct instruction (Zimmerman, 1997). What is the minimal number of recognition vocabulary words needed to facilitate reading comprehension? One study suggests that 3,000 words (in word families) are needed (Laufer, 1989). Part of the problem with acquiring vocabulary is that word learning takes place in increments; although a single encounter with a word may provide some learning, 100 encounters may not spark in an English learner the native speaker's complex knowledge of the word and the way it is used in the culture. The real problem is achieving adequate, in-depth exposure to content-related vocabulary.

New vocabulary words can be introduced before a reading lesson, or meaning can be inferred from context during reading. Explicit work with new vocabulary words, though, is usually reserved for the after-reading phase. Students can study words by means of the *word element approach,* isolating roots, prefixes, and suffixes and using word families to expand a new word into its host of relations (e.g., the words *biology, sociology,* and *psychology* are relatives of *anthropology*). Or students can practice *specific vocabulary-acquisition strategies,* such as inferring from context (finding synonyms in apposition, making use of a subsequent list of examples of a new word, or using a dictionary).

Students can practice *acquiring technical words* by using a glossary, sidebar, chart, or graphs. Worksheets or other kinds of practice can help students recognize meaning. Students can practice *word formation* through compounding (*room + mate = roommate*), blending (*motor hotel = motel*), and making acronyms (*self-contained underwater breathing apparatus = scuba*). However, moving a new word from students' acquisition vocabulary (used in reading or listening) to their production vocabulary (used in writing or speaking) requires far more guided practice.

**Contextual Redefinition**    Learning to use context to increase comprehension while reading is an important skill that proficient readers use. Contextual redefinition shows students the importance of context in gaining meaning. This is a useful learning strategy for beginning, below-grade-level, and above-grade-level readers because the context can be used to define terms they may not know and encourage them to use prior knowledge to find meaning even when there are no dictionaries readily available.

The teacher can select a few essential words students will encounter in the text, present these in isolation, and then have students offer suggestions about their meaning. The teacher can then provide a context for each of the words, with clues of definition. Students offer suggestions about the meanings and work in groups to consult dictionaries. This activity builds reading, writing, comprehension, listening, and speaking skills; encourages a natural and holistic view of language learning; and provides multiple opportunities for English learners to use and hear language in a variety of settings.

## Reading Processes

**Before Reading**    "Into" activities activate students' prior knowledge by drawing from their past experiences, or help students develop background knowledge through new experiences. Films, texts, field trips, visual aids, and graphic organizers can clarify meaning and help students anticipate the work. Brainstorming ideas about a topic is one way to activate prior knowledge. Some teachers have students make predictions about the content of a story. Students can discuss what happened later in the book to confirm or disprove their original predictions.

Background knowledge can be activated or developed through classroom activities that include all of the language processes. Two such activities are brainstorming and K-W-L (What do I **K**now? What do I **W**ant to learn? What have I **L**earned?). Asking, "What do I know?" allows students to place new knowledge in the context of their own episodic memories and existing concepts.

During brainstorming and K-W-L, all ideas should be accepted. Once ideas are exhausted, the students and teacher together can organize the list, grouping and selecting appropriate category labels to create a beginning model from which they can work and learn.

K-W-L not only taps into what students already know but also draws from them what they would like to learn. The students list everything they know about a topic. They then tell the teacher what they would like to learn. The chart is kept up throughout the duration of the unit, and students refer to it from time to time. When the unit is completed, they return to the chart and talk about what they have learned. By starting each topic or unit with an activity that actively engages students in reviewing their own experiences relevant to the topic, the teacher gains valuable insights.

**During Reading**   "Through" activities help students as they work with the text. Reading aloud is a useful strategy that gives the students an opportunity to hear a proficient reader, to get a sense of the format and story line, and to listen to the teacher "think aloud" about the reading. In the think-aloud, teachers can model how they monitor a sequence of events, identify foreshadowing and flashbacks, visualize a setting, analyze character and motive, comprehend mood and theme, and recognize irony and symbols.

Teachers using literature in their classrooms may find that English-language literature does not elicit the same responses from English learners as from native English speakers. By selecting materials judiciously, slowing the pace slightly, portioning work into manageable chunks, and increasing the depth of each lesson, the teacher can ensure that English learners have a fulfilling experience with literature.

Students can perform the actual reading through a variety of methods. Table 6.6 offers some reading methods for in-class use across a variety of grade levels.

To sustain students' interest in a longer work of literature, class time can be used to review the narrative to date and discuss students' understanding of the assigned reading. A preview of the next reading can feature interesting aspects of the new passage. In *Literature in the Language Classroom,* Collie and Slater (1987) suggested ways a teacher can structure literature homework:

- *Gap Summary* is a technique in which the teacher provides an almost-complete and simply phrased description of the main points of the section assigned for home reading. Gaps are usually key words or expressions that only a reading of the passage can reveal.
- *Character Diary* is an ongoing record of what each character is feeling that helps students step within the character.
- *What's Missing* encourages students to make inferences about missing aspects of the story: What were the characters like at school? What were their favorite subjects? Did they have friends? Were they close to their parents?
- *Story Mapping* is a way for students to use a graphic organizer to follow the events in the plot. Younger students can chart "What Happens Next." Older students can use the categories Characters, Intent, Opposition, and Resolution.

**After Reading**   "Beyond" activities are designed to extend the students' appreciation of literature, usually in another medium.

**TABLE 6.6** In-Class Reading Methods for English Learners

| Method | Description |
|---|---|
| Page and Paragraph | Teacher or fluent reader reads a page, then English learner reads a paragraph, then group discusses what has been read. |
| Equal Portions | Students work in pairs and each reads aloud the same amount of text. |
| Silent with Support | Students read silently in pairs and can ask each other for help with a difficult word or phrase. |
| Choral Reading | Passage is divided into sections, and various parts of the audience read various sections. |
| Radio Reading | One student reads while others close their books and listen. After reading, the reader can question each student about what was read. |
| Repeated Reading | Students read silently a book that has been read aloud, or independently reread books of their choice. |
| Interactive Read-Aloud | Students can join in on repetitious parts or take parts of a dialogue. |
| Echo Reading | For rhythmic text, students echo or repeat lines. |
| Cloze Reading | When reading Big Books, teacher covers certain words and students try to guess word in context. |
| Nonprint Media Support | Students can follow along with a taped version of the book. |

*Source:* Hadaway, Vardell, & Young (2002).

- Poems can be written and shared with other classes or parents at a Poetry Night.
- Reviews of literature works can be written for the school or classroom newspaper.
- Letters to authors or to pen pals encourage students to express their reactions to certain pieces of literature.
- Students can be movie critics and view the film representation of a text studied in class, comparing the differences, pros, and cons of the two media.
- Favorite parts of selections can be rewritten as a play and enacted for other classes.
- Using reminder sheets, students in pairs can restate to each other various parts of what they have read (cued retelling).
- Students can plan a mock television show—for example, a game show—in which a host asks contestants to answer questions or to act as characters or objects in the story.

One instructor started an ESL book club, with special bookmarks and regular meeting times (ESL Meet), at which students present book reviews or recommend books to one another. About six to ten students attend the meetings, with about twenty-five to thirty active club members (Suresh, 2003).

## Developing Reading Comprehension

Comprehension is the key to meaning. Readers generally form some initial hypothesis about the content or main idea of a book or a reading passage based on their expectations, title, first sentence, previous knowledge of genre, or other clues. Reading further, the reader modifies the initial prediction (Gunning, 2005). Getting the gist of a reading passage is the most important skill a reader can develop, because getting the main idea makes further reading more purposeful, facilitates recall, and helps to make sense of the supporting details.

## CLASSROOM GLIMPSE: Daily Reading Interventions

*Based on observations during the previous school year of those children who had made unexpected progress in reading skills, Mrs. Greaver-Pohzehl, a second-grade teacher, devised a new program involving the use of volunteers and a take-home reading program.*

*In the classroom, the students received daily directed, guided reading instruction with the teacher or a classroom aide to introduce and discuss new texts and build comprehension. Parent volunteers, trained to provide appropriate prompts for struggling readers, provided additional daily opportunities for children to reread texts for fluency, practice spelling words, and develop phonemic awareness through games and activities. Each child received a tape recorder and checked out books to read or tapes to listen to at home with a parent.*

*By the end of the year every child in the program made progress—all of them advanced at least two reading divisions on the district's literacy scale; developed a greater range of reading and writing skills; developed a stronger, more fluent voice while reading; and showed positive attitudes toward reading and writing. (Greaver & Hedberg, 2001)*

**Teaching of Reading Matched to Proficiency Levels**    Teaching reading to English learners implies that reading activities can be matched to the language-proficiency level of the student. Omaggio (1986) provided strategies that she considers appropriate for several proficiency levels. These separate beginning from intermediate and advanced levels.

## BEST PRACTICE: Reading Strategies for Students at Different Levels of Proficiency

*Novice:* anticipating/predicting, skimming, scanning, extracting specific information, contextual guessing, prereading activities, simple fill-in-the-blanks

*Intermediate/Advanced:* Comprehension checks, guessing from context, clue searching, making inferences, scrambled stories, extracting specific information, skimming, scanning, paraphrasing, note taking/outlining, passage completion, understanding idioms, understanding discourse structures, understanding linking words. (Omaggio, 1986, pp. 153–155)

**TABLE 6.7** Strategies That Readers Can Use When Comprehension Fails

| Strategy | Description |
| --- | --- |
| Rereading: Text-Based Answers | *Text-based* means one can skim the text and find the answer. (1) |
| "Right There" Answers | Answer is easily found in the book. (2) |
| "Think and Search" Answers | Reader needs to put together different parts of the reading to obtain a solution. (2) |
| Rereading: Reader-Based Answers | *Reader based* means the reader must infer the answer: Look for clues from text. (1) |
| "Author and You" Answer | Solution lies in a combination of what is in the story plus the reader's experience. (2) |
| "On My Own" Answers | Answer comes from one's own experience. (2) |
| Visual Imagery | Before rereading, students discuss what pictures come to mind. Younger children can draw these pictures, and older children can use verbal description. Ask students to form mental images while rereading. (3) |
| Think-Aloud | Students self-monitor comprehension by asking, "Does this make sense?" as they read. What question can they ask that will help them focus on what they need in order for it to make sense? (1) |
| Suspending Judgment | Read ahead when a new concept is not well explained, seeking information to develop clarity. (1) |
| Reciprocal Teaching | Students predict, summarize, ask questions, and suspend judgment, using these techniques with one another. (4) |
| Mine, Yours, and Ours | Students make individual summaries and compare with a partner, then write a joint paragraph outlining their similarities and differences. (5) |
| Summary Pairs | Students read aloud to each other and summarize what they have read. (5) |
| Shrinking Stories | Students write their own versions of a passage in 25 words or less. (6) |
| Simply Put | Students rewrite a selection so that students two or three years younger might understand it. (6) |

*Sources:* (1) Barr & Johnson (1997); (2) Raphael (1986); (3) Gamrel & Bales (1986); (4) Palinscar & Brown (1984); (5) Lipton & Hubble (1997); (6) Suid & Lincoln (1992).

**Strategies When Comprehension Fails**   Too often, students do not know what to do when they cannot comprehend a text. Table 6.7 presents several strategies that are useful when comprehension fails.

Each of these strategies can be developed using a variety of reading selections. When introducing a new comprehension strategy, the teacher explains when the strategy is useful, models the process, and then gives the students guided practice.

**Text Genres**    Readers must become familiar with the features, structures, and rhetorical devices of different types of texts, such as narrative, descriptive, and analytic. For example, a government document presents a formal, official point of view, whereas a personal or family story conveys the subject from a different, more intimate perspective. Even samples from the same type of content—storytelling, for example—feature various genres, such as folktales, myths, legends, and autobiographies. Scientific writing includes varied genres—peer-reviewed academic journals, "high-brow" general magazines (e.g., *Nature*), popular magazines (e.g., *Wired*), science fiction, and even comic books. Students need to be taught text processing techniques (how to take notes, how to reread text for answers to study questions, how to read charts and picture captions) and then held to a high level of recall about the information they read (Anderson & Gunderson, 2004).

*Multicultural literature* helps students see life from a variety of points of view, compare cultures on different aspects of life, and see their own culture represented in the curriculum. Anthologies of multicultural literature present a wealth of materials, some grouped thematically (see Harris, 1997; Monroe, 1999). *Multicultural Voices in Contemporary Literature* (Day, 1994) presents thirty-nine authors and illustrators from twenty different cultures. A follow-up book, *Latina and Latino Voices in Literature for Children and Teenagers* (Day, 1997), has biographies of thirty-eight authors, with synopses of their work, as well as an extensive list of resources for books in English on Latino themes. Day (2003) is a follow-up extending the Latina and Latino theme.

**Grade-Level-Appropriate Texts**    Students read at grade level for schooling purposes, but they can also read below grade level for entertainment and above grade level with assistance. Many classrooms have "leveled" books so that students' frustration level can be allayed. However, mentoring is essential to help students grow.

Several sources are available that suggest *age-level-appropriate reading material.* Public libraries have detailed reference books that list thousands of children's books, including the Caldecott and Newbery Medal books. Sometimes a school will send out a list of recommended books to every family. At one school, fourth graders prepared their own list of books and duplicated it for every child in the school. Generally speaking, children respect the teacher's recommendations, but if a recommended book is not grade-level appropriate, the young reader may become discouraged.

**Critical Thinking**    An important aspect of schooling in a democracy is the ability to think for oneself—to analyze ideas, separate fact from opinion, support opinions from reading, make inferences, and solve problems. Critical thinking can create self-understanding because a person might approach significant issues in life differently with the acquisition of analytic skills.

Thinking skills are an important part of reading comprehension. Identifying fact and opinion, identifying cause and effect, using a text to draw conclusions and make inferences, and evaluating the credibility of text are among the skills incorporated into high-quality reading lessons. The four-volume set *Critical Thinking Handbook* (grades K–3, 4–6, 7–9, and high school) presents lesson plans that have been remodeled to include critical thinking strategies (available from the Center for Critical Thinking at Sonoma State University, online at www.sonoma.edu/cthink).

**Creative Thinking and Risk Taking**    Creativity is a part of cognition and should not be confined to music and art classes. During problem solving and project-based learning, for example, once the requirements of a problem or project have been surveyed and the goals determined, creative thinking can be used to generate possible solutions. Creative thinking can be used in every reading lesson to generate alternatives and to expand the point of view of reading comprehension: What if the main character were female rather than male? What if the book were set in the seventeenth century rather than in the modern era? What if the setting were Thailand rather than the United States? Can we imagine a different outcome?

This focus opens the door to a fertile terrain, the imaginary, a world in which possibilities are unlimited and constraints of reality do not pinch. In addition, use of the imaginary can stimulate scholars to explore other cultures, other times in history, and nonhuman worlds, such as in science fiction, myths, or animal tales.

The genre of brain puzzles is also mentally stimulating. Books of such puzzles can be found at major bookstores and are fun to use to keep young brains alert.

Both critical and creative thinking are integral parts of the human mind that enrich any part of the curriculum. Thinking is the key to the creation of meaning, during which children learn to react not just in response to the immediate, real world before them, but also in accord with their internal world, the world of ideas. Channeling the power of thought is an important part of language education in the context of cognitive development.

**Language Experience Approach**   A language development activity that encourages students to respond to events in their own words is the language experience approach (LEA). As a student tells a story or relates an event, the teacher writes it down and reads it back so that students can eventually read the text for themselves. Because the students are providing their own phrases and sentences, they find the text relevant and interesting and generally have little trouble reading it. The importance of LEA in developing the language of English learners cannot be overemphasized. Its advantages include the following:

- LEA connects students to their own experiences and activities by having them express themselves orally.
- LEA reinforces the notion that sounds can be transcribed into specific symbols and that those symbols can then be used to re-create the ideas expressed.
- LEA provides texts for specific lessons on vocabulary, grammar, writing conventions, structure, and more.

## CLASSROOM GLIMPSE: Using LEA after Reading

*Sixth-grade teacher Laura Bowen used LEA to help reinforce key concepts after her students read about the Qin dynasty.*

*After finishing the lesson on the Qin dynasty, I had my class brainstorm key ideas. I wrote their points on the board and then asked them to tell a story about a fictional family of three living during that era. The only restriction was that they had to keep in mind the key points. Their story follows:*

> *Chang, Li, and their son, Wei, lived during the Qin dynasty. Li was excited because Chang was able to buy the family some land. A few days later, Chang was taken by the emperor to go build the Great Wall. Li and Wei were sad. They did not like the emperor, because he had strict laws and punishments. Chang died on the long walk to the Great Wall. Li and Wei grew crops so they could survive. They hoped a new and better emperor would come and overthrow the mean one.*

*After the class finished their story, they read it aloud many times. This experience helped them to personalize history.*

**Directed Reading–Thinking Activity**    Students need to understand that proficient readers actively work with text by making predictions as they read. Directed reading–thinking activity (DR–TA) is a teacher-guided activity that leads students through the prediction process until they are able to do it on their own. The teacher asks students to make predictions and then read to confirm or disconfirm their ideas. The key to successful DR–TA lessons is for students to update their ideas as new information is revealed.

## Developing Literary Response and Analysis Skills

Students of literature need to acquire a set of literary response skills in order to fully appreciate fiction, nonfiction, and other creative work. Literary criticism consists of analysis of plot, character, theme, and creative language use. These skills are described and levels provided in the ELD and ELA frameworks.

To help develop a community of readers and help students understand the richness of the literacy experience, teachers engage them in literature response groups. After having read a piece of literature, the teacher and a small group meet to discuss the piece. Each student is given an opportunity to express ideas about the story before a general discussion begins. The teacher listens and, after each student has had a turn, opens the discussion with a thought-provoking question.

As points are made, the teacher guides the students to deeper understandings by, for example, asking them to support their point with words from the text and asking what words or devices the author used to invoke a mood, establish a setting, describe a character, move the plot along, and so on.

## CLASSROOM, GLIMPSE: A Literature Response Group

*Teacher Christina Dotts describes how literature response groups worked in her second-grade classroom. The students had read Tomi dePaola's* Now One Foot, Now the Other *(1981).*

> *In planning this lesson, I was a bit apprehensive about the students' overall reaction to this type of discussion. However, I found that they enjoyed discussing the story in a more intimate setting as opposed to a whole-class discussion. These second graders were indeed up to the challenge of using higher-order thinking skills. One of my objectives was for the students to verbalize their thoughts and convey meaning. They needed practice in doing so. I discovered my students had definite ideas about major issues—illness, hospitals, family members, working, being responsible, and being good friends. Their concerns were very important in their lives, and this piece of literature and forum for discussion provided an opportunity for them to talk about these concerns. Students felt proud to lead discussions and exercise their leadership skills.*

## Secondary-Level Content Reading

Reading in the content areas in high school is addressed according to specific disciplines in Chapter 7. However, there are fundamental reading adaptations that teachers of English learners can make in their planning and instruction (see Box 6.3).

---

**Box 6.3**  Generic Reading Adaptations for English Learners at the Secondary Level

- Use read-alouds.
- Create a print-rich environment.
- Accommodate students' interests and backgrounds.
- Read, read, read.
- Use systematic, varied strategies for recognizing words.
- Use a variety of reading methods to raise interest.
- Integrate language activities.
- Activate students' prior knowledge.
- Provide authentic purpose, materials, and audiences in the development of oracy and literacy.
- Construct, examine, and extend meaning.
- Provide explicit instruction of what, when, and why.
- Provide opportunities for students to take control of the reading process.

---

Despite the success of approaches based on social constructionism, a generation of students is being taught how to read through a series of controlled, behaviorally based lessons. Such programs as Reading Mastery, Open Court, and Direct Instruction employ teacher-centered methods in step-by-step curricula that follow highly structured, interactive scripts (Groves, 2001). Reading Mastery requires students to be grouped in precisely measured skill levels, and Open Court expects teachers to follow an exact script verbatim day by day to reinforce skills. Only time will tell if the students taught in this manner learn to read both for academics and for enjoyment. Groves makes the point that gifted students are not taught in such a prescriptive manner. It may be that being taught to read in this didactic manner is yet another social-class marker in the United States.

### Writing and the English Learner

Hand in hand with reading goes writing. Writing is no longer an activity that can be postponed until English learners can speak fluently: "Child ESL learners, early in their development of English, can write English and can do so for various purposes" (Hudelson, 1984, p. 221). Writing in English is not only a key to academic success but also an outlet for self-expression.

Although much has been written about the writing process, it is more accurate to use the term *writing processes*. Most writers do not simply draft, revise, edit, and publish. Instead, the process is recursive, with much travel back and forth from drafting to redrafting, from editing to redrafting, from revising to redrafting, and so forth. Many teachers teach a five-step writing process, but in reality, in a classroom with a rich learning environment, students are in various stages simultaneously. If teachers honor the reality of the learning process, rather than try to impose a lockstep system, the mind stays engaged throughout the struggle to "write down" and clarify thinking.

## Generation 1.5 and College Writing

Students who are still in the process of acquiring English are entering colleges and universities at an unprecedented rate. The good news is that English learners are being encouraged to pursue higher education. The bad news is that few are ready to perform college-level work. In the California State University system of twenty-two campuses, for example, 46 percent of the 36,655 first-year students who enrolled in the fall of 2001 failed the English Placement Test and therefore could not enroll in English 101 (Tresaugue, 2002). Why are so many students unprepared for college writing?

Many first-year college students are Generation 1.5 students, U.S.-educated English-language learners who immigrated to the United States while they were in elementary or high school, or who were born in the United States but grew up speaking a language other than English at home. These students are diverse in terms of their prior educational experience, native- and English-language proficiency, language dominance, and academic literacy. They have learning needs that differ from other English learners and can benefit from targeted intervention in academic writing and other skills.

Students' prior academic work and social situation may hamper their ability to participate in discourse at the university level. To become insiders in the world of academic culture, students must learn to write essays that express their personal values, experiences, knowledge, and questions. In this way, students can discover an "enlarging horizon that every discourse can open to [their] view," and "gradually enter the community of 'knowers' while retaining their own voice" (Spellmeyer, 1989, p. 274).

## Writing as a Social Construction

Writing is no longer seen as a lone pursuit of the individual. Farr (1994) studied the motivation of a group of Mexican immigrants in Chicago. The motivation for many students to improve their writing is not so much internal or intrinsic, but rather lies embedded in the social context in which the writing takes place.

Rodby (1999) described case studies of ELD students who were more or less able to draw on multiple and overlapping systems of support from work, home, church, clubs, peer interactions, faculty, and social/cultural systems to revise their writing in a pre-first-year English class. These students are examples of the way their social contexts influenced their literacy behavior, which in turn influenced their academic potential. Therefore, interventions to improve their writing must be sensitive to context and culture.

## Stages of Writing Development for Young English Learners

Writing behavior on the part of children who are native speakers of English reflects a series of developmental stages, starting with *scribbling and drawing*. Then, at the *prephonemic* stage, the writer uses real letters, but the meaning stands for whole ideas. Moving on to the *early phonemic* stage, the writer uses letters—usually consonants—to stand for words, and at the letter-naming stage, vowels may accompany the consonants in an attempt to approximate phonemic sequences. As the writer goes through a *transitional* phase as he or she moves toward *conventional* spelling, the child uses "invented" or "temporary" spelling to convey meaning. If children are held to correct spelling, they write much less (Hadaway, Vardell, & Young, 2002).

The actual spelling that children write is a fascinating indicator of their thinking and their emotions, as well as their progress in learning conventional forms. Kress (2000) looked at one child's form, *dided* ("died"), and speculates that the child is struggling with overregularization of past tense, while another child, Emily, prints the upper case *E* with four horizontal strokes, perhaps an indication that this letter carries extra signification as the first letter of her name. Emergent spelling, whether it stems from first- or second-language acquisition, is a rich source of knowledge about intellectual and interlanguage development.

Beginning English learners usually enter English in the transitional phase; that is, they generally catch on to the sound–symbol principle of the alphabet, even if their own language is ideographic. The more similar their home language alphabet is to the English alphabet, the more easily their writing skills will transfer to English. Word banks can be a rich source of vocabulary building; students can collect words on index cards and alphabetize them, classify them, illustrate them, or nominate them for Word of the Week contests (Lipton & Hubble, 1997). Beginning students can engage in interactive journal writing with their teacher, or complete simple frame sentences such as "I like _____ because _____." They can copy words and sentences, or they can make their own books by copying and illustrating simple books (Hadaway et al., 2002).

Intermediate English learners increase their vocabulary as they attempt more complex sentences while writing. They can try their hand at various genres of personal and expressive writing, such as letter writing, as well as various types of academic writing such as note taking, short essays, and lists. Exercises in sentence combining help English learners extend the length and variety of their writing. Students at this level of English acquisition are struggling with the correct forms of plural nouns, pronouns, verb tenses, and subject–verb agreement. Many errors are at the sentence level, such as the correct use of adverb and adjective phrases and clauses, sentence fragments and run-on constructions, and collocation errors (verb + preposition combinations are not accurate) (Leki, 1992).

Advanced English learners write responses to many academic assignments, such as personal or literary essays and written work on worksheets, laboratory manuals, and test questions. Their writing may feature many of the issues with which native speakers struggle, such as topic focus, parallel sentence structure, and paragraph cohesion.

## Handwriting in English

The era has passed when handwriting was neglected. All students, but particularly English learners with primary languages that are nonalphabetic, need to learn the basics of letter formation, letter size and proportion, spacing, slant, alignment, and line quality (Barbe, Wasylyk, Hackney, & Braun, 1984). Letters are best learned when sorted by shape, with the line letters first (l, t, i, L, T, I, E, F, H), followed by angle (k, v, w, x, y, z, A, K, M, N, V, W, X, Y, Z); circle/line (o, a, b, d, p, q, O, Q); open circle (c, e, C, G); line/half-circle (B, D, P, R); curved (h, m, n, u, U); partial curve (f, r, j, g, J); and S-curve (s, S). TPR can be used to link physical actions with demonstrated commands to orient students to the forms of letters (Boyd-Batstone, 2006).

## The Writing Workshop

In the workshop environment, students are free to talk with one another as they write. English learners can draw on other students, not just the teacher, as a resource, and can in turn use their own experiences to enrich their writing and that of their peers. The teacher's role, then, becomes that of facilitator and listener.

Writing can be fun if students write collaboratively. Students can brainstorm and share ideas and then write these ideas in a list form that resembles poetry. One useful convention is the phrase "I used to _____ but now _____." Once the story is completed, it can be copied onto a chart and used for reading practice. This is a version of the language experience approach that connects students to their own experiences and activities by having them express themselves orally.

Students may enjoy writing buddy journals, a kind of diary in which a pair of students write back and forth to each other (Bromley, 1989). The teacher models this by suggesting sample topics and perhaps putting a daily journal entry on the board: "Today I feel excited about the field trip. I got up extra early to find something to pack in my lunch!" (The buddy journals are not as private as a teacher–student dialogue journal might be, because every two weeks or so the students change buddies, and the new buddies have access to previous entries.)

The process approach to writing involves several stages: the planning or prewriting stage, the writing stage, and the feedback/editing stage.

### The Writing Process: Prewriting

During *prewriting*, students are involved in oral language experiences that develop their need and desire to write. These activities may include talking and listening about shared experiences, reading literature, brainstorming, or creating role-playing or other fantasy activities. Mind mapping encourages students to generate and organize their ideas graphically on chart paper or on the chalkboard. Some classes may use *Inspiration*, a computer program that facilitates idea generation.

The prewriting phase helps to generate, incubate, explore, test, and integrate ideas. Most writers find it often helps to talk about a topic, bouncing ideas off others, benefiting from the questions others ask as they shape and explore ideas. Not only does this help students build a representation of the topic about which they are writing, but also the challenges, prompts, and questions from collaborators help to fashion a working representation of the assignment or task (Flower, 1994).

Some writers experience prolonged silent periods, whereas others report heightened emotional states or sudden bursts of productivity. The best writing springs from creative sources within the person that may manifest as the individual becomes "distracted, preoccupied, or temperamental. If new ideas are bubbling, the individual may become restless, excitable, emphatic even, while lack of manifest progress may result in gloom and despondency" (Smith, 1982, p. 126). The most profound education reaches deep into the individual, and in reaching deeply, evokes emotional reaction. Teachers who respect this passion sympathize with its companion emotions. The alternative? Apathy.

### The Writing Process: Drafting

The drafting stage involves quickly capturing ideas. There may be several false starts, changes of mind, and search for more ideas. Writers do the best they can in spelling, vocabulary, and syntax, without a concern for accuracy. This is followed by revision. Students share and discuss the content and clarity of their writing, drawing on the teacher as a resource for advice and support. This helps students to expand their thinking and communicate more expressively before editing perfects the form and grammar.

A *word wall* or *word bank* is useful for English learners, providing a visual representation of words they may need to draw on while writing. For example, a pictorial word wall for a unit on fairy tales might include matched pictures and the printed words *queen, king, castle, crown,* and other words that a writer might need to use. This helps English learners to be more fluent as they draft their ideas.

**Self-Correction and Revision**  Writers face similar problems as they draft. Gregory and Kuzmich (2005) suggest that the following components can be used for student self-assessment:

> *Ideas:* Is my message clear? Do I know enough about my topic? Did I try hard to make it interesting?
>
> *Organization:* Does the paper have a good beginning? Are things told in a logical order? Does the paper end well?
>
> *Conventions:* Are there paragraphs? Are words spelled correctly? Did I use appropriate capitalization and punctuation?
>
> *Voice:* Does the writing sound like me? Are the thoughts clear to the reader? Will the reader be interested?

**Feedback through Peer Response and Writing Conferences**  Students can give one another feedback through formal "sharing" meetings, organized by the teacher, in which students read their work and ask peers for comments; or they can be informal, student-initiated interactions. Peer response can be more valuable than teacher feedback in helping writers analyze their own drafts (Reid, 1993). To be useful, peer responding must be modeled and taught as part of the writing process from the beginning so that students are aware of writing for their peers as well as for the teacher.

One way to shape peer response is to provide students with a peer review sheet that is specifically designed for the writing prompt or the evaluation criteria for the final paper (Campbell, 1998). These might include the following:

- Is the title specific, related to the central idea?
- Does the introductory paragraph preview the entire paper?
- Is the thesis clearly stated? Does it tie the ideas together?
- Are paragraphs logically organized? Are claims supported by evidence?
- Is there a clear differentiation between writer's ideas and those of other authors?
- Is there a concluding paragraph discussing the significance of the ideas?
- Is there appropriate grammar and usage?

Peer response to writing is not editing. It should include feedback about the content, point of view, and tone of the work. This helps students focus on the communicative content of the writing and draws them together in a more respectful sharing of the messages they intend.

Individual writing conferences with the teacher are interviews in which the teacher listens to each student talk about the work in progress, commenting and asking questions to help the student organize and focus the writing. This questioning also helps the teacher understand the student's topic and focus. Ideally, the tone of the conference makes it clear that the writer is in charge. The writer speaks first to set the agenda and communicate the intended meaning. The teacher may then query specific sections ("What is the main point of this part?") and offer suggestions as alternatives.

**The Writing Process: Editing**    Editing takes place after the message is intact, to "fix up" errors or mistakes in usage and spelling. Students who learn to self-edit can examine their own writing critically and improve it. The teacher's proofreading is useful only if the students can use it to improve their own writing.

If a perfected version is not necessary, students may archive their rough drafts in a portfolio, without rewriting. If, however, the writing is published or publicly shared, and students are to achieve the pride of authorship, accuracy in such areas as spelling is more warranted.

**Error Correction**    In the early stages of writing English, fluency is a much more vital goal than accuracy. With English learners, the teacher must consider the level of their general language proficiency before decisions about error correction can be made. Law and Eckes (2000) suggested that with younger children and newcomers, one should encourage expression of ideas without correcting grammar. Writers should be rewarded for their courage in trying new formats and more complicated sentence syntax, with encouragement for risk taking. Error correction is a process in which attention is paid to the communication of meaning and the learner is guided toward self-correction.

Proofreading marks should be simple and consistent. Moreover, teachers may wish to use *restrictive correcting,* a focus on only a few types of errors at one time (Bartram & Walton, 1994, p. 80). Some instructors set certain standards of submission before accepting a paper, such as requiring that a word-processed paper be electronically spellchecked.

**Publishing**    Ways of publishing can vary: A play is performed, a story is bound into a book for circulation in the class library, a poem is read aloud, an essay is posted on a bulletin board, a video is made of a student reading aloud, a class newspaper is circulated to the community. Desktop publishing software has made more readily accessible the look of professional typesetting and layout, usually using a simple page layout computer program combined with a word processor. When printed, the class newspaper can circulate to the school and community.

## Issues with ESL Writing

*Selecting a topic* can sometimes be a concern for English learners. Not all writers find a topic of a personal nature, such as childhood experiences, particularly fruitful for generating ideas. Being familiar with a topic is no guarantee of writing ease. Just because a topic is popular with native English speakers is no guarantee that the topic will enable English learners.

*Establishing a tone* may be difficult for English learners, especially at the young adult level. Tones to avoid are flippancy (disrespectful levity), sarcasm (contemptuous remarks), sentimentality (shallow feeling), self-righteousness (taking on a special claim to virtue), belligerence (trying to bully the reader into agreement), and apology ("poor little me") (Packer & Timpane, 1997).

*Issues of plagiarism* may be difficult to convey. Students may feel pressure to help others by letting them copy, they may have different "rules" about using others' work in their own cultures, or they may simply work together in a way that results in identical copies of student work. At a deeper level, however, plagiarism may occur because English learners feel coerced into writing in English, either due to social, academic, or economic demands on their lives, or to feeling a lack of ownership over English (Pennycook, 1998). The best solution to the problem of plagiarism is to give students support and accurate feedback at various stages in their writing, and to offer specific guidelines and training in using "textual borrowing" strategies (Bloch, 2001; Barks & Watts, 2001, p. 246).

*The use of dictionaries and the use of the library* are two areas in which English learners may need guidance and direction. Many students rely on bilingual dictionaries, which in their brevity do not always supply accurate translations. Teaching dictionary skills explicitly can be of great help to students, especially those whose first language is written in the same alphabet as English (see Feuerstein & Schcolnik [1995], for an example of such instruction). International students sometimes rely on pocket translating devices, which do not always supply accurate translations.

English learners may not be familiar with the use of a library, especially if such resources are not available in their native culture. Students who know how to use a library may simply need special training to be able to make use of the library's features, such as the electronic card catalog. In other cases, students may have come to rely on the libraries within their own families, if they are among the elite, or they may never have had occasion use a library. They will require more help in learning to navigate in a library. Table 6.8 summarizes adaptations in writing for English learners.

 In summary, current approaches to literacy and oracy instruction vary in emphasis, but the best teaching supports the following principles: (1) integration of language and content teaching, (2) use of authentic language and materials, (3) recognition of student diversity and learning styles, (4) development of cognitive strategies, (5) use and support of students' first languages and cultures, (6) importance of interaction and collaborative learning, and (7) student engagement in purposeful learning tasks.

## VIDEO WORKSHOP:   "Writing Strategies"

In this video, a teacher demonstrates Guided Writing as an effective strategy for developing literacy in English language learners. She uses sentences the students have written to help them learn effective paragraph writing strategies.

To access the video, log on to MyLabSchool at www.mylabschool.com, enter Assignment ID **ENV3** into the **Assignment Finder**, and select the video entitled "Writing Strategies." Watch the video, complete the questions that follow, and e-mail your responses to your professor for credit.

**(î)mylabschool™**

**TABLE 6.8**    Adaptations in Writing for English Learners

| Writing Strategies | Description |
| --- | --- |
| Write. Write. Write. | Provide students with a wide variety of opportunities to write and share their writing.<br>Write in all subject areas.<br>Encourage students to use and practice writing across the curriculum. |
| Use authentic writing. | Use tasks that have real purpose and real audiences. |
| Use examples of good writing. | Provide access to a variety of written materials and examples of good writing.<br>Make the expression of thoughts and ideas the primary goal, with correctness of form secondary. |
| Model writing as a process. | Writing is developmental and takes time; steps in writing are made visible and practiced. |
| Use writing conferences. | Confer individually with students on a regular basis to enhance students' self-assessment of their own writing skills and their understanding of the processes. |
| Teach students "how to write." | Provide explicit instruction, often in the form of mini-lessons, demonstrating what students are expected to do in their writing. |
| Allow time to learn supportive skills. | Reinforce writing skills such as prewriting, planning, drafting, revising, and editing on a daily basis; establish a routine for these behaviors and encourage students to use their own strategies, move naturally between states, and work at their own pace. |
| Provide clear criteria for evaluation. | Foster independence and responsibility by providing criteria (e.g., rubrics, exemplars) students can use to evaluate their own writing. |
| Include contextual instruction in grammar. | Grammar is taught within the context of writing, not in isolation, and also emphasizes strategies consistent with individual learner needs. |
| Use the inquiry method. | Use structured assignments based on inquiry to help students produce writing that expands strategy use, accommodates a variety of purposes and audiences, and addresses increasingly complex topics. |
| Use writing portfolios. | Use portfolios to monitor and evaluate students' writing abilities in different genres and to provide students with greater responsibility for their progress as writers through self-assessment of their own work. |
| Involve students in the evaluation process. | Students are held accountable for their own growth and employ multiple measures to assess literacy skills. |

# CHAPTER SEVEN

# Planning and Implementing SDAIE-Based Content Instruction

## PLANNING SDAIE LESSONS

When instruction is delivered in English and the student has not achieved advanced proficiency in English, a fundamental chasm undermines learning. This gulf between instruction and comprehension cannot be bridged by reducing the standards of expectation for the student—it must be overcome by adapting instruction to the student's second-language acquisition level by using specially designed academic instruction in English (SDAIE). This chapter addresses pedagogy for English learners by focusing on SDAIE-enhanced curriculum design and lesson delivery, cognitive academic language proficiency, and use of learning strategies as core elements in teaching English-language development and content area knowledge.

SDAIE is an approach used in multilinguistic content classrooms to provide language support to students while they are learning academic subjects, rather than expecting them to "sink or swim" in a content class designed for native English speakers. This can take place either in mainstream classes made up of native English speakers mixed with non-native English speakers of intermediate proficiency, or in classes consisting solely of non-native speakers who operate at similar English proficiency levels (Echevarria, Vogt, & Short, 2004).

Planning affords teachers the opportunity to adapt lessons for English learners so instruction is understandable and interactive. An SDAIE lesson plan follows a fairly predictable format. Box 5.3 describes the five main parts of the SDAIE lesson.

SDAIE combines second-language acquisition principles with elements of quality teaching so students can improve listening, speaking, reading, and writing as they study an academic subject. SDAIE is the preferred method used by both middle and high schools when primary-language instruction is not available or is offered in only one primary language.

Instead of organizing this chapter by content area—treating only mathematics in its own section, for example—I have organized this material by the main parts of the SDAIE lesson. By viewing the same SDAIE principle across several content domains, it is easier to grasp the concept.

### Setting Objectives

Knowledge and language cannot be separated—language is the brain's input device, whether verbal or figural (pictures, numbers, graphs). Content instruction (mathematics, social studies, literature, science, physical education, visual arts, music, and performance arts) takes place using language as the medium, so language objectives are an integral part of content instruction. To maintain grade-level content objectives and sustain the academic expectations for achievement, both language and content objectives are included in SDAIE lessons. Moreover, the current emphasis on cognitive teaching mandates that learning strategy objectives be included as well. This gives every SDAIE lesson a three-part focus.

**Standards-Based Content Objectives**    The teacher first specifies learning goals using standards documents, usually in the form of school-district curriculum programs. The teacher divides the overall goals for the year into units, then into specific lessons, and then into the content area objectives for each lesson.

Teachers usually sequence content objectives to match the material in mandated textbooks. The challenge is to use concrete means to introduce abstract ideas (teaching with hands-on materials, visuals, and demonstrations to lead into those ideas that are difficult to demonstrate or that require more oral or written skills).

Table 7.1 displays content domains, typical content standards topics, and matching objectives. The idea is to accomplish one content objective in one lesson.

**Content-Related Language Objectives**    The language objectives of an SDAIE lesson are drawn from the ELD standards. Because students in a class are usually at various CELDT levels—even a single student usually scores at different CELDT levels on listening/speaking, reading, and writing—the teacher plans for differentiated instruction by incorporating more than one level of language skill in each lesson. The language objective must also address the language needed to accomplish the content objective. In other words, if the lesson features a science laboratory objective, the language objective is integrated with laboratory activity—for example, making observations orally and recording data by writing in a lab manual.

*The CALLA Handbook* (Chamot & O'Malley, 1994) is a valuable resource for helping teachers understand the language demands of various disciplines. Each of the chief subjects—science, mathematics, social studies, and literature and composition—is the focus of a chapter in which the authors specifically address language demands.

Table 7.2 illustrates the alignment of content and language objectives for two CELDT levels. This demonstrates differentiated instruction.

**Content-Integrated Learning Strategy Objectives**    Learning strategies help students learn *how* to learn. This includes a range of knowledge, including learning how to use graphic organizers to generate or evaluate ideas; learning how to plan, self-monitor, and self-evaluate; acquiring academic vocabulary, study skills, and reading strategies; or improving group work, social skills, and emotional self-motivation or self-control.

## CLASSROOM GLIMPSE: Planning for SDAIE Science

*In a sheltered (SDAIE) seventh-grade science class, students improve their English language skills while studying about the universe. The teacher's primary goal is for students to understand the content materials (in this case, about the origin of the universe). But she also spends some time helping students with language-related issues (e.g., academic vocabulary, reading skills) that pertain to the science unit they are studying. The exposure to higher-level language (through the content materials) and the explicit focus on language issues by the teacher set the stage for successful language acquisition. (Brinton, 2003, p. 203)*

**TABLE 7.1**  Content Domains, Content Standards, Typical Topics, and Matching Objectives (Sources for standards are in parentheses)

| Content Domains | Content Standard | Typical Topic | Matching Objective |
|---|---|---|---|
| Mathematics | (Gr. 7) (Algebra and Functions). Students express quantitative relationships by using algebraic expressions, equations, inequalities, and graphs. (1) | Finding the unknown | Identify orally or in writing the pre-algebra concept of finding the unknown. |
| Social Studies | (Gr. 6) (World History and Geography: Ancient Civilizations). 6.2. Students analyze the geographic, political, economic, religious, and social structures of the early civilizations of Mesopotamia, Egypt, and Kush. (2) | Religion of Egypt | Identify Egyptian gods from tomb paintings. |
| Literature | (Gr. 11 & 12) (Literary Response and Analysis). 3.4. Analyze ways in which poets use imagery, personification, figures of speech, and sounds to evoke readers' emotions. | Analyze poem | Analyze "We Real Cool" by Gwendolyn Brooks (Brooks, 1944) for plot, language, and theme. |
| Science | (Gr. 1) (Life Sciences). 2b. Students know both plants and animals need water, animals need food, and plants need light. (4) | Plants need light | Expose plants to different conditions of light to observe consequences. |
| Physical Education | (High school course 1, Standard 2). 2.7. Develop and implement a one-month personal physical fitness plan. (5) | Personal physical fitness | Compare two kinds of exercise that could become part of a one-month personal physical fitness plan. |
| Visual Arts | (Gr. 4) (Aesthetic Valuing). 4.3. Describe how using the language of the visual arts helps to clarify personal responses to works of art. (6) | Interpreting a painting | Compare personal responses to Picasso's *Las Meninas* with Renoir's *The Luncheon of the Boating Party at Bougival.* |
| Music | (Gr. 5) (Historical and Cultural Context). 3.2. Identify different or similar uses of musical elements in music from diverse cultures. (7) | Comparing music from different cultures | Contrast the use of drums in three cultural contexts: Brazil, Nigeria, and the United States. |

*(Continued)*

**TABLE 7.1** (*Continued*)

| Content Domains | Content Standard | Typical Topic | Matching Objective |
|---|---|---|---|
| Performance Arts | (Gr. 3) (Creative Expression). 2.2. Create for classmates simple scripts that demonstrate knowledge of basic blocking and stage areas. (8) | Staging a play | In groups, students will act out a scene from the Chinese fable *The Magic Sieve.* |

*Sources:* (1) California Department of Education (1997); (2) www.cde.ca.gov/be/st/ss/hstgrade6.asp; (3) www .cde.ca.gov/be/st/ss/enggrades11-12.asp (English Language Arts Content Standards); (4) www.cde.ca.gov/be/ st/ss/scgrade1.asp; (5) California Department of Education (2004a); (6) http://www.cde.ca.gov/be/st/ss/ vagrade8.asp; (7) http://www.cde.ca.gov/be/st/ss/mugrade5.asp; (8) www.cde.ca.gov/be/st/ss/thgrade3.asp. Brooks, G. (1944). *Selected poems.* New York: Harper & Row.

## Selecting and Modifying Materials

Selecting materials involves an initial choice by the teacher whether to have one main content source or a package of content-related materials (chapters from various texts, video- and audio-tapes, magazine and newspaper articles, encyclopedia entries, literary selections, Internet sources, software programs, etc.). Regardless of what is chosen, the teacher must consider two criteria: Are the content objectives for the lesson adequately presented by the material? Is the material comprehensible to English learners?

The following list enumerates items to consider when selecting materials:

- The information is accurate, up-to-date, and thorough.
- The tasks required of students are appropriate to the discipline and promote critical thinking.
- The text is clearly organized and engaging, with attractive print and layout features that assist students' comprehension.
- The text appeals to a variety of learning styles.
- Sources represented in the text include various literary genres (e.g., narrative, descriptive, analytic).
- The language of the text is straightforward, without complex syntactic patterns, idioms, or excessive jargon.
- New content vocabulary is clearly defined within the text or in a glossary.
- Diagrams, graphs, and charts are clearly labeled and complement and clarify the text.

Content area teachers must also use primary-language resources, such as dictionaries, books, software programs, Internet sites, encyclopedias, textbooks, and illustrated charts as well as people resources, such as cross-age tutors, parents, and community volunteers, in helping students to understand concepts. English learners in the content class are continually exposed to new content material and often find primary-language sources helpful.

Modifying materials may be necessary to help English learners comprehend connected discourse. One of the following approaches may be helpful:

**TABLE 7.2**    Content and Language Objectives for Two CELDT Levels in Two Content Areas (Sources for standards are in parentheses)

| Content Standard | Content Objective | Language Standards | Language Objectives |
|---|---|---|---|
| *Life Sciences (Grade 1)* | | | |
| 2b. Students know both plants and animals need water, animals need food, and plants need light. (1) | Expose plants to different conditions of light to observe consequences. | (Beginning). Responds to simple directions and questions using physical actions <br><br>(Intermediate). Participates in instructional conversations using expanded vocabulary | (Beginning). Working in a group, students will follow verbal directions to set up a plant-light exposure experiment. <br><br>(Intermediate). Students will discuss in a group how to set up an observation sheet for plant-light exposure experiment. |
| *Physical Education (High School Course 1, Standard 2)* | | | |
| 2.7. Develop and implement a one-month personal physical fitness plan. (2) | Compare two kinds of exercise that could become part of a one-month personal physical fitness plan. | (Early Intermediate). Uses writing to convey meaning <br><br>(Early Advanced). Produces independent writing using consistent grammatical forms, mechanics, and word order. | (Early Intermediate). Students will list three reasons for and three reasons against two types of exercise for their personal fitness plan. <br><br>(Early Advanced). Students will write a comparison paragraph giving three reasons for and three reasons against two types of exercise for their personal fitness plan. |

*Sources:* (1) California Department of Education (1997); (2) California Department of Education (2004a).

- Supply an advance organizer for the text that highlights the key topics and concepts in outline form, as focus questions, or as concept maps.
- Change the modality from written to oral. By reading aloud, the teacher can also model the process of posing questions while reading to show prediction strategies used when working with text (see the discussion of directed reading–thinking activity in Chapter 6).
- Selected passages can be tape-recorded for students to listen to as they read along in the text.
- By working in groups, students can share their notes and help one another complete missing parts or correct misunderstood concepts.

## DIFFERENTIATED INSTRUCTIONAL DELIVERY IN THE CONTENT DOMAINS

Planning instructional objectives aligned with content standards is completed; planning now moves to consideration of the needs of the English learner. The following sections address the issue of making instruction meaningful to the learner using various facets of SDAIE.

### Bridging: Accessing Prior Knowledge and Building Schemata

All learning builds on what has been previously learned, because the brain uses schemata to think. When exposed to new information, students access what is already known to them. If little prior knowledge exists, the teacher must supply background knowledge so that instruction can make sense.

## BEST PRACTICE: Ways "into" Literature

Before reading a work of literature, the teacher can employ various ways to access prior knowledge:

- *Anticipation/reaction guides:* A short list of statements to which students agree or disagree
- *Pictures, art, movies:* Visual cues to build a feeling for the setting
- *Physical objects:* Items relating to the reading selection that students identify and discuss
- *Selected read-alouds:* Passages that pique students' interest in the selection

**Assessing What Is Known**    Before teaching, one must assess students' prior knowledge of the concepts and vocabulary that will be presented in the lesson in order to establish a starting point for the lesson, help students to review and stabilize their background information, and avoid spending instructional time on what is already known. Assessments can include a quick written pretest, informal survey, show of hands, pair/share (students discuss in pairs, then tell the whole class), teacher-led oral review, or a student quickwrite of some key points.

Sometimes what is already known is a mishmash of media images and hearsay that must be clarified. At other times, students may not be familiar with, or may disagree with, commonly held beliefs of the mainstream culture.

> [S]tudents bring much more background knowledge to the study of history than we sometimes credit them with. History is, after all, not confined to historians. The media also interpret historical events. . . . [T]here are also persistent historical myths and legends held dear by parts of the larger culture—Betsy Ross sewing the first flag, Columbus discovering a new world, and so forth. For some students, these images are comforting; others may feel excluded by the popular culture's mythologies. (Levstik & Barton, 2001, p. 25)

## BEST PRACTICE: Some Questions to Ask before Beginning

Sometimes students can write down their prior knowledge. Before beginning a new topic, students can interview each other in pairs to ask the following questions:

- Have you ever read or heard anything about this topic?
- Can you tell me about a similar topic that you think will help us learn about this one?
- If you were a reporter and could talk to someone about this topic, who would you seek out? (Adapted from Fisher, Brozo, Frey, & Ivey, 2007)

## CLASSROOM GLIMPSE: Interest-Generating Questions

*Mr. Gruen, a seventh-grade science teacher, wrote the following statement on the board: "It's only a matter of time before Earth will be hit by a large object from space." He then asked students to find a partner and think of three question they would most like answered about this statement. After-ward, he gathered the questions and wrote them on the board, placing a star next to the ones that were similar so students could see common themes of interest. This is part of a larger sequence known as Student Questions for Purposeful Learning (SQPL) (Ediger & Pavlik, 1999; Guthrie & Wigfield, 2000). (Adapted from Fisher et al., 2007, p. 113)*

**Building Background Schemata**    Teachers can provide new experiences that arouse interest in and draw attention to a topic, including field trips, guest speakers, fiction and nonfiction films, experiments, classroom discovery centers, music and songs, poetry and other literature, and computer simulations. To deepen these experiences, the teacher can guide the students to talk and write about them.

## CLASSROOM GLIMPSE: New Experiences to Build Background Knowledge

*The firsthand experiences of a field trip piqued the interest of Dorothy Taylor's students in Virginia history and prepared them for the unit she had planned about colonial America.*

*In the fall, all of the fourth-grade classes in the school went on a field trip to Jamestown, Virginia. The children returned from their trip eager to talk about what they had learned. The field trip and students' enthusiasm were a perfect introduction to the social studies unit on the hardships faced by the Jamestown colonists. The students shared with one another what they knew about Jamestown and colonial America and added to their knowledge and vocabulary by reading and watching a video. (Taylor, 2000, pp. 53–55)*

Teachers who are familiar with the background of the students can elicit beliefs, obser-vations, and questions using students' everyday knowledge and cultural patterns.

## BEST PRACTICE: The Cheche Konnen Science Project

Case studies in classrooms with low-income students from African-American, Haitian, and Latino backgrounds found ways that students deployed "sense-making practices—deep questions, vigorous argumentation, situated guesswork, embedded imagining, multiple perspectives, and innovative uses of everyday words" (Lee, 2005, p. 504)—to construct new meanings that were productive bridges to scientific practices. The teachers in the Cheche Konnen project tapped students' linguistic and cultural experiences to link their prior experiences to instruction, letting students draw on the forms of reasoning they employ in their daily lives as intellectual resources in science learning (Rosebery, Warren, & Conant, 1992; Warren, Ballenger, Ogonowski, Rosebery, & Hudicourt-Barnes, 2001).

**Contextualization**    When students are asked to learn a new concept, the use of materials, resources, and activities can provide contextualization. The verbal presentation of a lesson is supplemented by the use of manipulatives, realia, media, and visual backup as teachers write key words and concepts on the chalkboard or butcher paper, and use graphs, pictures, maps, and other physical props to communicate. By presenting concepts numerous times through various means and in a rich visual, auditory (for example, software programs and Internet sources that offer sounds and experiences), and kinesthetic (drama and skits, "gallery" walks) environment, teachers provide lessons that also appeal to students' different learning styles.

Teachers can contextualize mathematics instruction by having sports fans calculate batting average, points per game, or average speed; students who shop with their parents can help to keep purchases within budget by determining the best-priced item. Many activities in mathematics lend themselves to multicultural reference. Systems of numeration and measurements that originated in ancient civilizations (e.g., Egypt, Inca, Aztec, Maya) can be explored and contrasted (Hatfield, Edwards, Bitter, & Morrow, 2004). Many countries around the world use the metric system, and English learners may have expertise in this system that they could share.

## CLASSROOM GLIMPSE: Cultural Contextualization

*Linda Arieto, a Puerto-Rican American who grew up in a low-income community in the Bronx, shared a great deal in terms of language, culture, race, and class background with her students at Peter Towns Elementary. She was skillful using and responding to multiple varieties of language familiar to her students, such as Puerto-Rican Spanish, Puerto-Rican English, Black English vernacular, and Standard English. In the area of mathematics, she consistently found and used lessons in the text that made sense to her students' cultural backgrounds and urban experiences. She used dominoes as math manipulatives, for example, because they correspond to a game that is popular in Caribbean culture. (Remillar & Cahnmann, 2005, pp. 178–179)*

One example of contextualization is the effort to organize science instruction around common science themes (e.g., nature of matter or magnetic energy) or societal issues (e.g., water pollution, drug addiction) that could make scientific knowledge relevant to students' lives. This makes science more approachable, allowing for more understanding and reflection, and permits key vocabulary to be used again and again.

### Vocabulary Front-Loading

Building vocabulary concept by concept is integral to content teaching. Several strategies are useful in helping English learners acquire vocabulary. Not all vocabulary can be learned when it is pretaught; it can be presented before a lesson, but it must also be repeated again and again during the lesson as well as afterward, for purposes of long-term memory. The following are strategies central to vocabulary retention.

To encourage *visual cueing*, teachers can post key terms on the bulletin board throughout a unit, offer key terms in test questions to be used in short-answer responses, color or highlight new words, and try to connect a concrete image with the term. Teachers cue *episodic memory* by having students role-play the meaning of key terms, demonstrate or model new ideas, and have students create semantic maps, posters, or collages to make key ideas more memorable. To promote *verbal rehearsal*, teachers can praise the use of key terms during student discussions, require key terms to be used during oral presentations, and use a pointer to refer to key terms during lectures (Gregory & Kuzmich, 2005).

### BEST PRACTICE: Vocabulary Development across Proficiency Levels

Instructors of English learners should not assume that all vocabulary instruction must be concrete. Each particular word calls for a unique balance of concrete (real objects, meaningful movement [TPR], modeling, actual experience), symbolic (pictures, charts, icons, maps, models, graphic organizers), or abstract representation (verbal-only explanations orally or in print). Boyd-Batstone (2006) recommends a three-part checklist to judge the best way to teach or depict a new word: (1) Can a real object or experience be used? (2) Is a visual model useful? (3) Can an abstract term be "unpacked" (using word origin, related roots, cognates, primary-language translation, or metaphors)?

### CLASSROOM GLIMPSE: Teaching the Word *Metamorphosis*

*Ny Ha took considerable care to teach her third-grade students the term metamorphosis. She brought in a fishbowl with tadpoles and students observed and recorded the change of life cycle. She provided numerous picture books as well as computer programs that showed sequential pictures. Students made semantic maps of the concept. They made life cycle collages. They looked at models of caterpillars undergoing change. They used Kidspiration to generate mind maps using pictorial clip art. In the end, Ny thinks they "got it"! (Adapted from Boyd-Batstone, 2006)*

### Strategic Teaching Using Multimodalities

Students can be provided with cognitively engaging input (both oral and written) in ways that appeal to their learning styles and preferences. Many students need to see, hear, smell, touch, and feel knowledge all at the same time!

## CLASSROOM GLIMPSE: Supplementing the Verbal Presentation

*In a middle school life science class, when teaching about flowers, Ms. Chen refers students to the explanation in the text (paragraph form), to a diagram of a flower in the text (graphic form), to a wall chart with a different flower (pictorial form), to a text glossary entry (dictionary form), and to actual flowers that students can examine. Through these numerous media, the concepts "petal," "stamen," "pistil," and "sepal" are understood and provide a basis for future study about life-forms. The teacher's task here is to ensure that these multiple sources are organized to communicate clearly and distinguish each concept.*

### Access to Cognitive Academic Language Across the Content Areas

Each academic subject makes distinct demands on the student. For example, mathematics uses discourse that is unlike natural language. Readers may find confusing the tendency to interrupt for the inclusion of formulae. Such texts require a reading rate adjustment because they must be read more slowly and require multiple readings. Charts and graphs are an integral part of the text, not a supplement, and technical language has precise meaning. Besides the key words and phrases heard in lesson presentations, there are also key direction words that students need to know, such as *analyze, compare, contrast, define, describe, discuss, explain, evaluate, illustrate, justify, state,* and *summarize.*

**The Language of Mathematics**    Language difficulties for English learners lie in vocabulary, syntax, semantics, and discourse. Vocabulary in mathematics includes technical words such as *numerator, divisor,* and *exponent.* Words such as *regroup, factor,* and *table* have a meaning different from everyday usage. Two or more mathematical concepts may combine to form a different concept: *line segment, cross multiply.* A variety of terms can signal the same mathematical operation: *Add, and, plus, sum, combine,* and *increased by* all represent addition (Dale & Cuevas, 1992). Sentence structures may involve complex syntax: "____ is to ____ as ____ is to ____" and "____ is ____ percent of ____." Statements must be translated into logical symbols before problems can be completed, posing additional linguistic difficulty.

Problems with meaning (semantics) occur when natural language becomes the language of mathematics. For example, in the problem "Five times a number is two more than ten times the number," students must recognize that "a number" and "the number" refer to the same quantity. However, in the problem "The sum of two numbers is 77. If the first number is ten times the other, find the number," students need to know they are dealing with two numbers. Technical language has precise, codified meaning and must be learned in context.

Abbreviations and other math symbols may need to be interpreted. For example, *ft* for foot or the use of the apostrophe may be confusing for students, especially those who were previously educated in the metric system. Vocabulary charts that include the use of abbreviations and symbols can be placed around the classroom to help students remember. Teachers must be aware of these language differences and mediate the transition in learning a new language to express mathematical concepts.

## CLASSROOM GLIMPSE: Embodying the Language of Ratio

*In a lesson on fractions, Mr. Goodall asked three students to come to the front of the class for a demonstration. One student measured the height and arm spread of a second student while the third student wrote the measurements on the board. The students used these numbers to express the relationships both as a ratio and as a percentage. (Adapted from Weiss & Pasley, 2004, p. 25)*

**The Language of Science**   The four major language areas (vocabulary, syntax, semantics, discourse features) detailed in the section on mathematics are also relevant for science. Students not only have to learn scientific definitions of some common words they may already know (e.g., *energy, sense, work*), but they must also learn complex syntactic structures, which include passive voice, multiple embeddings, and long noun phrases (Pérez & Torres-Guzmán, 2002).

A number of types of text structures are common in science content materials. The *cause/effect* structure links reasons with results or actions with their consequences. The *compare/contrast* structure examines the similarities and differences between concepts. The *time-order* structure shows a sequential relationship over the passage of time (Pérez & Torres-Guzmán, 2002). To assist in their comprehension, students can receive special training in following written instructions for procedures or experiments.

English-language development must be an objective in all science instruction. Teachers should review vocabulary terms to be used in a lesson before beginning, including the names of equipment and activities that will be used; scientific definitions of some common words (e.g., *energy, speed, work*); and new content words (e.g., *acceleration, inertia*). Students need to be taught text processing techniques (how to take notes, how to reread text for answers to study questions, how to read charts and picture captions) and then held to a high level of recall about the information they read (Anderson & Gunderson, 2004). To assist their learning scientific language, students can receive special training in following written instructions for procedures or experiments and in using glossaries.

## BEST PRACTICE: Developing Scientific Language

- Provide appropriate contexts for new vocabulary, syntactic structures, and discourse patterns. Isolated lists or exercises do not appear to facilitate language acquisition.
- Engage students in hands-on activities in which they discuss concepts in a genuine communicative context.
- Promote activities in which students actively debate with one another about the truth of a hypothesis or the meaning of data gathered.
  (Adapted from Carrasquillo & Rodríguez, 2002; Kessler et al., 1992)

**The Language of Social Studies**   Because history itself has taken place in many languages, a strong social studies curriculum builds on dual-language skills. Students can use communication skills in two languages to gather oral histories from their families and communities. Their own family histories can teach them firsthand about complex historical issues. For more information about oral history projects, read "Junior Historians: Doing Oral History with ESL and Bilingual Students" (Olmedo, 1993).

As a discipline, social studies is concept-rich in ideas that may be difficult to depict in visuals. Student interaction is necessary if students are to acquire concepts and then be able to apply them in situations different from the one in which they acquired them. Inquiry skills that are used first in the classroom and then in the community help students practice what they are learning in authentic situations (Sunal & Haas, 2005).

**The Language of Music**    Music is a universal language. All cultures make music and express their cultural heritage in the sounds they select to make their music. However, music has its own language and requires particular understanding before an individual can become a proficient performer. For example, words such as *jazz, pitch, atonality,* and *folk music* are important technical concepts specific to music; if not taught within the proper context, they may pose a challenge for many English learners.

Music can also be used to teach concepts in other content domains. A first-grade lesson teaches opposites through music. Students listen to a story about opposites, discuss opposites, and find opposites in music, using the books *Elmo's Big Lift and Look Book* and *Pooh Popping Opposites* and the music tapes *Down on Grandpa's Farm* and *Lullaby and Goodnight.* After a warm-up in which the teacher asks students "What are opposites?" and "How do we find them?," the teacher reads books that illustrate opposites, asks students for some more examples of opposites, and states some things that are not opposites. Then the teachers plays tapes of songs that show opposites: fast/slow, number of instruments or people singing, etc.). For assessment, students listen to two more tape selections and write the opposites found (Graves, 1996).

**Language in the Visual Arts**    Artists have specific ways of doing art, and there is a language to express those ways. Part of an effective visual arts education is that teachers expose students to appropriate language that describes artistic expression and creates a common language in the community of artists. Part of effective teaching, particularly with English learners, is explicit teaching of words such as *movement, medium,* or *organic.* Art lends itself to contextualization of terms but still requires careful and skillful teaching to connect language and art.

## Modifying Language without Simplification in Content Delivery

In addition to contextualizing the content of a lesson, teachers of English learners must also make accessible the organization and management procedures in the classroom. During the lesson, verbal markers provide structure so that students can understand what is expected of them. To help with directions, teachers can determine the ten most frequently used verbal markers and provide mini-TPR-type lessons to help students learn them. This provides a bond between teacher and students as the students recognize and appreciate the teacher's attempts to include them and know something about their language.

## CLASSROOM GLIMPSE: Lecturing with Key Markers

*In reviewing for the final examination in American history in the eighth grade, Mrs. Farrell emphasized key points using specific verbal markers, such as* now, note this, for instance, *or* in conclusion, *to cue students to material that was especially important. Terms such as* first, second, *and* last *clearly marked the steps of a timeline. To help the English learners with these verbal markers, she provided them with a list and asked them to listen for the terms during the review. This helped students overcome the anxiety about following her lecture in preparing for the exam.*

**Modeling with Explanation**  Demonstrating new concepts can involve hands-on, show-and-tell explanations in which students follow a careful sequence of steps to understand a process. This can include having students work with materials at their seats as an accompaniment to the demonstration. The teacher ensures that the demonstration illustrates the concept clearly and that there is a one-to-one correspondence between the teacher's words and the demonstration. The teacher is prepared to demonstrate again as needed. In addition, the teacher continues to use the chalkboard, overhead, butcher paper, or computer to write key terms, concepts, and sequential elements.

## BEST PRACTICES: Strategies for Comprehensibility

- Use sentence structures that expand the students' output by supplying needed phrases and vocabulary.
- Use gestures to convey instructions.
- Concentrate on understanding and communicating rather than on error correction.
- Provide alternative grouping procedures so that students can share their understanding with one another and with the teacher.
- Maintain consistent classroom procedures and routines from one day to the next.

### Scaffolded Content Instruction

Each content domain has particular ways of presenting content, including differences between elementary and secondary methods. Scaffolded teaching approaches in various content areas are presented as follows by level.

**Elementary Mathematics**  Adapting math instruction for English learners takes many forms. Table 7.3 contrasts math centers set up to teach multiplication that are designed for the mainstream classroom and then adapted for English learners.

**Secondary Mathematics: The Three-Phase Pattern**  Many mathematics teachers follow a three-phase pattern. The first phase involves the introduction, demonstration, and explanation

**TABLE 7.3**   Adapting Math Centers for English Learners: Multiplication Station Activities

| Unadapted Center | Suggested Adaptations |
| --- | --- |
| 1. Shopping Spree: Students look at a menu of items to buy. Their task is to spend exactly $25. | Directions can be in pictorial form. |
| 2. Circles and Stars: Students play a multiplication game with a partner by rolling 1 die to determine how many circles to draw and then rolling a different colored die to draw the number of stars in each circle. They record the number, sentence, and product. | A peer or older tutor can be stationed at the center to explain directions in L1. |
| 3. Patterns of Multiples: Students place number tiles on a 0–99 chart to explore patterns of multiples. | Students of various English levels can work together. |
| 4. Comparison Game: Students draw two cards from a standard deck of cards in which the face cards have been removed and the ace is equal to one. They record their multiplication number sentence and product. Their partner repeats the process above. Finally, they spin a "more or less" spinner to determine the winner for that round. | A pair of students can observe while another pair plays until they get the idea. |
| 5. 4 in a Row: Students spin spinners to determine the product of two numbers and then cover the product on a hundreds board. The winner is the first person to cover 4 squares in a row. If the number is already covered, the student doesn't play that turn. | Instructions can be written in the primary language(s). |

*Source:*  http://mathforum.org/t2t/message.taco?thread=5024&message=4.

of the concept or strategy by the teacher, followed by an interactive questioning segment, in which the teacher establishes how well students are grasping the concept. The second phase involves guided practice, in which students make the transition from "teacher regulation" to student "self-regulation" (Belmont, 1989). Supporting techniques can include coaching, prompting, cueing, and monitoring student performance. The third phase allows students to work independently. If students are having difficulty during independent practice, they can receive more guided practice.

Further research in secondary mathematics teaching suggests the importance of teachers making the short- and long-term goals clear, as well as of explaining to students the usefulness of each mathematical concept. Projects are very effective, although long projects need to be used with discretion. Table 7.4 shows additional strategic approaches to teaching mathematics to English learners.

## CLASSROOM GLIMPSE: Modified Questions in Mathematics

*The teacher's use of language in mathematics can be tailored to elicit different responses from students in various stages of language acquisition. For example, when teaching triangle shapes, the teacher may ask a beginning English learner the question, "Show me the right triangle"; to intermediate students, "What do we call this shape?"; and for advanced students, "What makes a right triangle?"*

**TABLE 7.4**   Mathematics Teaching Strategies for English Learners

| Teaching Strategy | Description |
| --- | --- |
| Encourage exploration. | Plans activities that facilitate and explorations and investigations of mathematical concepts, promote the construction of mathematical knowledge, and nurture students' curiosity and stimulate creativity |
| Use manipulatives. | Manipulatives help make abstract concepts concrete and hands-on; this tends to be particularly useful as students are building their mathematical CALP, because manipulatives provide a context for making conceptual understanding easier. |
|  | With manipulatives students "see" and "touch" connections between different representations of mathematical ideas (concrete, graphic, symbolic, linguistic), understand, and internalize. |
| Use real-world problem-solving activities. | Using mathematics as it applies to daily life and to solve real-life problems makes it interesting and meaningful, and students internalize and retain mathematical concepts much better. |
| Encourage oral and written expression. | Mathematics requires specific language and CALP, and students should be provided opportunities to practice and express their mathematical knowledge orally and in writing. |
| Offer an enriched curriculum and challenging activities. | Mathematics is a discipline with its own CALP characterized by specific experiences and abilities involving inquiry, problem solving, and higher thinking. |
|  | Teachers can design curriculum that sets high expectations for students who learn to think like mathematicians and move away from repetitive drill and memorization of formulas without a context. |
| Use a variety of problem-solving experiences. | The drill-and-practice approach to mathematics should not be the staple of a mathematics curriculum. Teachers should plan challenges that stimulate higher-order thinking and problem solving, and that are nonroutine and open-ended. For example, provide math problems that may have various correct solutions and answers, problems with multiple interpretations, and problems that are not exclusively reading or writing based, with answers that can be represented in multiple ways. |

*Source:* Balderrama & Díaz-Rico (2006).

**Elementary Science**   The important thing in science instruction is to adopt a problem-solving approach featuring problems that are both comprehensible and interesting. Students can be assisted to solve problems in science by developing a personal set of learning strategies. Teachers can help students describe the thinking they used to come up with a solution.

Students can also share with one another their processes, resulting in multiple ways of approaching a problem. Teachers can share with students the biographies of famous scientists, showing the perseverance it took to solve the problems they addressed. Teachers can also praise students' use of innovative techniques.

**Secondary Science**    Alternative means of representing information is important in secondary science instruction. Students need complex information scaffolded in many ways—and they need to learn to do this scaffolding for themselves. T-charts and other graphic organizers are ways to train students to translate verbal information from texts and lectures into mental structures for purposes of memorization as well as understanding. Pictures are important sources of information, whether from texts or supplementary sources. A set of probing questions about visual graphics helps students use their senses to sharpen their visual input mode. In summary, any method of noting details, organizing these details, and creating and testing hypotheses furthers the goals of science inquiry.

**Elementary Literature**    Many graphic organizers are available for use in scaffolding literature instruction: character trait charts, sequence-of-events charts, cause-and-effect charts, setting description charts, and so forth. One key aspect of scaffolding literature that can be used in other content areas is the *cognitive apprentice model*. Children learn to read from teachers, but they also learn from teachers to enjoy reading. Teachers can model why they like certain genres, why a certain turn of phrase is delightful, why a plot is compelling, and so forth. Students then become the apprentices of teachers' thinking about literature—an apprenticeship in literature appreciation. This is the core of scaffolding in reading instruction. Without learning to love reading, students will be unreceptive to all other techniques.

**Secondary Literature**    Building on the love of reading that is the foundation of elementary instruction, students at the secondary level must balance consumption with production. It is one thing to read poetry and entirely another to write it, to struggle firsthand with the freshness of images, the discipline of meter, the lure of rhyme. To appreciate literature, one must be willing to dive in, to create and re-create in the leading genres of the day. Therefore, scaffolding literature is intrinsically bound up with creative production of language.

Integral to production of language is scaffolded creativity in the primary language. Students who create in two languages are addressing a peer audience that appreciates the effort. Even students with a primary language not understood by peers can share the poetic sound and meaning (in translation). All creativity stimulates the common underlying proficiency that makes language a human treasure.

**Elementary Social Studies**    Scaffolded social studies starts with the timeline and the map as the basic graphic organizers. Students need a firm understanding of when and where events took place. Any mental device is useful that helps students visualize when and where. If the computer program Google Earth can be displayed from the computer screen onto a large surface at the beginning of each lesson, students can start "zoomed in" at their own school and then "zoom out" to the picture of the earth in space, move the map to the location of the day's lesson in history or geography, and then "zoom in" to locate any feature under discussion. This grounds students in their own place before making the transition to another.

**Secondary History/Social Science**   The reading load in secondary history often needs to be scaffolded. Bradley and Bradley (2004, n.p.) offered several useful methods to help students monitor their comprehension during reading.

- *Analyzing captions:* Look at the picture captions and ask, "How does this tie into the reading?"
- *Turning subheads into questions:* By rephrasing a subheading into a question, readers are able to predict upcoming content.
- *Making margin notes:* Using small sticky notes, students write new vocabulary words they encounter—even words not in the content glossary.
- *Students reading to each other.*

A useful scaffolding technique for secondary social studies is the question–answer relationships (QAR) model (Raphael, 1986). This strategy describes four kinds of questions: Right There (direct quote from the text), Think and Search (the answer must be inferred from several text passages), Author and You (text integrated with personal experience), and On Your Own (drawn from personal experiences). Each question requires a different set of text processing or thinking resources. This method can be taught in one lesson, and thereafter students can learn to classify questions and locate answers independently.

## BEST PRACTICE: Teaching Note-Taking Skills

Better note takers achieve better academically in middle and high school (Faber, Morris, & Lieberman, 2000). Here are tips on taking better notes:

- Date and title notes at the top of the page.
- Split the page: Keep lecture notes on the left side and organizational and summary notes on the right side.
- Skip lines to show change of topic.
- Use the same organization as the lecturer to number subpoints or mark details.
- Use underlining, circling, or highlighting to indicate important ideas. (Adapted from Stahl, King, & Henk, 1991)

## CLASSROOM GLIMPSE: Collaboration in Middle School Social Studies

*At Gerona Middle School (pseudonym) in a medium-sized California agricultural town, more than half of the students are English learners, some from migrant labor families. The majority of students are academically underprepared according to their scores on standardized tests.*

*In a recent unit about the Crusades, students wrote expository essays in which they described, justified, and persuaded. At the end of each group activity and each unit, students wrote a final essay, making connections between their group activities and the central theme of the unit. Content area and language arts teachers coordinated interdisciplinary responsibility for this writing. This is known as sustained-content instruction. (Adapted from Bunch, Abram, Lotan, & Valdés, 2001)*

## Guided and Independent Practice That Promotes Students' Active Language Use

**Guided Practice**    Teachers working in mixed-ability classrooms can plan group activities that help students in different ways. Students can work in homogeneous groups when the goal of the activity is accuracy and in heterogeneous groups when the goal is fluency. For example, to develop accuracy, first-grade students can listen to a reading of the Chinese folktale "The Magic Sieve." A group of beginning students can retell the story using pictures and then talk about the pictures. Intermediate students can retell the story to the teacher or a cross-age tutor. The teacher writes their story for them, and then students can reread, illustrate, and rearrange the story from sentence strips. A group of more proficient students can create a new group story.

At the secondary level, as students work in class, teachers can use various strategies to guide their learning. Groups of students can work together to create visual summaries or chapter reviews of textbook content. Specific students can each take on the persona of a literary character or historic personage and provide background for other students' questions throughout the reading. Charts, graphs, pictures, and symbols can trace the development of images, ideas, and themes.

## BEST PRACTICE: Guided Practice in Reading Literature

Scaffolded activities help students as they work with text. Reading aloud to students as they follow along can give the students an opportunity to hear a proficient reader, get a sense of the format and story line, and listen to the teacher think aloud about the reading. In the think-aloud, teachers can model how they monitor a sequence of events, identify foreshadowing and flashback, visualize a setting, analyze character and motive, comprehend mood and theme, and recognize irony and symbolism. To help students develop a sense of inflection, pronunciation, rhythm, and stress, a commercial tape recording of a work of literature can be obtained for listening and review, or native-English-speaking students or adult volunteers may be willing to make a recording.

**Maintaining the First Language in Guided Practice**    Students can be encouraged to use and develop their native language during guided practice. Teachers can use several strategies that support students' first language within the context of the classroom program. Aides and tutors can help explain difficult passages and help students summarize their understanding. Native-language books, magazines, films, and other materials relating to the topic or theme of the lesson can support and even augment students' learning. Students can also maintain reading logs or journals in their native language.

## CLASSROOM GLIMPSE: Primary-Language Poetry

*Judith Casey (2004) encourages students to share their native language with their classmates during a poetry activity.*

*Ms. Casey invites students to bring in and read aloud a poem in their L1. On Poetry Day, the atmosphere of the class is charged. No one knows exactly what to expect, but the students are excited. Amazingly, hearing one another read in their L1 lets the students see each other in a new light. The class is forever changed as students recognize the value, contributions, and abilities of their classmates. (pp. 51–52)*

**Independent Practice**   Computers and other resources can be used to extend practice in various content domains. Many English learners are unfamiliar with the basic tools associated with mathematics (rulers, protractors, calculators, computers, etc.) (Buchanan & Helman, 1997). After demonstrating each, teachers can provide students with real-life opportunities to use them. For example, students are told that the playground needs to be repaved. They first have to estimate the area, then check their estimates with the actual tools (using both standard and metric measuring instruments, as they will not know which system the parking company uses), and then use calculators to find the percentage of error in their estimates. Computer programs can also be used to provide estimates and calculations.

## BEST PRACTICE: Independent Reactions to Works of Literature

- Authentic written responses encourage students to reflect on the piece of literature and to express their interpretations to an audience beyond the classroom.
- Students write poems and share them with other classes or parents at a Poetry Night.
- Student journalists write reviews of literature works for the school or classroom newspaper or act as movie critics and review the film version of a text studied in class. They can then compare the differences and draw conclusions about the pros and cons of the different media.
- Students write letters to authors to express their reactions to the story or to pen pals recommending certain pieces of literature.
- Favorite parts of selections can be rewritten as a play and enacted for other classes as a way to encourage other students to read that piece of literature.
- Students can plan a mock television game show and devise various formats that include ideas from the literature studied.

## BEST PRACTICE: Independent Questioning Strategies

"Question swap" (Gregory & Kuzmich, 2005) is a useful device for helping students personalize social studies. For any given topic, students write out two questions each (with answers) and then swap one question with the first partner, each writing out answers. The questioners then do the same with the second question. This process restructures information from verbal input to mental schemata. The questions are the scaffold. The teacher should gather up the questions and answers at the end and skim quickly to clear up any misrepresentation.

### Resources for Independent Practice

Across the content areas, teachers can help make resources available for students as they approach learning tasks autonomously. This helps students take responsibility for their own learning.

## CLASSROOM GLIMPSE: Using Multiple Resources for Independent Research

*Students studying a fifth-grade unit on settlement of the West can examine the legal issues involved in the Treaty of Guadalupe-Hidalgo, compare the various cultures that came into contact in the Southwest, delve into the history of land grant titles, and pursue many more issues of interest. Through filmstrips, films, videos, computer simulations, literature, nonfiction texts, and oral discussions, students develop conceptual knowledge. Such a unit incorporates history, geography, sociology, economics, values, information-seeking skills, group participation, and perhaps dramatic skills as students act out the signing of treaties and other cultural events.*

**Math Resources for Elementary English Learners**   Almost all math programs at the primary level are supported by sets of manipulative materials; however, manipulatives are not a magic substitute for intensive, multimodal instruction that ensures all students acquire mathematics concepts at every stage. The World Wide Web is a vast source of problems, contests, enrichment, and teacher resources to supplement classroom instruction. Mentors who represent diverse linguistic and cultural groups within the school system, volunteers from the community, or experts who agree to respond to questions by e-mail can all help students.

Family Math is a program that focuses on families learning mathematics together in support of the elementary math curriculum. Adults and children come to Family Math classes together once a week for several weeks, doing activities in small groups, with two or three families working together. As a follow-up, family members use inexpensive materials found in the home (bottle caps, toothpicks, coins) to practice ideas that were presented in class. Materials are presented in English and Spanish (online at www.lhs.berkeley.edu/equals/FMnetwork.htm).

**Math Resources for Secondary English Learners**   The Internet provides numerous sites that are both resources for teachers and opportunities for students to practice mathematical skills. Table 7.5 features several websites recommended by some of the mathematics teachers with whom I work, including their descriptions of how these sites help them in working with English learners.

**Internet Social Studies Resources for English Learners**   Classroom teachers can combine the enormous range of resources from the Internet with other instructional resources and methods. Field trips via the Internet include visiting the White House (www.whitehouse.gov), exhibitions of African and pre-Columbian Native-American art (www.artic.edu), or the Egyptian pyramids (www.pbs.org/wgbh/nova/pyramid). Many of the virtual field trip sites are designed specifically for education, featuring lesson plans and interactive student activities (see www.internet4classrooms.com/social.html). Students can create their own virtual field trips of local historical sites, or even of their school. To see what a group of students in grades 3–12 did with a five-day virtual journey across the world, visit www.win4edu.com/minds-eye/journey. Table 7.6 offers selected websites for teaching secondary social studies to English learners.

**TABLE 7.5**  Websites for Teaching Secondary Mathematics to English Learners

| Website | Description |
|---|---|
| http://matti.usu.edu/nlvm/ nav/vlibrary.html | Provides manipulatives as a visual demonstration of concepts taking place in the class. The graph is an excellent tool; one can graph several lines on the same Cartesian plane and see the variations made by changing a coefficient. |
| www.purplemath.com/ modules/translat.htm | Translates word problems into algebraic expressions. When English learners are faced with word problems, it is rarely one word that gives them problems, but more often a phrase. That phrase is usually the key to setting up the problem. The website provides a step-by-step account of how to set up these problems. |
| www.enc.org/topics/ equity/articles | Addresses the cultural aspects of teaching mathematics. It identifies characteristics of learners from different cultures and the common misconception that mathematics can be taught without taking culture into account. |

*Source:* Balderrama & Díaz-Rico (2006).

## CLASSROOM GLIMPSE: A Historic Website

*Ms. Rosie Beccera Davies's third-grade class at Washington Elementary School in Montebello, California, made a historical website for their community, beginning with the Gabrielino (Tongva) Indians, and including many local historical sites.*

**TABLE 7.6**  Websites for Teaching Secondary Social Studies to English Learners

| Website | Description |
|---|---|
| www. DiscoverySchool.com | An excellent supplement to world history videos. The site offers vocabulary words and terms used in the video, rubrics, and a list of additional resources. The vocabulary terms are integral in terms of providing scaffolding for English learners. (Recommended by J. Kabel, high school social sciences teacher, Palm Desert, CA) |
| http://atozteacherstuff.com/ | Contains many ELD lessons specifically designed for all content areas. I found several excellent lessons that I can use for my English learners in U.S. history and government. |
| www/eduref.org/virtual/ lessons | An easy to use (clean and uncluttered) site, containing a thorough resource guide and question archives for easy reference. The site also contained several pages of social studies lessons for English learners (Recommended by J. Johnson, a social studies alternative high school teacher in San Bernardino, CA) |

**Science Resources outside of the School**    The school science program often extends beyond the walls of the school to the resources of the community. Teachers can work with local personnel, such as those at science-rich centers (museums, industries, universities, etc.), to plan for the use of exhibits and educational programs that enhance the study of a particular topic. In addition, the physical environment in and around the school can be used as a living laboratory for the study of natural phenomena in project-based and service-learning activities.

A wide diversity of scientists has made significant contributions to scientific knowledge in the United States. Studying these role models promotes respect by all students for the accomplishments of people of many different backgrounds and helps students who share the culture of the scientists to imagine a successful career in science.

**Resources for Music**    When adapting music lessons for English learners, primary-language music audiotapes are available through Shen's Books at www.shens.com, including tapes in Spanish, Hmong, Vietnamese, Cambodian, Korean, Japanese, and Mandarin, as well as tapes from cultures other than the native cultures of the students.

Technology is increasingly an important resource in music education. The most powerful application for music education may be the use of computers, allowing students to improvise, make arrangements, and access vast libraries of recorded music. When instruments are connected to electronic instruments and computers, they can be used to record, transcribe, and even permit practice performances.

Musical and cultural resources abound in all communities, and skillful music educators tap into these resources by working with parents, churches, and other civic organizations. Local musicians, professionals, music faculty at local universities, family members, and students at colleges and universities can conduct sessions and workshops in conjunction with the regular instructional program.

Many students from low-income homes, including English learners, cannot afford instruments and therefore are not able to participate in the music program. Teachers should work together with parents and community groups to have a set of instruments students can borrow until they purchase an instrument.

### Formative Assessment and Reteaching Content

The hands-on nature of problem solving in science can naturally align with performance-based assessment. By performing actual science activities, students are actively demonstrating the skills for which assessment holds them responsible. The use of formative assessment involves teachers in the role of offering guidance and feedback so the given skills can be accomplished.

## CLASSROOM GLIMPSE: Checking Exit Comprehension in Science

*Mr. Petersen uses the strategy Exit Slips just before students leave their middle school science class. He provides students with a preprinted prompt, such as "I'm still not clear about . . . ," to help them pinpoint what is still fuzzy for them about the day's lesson. Students can reflect on what they have just learned, show their thinking process, and prepare for continued learning on the topic. Teachers can use this information to select what to revisit, elaborate, or expand on in the next lesson. (Adapted from Fisher et al., 2007)*

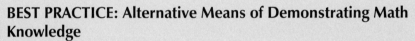

## Summative Assessment of Content Lessons

Multiple strategies can be used to assess students' mastery of language objectives and grade-level content objectives across diverse content domains.

**Assessment in Mathematics**  Although traditional assessment in mathematics focuses on the mastery of algorithms, many alternative forms of assessment can be used to measure mathematical thinking and problem solving. Authentic assessment allows the teacher to assess mathematics understanding while students are actively engaged in such learning as running a school store or simulating trade on the stock market. Assessments should allow for differences in understanding, creativity, and accomplishment. Students should be encouraged to explain their reasoning both orally and in writing. Flexible expectations allow different pacing for students with basic versus advanced math skills.

## BEST PRACTICE: Alternative Means of Demonstrating Math Knowledge

Students can . . .

- Produce or find three different drawings for the number *x*.
- Write three story problems that have the number *x* as an answer.
- Make up a pattern and explain it.
- Interview ten people to find out the favorite ice cream flavors and then invent a way to show this information to the class.

*Source:* Adapted from Rowan & Bourne (1994).

**Assessment in Visual and Performing Arts**  Instruction and assessment go hand in hand in the visual and performing arts. The teacher and the artist interact and collaborate in ongoing feedback, with self-monitoring and self-assessment being a part of the daily experience. Portfolios are very common assessment tools used by artists in the performing arts because they track individual growth. They can help high school students, for example, apply for college entrance to an art institute, or apply for employment in the visual arts.

Student exhibitions are also a way in which teachers can create safe opportunities for assessment, whereby peers and other adults give feedback on completed works or works-in-progress. These exhibitions can take place in the classroom, and rubrics can be developed by the class to evaluate basic elements in a work.

 *Members of the community can share cultural activities such as music and art with students.*

## BEST PRACTICE:  Assessment as Musical Performance

Showcasing musical talent by means of group and individual performance is a time-honored assessment of musical involvement. The excitement of performance and the responsibility of individuals toward their peers and their audience teach maturity and poise. Bridging cultural gaps by offering music in many languages helps to involve the families and community in preparing for, attending, and enjoying concerts.

**Assessment in Social Studies**    Assessment of all students must be equitable in a social studies program. English learners can show proficiency in multiple ways: portfolios, performance assessments, written reports, role-plays, and research projects. When high-stakes educational decisions for individual students are made, the decisions should be based on a variety of assessments, rather than on a single test score. Assessments of students in social studies should be designed and used to further the goal of educating students to be active citizens in a democratic society (see Chapter 3 for more on assessment).

Table 7.7 presents strategies for adapting curricula in secondary school studies. Similar strategies may apply in other content areas. These strategies represent a sample of SDAIE methods.

**TABLE 7.7**　Strategies for Adapting Curricula in Secondary Social Studies

| Strategy | How It Helps |
| --- | --- |
| Identify similarities and differences | Helps students compare, create metaphors, and use analogies (comparing the U.S. Cabinet to a school can clarify the concept of analogy); builds vocabulary, comprehension. |
| Historical investigation | Gives students an active role in understanding history and allows them to pursue a question using strategies that work for them; focuses on students' interests; allows students flexibility; encourages self-monitoring of progress. |
| Inventions | Inventions are/have been an important part of U.S. history; students are able to demonstrate comprehension, knowledge, and creativity within a historical framework while reliving history. |
| Role-playing | Adolescents are quite dramatic and like to be in "someone else's shoes"; students learn about others' perspectives while using language, gestures, and body language to show their understanding. |
| Group work | Collaborative projects or assignments help students to solve problems together as they hear and use history-related CALP in a low-anxiety environment; structured group work addresses status issues so that "everyone participates, no one dominates" and English learners have chances to talk. |
| Decision making | This provides for contemplation and discussion of concepts central to many historical issues; provides students a chance to hear and use language to make decisions. |
| "What if" stories | Help students use language to create hypothetical predictions about history: for example, what if Columbus had not sailed to America? |
| Puzzles, riddles | Students see representations of historical concepts in different formats that engage and incorporate multiple intelligences. |
| Explanations with concrete referents | Help students understand abstract concepts. |
| Alternative representation formats | Different ways of presenting facts; for example, graphic organizers, maps, tables, charts, and graphs can reduce verbiage and identify key concepts in a lesson; this also models the different means historians use to gather evidence. |
| Summarizing and note taking | An important skill of historians; allows students to make sense of extensive text and lecture by listening for key words and identifying relevant information. |
| Preteach assignments | Helps students anticipate key concepts before reading assignment. |
| Prepare for exams | Teacher can model how to use textbook features such as chapter goals and overviews, summaries, and glossaries; this also helps students self-monitor comprehension and progress. |
| Provide learning, reading, and study support | Helps students process text and use language to voice their ideas; puts them in role of experts. Teachers arrange jigsaw groups to read text, assigning students to groups and making groups of students experts on specific portions of reading; students read and discuss together; teacher reviews and addresses specific issues with the entire class. |
| Word association | Vocabulary enrichment; teaching students to hear a word and associate it with an image helps comprehension and retention. |
| Listen for specific information | Teaches students explicitly what is important in a lecture, text, or historical document; students use teacher-created graphic organizers or use fill-in-the-blank lecture notes. |

## ▓▓ INSTRUCTIONAL NEEDS BEYOND THE CLASSROOM

To be successful in their academic courses, English learners often need assistance from organizations and volunteers outside of the classroom. This assistance can come from academic summer programs, additional instructional services such as after-school programs and peer tutoring, and Dial-a-Teacher for homework help in English and in the primary language. Support in the affective domain may include special home visits by released time teachers, counselors, or outreach workers and informal counseling by teachers. Monitoring of academic progress by counselors helps to encourage students with language needs.

### BEST PRACTICE:  Meeting Instructional Needs beyond the Classroom

Escalante and Dirmann (1990) explicated the main components of the Garfield High School Advanced Placement (AP) calculus course in which Escalante achieved outstanding success in preparing Hispanic students to pass the AP calculus examination. Escalante's success was not due solely to outstanding classroom teaching; he was the organizer of a broad effort to promote student success. In his classroom, he set the parameters: He made achievement a game for the students, the "opponent" being the Educational Testing Service's examination; he coached students to hold up under the pressure of the contest and work hard to win; and he held students accountable for attendance and productivity. But beyond this work in the classroom was the needed community support.

Community individuals and organizations donated copiers, computers, transportation, and souvenirs such as special caps and team jackets. Parents became involved in a campaign against drug use. This helped Escalante emphasize proper conduct, respect, and value for education. Past graduates served as models of achievement. They gave pep talks to students and acted as hosts in visits to high-tech labs. The support from these other individuals combined to give students more help and encouragement than could be provided by the classroom teacher alone. Students saw concentrated, caring, motivated effort directed toward them—something they had rarely before experienced. The results were dramatized in the unforgettable feature film *Stand and Deliver*.

Escalante's successful AP calculus program at Garfield High School involved much more than excellent classroom instruction. It is not surprising that the key features of SDAIE were incorporated in his teaching: content and language teaching, the latter through an extensive attention to specific mathematics vocabulary; connections between the math curriculum and the students' lives and development of appropriate schemata when background was lacking; comprehensibility through use of realia and visual support for instruction and modification of teacher talk; interaction with one another through cooperative learning; and teacher attitude, a positive coaching approach that conveyed high expectations. This is the instructional enhancement that opens the door to success for English learners.

**VIDEO WORKSHOP:** "Teaching English Language Learners"

In this video, a teacher explains and then demonstrates some of her own effective techniques for teaching in a multicultural classroom. Then, a physical education teacher talks about his own success in just spending some extra time explaining rules to children with limited English proficiency.

To access the video, log on to MyLabSchool at www.mylabschool.com, enter Assignment ID **ENV2** into the **Assignment Finder**, and select the video entitled "Teaching English Language Learners." Watch the video, complete the questions that follow, and e-mail your responses to your professor for credit.

**mylabschool**
Where the classroom comes to life!

# CHAPTER EIGHT

# Culture and Cultural Diversity and Their Relationship to Academic Achievement

## ▧ CULTURAL CONCEPTS AND PERSPECTIVES

People used to think of culture as Culture, as in "highbrow" activities such as going to the opera or symphony, or as Exotic Culture, such as viewing a display of African masks. But culture is more than performing traditional rites or crafting ritual objects. Culture, though largely invisible, influences the way people think, talk, and act—the very way people see the world.

Cultural patterns are especially evident in schools because home and school are the chief sites where the young are acculturated. If we accept the organization, teaching and learning styles, and curricula of the schools as natural and right, we may not realize that these patterns are cultural; they seem natural and right only to the members of the culture who created them. As children of nondominant cultures enter the schools, however, they may find the organization, teaching and learning styles, and curricula to be alien, incomprehensible, and exclusionary.

Fortunately, teachers can learn to see clearly the key role of culture in teaching and learning. They can incorporate culture into classroom activities in superficial ways—as a group of artifacts (baskets, masks, distinctive clothing), as celebrations of holidays (Cinco de Mayo, Martin Luther King Jr. Day), or as a laundry list of stereotypes and insensitivities to be avoided. These ways of dealing with culture are limiting but useful as a starting point.

However, teachers can also gain a more insightful view of culture and cultural processes and use this understanding to move beyond the superficial. To be knowledgeable as an intercultural educator is to understand that observable cultural items are but one aspect of the cultural web—the intricate pattern that weaves and binds a people together. Knowing that culture provides the lens through which people view the world, teachers can look at the "what" of a culture—the artifacts, celebrations, traits, and facts—and ask "why?" Knowledge of the deeper elements of culture—beyond aspects such as food, clothing, holidays, and celebrations—can give teachers a crosscultural perspective that allows them to educate students to the fullest extent possible.

### What Is Culture?

Does a fish understand water? Do people understand their own culture? Teachers are responsible for helping to pass on cultural knowledge through the schooling process. Can teachers step outside their own culture long enough to see how it operates and to understand its effects on culturally diverse students? A way to begin is to define culture.

**Defining Culture**   The term *culture* is used in many ways. It can refer to activities such as art, drama, and ballet or to items such as pop music, mass media entertainment, and comic books. The term *culture* can be used for distinctive groups in society, such as adolescents and their culture. It can be used as a general term for a society, such as the "French culture." Such uses do not, however, define what a culture is. As a field of study, culture is conceptualized in various ways (see Table 8.1).

**TABLE 8.1**   Definitions of Culture

| Definition | Source |
| --- | --- |
| The sum total of a way of life of a people; patterns experienced by individuals as normal ways of acting, feeling, and being. | Hall (1959) |
| That complex whole that includes knowledge, belief, art, morals, law, and custom, and any other capabilities acquired by humans as members of society. | Tylor (in Pearson, 1974) |
| A dynamic system of symbols and meanings that involves an ongoing, dialectic process in which past experience influences meaning, which in turn affects future experience, which in turn affects subsequent meaning, and so on. | Robinson (1985) |
| Mental constructs in three basic categories: *shared knowledge* (information known in common by members of the group), *shared views* (beliefs and values shared by members of a group), and *shared patterns* (habits and norms in the ways members of a group organize their behavior, interaction, and communication). | Snow (1996) |
| Partial solutions to previous problems that humans create in joint mediated activity; the social inheritance embodied in artifacts and material constituents of culture as well as in practices and ideal symbolic forms; semi-organized hodgepodge of human inheritance. Culture is exteriorized mind and mind is interiorized culture. | Cole (1998) |
| Frames (nationality, gender, ethnicity, religion) carried by each individual that are internalized, individuated, and emerge in interactions. | Smith, Paige, & Steglitz (1998) |
| People are never merely passively subordinated, never totally manipulated, never entirely incorporated. People are engaged in struggles with, within, and sometimes against real tendentious forces and determinations in their efforts to appropriate what they are given. Consequently, their relations to particular practices and texts are complex and contradictory. . . . If people's lives are never merely determined by the dominant position, and if their subordination is always complex and active, understanding culture requires us to look at how practices are actively inserted at particular sites of everyday life and how particular articulations empower and disempower their audiences. | Grossberg (1988, pp. 169–170) |
| [T]he social bond is a weave of crisscrossing threads of discursive practices, no single one of which runs continuously throughout the whole. Individuals are the nodes or "posts" where such practices intersect and, so, they participate in many simultaneously. It follows that social identities are complex and heterogeneous. | Fraser & Nicholson (1988, pp. 88–89) |

The definitions in Table 8.1 have common factors but they vary in emphasis. Early cultural theorists emphasize the way an individual is immersed in culture, even unknowingly; whereas postmodern definitions (see Grossberg, 1988, and Fraser and Nicholson, 1988) make the point that the individual plays an active role in shaping his or her cultural ambiance, and must continually remake a cultural identity (using language and power) to adapt to shifting circumstances. The following definition of culture combines the ideas in Table 8.1 with other contemporary notions:

> Culture is the explicit and implicit patterns for living, the dynamic system of commonly agreed-upon symbols and meanings, the deep structure of knowledge, belief, art, morals, law, customs, behaviors, traditions, and/or habits that are shared and make up the total way of life of a people, as negotiated by individuals in the process of constructing a personal identity.
>
> To understand culture, one must look beyond the obvious to understand how values, codes, beliefs and social relations are continually being reshaped by shifting parameters of place, identity, history, and power. Rather than individuals being excluded for differing from cultural norms, people with dissonant, flexible, complex, and hybrid racial and ethnic identities struggle to generate new meanings within accommodating contexts as they use experimentation and creativity to rework existing configurations of knowledge and power and thus extend the possibilities of being human, even in the face of an uncertain outcome.

The important idea is that culture involves both observable behaviors and intangibles such as beliefs and values, rhythms, rules, and roles. The concept of culture has evolved over the last fifty years away from the idea of culture as an invisible, patterning force to that of culture as an active tension between the social "shortcuts" that make consensual society possible and the contributions and construction that each individual creates while living in society. To mix metaphors, culture is not only the filter through which people see the world but also the raw dough from which each person fashions a life that is individual and satisfying.

Because culture is all-inclusive, it includes multiple aspects of life. Snow (1996) listed a host of components (see Table 8.2).

## Key Concepts about Culture

To understand culture, one cannot simply total a list of traits—there is wholeness about cultures, with various aspects overlapping and integrated with other aspects. Cultures cannot be taught merely by examining external features such as art and artifacts, although those may be a useful starting point. Even traveling to a country may not engender a deeper understanding of that country's culture(s). To understand a culture, one must examine the living patterns and values of the people living in that culture. Despite the aspects of diverse cultures that may seem unique, cultures have various elements in common.

**Culture Is Universal**    Everyone in the world belongs to one or more cultures. Each culture provides organized ways to carry out and interpret such experiences as serving food, speaking to children, marrying, and so forth. Because humans have similar needs, cultures must meet these needs, albeit in diverse ways.

**Culture Simplifies Living**    Social behaviors and customs offer structure to daily life that minimizes interpersonal stress. Cultural patterns are routines that free humans from endless negotiation about each detail of living. Culture helps to unify a society by providing a common base of communication and social customs.

**TABLE 8.2** Components of Culture

| Component | Example | Component | Example |
|---|---|---|---|
| Daily life | Animals | Interacting | Chatting |
| | Clothing | | Eating |
| | Daily schedule | | Drinking |
| | Food | | Gift giving |
| | Games | | Language learning |
| | Hobbies | | Parties |
| | Housing | | Politeness |
| | Hygiene | | Problem solving |
| | Jobs | Society | Business |
| | Medical care | | Cities |
| | Plants | | Economy |
| | Recreation | | Education |
| | Shopping | | Farming |
| | Space | | Industry |
| | Sports | | Government and politics |
| | Time | | Languages and dialects |
| | Traffic and transport | | Law and order |
| | Travel | | Science |
| The cycle of life | Birth | | Social problems |
| | Children | The nation | Holidays |
| | Dating/mating | | Geography |
| | Marriage | | History |
| | Divorce | | Famous people |
| | Friends | | National issues |
| | Old age | | Stereotypes |
| | Funerals | Creative arts | Arts |
| | Rites of passage | | Entertainment |
| Values | Philosophy | | Literature |
| | Religion | | Music |
| | Beliefs | | Television |

*Source:* Snow, D. (1996). More than a native speaker. Alexandria, VA: TESOL.

**Culture Is Learned in a Process of Deep Conditioning** Cultural patterns are absorbed unconsciously from birth, as well as explicitly taught by other members. The fact that cultural patterns are deep makes it difficult for the members of a given culture to see their own culture as learned behavior.

**Culture Is Demonstrated in Values**    Every culture holds some beliefs and behaviors to be more desirable than others, whether these be about nature, human character, material possessions, or other aspects of the human condition. Those members of the culture who exemplify these values are rewarded with prestige or approval.

**Culture Is Expressed Both Verbally and Nonverbally**    Although language and culture are closely identified, nonverbal components of culture can be just as powerful in communicating cultural beliefs, behaviors, and values. Images, gestures, and emotions are as culturally conditioned as words. In the classroom, teachers may misunderstand a student's intent if nonverbal communication is misinterpreted.

## CLASSROOM GLIMPSE: Nonverbal Miscommunication

*Ming was taught at home to sit quietly when she was finished with a task and wait for her mother to praise her. As a newcomer in the third grade, she waited quietly when finished with her reading assignment. Mrs. Wakefield expected Ming to take out a book to read or to begin another assignment when she completed her work. She made a mental note: "Ming lacks initiative."*

**Societies Represent a Mix of Cultures**    The patterns that dominate a society form the *macroculture* of that society. Within the macroculture, a variety of *microcultures* (subcultures) coexist, distinguished by characteristics such as gender, socioeconomic status, ethnicity, geographical location, social identification, and language use.

   Generational experiences can cause the formation of microcultures. For example, the children of Vietnamese who immigrated to the United States after the Vietnam War often became native speakers of English, although their parents often spoke little English. This separated the two generations by language. Similarly, Mexicans who migrate to the United States may find that their children born in the United States do not consider themselves Mexicans but instead identify with other terms such as *Chicano*.

### DID YOU KNOW?
#### Generation of Japanese Immigrants
The first generation of Japanese immigrants, who often referred to themselves as *issei* or first generation, came to the United States starting about 1900. These were, for the most part, young men who worked as agricultural laborers or skilled craftsmen. Often seen as a threat by European Americans, these immigrants were often the targets of discrimination. This prejudice came to a head after the attack by the Japanese on Pearl Harbor in 1941, when the *issei* were divested of their property and removed to relocation camps. After the war, their children, the *nisei* generation, assumed a low ethnic profile, perhaps as a response to the treatment of their parents. (Leathers, 1967)

**Most Societies Have a Mainstream Culture**    The term *mainstream culture* refers to those individuals or groups who share values of the dominant macroculture. In the United States, the macroculture's traditions and cultural patterns—the mainstream culture—have largely been determined by European Americans who constitute the middle class. Mainstream American culture is characterized by the following values (Gollnick & Chinn, 2002):

- Individualism and privacy
- Independence and self-reliance
- Equality
- Ambition and industriousness
- Competitiveness
- Appreciation of the good life
- Perception that humans are separate from, and superior to, nature

**Culture Is Both Dynamic and Persistent**   Some features of human cultures are flexible and responsive to change, and other features last thousands of years without changing. Values and customs relating to birth, marriage, medicine, education, and death seem to be the most persistent, for humans seem to be deeply reluctant to alter those cultural elements that influence labor and delivery, marital happiness, health, life success, and eternal rest.

**Culture Is a Mix of Rational and Nonrational Elements**   Much as individuals living in western European post-Enlightenment societies may believe that reason should govern human behavior, many cultural patterns are passed on through habit rather than reason. People who bring a real tree into their houses in December—despite the mess it creates—do so because of centuries-old Yule customs. Similarly, carving a face on a hollow pumpkin or hiding colored eggs are hardly rational activities. Other customs persist because they provide workable solutions to persistent problems, such as assigning postal numbers to houses on a street.

**Cultures Represent Different Values**   The fact that each culture possesses its own particular traditions, values, and ideals means that each culture of a society judges right from wrong in a different way. Actions can be judged only in relation to the cultural setting in which they occur. This point of view has been called *cultural relativism*. In general, the primary values of human nature are universal—for example, few societies condone murder. However, sanctions relating to actions may differ. The Native-American cultures of California before contact with Europeans were peace loving to such an extent that someone who took the life of another would be ostracized by the tribe. In contrast, the U.S. macroculture deems it acceptable for soldiers to kill in the context of war.

## CLASSROOM GLIMPSE: Clashing Values about Reading Fiction

*Jerome Harvey gave out library prizes in the sixth grade for ROAR (Required Outside Additional Reading). Students competed with one another to see how many pages they could read and report during the contest period. Min-Yi Chen, one of the outstanding readers in class, ranked near the bottom in number of pages. Mr. Harvey brought this up with the Chens at the fall parent–teacher conference. "Well," said Mr. Chen, "Reading of stories is a waste of time—we expect her to go to summer math camp, and the entrance exam is in January. She will be working two or three hours per night on that." Mr. Harvey wonders if he should quit urging Min-Yi to read on her own.*

**Culture Affects People's Attitudes toward Schooling**    Educational aspiration affects the attitude people have toward schooling, what future job or profession they desire, the importance parents ascribe to education, and how much investment in education they are willing to make. The son of blue-collar workers, for example, might not value a college education because his parents, who have not attained such an education, have nevertheless prospered, whereas the daughter of a recent, low-wage immigrant may work industriously in school to pursue higher education and a well-paid job. Cultural values also affect the extent to which families are involved in their children's schooling and the forms this involvement takes. Family involvement is discussed in Chapter 9.

## BEST PRACTICE: Working with Aspirations about Schooling

In working with English learners, teachers will want to know the following:

- What educational level does the family and community desire for the student?
- What understanding do family members have about the connection between educational level attained and career aspiration?
- What link does the family make between current effort and career aspiration?

**Culture Governs the Way People Learn**    Any learning that takes place is built on previous learning. Students have learned the basic patterns of living in the context of their families. They have learned the verbal and nonverbal behaviors appropriate for their gender and age and have observed their family members in various occupations and activities. They have observed community members cooperating to learn in a variety of methods and modes. Their families have given them a feeling for music and art and have shown them what is beautiful and what is not. Finally, they have learned to use language in the context of their homes and communities, and they can express their needs, desires, and delights.

The culture that students bring from the home is the foundation for their learning in school. Although certain communities exist in relative poverty—that is, they are not equipped with middle-class resources—poverty should not be equated with cultural deprivation. Every community's culture incorporates vast knowledge about successful living. Teachers can use this cultural knowledge to organize students' learning in schools.

Culture appears to influence the way individuals select strategies and approach learning (Shade & New, 1993). For example, students who live in a farming community may have sensitive and subtle knowledge about weather patterns, and this may predispose students to value learning in the classroom that helps them better understand natural processes such as climate. These students may prefer kinesthetic learning that builds on the same kind of learning that has made it possible for them to sense subtleties of weather. In a similar manner, Mexican-American children from traditional families who are encouraged to view themselves as an integral part of the family may prefer social learning activities.

Acting and performing are the focus of learning for many African-American children. Children observe other individuals to determine appropriate behavior and to appreciate the performance of others. In this case, observing and listening culminates in an individual's performance before others (Heath, 1999). In contrast, reading and writing may be primary learning modes for other cultures. Traditionally educated Asian students equate the printed page with learning and often use reading and writing to reinforce learning. Despite these varying approaches, all cultures lay out the basic design for learning for their members.

**Ethnocentrism versus Cultural Relativism**   Individuals who grow up within a macroculture and never leave it may act on the assumption that their values are the norm. When encountering other cultures, they may be unable or unwilling to recognize that alternative beliefs and behaviors are legitimate within the larger society. Paige (1999) defined this ethnocentrism as when "people unconsciously experience their own cultures as central to reality. They therefore avoid the idea of cultural difference as an implicit or explicit threat to the reality of their own cultural experience" (p. 22).

In contrast, when in a state of cultural relativism, people recognize that all behavior exists in a cultural context, including their own. They recognize the limitation this places on their experience, and they therefore seek out cultural diversity as a way of understanding others and enriching their own experience of reality (Paige, 1999). When people adopt a culturally relative point of view, they are able to accept that a different culture might have different operating rules, and they are willing to see that in a neutral way, without having to judge their own culture as inferior or superior by comparison.

**Cultural Relativism versus Ethical Relativism**   Accepting the fact that a person from another culture may have different values does not mean that from a culturally relative point of view one must always agree with the values of a different culture—some cultural differences may be judged negatively—but the judgment is not ethnocentric in the sense of denying that such a difference could occur. Cultural relativism is not the same as ethical relativism—saying "cultures have different values" is not the same as saying "morally and ethically, anything goes" (all behavior is acceptable in all contexts). One does not have to abandon one's own cultural values to appreciate the idea that not all cultures share the same values.

**Cultural Pluralism**   The idea that a society can contain a variety of cultures is a pluralist viewpoint. There are two kinds of pluralist models—*pluralist preservation* holds that a society should preserve all cultures intact, with diversity and unity as equal values, whereas *pluralistic integration* is the belief that a society should have consensus about core civic values. Both these positions contrast with the idea that a society should be composed of a monoculture, with all diversity assimilated (the "melting pot" model) (National Center for Culturally Responsive Educational Systems, 2006).

Individually, some people are *bicultural,* able to shift their cultural frames of reference and intentionally change their behavior to communicate more effectively when in a different culture. However, just because people are raised in two cultures does not necessarily give them the ability to understand themselves or to generalize cultural empathy to a third culture.

Even in a society in which members of diverse cultural groups have equal opportunities for success, and in which cultural similarities and differences are valued, ethnic-group identity differences may lead to intergroup conflict. A dynamic relationship between ethnic groups is inevitable; each society must find healthy ways to mediate conflict. In a healthy society, strength of the society is founded on a basic willingness to work together to resolve conflicts. Schools can actively try to foster interaction and integration among different groups. Integration creates the conditions for cultural pluralism.

## CLASSROOM GLIMPSE: High School Apartheid?

*Marshall Cox teaches tenth-grade World Cultures in a Los Angeles high school. The high school is situated in a neighborhood that is mixed Hispanic and African-American families and has a science magnet program that attracts high-achieving science students from various other parts of the city. The science students, mostly Asian and European Americans, socialize with their own groups during school and at lunch, as do students of the other ethnicities. Even in his World Cultures classes, which are not specific to the regular or magnet program, students from the two programs attend classes at separate times. As part of his responsibilities as a World Cultures teacher, Marshall would like to see students from the various ethnicities communicate interculturally more often. Should he try to be proactive? If so, what can he do?*

**Cultural Congruence**   In U.S. schools, the contact of cultures occurs daily. Students from families whose cultural values are similar to those of the European-American mainstream culture may be relatively advantaged in schools, such as children from those Asian cultures who are taught that students sit quietly and attentively—behavior that is rewarded in most classrooms. In contrast, African-American students who learn at home to project their personalities and call attention to their individual attributes (Gay, 1975) may be punished for acting out. The congruence or lack thereof between mainstream and minority cultures has lasting effects on students.

Teachers, who have the responsibility to educate students from diverse cultures, find it relatively easy to help students whose values, beliefs, and behaviors are congruent with U.S. schooling but often find it difficult to work with others. The teacher who can find a common ground with diverse students will promote their further education. Relationships between individuals or groups of different cultures are built through commitment, a tolerance for diversity, and a willingness to communicate. The teacher, acting as intercultural educator, accepts and promotes cultural content in the classroom as a valid and vital component of the instructional process and helps students to achieve within the cultural context of the school.

**The Impact of Physical Geography on Cultural Practices**   A social group must develop the knowledge, ideas, and skills it needs to survive in the kind of environment the group inhabits. The geographical environment or physical habitat challenges the group to adapt to or modify the world to meet its needs. When the Native Americans were the sole inhabitants of the North American continent, a wide variety of cultures existed, a necessary response to the variety in the environment. The Iroquois were a village people who lived surrounded by tall wooden palisades. The Chumash, in contrast, lived a leisurely seashore existence on the California coast where fishing was plentiful and the climate moderate. Still a third group, the Plains Indians, were a nomadic people who followed the bison. Each group's culture was adapted for success in its own specific environment.

Classrooms constitute physical environments. These environments have an associated culture. In a room in which the desks are in straight lines facing forward, participants are acculturated to listen as individuals and to respond when spoken to by the teacher. This may be a difficult environment for a young Pueblo child whose learning takes place largely in the communal courtyards outside comfortable adobe dwellings and who is taught the traditional recipes by a mother or grandmother, or the secrets of tribal lore in an underground kiva by the men of the village. The physical environments in which learning takes place vary widely from one culture to another.

**Intragroup and Intergroup Cultural Differences**   Even among individuals from the same general cultural background, there are intragroup differences that affect their worldviews. Some student populations have very different cultures despite a shared ethnic background. Such is the case at Montebello High School in the Los Angeles area:

> Students at Montebello . . . may look to outsiders as a mostly homogeneous population—93 percent Latino, 70 percent low-income—but the 2,974 Latino students are split between those who are connected to their recent immigrant roots and those who are more Americanized. On the "TJ" (for Tijuana) side of the campus, students speak Spanish, take ESL classes, and participate in soccer, *folklorico* dancing, and the Spanish club. On the other side of campus, students speak mostly English, play football and basketball, and participate in student government. The two groups are not [mutually] hostile . . . but, as senior Lucia Rios says, "it's like two countries." The difference in values between the two groups stems from their families' values—the recent immigrants are focused on economic survival and do not have the cash to pay for extracurricular activities. . . . Another difference is musical taste (soccer players listen to Spanish music in the locker room, whereas football players listen to heavy metal and rap). (Hayasaki, 2004, pp. A1, A36–A37)

In the preceding example, the immigrants who had arrived within the last three to five years still referred to Mexico as home. Most of these students were monolingual in Spanish, with varying levels of English proficiency. In contrast, the Mexican-American students who were U.S.-born were English speakers—although they had Mexican last names, they were strongly acculturated into mainstream U.S. values and manifested few overt cultural symbols. Each of these groups could be considered a microculture within the larger microculture of people of Mexican descent living within the United States.

In this case, social identification and language usage, as well as dress, were the markers of the distinct microcultures. As immigrants enter American life, they make conscious or unconscious choices about which aspects of their culture to preserve and which to modify. These decisions are a response to cultural contact.

## Looking at Culture from the Inside Out

**External Elements of Culture**   External elements of culture (e.g., shelter, clothing, food, arts and literature, religious structures, government, technology, language) are relatively easily identified as cultural markers. Certainly young immigrant children would feel comfortable if external elements of their home culture were prominently displayed in the classroom or school. A display of Mexican-style paper cutouts as decoration in a classroom, for example, usually would be viewed in a positive way and not as a token of superficial cultural appropriation.

Indeed, external elements of culture are visible and obvious, to the extent that these are often used as symbols of cultural diversity. How many times does a printed flyer for a Chinese guest speaker have to display a bamboo border before this becomes hackneyed? These visible markers are "ethnic," as in "ethnic food." When one goes out for "ethnic food," does one eat roast beef and potatoes—quintessentially British food? When these external symbols are marked only for minorities, the mainstream culture thinks of itself as "culturally neutral,"

*Bringing the students' culture into the classroom can motivate students to value their heritage.*

whereas those displaying external elements of microcultures are considered "ethnic." Thus, European-American culture is maintained as the norm.

**Internal Elements of Culture**    Internal elements of culture (e.g., values, customs, worldview, mores, beliefs and expectations, rites and rituals, patterns of nonverbal communication, social roles and status, gender roles, family structure, patterns of work and leisure) are harder to identify as cultural markers because they are intangible. Yet these can be as persistent and emotionally loaded as external symbols such as flags or religious icons. In fact, behaviors and attitudes that are misinterpreted can be considered potentially more damaging than misunderstandings about overt symbols, especially with people from cultures that are skilled in reading subtle behavior signals.

## CLASSROOM GLIMPSE: Do You Think I'm Dumb?

*In an English-language development class with beginning middle school English learners, Iris Schaffer pointed to a picture with birds on a tree. "Is this a bird or a tree?" she asked. "How many leaves are there on the ground? What is the color of the leaves?"*

*From the student's facial expressions and voice tones, a visitor noted that they were bored to death and showed little interest in learning. To be asked these types of questions at their age could be insulting. The question was, why didn't the teacher know the students were bored? Were their behaviors and attitudes too subtle for the teacher to read? Was she unable to read these internal elements of culture? (Adapted from Fu, 2004, pp. 9–10)*

## Cultural Diversity: Historical and Contemporary Perspectives

The rhetoric seeking to explain school failure of minority children has changed over the years. Because racial explanations have largely failed—although even as late as the turn of the twenty-first century, several psychologists tried to resurrect racial inferiority theory—there have been attempts to find other explanations based more on cultural than racial differences.

**From Racial Inferiority to Cultural Inferiority**   After Binet's research on intelligence at the turn of the twentieth century, researchers became convinced that inherited racial differences were an explanation for the differential success of students. This became a rationale for unequal school facilities. The genetic inferiority argument, now discredited, assumes that certain populations do not possess the appropriate genes for high intellectual performance.

After the 1954 *Brown v. Board of Education* decision officially signaled the end of segregated schools, the continued lack of school achievement on the part of racial minorities in the United States was attributed not to racial differences but to the fact that families originating in poor, working-class, urban areas were holders of a culture that was inherently inferior (Josephs, 2004). This was a *cultural deprivation* or *cultural deficit* model—essentially, it blamed the poor for the lack of resources in the home. Conveniently, it could be used to blame cultural minorities as well as racial minorities.

**Cultural Incompatibility Theory**   The next theory, that of *cultural incompatibility* or *cultural mismatch*, denied the implication of an inherent inferiority in minority cultures but posited that the difference in home culture versus school culture was one of the reasons minority students do poorly (Irvine, 1990). The cultural mismatch perspective maintains that cultures vary and that some of the skills learned in one culture may transfer to a second, but that other skills will be of little value or, worse, will interfere with assimilation to the new culture.

Cultural mismatch was quickly generalized from its origin in race theory to all cultural differences, including those involving language. Furthermore, unlike cultural deprivation theory, it placed no explicit value judgment on the culture of either the school or the home. This theory of cultural incompatibility stated that when teachers and students do not share the same culture, the different cultural behaviors performed by the other are open to misinterpretation because neither party realizes they may be operating on different cultural codes.

The concept that minority students experience a cultural dissonance between their home culture and their school culture is well documented (Heath, 1999). Unfortunately, this theory has left the onus to teachers to change conditions within the classroom to accommodate the students' cultures, which has proved to be difficult when students from many cultures are schooled in the same room. The result has been "business as usual," with the culture of the schools remaining intact and the expectation remaining that the culture of the home will change.

**The Contextual Interaction Model**   The contextual interaction explanation posits that achievement is a function of the interaction between two cultures—that the values of each are not static but instead adapt to each other when contact occurs. This is the origin of the idea that teachers should accommodate instruction to students as they acculturate.

**Issues of Power and Status**   In classrooms during the monolingual era, students spoke one language or remained silent. The institution controlled the goals and purposes of students' second-language acquisition. There was no question who had the power—the teacher, the authorities, and the language sanctioned by the school (see Darder, 1991; McCarty, 2005).

In retrospect, theories of cultural incompatibility were too narrowly focused on the student, the school, and the home, ignoring the larger issue of inequity of resources in society. The "cure" for school failure in the cultural dissonance model was to align the cultures of the home and school more congruently—and because teachers and schools could not accomplish that mission in the short time allotted for teacher multicultural education, the burden was put again to the families to assimilate more rapidly. Hence the classic emphasis put on the individual to transcend his or her social class.

As soon as the limitations of this liberalist model became apparent, a conservative administration instituted rigorous testing, setting into motion the specter of failure not only for individuals but also for entire schools in minority communities. This distracted schools from the mission of cultural congruence and left the issues unresolved, emphasizing instead standardized testing.

**The Impact of Ethnic Politics**    In the postmodern shift, power circulates, just as dual-language acquisition circulates power between peoples and among cultures. Instead of the pretense that power is nonnegotiable, unavailable, and neutral, communities sought to gain the power to speak, to use a public voice toward their self-determined ends. This resulted in the movement toward charter schools, by which families can choose to exit the public schools. Over 2,200 charter schools now operate in many poor and working-class communities, educating over 750,000 children nationwide (Center for Educational Reform, 2000).

Some charter schools have done a better job than the public schools of fostering ethnic pride. One student from a small middle school in Oakland, California, put it this way:

> It was just really like a community setting . . . like we were learning at home . . . with a bunch of our friends. They had really nice teachers who were, you know, mostly Chicano and Chicana. . . . We could relate to them. They know your culture, your background. [They] talk to your parents and your parents trust them. It's like a family. (Wexler & Huerta, 2002, p. 100)

The pursuit of local schools that reflect the values of the parent community has led to serious alternatives to the dream of the public school that can educate all children with equity under one roof. Many advocates of charter schools no longer believe that the children of diversity can wrest a high-quality education from neighborhood schools that are underfunded and mediocre. The notion of empowerment has taken many ethnic communities down the path of separatism (Fuller, 2003).

## Political and Socioeconomic Factors Affecting English Learners and Their Families

By the year 2010, one of every three Americans will be African American, Hispanic American, or Asian American. This represents a dramatic change from the image of the United States throughout its history. Immigration, together with differing birthrates among various populations, is responsible for this demographic shift. Along with the change in racial and ethnic composition has come a dramatic change in the languages spoken in the United States and the languages spoken in U.S. schools.

These changing demographics are seen as positive or negative depending on one's point of view. Some economists have found that immigrants contribute considerably to the national economy by filling low-wage jobs, spurring investment and job creation, revitalizing once-decaying communities, and paying billions annually in taxes. Unfortunately, the money generated from federal taxes is not returned to the local communities most affected by immigration to pay for schools, hospitals, and social services needed by newcomers (Shuit & McConnell, 1992). The resultant stress on these services may cause residents to view newcomers negatively.

In the midst of changing demographics in the United States, immigrants and economically disadvantaged minorities within the country face such challenges as voting and citizenship status; family income, employment, and educational attainment; housing; and health care availability.

**Culture and Gender Issues**   Parents of English learners often work long hours outside the home, and some families simply are unable to dedicate time each evening to help students complete school assignments. Many young people find themselves working long hours outside the home to help support the family or take care of siblings while parents work double shifts. The role of surrogate caretaker often falls disproportionately on young women, compromising their academic potential. Some immigrant families favor the academic success of sons over daughters, to the dismay of teachers in the United States who espouse equality of opportunity for women. This issue may be more acute as high school students contemplate attending college.

Other issues have emerged as immigrants enter U.S. schools from ever-more diverse cultures. Some girls from traditional cultures are forbidden by their families to wear physical education attire that reveals bare legs. Male exchange students from Muslim cultures may be uncomfortable working in a mixed-gender cooperative learning group in the classroom. Parents who have adopted children from the People's Republic of China may request heritage-language services from the local school district. Multiple issues of language and culture complicate schooling for English learners.

**Poverty among Minority Groups**   A key difficulty for many minorities is that of poverty. Almost one-quarter (24 percent) of African Americans and over one-fifth (22 percent) of Hispanic Americans live in poverty (U.S. Census Bureau, 2004a). Worse, Blacks and Hispanics are even more likely not to be simply poor, but to be *extremely* poor—with incomes under half the poverty level of Whites. In fact, at 16.1 percent, the share of the Black population that is extremely poor is over four times that of non-Hispanic Whites (3.7 percent) and well above that of Hispanics (10.5 percent) (Henwood, 1997).

Poverty hits minority children particularly hard. In 2003, 12.9 million children in the United States lived below the poverty line, and more than one out of every six American children (17.6 percent) were poor. In numbers, 4.2 million poor children are non-Hispanic White, 3.9 million are Black, and 4.1 million are Hispanic. However, the proportion of minority children who are poor is higher: 34.1 percent of Black children, 29.0 percent of Latino children, 12.5 percent of Asian children, and 9.8 percent of non-Hispanic White children.

Poverty does not mean merely inadequate income; rather, it engenders a host of issues, including underemployment, insufficient income and jobs with limited opportunity, homelessness, lack of health insurance, inadequate education, and poor nutrition. Poor children are at least twice as likely as non-poor children to suffer stunted growth or lead poisoning or to be kept back in school. They score significantly lower on reading, math, and vocabulary tests when compared with similar non-poor children (Children's Defense Fund, 2005). However, not all poverty can be linked to these difficulties; some minorities continue in poverty because of social and political factors in the country at large, such as racism and discrimination.

Poverty affects the ability of the family to devote resources to educational effort and stacks the deck against minority student success. Demographic trends ensure that this will be a continuing problem in the United States. Almost three-quarters (74.0 percent) of the Hispanic population are under thirty-five years of age, compared with a little more than half (51.7 percent) of the non-Hispanic White population. The average Hispanic female is well within childbearing age, and Hispanic children constitute the largest growing school population. Therefore, the educational achievement of Hispanic children is of particular concern.

## Educational Issues Involving English Learners beyond the Classroom

What obligation does a community have toward non-English-speaking children? When education is the only means of achieving social mobility for the children of immigrants, these young people must be given the tools necessary to participate in the community at large. When school dropout rates exceed 50 percent among minority populations, it seems evident that the schools are not providing an adequate avenue of advancement. Clearly, some English learners do succeed: Asian-American students are overwhelmingly represented in college attendance, whereas Hispanics are underrepresented.

Individual states are addressing the obligation to educate all students by adhering to content standards documents, written by mandate of the 2001 No Child Left Behind legislation. Nevertheless, children continue to receive different treatment in the public schools. The structure of schooling creates equity problems, all the way from segregative tracking procedures to the day-to-day operation of classrooms, in which some students' voices are heard while others are silenced. These structural components of schools must be addressed lest the belief continue that achievement problems reside solely within students.

In schools, underachievement, the "overachievement" myth, segregation, overreferral to special education, lack of access to the core curricula, and little support for the home language are key concerns. These phenomena may occur because of the ways in which schools and classrooms promote unequal classroom experiences for students. In response to the perception that some students underachieve or overachieve or drop out or are pushed out, schools have designed various mechanisms to help students succeed. Some of these have been successful, others problematic.

The economy of the United States in the future will rest more on Asian-American and Hispanic-American workers than at present. As a consequence, the education of these populations will become increasingly important. Consider that in 2000, 38.8 percent of students enrolled in public elementary and secondary schools were minorities—an increase of 30 percent from 1986, largely due to the growth in the Hispanic population (National Center for Education Statistics [NCES], 2002).

Of these minorities, 87.6 percent of Asian Americans have a high school degree and 49.8 percent have bachelor degrees. In contrast, only 57 percent of Hispanics have high school diplomas and 11.4 percent have college degrees. Eighty-five percent of non-Hispanic Whites, on the other hand, have high school diplomas and over a quarter (27.6 percent) have bachelor degrees (U.S. Census Bureau, 2004a). With these numbers, the extent of the problem becomes clearer.

**Underachievement—Retention, Placement, and Promotion Policies**   Unfortunately, some students are at risk of retention due to underachievement almost immediately on entering school. In 1995, of the 13.7 percent of children who spoke a language other than English in the home, one student in ten (10 percent) was retained at least one grade. (The same percentage was also true for children who speak English at home.) However, retention rates for English learners differed according to language: Spanish, 10.4 percent; other European, 4.3 percent; Asian, 2.4 percent; other, 6.6 percent (NCES, 2000). Thus, Spanish-speaking students are much more at risk of school failure than Asians. On the other side of the coin, students are also differentially distributed in Advanced Placement courses, a type of "in-house" promotion.

*Tracking* offers very different types of instruction depending on students' placement in academic or general education courses. To justify this, educators have argued that tracking is a realistic, efficient response to an increasingly diverse student population. However, tracking has been found to be a major contributor to the continuing gaps in achievement between minorities and European Americans (Oakes, 1985, 1992).

**Underachievement—ELD as Compensatory Education**   The impetus behind the success of the original Bilingual Education Act was that language-minority students needed compensatory education to remediate linguistic "deficiencies." However, compensatory programs are often reduced in scope, content, and pace, and students are not challenged enough, nor given enough of the curriculum to be able to move to mainstream classes.

The view that ELD is compensatory education is all too common. As a part of ELD programs, a portion of the instructional day is usually reserved for ELD instruction. Too often the ELD instruction is given by teaching assistants who have not had professional preparation in ELD teaching, and the instruction has consisted of skill-and-drill worksheets and other decontextualized methods.

*Inclusion* of English learners in mainstream classrooms and challenging educational programs is now the trend. In a study of good educational practice for LEP students, researchers found numerous schools that have successfully been educating English learners to high standards (McLeod, 1995). In these schools, programs for English learners were an integral part of the whole school program, neither conceptually nor physically separate from the rest of the school.

> The exemplary schools have devised creative ways to both include LEP students centrally in the educational program and meet their needs for language instruction and modified curriculum. Programs for LEP students are so carefully crafted and intertwined with the school's other offerings that it is impossible in many cases to point to "the LEP program" and describe it apart from the general program. (McLeod, 1995, p. 4)

Several reform efforts have attempted to dismantle some of the compensatory education and tracking programs previously practiced in schools. These have included accelerated schools, cooperative learning, restructured schools, and "untracking." A particularly noteworthy high school program is Advancement Via Individual Determination (AVID). This "untracking" program places low-achieving students (who are primarily from low-income and ethnic or language-minority backgrounds) in the same college preparatory academic program as high-achieving students (who are primarily from middle- or upper-middle-income and "Anglo" backgrounds) (Mehan & Hubbard, 1999).

**Underachievement—Dropping Out of High School**    An unfortunate and direct result of being schooled in an unfamiliar language is that some students begin falling behind their expected grade levels, putting them at risk eventually. Students who repeat at least one grade are more likely to drop out of school. Every year across the country, a dangerously high percentage of students—disproportionately poor and minority—disappear from the educational pipeline before graduating from high school. Nationally, only about 68 percent of all students who enter ninth grade will graduate "on time" with regular diplomas in twelfth grade.

Whereas the graduation rate for White students is 75 percent, only approximately half of Latino students earn regular diplomas alongside their classmates. Even though California reports a robust overall graduation rate of 86.9 percent, researchers at the Harvard Civil Rights Project have claimed that this figure dramatically underestimates the actual numbers of dropouts, and that graduation rates in individual districts and schools—particularly those with high minority concentrations—remain at crisis-level proportions.

An independent study by Dr. Julie Mendoza of the University of California All Campus Consortium on Research for Diversity (UC/ACCORD) finds that in the Los Angeles Unified School District (LAUSD) the exodus of Los Angeles youth from school is especially pronounced between grades 9 and 10; only 48 percent of Black and Latino students who start ninth grade complete grade 12. Of the Black and Latino youth who complete high school in LAUSD, only one in five has met the curriculum requirements to qualify for admission to a four-year public university in California (Losen & Wald, 2005).

An important marketplace repercussion from dropout statistics is the differential rate of employment of these two groups: Sixty-one percent of high school dropouts are in the labor force versus 80 percent of graduates who were not in college (Kaufman, Alt, & Chapman, 2004).

## CLASSROOM GLIMPSE: Segregation and Dropping Out

*The predominantly Puerto-Rican community in North Philadelphia is located in an economically depressed part of the city that is plagued by many of the problems of low-income urban neighborhoods across the United States. Latinos make up between 85 and 99 percent of the total student population in this community, and the Latino dropout rate is disproportionately high in the district. According to a Harvard University report that examined issues of racial justice in the United States, such segregation of Latinos in poorly performing schools in low-income neighborhoods is relatively common across the nation. In fact, it is pervasive in cities in the Northeast (Harvard Civil Rights Project, online at www.civilrightsproject.harvard.edu/research/reseg03/resegregation03.php). (Freeman, 2004, p. 88)*

Noting the alarmingly high percentage of Hispanic dropouts, U.S. Secretary of Education Richard W. Riley in 1995 initiated a special project to study issues related to the problem. In its final report, *No More Excuses,* the Hispanic Dropout Project (1998) explicated the continuing stereotypes, myths, and excuses that surround Hispanic-American youth and their families:

What we saw and what people told us confirmed what well-established research has also found: Popular stereotypes—which would place the blame for school dropout on Hispanic students, their families, and language background, and that would allow people to shrug their shoulders as if to say that that was an enormous, insoluble problem or one that would go away by itself—are just plain wrong. (p. 3)

The Hispanic Dropout Project (1998) found that teachers may make one of two choices that undermine minority students' school achievement: either to blame the students and their families for school failure or to excuse the students' poor performance, citing factors such as low socioeconomic status or lack of English proficiency. This latter attitude, although well meaning, is particularly harmful as it does not allow students access to cognitively demanding instruction (Lockwood, 2000).

The three recommendations the Hispanic Dropout Project (1998) report made for teachers are consistent with the principles, concepts, and strategies outlined in this text: (1) Provide high-quality curriculum and instruction—methods and strategies provided in Part II of this book; (2) become knowledgeable about students and their families, as discussed in Part III; and (3) receive high-quality professional development—an ongoing task in which this entire text can be an impetus. The online *Transforming Education for Hispanic Youth: Exemplary Practices, Programs, and Schools* (Lockwood & Secada, 1999) provided more in-depth information about, and examples of, exemplary schools for Hispanic-American youth.

**Underachievement—Difficulties in Higher Education**   Several measures of achievement reveal discrepancies in the achievement of Whites in comparison with ethnic minorities. Ethnic minority groups, except for Asian Americans, attain lower levels of higher education. Of college students in 1996, Latinos represented 11.7 percent of community college students and only 5.7 percent in four-year institutions. In 2001, of the 62 percent of high school graduates who attended college, 54.6 percent were White and only 5.6 percent were of Hispanic origin (National Center for Education Statistics [NCES], 2005).

As of 2003, young Blacks and Hispanics (ages eighteen to twenty-four) participated in postsecondary education at a lower rate than Whites: Blacks at 26 percent, Hispanics at 22 percent, compared to 38 percent for Whites. Participation rates for Hispanic young men have declined since 1974 (NCES, 2005). Only about one in six Latinos who attend college ultimately graduates (Thernstrom & Thernstrom, 2003). Low educational levels have resulted in poor subsequent incomes and a lower likelihood of attaining high-prestige occupations.

**Underachievement—Difficulties Attaining Management Status**   Hispanic Americans represent only a small number of faculty members and administrators in higher education; they hold 3.3 percent of such positions (NCES, 2003). Whether due to English-language limitations or other structural problems in society, Latino men hold only 0.7 percent of top management positions in U.S. society, and Latinas only 0.1 percent (Cockcroft, 1995).

It is unclear whether underachievement is the real problem. The real problem may be racism—even ethnic minorities who achieve in school may not be able to attain positions of responsibility in society. It is equally unclear to what extent English proficiency—or lack of it—is linked to underachievement and discrimination.

**The "Overachievement" Myth**    A pernicious view ascribes exceptional achievement to a specific group, Asian Americans. The term *model minority* has been coined for Asian Americans, connoting a supergroup whose members have succeeded in U.S. society despite a long history of racial oppression. Asian-American students are seen as academic superstars who win academic distinction and are overrepresented in elite institutions of higher education (Suzuki, 1989).

This stereotype plays out in at least two ways with equally damaging results. First, ascribing a "whiz kid" image to students can mask their individual needs and problems and lead the teacher to assume a student needs little or no help. This may ultimately lead to neglect, isolation, delinquency, or inadequate preparation for the labor market among these students (Feng, 1994).

Second, lumping all Asian Americans together into this stereotype ignores the different cultural, language, economic, and immigration statuses of the various groups and severely limits those most in need of help. Among Southeast Asian students, the Khmer and the Lao tend to have a grade point average (GPA) below that of White majority students, whereas Vietnamese, Chinese-Vietnamese, Japanese, Korean, Chinese, and Hmong students tend to have well above this GPA (Trueba, Cheng, & Ima, 1993).

One factor that may contribute to academic success for certain minority groups is the groups' views about the place of education for the group. For example, the success of the Punjabi (Sikhs from rural northwest India who have settled mainly in northern California) may be due to the group's resistance to assimilation into mainstream society and to the strong family support for students who are harassed or who experience other cultural conflicts in the schools (Gibson, 1987).

Another factor may be bias toward viewing the group as academically successful—school personnel may act toward Asian Americans in ways that support the model minority attribution. The behavior of Chinese students may be more in accord with teachers' expectations than, for example, that of Hispanic-American students. Asian-American students may comply with authority, but this compliance may afford them less opportunity to acquire the networking and social skills needed to advance in the workplace.

## BEST PRACTICE: Countering the Model Minority Myth

To avoid reenacting the model minority myth in the classroom:

- Treat students as individuals.
- Do not ascribe high or low expectations based on national origin or ethnicity.
- Recognize that Asian/Pacific Island-American students speak different languages and come from different cultural areas.
- Take time to learn about the languages and cultures of students to appreciate their differences. (Nash, 1991)

"Asian-American Children: What Teachers Should Know" (Feng, 1994) provides general information about Asian-American students and a list of practices to help teachers become more knowledgeable about Asian cultures. Equally helpful is O'Connor's (2004) "Understanding Discrimination against Asian Americans."

**Segregated Schools**   Although during the 1970s and 1980s districts were working at deseg-regating their schools, the 1990s witnessed an increasing number of court cases that released districts from these efforts (Weiler, 1998). Inequity follows segregation. In a study in the Boston metro area, "97 percent of the schools with less than a tenth white students faced concentrated poverty compared to 1 percent of the schools with less than a tenth minority students" (Orfield & Lee, 2005, n.p.) In addition, segregation makes it difficult for English learners to be grouped with native speakers of English during the school day.

Minority students typically live in racially isolated neighborhoods and are more likely to attend segregated schools. Over one-third (38 percent) of Hispanic students and Black stu-dents (37 percent) attended schools with minority enrollments of 90 to 100 percent. Seventy-seven percent of Hispanics and 71 percent of Blacks were enrolled in schools where minorities constitute 50 percent or more of the population.

Therefore, nearly a half-century after *Brown v. Board of Education*, a student who is Black, Latino, or Native American remains much less likely to succeed in school. A major fac-tor is a disparity of resources—inner-city schools with large minority populations have been found to have higher percentages of first-year teachers, higher enrollments, fewer library resources, and less in-school parental involvement, all characteristics that have been shown to relate to school success (U.S. Government Accounting Office, 2002).

**Overreferral to Special Education**   Referrals and placements in special education have been disproportionate for culturally and linguistically different students. Various explanations have been offered for this overreferral: language problems, poor school progress, academic or cogni-tive difficulties, low level of acculturation, inadequate assessment, or special learning problems (Malavé, 1991). Biased assessment can result in negative evaluation of English learners, espe-cially when tests are given in English to students who have not had sufficient exposure to English, include language or concepts that favor the middle-class native English speaker, or are predicated on models of cultural deprivation or other deficit models (Valenzuela & Baca, 2004).

**Access to Core Curricula**   Access to the core curriculum is essential for English learners to make adequate progress in school. This means that ELD activities cannot stand in the way of other academic subjects. A student who is pulled out of the class to receive ESL services, for exam-ple, cannot miss social studies class. Nor can a student who arrives in a large urban high school without adequate English proficiency be denied an appropriate mathematics curriculum. Meet-ing the needs of English learners with SDAIE instruction is a challenge that must be addressed.

Issues of race and class are compounded by issues of language in U.S. schools. For exam-ple, compared to White and Asian students, Latino students are less likely to be placed in edu-cation tracks with rigorous curricula that prepare them for college (Haycock, Jerald, & Huang, 2001). Only one in five eighth-grade Latino students takes algebra, compared to one in four for Whites (The Education Trust, 1998). Among seventeen-year-olds, only 8 percent of Hispanics have taken precalculus or calculus, compared with 15 percent of Whites (NCES, 2000).

**Little Support for the First Language**   In U.S. schools, second-language and foreign lan-guage learning are neglected in the core curriculum, unlike, for example, in European schools, in which many elementary children are given foreign language classes. U.S. students who are already proficient in a heritage language bring a rich resource to academia that is being tapped in the two-way immersion programs. Foreign language in the elementary school (FLES) is an academic subject in the United States in elite schools (private schools in New York and Washington, D.C., for example), where French (or, less commonly, Japanese) is offered, as well as in privileged environments such as the wealthy suburbs of New York, Boston, San Francisco, and Minneapolis and in university towns such as Chapel Hill, North Carolina, and Austin, Texas.

Yet the urban school districts that do not support maintenance programs in heritage languages are causing students to lose the very language resources that are difficult to reestablish as foreign languages at the high school level. Access to the core curriculum is the right of all learners—and in the case of English learners, that core curriculum should include language classes in the heritage as well as perhaps a third language.

The issues just outlined offer some examples of the complexity involved in educating students of diverse primary languages and cultures. The current emphasis on standards heightens the tensions inherent in such a project. On the positive side, students have a right to a high standard of rich, challenging instruction no matter what linguistic and cultural resources they bring to schooling. On the other hand, the emphasis on high standards must be matched with allocation of funds so that teachers are given the resources they need to accomplish these lofty goals.

The conclusion is inescapable: The educational system of the United States has been fundamentally weak in serving the fastest growing school-age populations. Today's minority students are entering school with significantly different social and economic backgrounds from those of previous student populations and therefore require educators to modify their teaching approaches to ensure that these students have access to the American dream.

These issues involving the education of English learners will not be resolved solely through the efforts of individual teachers, but require a determined effort on the part of educators as a social movement to reverse discriminatory educational policies and achieve full funding for the educational services that English learners deserve. This will require reversal of the damaging educational politics of neoliberalism of the past twenty years (Anyon, 1994).

## CULTURAL CONTACT

Since the 1980s, an unprecedented flow of immigrants and refugees has entered the United States. One of the impacts of this immigration is that many school districts not only have students speaking three or more languages in a single classroom, but they also have students who speak the same non-English language but who come from different cultures. School officials have found, for example, that many immigrants from Central America do not follow the same pattern of school performance as Mexican-American students. These demographic issues provoke the question, can we understand how to increase the school success of all students by studying the process of cultural contact?

As immigrants enter American life, they make conscious or unconscious choices about which aspects of their culture to preserve and which to modify, and these decisions affect learning. The contact between the home culture and the school culture affects schooling. The immigrant culture can be swallowed up (*assimilation*), immigrants can adapt to the dominant culture (*acculturation*), both may adapt to each other (*accommodation*), or they may coexist (*pluralism* or *biculturalism*). Contact between cultures is often fraught with misunderstanding, but it can also be positive and enriching. Means of mediation or resolution must be found to help students benefit from one anothers' cultural knowledge, as well as alleviate cultural conflict.

## Fears about Cultural Adaptation

Pryor (2002) captured the nature of immigrant parents' concerns about their children's adjustment to life in the United States:

> In the United States, some immigrant parents live in fear that their children will be corrupted by what they believe to be the materialistic and individualistic dominant culture, become alienated from their families, and fall prey to drugs and promiscuity. One Jordanian mother stated, "I tell my son (who is 8 years old) not to use the restroom in school. I tell him it is because he might catch germs there that he could bring home, and make the whole family ill. I really am afraid he may get drugs from other kids in the restroom." (p. 187)

Many immigrant parents are overwhelmed with personal, financial, and work-related problems; they may miss their homelands and family members abroad and have few resources to which to turn for help. They struggle to maintain their dignity in the face of humiliation, frustration, and loneliness. In the process of coming to terms with life in a foreign country, they may be at odds with the assimilation or acculturation processes their children are experiencing, causing family conflict.

## Processes of Cultural Contact

**Assimilation**   *Cultural assimilation* is the process by which individuals adopt the behaviors, values, beliefs, and lifestyle of the dominant culture, neglecting or abandoning their own culture in the process. *Structural assimilation* is participation in the social, political, and economic institutions and organizations of mainstream society. It is structural assimilation that has been problematic for many immigrants, especially for groups other than White Protestant immigrants from northern and western Europe.

Individuals may make a choice concerning their degree of cultural assimilation. However, the dominant society determines the extent of structural assimilation. These two related but different concepts have important consequences in classrooms. Teachers may be striving to have students assimilate but be blind to the fact that some of their students will not succeed because of attitudes and structures of the dominant society.

**Acculturation**   When individuals *acculturate*, they adapt to a second culture without necessarily giving up their first culture. It is an additive process in which individuals' rights to participate in their own heritage is preserved (Finnan, 1987). Schools are the primary places in which children of various cultures learn about the mainstream culture. According to Cortés (1993):

> Acculturation . . . should be a primary goal of education. Schools have an obligation to help students acculturate because additive acculturation contributes to individual empowerment and expanded life choices. But schools should not seek subtractive assimilation, which can lead to personal and cultural disempowerment by eroding students' multicultural abilities to function effectively both within the mainstream and within their own ethnic milieus. Although assimilation is acceptable, it should be regarded as a student's choice and not as something for the school to impose. (p. 4)

**Accommodation**    A two-way process, *accommodation* happens when members of the mainstream culture change in adapting to a minority culture, the members of which in turn accept some cultural change as they adapt to the mainstream. Thus, accommodation is a mutual process. To make accommodation a viable alternative in schools, teachers need to demonstrate that they are receptive to learning from the diverse cultures in their midst.

## CLASSROOM GLIMPSE: Accommodating Students' Culture

*[I]n non-[American]-Indian classes students are given opportunities to ask the teacher questions in front of the class, and do so. Indian students are given fewer opportunities for this because when they do have the opportunity, they don't use it. Rather, the teacher of Indians allows more periods in which she is available for individual students to approach her alone and ask their questions where no one else can hear them. (Philips, 1972, p. 383)*

**Biculturalism**    Being able to function successfully in two cultures constitutes biculturalism. Darder (1991) defined *biculturalism* as

> a process wherein individuals learn to function in two distinct sociocultural environments: their primary culture, and that of the dominant mainstream culture of the society in which they live. It represents the process by which bicultural human beings mediate between the dominant discourse of educational institutions and the realities they must face as members of subordinate cultures. (pp. 48–49)

Everyone is to some extent bicultural. At a minimum level, everyone who works outside the home functions daily in two cultures—personal (home) and professional (work). For some individuals, the distance between the cultures of work and home are almost indistinguishable, whereas for others the distance is great. For example, Native-American children who were sent to Bureau of Indian Affairs boarding schools often experienced great difficulties in adjusting to the disparate cultures of home and school.

What is it like to be bicultural in the United States? Bicultural people are sometimes viewed with distrust. Even parents may feel threatened by their bicultural children. Appalachian families who moved to large cities to obtain work often pressured their children to maintain an agrarian, preindustrial lifestyle, a culture that is in many ways inconsistent with urban environments (Pasternak, 1994). Similarly, families from rural Mexico may seek to maintain traditional values even as their children adopt behaviors from the macroculture. The process of becoming bicultural is not without stress, especially for students who are expected to internalize dissimilar, perhaps conflicting values.

### Psychological and Social–Emotional Issues Involving Cultural Contact

**Phases of Acculturation**    Reactions to a new culture vary, but there are distinct stages of emotional ups and downs in the process of experiencing a different culture: Typical emotions and behaviors begin with elation or excitement, move to anxiety or disorientation, and culminate in some degree of adjustment (Levine & Adelman, 1982). Students go through these same emotional stages, with varied intensity depending on the degree of similarity between home and school cultures, the individual child, and the teacher.

The first state, *euphoria* or the *honeymoon period*, may result from the excitement of and fascination with the customs, foods, and sights of the new culture. The next stage, *culture shock* or *cultural fatigue*, may follow as the newcomer is increasingly frustrated by disorienting cultural cues. Deprivation of the familiar may cause a loss of self-esteem, depression, anger, or withdrawal. The severity of this shock will vary as a function of the personality of the individual, the emotional support available, and the perceived or actual differences between the two cultures.

The final stage, *adjustment* or *adaptation* to the new culture, can take months or years. Ideally, the newcomer borrows habits, customs, and characteristics from the new culture, resulting in a feeling of comfort in negotiating everyday activities such as going to school and shopping. On the other hand, individuals who do not adjust may feel lonely, frustrated, and repulsed by aspects of the new culture. Eventually, successful adaptation results in newcomers being able to actively express themselves and to create a full range of meaning in the situation. (See Box 8.1.)

In the classroom, students may show culture shock as withdrawal, depression, or anger. Mental fatigue may result from continually straining to comprehend the new culture. Individuals may need time to process personal and emotional as well as academic experiences. The teacher must take great care to not belittle or reject a student who is experiencing culture shock.

### Resolving Problems of Cultural Contact

Students experiencing cultural conflict may meet racism and anti-immigration sentiment and behaviors ranging from subtle innuendos, to verbal abuse and threats, to physical violence. Schools are crucial to the resolution of hate crime because the young are perpetrators and the schools are staging grounds. Policies, curricula, and antiracism programs are needed to moderate conflicts when cultures come into contact.

**The Culturally Receptive School**   In general, research suggests that substantive changes in attitudes, behaviors, and achievement occur only when the entire school adopts a multicultural atmosphere. In such schools, all students learn to understand cultures different from their own.

---

### Box 8.1   Example of Concept: Language and Culture Shock

Zacarian (2004) related the story of one student experiencing language and culture shock and the effect it had on his personality: "One student, whom I'll call Jin, shared some powerful feelings with his classmates. Through his tutor, he stated that he had been very popular in China, made friends easily, and loved to be with his friends. However, after a few weeks of attempting to ask short questions in English and not being able to understand the responses he received he had found it increasingly painful and frustrating to try to speak English. 'From being popular and having a lot of friends,' Jin stated through his translator, 'to being silenced by my lack of English is terrible for me.'" (pp. 12–13)

Minority students do not internalize negativity about their culture and customs. Cooperative learning groups and programs that allow interaction between students of diverse backgrounds usually result in fewer incidents of name-calling and ethnic slurs as well as in improved academic achievement (Nieto, 2004).

When the languages and cultures of students are highly evident in their schools and teachers refer to them explicitly, they gain status. Schools that convey the message that all cultures are of value—by displaying explicit welcome signs in many languages, by attempts to involve parents, by a deliberate curriculum of inclusion, and by using affirmative action to promote hiring of a diverse faculty—help to maintain an atmosphere that reduces interethnic conflict.

**Strategies for Conflict Resolution**     If interethnic conflict occurs, taking immediate, proactive steps to resolve the conflict is necessary. The Conflict Resolution Network online at www.crnhq.org/twelveskills.html recommends a twelve-skill approach. Table 8.3 presents a scenario in which conflict resolution is needed and describes the twelve skills applied to the scenario.

## BEST PRACTICE: Conflict Resolution in New Jersey

Real estate development in the West Windsor–Plainsboro School District in the 1980s and 1990s brought a diverse population into one rural area. Increasing incidents of racial unrest in the schools and in the community at large caused school administrators to begin a program of conflict resolution in K–12 classrooms. Among its components were the following:

- A peacemaking program at the elementary level to teach children how to solve problems without resorting to aggression
- Training for middle school students in facilitating positive human relations
- A ninth-grade elective course in conflict resolution
- An elective course for grades 11 and 12 students to prepare student mediators for a peer-mediation center
- An annual "human relations" retreat for student leaders and teachers that encouraged frank conversations about interpersonal and race relations
- A planned welcome program for newcomers at the school to overcome feelings of isolation
- A minority recruitment program for teachers
- Elimination of watered-down, nonrigorous academic courses in lieu of challenging courses, accompanied by a tutoring program for academically underprepared high school students

Within three years, the number of incidences of vandalism, violence, and substance abuse in the school district was reduced considerably. The people of West Windsor and Plainsboro "accomplished much in their quest to rise out of the degradation of bigotry" (Bandlow, 2002, pp. 91–92; also Prothrow-Smith, 1994).

Explicit training for elementary students in negotiation and mediation procedures has proved effective in managing conflict, especially when such programs focus on safely expressing feelings, taking the perspective of the other, and providing the rationale for diverse points

**TABLE 8.3** Applying the Twelve-Skill Approach to Interethnic Conflict

Scenario: A group of four white girls in tenth grade had been making fun of Irena and three of her friends, all of whom were U.S.-born Mexican Americans. One afternoon Irena missed her bus home from high school, and the four girls surrounded her when she was putting books in her locker. One girl shoved a book out of the stack in her hands. Irena shoved her back. Just then, a teacher came around the corner and took Irena to the office for discipline. The assistant principal, Ms. Nava, interviewed Irena to gain some background on the situation. Rather than dealing with Irena in isolation, Ms. Nava waited until the next day, called all eight of the girls into her office, and applied the twelve-skill approach to conflict resolution.

| Skill | Application of Skills to Scenario |
|---|---|
| 1. The win–win approach: Identify attitude shifts to respect all parties' needs. | Ms. Nava asked each girl to write down what the ideal outcome of the situation would be. Three of the girls had written "respect." Ms. Nava decided to use this as a win–win theme. |
| 2. Creative response: Transform problems into creative opportunities. | Each girl was asked to write the name of an adult who respected her and how she knew it was genuine respect. |
| 3. Empathy: Develop communication tools to build rapport. Use listening to clarify understanding. | In turn, each girl described what she had written. The other girls had to listen, using eye contact to show attentiveness. |
| 4. Appropriate assertiveness: Apply strategies to attack the problem, not the person. | Ms. Nava offered an opportunity for members of the group to join the school's Conflict Resolution Task Force. She also warned the group that another incident between them would result in suspension. |
| 5. Cooperative power: Eliminate "power over" to build "power with" others. | Each girl was paired with a girl from the "other side" (cross-group pair) to brainstorm ways in which teens show respect for one another. |
| 6. Managing emotions: Express fear, anger, hurt, and frustration wisely to effect change. | Ms. Nava then asked Irena and the girl who had pushed her book to tell their side of the incident without name-calling. |
| 7. Willingness to resolve: Name personal issues that cloud the picture. | Each girl was asked to name one underlying issue between the groups that this incident represented. |
| 8. Mapping the conflict: Define the issues needed to chart common needs and concerns. | Ms. Nava mapped the issues by writing them on a wall chart as they were brought forth. |
| 9. Development of options: Design creative solutions together. | Still in the cross-group pairs from step 5, each pair was asked to design a solution for one of the issues mapped. |
| 10. Introduction to negotiation: Plan and apply effective strategies to reach agreement. | Ms. Nava called the girls into her office for a second day. They reviewed the solutions that were designed and made a group plan for improved behavior. |
| 11. Introduction to mediation: Help conflicting parties move toward solutions. | Each cross-group pair generated two ideas for repair if the above plan failed. |
| 12. Broadening perspectives: Evaluate the problem in its broader context. | The eight girls were asked if racial conflict occurred outside their group. Ms. Nava asked for discussion: Were the same issues they generated in this conflict responsible for other conflicts? |

*Source:* Adapted from www.crnhq.org.

of view (Johnson, Johnson, Dudley, & Acikgoz, 1994). Especially critical is the role of a mediator in establishing and maintaining a balance of power between two parties in a dispute, protecting the weaker party from intimidation, and ensuring that both parties have a stake in the process and the outcome of mediation.

Perhaps the best way to prevent conflict is to include a variety of cultural content and make sure the school recognizes and values cultural diversity. If conflict does occur, however, there are means to prevent its escalation. Teachers should be aware of conflict resolution techniques before they are actually needed.

## BEST PRACTICE: Resolving Conflicts in the Classroom

- To defuse a problem:
  - ✓ Talk to students privately, encouraging the sharing of perceptions on volatile issues.
  - ✓ Communicate expectations that students will be able to resolve their differences.

- If confrontation occurs:
  - ✓ Resolve to be calm in the face of verbalized anger and hostility.
  - ✓ Set aside a brief period for verbal expression.
  - ✓ Allow students to vent feelings as a group.
  - ✓ Do not tolerate violence or personal attacks.

Programs that teach about "group differences," involve exhortation or mere verbal learning, or are designed merely to "reduce prejudice" are usually not effective, because to achieve a long-term change in attitudes, a change in behavior must come first. Schools that are committed to increasing intercultural communication can make cultural contact a positive experience for everyone involved.

# CULTURAL DIVERSITY IN THE UNITED STATES AND CALIFORNIA

## The Demographics of Change

Throughout the United States, 47 million people (18 percent of the population) speak a language other than English at home (U.S. Census Bureau, 2003). In the 2000 census, almost 23 million people in the United States reported that they *do not* speak English well. Although the largest percentage of non–English speakers (37 percent) lives in the West, English learners and their families are increasingly living in places such as the Midwest (9 percent) and the South (15 percent) that have not previously needed to hire English-language development (ELD) teachers. The majority of English learners in the United States are Spanish-speaking (28.1 million); this represents an increase of 62 percent over the decade 1990–2000.

Again according to the 2000 census, almost 3 million school-age children spoke Spanish as a native language—more than three-quarters (76.9 percent) of English learners in schools. No other native language exceeded 3 percent. The five most common languages after Spanish

**TABLE 8.4**   States with the Highest Percent of Population Speaking a Language Other Than English

| State | Population of Non-English-Language Speakers (in millions) | Percent of the State's Population |
|---|---|---|
| California | 12.4 | 39.5 |
| New Mexico | 0.5 | 36.5 |
| Texas | 6.0 | 31.2 |
| New York | 5.0 | 28.0 |
| Hawaii | 0.3 | 26.6 |
| Arizona | 1.2 | 25.9 |
| New Jersey | 2.0 | 25.5 |

were Vietnamese (2.4 percent), Hmong (1.8 percent), Korean (1.2 percent), Arabic (1.2 percent), and Haitian Creole (1.1 percent) (Hopstock & Stephenson, 2003).

California had the largest population percentage of non-English-language speakers, followed by New Mexico, Texas, New York, Hawai'i, Arizona, and New Jersey (see Table 8.4). Other states—Florida (3.5 million), Illinois (2.2 million), and Massachusetts (1.1 million)—also have large populations of non-English-language speakers. The largest percentage increase from 1990 to 2000 occurred in Nevada, where the number increased by 193 percent. In California, English learners increased 44 percent in the decade 1992–2002.

The National Clearinghouse for English Language Acquisition and Language Instruction Educational Programs (NCELA) put the number of children of school age with a home language other than English at 9,779,766—one of every six children. Of these language-minority students, almost half (or 4,747,763) do not yet have sufficient proficiency in English to be able to succeed academically in traditional all-English-medium classrooms (NCELA, 2004). Los Angeles Unified School District leads all other school districts in the nation in the number (299,232) of English learners (in 2002–2003), the number of languages (56), and the percent of total enrollment (40 percent); followed by New York City; Dade County, Florida; Chicago; Houston; Dallas; San Diego; and Long Beach, California. In 2004, California led the states in need for English learner services at the K–12 level with a school enrollment of approximately 1.6 million English learners (California Department of Education, 2004b).

These population demographics indicate that all states need to provide services for English learners, with the need greatest in California, New Mexico, New York, and Texas, serving Hispanics or Asian/Pacific Islanders. The linguistic and cultural variety of English learners suggests that more and more teachers use ELD strategies and methods to serve as intercultural and interlinguistic educators—those who can reach out to learners from a variety of backgrounds and offer effective learning experiences.

## Migration and Immigration in the United States and California

The United States has historically been a nation of immigrants, but the nature and causes of immigration have changed over time. The earliest settlers to the east coast of North America came from England and Holland, whereas those to the south and west came mainly from

Spain. In the early eighteenth century, these settlers were joined by involuntary immigrants—slaves from Africa. The social upheavals and overpopulation that characterized nineteenth-century Europe and Asia brought more than 14 million immigrants to the United States in the forty-year period between 1860 and 1900. Immigration from the Pacific Rim countries was constrained by severe immigration restrictions until the last decades of the twentieth century.

However, imperialistic policies of the United States, primarily the conquest of the Philippines, Puerto Rico, Hawai'i, and the Pacific Islands, caused large influxes of these populations throughout the twentieth century. The wars in Southeast Asia and Central America throughout the 1970s and 1980s led to increased emigration from these areas. In the 1990s, immigrants arrived from all over the world. In 2000, 40 percent of all legal immigrants came from just five countries—Mexico, China, the Philippines, India, and Vietnam (Migration Policy Institute, 2004).

Immigrants have come to the United States for a variety of reasons: the desire for adventure and economic gain in a new world, the desire to flee religious and political persecution, or as a result of forcible abduction. These factors provided both attractive forces (pull) and expulsive forces (push). Later, U.S. foreign policy created connections with populations abroad that pulled certain groups to the United States. For example, the conquest of the Philippines at the turn of the century eventually resulted in significant Philippine immigration to the United States.

Immigration laws responded to both push and pull factors throughout the nineteenth and twentieth centuries, at times curtailing emigration from specific regions and at other times allowing increased immigration. Once in the United States, both immigrants and natives have historically been restless populations. Much of the history of the United States consists of the migration of groups from one part of the country to another.

## Contemporary Causes of Migration and Immigration

Migration is an international phenomenon. Throughout the world, populations are dislocated by war, famine, civil strife, economic change, persecution, and other factors. The United States has been a magnet for immigrants seeking greater opportunity and economic stability. Politics and religion as well as economics provide reasons for emigration. U.S. domestic and foreign policies affect the way in which groups of foreigners are accepted. Changes in immigration policy, such as amnesty, affect the number of immigrants who enter the country each year.

**Economic Factors**   The great disparity in the standard of living attainable in the United States compared to that of many developing countries makes immigration attractive. Self-advancement is uppermost in the minds of many immigrants and acts as a strong incentive despite the economic exploitation often extended to immigrants (e.g., lower wages, exclusion from desirable jobs). Immigrants may bring with them unique skills. On the whole, however, the economy of the United States does not have an unlimited capacity to employ immigrants in specialized niches.

Immigration policy has corresponded with the cycles of boom and bust in the U.S. economy. The Chinese Exclusion Act of 1882 stopped immigration from China to the United States because of the concern that Chinese labor would flood the market. The labor shortage in the western United States that resulted from excluding the Chinese had the effect of welcoming Japanese immigrants who were good farm laborers. Later, during the Great Depression of the 1930s, with a vast labor surplus in the United States, the U.S. Congress severely restricted Philippine immigration, and policies were initiated to "repatriate" Mexicans back across the border.

> **Box 8.2**   Find Out More about Economic Factors:
> *US Immigration Facts*
>
> www.rapidimmigration.com/usa/1_eng_immigration_facts.html. This site provides general facts about recent U.S. immigration and then discusses immigrant entrepreneurs and economic characteristics of immigrants.

When World War II transformed the labor surplus of the 1930s into a severe worker shortage, the United States and Mexico established the Bracero Program, a bilateral agreement allowing Mexicans to cross the border to work on U.S. farms and railroads. However, despite the economic attractiveness of the United States, now, as then, most newcomers to this society experience a period of economic hardship (see Box 8.2).

**Political Factors**   Repression, civil war, and change in government create a push for emigration from foreign countries, whereas political factors within the United States create a climate of acceptance for some political refugees and not for others. After the Vietnam War, many refugees were displaced in Southeast Asia. Some sense of responsibility for their plight caused the U.S. government to accept many of these people into the United States, such as Cambodians who cooperated with the U.S. military: 6,300 Khmer in 1975; 10,000 Cambodians in 1979; and 60,000 Cambodians between 1980 and 1982 (Gillett, 1989a). In the 1980s, civil war caused the displacement of 600,000 Salvadorans, nearly 200,000 of whom were admitted to the United States through the Deferred Enforced Departure program (Gillett, 1989b).

Other populations, such as Haitians claiming political persecution, have been turned away from U.S. borders. U.S. policy did not consider them to be victims of political repression but rather of economic hardship—a fine distinction, in many cases, and here one might suspect that racial issues in the United States make it more difficult for them to immigrate. It would seem, then, that the grounds for political asylum—race, religion, nationality, membership in a particular social group, political opinion—can be clouded by confounding factors.

Religion complicates the political picture; many eastern European Jews, forced to emigrate because of anti-Semitic pogroms in the nineteenth century, came to the United States in great numbers. Unfortunately, during the 1930s and 1940s, Jews persecuted by Nazis were not free to emigrate or were not accepted as immigrants, and were killed. Under the communist regime in the former USSR, Russian Jews were allowed to emigrate in small numbers and were accepted into the United States. Current immigration policies permit refugees to be accepted on the basis of religion if the applicant can prove that persecution comes from the government or is motivated by the government.

In sum, people are pushed to the United States because of political instability or political policies unfavorable to them in their home countries. Political conditions within the United States affect whether immigrants are accepted or denied.

**Family Unification**   A primary motivation for many applications to the Bureau of Citizenship and Immigration Services (BCIS) in the Department of Homeland Security is family unification. Once settled, immigrants seek to bring family members. The risks associated with travel to the New World have made immigration a male-dominated activity since the early settlement of North America. Today's Mexican immigrant population consists largely of young men who have come to the United States without their families to work.

**Migration within the United States**   Today, many immigrants are sponsored by special-interest groups such as churches and civic organizations that invite them to reside in the local community. Once here, however, some groups find conditions too foreign to their former lives and eventually make a *secondary migration* to another part of the United States. For example, a group of Hmong families sponsored by Lutheran charities spent two years in the severe winter climate of the Minneapolis area before resettling in California. Hispanics, on the other hand, are migrating from cities in the Southwest, New York, and Miami toward destinations in the Midwest and middle South (Wilson, 1984). California, which had attracted 33 percent of these immigrants, recently has only received 22 percent (Migration Policy Institute, 2004).

For newly arriving immigrants, historical patterns are also changing. See the following Did You Know box.

**DID YOU KNOW?**
**Hispanic Migration**

Although Hispanics are the most urbanized ethnic/racial group in the United States (90 percent living in metropolitan areas in 2000), the nonmetro Hispanic population is now the most rapidly growing demographic group in rural and small-town America. By 2000, half of all nonmetro Hispanics lived outside traditional Southwest cities. Many of these Hispanics are newly arrived undocumented young men from rural, depressed areas of Mexico. In spite of their relatively low education levels and weak English skills, employment rates exceeded those of all other nonmetro Hispanics and non-Hispanic Whites. (Kandel & Cromartie, 2004)

**U.S. Immigration Laws and Policies**   Economic cycles in the United States have affected immigration policies, liberalizing them when workers were needed and restricting immigration when jobs were scarce. These restrictive immigration policies were often justified using overtly racist arguments.

The immigration laws of the 1920s (the National Origins Acts of 1924 and 1929) banned most Asian immigration and established quotas that favored northwestern European immigrants. The quota system, however, did not apply to Mexico and the rest of the Western Hemisphere. In 1943, Congress symbolically ended the Asian exclusion policy by granting ethnic Chinese a token quota of 100 immigrants a year. The Philippines and Japan received similar tiny quotas after the war.

The Immigration and Nationality Act Amendments of 1965 brought about vast changes in immigration policy by abolishing the national origins quota system and replacing it with a seven-category preference system for allocating immigrant visas, a system that emphasizes family ties and occupation. Although there is a per-country limit for these preference immigrants, certain countries are "oversubscribed" and hopefuls are on long waiting lists (People's Republic of China, India, Mexico, and the Philippines). An additional provision in the 1965 act was the diversity immigrant category, in which 55,000 immigrant visas can be awarded each

---

**Box 8.3**   Find Out More about Immigration Legislation

*Executive Summary: U.S. Immigration: A Legislative History* www.prcdc.org/summaries/
usimmighistory/usimmighistory.html. This site contains a bulleted listing of U.S. immigration from 1790 to President George W. Bush's proposed immigration reform, as well as pie
charts of countries of origin during various periods and graphs of the U.S. foreign-born
population.

---

fiscal year to permit immigration opportunities for persons from countries other than the
principal sources of current immigration to the United States.

On May 25, 2006, the U.S. Senate voted to approve the Comprehensive Immigration
Reform Act of 2006, a massive and complex bill that is one of the most sweeping immigration reform proposals ever to be passed by Congress, containing multiple provisions
focused on both border security and immigration policy reform. However, the immigration
reform bill passed in the House—the Border Protection, Antiterrorism, and Illegal Immigration Control Act of 2005—is substantially different from the Senate bill, as it focuses on
border security. Many conservative leaders in the House have voiced their opposition to
immigration reform measures that would feature such pathways to citizenship and guest
worker programs (see Box 8.3).

**Legal Status**   Many immigrants are *documented*—legal residents who have entered the
United States officially and live under the protection of legal immigration status. Some of these
are officially designated *refugees*, with transitional support services and assistance provided by
the U.S. government. Most immigrants from Cambodia, Laos, Vietnam, and Thailand have
been granted refugee status. *Undocumented* immigrants are residents without any documentation who live in fear of being identified and deported.

Being in the United States illegally brings increased instability, fear, and insecurity to
school-age children because they and their families are living without the protection, social
services, and assistance available to most immigrants. With the passage of the Immigration
Reform and Control Act in 1986, however, undocumented children are legally entitled to
public education.

**Resources Available to Immigrants**   The Emergency Immigrant Education Program
(EIEP) (No Child Left Behind, Title III, subpart 4) provides assistance to school districts whose
enrollment is affected by immigrants. The purpose of the program is to provide high-quality
instruction to immigrant children and youth, to help them with their transition into U.S. society, and to help them meet the challenging academic content and student academic achievement standards (NCLB, sec. 3241).

In addition, the immigrant communities themselves have networks of linguistic, financial, and social support, such as the extensive Taiwanese communities of the San Gabriel Valley
in Southern California, the Afghan community in the San Francisco Bay area, and the Muslim
communities of Michigan. These communities have primary-language activities throughout
the year, as well as hosting websites for the immigrant community.

## The Cultural and Linguistic Challenges of Diversity

No other country in the world faces a diversity challenge as great as that of the United States. At any given time, almost one-fifth of the population speaks another language, with issues of primary-language maintenance and loss. New refugees are suffering culture shock, undocumented immigrants are living in fear of apprehension, and other non-residents are seeking support networks and services. Worse, many immigrants face bias and discrimination.

**Issues of Bias and Discrimination in the United States**    If diversity is recognized as a strength, educators will "avoid basing decisions about learners on inaccurate or stereotypical generalizations" (Manning, 2002, p. 207). Misperceptions about diversity often stem from prejudice, which can be diffused when various groups interact and come to know one another more deeply. But discrimination also stems from fear; dominant groups are afraid to lose power, and they benefit from the disadvantage of the subordinated.

The United States is a diverse country, with vast disparities among its residents in social class, age, gender, occupation, education level, geographic isolation, race, U.S.-born versus immigrant status, sexual orientation, and handicapping condition. As long as schools privilege some students and subordinate others based not on an individual's gifts and talents but on external social factors, schools will not represent level playing fields.

**The Dynamics of Prejudice**    One factor that inhibits intercultural communication is prejudice, which takes various forms: excessive pride in one's own ethnic heritage, country, or culture so that others are viewed negatively; ethnocentrism, in which the world revolves around oneself and one's own culture; prejudice against members of a certain racial group; and stereotypes that label all or most members of a group. All humans are prejudiced to some degree, but it is when people act on those prejudices that discriminatory practices and inequalities result.

Allport (1954) offered several explanations for the phenomenon of prejudice: historical, sociocultural (for example, the pressures of urban life have caused people to depersonalize and discriminate against minorities), psychological (all groups discriminate against nonmembers), social learning theory (people learn prejudice from others around them), and psychodynamic (people are prejudiced because prejudice acts as a release from personal frustration). Yet a simpler, more global explanation for prejudice is that it is based on fear—fear of the unknown, fear of engulfment by foreigners, or fear of contamination from dissimilar beliefs or values.

A closer look at various forms of prejudice, such as racism and stereotyping, as well as resulting discriminatory practice, can lead to an understanding of these issues. Teachers can then be in a position to adopt educational methods that are most likely to reduce prejudice.

**Racism**    The view that one race is superior to another is racism. For example, one sixteenth-century justification for genocide in the New World was that Native Americans were not human. Racism can also be cultural when one believes that the traditions, beliefs, language, artifacts, music, and art of other cultures are inferior. On the basis of such beliefs, racists justify discriminating against or scapegoating other groups. Racism may be expressed in hate crimes, which are public expressions of hostility directed at specific groups or individuals (harassment, scrawling graffiti on people's homes, burning crosses on lawns, etc.) or, at the extreme, assaults and murder directed toward minorities.

*Youth at the Edge*, a report by the Southern Poverty Law Center (1999), described a frustrated, marginally employed, and poorly educated underclass of disenchanted youth in the United States who are susceptible to hate groups and seek out scapegoats to harass such as immigrants, particularly those of color. The availability of information on the Internet has unfortunately encouraged sites that foment racial hatred. Schools are often prime sites in which hate crimes are committed. This fact underscores the urgency of educators' efforts to understand and combat racism.

**Stereotypes**  Often resulting from racist beliefs, stereotypes are preconceived and oversimplified generalizations about a particular group, race, or gender. The danger of stereotyping is that people are not considered as individuals but are categorized with all other members of a group. A person might believe that a racial group has a global trait and subsequently everyone from that group is judged in this stereotypical way. Conversely, a person might judge an entire group on the basis of an experience with a single individual. Whether positive or negative, a stereotype results in a distorted perspective.

## CLASSROOM GLIMPSE: Educating against a Stereotype

*Mrs. Abboushi, a third-grade teacher, discovers that her students hold many misconceptions about the Arab people. To present an accurate and more rounded view of the Arab world, she has students read* Ibrahim *(Sales, 1989),* The Day of Ahmed's Secret *(Heide & Gilliland, 1990), and* Nadia, the Willful *(Alexander, 1983).*

*After reading and interactively discussing the books, students are divided into groups. Each group is assigned a different book. Students prepare a Cultural Feature Analysis chart that includes the cultural features, setting, character and traits, family relationships, and message of their book. Groups share their information and Mrs. Abboushi records the information on a large summary chart. During the follow-up discussion, students discover that not all Arabs live the same way, dress the same way, or look the same way. They recognize the merging of traditional and modern worlds, the variability in living conditions, customs and values, architecture, clothing, and modes of transportation. (Diamond & Moore, 1995, pp. 229–230)*

**Teaching against Racism**  Students and teachers alike must raise awareness of racism in the attempt to achieve racial equality and justice. Actively listening to students in open discussion about racism, prejudice, and stereotyping can increase teachers' understanding of how students perceive and are affected by these concepts. School curricula can be used to help students be aware of the existence and impact of racism. Science and health teachers can debunk myths surrounding the concept of race. Content area teachers can help students develop skills in detecting bias.

## BEST PRACTICE: Antiracist Activities and Discussion Topics

- Understand the origins of racism and why people hold racial prejudices and stereotypes.
- Be able to identify racist images in the language and illustrations of books, films, television, news media, and advertising.
- Be able to identify current examples of racism in the immediate community and society as a whole.
- Identify specific ways of developing positive interracial contact experiences.
- Extend the fight against racism into a broader fight for universal human rights and respect for human dignity.

*Source:*   Adapted from Bennett (2003, pp. 370–373).

**Programs to Combat Prejudice and Racism**   The Southern Poverty Law Center distributes *Teaching Tolerance* magazine, a free resource sent to over 600,000 educators twice a year that provides antibias strategies for K–12 teachers. Carnuccio (2004) describes the Tolerance.org website, a Web project of the Southern Poverty Law Center (available at www.splcenter.org), as an "extremely informative resource":

> The project has done an excellent job of collecting and disseminating information on the advantages of diversity. . . . *Planet Tolerance* has stories for children to read and listen to and games for them to play. Teens can find ideas on how to bring diverse groups together in their schools. Teachers' pages feature articles, films and books to order, lesson ideas, and a forum in which to share ideas with other teachers. *101 Tools for Tolerance* suggests a variety of ideas for community, workplace, school, and home settings. *Parenting for Tolerance* offers ways for parents to guide their children to develop into tolerant adults. (p. 59)

**Institutional Racism**   Classroom teaching that aims at detecting and reducing racism may be a futile exercise when the institution itself—the school—promotes racism through its policies and practices, such as underreferral of minority students to programs for gifted students or failing to hire minority teachers in classrooms where children are predominantly of minority background. There may be no intent to discriminate on the part of an institution such as a school; however, interactions with minority students may reflect unquestioned negative assumptions about the abilities or participation of these students.

Teachers do not have to look far to encounter educational practices that are imbued with racial, ethnic, and class privilege. How does one identify institutional racism? One way is to profile the racial and ethnic composition of school staff, of academic "tracks," and of school activities. The following questions help to clarify the issue of institutional racism:

- Do the racial demographics of the teaching staff match that of the students?
- As English learners come to school, do they meet only maintenance personnel and cafeteria workers who speak their language?
- Does the school offer English learners equal access to an academic curriculum, including classes for the gifted and talented?

- Does the school provide equality in resources to support and enrich learning for all students?
- Do school clubs recruit effectively from all races and cultures of the student body, or are English learners segregated into "culture" clubs while native speakers of English staff the more high-status activities such as the school yearbook, newspaper, and student leadership clubs?
- Are family members of all students provided equal opportunities for involvement in school-level activities, or is the only parent organization available designed for middle-class parents who are English literate and have flexible work schedules that enable them to participate in school functions and fundraisers during the school day?

**Classism**   In the United States, racism is compounded by classism, discrimination against the poor. Although this classism is often directed against linguistic and cultural minorities—in the American imagination, a typical poor person is urban, black, and young—portraying poverty that way makes it easier to stigmatize the poor (Henwood, 1997).

Classism has engendered its own stereotype against poor European Americans—for example, the stereotyped white indigent who is called, among other things, "white trash" ("the white trash stereotype serves as a useful way of blaming the poor for being poor") (Wray & Newitz, 1997, p. 1). Poor whites, who outnumber poor minorities, may bear the brunt of a caste-like status in the United States (Ogbu, 1978) as much as do linguistic and cultural minorities.

**Discrimination**   Discrimination refers to actions that limit the social, political, or economic opportunities of particular race, language, culture, gender, and/or social-class groups and legitimize the unequal distribution of power and resources. Blatant, legally sanctioned discrimination may be a thing of the past, but de facto segregation continues—most students of color are still found in substandard schools, taught by faculty who have less experience and academic preparation, do not share the ethnic background of their students, and may not communicate well with these students (Ortiz, 1988). Teachers may communicate low expectations to minority students.

In the past, those in power often used physical force to discriminate. Those who did not go along were physically punished for speaking their native language or adhering to their own cultural or ethnic customs. With the spread of literacy, discrimination took the form of internalized shame and guilt, leading minorities to become ashamed of their parents and origins. Skutnabb-Kangas (1981) cited a variety of examples of this *symbolic-structural violence* against minority students in Swedish and Norwegian schools:

> The headmaster said, "You have a name which is difficult for us Swedes to pronounce. Can't we change it?" "Well, I suppose I'd better change it," I thought. (p. 316)

> I love my parents and I respect them but what they are and everything they know counts for nothing. (p. 317)

Students experiencing racism and anti-immigration sentiment from peers in their environment, together with the increasing involvement of young adults on and off campus, is a disturbing trend on today's campuses. Policies, curricula, and antiracism programs are needed to prevent and control hate crimes. Hand in hand with sanctions for such negative behavior, students need training in intercultural communication.

**Fighting for Fairness and Equal Opportunity**    Schools in the United States have not been level playing fields for those of nonmainstream cultures. Teachers can remedy this in both academic and extracurricular areas. According to Manning (2002), teachers should

> consider that all learners deserve, ethically and legally, equal access to curricular activities (e.g., higher-level mathematics and science subjects) and opportunities to participate in all athletic activities (e.g., rather than assuming all students of one race will play on the basketball team and all students of another race will play on the tennis or golfing teams). (p. 207)

Cultural fairness can extend to the social and interpersonal lives of students, those daily details and microinteractions that also fall within the domain of culture. Teachers who invest time in getting to know their students, as individuals as well as cultural beings, address issues of fairness through a personal commitment to equality of treatment and opportunity.

# INTERCULTURAL COMMUNICATION

Exchange that takes place between individuals of different cultures is known as intercultural communication. Channels of communication are verbal and nonverbal.

## Cultural Diversity in Nonverbal Communication

Nonverbal communication is just as important as verbal communication. Educators are oriented toward verbal means of expression and are less likely to accord importance to the "silent language." However, more than 65 percent of the social meaning of a typical two-person exchange is carried by nonverbal cues (Birdwhistell, 1974). Body movements, gestures, and facial expressions can enhance a message or constitute a message in itself. *Physical appearance* is an important dimension of the nonverbal code during initial encounters. *Paralanguage*, the nonverbal elements of the voice, is an important aspect of speech that can affirm or belie a verbal message. *Proxemics*, the communication of interpersonal distance, varies widely across cultures. Last but not least, *olfactics*—the study of interpersonal communication by means of smell—constitutes a factor that is powerful yet often overlooked.

**Body Language**    The way one holds and positions oneself—one's body language—is one way a teacher communicates authority in the classroom. To become the focus of attention, a teacher stands in front of the room and, by passing from desk to desk while students are working, communicates individual attention to students' needs. In turn, students communicate that they are paying attention with eyes up front; if they act industrious (busily writing or quietly reading a book), they are often seen as more effective academically. Thus, body language helps to shape and maintain one's image in the eyes of others.

In a parent conference, however, cultural differences in body language may impede communication. In traditional cultures, a guest is formally ushered into the classroom and not merely waved in with a flick of the hand. Parents from a culture that offers elaborate respect for the teacher may become uncomfortable if the teacher slouches, moves his or her chair too intimately toward the parent, or otherwise compromises the formal nature of the interchange. In contrast, welcoming body language enhances communication.

**Gestures and Facial Expressions**    Expressive motions or actions made with hands, arms, head, or even the whole body are culturally based signs that are often misunderstood. "Yes" is generally signaled by a nod of the head, but in some cultures a shake of the head means "yes." This can be particularly unnerving for teachers if they constantly interpret the students' head-shakes as rejection rather than affirmation. Facial expressions are also easily misinterpreted. Through the use of eyebrows, eyes, cheeks, nose, lips, tongue, and chin, people nonverbally signal any number of emotions, opinions, and moods. Although some facial expressions of happiness, sadness, anger, fear, surprise, disgust, and interest appear to be universal across cultures, other expressions are learned.

**Eye Contact**    Another communication device that is highly variable and frequently misunderstood is eye contact. Both insufficient and excessive eye contact create feelings of unease. Generally, children in European-American culture are taught to look people in the eye when addressing them. In some cultures, however, children learn that respect is conveyed by looking down when addressed, and a teacher may incorrectly interpret a student's downcast eyes as an admission of guilt. The teacher may need to explain to the student that in English the rules of address call for different behavior.

**Distance between Speakers**    Personal space is an aspect of social customs that differs according to cultural experience. Personal space varies: In some cultures, individuals touch one another frequently and maintain high degrees of physical contact; in other cultures, touch and proximity cause feelings of tension and embarrassment. The following incident and thousands of others, which may be unpredictable, puzzling, uncomfortable, or even threatening, occur in situations in which cultural groups come into contact.

## CLASSROOM GLIMPSE: Personal Space

*"Teacher," Maria said to me as the students went out for recess. "Yes, Maria?" I smiled at this lively Venezuelan student and we launched into conversation. The contents of this talk are now lost on me, but not the actions. For as we talked, we slowly moved, she forward, me backward, until I was jammed up against the chalkboard. And there I remained for the rest of the conversation, feeling more and more agitated. She was simply too close.*

*Because I knew the different cultural norms under which Maria and I were operating—the fact that the requirement for space between interlocutors is greater for me as a North American than for her as a South American—I did not ascribe any negative or aggressive tendencies to her. But knowing the norm difference did not lessen my anxiety. What it afforded me was the knowledge that we were behaving differently and that such differences were normal for our respective groups. (Kathryn Weed quoted in Díaz-Rico & Weed, 2006, p. 261)*

> ## BEST PRACTICE: Accommodating Different Concepts of Personal Space
>
> - If students from the same culture (one with a close personal space) and gender have a high degree of physical contact and neither seems bothered by this, the teacher does not have to intervene.
> - The wise teacher accords the same personal space to students no matter what their culture (e.g., does not touch minority students more or less than mainstream students).
> - Students from affluent families should not bring more "stuff" to put in or on their desks than the average student.

## Cultural Diversity in Verbal Communication

Whether oral or written, verbal communication constitutes the other half of intercultural interaction. Aside from first- and second-language differences, a world of patterns and practices surrounds oral and written expression.

**Diversity in Oral Discourse**   In learning a second language, students (and teachers) often focus on the form. Frequently ignored are the ways in which that second language is used (see the section on pragmatics in Chapter 1). The culture that underlies each language prescribes distinct patterns and conventions about when, where, and how to use the language. Heath's (1999) *Ways with Words* noted that children in "Trackton," an isolated African-American community in the South, were encouraged to use spontaneous verbal play, rich with metaphor, simile, and allusion. In contrast, the children of "Roadville," a lower-middle-class European-American community in the South, used language in more restricted ways, perhaps because of habits encouraged by a fundamentalist religious culture.

Using language to satisfy material needs, control the behavior of others, get along with others, express one's personality, find out about the world, create an imaginative world, or communicate information seems to be universal among language users. How these social functions are accomplished, however, varies greatly among cultures. For example, when accidentally bumping someone, Americans, Japanese, Koreans, and Filipinos would say, "Excuse me" or "Pardon me." The Chinese, however, would give an apologetic look. Within a family, Hispanics often say "thank you" nonverbally for acts of service, whereas European-American children are taught that a spoken "thank you" is necessary, especially to a family member.

**The Role of Silence**   People throughout the world employ silence in communicating. Silence can in fact speak loudly and eloquently. The silence of a parent in front of a guilty child is more powerful than any ranting or raving. As with other language uses, however, silence differs dramatically across cultures. In the U.S. mainstream culture, silence is interpreted as expressing embarrassment, regret, obligation, criticism, or sorrow (Wayne in Ishii & Bruneau, 1991). In Asian cultures, silence is a token of respect. Particularly in the presence of the elderly, being quiet honors their wisdom and expertise. Silence can also be a marker of personal power. In many Eastern cultures, women view their silent role as a symbol of control and self-respect. In many Native-American cultures, silence is used to create and communicate rapport in ways that language cannot.

## CLASSROOM GLIMPSE: The Role of Silence

*In a research project that took place in several Ogala Sioux classrooms, a central factor was the withdrawal of the Sioux students. Teachers were faced with unexpectedly intense, sometimes embarrassingly long periods of silence. They cajoled, commanded, badgered, and pleaded with students, receiving an inevitable monosyllabic or nonverbal response. Yet outside the classroom, these children were noisy, bold, and insatiably curious. The lack of verbal response from students frustrated teachers. The solution? The teachers involved themselves in the daily life of the community and reduced the isolation of the school from the values of the community. They went so far as to locate classrooms in community buildings. In a different context, students were more willing participants. (Dumont, 1972)*

**The Nature of Questions**   Intercultural differences exist in asking and answering questions. In middle-class European-American culture, children are exposed early on to their parents' questioning. While taking a walk, for example, a mother will ask, "See the squirrel?" and later, "Is that a squirrel? Where did that squirrel go?" It is obvious to both parent and child that the adult knows the answer to these questions. The questions are asked to stimulate conversation and to train children to focus attention and display knowledge. In the Inuit culture, on the other hand, adults do not question children or call their attention to objects and events in order to name them (Crago, 1993).

Responses to questioning differ across cultures as well. Students from non-Western cultures may be reluctant to attempt an answer to a question if they do not feel they can answer absolutely correctly. These students may not share the European-American value of answering questions to the best of their ability regardless of whether that "best" answer is absolutely correct, nor will students from many Eastern countries speak up when they do not understand or ask questions solely to demonstrate intelligence.

**Discourse Styles**   Cultures may differ in ways that influence conversations: the way conversations open and close, the way people take turns, or the way messages are repaired to make them understandable. Those who have traveled to a foreign country recognize that a small interaction such as answering the telephone may have widely varying sequences across cultures. Sometimes callers give immediate self-identification, sometimes not; sometimes greetings are followed with "how are you" sequences. Deviations from these routines may be cause to terminate a conversation in the earliest stages. Differences in discourse may be stressful for second-language learners.

## CLASSROOM GLIMPSE: Classroom Discourse Patterns

*Discourse in the classroom can be organized in ways that involve children positively—in ways that are culturally compatible. A group of Hawai'ian children, with the help of an encouraging and participating adult, produced group discourse that was co-narrated, complex, lively, imaginative, and well connected. Group work featured twenty-minute discussions of text in which the teacher and students mutually participated in overlapping, volunteered speech and in joint narration (Au & Jordan, 1981). In contrast, Navajo children in a discussion group patterned their discourse after the adults of their culture. Each Navajo student spoke for an extended period with a fully expressed statement, and other students waited courteously until a clear end was communicated. Then another took a similar turn. In both communities, children tended to connect discourse with peers rather than with the teacher functioning as a central "switchboard." If the teacher acted as a central director, students often responded with silence. (Tharp, 1989)*

---

**DID YOU KNOW?**
**How Students Tell You They Don't Understand**

Arabic (men): *Mish fahem*

Arabic (women): *Mish fahmeh*

Armenian: *Yes chem huskenur*

Chinese (Cantonese): *Ngoh m-ming*

Chinese (Mandarin): *Wo bu dung*

Persian: *Man ne'me fah'mam*

Japanese: *Wakarimasen*

Korean: *Juh-neun eehae-haji mot haget-ssum-nida*

Russian: *Ya nye ponimayu*

Spanish: *No comprendo*

Vietnamese: *Toi khong hieu*

In addition to ways to say "I don't understand" in 230 languages, J. Runner's webpage has translations in many languages for the following phrases: "Hello, how are you?," "Welcome," "Good-bye," "Please," "Thank you," "What is your name?," "My name is . . . ," "Do you speak English?," "Yes," and "No." There is also a link to Internet language resources; see www.elite.net/~runner/jennifers/understa.htm.

*Source:* Runner (2000).

---

**Oral versus Written Language**    In studying oral societies, researchers have noted that the structure and content of messages tend to be narrative, situational, and oriented toward activity or deeds, although abstract ideas such as moral values are often implicit. In contrast, the style represented by literacy is conceptual rather than situational. Words are separate from the social context of deeds and events, and ideas can be extracted from written texts. In an oral society, learning takes place in groups because narration must have an audience. This contrasts with a literate society, in which reading and writing can be solitary experiences. Separation from the group appears to be one of the burdens of literacy. In an oral society, much reliance is placed on memory, as this is the principal means of preserving practices and traditions (Ong, 1982).

**Cultural Differences in Written Discourse**    Oracy is the foundation of languages. Written expression is a later development. In fact, of the thousands of reported languages in use, only seventy-eight have a written literature (Edmonson, 1971). Research has suggested that acquiring literacy involves more than learning to read and write. Thinking patterns, perception, cultural values, communication style, and social organization can be affected by literacy.

Many features of written language have to be learned in school. The style of argumentation, the use of voice and formality level, and the organizational structure used in writing are unique to each culture. This is a part of acquiring cognitive academic language proficiency.

## Strategies for Intercultural Communication in the School and Classroom

Communicating with students from other cultures is more than learning a few phrases in the second language and expecting the students and families to stretch more than halfway. Much can be done to adapt one's communication styles and habits to make others more comfortable and to get one's message across.

**Teaching Styles**   The way teachers are taught to teach is a reflection of the expectations of U.S. culture. Teachers raised in a mainstream culture have elements of that culture embedded in their personal teaching approach. The selection of a particular teaching method reflects cultural values more than it argues for the superiority of the method. Some of these elements may need to be modified to meet the needs of students from other cultures. As a beginning step, a teacher can examine his or her teaching style to evaluate whether, for example, it is student centered or subject centered, or whether students are encouraged to work alone or cooperatively.

Even in monocultural classrooms, the teacher's style is more in accordance with some students than with others. Flexibility becomes a key to reaching more students. In a multicultural classroom, this flexibility is even more crucial. With knowledge of various teaching styles, teachers can examine their own style, observe students' reactions to that style, ask questions about a teacher's expected role and style in the community, and modify their style as necessary.

**Teacher–Student Interactions**   The teacher–student interaction is culturally mandated in general ways, although individuals may vary. Students who have immigrated may bring with them varying notions of teacher–student interactions. For example, in some cultures, learning takes place in an absolutely quiet classroom where the teacher is in complete control and authority is never questioned. In other cultures, students talk among themselves and are able to engage with teachers in cooperative planning. Attitudes toward authority, teacher–student relationships, and teacher expectations of student achievement vary widely. Yet the heart of the educational process is in the interaction between teacher and student. This determines the quality of education the student receives.

In some parts of the world, it is acceptable to call a teacher by the first name, indicating that relations between teachers and students are warm, close, and informal. Other cultures may be wary of a teacher's motives and take a long time to share a feeling of rapport.

Differences in the culture of the teacher and the student may cause miscommunication. Language and word choice are other factors making intercultural communication challenging. Words that may seem harmless in one context may have a subculture connotation. Teachers have to be equally careful both to use appropriate terms of address and reference when communicating with students and to be aware of terms that are used in the classroom that might have an incendiary effect.

## BEST PRACTICE: Encouraging Positive Relationships

Although it may appear daunting to be able to accommodate the various teacher–student relations represented by different cultural groups in a classroom, there are several ways teachers can improve rapport with their students:

- Express care and respect equally to all students.
- Openly communicate acceptance of students and be accessible to them.
- In classroom discussions and in private, encourage students to talk about their lives, feelings (including the sometimes tragic details), and expectations for learning.
- Understand that you are not only helping students academically but also that you may be helping families adjust. (Lemberger, 1999)

**Power and Authority**   Most students expect power and authority to be vested in the teacher, and teachers expect respect from students. Respect is communicated verbally and nonverbally and is vulnerable to cultural misunderstanding. In the United States, respect is shown to teachers by looking at them, but in some cultures looking at the teacher is a sign of disrespect. Moreover, students are expected to raise their hands in North American classrooms if they wish to ask or answer a question. Vietnamese culture, on the other hand, does not have a way for students to signal a desire to talk to a teacher; students speak only after the teacher has spoken to them (Andersen & Powell, 1991).

## BEST PRACTICE: Understanding Behaviors Related to Power and Authority

- Seek alternative explanations to unexpected behavior rather than interpreting the behavior according to your own cultural framework.
- Ask "Why is this behavior occurring?" Rather than "What is the matter with this child?" (Cushner, 1999, p. 75)

### Teaching Intercultural Communication

Students are often fascinated by cultural difference. Because this content is not on standardized tests, teachers may be reluctant to spend time on such a topic. However, the "teachable moment" occurs whenever a cultural difference is relevant to a classroom occurrence.

Multicultural literature and other facets of a multicultural curriculum are useful ways to teach about culture. Practicing intercultural communication skills—listening and speaking in a culturally sensitive way—is a daily occurrence.

A classroom bulletin board display area may be put to good use throughout the school year, with one half devoted to cultural artifacts, language, numbering systems, and other external elements of culture. The other half might display key ideas about culture such as ideas about personal space, nonverbal language, and other concepts that students can acquire. This keeps the issue of cultural diversity open and available as food for thought.

# ▨▨ INVESTIGATING OURSELVES AS CULTURAL BEINGS

Teachers who function as intercultural educators acquire a sense of the difficulties faced by English learners. However, many prospective teachers initially are unaware of their own cultural values and behaviors and how these might be at odds with the home cultures of students.

The most powerful means of learning about culture is learning about ourselves and our own culture. Those who are willing to engage in self-assessment activities are often richly rewarded with a deeper understanding of their professional and personal lives. The goal of such assessment is to enable prospective teachers to sustain intercultural contact, foster culturally responsive pedagogy, and develop the skills of advocacy for, and appreciation of, English learners. Understanding ourselves builds the foundation for understanding others.

## The Personal Dimension

For intercultural educators, self-reflection is vital. By examining their own attitudes, beliefs, and culturally derived beliefs and behaviors, teachers begin to discover what has influenced their value systems. Villegas and Lucas (2002) summarized this self-reflection in eight components (see Table 8.5)

## Cultural Self-Study

Self-study is a powerful tool for understanding culture. A way to begin a culture inquiry is by investigating one's personal name. For example, ask, "Where did I get my name? Who am I

**TABLE 8.5**   Components of the Personal Dimension of Intercultural Education

| Component | Description |
| --- | --- |
| Engage in reflective thinking and writing. | Awareness of one's actions, interactions, beliefs, and motivations—such as racism—can catalyze behavioral change. |
| Explore personal and family histories by interviewing family members. | Exploring early cultural experiences can help teachers better relate to individuals with different backgrounds. |
| Acknowledge group membership. | Teachers who acknowledge their affiliation with various groups in society can assess how this influences views of and relationships with other groups. |
| Learn about the experiences of diverse groups by reading or personal interaction. | Learning about the histories of diverse groups—from their perspectives—highlights value differences. |
| Visit or read about successful teachers. | Successful teachers of children from diverse backgrounds serve as exemplary role models. |
| Appreciate diversity. | Seeing difference as the norm in society reduces ethnocentrism. |
| Participate in reforming schools. | Teachers can help reform monocultural institutions. |

*Source:* Adapted from Villegas & Lucas (2002).

named for? In which culture did the name originate? What does the name mean?" Continue the self-examination by reviewing favorite cultural customs, such as holiday traditions, home decor, and favorite recipes.

More difficult self-examination questions address the mainstream U.S. values of individual freedom, self-reliance, competition, individualism, and hard work. One can ask oneself the following questions: If someone in authority tells me to do something, do I move quickly or slowly? If someone says, "Do you need any help?" do I usually say, "No, thanks. I can do it myself'?" Am I comfortable promoting myself (for example, talking about my achievements in a performance review)? Do I prefer to work by myself or on a team? Do I prefer to associate with high achievers and avoid spending much time with people who do not work hard?

These and other introspective questions help to pinpoint cultural attitudes (see Box 8.4). Without a firm knowledge of one's own beliefs and behaviors, it is difficult to contrast the cultural behaviors of others. However, the self-examination process is challenging and ongoing. It is difficult to observe one's own culture.

## Box 8.4  Cultural Self-Study: Self-Exploration Questions

- Describe yourself as a preschool child. Were you compliant, curious, adventuresome, goody-goody, physically active, nature loving? Have you observed your parents with other children? Do they encourage open-ended exploration, or would they prefer children to play quietly with approved toys? Do they encourage initiative?

- What was the knowledge environment like in your home? What type of reading did your father and mother do? Was there a time when the members of the family had discussions about current events or ideas and issues? How much dissent was tolerated from parental viewpoints? Were children encouraged to question the status quo? What was it like to learn to talk and think in your family?

- What kind of a grade school pupil were you? What is your best memory from elementary school? What was your favorite teacher like? Were you an avid reader? How would you characterize your cognitive style and learning style preferences? Was the school you attended ethnically diverse? What about your secondary school experience? Did you have a diverse group of friends in high school?

- What is your ethnic group? What symbols or traditions did you participate in that derived from this group? What do you like about your ethnic identity? Is there a time now when your group celebrates its traditions together? What was the neighborhood or community like in which you grew up?

- What was your experience with ethnic diversity? What were your first images of race or color? Was there a time in your life when you sought out diverse contacts to expand your experience?

- What contact do you have now with people of dissimilar racial or ethnic backgrounds? How would you characterize your desire to learn more? Given your learning style preferences, how would you go about this?

## Participating in Growth Relationships

Self-study is only one means of attaining self-knowledge. Teachers who form relationships with individuals whose backgrounds differ from their own, whether teacher colleagues or community members, can benefit from honest feedback and discussions that help to expand self-awareness. Intercultural educators are not free from making mistakes when dealing with students, family and community members, and colleagues whose cultures differ from their own. The only lasting error is not learning from these missteps or misunderstandings.

Exploring culture and cultural diversity is a lifelong endeavor. Many people experience this only after retirement, in traveling around the world as tourists. How lucky intercultural educators are, to be exposed to cultural diversity on a daily basis and have the opportunity to learn intercultural communication as they teach!

### VIDEO WORKSHOP: "The Importance of Culture"

In this video, an educator explains the close relationship between culture and language. ESL students are not only learning a second language, she says, but also a second culture. In many cultures, culture is also related to morality. The video discusses how important it is that students are made to feel that their culture is important.

To access the video, log on to MyLabSchool at www.mylabschool.com, enter Assignment ID **ENV2** into the **Assignment Finder**, and select the video entitled "The Importance of Culture." Watch the video, complete the questions that follow, and e-mail your responses to your professor for credit.

**mylabschool**™
Where the classroom comes to life!

# CHAPTER NINE

# Culturally Inclusive Instruction

## THE ROLE OF CULTURE IN THE CLASSROOM AND SCHOOL

Culture influences every aspect of school life. Becoming an intercultural educator requires not only specific knowledge about the culture(s) of the students but also general knowledge about how to use that knowledge appropriately in specific contexts. Students from a nonmainstream culture are acquiring a mainstream classroom culture that may differ markedly from their home culture. Intercultural educators who understand students' cultures design instruction to meet children's learning needs.

### Acknowledging Students' Differences

Imagine a classroom of thirty students, each with just one unique fact, value, or belief included in the more than fifty categories presented in Table 8.2 ("Components of Culture"). Yet this dizzying array of uniqueness is only the tip of the iceberg, because within each of these categories individuals can differ. Take, for example, the category "food" under "daily life" in Table 8.2. Each student in a classroom of thirty knows a lot about food. What they know, however, depends largely on what they eat every day.

Culture includes diversity in values, social customs, rituals, work and leisure activities, health and educational practices, and many other aspects of life. Each of these can affect schooling. The areas that most directly affect schooling are discussed as follows, including ways that teachers can respond to these differences in adapting instruction.

### The Alignment of Home and School

Teachers who are members of the mainstream culture and who have an accommodating vision of cultural diversity recognize that they need to adapt culturally to CLD students, just as these individuals, in turn, accept some cultural change as they adapt to the mainstream. In this mutual process, teachers who model receptiveness to learning from the diverse cultures in their midst help students to see this diversity as a resource.

All the influences that contribute to the cultural profile of the family and community affect the students' reactions to classroom practices. Students whose home culture is consistent with the beliefs and practices of the school are generally more successful in school. However, different cultures organize individual and community behavior in radically different ways—ways that, on the surface, may not seem compatible with school practices and beliefs. To understand these differences is to be able to mediate for the students by helping them bridge relevant differences between the home and the school cultures.

Cultural accommodation is a two-way exchange. Obviously, a single teacher cannot change the culture of an entire school; similarly, families cannot change the deep structure of their values solely for the sake of their children's school success. Flexibility and awareness of cultural differences go a long way toward supporting students and defusing misunderstanding.

## The Value System of the Teacher and Cultural Accommodation

Because culture plays such an important role in the classroom and the school, the degree to which home and school are congruent can affect the student's learning and achievement. Some of this congruence—this alignment of the cultures of home and school—depends on what teachers see as important. Because over 80 percent of teachers represent mainstream culture, the following information contrasts U.S. mainstream values with those that might differ.

**What Are Values?**   Values are "beliefs about how one ought or ought not to behave or about some end state of existence worth or not worth attaining" (Bennett, 2003, p. 64). Values are particularly important to people when they educate their young, because education is a primary means of transmitting cultural knowledge. Parents in minority communities are often vitally interested in their children's education even though they may not be highly visible at school functions.

**Values about Time**   Cultures cause people to lead very different daily lives. These customs are paced and structured by deep habits of using time and space. For example, *time* is organized in culturally specific ways.

## CLASSROOM GLIMPSE: Cultural Conceptions about Time

*Adela, a Mexican-American first-grade girl, arrived at school about twenty minutes late every day. Her teacher was at first irritated and gradually exasperated. In a parent conference, Adela's mother explained that braiding her daughter's hair each morning was an important time for the two of them to be together, even if it meant being slightly late to school. This family time presented a values conflict with the school's time norm.*

Other conflicts may arise when teachers demand abrupt endings to activities in which children are deeply engaged or when events are scheduled in a strict sequence. In fact, schools in the United States are often paced very strictly by clock time, whereas family life in various cultures is not regulated in the same manner. Moreover, teachers often equate speed of performance with intelligence, and standardized tests are often a test of rapidity. Many teachers find themselves in the role of "time mediator"—helping the class adhere to the school's time schedule while working with individual students to help them meet their learning needs within the time allotted.

## BEST PRACTICE: Accommodating to Different Concepts of Time and Work Rhythms

- Provide students with choices about their work time and observe how time spent on various subjects accords with students' aptitudes and interests.
- If a student is a slow worker, analyze the work rhythms. Slow yet methodically accurate work deserves respect, but slow and disorganized work may require a peer helper.
- If students are chronically late to school, ask the school counselor to meet with the responsible family member to discuss a change in morning routines.

**Values about Space**    Another aspect about which values differ according to cultural experience is the concept and experience of space. Just as attitudes toward personal space vary among cultures, a cultural sense of space influences in which rooms and buildings people feel comfortable. Large cavernous classrooms may be overwhelming to students whose family activities are carried out in intimate spaces. The organization of the space in the classroom sends messages to students, such as how free they are to move about the classroom and how much of the classroom they "own." Both the expectations of the students and the needs of the teacher can be negotiated to provide a classroom setting in which space is shared.

## CLASSROOM GLIMPSE: Discomfort in the Classroom Space

*The classroom . . . was terribly huge and smelled of medicine like the village clinic I feared so much. Those fluorescent light tubes made an eerie drone. Our confinement to rows of desks was another unnatural demand made on our active little bodies. . . . We all went home for lunch since we lived a short walk from the school. It took coaxing, and sometimes bribing, to get me to return and complete the remainder of the school day. (Suina, 1985, n.p.)*

**Values about Dress and Appearance**    Sometimes values are about externals, such as dress and personal appearance. For example, a third-grade girl wearing makeup is communicating a message that some teachers may consider an inappropriate indicator of premature sexuality, although makeup on a young girl may be acceptable in some cultures.

## BEST PRACTICE: Culturally Influenced School Dress Codes

- Boys and men in some cultures (rural Mexico, for example) wear hats. Classrooms need to have a place for these hats during class time and provision for wearing the hats during recess.
- Schools that forbid "gang attire" yet permit privileged students to wear student council insignia (sweaters with embroidered names, for instance) should forbid clique-related attire for all.

- A family–school council with representatives from various cultures should be responsible for reviewing the school dress code on a yearly basis to see if it meets the needs of various cultures.

**Rites, Rituals, and Ceremonies**   Each culture incorporates expectations about the proper means for carrying out formal events. School ceremonies—for example, assemblies that begin with formal markers such as the Pledge of Allegiance and a flag salute—should have nonstigmatizing alternatives for those whose culture does not permit participation.

Rituals in some elementary classrooms in the United States are relatively informal. For example, students can enter freely before school and take their seats or go to a reading corner or activity center. Students from other cultures may find this confusing if they are accustomed to lining up in the courtyard, being formally greeted by the principal or head teacher, and then dismissed in their lines to enter their respective classrooms.

A traditional Hawai'ian custom was for students to chant outside the classroom door and listen for the teacher's welcome chant from within. In Japan before 1945, bowing to Emperor Hirohito's portrait was a normal way of starting the school day for millions of children. In U.S. classrooms, a bell normally rings to start the school day, but individual class periods at the elementary level do not usually have formal signals to cue transitions.

**DID YOU KNOW?**
**Classroom Behavior in Laos**

In Laos, when it is time for recess or lunch break, students rise and stand by their seats, waiting for permission to leave the room. When passing the teacher, students clasp their hands in front of their faces in a ritual of respect (Bliatout, Downing, Lewis, & Yang, 1988).

## BEST PRACTICE: Accommodating School Rituals

- Teachers might welcome newcomers with a brief explanation of the degree of formality expected of students.
- School seasonal celebrations are increasingly devoid of political and religious content. The school may, however, permit school clubs to honor events with extracurricular rituals.
- Teachers might observe colleagues from different cultures to view the rituals of family–teacher conferences and adapt their behavior accordingly to address families' cultural expectations.
- Greeting and welcome behaviors during parent conferences vary across cultures. The sensitive teacher understands how parents expect to be greeted and incorporates some of these behaviors in the exchange.

**Values about Work and Leisure**   Crosscultural variation in work and leisure activities is a frequently discussed value difference. Many members of mainstream U.S. culture value work over play; that is, one's status is directly related to one's productivity, salary, or job description. Play, rather than being an end in itself, is often used in ways that reinforce the status achieved through work. For example, teachers may meet informally at someone's home to bake holiday dishes, co-workers form bowling leagues, and alumni enjoy tailgate parties before attending football games; one's work status governs who is invited to attend these events.

Young people in the mainstream U.S. culture, particularly those in the middle class, are trained to use specific tools of play, and their time is structured to attain skills (e.g., organized sports, music lessons). In contrast, other cultures do not afford children structured time to play but instead expect children to engage in adult-type labor at work or in the home. In still other cultures, such as that of the Hopi Nation in Arizona, children's playtime is relatively unstructured, and parents do not interfere with play. Cultures also vary in the typical work and play activities expected of girls and of boys. All these values have obvious influence on the ways children work and play at school (Schultz & Theophano, 1987).

In work and play groups, the orientation may be *individual* or *group*. The United States is widely regarded as a society in which the individual is paramount. This individualism often pits students against one another for achievement. In contrast, many Mexican immigrants from rural communities have group-oriented values and put the needs of the community before individual achievement. Families may, for example, routinely pull children from school to attend funerals of neighbors in the community; in mainstream U.S. society, however, children would miss school only for the funerals of family members.

▌ DID YOU KNOW?
**Cooperation and Competition in Japan**

In Japan, individuals compete fiercely for admission to prestigious universities, but accompanying this individual competitiveness is a sense that one must establish oneself within a group. Competition in the Japanese classroom is not realized in the same way as in U.S. schools; being singled out for attention or praise by teachers may result in embarrassment. (Furey, 1986)

## BEST PRACTICE: Accommodating Diverse Ideas about Work and Play

- Many high school students arrange class schedules in order to work part time. If a student appears chronically tired, a family–teacher conference may be needed to review priorities.
- Many students are overcommitted to extracurricular activities. If grades suffer, students may be well advised to reduce activities to regain an academic focus.
- Out-of-school play activities should not be organized at the school site, such as passing out birthday party invitations that exclude some students.

**Values about Medicine, Health, and Hygiene**    Health and medicine practices involve deep-seated beliefs because the stakes are high: life and death. Each culture has certain beliefs about sickness and health, beliefs that influence the interactions in health care settings. Students may have problems—war trauma, culture shock, poverty, addiction, family violence, crime—that their culture treats in particular culturally acceptable ways. When students come to school with health issues, teachers need to react in culturally compatible ways.

Miscommunication and noncooperation can result when teachers and the family view health and disease differently (Witte, 1991). For example, community health practices, such as the Cambodian tradition of coining (in which a coin is dipped in oil and then rubbed on a sick person's back, chest, and neck), can be misinterpreted by school officials who, seeing marks on the child, swiftly call Child Protective Services.

## CLASSROOM GLIMPSE: Exotic Family Health Practice?

*One of Ka's uncles called to explain that his nephew was sick and would miss school another two days. Lenny had read that the Hmong were animists and believed sickness was often caused by evil spirits who lured the soul from the body. Getting well sometimes required an animal sacrifice and a healing ceremony with a shaman who found and returned the runaway soul. Lenny wished the boy well and then asked about the nature and course of Ka's illness, fully expecting the evil spirit, animal sacrifice, and shaman scenarios. "Strep throat," answered the uncle, "but we went to the hospital and got antibiotics." (Cary, 2000, p. 19)*

## BEST PRACTICE: Health and Hygiene Practices

- Families who send sick children to school or, conversely, keep children home at the slightest ache may benefit from a conference with the school nurse.
- All students can profit from explicit instruction in home and school hygiene.

**Values about Economics, Law, Politics, and Religion**   The institutions that support and govern family and community life have an influence on behavior and beliefs. The economic institutions of the United States are diverse, ranging from small business enterprises to large corporate or government agencies. These institutions influence daily life in the United States by means of a complex infrastructure. The families of English learners may fit in anywhere along this continuum.

Interwoven into this rich cultural-economic-political-legal texture are religious beliefs and practices. In the United States, religious practices are heavily embedded but formally bounded—people argue over Christmas trees in public schools but there is almost universal acceptance of increased consumer spending at the close of the calendar year. Religious beliefs underlie other cultures even more fundamentally.

Immigrants with Confucian religious and philosophical beliefs, for example, subscribe to values that mandate a highly ordered society and family through the maintenance of proper social relationships. In Islamic traditions, the Koran prescribes proper social relationships and roles for members of society. When immigrants with these religious beliefs encounter the largely secular U.S. institutions, the result may be that customs and cultural patterns are challenged, fade away, or cause conflict within the family (Chung, 1989).

## BEST PRACTICE: Accommodating Economic, Legal, Political, and Religious Practices

- On a rotating basis, teachers could be paid to supervise after-school homework sessions for students whose parents are working multiple jobs.
- Schools can legally resist any attempts to identify families whose immigration status is undocumented.
- Schools should not tolerate messages of political partisanship.
- Permission for religious garb or appearance (e.g., Islamic head scarves, Sikh ritual knives, Hassidic dress) should be a part of the school dress code.

**Values and Expectations about Education**    In the past, educational systems were designed to pass on cultural knowledge and traditions, which constituted much the same learning that parents taught their children. Students come to school steeped in the learning practices of their own family and community. They come with expectations about learning and generally expect that they will continue to learn the same way in school. However, many of the organizational and teaching practices of the school may not support the type of learning to which students are accustomed.

For example, Indochinese students expect to listen, watch, and imitate. They may be reluctant to ask questions or volunteer answers and may be embarrassed to ask for the teacher's help or reluctant to participate in individual demonstrations of a skill or project. For immigrant children with previous schooling, experience in U.S. classrooms may engender severe conflicts. Teachers who can accommodate these students' proclivities can gradually introduce student-centered practices while supporting an initial dependence on the teacher's direction.

### DID YOU KNOW?
**Overcoming Passivity**

Polynesian students newly arrived from the South Pacific may have experienced classroom learning as a relatively passive activity. They expect teachers to give explicit instruction about what to learn and how to learn it. When these students arrive in the United States and encounter teachers who value creativity and student-centered learning, they may appear passive as they wait to be told what to do. (Funaki & Burnett, 1993)

## BEST PRACTICE: Accommodating Culturally Based Educational Expectations

Teachers who seek to understand the value of education within the community can do the following:

- Invite classroom guests from the community to share methods for teaching and learning that are used in the home (e.g., modeling and imitation, didactic stories and proverbs, direct verbal instruction).

- Pair children from cultures that expect passive interaction with teachers (observing only) with more participatory peers to help the former learn to ask questions and volunteer.
- In communities with a high dropout rate, support the systematic efforts of school counselors and administrators to help families accommodate their beliefs to a more proactive support for school completion and higher education.

**Values about Roles and Status**    Cultures differ in the roles people play in society and the status accorded to these roles. For example, in the Vietnamese culture, profoundly influenced by Confucianism, authority figures are ranked in the following manner: The father ranks below the teacher, who ranks only below the king (Chung, 1989). Such a high status is not accorded to teachers in U.S. society, where, instead, medical doctors enjoy this type of prestige. Such factors as gender, social class, age, occupation, and education level influence the manner in which status is accorded to various roles. Students' perceptions about the roles possible for them in their culture affect their school performance.

**Values about Gender**    In many cultures, gender is related to social roles in a similar way. Anthropologists have found men to be in control of political and military matters in all known cultures. Young boys tend to be more physically and verbally aggressive and to seek dominance more than girls do. Traditionally, women have had the primary responsibility for child-rearing, with associated tasks, manners, and responsibilities. Immigrants to the United States often come from cultures in which men and women have rigid and highly differentiated gender roles. The gender equality that is an ostensible goal in U.S. classrooms may be difficult for students of these cultures.

## CLASSROOM GLIMPSE: To Mentor or Not to Mentor?

*Chad is a journalism teacher in a large urban high school and the advisor of the school newspaper. Khalia is a young woman who enrolled in a beginning journalism class as a junior. Although English was not her first language, she showed unusual ability and creativity in writing the stories to which she was assigned. Chad routinely advises students on their vocational choice, writes letters of recommendation for them when they apply to college, and encourages those who want to further their education. Khalia has confided in him that her parents have discouraged her from attending college. Khalia does not want to marry immediately after high school and has asked Chad's help in applying to college. Should Chad help Khalia?*

## BEST PRACTICE: Gender-Role Expectations

- Monitor tasks performed by boys and girls to ensure they are the same.
- Make sure that boys and girls perform equal leadership roles in cooperative groups.
- If families in a given community provide little support for the scholastic achievement of girls, a systematic effort on the part of school counselors and administrators may be needed to help families accommodate their beliefs to a more proactive support for women.

**Values about Social Class**    Stratification by social class differs across cultures. Cultures that are rigidly stratified, such as India's caste system, differ from cultures that are not as rigid or that, in some cases, border on the anarchic, such as continuously war-torn countries. The belief that education can enhance economic status is widespread in the dominant culture of the United States, but individuals in other cultures may not have similar beliefs.

In general, individuals and families at the upper socioeconomic levels are able to exert power by sitting on college, university, and local school boards and thus determining who receives benefits and rewards through schooling. However, middle-class values are those that are generally incorporated in the culture of schooling. The social-class values that children learn in their homes largely influence not only their belief in schooling but also their routines and habits in the classroom.

## BEST PRACTICE: Accommodating the Influence of Social Class on Schooling

- Students who are extremely poor or homeless may need help from the teacher to store possessions at school.
- A teacher who receives an expensive gift should consult the school district's ethics policies.
- A high grade on a school assignment or project should not depend on extensive family financial resources.

**Values about Age-Appropriate Activities**    Age interacts with culture, socioeconomic status, gender, and other factors to influence an individual's behavior and attitudes. In various cultures, expectations about appropriate activities for children and the purpose of those activities differ. Middle-class European Americans expect children to spend much of their time playing and attending school rather than performing tasks similar to those of adults. Cree Indian children, on the other hand, are expected from an early age to learn adult roles, including contributing food to the family. Parents may criticize schools for involving children in tasks that are not related to their future participation in Cree society (Sindell, 1988).

Cultures also differ in their criteria for moving through the various (culturally defined) life cycle changes. An important stage in any culture is the move into adulthood, but the age at which this occurs and the criteria necessary for attaining adulthood vary according to what adulthood means in a particular culture. Rural, traditional families in many countries expect young men and women to be socially mature when they enter high school; whereas other families, for example, middle-class families in Taiwan, expect a much longer period of adolescence.

## BEST PRACTICE: Accommodating Beliefs about Age-Appropriate Activities

- Child labor laws in the United States forbid students from working for pay before a given age. However, few laws govern children working in family businesses. If a child appears chronically tired, the school counselor may need to discuss the child's involvement in a family business with a responsible family member.

- Cultural groups in which girls are expected to marry and have children at the age of fifteen or sixteen (e.g., Hmong) may need access to alternative schools.
- If a student misses school because of being expected to accompany family members to social services to act as a translator or to stay at home as a babysitter, the school counselor may be able to intervene to help families find other resources.

**Values about Occupations**   In the United States, occupation very often determines income, which in turn is a chief determinant of prestige in the culture. Other cultures, however, may attribute prestige to those with inherited status or to those who have a religious function in the culture. Prestige is one factor in occupational choices. Other factors can include cultural acceptance of the occupation, educational requirements, gender, and attainability. Students therefore may not see all occupations as desirable for them or even available to them and may have mixed views about the role education plays in their future occupation.

Some cultural groups in the United States are engaged in a voluntary way of life that does not require public schooling (e.g., the Amish). Other groups may not be adequately rewarded in the United States for school success but expect to be rewarded elsewhere (e.g., children of diplomats and short-term residents who expect to return to their home country). Still other groups may be involuntarily incorporated into U.S. society and relegated to menial occupations and ways of life that do not reward and require school success (e.g., Hispanics in the Southwest). As a result, they may not apply academic effort (Ogbu & Matute-Bianchi, 1986).

## BEST PRACTICE: Accommodating Occupational Aspirations

- At all grade levels, school subjects should be connected with future vocations.
- Role models from minority communities can visit the classroom to recount stories of their success. Successful professionals and businesspeople can visit and explain how cultural diversity is supported in their place of work.
- Teachers should make available at every grade an extensive set of books on occupations and their requirements, and discuss these with students.

**Values about Child-Rearing**   The way in which families raise their children has significant implications for schools. Factors such as who takes care of children, how much supervision they receive, how much freedom they have, who speaks to them and how often, and what they are expected to do affect students' behavior on entering schools. Many of the misunderstandings that occur between teachers and students arise because of different expectations about behavior, and these different expectations stem from early, ingrained child-rearing practices. In Hmong society, for example, family values are placed above individual concerns. Children spend the majority of every day in close physical proximity to their parents. Parents carry and touch their children more than is common in Western cultures (Bliatout et al., 1988).

Because the largest group of English learners in California is of Mexican ancestry, teachers who take the time to learn about child-rearing practices among Mexican immigrants can help students adjust to schooling practices in the United States. An excellent source for this cultural study is *Crossing Cultural Borders* (Delgado-Gaitan & Trueba, 1991).

**Food Preferences**   As the numbers of school-provided breakfasts and lunches increase, food preferences are an important consideration. Furthermore, teachers who are knowledgeable about students' dietary practices can incorporate their students' background knowledge into health and nutrition instruction.

Besides customs of what and when to eat, eating habits vary widely across cultures, and "good" manners at the table in some cultures are inappropriate or rude in others. For example, the Indochinese consider burping, lip smacking, and soup slurping to be common behaviors during meals, even complimentary to hosts. Cultural relativity is not, however, an excuse for poor or unhygienic eating, and teachers do need to teach students the behaviors that are considered good food manners in the U.S. mainstream context.

## BEST PRACTICE: Dealing with Food Preferences

- In addition to knowing in general what foods are eaten at home, teachers will want to find out about students' favorite foods, taboo foods, and typical foods.
- Eating lunch with students, even on a by-invitation basis, can provide the opportunity to learn about students' habits.
- If a student's eating habits alienate peers, the teacher may need to discuss appropriate behaviors.

**Valuing Humanities and the Arts**   In many cultures, crafts performed at home—such as food preparation; sewing and weaving; carpentry; home building and decoration; religious and ritual artistry for holy days, holidays, and entertaining—are an important part of the culture that is transmitted within the home. Parents also provide an important means of access to the humanities and the visual and performing arts of their cultures. The classroom teacher can foster an appreciation of the works of art, architecture, music, and dance that have been achieved by students' native culture by drawing on the resources of the community and then sharing these with all members of the classroom.

**Cooperation versus Competition**   Many cultures emphasize cooperation over competition. Traditional U.S. classrooms mirror middle-class European-American values of competition: Students are expected to do their own work; are rewarded publicly through star charts, posted grades, and academic honors; and are admonished to do their individual best. In the Cree Indian culture, however, children are raised in a cooperative atmosphere, with siblings, parents, and other kin sharing food as well as labor (Sindell, 1988). In the Mexican-American culture, interdependence is strength; individuals have a commitment to others, and all decisions are made together. Those who are successful have a responsibility to others to help them succeed.

A classroom structured to maximize learning through cooperation can help students extend their cultural predilection for interdependence. This interdependence does not devalue the uniqueness of the individual. The Mexican culture values *individualismo*, the affirmation of an individual's intrinsic worth and uniqueness aside from any successful actions or grand position in society (deUnamuno, 1925). A workable synthesis of individualism versus interdependence would come from classroom activities that are carried out as a group but that affirm the unique gifts of each individual student.

## Adapting to Students' Culturally Supported Facilitating or Limiting Attitudes and Abilities

A skilled intercultural educator recognizes that each culture supports distinct attitudes, values, and abilities. These may facilitate or limit the learning situation in U.S. public schools. For example, the cultures of Japan, China, and Korea, which promote high academic achievement, may foster facilitating behaviors such as the ability to listen and follow directions, attitudes favoring education and respect for teachers and authorities, attitudes toward discipline as guidance, and high-achievement motivation. However, other culturally supported traits may hinder adjustment to the U.S. school, such as lack of experience participating in discussions; little experience with independent thinking; strong preference for conformity, which inhibits divergent thinking; and distinct sex-role differentiation, with males more dominant.

Mexican-American cultural values encourage cooperation; affectionate and demonstrative parental relationships; children assuming mature social responsibilities such as child care and translating family matters from English to Spanish; and eagerness to try out new ideas. All of these values facilitate classroom success. On the other hand, such attitudes as depreciating education after high school, especially for women; explicit sex-role stereotyping favoring limited vocational roles for women; emphasis of family over the achievement and life goals of children; and dislike of competition may work against classroom practices and hinder classroom success (Clark, 1983).

Accommodating school routines is a schoolwide responsibility that is furthered when the principal sets the tone of appreciation and support for cultural diversity. Much can also be done by individual teachers in the classroom to set high standards of achievement that students and family members can support.

## EDUCATING STUDENTS ABOUT DIVERSITY

Both mainstream students and CLD students benefit from education about diversity, not only cultural diversity but also diversity in ability, gender preference, and human nature in general. This engenders pride in cultural identity, expands the students' perspectives, and adds cultural insight, information, and experiences to the curriculum.

### Global and Multicultural Education

ELD teachers, as well as mainstream teachers who teach English learners, can bring a global and multicultural perspective to their classes.

> Language teachers, like teachers in all other areas of the curriculum, have a responsibility to plan lessons with sensitivity to the racial and ethnic diversity present in their classrooms and in the world in which their students live. . . . [Students] can learn to value the points of view of many others whose life experiences are different from their own. (Curtain & Dahlberg, 2004, p. 244)

Table 9.1 lists some cultural activities that Curtain and Dahlberg recommended for adding cultural content to the curriculum.

TABLE 9.1 Sample Cultural Activities for Multicultural Education

| Activity | Suggested Implementation |
| --- | --- |
| Visitors and guest speakers | Guests can share their experiences on a variety of topics, using visuals, slides, and hands-on materials. |
| Folk dances, singing games, and other kinds of games | Many cultures can be represented; cultural informants can help. |
| Field trips | Students can visit neighborhoods, restaurants, museums, or stores that feature cultural materials. |
| Show-and-tell | Students can bring items from home to share with the class. |
| Read fables, folktales, or legends | Read in translation or have a visitor read in another language. |
| Read books about other cultures | Age-appropriate fiction or nonfiction books can be obtained with the help of the school or public librarian. |
| Crosscultural e-mail contacts | Students can exchange cultural information and get to know peers from other lands. |
| Magazine subscriptions | Authentic cultural materials—written for adults or young people—give insight about the lifestyles and interests of others. |

*Source:* Curtain & Dahlberg (2004).

There is a clear distinction between multiculturalism and globalism, although both are important features of the school curriculum: "Globalism emphasizes the cultures and peoples of other lands, and multiculturalism deals with ethnic diversity within the United States" (Ukpokodu, 2002, pp. 7–8).

**▌ DID YOU KNOW?**
**Studying Cultures Here and There**

James Banks explained the difference between studying the cultures of other countries and studying the cultures within the United States. According to Banks, many teachers implement a unit on the country of Japan but avoid teaching about Japanese internment in the United States during World War II. (Brandt, 1994)

## The Multicultural Curriculum: From Additive to Transformative

The goal of multicultural education is to help students "develop cross-cultural competence within the American national culture, with their own subculture and within and across different subsocieties and cultures" (Banks, 1994, p. 9). Banks introduced a model of multicultural education that has proved to be a useful way of assessing the approach taken in pedagogy and curricula. The model has four levels, represented in Table 9.2 with a critique of strengths and shortcomings taken from Jenks, Lee, and Kanpol (2002).

Similar to Banks's superficial-to-transformative continuum is that of Morey and Kilano (1997). Their three-level framework for incorporating diversity identifies as "exclusive" the stereotypical focus on external aspects of diversity (what they called the four *f*'s: food, folklore, fun, and fashion); as "inclusive" the addition of diversity into a curriculum that, although enriched, is fundamentally the same structure; and as "transformed" the curriculum that is built on diverse perspectives, equity in participation, and critical problem solving. Thus, it is clear that pouring new wine (diversity) into old bottles (teacher-centered, one-size-fits-all instruction) is not transformative.

**TABLE 9.2**   Banks's Levels of Multicultural Education, with Critique

| Level | Description | Strengths | Shortcomings |
|---|---|---|---|
| Contributions | Emphasizes what minority groups have contributed to society (examples: International Food Day, bulletin board display for Black History Month). | Attempts to sensitize the majority white culture to some understanding of minority groups' history. | May amount to "cosmetic" multiculturalism in which no discussion takes place about issues of power and disenfranchisement. |
| Additive | Adding material to the curriculum to address what has been omitted (reading *The Color Purple* in English class). | Adds to a fuller coverage of the American experience, when sufficient curricular time is allotted. | May be an insincere effort if dealt with superficially. |
| Transformative | An expanded perspective is taken that deals with issues of historic, ethnic, cultural, and linguistic injustice and equality as a part of the American experience. | Students learn to be reflective and develop a critical perspective. | Incorporates the liberal fallacy that discussion alone changes society. |
| Social Action | Extension of the transformative approach to add students' research/action projects to initiate change in society. | Students learn to question the status quo and the commitment of the dominant culture to equality and social justice. | Middle-class communities may not accept the teacher's role, considering it as provoking students to "radical" positions. |

*Sources:* Model based on Banks (1994); strengths and shortcomings based on Jenks, Lee, & Kanpol (2002).

## CLASSROOM GLIMPSE: Transformative Multicultural Education

*Christensen (2000) described how her students were moved to action:*

> One year our students responded to a negative newspaper article, about how parents feared to send their children to our school, by organizing a march and rally to "tell the truth about Jefferson to the press." During the Columbus quincentenary, my students organized a teach-in about Columbus for classes at Jefferson. Of course, these "spontaneous uprisings" only work if teachers are willing to give over class time for the students to organize, and if they've highlighted times when people in history resisted injustice, making it clear that solidarity and courage are values to be prized in daily life, not just praised in the abstract and put on the shelf. (pp. 8–9)

### Validating Students' Cultural Identity

"An affirming attitude toward students from culturally diverse backgrounds significantly impacts their learning, belief in self, and overall academic performance" (Villegas & Lucas, 2002, p. 23). Cultural identity—that is, having a positive self-concept or evaluation of oneself and one's culture—promotes self-esteem. Students who feel proud of their successes and abilities, self-knowledge, and self-expression, and who have enhanced images of self, family, and culture, are better learners.

Of course, the most powerful sense of self-esteem is the result not solely of one's beliefs about oneself but also of successful learning experiences. Practices of schooling that damage self-esteem, such as tracking and competitive grading, undermine authentic cooperation and a sense of accomplishment on the part of English learners.

**Classroom Practices That Validate Identity**   Siccone (1995) described the activity Name Interviews in which students work in pairs using a teacher-provided questionnaire: "What do you like about your name? Who named you? Were you named for someone? Are there members of your family who have the same name?" This activity can be adapted for both elementary and secondary classrooms. Díaz-Rico (2004) suggested that interested teachers might ask students to provide initial information about cultural customs in their homes, perhaps pertaining to birthdays or holidays. Through observations, shared conversations during lunchtime or before or after school, and group participation, teachers can gain understanding about various individuals and their cultures.

Educators who form relationships with parents can talk about the students' perception of their own identity. Teachers can also ask students to interview their parents about common topics such as work, interests, and family history and then add a reflective element about their relationship and identification with these aspects of their parents' lives.

**Instructional Materials That Validate Identity**   Classroom texts are available that offer literature and anecdotal readings aimed at the enhancement of identity and self-esteem. *Identities: Readings from Contemporary Culture* (Raimes, 1996) includes readings grouped into chapters titled "Name," "Appearance, Age, and Abilities," "Ethnic Affiliation and Class," "Family Ties," and so forth. The readings contain authentic text and may be best used in middle or high school classes.

The use of multicultural literature can enhance cultural and ethnic identity, but this is not always the case. In 1976 a committee of Asian-American book reviewers formed the Asian-American Children's Book Project under the aegis of the Council for Interracial Books for Children. Their main objective was to evaluate books and identify those that could be used effectively in educational programs.

When they had evaluated a total of sixty-four books related to Asian-American issues or characters, they concluded that most of the existing literature was "racist, sexist, and elitist and that the image of Asian Americans present [in the books] is grossly misleading" (Aoki, 1992, p. 133). The criticism was that these books depicted "Orientals" as slant-eyed, black-haired, quietly subservient people living lives far removed from those of mainstream Americans. The challenge, then, is to represent ethnic characters in a more realistic way.

A book that is useful for a comparison of Asian cultural values with those of mainstream American culture is Kim's (2001) *The Yin and Yang of American Culture.* This book presents a view of American culture—its virtues and vices—from an Eastern perspective and may stimulate discussion on the part of students. *Exploring Culturally Diverse Literature for Children and Adolescents* (Henderson & May, 2005) helps readers understand how stories are tied to specific cultural and sociopolitical histories.

### Promoting Mutual Respect among Students

The ways in which we organize classroom life should make children feel significant and cared about—by the teacher and by one another. Unless students feel emotionally and physically safe, they will be reluctant to share real thoughts and feelings. Classroom life should, to the greatest extent possible, prefigure the kind of democratic and just society we envision and thus contribute to building that society. Together, students and teachers can create a "community of conscience," as educators Asa Hillard and George Pine call it (Christensen, 2000, p. 18). Mutual respect is promoted when teachers listen as much as they speak, when students can build on their personal and cultural strengths, when the curriculum includes multiple points of view, and when students are given the chance to genuinely talk to one another about topics that concern them. The instructional conversation is a discourse format that encourages in-depth conversation, a lost art in today's world (see Chapters 2 and 6).

## ◼◼ LEARNING ABOUT STUDENTS' CULTURES

Teachers can use printed, electronic, and video materials, books, and magazines to learn about other cultures. However, the richest source of information is local—the life of the community. Students, parents, and community members can provide insights about values, attitudes, and habits. One method of learning about students and their families, ethnographic study, has proved useful in illuminating the ways that students' experiences in the home and community compare with the culture of the schools.

### Ethnographic Techniques

Ethnography is an inquiry process that seeks to provide cultural explanations for behavior and attitudes. Culture is described from the insider's point of view, as the classroom teacher becomes not only an observer of the students' cultures but also an active participant (Erickson, 1977; Mehan, 1981; Robinson, 1985). Parents and community members, as well as students, become sources for the gradual growth of understanding on the part of the teacher.

For the classroom teacher, ethnography involves gathering data in order to understand two distinct cultures: the culture of the students' communities and the culture of the classroom. To understand the home and community environment, teachers may observe and participate in community life, interview community members, and visit students' homes. To understand the school culture, teachers may observe in a variety of classrooms, have visitors observe in their own classroom, audio- and videotape classroom interaction, and interview other teachers and administrators.

**Observations**    Ideally, initial observations of other cultures must be carried out with the perspective that one is seeing the culture from the point of view of a complete outsider. Of course, when observing interactions and behaviors in another culture, one always uses the frame of reference supplied by one's own culture. This stance gradually changes as one adopts an ethnographic perspective.

Observers need to be descriptive and objective and make explicit their own attitudes and values in order to overcome hidden sources of bias. This requires practice and, ideally, some training. However, the classroom teacher can begin to observe and participate in the students' culture, writing up field notes after participating and perhaps summing up the insights gained in an ongoing diary that can be shared with colleagues. Such observation can document children's use of language within the community; etiquettes of speaking, listening, writing, greeting, and getting or giving information; values and aspirations; and norms of communication.

When analyzing the culture of the classroom, teachers might look at classroom management and routines; affective factors (students' attitudes toward activities, teachers' attitudes toward students); classroom talk in general; and nonverbal behaviors and communication. In addition to the raw data of behavior, the thoughts and intentions of the participants can also be documented.

**Interviews**    Interviews can be divided into two types: structured and unstructured. Structured interviews use a set of predetermined questions to gain specific kinds of information. Unstructured interviews are more like conversations in that they can range over a wide variety of topics, many of which the interviewer would not necessarily have anticipated. As an outsider learning about a new culture, the classroom teacher would be better served initially by using an unstructured interview, beginning with general questions and being guided in follow-up questions by the interviewees' responses. The result of the initial interview may in turn provide a structure for learning more about the culture during a second interview or conversation. A very readable book about ethnography and interviewing is *The Professional Stranger: An Informal Introduction to Ethnography* (Agar, 1980).

**Home Visits**    Home visits are one of the best ways in which teachers can learn what is familiar and important to their students. The home visit can be a social call or a brief report on the student's progress that enhances rapport with students and parents. Scheduling an appointment ahead of time is a courtesy that some cultures may require and provides a means for the teacher to ascertain if home visits are welcome. The visit should be short (twenty to thirty minutes) and the conversation positive, especially about the student's schoolwork. Viewing the child in the context of the home provides a look at the parent–child interaction, the resources of the home, and the child's role in the family.

## CLASSROOM GLIMPSE: A Home Visit

*Hughes describes the result of one home visit:*

> *Years ago a child named Nai persuaded her parents to let me visit them. Many people lived in the small apartment. One of the men spoke a little English as I tried a few Mien phrases that drew chuckles and good will. I ate with them. Recently a community college student dropped in at our school. "Nai!" I cried, delighted. . . . "How's your family?" "They OK." "I enjoyed my visit with them," I said. She smiled. "My parents . . . they talk still about 'that teacher,' they call you."* (Hughes, 2004, p. 10)

### Students as Sources of Information

Students generally provide teachers with their initial contact with other cultures. Through observations, one-on-one interaction, and group participatory processes, teachers gain understanding about various individuals and their cultural repertoire. Teachers who are good listeners offer students time for shared conversations by lingering after school or opening the classroom during lunchtime. Questionnaires and interest surveys are also useful. Cary (2000) called this information about students their "outside story": "The outside story unfolds away from school and is built from a thousand and one experiences hooked to home and home country culture—family structure, language, communication patterns, social behavior, values, spirituality, and worldview" (p. 20).

Cary's *Working with Second Language Learners: Answers to Teachers' Top Ten Questions* (2000) details one teacher's exploration of the culture and homeland of a Hmong student, Ka Xiong. Lenny Rossovich, the teacher of the new fifth grader, used every resource from a school encyclopedia, websites (including the Hmong homepage [see Table 9.3]), the local library, and one of Ka's uncles to learn more about the Hmong culture. Lenny even took a few Hmong language lessons on the Web. Lenny's adventure toward understanding his student is an engrossing model.

### Families as Sources of Information

Family members can be sources of information in much the same way as their children. Rather than scheduling one or two formal conferences, PTA open house events, and gala performances, the school might encourage family participation by opening the library once a week after school. This offers a predictable time during which family members and teachers can casually meet and chat. Families can also be the source for information that can form the basis for classroom writing. Using the language experience approach, teachers can ask students to interview their family members about common topics such as work, interests, and family history. In this way, students and family members together can supply knowledge about community life.

## Community Members as Sources of Information

Community members are an equally rich source of cultural knowledge. Much can be learned about a community by walking or driving through it, or stopping to make a purchase in local stores and markets. Other teachers may ask older students to act as tour guides. During these visits, the people of the neighborhood can be sources of knowledge about housing, places where children and teenagers play, places where adults gather, and sources of food, furniture, and services.

Through community representatives, teachers can begin to know about important living patterns of a community. A respected elder can provide information about the family and which members constitute a family. A religious leader can explain the importance of religion in community life. Teachers can also attend local ceremonies and activities to learn more about community dynamics.

## The Internet as an Information Source about Cultures

Websites proliferate that introduce the curious to other cultures. Webcrawler programs assist the user to explore cultural content using key word prompts. Table 9.3 lists websites with information about cultures commonly found in U.S. schools.

# ▓▓▓ CULTURALLY INCLUSIVE LEARNING ENVIRONMENTS

Culturally responsive accommodations help teachers maintain culturally inclusive learning environments. But what characteristics of classroom and school environments facilitate culturally responsive accommodations to diverse communities?

## What Is a Culturally Supportive Classroom?

A variety of factors contribute to classroom and school environments that support cultural diversity and student achievement. The most important feature of these classrooms is the expectation of high achievement from English learners while supporting them culturally, intellectually, and emotionally toward the attainment of this goal. Communicating these expectations requires specific educational programs that draw attention to the hidden curriculum of the school, quality of interaction between teachers and students, diverse learning styles, the use of the community as a resource, and a commitment to democratic ideals in the classroom (Gollnick & Chinn, 2002). Such factors as culturally accommodating schooling, supporting students' culture(s) and language(s), and conflict resolution have already been discussed. High expectations, active student learning, and use of critical thinking and critical consciousness are explored in turn, followed by ways to involve the family and community.

**High Expectations for All Students** Expectations for student achievement are also a feature of culturally responsive schooling. Teachers need to challenge students to strive for excellence as defined by their potential. Teachers tread a fine line between expecting too much of their students, causing frustration on students' part through stress and overwork, and expecting too little by watering down the curriculum, leading to boredom and low academic achievement.

**TABLE 9.3**    Websites Featuring Cultures Found in U.S. Schools

| Culture | Website | Description |
|---|---|---|
| Armenia | www.loc.gov/rr/international/amed/ armenia/resources/armenia-culture.html | Portal to the Armenian culture and diaspora, including music, history, art, and film |
| China | chineseculture.about.com/ | Comprehensive! |
| Philippines | pinas.dlsu.edu.ph/culture/culture.html | Portal to many other Filipino websites |
| Guatemala | | |
| Hmong | www.hmongcenter.org/ | A virtual museum of Hmong artifacts, online arts exhibit, bibliography about the Hmong, educational resources, and lesson plans |
| India | www.culturopedia.com/ | "Treasure house" of India's culture and heritage |
| Iran | www.iranvision.com/ | A user-friendly contemporary point of view |
| Japan | www.japan-zone.com/culture/index.shtml | Comprehensible overview |
| Laos | www.laoheritagefoundation.org/ | Introduction to Lao culture, history, and performing arts |
| Mexico | www.mexican-embassy.dk/history.html | Overview of Mexico's history and traditions |
| Russia | www.goehner.com/russinfo.htm | Comparisons between U.S. and Russian cultures |
| El Salvador | www.student.nvcc.edu/home/ycoreas/culture /index.htm | Survey of El Salvador in digest form— concise yet comprehensive |
| South Korea | www.sogang.ac.kr/~burns/cult96/cult96-index .html | Short essays on aspects of Korean culture from the university student's perspective prepared by students of Sogang University to introduce their culture to peers around the world |
| Tonga | www.answers.com/topic/culture-of-tonga | Survey of Tongan culture, including religion, art, food, clothing, and dance |
| Ukraine | www.infoukes.com/culture/ | General source for many aspects of Ukranian culture |
| Vietnam | ethnomed.org/cultures/vietnamese/ vietnamese_cp.html | Geography, history, politics, and cultural values and etiquette |

Many students' abilities are underestimated because their second-language skills do not adequately convey their talents. Sometimes unfamiliarity with the students' culture compounds the language barrier. Ongoing formative assessment, combined with a sensitive awareness of students' needs and a willingness to be flexible, help the teacher monitor and adjust the instructional level to students' abilities.

Teachers' behavior varies with the level of expectation held about the students. Students of whom much is expected are given more frequent cues and prompts to respond to, are asked more and harder questions, are given a longer time to respond, are encouraged to provide more elaborate answers, and are interrupted less often (Good & Brophy, 1984). Teachers tend to be encouraging toward students for whom they have high expectations. They smile at these students more often and show greater warmth through nonverbal responses such as leaning toward the students and nodding their head as students speak (Woolfolk & Brooks, 1985).

Some teachers expect more from Asian Americans than from other minorities because of the "model minority" myth. Acting toward students on the basis of these stereotypes is a form of racism, which is detrimental to all. The online report *Expectations and Student Outcomes* (Cotton, 1989, www.nwrel.org/scpd/sirs/4/cu7.html) is a useful resource for learning about how inappropriate expectations are formed and how differential expectations are communicated to students.

Students' responses to teacher expectations seem to be highly influenced by cultural background and home discourse patterns. Sato (1982) found that Asian students initiated classroom discourse less often than English learners from other countries. Some cultures encourage students to set internal standards of worth, and peer pressure devalues dependence on teachers for approval.

**Motivating Students to Become Active Participants in Their Learning**   Learner autonomy is a key element of constructivist learning, in which teachers help students to construct new knowledge, providing scaffolds between what students already know and what they need to learn. Learner autonomy is the learner's ability and willingness to study due to the individual's own volition. This autonomy is the basis for self-managed, self-motivated instruction. Such autonomy is more than a preference or strategy by the learner; it must be supported in a systematic way by the teacher and curriculum for the learner to benefit. Therefore, a major aim of classroom instruction should be to equip learners with learning skills they can employ on their own. These include the following:

- Efficient learning strategies
- Identification of students' preferred ways of learning
- Skills needed to negotiate the curriculum
- Encouragement to set their own learning objectives
- Support for learners to set realistic goals and time frames
- Skills in self-evaluation (Nunan, 1989, p. 3)

Student autonomy is at risk in the climate of coercive adherence to standardized test scores as the sole criterion of effective instruction. Certainly, in democratic schooling, there is a place for choice in topics and freedom to voice divergent views (Giroux & McLaren, 1996).

**Encouraging Students to Think Critically and Become Socially and Politically Conscious**
"Sociocultural consciousness means understanding that one's way of thinking, behaving, and being is influenced by race, ethnicity, social class, and language" (Kea, Campbell-Whatley, & Richards, 2004, p. 4). Students as well as teachers need to have clarity of vision about their sociocultural identities and their role in the institutions that maintain social and economic distinctions based on social class and skin color.

Political and social consciousness is hard-won. It requires teachers to offer students a forum in which to discuss social and political events without partisan rancor, to investigate issues in the national and local press that are open to multiple perspectives, and to find a way to support students' voices about their lives and feelings. Bulletin boards on which student writing can be posted, weekly current event discussions, and class newsletters are projects that can encourage autonomous student thinking, writing, and discussion.

An important aspect of schooling in a democracy is the ability to think for oneself, analyze ideas, separate fact from opinion, support opinions from reading, make inferences, and solve problems. The ability to think critically can enhance self-understanding and help students approach significant issues in life with analytic skills. Critical thinking includes the ability to look for underlying assumptions in statements, to detect bias, to identify illogical connections between ideas, and to recognize attempts to influence opinion by means of propaganda. These skills are fundamental to the clear thinking required of autonomous citizens in a democracy.

## FAMILY AND COMMUNITY INVOLVEMENT

Family and community involvement supports and encourages students and provides opportunities for families and educators to work together in educating students. Families need to become involved in different settings and at different levels of the educational process. Family members can help teachers establish a genuine respect for their children and the strengths they bring to the classroom. They can work with their own children at home or serve on school committees. Collaborative involvement in school restructuring includes family and community members who help set goals and allocate resources.

### Value Differences in Family and Community Support for Schooling

Family involvement in the school is influenced by cultural beliefs. The U.S. system was developed from small, relatively homogeneous local schools with considerable community and parental control. The pattern of community and parental involvement continues today with school boards, PTAs, and parent volunteers in the schools. This pattern is not universal outside the United States. For example, in traditional Cambodia, village families who sent their children to schools in cities had no means of involving themselves in the school (Ouk, Huffman, & Lewis, 1988).

In cultures in which teachers are accorded high status, parents may consider it improper to discuss educational matters or bring up issues that concern their children. Other factors that make family involvement difficult are school procedures such as restrictive scheduling for family–teacher conferences and notification of parents that students' siblings are not welcome at school for conferences and other events. These procedures tend to divide families and exclude parents. School staff members can involve the community by talking with parents and community liaisons to work out procedures that are compatible with cultural practices.

### Issues in Family Involvement

Schools that have grappled with how to increase parental involvement have encountered many of the same issues (Bermúdez & Márquez, 1996; Young & Helvie, 1996). Ovando and Collier

(1998, pp. 301–309) organized these issues around five areas: language; survival and family structure; educational background and values; knowledge about education and beliefs about learning; and power and status. From each area arise questions that serve as guides for school personnel as they build collaborations with parents. These questions, and some strategies that address these issues, are presented in Table 9.4.

### Myths about Families and Other Communication Barriers

Often teachers think that families of English learners are not interested in what happens in schools because they are not visible at parent meetings or traditional parent–school activities. However, surveys of parents show that an overwhelming number express interest in being involved in school events, activities, and decisions. At the same time, they report that they are often not consulted about the type of involvement, scheduling of activities, or location of events. These reports show that the so-called lack of interest myth that circulates in low-achieving schools may be due to poor communication between home and school.

### Enhancing Home–School Communication

If the teacher does not speak the same language as the family, nonverbal messages assume an increased importance. Teachers who meet family members informally as they arrive to drop off their child, at a classroom open house, or during other school events should strive to have their body language be "warm" rather than cold. Teachers can show respect toward family members by, for example, rising as guests enter the room, greeting guests at the door, and accompanying them to the door when they leave.

Any notes, letters, or newsletters sent home need to be translated into the home language. If communication sent home is positive, there is more chance it will be read. Many teachers establish a positive communication pattern by sending a consistent stream of "happy grams" describing what a student has done well. However, if a student has a problem in class, communication between home and school must be consistent and sustained. Any program of home–school communication is first based on having established a rapport with parents in person.

Teachers have modified a wide range of classroom behaviors through the use of school-to-home notes. The most effective notes are those that focus on the improvement of academic productivity, such as the amount or quality of completed classwork or homework. Work completion and accuracy are goals for all students, and when students are rewarded for increased outcomes, research shows that improvements in classroom conduct occur simultaneously. After all, few children can complete their work accurately and have time to misbehave. In contrast, a focus on disruptiveness does not cause an improvement in academic performance (Kelley, 1990).

### Family–Teacher Conferences

Preparation for meetings with families enhances success. The concerned teacher makes sure that scheduled times are convenient for family members and prepares a portfolio of the student's successes. The conference might begin with a limited amount of small talk, especially if there has been a recent notable family event. Then the teacher reviews the student's performance, using the portfolio or other evidence of student work. Showing an anonymous example

**TABLE 9.4** Strategies for Teachers Based on Questions Regarding Parent–School Relationships

| Area of Concern | Questions | Strategies for Teachers |
|---|---|---|
| Language | How does educators' language (jargon?) affect home–school communication? | Translate jargon into plain English and then into home language. |
| | Do community members support using the home language in school? | Advocate maintenance of the home language in all parent communication. |
| Family structure | How do the struggles of day-to-day survival affect the home–school partnership? | Arrange conferences at convenient times for working families. |
| | How will differences in family structure affect the relationship? | Speak about "families" rather than "parents." Accept the relationships that exist. |
| Educational background, attitudes toward schooling | Do school expectations match the parents' educational backgrounds? | Discover the parents' aspirations for their children. Do everything possible to have the school and family agree on high standards. |
| | What do educators assume about the attitudes of parents toward schooling? | Ensure that communication with school is always honest and positive. |
| Knowledge and beliefs about education | How do parents learn about school culture, their role in U.S. schools, and the specific methods being used in their child's classroom? Would they be comfortable reinforcing these methods at home? | Family education events, family literacy classes, primary-language written and oral information, formal and informal teacher–family talks, and family tutoring training are a part of the picture. |
| | How do parents and teachers differ in the perception of the home–school relationship? | Not only do teachers inform parents, but also interest and communication are fully two-way. |
| Power and status | How does the inherent inequality of the educator–layperson relationship affect the partnership? | Try to have a "family space" at the school. Parents should be informed and involved in decisions. |
| | Do programs for parents convey a message of cultural deficiency? | The funds of knowledge approach affirms and respects the knowledge of the home. |
| | To what degree are language-minority community members a part of the school in instructional and administrative positions? | Bilingual speakers are paid well and are considered respected assets to the school as well as to the classroom. |

*Source:* Adapted from Ovando & Collier (1998, pp. 301–309).

of a grade-level performance may make it easier for family members to put their child's performance in perspective. Listening to family members helps the teacher get a more complete view of the child. If a plan for improvement needs to be drawn up, specific steps are identified, as well as a time in the near future to compare notes on the child's progress.

**The Use of an Interpreter**   Having a translator facilitate parent conferences shows respect for the home language of families. During the conference, the interpreter usually translates the client's words as closely as possible to give a sense of the client's concepts, emotional state, and other important information. Despite the language difference, the teacher can watch nonverbal, affective responses and, by observing facial expressions, voice intonations, and body movements, extend communication.

**Tracking Contact with the Family**   All family contact should be documented in an activity log, including date, subject, and parents' reactions. In this way, school administrators can see what communication efforts have been made.

**Three-Way Conferences**   Including the student in the family–teacher conference invites family members into a dialogue about their child's schooling. Students can use this opportunity to demonstrate what they know, share their accomplishments, and set new learning goals. Teachers act as guides by clarifying ideas and issues and responding to specific questions (Davies, Cameron, Politano, & Gregory, 1992). In this way, students are encouraged to follow through on their self-regulated learning.

### How Families Can Assist in a Child's Learning

Schools that have a take-home library of print- and media-based materials encourage learning activities outside of school. In a dual-language setting, families can work with their children in either language.

**If the Family Is Not Supportive**   Families may not support learning in two languages. For example, Watahomigie (1995) described parents' negative reaction on the Hualapai Indian reservation in Peach Springs, Arizona, when educators proposed that schools establish a Hualapai–English bilingual program. The parents had been told for over 100 years that the native language was unimportant, and they did not believe that such instruction would benefit their children. A high-tech approach was eventually successful, built on efforts to convince parents of its value.

**Family Literacy Projects**   In Fresno, California, the Hmong Literacy Project was initiated by parents to help students appreciate their cultural roots, preserve oral history, and maintain the culture through written records. Parents asked for literacy lessons in Hmong (a language that has been written for only about thirty years) and in English. The program helped families to develop not only literacy skills but also skills in math and computers, which then allowed them to help their children academically. The Hmong Parents Newsletter increased communication between the school and the community, leading to greater parent participation in school activities (Kang, Kuehn, & Herrell, 1996).

A different type of program is the Parent Resource Center in Texas, affiliated with the University of Houston–Clear Lake. It provides a system of social and educational support for language-minority parents. Based on a needs assessment, the parent community identified four priorities: (1) ESL instruction, (2) strategies to help their children at home, (3) understanding the school system, and (4) understanding their rights and responsibilities as parents (Bermúdez & Márquez, 1996).

### Internet Resources for Family Involvement

Websites are available that feature various models of family involvement: www.ncrel.org/sdrs/areas/issues/envrnmnt/famncomm/pa100.htm, www.rci.rutgers.edu/~cfis/, www.ed.gov/pubs/FamInvolve/index.html, www.ncpie.org/, and www.ericdigests.org/1999-1/father.html.

### A Model of Home–School Relationships

Faltis (2001) provided a four-level sequence for home–school relationships based on an earlier model proposed by Rasinski and Fredericks (1989). Although teachers may not be able to reach the highest level of parental involvement at a particular school site, the model presents an overall view of the possibilities. This reciprocal process is summarized in Table 9.5.

Box 9.1 offers a host of tactics for involving parents in learning, ranging from providing information to learning from them about their views on education. These suggestions are drawn from Jones (1991) and Díaz-Rico and Weed (2006), among other sources, including Fredericks and Rasinski (1989). Rather than include a separate list of suggestions from each source, I have amalgamated them in categories.

### Family Members as Cultural Mediators

Family members play an important role as "brokers" or go-betweens who can mediate between the school and the home to solve cultural problems and create effective home–school relations (Arvizu, 1992).

## CLASSROOM GLIMPSE: A Parent Fosters Cultural Pride

*One Chinese-American parent successfully intervened in a school situation to the benefit of her daughter and her classmates.*

> *After my daughter was teased by her peers because of her Chinese name, I gave a presentation to her class on the origin of Chinese names, the naming of children in China, and Chinese calligraphy. My daughter has had no more problems about her name. What is more, she no longer complains about her unusual name, and she is proud of her cultural heritage. (Yao, 1988, p. 224)*

Whether parents are willing to come to school is largely dependent on their attitude toward school, a result in part of the parents' own school experiences. This attitude is also

**TABLE 9.5** A Two-Way Parent–School Involvement Model

| Level of Involvement | Description of Activity |
|---|---|
| I. Teacher–parent contact | The teacher learns about parents' daily experiences and initiates positive home–school contact and dialogue by chatting, making home visits, talking with community workers, and arranging for after-school homework help or tutoring to promote students' success. |
| II. Sharing information in the home about schooling | The teacher keeps the parents informed (in the home language, if possible) about important school and community events and meetings, changes in school schedules, help available from community-based organizations, and sources of academic support, using such means as student-produced newsletters, personal notes, telephone calls, and other notices. |
| III. Participation at home and school | Parents, caregivers, and other concerned adults are welcomed and encouraged to come to class and to attend school meetings and social events. Parents may linger in the morning to watch reading and writing take place, or to see a little poetry reading, especially if it takes place in the home language. Students may be assigned to find out about knowledge their families have about planting, banking, etc., and then teachers can find a way to use and elaborate on this information in class. |
| IV. Parental empowerment in curricular decisions | After the success of the previous three levels, teachers support parents who become involved as colleagues in professional activities and decisions. Some parents form advisory committees, start community tutoring centers, and find multiple means to influence school policy and support academic learning outside of the classroom. The role of the teacher is to encourage and work with parents to make these possible. |

*Source:* Faltis (2001).

a result of the extent to which they are made welcome by the schools. Invitational barriers can exclude parents as well as students. On the other hand, teachers who are willing to reach out to parents and actively solicit information from them about their children and their hopes for their children's schooling are rewarded with a richer understanding of students' potential.

## Box 9.1    Strategies to Involve Parents in Schooling

### Providing Information

- Informally chat with parents as they pick up their child after school.
- Use the telephone as an instrument of good news.
- Videotape programs for parents.
- Operate a parent hot line.
- Encourage parent-to-parent communication.
- Hold parent workshops on helping their children with reading skills.
- Offer materials in the home language.
- Provide bilingual handouts that describe programs available through the school.
- Make available a list of parental rights under the Bilingual Education Act.
- Send home personal handwritten notes, using a translator if necessary.
- Send home notes when students are doing well.
- Create parent–student handbooks.
- Have students write classroom newsletters.
- Welcome new families with packets delivered to the home.

### Ways to Showcase English Learners

- Enter students in poetry, essay, or art contests or exhibits sponsored by community or professional organizations.
- Offer to train students how to read aloud at libraries or children's centers.
- Encourage dual-language proficiency as a mark of prestige in school.

### Ways to Bring Parents to School

- Encourage parents to come to class to make crafts with students or to discuss culture, calligraphy, or family history.
- Find out if parent conferences or meetings conflict with work schedules.
- Ensure that siblings are welcome at parent conferences or meetings.
- Provide babysitting services for parent conferences.
- Maintain a friendly school office.
- Establish an explicit open-door policy so parents will know they are welcome; include welcoming signs in primary language.
- Suggest specific ways parents can help to promote achievement.
- Help parents to obtain remedial help if necessary in a timely way.
- Make meetings into social events, with food, dramatic, or musical performances if time permits.
- Hold student–teacher–family breakfasts once a month.
- Schedule primary-language speakers at school events.
- Recognize parents for involvement at award ceremonies, send thank-you notes, and speak positively of parents to their child.

*(Continued)*

## Box 9.1    (*Continued*)

**What Teachers Can Learn from Parents**

- Ideas of better ways to communicate.
- A richer understanding of the student's role(s) in the family.
- The hopes that parents have for schooling.
- Students' hobbies, interests, and strengths.

**Homework Tips for Parents (adapted from Jones, 1991)**

- Set aside a family quiet time when each person has homework or other activities to do that demand concentration.
- Have a regular means for finding out what assignments to expect.
- Make sure there is a place set aside for homework; provide paper, pencils, adequate lighting, etc.
- Check with the child to see if he or she understands the assignment. If needed, work through a problem. Have someone to call for help if necessary.
- Check the completed assignment with the child.
- Praise the work or offer constructive improvements.

**Workshops and Parent Support Groups (adapted from Jones, 1991)**

- Make-it-and-take it workshops to construct home learning materials
- Family Learning Center—school library or computer center is open several nights a week with learning activities for all ages
- Learning Fairs—single-topic sessions held in the evening
- Parent support groups hosted by community members
- Family Room—a room at school set aside for families to drop in and participate in informal activities, play with toys, and talk with other parents
- Child and adolescent development talks
- Special topic workshops on reading, math, study skills, self-esteem, etc.

## The Home–School Connection

Parents and older siblings can be encouraged to work with preschool and school-age children in a variety of activities. Teachers can encourage home language with children in ways that build underlying cognitive skills. Family members can sit with the child to look at a book, pointing to pictures and asking questions; they can read a few lines and let the child fill in the rest, or let the child retell a familiar story. Children can listen to adults discuss something or observe reading and writing in the primary language. Schools can assist communities with implementing literacy or cultural classes or producing a community primary-language newspaper. The school can also educate students and parents on the benefits of learning the home language of the parents and can find ways to make dual-language proficiency a means of gaining prestige at school (Ouk et al., 1988).

Families and community volunteers can provide tutoring and language enrichment.

## CLASSROOM GLIMPSE: The Publishing Party

*One teacher describes the success of a nonfiction Publishing Party hosted by the students. Parents and many extended family members came, as did neighbors and youth organization leaders with whom the students were involved. At various places around the room, reports were visible with yellow comment sheets. Visitors could sit at a desk or table, read, and comment on what they had read.*

*Language was not a barrier. Many parents encouraged their children to read to them in English and translate the stories into the native language. They were proud of the English their child had learned and proud that the child remembered the native language well enough to translate. . . . Everywhere I looked, I saw proud children beaming as they showed their work off to the people they cared about and who cared about them. (Cho Bassoff, 2004, para. 9, 10)*

### Involving the Family and Community in School Governance

Encouraging parents to participate in school activities is vital. The extra step of sending parents letters, reports, and notices in their home language helps to build rapport and extend a welcome to the school. These language policies constitute the daily message that home languages are important and valued. Parents can receive the message that they are valued in many ways:

- Representative parent committees can advise and consent on school practices that involve English learners.
- School facilities can be made available for meetings of community groups.
- Frequent attendance at school board meetings sends the message that the meetings are monitored by those who support English learners' achievement.
- Running for a seat on the school board brings power directly to the community.

This chapter has emphasized the important role that teachers can play in learning about their students' communities and cultures and in reducing the culture shock between home and school by working actively toward the creation of culturally compatible instruction. The best way for a teacher to understand culture is first to understand himself or herself and the extent to which U.S. mainstream cultural values are explicitly or implicitly enforced during instruction. A teacher who understands his or her own teaching and learning styles can then ask to what extent each student is similar or dissimilar. This goes a long way toward understanding and honoring individual differences.

The teacher can then use direct personal observation of social behavior to construct an image of students' cultures from the perspective of the members of those cultures. This understanding can be used to organize classroom activities in ways that are comfortable and promote learning. Thus, an understanding of cultural diversity leads to engagement in the struggle for equity and then to a commitment to promoting educational achievement for all students. In a multicultural classroom, there may be no single best way for teachers to teach or for students to learn. A variety of activities—ones that appeal to different students in turn—may be the most effective approach. The observation cycle continues as teachers watch students to see *which* approaches meet *whose* needs. The key for the intercultural educator is to be sensitive, flexible, and open.

## VIDEO WORKSHOP: "Family Literacy Program"

In this video, the director of a family literacy program explains the benefits of such a program for families who speak English as a second language. In the program, parents visit the school regularly to participate in activities of their children's choosing.

To access the video, log on to MyLabSchool at www.mylabschool.com, enter Assignment ID **ENV3** into the **Assignment Finder**, and select the video entitled "Family Literacy Program." Watch the video, complete the questions that follow, and e-mail your responses to your professor for credit.

**ⓒmylabschool™**
Where the classroom comes to life!

# BIBLIOGRAPHY

Adams, M. J. (1990). *Beginning to read: Thinking and learning about print.* Cambridge, MA: MIT Press.

Adamson, H. D. (1993). *Academic competence.* New York: Longman.

Addison, A. (1988, November). Comprehensible textbooks in science for the nonnative English-speaker: Evidence from discourse analysis. *The CATESOL Journal, 1*(1), 49–66.

Adger, C. (2000). School/community partnerships to support language minority student success. *CREDE Research Brief #5.* Santa Cruz, CA: Center for Research on Education, Diversity and Excellence. Accessed July 7, 2006, from www.crede.org/products/print/research_briefs/rb5.shtml

Af Trampe, P. (1994). Monitor theory: Application and ethics. In R. Barasch & C. James (Eds.), *Beyond the monitor model.* Boston: Heinle and Heinle.

Agar, M. (1980). *The professional stranger: An informal introduction to ethnography.* Orlando, FL: Academic Press.

Agor, B. (Ed.). (2000). *Integrating the ESL standards into classroom practice: Grades 9–12.* Alexandria, VA: Teachers of English to Speakers of Other Languages (TESOL).

Alcaya, C., Lybeck, K., Mougel, P., & Weaver, S. (1995). *Some strategies useful for speaking a foreign language.* Unpublished manuscript, University of Minnesota.

Alexander, S. (1983). *Nadia, the willful.* New York: Dial.

Altman, L. J. (1993). *Amelia's road.* New York: Lee and Low Books.

Allen, E., & Vallette, R. (1977). *Classroom techniques. Foreign languages and English as a second language.* San Diego, CA: Harcourt Brace Jovanovich.

Allport, G. (1954). *The nature of prejudice.* Garden City, NY: Doubleday Anchor.

Amselle, J. (1999). Dual immersion delays English. *American Language Review, 3*(5), 8.

Andersen, J., & Powell, R. (1991). Intercultural communication and the classroom. In L. Samovar & R. Porter (Eds.), *Intercultural communication: A reader* (6th ed.). Belmont, CA: Wadsworth.

Anderson, J., & Gunderson, L. (2004). You don't *read* a science book, you *study* it: An exploration of cultural concepts of reading. Accessed July 24, 2006, from www.readingonline.org/electronic/elec_index.asp?HREF=anderson/index.html

Antuñez, B. (2002). *Reading and English language learners.* Accessed July 25, 2006, from www.colorincolorado.org/articles/antunez_readindandells.php

Anyon, J. (1994). The retreat of Marxism and socialist feminism: Postmodern and poststructural theories in education. *Curriculum Inquiry, 24,* 115–133.

Aoki, E. (1992). Turning the page: Asian Pacific American children's literature. In V. J. Harris (Ed.), *Teaching multicultural literature in grades K–8.* Norwood, MA: Christopher-Gordon Publishers.

Arvizu, S. (1992). Home-school linkages: A cross-cultural approach to parent participation. In M. Saravia-Shore & S. Arvizu (Eds.), *Cross-cultural literacy: Ethnographies of communication in multiethnic classrooms.* New York: Garland.

Asher, J. (1982). *Learning another language through actions: The complete teachers' guidebook.* Los Gatos, CA: Sky Oaks.

Asian Pacific Fund. (2003, Fall/Winter). *Asian outlook: Bay area people in need.* San Francisco: Author. Accessed August 2, 2006, from www.asianpacificfund.org/resources

Au, K., & Jordan, C. (1981). Teaching reading to Hawaiian children: Finding a culturally appropriate solution. In H. Trueba, G. Guthrie, & K. Au (Eds.), *Culture and the bilingual classroom: Studies in classroom ethnography.* Rowley, MA: Newbury House.

Babbitt, N. (1976). *Tuck Everlasting.* New York: Bantam Books.

Baker, C. (1993). *Foundations of bilingual education and bilingualism.* Clevedon, UK: Multilingual Matters.

Baker, C. (2001). *Foundations of bilingual education and bilingualism* (3rd ed.). Clevedon, UK: Multilingual Matters.

Balderrama, M. V., & Díaz-Rico, L. T. (2006). *Teacher performance expectations for educating English learners.* Boston: Allyn & Bacon.

Bandlow, R. (2002). Suburban bigotry: A descent into racism & struggle for redemption. In F. Schultz (Ed.), *Annual editions: Multicultural education 2002–2003* (pp. 90–93). Guilford, CT: McGraw-Hill/Dushkin.

Banks, J. (1991). A curriculum for empowerment, action, and change. In C. Sleeter (Ed.), *Empowerment through multicultural education*. Albany: State University of New York Press.

Banks, J. (1994). *An introduction to multicultural education*. Boston: Allyn & Bacon.

Barbe, W. B., Wasylyk, T. M., Hackney, C. S., and Braun, L. A. (1984). *Zaner-Bloser creative growth in handwriting (grades K–8)*. Columbus, OH: Zaner-Bloser.

Barks, D., & Watts, P. (2001). Textual borrowing strategies for graduate-level ESL students. In D. Belcher and A. Hirvela (Eds.), *Linking literacies: Perspectives on L2 reading-writing connections* (pp. 246–267). Ann Arbor, MI: The University of Michigan Press.

Barr, R. & Johnson, B. (1997). *Teaching reading and writing in elementary classrooms* (2nd ed.). New York: Longman.

Bartolomé, L. I. (1994). Beyond the methods fetish: Toward a humanizing pedagogy. *Harvard Educational Review, 64*(2), 173–194.

Barton, D., Hamilton, M., & Ivanič, R. (2000). Introduction. In D. Barton, M. Hamilton, & R. Ivanič (Eds.), *Situated literacies* (pp. 1–15). London and New York: Routledge.

Bartram, M., & Walton, R. (1994). *Correction: A positive approach to language mistakes*. Hove, UK: Language Teaching Publications.

Bassano, S., & Christison, M. A. (1995). *Community spirit: A practical guide to collaborative language learning*. San Francisco: Alta Book Center.

Bell, C. (2002). Secondary level report—Explaining SDAIE to colleagues. *CATESOL News, 34*(3), 15.

Belmont, J. M. (1989). Cognitive strategies and strategic learning: The socioinstructional approach. *American Psychologist, 44*, 142–148.

Bembridge, T. (1992). A MAP for reading assessment. *Educational Leadership, 49*(8), 46–48.

Bennett, C. (1990). *Comprehensive multicultural education: Theory and practice* (2nd ed.). Boston: Allyn & Bacon.

Bennett, C. (2003). *Comprehensive multicultural education: Theory and practice* (5th ed.). Boston: Allyn & Bacon.

Benson, V. A. (1999). Syl/la/bles and linking. In N. Shameem & M. Tickoo (Eds.), *New ways in using communicative games* (pp. 18–19). Alexandria, VA: Teachers of English to Speakers of Other Languages.

Bergman, J. L., & Schuder, T. (1993). Teaching at-risk students to read strategically. *Educational Leadership, 50*(54), 19–23.

Berk, L. E., & Winsler, A. (1995). *Scaffolding children's learning: Vygotsky and early childhood education*. Washington, DC: National Association for the Education of Young Children.

Bermúdez, A., & Márquez, J. (1996). An examination of a four-way collaborative to increase parental involvement in the schools. *The Journal of Educational Issues of Language Minority Students, 16*. Accessed July 7, 2006, from www.ncela.gwu.edu/pubs/jeilms/vol16/jeilms1601.htm

Bielenberg, B., & Wong Fillmore, L. (2004/2005). The English they need for the test. *Educational Leadership, 62*(4), 45–49.

Birdwhistell, R. (1974). The language of the body: The natural environment of words. In A. Silverstein (Ed.), *Human communication: Theoretical explorations*. Hillsdale, NJ: Erlbaum.

Bitter, G., Pierson, M., & Burvikovs, A. (2004). *Using technology in the classroom* (6th ed.). Boston: Allyn & Bacon.

Blair, R. W. (Ed.). (1982). *Innovative approaches to language teaching*. Boston: Heinle & Heinle.

Bliatout, B., Downing, B., Lewis, J., & Yang, D. (1988). *Handbook for teaching Hmong-speaking students*. Folsom, CA: Folsom Cordova Unified School District, Southeast Asia Community Resource Center.

Bloch, J. (2001). Plagiarism and the ESL student: From printed to electronic texts. In D. Belcher & A. Hirvela (Eds.), *Linking literacies: Perspectives on L2 reading-writing connections* (pp. 209–228). Ann Arbor: The University of Michigan Press.

Bosher, S. (1997). Language and cultural identity: A study of Hmong students at the postsecondary level. *TESOL Quarterly, 31*(3), 593–603.

Bourdieu, P. (1977). *Reproduction in society, education, and culture* (with J. Passeron). Los Angeles: Sage.

Boyd-Batstone, P. (2006). *Differentiated early literacy for English language learners: Practical strategies*. Boston: Pearson.

Bradley, K. S., & Bradley, J. A. (2004). Scaffolding academic learning for second language learners. Accessed July 31, 2006, from http://iteslj.org/Articles/Bradley-Scaffolding/

Brandt, R. (1994). On educating for diversity: A conversation with James A. Banks. *Educational Leadership, 51*, 28–31.

Brend, R. M. (1975). Male-female intonation patterns in American English. In B. Thorne & N. Henley (Eds.), *Language and sex: Differences and dominance*. Rowley, MA: Newbury House.

Brinton, D. (2003). Content-based instruction. In D. Nunan (Ed.), *Practical English language teaching.* New York: McGraw-Hill.

Brinton, D., & Master, P. (Eds.). (1997). *New ways in content-based instruction.* Alexandria, VA: Teachers of English to Speakers of Other Languages (TESOL).

Brisk, M. E., & Harrington, M. M. (2000). *Literacy and bilingualism.* Mahwah, NJ: Erlbaum.

Bromberg, M., Liebb, J., & Traiger, A. (2005). *504 absolutely essential words* (5th ed.). Hauppage, NY: Barron's.

Bromley, K. D. (1989). Buddy journals make the reading-writing connection. *The Reading Teacher, 43*(2), 122–129.

Brown, D. (1987). *Principles of language learning and teaching* (2nd ed.). Englewood Cliffs, NJ: Prentice Hall.

Brown, D. (2000). *Principles of language learning and teaching* (4th ed.). Englewood Cliffs, NJ: Prentice Hall.

Bruner, J. (1986). *Actual minds, possible worlds.* Cambridge: Harvard University Press.

Brutt-Griffler, J., & Samimy, K. K. (1999). Revisiting the colonial in the postcolonial: Critical praxis for the nonnative-English-speaking teachers in a TESOL program. *TESOL Quarterly, 33*(3), 413–431.

Buchanan, K., & Helman, M. (1997). Reforming mathematics instruction for ESL literacy students. *ERIC Digest.* Retrieved Oct. 15, 2004, from www.cal.org/resources/digest/buchan01.html

Bunch, G. C., Abram, P. L., Lotan, R. A., & Valdés, G. (2001). Beyond sheltered instruction: Rethinking conditions for academic language development. *TESOL Journal, 10*(2/3), 28–33.

Bunting, E. (1988). *How many days to America?* New York: Clarion.

Burgstahler, S. (2002). *Universal design of instruction.* Retrieved July 7, 2006, from www.washington.edu/doit/Brochures/Academics/instruction.html

Burely-Allen, M. (1995). *Listening: The forgotten skill.* New York: John Wiley & Sons.

Byrd, P., & Benson, B. (1994). *Problem-solution: A reference for ESL writers.* Boston: Heinle & Heinle.

Caine, R. N., Caine, G., McClintic, C., & Klimek, K. (2004). *Brain/mind learning principles in action: The fieldbook for making connections, teaching, and the human brain.* Thousand Oaks, CA: Sage.

California Department of Education. (1992). *Handbook for teaching Korean-American students.* Sacramento: Author.

California Department of Education. (1997). *English/language arts standards.* Sacramento: Author. Accessed July 18, 2006, from www.cde.ca.gov/be/st/ss/engmain.asp

California Department of Education. (1999). *English language development standards.* Sacramento: Author. Online at www.cde.ca.gov/statetests/eld/eld_grd_span.pdf

California Department of Education. (2004a). *Physical education model content standards for California public schools.* Sacramento: Author.

California Department of Education. (2004b). *English learner students.* Accessed August 4, 2006, from www.cde.ca.gov/re/pn/fb/yr04english.asp

California Department of Education. (2006a). *Reading/language arts framework for California public schools* (draft). Sacramento: Author. Accessed July 18, 2006, from www.cde.ca.gov/ci/rl/cf/index.asp

California Department of Education (CDE). (2006b). *Number of English learners by language.* Accessed May 11, 2006, from http://data1.cde.ca.gov/dataquest/LEPbyLang1.asp

California Department of Education (CDE). (2006c). *The science content standards for kindergarten through grade five.* Accessed August 4, 2006, from www.cde.ca.gov/re/pn/fd/sci-frame-dwnld.asp

Cameron, A. (1988). *The most beautiful place in the world.* New York: Random House.

Campbell, C. (1998). *Teaching second language writing: Interacting with text.* Pacific Grove, CA: Heinle & Heinle.

Canale, M. (1983). From communicative competence to communicative language pedagogy. In J. Richards & R. Schmidt (Eds.), *Language and communication.* New York: Longman.

Cantlon, T. L. (1991). *Structuring the classroom successfully for cooperative team learning.* Portland, OR: Prestige Publishers.

Carnuccio, L. M. (2004). Cybersites. *Essential Teacher, 1*(3), 59.

Carrasquillo, A., & Rodríguez, V. (2002). *Language minority students in the mainstream classroom.* Clevedon, UK: Multilingual Matters.

Cary, S. (2000). *Working with second language learners: Answers to teachers' top ten questions.* Portsmouth, NH: Heinemann.

Casey, J. (2004). A place for first language in the ESOL classroom. *Essential Teacher, 1*(4), 50–52.

CATESOL. (1998). *CATESOL position statement on literacy instruction for English language learners, grades*

*K–12.* Retrieved July 24, 2006, from www.catesol.org/literacy.html

Celce-Murcia, M., & Olshtain, E. (2001). *Discourse and context in language teaching.* Cambridge: Cambridge University Press.

Center for Educational Reform. (2000). *National charter school directory* (7th ed.). Washington, DC: Author.

Chambers, J., & Parrish, T. (1992). *Meeting the challenge of diversity: An evaluation of programs for pupils with limited proficiency in English: Vol. 4. Cost of programs and services for LEP students.* Berkeley, CA: BW Associates.

Chamot, A. U., & O' Malley, J. (1994). *The CALLA handbook: Implementing the cognitive academic language learning approach.* Boston: Addison-Wesley.

Chan, L. (2004). The inexorable rise in demand for qualified ESL teachers. *Language, 3*(6), 30–31.

Chandler, D. (2005) *Semiotics for beginners.* Retrieved June 27, 2006, from www.aber.ac.uk/media/Documents/S4B/semiotic.html

Chaney, A. L., & Burk, T. L. (1998). *Teaching oral communication in grades K–8.* Boston: Allyn & Bacon.

Chard, D. J., Pikulski, J. J., & Templeton, S. (n.d.). From phonemic awareness to fluency: Effective decoding instruction in a research-based reading program. Accessed July 24, 2006, from www.eduplace.com/state/pdf/author/chard_pik_temp.pdf

Cheng, L. (1987). English communicative competence of language minority children: Assessment and treatment of language "impaired" preschoolers. In H. Trueba (Ed.), *Success or failure? Learning and the language minority student.* Boston: Heinle and Heinle.

Chesterfield, R., & Chesterfield, K. (1985). Natural order in children's use of second language learning strategies. *Applied Linguistics, 6,* 45–59.

Children's Defense Fund. (2005). *The state of America's children.* Retrieved August 2, 2006, from http://cdf.convio.net/site/PageServer?pagename=research_publications

Cho Bassoff, T. (2004). Compleat Links: Three steps toward a strong home-school connection. *Essential Teacher, 1*(4). Retrieved August 3, 2006, from www.tesol.org/s_tesol/sec_document.asp?CID=65&DID=2586

Christensen, L. (2000). *Reading, writing, rising up: Teaching about social justice and the power of the written word.* Milwaukee, WI: Rethinking Schools.

Chung, H. (1989). *Working with Vietnamese high school students.* San Francisco: New Faces of Liberty/SFSC.

Cipollone, N., Keiser, S. H., & Vasishth, S. (1998). *Language files* (7th ed.). Columbus: Ohio State University Press.

Clark, B. (1983). *Growing up gifted: Developing the potential of children at home and at school* (2nd ed.). Columbus, OH: Merrill.

Cloud, N., Genesee, F., & Hamayan, E. (2000). *Dual language instruction.* Boston: Heinle & Heinle.

Cockcroft, J. D. (1995). *Latinos in the struggle for equal education.* Danbury, CT: Franklin Watts.

Coehlo, E., Winer, L., & Olsen, J. W-B. (1989). *All sides of the issue: Activities for cooperative jigsaw groups.* Hayward, CA: Alemany Press.

Cogan, D. (1999). What am I saying? In N. Shameem & M. Tickoo (Eds.), *New ways in using communicative games* (pp. 22–23). Alexandria, VA: Teachers of English to Speakers of Other Languages.

Cohen, E. (1994). *Designing groupwork: Strategies for the heterogeneous classroom.* New York: Teachers College Press.

Cohn, D., & Bahrampour, T. (2006, May 10). Of U.S. children under 5, nearly half are minorities. *Washington Post,* A01.

Cole, K. (2003, March). *Negotiating intersubjectivity in the classroom: Mutual socialization to classroom conversations.* Presentation at the American Association for Applied Linguistics annual conference, Arlington, VA.

Cole, M. (1998). *Cultural psychology: Can it help us think about diversity?* Presentation, annual meeting, American Educational Research Association, San Diego.

Collie, J., & Slater, S. (1987). *Literature in the language classroom.* Cambridge: Cambridge University Press.

Collier, V. (1987). Age and rate of acquisition of second language for academic purposes. *TESOL Quarterly, 21*(4), 617–641.

Collier, V. P. (1995). Acquiring a second language for school. *Directions in Language & Education, National Clearinghouse for Bilingual Education, 1*(4). Accessed July 7, 2006, from www.ncela.gwu.edu/pubs/directions/04.htm

Contra Costa County Office of Education. (2006). Curriculum and instruction: Standards implementation. Accessed August 4, 2006, from www.cccoe.k12.ca.us/edsvcs/assessment.html

Cook, V. (1999). Going beyond the native speaker in language teaching. *TESOL Quarterly, 33*(2), 185–209.

Corley, M. A. (2003). *Poverty, racism, and literacy.* ERIC Clearinghouse on Adult, Career, and Vocational Education. ERIC Digest #243.

Cortés, C. (1993). Acculturation, assimilation, and "adduction." *BEOutreach, 4*(1), 3–5.

Costa, A. L., & Garmston, R. J. (2002). *Cognitive coaching: A foundation for renaissance schools* (2nd ed.). Norwood, MA: Christopher-Gordon.

Cotton, K. (1989). *Expectations and student outcomes.* Retrieved August 3, 2006, from www.nwrel.org/scpd/sirs/4/cu7.html

Crago, M. (1993). Communicative interaction and second language acquisition: An Inuit example. *TESOL Quarterly, 26*(3), 487–506.

Crawford, J. (1999). *Bilingual education: History, politics, theory, and practice* (4th ed.). Los Angeles: Bilingual Educational Services.

Crawford, J. (2004). *Educating English learners: Language diversity in the classroom* (5th ed.). Los Angeles: Bilingual Educational Services, Inc.

Crawford, J. (2006). National language amendment: Political blunder by Republicans. Accessed July 6, 2006, from http://ourworld.compuserve.com/home pages/JWCrawford/

Cummins, J. (1976). The influence of bilingualism on cognitive growth: A synthesis of research findings and explanatory hypothesis. *Working Papers on Bilingualism, 9,* 1–43.

Cummins, J. (1979). Linguistic interdependence and the educational development of bilingual children. *Review of Educational Research, 49*(2), 222–251.

Cummins, J. (1980). The cross-lingual dimensions of language proficiency. Implications for bilingual education and the optimal age issue. *TESOL Quarterly, 14*(2), 175–187.

Cummins, J. (1981a). Age on arrival and immigrant second language learning in Canada: A reassessment. *Applied Linguistics, 2*(2), 132–149.

Cummins, J. (1981b). The role of primary language development in promoting educational success for language minority students. In *Schooling and language minority students: A theoretical framework.* Sacramento: California State Department of Education.

Cummins, J. (1984). *Bilingualism and special education: Issues in assessment and pedagogy.* San Diego: College-Hill.

Cummins, J. (1989). *Empowering minority students.* Sacramento: California Association for Bilingual Education.

Cummins, J. (1996). *Negotiating identities: Education for empowerment in a diverse society.* Los Angeles: California Association for Bilingual Education.

Cummins, J. (2000a). Beyond adversarial discourse: Searching for common ground in the education of bilingual students. In P. McLaren & C. J. Ovando (Eds.), *The politics of multiculturalism and bilingual education* (pp. 126–147). Boston: The McGraw-Hill Companies.

Curtain, H., & Dahlberg, C. A. (2004). *Language and children—Making the match: New languages for young learners, grades K–8.* Boston: Allyn & Bacon.

Cushner, K. (1999). *Human diversity in action.* Boston: McGraw-Hill.

Daloğlu, A. (2005). Reducing learning burden in academic vocabulary development. *Teachers of English to Speakers of Other Languages EFLIS Newsletter, 5*(1).

Dale, P., & Poms, L. (2005). *English pronunciation made simple.* White Plains, NY: Pearson/Longman.

Dale, T., & Cuevas, G. (1992). Integrating mathematics and language learning. In P. Richard-Amato & M. Snow (Eds.), *The multicultural classroom.* White Plains, NY: Longman.

Danesi, M. (1985). *A guide to puzzles and games in second language pedagogy.* Toronto: Ontario Institute for Studies in Education.

Darder, A. (1991). *Culture and power in the classroom.* New York: Bergin and Garvey.

Davies, A., Cameron, C., Politano, C., & Gregory, K. (1992). *Together is better: Collaborative assessment, evaluation, and reporting.* Winnepeg, CAN: Peguis.

Day, F. A. (1994). *Multicultural voices in contemporary literature: A resource for teachers.* Portsmouth, NH: Heinemann.

Day, F. A. (1997). *Latina and Latino voices in literature for children and teenagers.* Portsmouth, NH: Heinemann.

Day, F. A. (2003). *Latina and Latino voices in literature: Lives and works.* Westport, CT: Greenwood Publishers.

De Boinod, A-J. (2006). *The meaning of tingo.* New York: Penguin.

DeGeorge, G. (1987–1988, Winter). Assessment and placement of language minority students: Procedures for mainstreaming. *NCBE Occasional Papers #3.* Retrieved March 23, 2005, from www.ncela.gwu.edu/pubs/classics/focus/03mainstream.htm

Delgado-Gaitan, C., & Trueba, H. (1991). *Crossing cultural borders: Education for immigrant families in America.* London: Falmer Press.

dePaola, T. (1981). *Now one foot, now the other.* New York: G. P. Putnam's Sons.

deUnamuno, M. (1925). *Essays and soliloquies.* New York: Knopf.

Diamond, B., & Moore, M. (1995). *Multicultural literacy.* White Plains, NY: Longman.

Díaz, R. M., Neal, C. J., & Vachio, A. (1991). Maternal teaching in the zone of proximal development: A comparison of low- and high-risk dyads. *Merrill-Palmer Quarterly, 37,* 83–108.

Díaz-Rico, L. T. (2004). *Teaching English learners: Strategies and methods.* Boston: Allyn & Bacon.

Díaz-Rico, L. T., & Dullien, S. (2004). *Semiotics and people watching.* Presentation, California Teachers of English to Speakers of Other Languages regional conference, Los Angeles, CA.

Díaz-Rico, L. T., & Weed, K. Z. (2006). *Crosscultural, language, and academic development handbook* (3rd ed.). Boston: Allyn & Bacon.

Dicker, S. (1992). Societal views of bilingualism and language learning. *TESOL: Applied Linguistics Interest Section Newsletter, 14*(1), 1, 4.

Donato, R. (1997). *The other struggle for equal schools: Mexican Americans during the Civil Rights Era.* New York: State University of New York Press.

Dudley-Marling, C., & Searle, D. (1991). *When students have time to talk.* Portsmouth, NH: Heinemann.

Dumont, R. (1972). Learning English and how to be silent: Studies in Sioux and Cherokee classrooms. In C. Cazden, V. John, & D. Hymes (Eds.), *Functions of language in the classroom.* New York: Teachers College Press.

Dunkel, P., & Lim, P. L. (1994). *Intermediate listening comprehension: Understanding and recalling spoken English.* Boston: Heinle & Heinle.

Dunkel, P. A., Pialorsi, F., & Kozyrev, J. (1996). *Advanced listening comprehension: Developing aural and note-taking skills.* Boston: Heinle & Heinle.

Dryfoos, J. (1998). *Safe passage: Making it through adolescence in a risky society.* New York: Oxford.

Echevarria, J., Vogt, M. E., & Short, D. (2004). *Making content comprehensible for English language learners: The SIOP model* (2nd ed.). Boston: Allyn & Bacon.

Ediger, A., & Pavlik, C. (1999). *Reading connections: Skills and strategies for purposeful reading.* New York: Oxford University Press.

Edmonson, M., (1971). *Lore: An introduction to the science of fiction.* New York: Holt, Rinehart and Winston.

Education Trust, The. (1998). *Education watch: The Education Trust 1998 state and national data book.* Washington, DC: Author.

Egan, K., & Gajdamaschko, N. (2003). Some cognitive tools of literacy. In A. Kozulin, B. Gindis, V. S. Ageyev, & S. M. Miller (Eds.), *Vygotsky's educational theory in cultural context* (pp. 83–98). Cambridge: Cambridge University Press.

Egbert, J. (2004). Access to knowledge: Implications of Universal Design for CALL environments. *CALL_EJ Online, 5*(2). Retrieved July 7, 2006, from www.tell.is .ritsumei.ac.jp/callejonline/journal/5-2/egbert.html

Egbert, J., & Hanson-Smith, E. (1999). *CALL environments: Research, practice, and critical issues.* Alexandria, VA: Teachers of English to Speakers of Other Languages.

Ehri, L. (1997). Learning to read and learning to spell are one and the same, almost. In C. Perfetti, L. Rieben, & M. Fayol (Eds.), *Learning to spell: Research, theory, and practice across languages* (pp. 237–269). Mahwah, NJ: Erlbaum.

Ellis, R. (1986). *Understanding second language acquisition.* Oxford: Oxford University Press.

Ellis, S. S., & Whalen, S. F. (1992). Keys to cooperative learning: 35 ways to keep kids responsible, challenged, and most of all, cooperative. *Instructor, 101*(6), 34–37.

Erickson, F. (1977). Some approaches to inquiry in school-community ethnography. *Anthropology and Education Quarterly, 8*(2), 58–69.

Escalante, J., & Dirmann, J. (1990). The Jaime Escalante math program. *Journal of Negro Education, 59*(3), 407–423.

Faber, J. E., Morris, J. D., & Lieberman, M. G. (2000). The effect of note taking on ninth grade students' comprehension. *Reading Psychology, 21,* 257–270.

Faltis, C. (1993). Critical issues in the use of sheltered content instruction in high school bilingual programs. *Peabody Journal of Education, 69*(1), 136–151.

Faltis, C. (2001). *Joinfostering* (3rd ed.). Upper Saddle River, NJ: Prentice Hall.

Farr, M. (1994). En los dos idiomas: Literacy practices among Chicago Mexicanos. In B. Moss (Ed.), *Literacy across communities* (pp. 1–9). Cresskill, NJ: Hampton Press.

Feng, J. (1994). Asian-American children: What teachers should know. *ERIC Digest.* Champaign, IL: Clearinghouse on Elementary and Early Childhood Education. Online at http://ericps.ed.uiuc.edu/eece/pubs

Feuerstein, T., & Schcolnik, M. (1995). *Enhancing reading comprehension in the language learning classroom.* San Francisco, CA: Alta.

Finnan, C. (1987). The influence of the ethnic community on the adjustment of Vietnamese refugees. In G. & L. Spindler (Eds.), *Interpretive ethnography of education: At home and abroad.* Hillsdale, NJ: Erlbaum.

Fischer, B., & Fischer, L. (1979, January). Styles in teaching and learning. *Educational Leadership, 36*(4), 245–251.

Fisher, D., Brozo, W. G., Frey, N., & Ivey, G. (2007). *50 content area strategies for adolescent literacy.* Upper Saddle River, NJ: Merrill/Prentice Hall.

Flood, J., Lapp, D., Tinajero, J., & Hurley, S. (1997). Literacy instruction for students acquiring English: Moving beyond the immersion debate. *The Reading Teacher,* 356–358.

Florida Department of Education. (2003). *Inclusion as an instructional model for LEP students.* Retrieved February 10, 2005, from www.firn.edu/doe/omsle/tapinclu.htm

Flower, L. (1994). *The construction of negotiated meaning: A social cognitive theory of writing.* Carbondale and Edwardsville, IL: Southern Illinois University Press.

Flynn, K. (1995). *Graphic organizers . . . helping kids think visually.* Cypress, CA: Creative Thinking Press.

Flynt, E. S., & Cooter, R. B. (1999). *The English-Español reading inventory for the classroom.* Upper Saddle River, NJ: Merrill/Prentice Hall.

Folse, K. S. (1996). *Discussion starters.* Ann Arbor: The University of Michigan Press.

Fosnot, C. T. (1989). *Enquiring teachers, enquiring learners: A constructivist approach for teaching.* New York: Teachers College Press.

Foucault, M. (1979). *Discipline and punish: The birth of the prison.* New York: Vintage Books.

Foucault, M. (1980). *Power/knowledge: Selected interviews and other writings 1971–1977.* New York: Pantheon Books.

Fraser, N., & Nicholson, L. (1988). Social criticism without philosophy: An encounter between feminism and postmodernism. In A. Ross (Ed.), *Universal abandon? The politics of postmodernism* (pp. 83–94). Minneapolis: University of Minnesota Press.

Freeman, R. (2004). *Building on community bilingualism.* Philadelphia: Caslon.

Freire, P. (1970). *Pedagogy of the oppressed.* New York: Seabury Press.

Frey, N., & Fisher, D. (2007). *Reading for information in elementary school: Content literacy strategies to build comprehension.* Upper Saddle River, NJ: Merrill/Prentice Hall.

Friend, M., & Bursuck, W. D. (2002). *Including students with special needs: A practical guide for classroom teachers.* Boston: Allyn & Bacon.

Friend, M., & Cook, L. (1996). *Interactions: Collaboration skills for school professionals.* White Plains, NY: Longman.

From the Classroom. (1991). Teachers seek a fair and meaningful assessment process to measure LEP students' progress. Fountain Valley, CA: *Teacher Designed Learning, 2*(1), 1, 3.

Fu, D. (2004). Teaching ELL students in regular classrooms at the secondary level. *Voices from the Middle, 11*(4), 8–15.

Fuller, B. (2003). Educational policy under cultural pluralism. *Educational Researcher, 32*(9), 15–24.

Funaki, I., & Burnett, K. (1993). *When educational systems collide: Teaching and learning with Polynesian students.* Presentation, annual conference, Association of Teacher Educators, Los Angeles.

Furey, P. (1986). A framework for cross-cultural analysis of teaching methods. In P. Byrd (Ed.), *Teaching across cultures in the university ESL program.* Washington, DC: National Association of Foreign Student Advisors.

Gamrel, L. B., & Bales, R. J. (1986). Mental imagery and the comprehension-monitoring performance of fourth- and fifth-grade poor readers. *Reading Research Quarterly, 21,* 454–464.

Gándara, P. (1997). *Review of research on instruction of limited English proficient students.* Davis, CA: University of California, Linguistic Minority Research Institute.

Gándara, P., Maxwell-Jolly, J., García, E., Asato, J., Gutiérrez, K., Stritkus, T., & Curry, J. (2000). *The initial impact of Proposition 227 on the instruction of English learners.* Davis, CA: University of California Linguistic Minority Research Center.

Gaouette, N. (2006, May 10). Latinos boost U.S. population. *Los Angeles Times,* A04.

García, S. B., & Ortiz, A. A. (2004). *Preventing disproportionate representation: Culturally and linguistically responsive prereferral interventions.* National Center for Culturally Responsive Educational Systems. Retrieved August 4, 2006, from www.nccrest.org/publications.html

García, E. (2000). *The best of times and the worst of times: Proposition 227 aftermath in California.* Tenth Annual Bilingual Education Institute, Arizona State University West, Phoenix.

Gardner, H. (1983). *Frames of mind: The theory of multiple intelligences.* New York: Basic Books.

Gardner, R., & Lambert, W. (1972). *Attitudes and motivation in second language learning.* Rowley, MA: Newbury House.

Garrison, D. (1990). Inductive strategies for teaching Spanish-English cognates. *Hispania, 73*(2), 508–512.

Gascoigne, C. (2002). *The debate on grammar in second language acquisition: Past, present, and future.* Lewiston, NY: Edwin Mellen Press.

Gass, S. (2000). *Interaction in classroom discourse.* Presentation, annual meeting, Teachers of English to Speakers of Other Languages, Vancouver, Canada.

Gass, S., & Selinker, L. (2001). *Second language acquisition.* Mahwah, NJ: Erlbaum.

Gay, G. (1975, October). Cultural differences important in education of Black children. *Momentum, 30–32.*

Genesee, F. (Ed.). (1999). *Program alternatives for linguistically diverse students.* Santa Cruz, CA: Center for Research on Education, Diversity and Excellence. Online at www.cal.org/crede/pubs/edpractice/Epr1.pdf

Gibson, M. (1987). Punjabi immigrants in an American high school. In G. & L. Spindler (Eds.), *Interpretive ethnography of education: At home and abroad.* Hillsdale, NJ: Erlbaum.

Gillett, P. (1989a). *Cambodian refugees: An introduction to their history and culture.* San Francisco, CA: New Faces of Liberty/SFSC.

Gillett, P. (1989b). *El Salvador: A country in crisis.* San Francisco, CA: New Faces of Liberty/SFSC.

Giroux, H. (1983). Theories of reproduction and resistance in the new sociology of education: A critical appraisal. *Harvard Educational Review, 53,* 257–293.

Giroux, H. A. (1988). *Teachers as intellectuals: Toward a pedagogy of critical learning.* New York: Bergin & Garvey.

Giroux, H., & McLaren, P. (1996). Teacher education and the politics of engagement: The case for democratic schooling. *Harvard Educational Review, 56*(3), 213–238.

Glaser, S., & Brown, C. (1993). *Portfolios and beyond: Collaborative assessment in reading and writing.* Norwood, MA: Christopher-Gordon.

Goldenberg, C. (2001, January 25). These steps can help us teach Johnny to read. *Los Angeles Times,* B11.

Goldenberg, C., & Gallimore, R. (1991). Changing teaching takes more than a one-shot workshop. *Educational Leadership, 49*(3), 69–72.

Gollnick, D. M., & Chinn, P. C. (2002). *Multicultural education in a pluralistic society* (6th ed.). Upper Saddle River, NJ: Merrill Prentice Hall.

Gombert, J. E. (1992). *Metalinguistic development.* Chicago: The University of Chicago Press.

González, N. E., Moll, L., & Amanti, C. (Eds.). (2005). *Funds of knowledge: Theorizing practices in households, communities, and classrooms.* Mahwah, NJ: Erlbaum.

Good, T., & Brophy, J. (1984). *Looking in classrooms* (3rd ed.). New York: Harper and Row.

Goodman, K. (1986). *What's whole in whole language?* Portsmouth, NH: Heinemann.

Goodwin, J., Brinton, D., & Celce-Murcia, M. (1994). Pronunciation assessment in the ESL/EFL curriculum. In J. Morley (Ed.), *Pronunciation pedagogy theory: New views, new directions.* Alexandria, VA: Teachers of English to Speakers of Other Languages.

Gopaul-McNicol, S., & Thomas-Presswood, T. (1998). *Working with linguistically and culturally different children.* Boston: Allyn & Bacon.

Gottlieb, M. (1995). Nurturing student learning through portfolios. *TESOL Journal, 5*(1), 12–14.

Graham, C. (1988). *Jazz chant fairy tales.* New York: Oxford University Press.

Graham, C. (1992). *Singing, chanting, telling tales.* Englewood Cliffs, NJ: Regents/Prentice Hall.

Grasha, A. F. (1990). Using traditional versus naturalistic approaches to assess learning styles in college teaching. *Journal on Excellence in College Teaching, 1,* 23–38.

Graves, K. (1996). Teaching opposites through music: Lesson plan. Online at www.lessonplanspage.com/MusicOpposites.htm

Greaver, M., & Hedberg, K. (2001). Daily reading interventions to help targeted ESL and non-ESL students. Retrieved July 24, 2006, from www.fcps.k12.va.us/DeerParkES/TchrResearch.html

Gregory, G. (2003). *Differentiating instructional strategies in practice: Training, implementation, and supervision.* Thousand Oaks, CA: Corwin.

Gregory, G. H., & Kuzmich, L. (2005). *Differentiated literacy strategies for student growth and achievement in grades 7–12.* Thousand Oaks, CA: Corwin.

Grognet, A., Jameson, J., Franco, L., Derrick-Mescua, M. (2000). *Enhancing English language learning in elementary classrooms study guide.* McHenry, IL: Center for Applied Linguistics and Delta Systems.

Grossberg, L. (1988). Putting the pop back into postmodernism. In A. Ross (Ed.), *Universal abandon? The politics of postmodernism* (pp. 167–190). Minneapolis: University of Minnesota Press.

Groves, M. (2000, January 26). Vast majority of state's schools lag in new index. *Los Angeles Times,* pp. 1, 14.

Groves, M. (2001, August 20). "Direct instruction" paying off. *Los Angeles Times,* B1, B8.

Gunning, T. G. (2005). *Creating literacy: Instruction for all students* (5th ed.). Boston: Allyn & Bacon.

Guthrie, J., & Wigfield, A. (2000). Engagement and motivation in reading. In M. Kamil, P. Mosenthal, P. D. Pearson, & R. Barr (2002). *Handbook of reading research* (Vol. 3, pp. 403–422). Mahwah, NJ: Erlbaum.

Gutierrez, A. S., & Rodríguez, A. P. (2005). *Latino student success (K–20): Local community culture and context.* Spring 2005 Colloquium of the Maryland Institute for Minority Achievement and Urban Education, Baltimore, MD.

Hadaway, N. L., Vardell, S. M., & Young, T. A. (2002). *Literature-based instruction with English language learners, K–12.* Boston: Allyn & Bacon.

Hafernik, J. J., Messerschmitt, D. S., & Vandrick, S. (2002). *Ethical issues for ESL faculty.* Mahwah, NJ: Erlbaum.

Hakuta, K. (1986). *Mirror of language.* New York: Basic Books.

Hakuta, K., Butler, Y. G., & Witt, D. (2000). *How long does it take English learners to attain proficiency?* Santa Barbara: University of California Linguistic Minority Research Institute Policy Report 2000–1.

Hall, E. (1959). *The silent language.* New York: Anchor Books.

Halliday, M. (1975). *Learning how to mean: Explorations in the development of language.* London: Edward Arnold.

Halliday, M. (1978). *Language as a social semiotic.* Baltimore, MD: University Park Press.

Hamayan, E. (1994). Language development of low-literacy students. In F. Genesee (Ed.), *Educating second language children.* Cambridge: Cambridge University Press.

Hamers, J. F., & Blanc, M. A. H. (1989). *Bilinguality and bilingualism.* Cambridge: Cambridge University Press.

Han, Z. (2004). *Fossilization in adult second language acquisition.* Clevedon, UK: Multilingual Matters.

Hancock, C. (1994). Alternative assessment and second language study: What and why? *ERIC Digest.* Online at www.cal.org/ericcll/digest/hancoc01.html

Harel, Y. (1992). Teacher talk in the cooperative learning classroom. In C. Kessler (Ed.), *Cooperative language learning.* Englewood Cliffs, NJ: Prentice Hall.

Harris, T. L., & Hodges, R. E. (1995). *The literacy dictionary: The vocabulary of reading and writing.* Newark, DE: International Reading Association.

Harris, V. (1997). *Teaching multicultural literature in grades K–8.* Norwood, MA: Christopher-Gordon.

Hatfield, M. M., Edwards, M. T., Bitter, G., & Morrow, J. (2004). *Mathematics methods for elementary and middle school teachers.* Hoboken, NJ: John Wiley & Sons.

Hayasaki, E. (2004, December 3). Cultural divide on campus. *Los Angeles Times*, A1, A36, A37.

Haycock, K., Jerald, C., & Huang, S. (2001). *Thinking K–16, closing the gap: Done in a decade.* Washington, DC: The Education Trust.

Haynes, J. (2004). What effective classroom teachers do. *Essential Teacher, 1*(5), 6–7.

Heath, S. B. (1999). *Ways with words: language, life and work in communities and classrooms* (2nd ed.). Cambridge: Cambridge University Press.

Heide, F., & Gilliland, J. (1990). *The day of Ahmed's secret.* New York: Lothrop, Lee, & Shepard.

Heinle & Heinle. (2002). *Launch into reading, Level I: Teacher's resource book.* Boston: Author.

Heilman, A. W. (2002). *Phonics in proper perspective.* Upper Saddle River, NJ: Merrill Prentice Hall.

Henwood, D. (1997). Trash-o-nomics. In M. Wray, M. Newitz, & A. Newitz, (Eds.), *White trash: Race and class in America* (pp. 177–191). New York and London: Routledge.

Henderson, D., & May, J. (2005) *Exploring culturally diverse literature for children and adolescents.* Boston: Pearson.

Herrell, A. L. (2000). *Fifty strategies for teaching English language learners.* Upper Saddle River, NJ, and Columbus, OH: Merrill Prentice Hall.

Herring, S. (1996). *Computer-mediated communication: Linguistic, social, and cross-cultural perspectives.* Amsterdam/Philadelphia: John Benjamins Publishing.

Hetherton, G. (1999). Headline news. In N. Shameem & M. Tickoo (Eds.), *New ways in using communicative games* (67–68). Alexandria, VA: Teachers of English to Speakers of Other Languages.

Hispanic Dropout Project. (1998). *No more excuses: The final report of the Hispanic Dropout Project.* Washington, DC: U.S. Department of Education, Office of the Under Secretary. Online at www. senate.gov/~bingaman/databw.pdf

Hodgkinson, H. L. (1998). Demographics of diversity for the 21st century. *The Education Digest, 64*(1), 4–7.

Hopstock, P. J., & Stephenson, T. (2003). Descriptive study of services to LEP students and LEP students with disabilities. Washington, DC: U.S. Department of Education. Retrieved August 4, 2006, from www.ncela.gwu.edu/resabout/research/descriptive studyfiles/native_languages1.pdf

Horwitz, E., Horwitz, M., & Cope, J. (1991). Foreign language classroom anxiety. In E. Horwitz & D. Young (Eds.), *Language anxiety: From theory and research to classroom implications* (pp. 27–36). Englewood Cliffs, NJ: Prentice Hall.

Hudelson, S. (1984). Kan yu ret an rayt in Ingles: Children become literate in English as a second language. *TESOL Quarterly, 18,* 221–238.

Hughes, J. (2004). On bridge making. *Essential Teacher, 1*(1).

Huizenga, J., & Thomas-Ruzic, M. (1992). *All talk: Problem solving for new students of English.* Boston: Heinle & Heinle.

Huntley, H. (2006). *Essential academic vocabulary: Mastering the complete academic word list.* Boston: Houghton Mifflin.

Hymes, D. (1972). On communicative competence. In J. Pride & J. Holmes (Eds.), *Sociolinguistics.* Harmondsworth, UK: Penguin.

International Reading Association. (1997). *The role of phonics in reading instruction: A position statement of the International Reading Association.* Newark, DE: Author.

Irujo, S. (Ed.). (2000). *Integrating the ESL standards into classroom practice: Grades 6–8.* Alexandria, VA: Teachers of English to Speakers of Other Languages (TESOL).

Irvine, J. J. (1990). *Black students and school failure.* Westport, CT: Greenwood Press.

Ishii, S., & Bruneau, T. (1991). Silence and silences in cross-cultural perspective: Japan and the United States. In L. Samovar & R. Porter (Eds.), *Intercultural communication: A reader* (6th ed.). Belmont, CA: Wadsworth.

Jametz, K. (1994). Making sure that assessment improves performance. *Educational Leadership, 51*(6), 55–57.

Jasmine, J. (1993). *Portfolios and other assessments.* Huntington Beach, CA: Teacher Created Materials.

Jenks, C., Lee, J. O., & Kanpol, B. (2002). Approaches to multicultural education in preservice teacher education: Philosophical frameworks and models for teaching. In F. Schultz (Ed.), *Annual editions: Multicultural education 2002–2003* (pp. 20–28). Guilford, CT: McGraw-Hill/Dushkin.

Jensen, E. (1998). *Teaching with the brain in mind.* Alexandria, VA: Association for Supervision and Curriculum Development.

Johns, K. (1992). Mainstreaming language minority students through cooperative grouping. *The Journal of Educational Issues of Language Minority Students, 11,* Boise, ID: Boise State University Press.

Johnson, D. W., & Johnson, R. (1994). Cooperative learning in second language classes. *The Language Teacher, 18,* 4–7.

Johnson, D. W., & Johnson, R. T. (1995). Why violence prevention programs don't work—And what does. *Educational Leadership, 52*(5), 63–68.

Johnson, D. W., Johnson, R., & Holubec, E. (1993). *Circles of learning: Cooperation in the classroom* (3rd ed.). Edina, MN: Interaction Book Company.

Johnson, D. W., Johnson, R. T., Dudley, B., & Acikgoz, K. (1994). Effects of conflict resolution training on elementary school students. *The Journal of Social Psychology, 134*(6), 803–817.

Jones, L. T. (1991). *Strategies for involving parents in their children's education.* Bloomington, IN: Phi Delta Kappa Educational Foundation.

Jordan, C., Tharp, R., & Baird-Vogt, L. (1992). "Just open the door": Cultural compatibility and classroom rapport. In M. Saravia-Shore & S. Arvizu (Eds.), *Cross-cultural literacy.* New York & London: Garland.

Josephs, K. M. (2004). African American language styles in Afrocentric schools. Accessed August 1, 2006, from www.swarthmore.edu/SocSci/ Linguistics/papers/ 2004/josephs.doc

Jussim, L. (1986). Self-fulfilling prophecies: A theoretical and integrative review. *Psychological Review, 93,* 429–445.

Kagan, S. (1998). *Cooperative learning smart card.* Kagan Cooperative Learning. Online at kaganonline.com

Kagan, S. (1999). *Teambuilding smart card.* Kagan Cooperative Learning. Online at kaganonline.com

Kame'enui, E. J., & Simmons, D. C. (2000). *Planning and evaluation tool for effective schoolwide reading programs.* Eugene, OR: Institute for the Development of Educational Achievement.

Kandel, W., & Cromartie, J. (2004). *New patterns of Hispanic settlement in rural America.* Retrieved January 16, 2005, from www.ers.usda.gov/publications/rdrr99/

Kang, H-W., Kuehn, P., & Herrell, A. (1996). The Hmong literacy project: Parents working to preserve the past and ensure the future. Retrieved July 7, 2006, from www.ncela.gwu.edu/pubs/jeilms/vol16/jeilms1602.htm

Kaufman, P., Alt, M. N., & Chapman, C. (2004). *Dropout rates in the United States: 2001* (NCES 2005-046). U.S. Department of Education. National Center for Education Statistics. Washington, DC: U.S. Government Printing Office. Retrieved August 4, 2006, from www.nces.ed.gov/pubs/205/2005046.pdf

Kea, C., Campbell-Whatley, G. D., Richards, H. V. (2004). *Becoming culturally responsive educators: Rethinking teacher education pedagogy.* National Center for Culturally Responsive Educational Systems. Retrieved

January 29, 2005, from www.nccrest.org/publications .html

Kealey, J., & Inness, D. (2007). *Shenanigames: Grammar-focused interactive ESL/EfL activities and games.* Brattleboro, VT: Prolingua.

Keefe, M. W. (1987). *Learning style theory and practice.* Reston, VA: National Association of Secondary School Principals.

Kehe, D., & Kehe, P. D. (1998). *Discussion strategies.* Brattleboro, VT: Prolingua Associates.

Kelley, M. L. (1990). *School-home notes: Promoting children's classroom success.* New York: Guilford Press.

Kessler, C., Quinn, M., & Fathman, A. (1992). Science and cooperative learning for LEP students. In C. Kessler (Ed.), *Cooperative language learning* (pp. 65–83). Englewood Cliffs, NJ: Regents/Prentice Hall.

Kim, E. Y. (2001). *The yin and yang of American culture.* Yarmouth, ME: Intercultural Press.

Kluge, D. (1999). A brief introduction to cooperative learning. ERIC Document Service (ED437840). Accessed August 4, 2006, from www.eric.ed.gov

Kozyrev, J. R. (1998). *Talk it up! Oral communication for the real world.* Boston: Houghton Mifflin.

Krashen, S. (1981). Bilingual education and second language acquisition theory. In *Schooling and language minority students: A theoretical framework.* Los Angeles, CA: Evaluation, Dissemination and Assessment Center, California State University, Los Angeles.

Krashen, S. (1982). *Principles and practice in second language acquisition.* Oxford: Pergamon.

Krashen, S. (1985). *The input hypothesis: Issues and implications.* New York: Longman.

Krashen, S. (2003). *Explorations in language acquisition and language use: The Taipei lectures.* Portsmouth, NH: Heinemann. Quote accessed on July 20, 2006, from www.coas.uncc.edu/linguistics/courses/6163/ should_we_teach_grammar.htm

Krashen, S., & Terrell, T. (1983). *The natural approach: Language acquisition in the classroom.* Oxford: Pergamon.

Kress, G. (2000). *Early spelling: Between convention and creativity.* London and New York: Routledge.

Kress, G. R., & Van Leeuwen, T. (1995). *Reading images: The grammar of visual design.* London: Routledge.

Laberge, D., & Samuels, S. J. (1974). Toward a theory of automatic information processing in reading. *Cognitive Psychology, 6,* 293–323.

Laufer, B. (1989). What percentage of text-lexis is essential for comprehension? In C. Lauren & M. Nordman (Eds.), *Special language: From humans thinking to thinking machines* (pp. 316–323). Clevedon, UK: Multilingual Matters.

Laufer, B., & Paribakht, S. (1998). The relationship between passive and active vocabularies: Effects of language learning contexts. *Language Learning, 48,* 365–391.

Lave, J., & Wenger, E. (1991). *Situated learning: Legitimate peripheral participation.* New York: Cambridge University Press.

Law, B., & Eckes, M. (2000). *The more-than-just-surviving handbook* (2nd ed.). Winnipeg, Canada: Peguis.

Leathers, N. (1967). *The Japanese in America.* Minneapolis: Lerner Publications.

LeCompte, M. (1981). The Procrustean bed: Public schools, management systems, and minority students. In H. Trueba, G. Guthrie, & K. Au (Eds.), *Culture and the bilingual classroom: Studies in classroom ethnography.* Rowley, MA: Newbury House.

Lee, O. (2005). Science education with English language learners: Synthesis and research agenda. *Review of Educational Research, 75*(4), 491–530.

Leistyna, P., Woodrum, A., & Sherblom, S. (Eds.). (1996). Glossary. In P. Leistyna, A. Woodrum, & S. A. Sherblom (Eds.), *Breaking free: The transformative power of critical pedagogy* (pp. 301–331). *Harvard Educational Review* Reprint Series #27. Cambridge, MA: Harvard University Press.

Leki, I. (1992). *Understanding ESL writers.* Portsmouth, NH: Boynton/Cook.

LeLoup, J., & Ponterio, R. (2000). *Enhancing authentic language learning experiences through Internet technology.* ERIC Digest; Online at www.cal.org/ericcll/ digest/0002enhancing.html

Lemberger, N. (1999). Factors affecting language development from the perspectives of four bilingual teachers. In I. Heath & C. Serrano (Eds.), *Annual editions: Teaching English as a second language* (2nd ed.). Guilford, CT: Dushkin/McGraw-Hill.

Lenneberg, E. (1967). *Biological foundations of language.* New York: John Wiley & Sons.

LePage, R. B., & Tabouret-Keller, A. (1985). *Acts of identity: Creole-based approaches to language and ethnicity.* Cambridge: Cambridge University Press.

Levine, D., & Adelman, M. (1982). *Beyond language: Intercultural communication for English as a second language.* Englewood Cliffs, NJ: Prentice Hall.

Levine, L. N. (2000). The most beautiful place in the world. In K. D. Samway (Ed.), *Integrating the ESL standards into classroom practice: Grades 3–5* (pp. 109–131).

Alexandria, VA: Teachers of English to Speakers of Other Languages (TESOL).

Levstik, L. S., & Barton, K. C. (2001). Doing history: Investigating with children in elementary and middle schools (2nd ed.). Mahwah, NJ: Erlbaum.

Lewis, G., & Bedson, G. (1999). *Games for children.* Oxford: Oxford University Press.

Lewis, M. (1997). *New ways in teaching adults.* Alexandria, VA: Teachers of English to Speakers of Other Languages.

Lindholm, K. (1994). Promoting positive cross-cultural attitudes and perceived competence in culturally and linguistically diverse classrooms. In R. A. DeVillar, C. Faltis, and J. Cummins (Eds.), *Cultural diversity in schools: From rhetoric to practice* (pp. 189–206). Albany: SUNY Press.

Lindholm-Leary, K. (2000). *Biliteracy for a global society: An idea book on dual language eEducation.* Washington, DC: National Clearinghouse for Bilingual Education.

Linse, C. (2006). Using favorite songs and poems with young learners. *English Teaching Forum, 44*(2), 38–40.

Linn, R. L. (2000). Assessments and accountability. *Educational Researcher, 29*(2), 4–26.

Lippi-Green, R. (1997). *English with an accent.* London and New York: Routledge.

Lipton, L., & Hubble, D. (1997). *More than 50 ways to learner-centered literacy.* Arlington Heights, IL: Skylight Professional Development.

Lockwood, A. T. (2000). *Transforming education for Hispanic youth: Broad recommendations for teachers and program staff.* Washington, DC: National Clearinghouse for Bilingual Education, 4. Retrieved January 28, 2005, from www.ncela.gwu.edu/pubs/issuebriefs/ib4.html

Lockwood, A. T., & Secada, W. G. (1999). *Transforming education for Hispanic youth: Exemplary practices, programs, and schools. NCELA Resource Collection Series, 12.* Accessed August 3, 2006, from www.ncela.gwu.edu/pubs/resource/hispanicyouth/hdp.htm

Long, M. H. (1987). Listening comprehension: Approach, design, procedure. In M. H. Long & J. C. Richards (Eds.), *Methodology in TESOL: A book of readings* (pp. 161–176). New York: Newbury House.

Long, M. (1980). *Input, interaction, and language acquisition.* Unpublished PhD dissertation, University of California, Los Angeles.

Losen, D., & Wald, J. (2005). *Confronting the graduation rate crisis in California.* Cambridge, MA: Final report, Harvard Civil Rights Project.

Lu, M-L. (2000). *Language development in the early years.* Bloomington, IN: ERIC Clearinghouse on Reading, English, and Communication Digest #154.

Lucas, T., & Wagner, S. (1999). Facilitating secondary English language learners' transition into the mainstream. *TESOL Journal, 8*(4), 6–13.

Lyons, C. A., & Clay, M. M. (2003). *Teaching struggling readers: How to use brain-based research to maximize learning.* Portsmouth, NH: Heinemann.

Macedo, D., & Freire, A. M. A. (1998). Foreword. In P. Freire (Ed.), *Teachers as cultural workers* (pp. ix–xix). Boulder, CO: Westview Press.

Maciejewski, T. (2003). *Pragmatics.* Retrieved August 4, 2006, from www.lisle.dupage.k12.il.us/maciejewski/social.htm

McCarty, T. L. (Ed.). (2005). *Language, literacy, and power in schooling.* Mahwah, NJ: Erlbaum.

McKenna, M. C., & Robinson, R. D. (1997). *Teaching through text: A content literacy approach to content area reading* (2nd ed.). New York: Longman.

McLaren, P. (1995). Critical multiculturalism, media literacy, and the politics of representation. In J. Frederickson (Ed.), *Reclaiming our voices: Bilingual education, critical pedagogy, and praxis* (pp. 99–138). Ontario, CA: California Association for Bilingual Education. New York: Longman.

McLaughlin, B. (1987). *Theories of second-language learning.* London: Arnold.

McLaughlin, B. (1990). "Conscious" versus "unconscious" learning. *TESOL Quarterly, 24*(4), 617–634.

McLeod, B. (1995). *School reform & student diversity: Lessons learned—Educating students from diverse linguistic and cultural backgrounds.* Retrieved January 28, 2005, from www.ncela.gwu.edu/pubs/ncrcdsll/srsd/schoolorg.htm

Maculaitis, J. (1988). *The complete ESL/EFL resource book: Strategies, activities, and units for the classroom.* Lincolnwood, IL: National Textbook Company.

Mahoney, D. (1999a). Shadow tableaux. In N. Shameem & M. Tickoo (Eds.), *New ways in using communicative games* (pp. 13–14). Alexandria, VA: Teachers of English to Speakers of Other Languages.

Mahoney, D. (1999b). Stress clapping. In N. Shameem & M. Tickoo (Eds.), *New ways in using communicative games* (pp. 20–21). Alexandria, VA: Teachers of English to Speakers of Other Languages.

Majors, P. (n.d.). Charleston County School District, Charleston, SC, Sample Standards-Based Lesson plan. Retrieved August 4, 2006, from www.cal.org/eslstandards/Charleston.html

Malavé, L. (1991). Conceptual framework to design a programme intervention for culturally and linguistically different handicapped students. In L. Malavé & G. Duquette (Eds.), *Language, culture and cognition* (pp. 176–189). Clevedon, UK: Multilingual Matters.

Mandlebaum, L. H., & Wilson, R. (1989). Teaching listening skills in the special education classroom. *Academic Therapy, 24,* 451–452.

Manning, M. L. (2002). Understanding diversity, accepting others: Realities and directions. In F. Schultz, (Ed.), *Annual editions: Multicultural education 2002/2003.* Guilford, CT: McGraw-Hill/Dushkin.

Mansour, W. (1999). Give me a word that . . . In N. Shameem & M. Tickoo (Eds.), *New ways in using communicative games* (pp. 103–104). Alexandria, VA: Teachers of English to Speakers of Other Languages.

Marinova-Todd, S., Marshall, D., & Snow, C. (2000). Three misconceptions about age and L2 learning. *TESOL Quarterly, 34*(1), 9–34.

Marlowe, B. A., & Page, M. L. (1999). Making the most of the classroom mosaic: A constructivist perspective. *Multicultural Education, 6*(4), 19–21.

Marton, W. (1994). The antipedagogical aspects of Krashen's theory of second language acquisition. In R. Barasch & C. James (Eds.), *Beyond the Monitor Model.* Boston: Heinle and Heinle.

Marzano, R. J. (1994). Lessons from the field about outcome-based performance assessments. *Educational Leadership, 51*(6), 44–50.

May, F. B., & Rizzardi, L. (2002). *Reading as communication* (6th ed.). Upper Saddle River, NJ: Merrill Prentice Hall.

Medina, M., Jr., & Escamilla, K. (1992). Evaluation of transitional and maintenance bilingual programs. *Urban Education, 27*(3), 263–290.

Mehan, H. (1979). *Learning lessons.* Cambridge, MA: Harvard University Press.

Mehan, H. (1981). Ethnography of bilingual education. In H. Trueba, G. Guthrie, & K. Au (Eds.), *Culture and the bilingual classroom: Studies in classroom ethnography.* Rowley, MA: Newbury House.

Mehan, H., & Hubbard, L. (1999). *Tracking untracking: Evaluating the effectiveness of an educational innovation.* Santa Cruz, CA: The National Center for Research on Cultural Diversity & Second Language Learning. Online at www.cal.org/crede/pubs/ResBreef3.pdf

Mehrabian, A. (1969). Communication without words. In *Readings in Psychology Today.* Del Mar, CA: CMR Books.

Migration Policy Institute. (2004). *A new century: Immigration and the US.* Accessed January 15, 2005, from www.migrationinformation.org/Profiles/display.cfm?ID=6

Miller, G. (1985). Nonverbal communication. In V. Clark, P. Eschholz, & A. Rosa (Eds.), *Language: Introductory readings* (4th ed.). New York: St. Martin's Press.

Miller, W. H. (1995). *Alternative assessment techniques for reading and writing.* West Nyack, NJ: The Center for Applied Research in Education.

Miller, L. (2004). Developing listening skills with authentic materials. Accessed July 21, 2006, from www.eslmag.com/modules.php?name=News&file=article&sid=20

Molina, H., Hanson, R. A., & Siegel, D. F. (1997). *Empowering the second-language classroom: Putting the parts together.* San Francisco: Caddo Gap Press.

Moll, L. C. (1992). Bilingual classroom studies and community analysis: Some recent trends. *Educational Researcher, 21*(2), 20–24.

Monroe, S. (1999). Multicultural children's literature: Canon of the future. Reprinted in *Annual editions 99/00: Teaching English as a second language.* Guilford, CO: Dushkin/McGraw-Hill.

Mora, J. K. (2000). Staying the course in times of change: Preparing teachers for linguistically diverse classrooms. *Journal of Teacher Education, 51*(5), 345–357.

Mora, J. K. (2002). Proposition 227's second anniversary: Triumph or travesty? Accessed June 30, 2006, from http://coe.sdsu.edu/people/jmora/Prop227/227YearTwo.htm

Morey, A., & Kilano, M. (1997). *Multicultural course transformation in higher education: A broader truth.* Boston: Allyn & Bacon.

Morgan, B. (1998). *The ESL classoom: Teaching, critical practice, and community development.* Toronto: University of Toronto Press.

Morgan, R. (1992). Distinctive voices—Developing oral language in multilingual classrooms. In P. Pinsent (Ed.), *Language, culture, and young children* (pp. 37–46). London: David Fulton Publisher.

Morley, J. (1999). Current perspectives on improving aural comprehension. *ESL Magazine, 2*(1), 16–19.

Moskowitz, G. (1978). *Caring and sharing in the foreign language classroom.* Cambridge, MA: Newbury House.

Moxley, J. M. (1994). *Becoming an academic writer: A modern rhetoric.* Lexington, MA: D.C. Heath.

Murray, D. E. (2000). Protean communication: The language of computer-mediated communication. *TESOL Quarterly, 34*(3), 397–421.

Nagy, W. E. (1997). On the role of context in first- and second-language vocabulary learning. In N. Schmitt & M. McCarthy (Eds.), *Vocabulary: Description, acquisition, pedagogy* (pp. 64–83). Cambridge, UK: Cambridge University Press.

Nagy, W. E., García, G. E., Durgunoglu, A., & Hancin-Bhatt, B. (1993). Spanish-English bilingual students' use of cognates in English reading. *Bilingual Research Journal, 18*, 83–97.

Nash, P. (1991). ESL and the myth of the model minority. In S. Benesch (Ed.), *ESL in America*. Portsmouth, NH: Boynton/Cook.

Natheson-Mejia, S. (1989). Writing in a second language. *Language Arts, 66*(5), 516–526.

Nation, I. S. P. (1990). *Teaching and learning vocabulary*. New York: Newbury House.

Nation, P. (1994). *New ways in teaching vocabulary*. Alexandria, VA: Teachers of English to Speakers of Other Languages.

National Center for Culturally Responsive Educational Systems, 2006. *Cultural pluralism*. Accessed July 31, 2006, from http://nccrest.edreform.net/subject/culturalpluralism

National Center for Education Statistics (NCES). (2000). *NAEP 1999 trends in academic progress: Three decades of student performance*. Washington, DC: U.S. Department of Education.

National Center for Education Statistics. (2002). *Percentage distribution of enrollment in public elementary and secondary schools, by race/ethnicity and state: Fall 1986 and fall 2000*. Retrieved August 3, 2005, from http://nces.ed.gov/programs/digest/d02/dt042.asp

National Center for Education Statistics. (2003). *Employees in degree-granting institutions, by race/ethnicity, primary occupation, sex, employment status, and control and type of institution: Fall 2001*. Accessed March 20, 2005, from http://nces.ed.gov/programs/digest/d03/tables/dt228.asp

National Center for Education Statistics (NCES). (2005). *Postsecondary participation rates by sex and race/ethnicity: 1974–2003*. Washington: Author.

National Clearinghouse for English Language Acquisition & Language Instruction Programs (NCELA). (2004). *ELLs and the No Child Left Behind Act*. Accessed August 2, 2006, from www.ncela.gwu.edu/about/lieps/5ellnclb.html

National Commission on Teaching and America's Future. (2002). Teacher shortage question unraveled: NCTAF challenges the nation to address the teacher retention crisis. Washington, DC: Author.

National Education Association. (1975). *Code of ethics of the education profession*. Washington, DC: Author.

Nelson-Barber, S. (1999). A better education for every child: The dilemma for teachers of culturally and linguistically diverse students. In Mid-continent Research for Education and Learning (McREL). (Ed.). *Including culturally and linguistically diverse students in standards-based reform: A report on McREL's Diversity Roundtable I* (pp. 3–22). Aurora, CO: Author.

Nemmer-Fanta, M. (2002). Accommodations and modifications for English language learners. In *Serving English language learners with disabilities: A resource manual for Illinois educators*. Retrieved February 9, 2005, from www.isbe.state.il.us/speced/bilingualmanual2002.htm

Nero, S. J. (1997). English is my native language . . . or so I believe. *TESOL Quarterly, 31*(3), 585–593.

Newman, J. M. (1985). What about reading? In J. M. Newman (Ed.), *Whole language: Theory in use* (pp. 99–100). Portsmouth, NH: Heinemann.

Nieto, S. (2004). *Affirming diversity* (4th ed.). New York: Longman.

No Child Left Behind (NCLB). (2001). Title III, Part A, Sec. 3102. Purposes (1). Accessed August 4, 2006, from www.ncela.gwu.edu/about/lieps/5_ellnclb.html

Nunan, D. (1989). *Designing tasks for the communicative classroom*. Cambridge: Cambridge University Press.

Nunan, D. (1991). *Language teaching methodology: A textbook for teachers*. New York: Prentice Hall.

Oakes, J. (1985). *Keeping track: How schools structure inequality*. New Haven, CT: Yale University Press.

Oakes, J. (1992). Can tracking research inform practice? Technical, normative, and political considerations. *Educational Researcher, 21*(4), 12–21.

O'Barr, W. M., & Atkins, B. K. (1980). Women's language or powerless language. In S. McConnell-Ginet, R. Borker, & N. Furman (Eds.), *Women and language in literature and society* (pp. 93–110). New York: Praeger.

O'Connor, T. (2004). Understanding discrimination against Asian-Americans. Accessed August 4, 2006, from http://faculty.ncwc.edu/toconnor/soc/355lect10.htm.

Odlin, T. (1989). *Language transfer: Cross-linguistic influence in language learning*. Cambridge: Cambridge University Press.

Office of English Language Acquisition, Language Enhancements and Academic Achievement for Limited English Proficient Students (OELA). (2003). *The growing numbers of limited English proficient students 1991/2–2001/02*. Washington, DC: Author.

Ogbu, J. (1978). *Minority education and caste: The American system in crosscultural perspective.* New York: Academic Press.

Ogbu, J., & Matute-Bianchi, M. (1986). Understanding sociocultural factors: Knowledge, identity, and school adjustment. In *Beyond language: Social and cultural factors in schooling language minority students.* Los Angeles: Evaluation, Dissemination and Assessment Center, California State University, Los Angeles.

Olmedo, I. M. (1993, summer). Junior historians: Doing oral history with ESL and bilingual students. *TESOL Journal, 2*(4), 7–9.

Omaggio, A. (1978). *Games and simulations in the foreign language classroom.* Washington, DC: Center for Applied Linguistics.

Omaggio, A. C. (1986). *Teaching language in context.* Boston: Heinle & Heinle.

O'Malley, J. M., & Pierce, L. V. (1996). *Authentic assessment for English language learners.* Menlo Park, CA: Addison-Wesley.

Ong, W. (1982). *Orality and literacy.* London: Methuen.

Orfield, T., & Lee, C. (2005). Why segregation matters: Poverty and educational inequality. Retrieved August 6, 2006, from www.civilrightsproject.harvard.edu/research/deseg/deseg05.php

Ortiz, A. A. (2002). Prevention of school failure and early intervention for English Language Learners. In A. J. Artiles & A. A. Ortiz (Eds.), *English language learners with special education needs: Identification, assessment, and instruction* (pp. 31–63). Washington, DC: Center for Applied Linguistics and Delta Systems.

Ortiz, F. (1988). Hispanic-American children's experiences in classrooms: A comparison between Hispanic and non-Hispanic children. In L. Weis (Ed.), *Class, race, and gender in American education.* Albany: State University of New York Press.

Ouk, M., Huffman, F., & Lewis, J. (1988). *Handbook for teaching Khmer-speaking students.* Sacramento: Spilman Printing.

Ovando, C., & Collier, V. (1998). *Bilingual and ESL classrooms: Teaching in multicultural contexts.* Boston: McGraw-Hill.

Oyama, S. (1976). A sensitive period for the acquisition of nonnative phonological system. *Journal of Psycholinguistic Research, 5,* 261–284.

Packer, N. H., & Timpane, J. (1997). *Writing worth reading: The critical process* (3rd ed.). Boston: Bedford Books.

Paige, R. M. (1999). Theoretical foundations of intercultural training and applications to the teaching of culture. In R. M. Paige, D. L. Lange, & Y. A. Yershova

(Eds.), *Culture as the core: Integrating culture into the language curriculum* (pp. 21–29). Minneapolis: Center for Advanced Research on Language Acquisition, University of Minnesota.

Palinscar, A. S., & Brown, A. L. (1984). Reciprocal teaching of comprehension-fostering and comprehension-monitoring activities. *Cognition and Instruction, 1,* 117–175.

Pappas, C. C., Kiefer, B. Z., & Levstik, L. S. (2006). *An integrated language perspective in the elementary school* (4th ed.). Boston: Allyn & Bacon.

Parks, S., & Black, H. (1990). *Organizing thinking: Graphic organizers.* Pacific Grove, CA: Critical Thinking Press & Software.

Pasternak, J. (1994, March 29). Bias blights life outside Appalachia. *Los Angeles Times,* A1, A16.

Pearson, R. (1974). *Introduction to anthropology.* New York: Holt, Rinehart and Winston.

Peim, N. (1993). *Critical theory and the English teacher.* London and New York: Routledge.

Pennycook, A. (1998). Text, ownership, memory, and plagiarism. In V. Zamel & R. Spack (Eds.), *Negotiating academic literacies: Teaching and learning across languages and cultures* (pp. 265–292). Mahwah, NJ: Erlbaum.

Peregoy, S., & Boyle, O. (2005). *Reading, writing, and learning in ESL* (4th ed.). Boston: Pearson.

Pérez, B., & Torres-Guzmán, M. (2002). *Learning in two worlds* (3rd ed.). New York: Longman.

Philips, S. (1972). Participant structures and communicative competence: Warm Springs children in community and classroom. In C. Cazden, V. John, & D. Hymes (Eds.), *Functions of language in the classroom.* New York: Teachers College Press.

Phillips, J. (1978). College of, by and for Navajo Indians. *Chronicle of Higher Education, 15,* 10–12.

Pinnell, G. S. (1985) Ways to look at the functions of children's language. In A. Jaggar & M. Smith-Burke (Eds.), *Observing the language learner.* Newark, DE: International Reading Association.

Porter, R. (1990). *Forked tongue: The politics of bilingual education.* New York: Basic Books.

Pratt, C., & Nesdale, A. R. (1984). Pragmatic awareness in children. In W. E. Tunmer, C. Pratt, & M. L. Herriman (Eds.), *Metalinguistic awareness in children* (pp. 105–125). Berlin: Springer Verlag.

Pridham, F. (2001). *The language of conversation.* New York and London: Routledge.

Prothrow-Smith, D. (1994, April). Building violence prevention into the classroom. *The School Administrator, 8*(12), 8–12.

Pruitt, W. (2000). Using story to compare, conclude, and identify. In B. Agor (Ed.), *Integrating the ESL standards into classroom practice: Grades 9–12* (pp. 31–49). Alexandria, VA: TESOL.

Pryor, C. B. (2002). New immigrants and refugees in American schools: Multiple voices. In F. Schultz (Ed.), *Annual editions: Multicultural education 2002/2003* (pp. 185–193). Guilford, CT: McGraw-Hill/Dushkin.

Raimes, A. (Ed.). (1996). *Identities: Readings from contemporary culture.* Boston: Houghton Mifflin.

Raphael, T. E. (1986). Teaching question answer relationships, revisited. *The Reading Teacher, 39,* 516–523.

Ramírez, J. (1992, winter/spring). Executive summary, final report: Longitudinal study of structured English immersion strategy, early-exit and late-exit transitional bilingual education programs for language-minority children. *Bilingual Research Journal, 16*(1&2), 1–62.

Rasinski, T., & Fredericks, A. (1989). Dimensions of parent involvement. *The Reading Teacher, 43*(2), 180–182.

Reid, J. M. (1993). *Teaching ESL writing.* Englewood Cliffs, NJ: Prentice Hall Regents.

Reid, J. M. (1995). Preface. In J. Reid (Ed.), *Learning styles in the ESL/EFL classroom* (pp. viii–xvii). Boston: Heinle and Heinle.

Remillar, J. T., & Cahnmann, M. (2005). Researching mathematics teaching in bilingual-bicultural classrooms. In T. L. McCarty (Ed.), *Language, literacy, and power in schooling* (pp. 169–187). Mahwah, NJ: Erlbaum.

Ricento, T. (1995). Language policy in the United States: An overview. In M. Herriman & B. Burnaby (Eds.), *Language policy in English dominant countries: Six case studies.* Clevedon, UK: Multilingual Matters.

Richard-Amato, P. (2003). *Making it happen* (3rd ed.). White Plains, NY: Longman.

Richard-Amato, P., & Snow, M. (1992). Strategies for content-area teachers. In P. Richard-Amato & M. Snow (Eds.), *The multicultural classroom.* White Plains, NY: Longman.

Riles, G. B. & Lenarcic, C. (2000). Exploring world religions. In B. Agor (Ed.), *Integrating the ESL standards into classroom practice: Grades 9–12* (pp. 1–29). Alexandria, VA: Teachers of English to Speakers of Other Languages (TESOL).

Rinvolucri, M. (1984). *Grammar games: Cognitive, affective and drama activities for EFL students.* Cambridge: Cambridge University Press.

Rivera, C. (2006, June 9). Charter school fights back. *Los Angeles Times.* Accessed July 7, 2006, from www.latimes .com/news/local/lame-charter9jun09,1,4660030.story? ctrack=1&cset=true

Robin, R. (2006). *Should we teach grammar?* Accessed July 20, 2006, from www.coas.uncc.edu/linguistics/ courses/6163/should_we_teach_grammar.htm

Robinson, G. (1985). *Crosscultural understanding.* New York: Pergamon Institute of English.

Rodby, J. (1999). Contingent literacy: The social construction of writing for nonnative English-speaking college freshman. In L. Harklau, K. M. Losey, & M. Siegal (Eds.), *Generation 1.5 meets college composition: Issues in the teaching of writing to U.S.-educated learners of ESL* (pp. 45–60). Mahwah, NJ: Erlbaum.

Rose, C. (1987). *Accelerated learning.* New York: Dell.

Rosebery, A. S., Warren, B., & Conant, F. R. (1992). Appropriating scientific discourse: Finding from language minority classrooms. *Journal of the Learning Sciences, 21,* 61–94.

Rowan, T., & Bourne, B. (1994). *Thinking like mathematics.* Portsmouth, NH: Heinemann.

Rumbaut, R. G. (1995). The new Californians: Comparative research findings on the education progress of immigrant children. In R. G. Rumbaut & W. A. Cornelius, *California's immigrant children: Theory, research, and implications for educational policy* (pp. 17–70). San Diego, CA: University of California, San Diego Center for U.S.-Mexican Studies.

Runner, J. (2000). *"I don't understand" in over 230 languages.* Accessed August 2, 2006, from www.elite.net/~runner/ jennifers/understa.htm

Sadker, M. P., & Sadker, D. M. (2003). Questioning skills. In J. Cooper (Ed.), *Classroom teaching skills* (7th ed., pp. 101–147). Boston: Houghton-Mifflin.

Sales, F. (1989). *Ibrahim.* New York: Lippincott.

Samway, K. D. (Ed.). (2000). *Integrating the ESL standards into classroom practice: Grades 3–5.* Alexandria, VA: Teachers of English to Speakers of Other Languages (TESOL).

Samway, K. D., & McKeon, D. (1999). *Myths and realities: Best practices for language minority students.* Portsmouth, NH: Heinemann.

Santa Ana, O. (2004). Giving voice to the silenced. *Language, 3*(8), 15–17.

Sato, C. (1982). Ethnic styles in classroom discourse. In M. Hines and W. Rutherford (Eds.), *On TESOL '81.* Washington, DC: TESOL.

Scarcella, R. (1990). *Teaching language minority students in the multicultural classroom.* Englewood Cliffs, NJ: Prentice Hall.

Scarcella, R., & Rumberger, R. W. (2000). Academic English key to long-term success in school. *University of*

*California Linguistic Minority Research Institute Newsletter, 9*(4), 1–2.

Schifini, A., Short, D., & Tinajero, J. V. (2002). *High point.* Carmel, CA: Hampton-Brown.

Schultz, J., & Theophano, J. (1987). Saving place and marking time: Some aspects of the social lives of three-year-old children. In H. Trueba (Ed.), *Success or failure?* Cambridge, MA: Newbury House Publishers.

Schumann, J. (1978). The acculturation model for second-language acquisition. In R. Gringas (Ed.), *Second language acquisition and foreign language teaching.* Washington, DC: Center for Applied Linguistics.

Schumann, J. (1994). Emotion and cognition in second language acquisition. *Studies in Second Language Acquisition, 16,* 231–242.

Scollon, R., & Scollon, S. W. (2003). *Discourses in place: Language in the material world.* London and New York: Routledge.

Selinker, L. (1972). Interlanguage. *IRAL, 10*(3), 209–231.

Selinker, L. (1991). Along the way: Interlanguage systems in second language acquisition. In L. Malavé & G. Duquette (Eds.), *Language, culture and cognition.* Clevedon, UK: Multilingual Matters.

Shade, B., & New, C. (1993). Cultural influences on learning: Teaching implications. In J. Banks & C. Banks (Eds.), *Multicultural education: Issues and perspectives.* Boston: Allyn & Bacon.

Shaffer, D. R. (1999). *Developmental psychology: Childhood & adolescence* (5th ed.). Pacific Grove, CA: Brook Cole Publishing Company.

Shannon, S. (1994). Introduction. In R. Barasch & C. James (Eds.), *Beyond the Monitor Model.* Boston: Heinle & Heinle.

Shoemaker, C., & Polycarpou, S. (1993). *Write ideas: A beginning writing text.* Boston: Heinle & Heinle.

Sholley, D. (2006). Two culture, one unique talent. *The Sun-San Bernardino County,* July 20, U1–U2.

Short, D. (1998). Secondary newcomer programs: Helping recent immigrants prepare for school success. *ERIC Digest.* Retrieved January 28, 2005, from http://searcheric.org/scripts/seget2.asp?db=ericft& want=http://searcheric.org/ericdc/ED419385.htm

Short, D. J., & Boyson, B. A. (2004). *Creating access: Language and academic programs for secondary school newcomers.* Santa Cruz, CA: Center for Research on Education, Diversity, & Excellence.

Short, D. J., & Echevarria, J. (1999). The sheltered instruction observation protocol: A tool for teacher-researcher collaboration and professional develop-

ment. *ERIC Digest.* Retrieved January 28, 2005, from http://searcheric.org/scripts/seget2.asp?db=ericf& want=http://searcheric.org/ericdc/ED436981.htm

Shuit, D., & McConnell, P. (1992, January 6). Calculating the impact of California's immigrants. *Los Angeles Times,* A1, A19.

Siccone, F. (1995). *Celebrating diversity: Building self-esteem in today's multicultural classrooms.* Boston: Allyn & Bacon.

SIL International. (2000). *Geographic distribution of living languages, 2000.* Accessed May 17, 2006, from www.ethnologue.com/ethno_docs/distribution.asp

Silver, H. F., Strong, R. W., & Perini, M. J. (2000). *So each may learn: Integrating learning styles and multiple intelligences.* Alexandria, VA: Association for Supervision and Curriculum Development.

Sindell, P. (1988). Some discontinuities in the enculturation of Mistassini Cree children. In J. Wurzel (Ed.), *Toward multiculturalism.* Yarmouth, ME: Intercultural Press.

Singleton, D. M., & Ryan, L. (2004). *Language acquisition: The age factor.* Clevedon, UK: Multilingual Matters.

Skutnabb-Kangas, T. (1981). *Bilingualism or not: The education of minorities.* (L. Malmberg & D. Crane, Trans.) Clevedon, UK: Multilingual Matters.

Slavin, R. E. (1991). A synthesis of research on cooperative learning. *Educational Leadership, 48,* 71–82.

Smallwood, B. A. (Ed.). (2000). *Integrating the ESL standards into classroom practice: Grades Pre-K–2.* Alexandria, VA: Teachers of English to Speakers of Other Languages (TESOL).

Smilkstein, R. (2002) *We're born to learn: Using the brain's natural learning process to create today's curriculum.* Thousand Oaks, CA: Sage Publications.

Smith, F. (1982). *Writing and the writer.* New York: Holt, Rinehart, & Winston.

Smith, F. (1983). *Essays into literacy.* Portsmouth, NH: Heinemann.

Smith, S. L., Paige, R. M., & Steglitz, I. (1998). Theoretical foundations of intercultural training and applications to the teaching of culture. In D. L. Lange, C. A. Klee, R. M. Paige, and Y. A. Yershova (Eds.), *Culture as the core: Interdisciplinary perspectives on culture teaching and learning in the language curriculum* (pp. 53–91). Minneapolis: Center for Advanced Research on Language Acquisition, University of Minnesota.

Smith, T. E. C., Polloway, E. A., Patton, J. R., & Dowdy, C. A. (2003). *Teaching children with special needs in inclusive settings* (4th ed.). Boston: Allyn & Bacon.

Snow, C., & Hoefnagel-Hoehle, M. (1978). The critical period for language acquisition: Evidence from second language learning. *Child Development, 49,* 1114–1118.

Snow, D. (1996). *More than a native speaker.* Alexandria, VA: TESOL.

Snow, M. A. (1993). Discipline-based foreign language teaching: Implications from ESL/EFL. In M. Krueger & F. Ryan (Eds.), *Language and content: Discipline- and content-based approaches to language study* (pp. 37–56). Lexington, MA: D.C. Heath.

Snow, M. A., & Brinton, D. M. (1988). Content-based language instruction: Investigating the effectiveness of the adjunct model. *TESOL Quarterly, 22*(3), 201–217.

Snow, C. E., Burns, S. M., & Griffin, P. (Eds.). (1998). *Preventing reading difficulties in young children.* Washington, DC: National Academy Press.

So, H. (2006, April 28). School interpreters' goal: Being word perfect. *Los Angeles Times,* B2.

Sonbuchner, G. M. (1991). *How to take advantage of your learning styles.* Syracuse, NY: New Readers Press.

Southern Poverty Law Center. (1999). *Youth at the edge.* Montgomery, AL: Author. Accessed August 2, 2006, from www.splcenter.org/intel/intelreport/article.jsp?aid=302

Spears, R. A. (1992). *Common American phrases.* Lincolnwood, IL: National Textbook Company.

Spellmeyer, K. (1989). A common ground: The essay in the academy. *College English, 51,* 262–276.

Spinelli, E. (1994). *English grammar for students of Spanish* (3rd ed.). Ann Arbor, MI: The Olivia and Hill Press.

Spring, J. (2001). The new Mandarin society? Testing on the fast track. *The Joel Spring Library* Accessed July 31, 2006, from www.mhhe.com/socscience/education/spring/commentary.mhtml

Stahl, N. A., King, J. R., & Henk, W. A. (1991). Enhancing students' notetaking through training and evaluation. *Journal of Reading, 34*(8), 614–622.

Stanovich, K. (1986). Matthew effects in reading: Some consequences in individual differences in the acquisition of literacy. *Reading Research Quarterly, 21,* 360–407.

Strehorn, K. (2001). The application of Universal Instructional Design to ESL teaching. *Internet TESL Journal.* Accessed July 7, 2006, from http://iteslj.org/Techniques/Strehorn-UID.html

Suid, M., & Lincoln, W. (1992). *Ten-minute whole language warm-ups.* Palo Alto, CA: Monday Morning Books.

Suina, J. (1985). . . . And then I went to school. *New Mexico Journal of Reading V*(2).

Sunal, C. S., & Haas, M. E. (2005). *Social studies for elementary and middle grades: A constructivist approach.* Boston: Allyn & Bacon.

Suresh, B. (2003). Get 'em hooked on books—Start an ESL book club. *CATESOL News, 30*(2), 14.

Suzuki, B. (1989, November/December). Asian Americans as the "model minority." *Change, 21,* 12–19.

Swartz, S., Klein, A. F., & Shook, R. E. (2002). *Interactive writing & interactive editing: Making connections between writing and reading.* Carlsbad, CA: Dominie Press.

Swartz, S. L., Shook, R. E., Klein, A. F., Moon, C., Bunnell, K., Belt, M., & Huntley, C. (2003). *Guided reading and literacy centers.* Carlsbad, CA: Dominie Press.

Swerdlow, J. L. (2001). Changing America. *National Geographic Magazine, 200*(3), 42–61.

Takahashi, E., Austin, T., & Morimoto, Y. (2000). Social interaction and language development in an FLES classroom. In J. K. Hall & L. S. Verplaetse (Eds.), *Second and foreign language learning through classroom interaction* (pp. 139–162). Mahwah, NJ: Lawrence Erlbaum.

Taylor, B. P. (1987). In M. H. Long and J. C. Richards (Eds.), *Methodology in TESOL: A book of readings* (pp. 45–60). New York: Newbury House.

Taylor, D. (2000). Facing hardships: Jamestown and colonial life. In K. Samway (Ed.), *Integrating the ESL standards into classroom practice* (pp. 53–55). Alexandria, VA: TESOL.

Tannen, D. (2001). *Discourse analysis.* In Linguistic Society of America, "Fields of Linguistics." Online at www.lsadc.org/web2/ fldcont.html

Tharp, R. (1989). Culturally compatible education: A formula for designing effective classrooms. In H. Trueba, G. Spindler, & L. Spindler (Eds.), *What do anthropologists have to say about dropouts?* New York: Falmer Press.

Tharp, R., & Gallimore, R. (1991). *The instructional conversation: Teaching and learning in social activity.* Washington, DC: National Center for Research on Cultural Diversity and Second Language Learning.

Thernstrom, A., & Thernstrom, S. (2003). *No excuses: Closing the racial gap in learning.* New York: Simon & Schuster.

Thomas, W., & Collier, V. (1997). *School effectiveness for language minority students.* Accessed August 4, 2006, from www.ncela.gwu.edu/pubs/resource/effectiveness/

Thonis, E. (1983). *The English-Spanish connection.* Los Angeles: Santillana.

Tresaugue, M. (2002, January 31). Back to the basics. *Riverside Press-Enterprise,* A1, A8.

Trueba, H. (1989). *Raising silent voices.* Boston: Heinle & Heinle.

Tunmer, W., & Nesdale, A. (1985). Phonemic segmentation skill and beginning reading. *Journal of Educational Psychology, 77,* 417–427.

Tinajero, J. V., & Schifini, A. (1997). *Into English.* Carmel, CA: Hampton-Brown.

Trueba, H. (1989). *Raising silent voices.* Boston: Heinle & Heinle.

Trueba, H., Cheng, L., & Ima, K. (1993). *Myth or reality: Adaptive strategies of Asian Americans in California.* Washington, DC: Falmer Press.

Tunmer, W. E., Herriman, M. L., & Nesdale, A. R. (1988). Metalinguistic abilities and beginning reading. *Reading Research Quarterly, 23*(2), 134–158.

Ukpokodu, N. (2002). Multiculturalism vs. globalism. In F. Schultz (Ed.), *Annual editions: Multicultural education 2002–2003* (pp. 7–10). Guilford, CT: McGraw-Hill/Dushkin.

U.S. Census Bureau. (2000). Hispanic population in the United States: Population characteristics. Accessed August 4, 2006, from www.census.gov/population/www/socdemo/hispanic/ho00.html

U.S. Census Bureau. (2001a). *The Asian and Pacific Islander population in the United States: March 1999* (Update) (PPL–131). Online at www.census.gov/population/www/socdemo/race/api99.html

U.S. Census Bureau. (2001b). *Census 2000 Supplementary Survey.* Washington, DC: Author.

U.S. Census Bureau. (2001c). *Census 2000 Supplementary Survey.* Washington, DC: Author.

U.S. Census Bureau. (2003). *Language use, English ability, and linguistic isolation for the population 5 years and over by state, 2000* (Summary File 3, Tables P19, PCT13, and PCT14). Washington, DC: Author.

U.S. Census Bureau. (2004a). Educational attainment in the U.S.: 2003. Accessed August 2, 2006, from www.census.gov/population/www/socdemo/educ-attn.html

U.S. Census Bureau. (2004b). Poverty tables 2003. Accessed August 2, 2006, from www.census.gov/hhes/poverty/poverty03/tables03.html

U.S. Department of Education. (1998). *Fall staff survey.* Online at http://nces.ed.gov/pubs2000

U.S. Government Accounting Office. (2002). Per-pupil spending differences between selected inner city and suburban schools varied by metropolitan area. Accessed August 2, 2006, from www.gao.gov/new.items/d03234.pdf

Valenzuela, J. S., & Baca, L. (2004). Procedures and techniques for assessing the bilingual exceptional child. In L. M. Baca & H. T. Cervantes (Eds.), *The bilingual special education interface* (4th ed., pp. 184–203). Upper Saddle River, NJ: Pearson Merrill/Prentice Hall.

Veeder, K., & Tramutt, J. (2000). Strengthening literacy in both languages. In N. Cloud, F. Genesee, & E. Hamayan (Eds.), *Dual language instruction.* Boston: Heinle & Heinle.

Verdugo Hills High School. (2004). *Redesignated students.* Accessed February 2, 2005, from www.lausd.k12.ca.us/Verdugo_HS/classes/esl/redes.htm

Villegas, A. M., & Lucas, T. (2002). Preparing culturally responsive teachers: Rethinking the curriculum. *Journal of Teacher Education, 53*(1), 20–32.

Vygotsky, L. (1981). The genesis of higher mental functions. In J. V. Wertsch (Ed.), *The concept of activity in Soviet psychology.* Armonk, NY: Sharpe.

Wallraff, B. (2000). What global language? *The Atlantic Monthly, 286*(5), 52–66.

Walqui, A. (1999). Assessment of culturally and linguistically diverse students: Considerations for the 21st century. In Mid-continent Research for Education and Learning (McREL) (Ed.), *Including culturally and linguistically diverse students in standards-based reform: A report on McREL's Diversity Roundtable I* (pp. 55–84). Aurora, CO: Author (online at http://www.mcrel.org/topics/productDetail.asp?topicsID=3&productID=56)

Ward, A. W., & Murray-Ward, M. (1999). *Assessment in the classroom.* Belmont, CA: Wadsworth.

Warren, B., Ballenger, C., Ogonowski, M., Rosebery, A., & Hudicourt-Barnes, J. (2001). Rethinking diversity in learning science: The logic of everyday language. *Journal of Research in Science Teaching, 38*(5), 529–552.

Warschauer, M. (1995). *E-mail for English teaching.* Alexandria, VA: Teachers of English to Speakers of Other Languages.

Warschauer, M., Shetzer, H., & Meloni, C. (2000). *Internet for English teaching.* Alexandria, VA: Teachers of English to Speakers of Other Languages.

Watahomigie, L. (1995). The power of American Indian parents and communiities. *Bilingual Research Journal, 19*(1), 99–115.

Weatherly, S. D. (1999). I'll buy it! In R. E. Larimer & L. Schleicher (Eds.), *New ways in using authentic materials in the classroom* (pp. 73–80). Alexandria, VA: Teachers of English to Speakers of Other Languages.

Weaver, C. (1988). *Reading process and practice.* Portsmouth, NH: Heinemann.

Weber, E. (2005). *MI strategies in the classroom and beyond.* Boston: Pearson.

Weiler, J. (1998). Recent changes in school desegregation. *ERIC Digest. Clearinghouse on Urban Education,* ED#419029. Accessed August 4, 2006, from www.ericfacility.net/ericdigests/ed419029.htm

Weiss, I. R., & Pasley, J. D. (2004, February). What is high-quality instruction? *Educational Leadership,* 24–28.

Wells, C. G. (1981). *Learning through interaction: The study of language development.* Cambridge: Cambridge University Press.

Wells, G. (1998). Using the tool-kit of discourse in the activity of learning and teaching. From Wells, G. (Ed.), *Dialogic inquiry* (pp. 231–266). Cambridge: Cambridge University Press.

Wells, G., & Chang-Wells, G. L. (1992). *Constructing knowledge together: Classrooms as centers of inquiry and literacy.* Portsmouth, NH: Heinemann.

Westling, D. L., & Koorland, M. A. (1988). *The special educator's handbook.* Boston: Allyn & Bacon.

Wexler, E., & Huerta, K. (2002). An empowering spirit is not enough: A Latino charter school struggles for leadership. In B. Fuller (Ed.), *Inside charter schools: The paradox of radical decentralizaion* (pp. 98–123). Cambridge, MA: Harvard University Press.

Whisler, N., & Williams, J. (1990). *Literature and cooperative learning: Pathway to literacy.* Sacramento: Literature Co-op.

Whitman, E. L. (1994). *Miss Nell fell in the well.* Kissimmee, FL: Learning Pyramid.

Wiese, A. M., & García, E. (1998). The Bilingual Education Act: Language minority students and equal educational opportunity. *Bilingual Research Journal, 22*(1). Retrieved on June 21, 2005, from http://brj.asu.edu/v221/articles/art1.html

Wiggins, G. P., & McTighe, J. (1998). *Understanding by design.* Alexandria, VA: Association for Supervision and Curriculum Development.

Wilson, W. (1984). The urban underclass. In L. Dunbar (Ed.), *Minority report.* New York: Pantheon Books.

Wilton, D. (2003). How many words are there in the English language? Retrieved May 19, 2006, from www.wordorigins.org/number.htm

Wink, J. (2000). *Critical pedagogy: Notes from the real world.* New York: Addison Wesley.

Witte, K. (1991). The role of culture in health and disease. In L. Samovar & R. Porter (Eds.), *Intercultural communication: A reader* (6th ed.). Belmont, CA: Wadsworth.

Wolfe, P., & Poynor, L. (2001). Politics and the pendulum: An alternative understanding of the case of whole language as educational innovation. *Educational Researcher, 30*(1), 15–20.

Wolfram, W. (1991). *Dialects and American English.* Englewood Cliffs, NJ: Prentice Hall.

Wolfram, W. (1995). Reexamining dialect in TESOL. *TESOL Matters, 5*(2), 1, 22.

Wong, M. S. (1998). *You said it! Listening/speaking strategies and activities.* New York: St. Martin's Press.

Woolfolk, A. (2003). *Educational psychology* (9th ed.). Boston: Allyn & Bacon.

Woolfolk, A., & Brooks, D. (1985). The influence of teachers' nonverbal behaviors on students' perceptions and performance. *Elementary School Journal, 85,* 514–528.

Wray, M., & Newitz, A. (1997). *White trash: Race and class in America.* New York and London: Routledge.

Yao, E. (1988). Working effectively with Asian immigrant parents. *Phi Delta Kappan, 70*(3), 223–225.

Yep, L. (1975). *Dragonwings.* New York: Harper and Row.

Young, M., & Helvie, S. (1996). Parent power: A positive link to school success. *Journal of Educational Issues of Language Minority Students, 16.* Accessed July 7, 2006, from www.ncela.gwu.edu/pubs/jeilms/vol16/jeilms1611.htm

Zacarian, D. (2004). I was lost before the end of the first minute. *Essential Teacher, 1*(3), 11–13.

Zacarian, D. (2005). Rainforests and parking lots. *Essential Teacher, 2*(1), 10–11.

Zacarian, D. (2006). Testing, testing. *Essential Teacher, 3*(2), 10–12.

Zahar, R., Cobb, T., & Spada, N. (2001). Acquiring vocabulary through reading: Effects of frequency and contextual richness. *Canadian Modern Language Review, 57*(4). Accessed July 24, 2006, from www.utpjournals.com/product/cmlr/574/574-Zahar.html

Zelman, N. (1996). *Conversational inspirations: Over 2000 conversation topics.* Battleboro, VT: Pro Lingua Associates.

Zimmerman, C. (1997). Do reading and interactive vocabulary instruction make a difference? An empirical study. *TESOL Quarterly, 31*(1), 121–140.

# NAME INDEX

Abram, P. L., 255
Acikgoz, K., 290
Adamson, H. D., 204
Addison, A., 197
Adelman, M., 289
Adger, C., 145
Af Trampe, P., 62
Agar, M., 328
Agor, B., 199
Alcaya, C., 212
Alexander, S., 299
Allen, E., 208
Allport, G., 298
Alt, M. N., 282
Altman, L. J., 164
Amanti, C., 60, 153
Amselle, J., 132
Andersen, J., 308
Anderson, J., 228, 249
Antuñez, B., 215
Anyon, J., 286
Aoki, E, 327
Arvizu, S., 337
Asato, J., 125, 130
Asher, J., 56
Atkins, B. K., 47
Au, K., 305
Austin, T., 54

Babbitt, N., 186
Baca, L., 285
Bahrampour, T., 1
Baird-Vogt, L., 39
Baker, C., 59
Balderrama, M. V., 5, 186, 253, 259
Bales, R. J., 227
Ballenger, C., 246
Bandlow, R., 290
Banks, J., 148, 324, 325
Barbe, W. B., 233
Barks, D., 237
Barr, R., 227
Bartolomé, L. I., 8
Barton, D., 216

Barton, K. C., 244
Bartram, M., 210, 236
Bassano, S., 169, 171, 174
Bedson, G., 58
Bell, C., 181
Belmont, J. M., 252
Belt, M., 110
Bembridge, T., 104
Bennett, C., 300, 313
Benson, B., 196
Benson, V. A., 209
Bergman, J. L., 217
Berk, L. E., 155
Bermúdez, A., 333, 337
Bielenberg, B., 94
Birdwhistell, R., 302
Bitter, G., 188, 246
Black, H., 160
Blair, R. W., 58
Blanc, M. A. H., 151
Bliatout, B., 315
Bloch, J., 237
Bosher, S., 44
Bourdieu, P., 199
Bourne, B., 262
Boyd-Batstone, P., 233, 247
Boyle, O., 217, 221
Boyson, B. A., 135
Bradley, J. A., 255
Bradley, K. S., 255
Brandt, R., 324
Braun, L. A., 233
Brend, R. M., 47
Brinton, D., 16, 138, 197, 240
Brisk, M. E., 161
Bromberg, M., 28
Bromley, K. D., 234
Brooks, D., 332
Brophy, J., 332
Brown, A. L., 227
Brown, C., 105
Brown, D., 57, 58, 75, 81
Brozo, W. G., 245, 261
Bruneau, T., 304

Bruner, J., 165
Brutt-Griffler, J., 9
Buchanan, K., 257
Bunch, G. C., 255
Bunnell, K., 110
Bunting, E., 142
Burely-Allen, M., 202
Burgstahler, S., 138, 139
Burk, T. L., 211
Burnett, K., 318
Burns, S. M., 215
Bursuck, W. D., 113
Burvikovs, A., 188
Butler, Y. G., 32, 137
Byrd, P., 196

Cahnmann, M., 246
Caine, G., 67, 68
Caine, R. N., 67, 68
California Department of Education
    (CDE), 2, 52, 91, 109, 165, 242,
    243, 293
California State Code of
    Regulations, 125
Cameron, A., 167
Cameron, C., 336
Campbell, C., 235
Campbell-Whatley, G. D., 332
Canale, M., 191
Cantlon, T. L., 169, 171, 174
Carnuccio, L. M., 300
Carrasquillo, A., 249
Cary, S., 317, 329
Casey, J., 256
CATESOL, 214
Celce-Murcia, M., 16, 33
Center for Educational Reform, 278
Chambers, J., 138
Chamot, A. U., 80, 110, 166, 240
Chan, L., 8
Chandler, D., 66
Chaney, A. L., 211
Chang-Wells, G. L., 60
Chapman, C., 282

Chard, D. J., 219
Cheng, L., 97, 284
Chesterfield, K., 58
Chesterfield, R., 58
Children's Defense Fund, 280
Chinn, P. C., 271, 330
Cho Bassoff, T., 341
Christensen, L., 326, 327
Christison, M. A., 169, 171, 174
Chung, H., 317, 319
Cipollone, N., 40, 50
Clark, B., 323
Clay, M. M., 67
Cloud, N., 127, 150
Cockcroft, J. D., 123, 283
Coehlo, E., 171
Cogan, D., 209
Cohen, E., 168
Cohn, D., 1
Cole, K., 5
Cole, M., 267
Collie, J., 224
Collier, V., 32, 125, 137, 138, 144,
    182, 333–334, 335
Conant, F. R., 246
Contra Costa County Office of
    Education, 99
Cook, L., 174
Cook, V., 51, 117
Cooter, R. B., 72
Cope, J., 76
Corley, M. A., 216
Cortés, C., 287
Costa, A. L., 184
Cotton, K., 332
Crago, M., 305
Crawford, J., 118, 119, 123, 128
Cromartie, J., 296
Cuevas, G., 156, 248
Cummins, J., 28, 32, 51, 53, 54, 64, 74,
    128, 129, 137, 145, 179, 200
Curry, J., 125, 130
Curtain, H., 323, 324
Cushner, K., 308

Dahlberg, C. A., 323, 324
Dale, P., 16, 19
Dale, T., 156, 248
Daloğlu, A., 29

Danesi, M., 58
Darder, A., 278, 288
Davies, A., 336
Day, F. A., 228
De Boinod, A-J., 26
DeGeorge, G., 97
Delgado-Gaitan, C., 321
dePaola, T., 230
Derrick-Mescua, M., 107, 108
deUnamuno, M., 322
Diamond, B., 299
Díaz, R. M., 155
Díaz-Rico, L. T., 5, 66, 166, 186, 205,
    208, 253, 259, 303, 326, 337
Dicker, S., 82
Dirmann, J., 264
Donato, R., 130
Dowdy, C. A., 114, 116
Downing, B., 315
Dudley, B., 290
Dudley-Marling, C., 149
Dullien, S., 66
Dumont, R., 305
Dunkel, P., 204
Durgunoglu, A., 150

Echevarria, J., 182, 239
Eckes, M., 236
Ediger, A., 245
Edmonson, M., 306
Education Trust, The, 285
Edwards, M. T., 246
Egan, K., 192
Egbert, J., 139, 189
Ehri, L., 219
Ellis, R., 62
Ellis, S. S., 172
Erickson, F., 84, 328
Escalante, J., 264
Escamilla, K., 134

Faber, J. E., 255
Faltis, C., 168, 337, 338
Farr, M., 232
Fathman, A., 168, 249
Feng, J., 284
Feuerstein, T., 237
Finnan, C., 287
Fisher, D., 245, 261

Flood, J., 221
Florida Department of Education,
    114
Flower, L., 234
Flynn, K., 155
Flynt, E. S., 72
Folse, K. S., 208
Fosnot, C. T., 60
Foucault, M., 34, 148
Franco, L., 107, 108
Fraser, N., 267, 268
Fredericks, A., 337
Freeman, R., 282
Freire, P., 8
Frey, N., 245, 261
Friend, M., 113, 174
From the Classroom, 107
Fu, D., 276
Fuller, B., 278
Funaki, I., 318
Furey, P., 316

Gajdamaschko, N., 192
Gallimore, R., 38, 213
Gamrel, L. B., 227
Gándara, P., 94, 125, 130
Gaouette, N., 3
García, E., 123, 125, 130
García, G. E., 150
García, S. B., 113
Gardner, H., 78
Gardner, R., 75
Garmston, R. J., 184
Garrison, D., 150
Gascoigne, C., 196
Gass, S., 55, 143, 193
Gay, G., 274
Genesee, F., 127, 135, 150
Gibson, M., 284
Gillett, P., 295
Gilliland, J., 299
Giroux, H., 8, 84, 332
Glaser, S., 105
Goldenberg, C., 213, 216
Gollnick, D. M., 271, 330
Gombert, J. E., 150, 151
González, N. E., 60, 153
Good, T., 332
Goodman, K., 66

Goodwin, J., 16
Gopaul-McNicol, S., 111
Gottlieb, M., 105
Graham, C., 202
Grasha, A. F., 78
Graves, K., 250
Greaver, M., 226
Gregory, G., 100
Gregory, G. H., 235, 247, 257
Gregory, K., 336
Griffin, P., 215
Grognet, A., 107, 108
Grossberg, L., 267, 268
Groves, M., 231
Gunderson, L., 228, 249
Gunning, T. G., 218, 219, 226
Guthrie, J., 245
Gutierrez, A. S., 130
Gutiérrez, K., 125, 130

Haas, M. E., 250
Hackney, C. S., 233
Hadaway, N. L., 225, 233
Hafernik, J. J., 7
Hakuta, K., 32, 120, 137
Hall, E., 42, 267
Halliday, M., 30, 56, 66
Hamayan, E., 127, 150, 221
Hamers, J. F., 151
Hamilton, M., 216
Han, Z., 70
Hancin-Bhatt, B., 150
Hancock, C., 104
Hanson, R. A., 145
Hanson-Smith, E., 189
Harel, Y., 35, 38, 143
Harrington, M. M., 161
Harris, T. L., 221
Harris, V., 228
Hatfield, M .M., 246
Hayasaki, E., 275
Haycock, K., 285
Haynes, J., 142
Heath, S. B., 272, 277, 304
Hedberg, K., 226
Heide, F., 299
Heilman, A. W., 13
Heinle & Heinle, 217
Helman, M., 257

Helvie, S., 144, 333
Henk, W. A., 255
Henderson, D., 327
Henwood, D., 279, 301
Herrell, A. L., 105, 188, 336
Herriman, M. L., 151
Herring, S., 188
Hetherton, G., 213
Hispanic Dropout Project, 282–283
Hodges, R. E., 221
Hodgkinson, H. L., 178
Hoefnagel-Hoehle, M., 71
Holubec, E., 168
Hopstock, P. J., 96, 293
Horwitz, E., 76
Horwitz, M., 76
Huang, S., 285
Hubbard, L., 282
Hubble, D., 227, 233
Hudelson, S., 231
Hudicourt-Barnes, J., 246
Huerta, K., 278
Huffman, F., 333, 340
Hughes, J., 329
Huizenga, J., 210
Huntley, C., 110
Huntley, H., 28, 29
Hurley, S., 221
Hymes, D., 57

Ima, K., 284
Inness, D., 23
International Reading Association, 221
Irujo, S., 199
Irvine, J. J., 277
Ishii, S., 304
Ivanič, R., 216
Ivey, G., 245, 261

Jameson, J., 107, 108
Jametz, K., 94, 164
Jasmine, J., 106
Jenks, C., 325
Jensen, E., 67
Jerald, C., 285
Johns, K., 168
Johnson, B., 227
Johnson, D. W., 87, 168, 290

Johnson, R. T., 87, 168, 290
Jones, L. T., 337, 340
Jordan, C., 39, 305
Josephs, K. M., 277
Jussim, L., 5

Kagan, S., 158, 160, 169, 171, 174
Kame'enui, E. J., 99
Kandel, W., 296
Kang, H-W., 336
Kanpol, B., 325
Kaufman, P., 282
Kea, C., 332
Kealey, J., 23
Keefe, M. W., 78, 79
Kehe, D., 209
Kehe, P. D., 209
Keiser, S. H., 40, 50
Kelley, M. L., 334
Kessler, C., 168, 249
Kiefer, B. Z., 148
Kilano, M., 325
Kim, E. Y., 327
King, J. R., 255
Klein, A. F., 110
Klimek, K., 67, 68
Kluge, D., 168
Koorland, M. A., 176
Kozyrev, J. R., 202, 204
Krashen, S., 56, 62, 63, 193
Kress, G., 66, 233
Kuehn, P., 336
Kuzmich, L., 235, 247, 257

LaBerge, D., 222
Lambert, W., 75
Lapp, D., 221
Laufer, B., 28, 222
Lave, J., 34, 60
Law, B., 236
Leathers, N., 270
LeCompte, M., 83
Lee, C., 136, 285
Lee, J. O., 325
Lee, O., 246
Leistyna, P., 8
Leki, I., 233
LeLoup, J., 188
Lemberger, N., 308

Lenarcic, C., 165
Lenneberg, E., 71
LePage, R. B., 44
Levine, D., 289
Levine, L. N., 167
Levstik, L. S., 148, 244
Lewis, G., 58
Lewis, J., 315, 333, 340
Lewis, M., 58
Liebb, J., 28
Lieberman, M. G., 255
Lim, P. L., 204
Lincoln, W., 227
Lindholm, K., 127, 131
Lindholm-Leary, K., 131
Linn, R. L., 103
Linse, C., 202
Lippi-Green, R., 45, 46, 47
Lipton, L., 227, 233
Lockwood, A. T., 283
Long, M., 60
Long, M. H., 202
Losen, D., 282
Lotan, R. A., 255
Lu, M-L., 50
Lucas, T., 98, 309, 326
Lybeck, K., 212
Lyons, C. A., 67

Maciejewski, T., 39
McCarty, T. L., 278
McClintic, C., 67, 68
McConnell, P., 279
McKenna, M. C., 155, 197, 198
McLaren, P., 216, 332
McLaughlin, B., 62, 63
McLeod, B., 281
McTighe, J., 98
Maculaitis, J., 58
Mahoney, D., 209, 213
Majors, P., 109
Malavé, L., 285
Mandlebaum, L. H., 115
Manning, M. L., 298, 302
Mansour, W., 213
Marinova-Todd, S., 71
Marlowe, B. A., 178
Márquez, J., 333, 337

Marshall, D., 71
Marton, W., 63
Marzano, R. J., 104
Master, P., 138
Matute-Bianchi, M., 83, 321
Maxwell-Jolly, J., 125, 130
May, F. B., 216, 220
May, J., 327
Medina, M., Jr., 134
Mehan, H., 35, 59, 282, 328
Mehrabian, A., 41
Meloni, C., 190
Messerschmitt, D. S., 7
Migration Policy Institute, 294, 296
Miller, G., 41
Miller, L., 204
Miller, W. H., 106
Molina, H., 145
Moll, L. C., 60, 153
Monroe, S., 228
Moon, C., 110
Moore, M., 299
Mora, J. K., 128, 129, 130
Morey, A., 325
Morgan, R., 149, 207
Morimoto, Y., 54
Morley, J., 206
Morris, J. D., 255
Morrow, J., 246
Moskowitz, G., 75
Mougel, P., 212
Murray, D. E., 188
Murray-Ward, M., 103

Nagy, W. E., 150, 222
Nash, P., 284
Natheson-Mejia, S., 150
Nation, I. S. P., 28, 29
Nation, P., 58
National Center for Culturally Responsive Educational Systems, 273
National Center for Education Statistics (NCES), 280, 281, 283, 285
National Clearinghouse for English Language Acquisition &

Language Instruction Programs (NCELA), 1, 293
National Commission on Teaching and America's Future, 8
National Education Association (NEA), 6
Neal, C. J., 155
Nelson-Barber, S., 94
Nemmer-Fanta, M., 113
Nero, S. J., 44
Nesdale, A., 151
New, C., 272
Newitz, A., 301
Newman, J. M., 222
Nicholson, L., 267, 268
Nieto, S., 77, 84, 134, 290
No Child Left Behind (NCLB), 6, 297
Nunan, D., 182, 332

Oakes, J., 281
O'Barr, W. M., 47
O'Connor, T., 284
Odlin, T., 150
Ogbu, J., 81, 83, 301, 321
Ogonowski, M., 246
Olmedo, I. M., 250
Olsen, J. W-B., 171
Olshtain, E., 33
Omaggio, A., 58, 226
O'Malley, J. M., 80, 104, 110, 166, 240
Ong, W., 306
Orfield, T., 136, 285
Ortiz, A. A., 113
Ortiz, F., 301
Ouk, M., 333, 340
Ovando, C., 138, 144, 333–334, 335
Oyama, S., 71

Packer, N. H., 236
Page, M. L., 178
Paige, R. M., 7, 267, 273
Palinscar, A. S., 227
Pappas, C. C., 148
Paribakht, S., 28
Parks, S., 160
Parrish, T., 138

Pasley, J. D., 249
Pasternak, J., 288
Patton, J. R., 114, 116
Pavlik, C., 245
Pearson, R., 267
Peim, N., 33, 148
Pennycook, A., 237
Peregoy, S., 217, 221
Pérez, B., 83, 249
Perini, M. J., 78
Philips, S., 59, 86, 288
Phillips, J., 59,
Pialorsi, F., 204
Pierce, L. V., 104
Pierson, M., 188
Pikulski, J. J., 219
Pinnell, G. S., 31
Politano, C., 336
Polloway, E. A., 114, 116
Polycarpou, S., 196
Poms, L., 16, 19
Ponterio, R., 188
Porter, R., 128
Powell, R., 308
Poynor, L., 214
Pratt, C., 151
Pridham, F., 35
Prothrow-Smith, D., 292
Pruitt, W., 186
Pryor, C. B., 287

Quinn, M., 168, 249

Raimes, A., 326
Ramírez, J., 128
Raphael, T. E., 227, 255
Rasinski, T., 337
Reid, J. M., 178, 179, 235
Remillar, J. T., 246
Richard-Amato, P., 77, 187
Richards, H. V., 332
Riles, G. B., 165
Rinvolucri, M., 23
Rivera, C., 133
Rizzardi, L., 216, 220
Robin, R., 193
Robinson, G., 267, 328
Robinson, R. D., 155, 197, 198

Rodby, J., 232
Rodríguez, V., 249
Rodriquez, A. P., 130
Rose, C., 80
Rosebery, A. S., 246
Rowan, T., 262
Rumbaut, R. G., 130
Rumberger, R. W., 32
Runner, J., 306
Ryan, L., 70

Sales, F., 299
Samimy, K. K., 9
Samuels, S. J., 222
Samway, K. D., 199
Santa Ana, O., 88
Sato, C., 332
Scarcella, R., 32, 102
Schcolnik, M., 237
Schifini, A., 32, 99, 187, 203, 217
Schuder, T., 217
Schultz, J., 316
Schumann, J., 67, 81–82
Scollon, R., 66
Scollon, S. W., 66
Searle, D., 149
Secada, W. G., 283
Selinker, L., 55, 62, 192, 193
Shade, B., 272
Shaffer, D. R., 50
Shannon, S., 63
Sherblom, S., 8
Shetzer, H., 190
Shoemaker, C., 196
Sholley, D., 203
Shook, R. E., 110
Short, D., 32, 99, 135, 136, 182, 217, 239
Shuit, D., 279
Siccone, F., 75, 326
Siegel, D. F., 145
SIL International, 11
Silver, H. F., 78
Simmons, D. C., 99
Sindell, P., 320, 322
Singleton, D. M., 70
Skutnabb-Kangas, T., 301
Slater, S., 224

Slavin, R. E., 168
Smallwood, B. A., 199
Smilkstein, R., 67
Smith, F., 66, 234
Smith, S. L., 7, 267
Smith, T. E. C., 114, 116
Snow, C., 71
Snow, C. E., 215
Snow, D., 267, 269
Snow, M. A., 138, 187, 197
Sonbuchner, G. M., 78
Southern Poverty Law Center, 299
Spears, R. A., 57
Spellmeyer, K., 232
Spinelli, E., 25
Stahl, N. A., 255
Stanovich, K., 150
Steglitz, I., 7, 267
Stephenson, T., 96, 293
Strehorn, K., 139
Stritkus, T., 125, 130
Strong, R. W., 78
Suid, M., 227
Suina, J., 314
Sunal, C. S., 250
Suresh, B., 225
Suzuki, B., 284
Swartz, S. L., 110

Tabouret-Keller, A., 44
Takahashi, E., 54
Tannen, D., 33
Taylor, B. P., 57
Taylor, D., 245
Templeton, S., 219
Terrell, T., 56
Tharp, R., 38, 39, 59, 306
Theophano, J., 316
Thernstrom, A., 283
Thernstrom, S., 283
Thomas, W., 137, 138
Thomas-Presswood, T., 111
Thomas-Ruzic, M., 210
Thonis, E., 150
Timpane, J., 236
Tinajero, J. V., 32, 99, 187, 203, 217, 221
Torres-Guzmán, M., 83, 249

Traiger, A., 28
Tramutt, J., 132
Tresaugue, M., 232
Trueba, H., 59, 284, 321
Tunmer, W., 151

Ukpokodu, N., 324
United States Census Bureau, 3, 200, 279, 281, 292
U.S. Government Accounting Office, 285

Vachio, A., 155
Valdés, G., 255
Valenzuela, J. S., 285
Vallette, R., 208
Vandrick, S., 7
Van Leeuwen, T., 66
Vardell, S. M., 225, 233
Vasishth, S., 40, 50
Veeder, K., 132
Verdugo Hills High School, 101
Villegas, A. M., 309, 326
Vogt, M. E., 182, 239
Vygotsky, L., 61, 147, 199

Wagner, S., 98
Wald, J., 282

Wallraff, B., 3
Walqui, A., 94, 105
Walton, R., 210, 236
Ward, A. W., 103
Warren, B., 246
Warschauer, M., 188, 190
Wasylyk, T. M., 233
Watahomigie, L., 336
Watts, P., 237
Weatherly, S. D., 172
Weaver, C., 66
Weaver, S., 212
Weber, E., 75
Weed, K. Z., 205, 208, 303, 337
Weiler, J., 285
Weiss, I. R., 249
Wells, C. G., 38
Wells, G., 60, 206
Wenger, E., 34, 60
Westling, D. L., 176
Wexler, E., 278
Whalen, S. F., 172
Whisler, N., 174
Whitman, E. L., 20
Wiese, A. M., 123
Wigfield, A., 245
Wiggins, G. P., 98

Williams, J., 174
Wilson, R., 115
Wilson, W., 296
Wilton, D., 26
Winer, L., 171
Wink, J., 61, 148
Winsler, A., 155
Witt, D., 32, 137
Witte, K., 317
Wolfe, P., 214
Wolfram, W., 43, 44, 45
Wong, M. S., 210
Wong Fillmore, L., 94
Woodrum, A., 8
Woolfolk, A., 77, 332
Wray, M., 301

Yang, D., 315
Yao, E., 337
Yep, L., 142
Young, M., 144, 333
Young, T. A., 225, 233

Zacarian, D., 86, 101, 208, 289
Zelman, N., 208
Zimmerman, C., 222

# SUBJECT INDEX

Academic achievement, 280–286
  of minorities, 130, 280–286
  teacher expectations and, 5–6, 43, 318, 330–331
Academic competence, 34
Academic subjects. *See* Content-area instruction
Accent, 45, 47
Acceptable yearly progress (AYP), 91
Accommodation, 286, 288, 313, 314, 315, 316, 318–319,
  323
Acculturation, 286
  model (Schumann), 81–82
  phases of, 288–289
Achievement tests, 97
Acquisition-learning hypothesis, 62, 193
Acronyms, 21
Activities
  age-appropriate, 320–321
  to enhance self-esteem, 74–75, 89, 131
Adapting instruction for CLD special learners, 112–116
Additive bilingualism, 51, 131–133
Address, forms of, 70
Advancement Via Individual Determination (AVID),
  281
Affective filter hypothesis, 63–64
Affixes, 21
African Americans, 7, 87, 127, 272, 278, 279, 282, 283,
  285, 304
African-American Vernacular English, 45
Age-appropriate activities, 320–321
Age for second-language acquisition, 70–71
Aide. *See* Paraprofessional educator
Alignment of home and school, 312
Ambiguity, 24
Annual measurable achievement objectives, under
  NCLB, 98
Anxiety, test, 102
Arabic language, 293
Armenia, 331
Articulation, point of, 15
Arizona, English learners in, 293
Asian Americans, 3, 272, 278, 280, 281, 283, 284
Asian immigrants, 3
Assessment. *See also* Testing; Tests
  appropriate, 107

authentic, 104, 105
biased, 102
classroom, 103
of content, 108–109
of English learners, 90–116
formative, 99, 185, 195, 260
and grading plan, 108
linking to curriculum, 104, 162
observation-based, 106
performance-based, 101
for placement, 96
portfolio, 105
purpose of, 90, 95–108
scaffolding, 111
standardized testing, 91–92
summative, 99, 185, 261
types of, 103–107
uses of, 90, 103
Assimilation, 286, 287
Assimilationist model, 128
Attitudes, learner, 77, 130
Audiolingualism, 55–56
Audiolingual strategy, 78–79
Authentic assessment, 104, 105

Background factors of second-language acquisition,
  69–74
  academic success, 73–74
  age, 70, 71
  assessed L2 level, 72
  first-language proficiency, 70–71
  likes/dislikes, 74
  previous L2 experience, 72
Backwards lesson planning, 98, 99
Basic interpersonal communication skills (BICS), 32,
  179, 180, 199–200, 201
Behaviorism, 55–56
Benchmark group, 99–100
Bias
  class, in tests, 102
  cultural, in tests, 102
  dialectical, in tests, 102
  and discrimination in the U.S., 298
  geographic, in tests, 102

Bias (*continued*)
  language-specific, in tests, 102
  recognizing, 82
Biculturalism, 286, 288
Bilingual education
  historical development of, 117–124
  legal issues in, 120–123
  maintenance or developmental, 131–133
  organizational models of, 158–166
  politics of, 127–129
  transitional or early-exit, 134
Bilingual Education Act of 1968, 12, 122, 124, 281
Bilingualism
  additive, 51, 131, 133
  cognitive advantages of, 128
  limited, 51
  subtractive, 51, 134, 135, 136
  types of, 51
Blacks. *See* African Americans
Blends, 21
Body language, 42, 302–303
Bound morphemes, 20, 21
Brain-based learning, 67, 68, 176–177
Bridging, 176–178, 244
*Brown v. Board of Education,* 136, 277, 285
Building schemata, 178, 245

California, English learners in, 2, 293
California English-Language Arts Standards, 95, 138, 165, 215
California English Language Development Standards, 91–95, 98, 99, 165, 215
California English Language Development Test (CELDT), 52, 53, 72, 73, 98, 100, 101, 136, 137, 152, 153, 240, 243
California Standards Test, 101
CALLA. *See* Cognitive Academic Language Learning Approach
Cambodia, Cambodians, 120, 260, 295
*Castañeda v. Pickard,* 123
Castelike minorities, 81
Central Americans, 3, 286
Checking for comprehension, 106–107, 143
Cherokee language (Tsalagi), 118, 119
Chicano, 190, 270
Chinese, Chinese Americans, 3, 126, 130, 260, 284, 294, 296, 304, 323, 331
Chinese Exclusion Act, 294

Chinese language (Mandarin), 3, 25
Chomsky, 57, 193
Civil Rights Act of 1964, 122, 126
Clarity of vision, 7–8, 88
Clarification checks, 184
Class bias, 102
Class discussions, 218
Classism, 101
Classrooms
  assessments, 107
  environment of, 87
  resolving conflict in, 292
Clipping, 21
Co-construction of meaning, 38
Code switching, 59, 152
Cognates, English–Spanish, 26–27
Cognitive Academic Language Learning Approach (CALLA), 80, 166, 240
Cognitive academic language proficiency (CALP), 32–33, 64, 65, 179–180, 192, 248
Cognitive factors of second-language acquisition, 69, 77–80
Collaboration, 171, 306, 333–335
  with paraprofessionals, 174–176
  in teaching, 174–176, 197, 255
Collaborative relations of power, 129
Common underlying proficiency (CUP), 53–54
Communication
  with families, 144–145
  intercultural, 307–308
  listening for, 203–204
  nonverbal, 41–42, 302–304
  role of silence in, 304
  verbal, and cultural diversity, 304–307
Communicative competence, 56, 191–192
Communicative games, 58
Communicative interaction, focus on, 191–193
Communicative strategies, 58
Community as sources of information, 330
Community involvement, 86, 333–342
Community of practice, 35
Community participation, 39, 341–342
Community partnership with schools, 145
Compensatory education, 281–282
Competency tests, 181, 185
Competition, values about, 316, 322
Comprehensibility, 251
Comprehensible input, 63
Comprehension, in science, 260–261

Comprehension checks, 106–107, 143
Comprehensive Immigration Reform Act of 2006, 297
Computer-Assisted Language Learning (CALL), 190
Computer-managed instruction, 189
Concept development, 28–29, 219–220
Concepts about print, 218
Concurrent validity, 202
Conductive hearing loss, 342
Conferences
   parent–teacher, 334, 336
   three-way, 336
Conflict resolution, 290–292
Connotations, 26
Constructivist views of learning, 60–61
Content-area instruction, 239–265
   differentiated instructional delivery for, 244–263
   instructional needs beyond the classroom, 264
   in literature, 224, 228, 241, 244
   in mathematics, 240, 241, 248, 249, 251, 252, 253,
     258, 259, 260, 261, 262
   in music, 241, 250, 260, 262
   in physical education, 241, 243
   resources for, 258–260
   in science, 240, 241, 243, 246, 243–254, 260
   in social studies, 241, 249–250, 254–255, 258, 259,
     260, 263
   visual and performing arts, 241, 250, 262
Content-Based ESL, 138, 197–199
   collaboration in, 191
   lesson planning in, 197
Content-integrated learning strategy, 240
Content objective, 109, 142, 162–164
Content-related language objective, 240
Content standards, 155, 164
Content validity, 102
Context-embedded communication, 179, 200
Context-reduced communication, 32
Contextual interaction model, 277
Contextualization, 143, 246
Contextual redefinition, 223
Contrastive analysis, 18, 25, 54–55
Conversation
   environments for, 208
   instructional, 38, 205, 212–214
Cooperation, values about, 316, 322
Cooperative learning, 87, 168–174
   challenges to, 172
   as a discourse alternative, 38
   guidelines for, 168–169

   instructional use of, 170–171
   jigsaw, 172, 173
Court cases, 121–123
Creative thinking, 228–229
Critical discourse analysis, 33
Critical period hypothesis, 71
Critical perspective, 4–5
Critical reflection, 186
Critical thinking, 228, 332–333
Crosscultural, language, and academic development
   (CLAD), 130
Cuban Americans, 3, 120, 121
Cultural accommodation, 286, 288, 313
Cultural adaptation, 287
Cultural assimilation, 286–287
Cultural concepts and perspectives, 266–286
Cultural conflict, 290–292
Cultural congruence, 274
Cultural contact, 286–292
   processes, 287–288
   psychological and socio-emotional issues in, 288–289
   resolving problems of, 289–292
Cultural contextualization, 246
Cultural deprivation myth, 120, 272, 277
Cultural differences in written discourse, 306–307
Cultural diversity, 277–278, 292–301
   educating students about, 323–327
   in nonverbal communication, 302–304
   intragroup and intergroup, 275
Cultural fairness, 302
Cultural identity and pride, 131, 148, 326–327, 337
Cultural incompatibility theory, 277
Culturally and linguistically diverse (CLD) students, 1,
   4, 87, 114–116, 312
Culturally inclusive learning environment, 330–333
Culturally receptive school, 209–210
Culturally supportive classroom, 330–333
Cultural mismatch, 277
Cultural observation, 328
Cultural pluralism, 273
Cultural relativism, 273
Cultural self-study, 309–310
Cultural values, 271, 313–322
Culture
   definitions of, 266–268
   external elements of, 275–276
   and gender issues, 279
   key concepts about, 268–275
   importance of, 311

Culture (*continued*)
    internal elements of, 276
    learning about students', 327–330
    mainstream, U.S., 244, 270, 275, 304, 312, 316
Culture shock, 112, 135, 281
Cummins's theories of bilingualism and cognition, 64
Curriculum
    calibration, 99
    design, 85
    multicultural, 324–327

Declaration of the Rights of Persons Belonging to
    National, Ethnic, Religious, and Linguistic
    Minorities of the General Assembly of the United
    Nations, 120
Decoding, 220
*Del Rio Independent School District v. Salvatierra,* 121
Demographic trends, 1–4, 292–293
Democracy, 333
Denotations, 26
Developmental bilingual education, 127
Developmental programs, 146
Dialects and language variation, 13–47
    attitudes toward, 45–46
    common features of, 44–45
    deeper syntactic cause for, 45
    and education of English learners, 43–44
    gender and, 47
    nonstandard, 44
    regional, 44
    social and ethnic differences in, 45
    social stratification, 44–45
    and style, 47
    vernacular and language teaching, 47
Directed reading activity, 198
Directed reading-thinking activity (DRTA), 198, 230
Direct instruction, 194
Direct teaching, 55, 56, 194
Disciplinary policies, 85
Discourse, 33–39
    academic, 33
    community patterns of, 39
    oral, in the classroom, 34–38, 305–306
    styles, 305
    written, 306–307
Discourse analysis, 33
Discourse competence, 191–192
Discrimination, 298, 301
Discussion, classroom, 210

Diversity
    challenges, 298–302
    educating about, 323–327
    in oral discourse, 304
Dress and appearance, 314
Dropout rates, 282
    segregation and, 150
Dual immersion, 167
Dual-language immersion. *See* Two-way (dual)
    immersion programs

Economics, values about, 317–318
Editing, 236
Educational expectations, 5–6, 43, 318, 330–331
Educational issues involving English learners, 280–286
Educational standards, 90–95, 108, 156–157, 217
Elementary and Secondary Education Act (ESEA), 120,
    122, 124
El Salvador, 331
Emergency Immigrant Education Program (EIEP), 297
Emergent literacy, 218, 219
Emergent spelling, 233
Empirical validity, 102
Empowerment, 129, 148
Enculturation, 246
English as a second language (ESL). *See* English-
    language development
English language
    cognates, with Spanish, 26–27
    dialects and English learners, 43–44
    intonation, 19
    neologisms, 22
    nonstandard, 44
    phonemes, 14, 15
    sound system, 13
    stops, 13
    standard, 43–44, 47
    syntax, 25
    prolonged exposure to, 20
English-Language Arts (ELA) Content Standards, in
    California, 95, 100
English-language development (ELD)
    and academic instruction, 140–144
    basic interpersonal communication skills in, 32, 179,
        180, 199–200, 201
    in content areas, 151
    content-based, 197–199
    employment in, 8–10
    grammar, 193–197

listening, 200–206
literacy, 214–238
in newcomer programs, 136
objectives, 109–110, 162, 163, 165
oracy, 199–214
planning for, 162–176
reading, 215–231
speaking, 206–214
standards for, 91–95, 98, 99, 108, 147, 155, 162–165, 206
writing, 231–238
English-Language Development Standards, in California. *See* California English-Language Development Standards
English learners
achievement of, 7, 87
definition of, 1
demographic trends in, 1–3
cognitive factors influencing, 15
demographic trends in, 3–5, 292–293
dialects and education of, 43–44
learning challenges, 4
motivation for school achievement, 4
profile of, 69
psychological factors influencing, 5–19
social-emotional factors influencing, 11–15
sociocultural factors influencing, 19–29
English-only movement, 128
Equal Education Opportunities Act (EEOA), 122
Equal opportunity, 302
Equity in schooling, 130
Error correction, 195, 210
Escalante, math program, 264
Ethical relativism, 273
Ethnocentrism, 273
Ethnography, 39, 327–330
European Americans, 7
Evaluative approach, 298
Exit procedures, 101
Expectations
educational, 5–6, 43, 318, 330–331
Expertise in content, 6
Explicit feedback, 194, 195
Explicit teaching of grammar, 194, 195
Eye contact, 42, 303

Facial expressions, 303
Family. *See also* Parents
acculturation, 81, 82

learning about, 329–330
as source of information, 329, 339
tracking contact with, 336
Family involvement in school, 86, 333–342
issues in, 333–334
strategies for, 339–340
Family literacy projects, 336–337, 342
Family–school relationships, 335
Family–teacher conferences, 334–335, 336
Family unification, 295–296
Family values and school values, 83
Federal legislation, 119–125. *See also* No Child Left Behind Act
Feedback, in the recitation pattern, 35, 36–37
Filipino, 304, 331. *See also* Tagalog
First language, role of in schooling, 50–51
First-language proficiency. *See also* Primary language
acquisition of, 49–51
support for, 84, 87, 145, 285–286
Fluency, in reading, 221–222
Food preferences, 322
Foreign language in elementary school (FLES), 286
Formative assessment, 99, 185, 195, 260
Front-loaded English, 136
Front-loaded vocabulary, 247
Funds of knowledge approach, 60, 153
Fully qualified under NCLB, 6, 129

Gender roles, 319–320
Generation 1.5, 232
Genre, 33, 38
Geographic bias, on tests, 102
German language, 118, 119
Gestures, 12, 303
Globalism, 323–324
Goals 2000, 90
*Gómez v. Illinois State Board of Education,* 123
Grading, 107–108
Grammar, 24, 193–196
instruction in, 194, 196
and writing, 196
Grammar-translation pedagogy, 54, 55, 194
Grammatical competence, 191
Graphic organizers, 155, 157, 158–162
applications of, 157–158
Groups, working in, 72, 168–174
Guatemala, 331
Guided practice, 184–185, 256–257

Haitians, Haitian creole, 293, 295

Handwriting, 233

Hawai'i, Hawai'ian language, 13, 293, 294

Health, values about, 316–317

Hegemony, 8

Heritage language, support for, 127. *See also* Primary
    language

Hispanic, Hispanic Americans, 2, 3, 127, 278, 279, 280,
    282–283. *See also specific ethnic
    groups*
    academic statistics on, 130
    demographics of, 1–3, 278–279
    migration of, 296
    naming practices, 20

Hispanic Dropout Project, 282–283

Hmong Literacy Project, 336

Hmong, Hmong students, 130, 260, 284, 293, 317

Holistic scoring, 211

Home language. *See* Primary language

Home language survey, 96

Home–school communication, 334, 340

Home–school partnerships, 86

Home visits, 328–329

Homework tips, 148, 340

Humanities and the arts, values about, 322

Hygiene, values about, 316–317


Identification procedures
    for English learners, 95–96, 97
    for special needs, 112–113

Identity, 326–327

Immersion. *See* Structured English immersion,
    Two-way (dual) immersion

Immigrants
    legal status of, 297
    resources available to, 297

Immigration and Nationality Act Amendments of 1965,
    226–227

Immigration in the U.S., 293–297
    causes of, 294–297
    economic factors in, 294–295
    family unification and, 295–296
    history of, 292–293
    legislation, 297
    political factors in, 295
    policies, 296–297

Immigration laws, U.S., 294, 296–297

Immigration Reform and Control Act, 228

Implicit learning, 196

Independent practice, 184–185, 257–258

India, 320, 331

Indigenous language rights, 124

Individuals with Disabilities Act (IDEA), 123

Infixes, 21

Inhibition, 75

Innateness hypothesis, 50

Input hypothesis, 63

Institutional racism, 88

Instruction. *See also* Content-area instruction
    cycle of, 162
    differentiated, 96, 99, 100, 107, 176–186, 244–265
    of literacy, 214–238
    modifying to CLD students, 113
    for oracy, 199–214
    organizing the environment to enhance, 167–168

Instructional Conversation (IC), 38, 205, 212–213

Instrumental motivation, 76

Integrated language arts, 148

Integrative motivation, 76

Integrity, teaching with, 4–8

Intensive group, 100

Interactionist model of second-language acquisition, 60

Interactive journal writing, 233

Intercultural communication, 302, 307–308

Intercultural educator, 7, 312, 342

Intercultural pragmatics, 42

Interethnic conflict. *See* Cultural conflict

Interlanguage theory, 62, 192–193

Internet, 188, 242, 258, 330

Internet resources for family involvement, 337

Interpreter, use of, 336

Intersubjectivity, 5

Interventions, 100, 110, 112–113, 226

Interviews
    to identify students, 96, 97
    to learn about culture, 328

Intonation, 16, 18, 19–20, 209
    teaching, 19–20, 209

Iran, 331

IRE, IRF. *See* Recitation pattern

Islamic traditions, 317


Japanese immigrants, 270, 296, 331

Japanese language, students, 121, 260, 284, 304, 316, 331

Jazz chants, 202, 205


*Keyes v. School District #1*, 123

Khmer, 284, 295

Korean, Korean Americans, 130, 260, 284, 293, 304, 322, 331
Krashen. *See* Monitor theory

Language
  academic, 30–31
  complexity of, 12–13
  dialects in, 43–48
  dynamics of, 12
  functions of, 30–33
  modification in SDAIE, 181–182, 183, 250–251
  shock, 112, 289
  structure and use, 11–48
  universals, 11–13
Language acquisition device (LAD), 56
Language Experience Approach (LEA), 157, 229
Language objective, in lesson planning, 108, 109–110, 162, 163, 165, 240
Language restrictionism, 117
Language-rich environment, 168
Language-specific bias, 102
Language structure and use, 11–48
  language universals, 11–13
  discourse, 33–39
  morphology, 20–33
  phonology, 13–20
  pragmatics, 39–43
  semantics, 26–30
  syntax, 23–25
Language transfer, 150–152
Language variation. *See* Dialects and language variation
Laos, Laotian students, 130, 284, 315, 331
Latinos, 2–3, 6, 7, 87, 130, 190, 279, 282, 283, 285.
    *See also* Hispanic Americans
Lau Remedies, 120, 122, 126–127
*Lau v. Nichols,* 122, 126–127
Learners. *See* English learners
Learning strategy objectives, 108–109, 110, 162–163, 164–167, 240
Learning styles, 78–80, 178–179
  adapting instruction for, 80, 178–179
  websites for, 80
Legal issues in bilingual education, 120–123
*Lemon Grove v. Álvarez,* 121
Lesson planning, 162–176, 177
Linguistic bias, 199
Linguistic racism, 88
Listening processes, 200–206
  after, 204

authentic tasks in, 266
  before, 204
  for beginning comprehension, 202
  for communication, 203–204
  comprehension by ELD level, 205
  during, 204
  to repeat, 202, 203
  strategies for additional mediation, 115
  to understand, 79–80
Listen-read-discuss, 198
Literacy
  classification of English learners for, 214
  content, 197
  emergent, 218, 219
  for English learners, 214–238
  foundations of, 147–162
  integration of content and, 88
  media, 214
  personal factors affecting development, 149–155
  primary language, 215
Literature instruction, 224, 228, 241, 244
  guided practice in reading, 256
  response to, 257
  scaffolding, 254
Literacy instruction and development, 214–236. *See also* Reading instruction
  across the curriculum, 155
  integrated with oracy, 148–149
  response and analysis skills, 230
  strategies for, 90–94
Literature response groups, 2320

Macroculture, 270
Mainstream culture, U.S., 244, 270, 275, 304, 312, 316
Mandarin. *See* Chinese language
Massachusetts Comprehensive Assessment System (MCAS), 101, 102
Mastery learning, 55, 56
Materials, 162
  culturally appealing, 187–188
  selecting and modifying, 187, 242
Mathematics instruction, 241
  assessment in, 261, 262
  language of, 248, 249
  resources for, 258, 259
  scaffolding in, 251, 252
  teaching strategies for, 253
May 25 memorandum, 120
Meaning, 222

Meaning-centered approaches, 66
Media literacy, 214
*Méndez v. Westminster School District,* 121
Medicine, values about, 316–317
Memory difficulties, 111
Mentoring, 319
Metacognitive deficits, 111
Metacognitive strategies, 10, 166
Metalearning, 185
Metalinguistic knowledge/awareness, 24, 150–151
Metastrategic knowledge, 149
Mexican Americans, 3, 83, 275, 286, 331, *See also*
    Hispanic Americans
    cultural values of, 314, 323
Mexican immigrants, 118, 270, 294, 295
*Meyer v. Nebraska,* 119, 121
Microcultures, 270, 275
Migration, 293–297
    secondary, 296
Minorities
    castelike, 61
    discrepancies in achievement, 130, 280–286
Modeling, 143, 251
Model minority myth, 284
Monitor hypothesis, 62–63
Monitor Model (Krashen), 57, 62–64, 193
Morphemes, 20–21
    bound, 20, 21
    use in teaching, 21–23
Morphology, 20–23
    changes over time, 21
    morphemes, 20–21
    word-formation processes, 21
Motivation, 75–76, 153, 332
Motor disorders, 111
Multicompetent language use, 51, 117
Multicultural classroom, 265, 342
Multicultural education, 323–326
Multiculturalism, 274–276
Multicultural materials, 187–188, 228
    transformative, 276
Multimedia, 185
Multimodalities, 247
Multiple intelligences, 78
Music instruction, 241
    assessment in, 262
    language of, 280
    resources for, 260
Muslim, 297. *See also* Islam

MyLabSchool, 48, 116, 190, 237, 265, 311, 342

Naming practices, 70
National Association for Bilingual Education, 9
National Clearinghouse for English Language
    Acquisition and Language Instruction Educational
    Programs (NCELA), 9
Native American languages, 124
Native Americans, 85, 86, 118, 119, 124, 146, 274, 285,
    304
    participation styles of, 85–86
Native-English-speaking (NES) students, 128, 13
Native language rights, 5
Native/non-native speaker interaction, 60
Natural Approach, 62, 91
Natural order hypothesis, 62
Navajo, 146
Neologisms, 22
Nevada, English learners in, 293
Newcomer programs, 135–137
New Jersey, English learners in, 293
New Mexico, English learners in, 293
New York Times Education News Feed, 116
No Child Left Behind (NCLB) Act, 6, 90, 91, 94, 98, 123,
    124–125, 129, 280
Nonnative English Speaking Teachers in TESOL
    (NNEST), 9
Nonverbal communication, 41–42, 302–304
    body language, 42, 302
    conceptions of time and, 42
    eye contact, 42, 303
    facial expressions, 302
    gestures, 42, 303
    personal space, 42, 303, 304
Nonverbal miscommunication, 270
Note-taking skills, 255

Objectives, in lesson planning, 108–110, 162–176
Observation-based assessment, 106
Observations
    anecdotal, 106
    cultural, 328
Occupation and income, values about, 321
Office for Civil Rights, 120
Open Court, 231
Oracy
    connected to community, 199
    in English-language development, 199–214
    integrated with literacy, 148–149

Oral history, 250
Oral practice, 208
Oral registers, 40
Oral versus written language, 306
Ourselves as cultural beings, 309–310
Overachievement myth, 284

Pacific Islands, Pacific Islanders, 3, 294
Paraprofessional educators, 174–176
Parental rights, 144–145
Parent Resource Center in Texas, 337
Parents. *See also* Family
    school involvement model, 338
    strategies for involvement, 339
Partial bilingualism, 51
Participation, culturally preferred styles of, 85
Partnerships. *See* Home–school partnerships
Patterned language, 182
Peer response in writing, 235
Perceptual disorders, 111
Performance arts instruction, 242, 262
Performance-based assessment, 104
Personal space, 42, 303, 304
Philippines, 119, 294, 296, 331
Philipino immigrants, 294
Phonemes, 13–15
    development of, 52
    English, 14
    in other languages, 15
Phonemic awareness, 150, 219
Phonemic sequences, 15
Phonics
    analytical method, 220
    limitations of, 216
    in literacy instruction, 221
Phonology, 12
    intonation, 18, 19
    phonemes, 13–15
    pitch, 16, 17–18, 40, 47
    stress, 16–17
Physical education instruction, 241, 243
Physical geography and cultural practices, 274
Pitch, 16, 17–18, 40, 47
Placement, 95–98
    assessment for, 96–97
    services after, 113–114
Placement tests, 96, 97, 98
Plagiarism, 237
Pluralism, 286

*Plyler v. Doe,* 1423
Poetry, 205, 225, 256
Political clarity, 7
Political consciousness, 332–333
Political factors, 87–88
Politics
    ethnic, 278
    values about, 317
Polynesian students, 318
Portfolio assessment, 105
Poverty, among minority groups, 3, 279–280
Power and authority, 308
Practicality, in testing, 103
Pragmatics, 39–43
    appropriate language, 39
    features of school programs, 42
    language contexts and register shifts, 39
Prefixes, 21, 22
Prejudice, 298
Prereading activities, 223–224
Prewriting stage, 234
Primary language
    instruction, 4, 8
    institutional support for, 84, 87, 145, 286
    literacy level, 149–150
    literacy transfer, 150–152
    as resource, 117
Primary-language poetry, 256–257
Prior knowledge, 177–178, 212, 218, 219, 244
Privileged students, 314
Pronunciation, 16–20. *See also* Phonology
    self-correction, 16
    teaching, 16, 18–20
Proposition 187, in California, 123
Proposition 227, in California, 123, 125–126, 129, 130
Psychological factors, 67, 69–80
    cognitive, 67, 69, 77–80
    social–emotional, 67, 69, 74–77
Publishing, 236, 341
Puerto Rico, Puerto Ricans, 3, 119, 121, 282, 294
Pull-out ELD, 137–138
Punjabi, 284

Questioning strategies, 37–38, 184, 257
Questionnaires of students' interests, 106
Questions
    differentiated by proficiency level, 101, 252
    for generating interest, 245

Questions (*continued*)
  nature of, 305
  about prior knowledge, 245

Racism, 298–299
  institutional, 300–301
  programs to combat, 299–300
  teaching against, 299
Reading. *See also* Literacy instruction
  adaptations, 231
  after (beyond), 224–225
  age-level-appropriate, 228
  aloud, 222
  before (into), 223–224
  comprehension, 226, 227
  content, 230–231
  during (while), 224
  fluency, 221–222
  grade-level appropriate, 228
  in-class methods, 225
  interventions, 226
  for meaning, 222
  process, 223–225
  purposes for, 216–217
  standards-based, 217
  strategies for additional mediation, 115–116
  strategies matched to proficiency level, 226
  text genres in, 228
Reading dysfunctions, 112
Reading/Language Arts Framework, in California, 95,
    96, 138
Reading Mastery, 231
Realia, 179
Receptive language disorders, 111
Recitation pattern, in the classroom, 35–38
Redesignation/Reclassification of English learners, 95, 101
Referrals, 96, 112–113
Reflective pedagogy, 185–186
Register, in the classroom, 35, 41
Register shifts, 40–41
Relationships, positive, 308, 311
Reliability, test, 103
Religion, values about, 317, 318
Resistance towards schooling, 83
Resources
  for independent practice, 257
  for math, 258
  for music, 260
  for science, 260

in SDAIE, 258–260
  for social studies, 258–259
  for spoken discourse, 208
Respect, 327
Response
  to literature, 257
  in the recitation pattern, 35, 36
Reteaching, 185
Retention/promotion policies, 281
*Ríos v. Read,* 122
Risk taking, 75
Rites rituals, and ceremonies, 315
Roles, in society, 319–320
Rubrics, 106, 110
Russian immigrants, 295, 331

Scaffolding
  assessments, 111
  strategies, 155–162, 181, 182, 184
Schema building, 178, 245
School, culturally receptive, 209–210
School–community partnerships, 145
School dress codes, 265–266
Schooling. *See also* Students
  achieving equity in, 130
  community involvement in, 86, 333–342
  culturally responsive, 262
  family involvement in, 291–294
  limited role of students in, 65
Schools
  academic achievement of minorities in, 130,
    280–286
  community partnership with, 145
Science instruction, 240, 241, 243, 246, 253–254.
  260–261
  assessment in, 260
  language of, 249
  planning for, 240
  resources for, 260–261
SDAIE. *See* Specially designed academic instruction in
    English
Secondary migration, 296
Second-language acquisition (SLA), 49, 51–88
  age for, 70, 71
  behaviorism, 55–56
  communicative competence, 57
  current theories of, 56–67
  factors that influence, 67–88
  grammar-translation methodology, 54, 55

historical theories of, 54, 55
interactionist model of, 60
interlanguage theory of, 62
meaning-centered approaches to, 66
monitor model of (Krashen), 62–64
semiotics, 66
social constructionist views of, 61
sociocultural models of, 59
teacher's role in, 69–70
Total Physical Response method, 66
Segregation, 83, 282, 285
Self-esteem, 74–75, 89, 131
building, 74–75, 131
Self-study, cultural, 309–310
Semantics, 26–30
Semantic shifts, 30
Semiotics, 66
Sensorimotor skills, 150
Separate underlying proficiency (SUP), 53–54
*Serna v. Portales Municipal Schools,* 122
Sheltered instruction. *See* Specially Designed Academic Instruction in English (SDAIE)
Sight words, 220
Sikhs. *See* Punjabi
Silence, role of, 304–305
Silent period, 37
Simultaneous dual-language acquisition, 51–52
Skill with print, 218
Social-affective strategies, 110, 166
Social class, values about, 320
Social class inequality, 84
Social constructionist views of second–language acquisition, 61
Social–emotional factors, 69, 64–77
Social–emotional functioning, 111
Social justice, 47–48
Social stratification, 87
Social studies instruction, 241, 249–250, 254–255, 260, 263
adapting curriculum in, 263
assessment in, 260
language of, 249–250
scaffolding instruction for, 254–255
resources for, 158, 259
Sociocultural and political factors, 69, 81–88
family acculturation and use of first and second languages, 81–82
family values and school values, 83–84
institutional support for primary language, 84

political factors, 87
sociocultural support for L1 in the classroom environment, 87
structures in schools that affect student learning, 84–88
Sociocultural models of second-language acquisition, 59–60
Socio-emotional factors, 69, 74–77
Sociolinguistic competence, 191
Space, personal, 42, 303, 304
Spanish language, 25, 26, 27, 260
Spanish-speaking English learners, 2–3, 17, 22, 127, 292
Speaking, 149, 206–214
activities for, 213
after, 211, 212
before, 209, 210, 212
developing oral proficiency, 207
formats for oral practice, 208
instructional conversation, 38, 205, 212–214
media literacy promoting, 214
resources for spoken discourse, 208
situations for, 207
while, 210, 212
Special education and CLD learners, 111–116
academic and learning problems in, 111–112
overreferral of, 285
referral process, 112–113
teaching strategies for, 113, 114–116
Specially Designed Academic Instruction in English (SDAIE), 8, 135, 136, 137, 147, 176–190, 239–265
bridging in, 176–178
comprehensibility, 140, 141, 143
connections, 141, 142–143
content objectives, 141, 142
interaction, 141, 142, 144
language contextualization in, 181
learning-style modalities in, 179
manipulatives in, 179
model for, 140–141
modifying language for, 181–182
in newcomer programs, 136–137
planning, 143, 239
principles of, 103–104
setting objectives for, 239–240
strategies, 181
in structured English immersion programs, 135
teacher attitude and, 142
Speech adjustment, teacher, 143
Speech emergence stage, 10

Speech register, 43
Speech sounds. *See* Phonology
Spelling, changes over time, 233
Spoken discourse. *See* Speaking
Stages of second-language acquisition, 73
Standard English, 44, 47
Standardized testing, 175–178, 186
  and remedial referral, 26
  value of, 23
Standards
  content, 90, 108
  delivery, 90
  performance, 90
Standards-based assessment and instruction, 90–95,
    156–157, 162–167, 217
Standards-based content objectives, 240
Stereotyping, 299
Story retelling, 210
Strategic competence, 191
Strategic group, 100
Stress (word), 16–17, 209
Structural linguistics, 545–55
Structured English immersion, 135, 136
Students
  high expectations for, 330–332
  cultures, learning about, 327–330
  educating about cultural diversity, 323–327
  motivating, 332
  role of, 85
  as sources of information, 329
Subtractive bilingualism, 134, 135, 136
Suffixes, 21, 22
Summative assessment, 99, 185, 261
Survey, interest, 106
Syllables, 37–38
  stressed, 36–37
Symbolic-structural violence, 301
Synonyms, 26
Syntactic proficiency, 23
Syntax, 23–25
  English contrasted with Chinese, 25
  English contrasted with Spanish, 25
  teaching, 24–25

Tagalog, 10
Taiwanese, 297
Teacher commitment, 190
Teacher expectations, 5–6, 43, 318, 330–331
Teacher-fronted classroom, 35, 38, 143

Teachers
  attitude towards students, 152, 264, 309
  as intercultural educators, 7, 312, 342
  limited role of, 86
  participating in growth relationships, 311
  self-study of, 309–311
Teachers of English to Speakers of Other Languages,
    Inc. (TESOL, Inc.), 9
Teacher–student interactions, 307
Teaching styles, 307
Team-teaching. *See* Collaboration
Technological resources, 188–190
Test accommodation, 108
Test anxiety, 102
Testing. *See* Assessment
Tests. *See* Assessment
Texas, English learners in, 293
Thinking critically, 228, 332–333
Time, concepts of, 42
Tone languages, 17
Tonga, 331
Total Physical Response (TPR), 56, 181, 183
Tracking, 84–85, 281
Transformational grammar, 57
Transitional bilingual education (TBE), 134
Treaty of Guadalupe Hidalgo, 119
Turn-taking, 41
Two-way (dual) immersion programs, 1, 117, 127–128,
    131–133, 286

Ukraine, 381
Underachievement, 281–283
Universal access to language arts curriculum, 95–96, 99,
    138
Universal Declaration of Human Rights,
    120
Universal Declaration of Linguistic Rights, 120
Universal instructional design, 138–139
Unz initiative. *See* Proposition 227 in California

Validity, test, 102
Values. *See also* Cultural values
  about age-appropriate activities, 320–321
  about child-rearing, 321
  about cooperation and competition, 316, 322
  about dress and appearance, 314
  about economics, law, politics, and religion, 317
  about education, 271, 318–319
  about food preferences, 321

about gender, 319
about health and hygiene, 316–317
about humanities and the arts, 322
about occupations, 321
about roles and status, 319
about social class, 320
about space, 314
about time, 314
about work and leisure, 315–316
Validation, identity, 326–327
Vietnamese, 130, 284, 331
Vietnamese immigrants, 270
Vietnamese language, 260, 293
Violence, symbolic-structural, 301
Visual arts instruction, 241
  assessment in, 262
  language in, 250
Vocabulary
  academic, 26–29
  acquiring, 28
  and concept development, 218–220
  content, 137
  front-loading, 247
  in reading, 222–223
  teaching, 28–29
  in writing, 233
Vygotsky, 61, 147, 199

Websites, 259
  for teaching, 258
White (race), 7
Whole language, 66
*Williams v. the State of California,* 123, 126, 129, 145
Word-formation processes, 38–39
Word order, 24
Word recognition, 221
Writing, 75
  adaptations for English learners, 238
  for college, 232
  drafting in, 234
  editing of, 236
  error correction in, 236
  feedback on, 235
  issues with ESL, 236–237
  prewriting, 234
  processes of, 231
  publishing, 236
  self-correction and revising in, 235
  strategies in, 237
  as a social construction, 232
  stages in, 232–233
  workshop, 234
Written expression skill deficits, 112

Zone of proximal development, 61